CHA

Essential English Grammar and Usage

CHAMBERS

Essential English Grammar and Usage

CHAMBERS
English

CHAMBERS
An imprint of Chambers Harrap Publishers Ltd
7 Hopetoun Crescent Edinburgh EH7 4AY

A CIP catalogue record for this book is available from the British Library.

ISBN 0550 14090 5

We have made every effort to mark as such all words which we believe to be trademarks. We should also like to make it clear that the presence of a word in the dictionary, whether marked or unmarked, in no way affects its legal status as a trademark.

The British National Corpus is a collaborative initiative carried out by Oxford University Press, Longman, Chambers Harrap, Oxford University Computing Services, Lancaster University's Unit for Computer Research in the English language, and the British Library. The project received funding from the UK Department of Trade and Industry and was supported by additional research grants fom the British Academy and the British Library.

Designed and typeset in Great Britain by Chambers Harrap Publishers Ltd.
Printed in the UK by Caledonian International Book Manufacturing Ltd, Glasgow

Contents

Contributors

Senior Editor
Penny Hands

Editors
Anne Seaton
Sandra Anderson

Publishing Manager
Elaine Higgleton

Preface

Chambers Essential English Grammar and Usage has been compiled to provide intermediate to upper-intermediate learners of English with an up-to-date, user-friendly guide to how English works.

The guide is organized into alphabetical order, treating three different types of entry. First, *lexical* entries explain how certain words in English are used. These may be words which are often confused with other words, or words which occur in many different structures or have several different meanings. Secondly, *topic* entries look at certain language areas like spelling, differences between American and British English, and comparatives and superlatives. Finally, entries explaining how to perform certain *functions* using language are treated. These cover such areas as apologizing, making compliments, and requesting and inviting, and are presented in distinctive double-page panels.

In-depth research using the British National Corpus® has enabled compilers to make some fascinating insights into the use of English in everyday conversation, public and private correspondence, the press, and TV and radio news. It has, for example, helped us to gain a greater understanding of how modal verbs are used as substitutes for words or even whole phrases, and in functional entries (presented in panels) we have been able to give specific information about the contexts in which people use certain expressions.

In addition, the corpus has been used extensively to provide material for examples. These examples serve to illustrate the explanation, to show collocation, to show context, and to enable users to see whether the structure is more commonly used in formal or informal English. Sometimes, material for examples is entirely authentic in that it is transferred directly from the corpus. However, in order to keep the examples clear and useful, the language has often been modified or graded.

We hope that learners will enjoy using this exciting new addition to the Chambers ELT range, with its user-friendly layout, clearly defined entries and its up-to-date, easy-to follow and comprehensive coverage of the structures and usage of the English language.

The Editors

Organization of entries

along, through

Entries dealing with the ways in which particular words are used are presented like this.

ALONG

You use **along** to express movement and position on or in long narrow things such as roads, paths and rivers:

He saw a coach coming along the road.
Tall trees used to grow along these lanes.

The word or words being explained appear in bold in the explanation.

ALONG OR THROUGH

With long narrow three-dimensional spaces such as tunnels, **along** and **through** are both possible, but **through** is preferred when the movement is not horizontal:

She turned and walked back along (or *through*) *the tunnel.*
It can take 72 hours for food to pass through the body.

Examples of real usage supported by the BNC® show the range of ways in which language items can be used.

ALREADY

1 When using **already** to refer to things that have happened at an earlier time, you use the perfect form of verbs:
He's already told me the whole story.

> ⓘ Notice that in AmE people use the simple past where BrE uses the perfect:
> BrE: *I've already told you.*
> AmE: *I already told you.*

American English (AmE) is given wide coverage. Contrasts are made with British English (BrE) usage.

Tinted notes give useful hints regarding common errors, and highlight interesting points of usage.

Divisions of entries are clearly signposted.

Entries dealing with language topics are presented like this.

comparatives and superlatives

This entry first explains the rules for the *formation* of comparative and superlative adjectives and adverbs, and then provides information on the *use* of comparatives and superlatives.

FORMATION – ADJECTIVES

Adjectives that form comparatives and superlatives are usually the *qualitative* or *gradable* kind (see **adjectives**), but the common colour adjectives also have comparatives and superlatives (*He had bluer eyes than his brother.*).

1 one-syllable adjectives

- the general rule:

  one-syllable adjectives form their comparative by adding **-er** and their superlative by adding **-est**:

bright	*bright**er***	*bright**est***
great	*great**er***	*great**est***
...	...	...

In topic entries, elements being explained appear in bold in examples, where appropriate.

abbreviations

1 There are four kinds of abbreviation:

- The initial letters of a group of words are pronounced as separate letters. There is usually a stress on the last letter. This kind of abbreviation is called an **initialism**:

  BBC /bi:bi:'si:/ = British Broadcasting Corporation
  USA /ju:ɛs'eɪ/ = United States of America

- The initial letters of a group of words are pronounced as a word. This is called an **acronym**:

  Nato /'neɪtoʊ/ = North Atlantic Treaty Organization

Pronunciation is shown where appropriate. An explanation of the phonetic symbols is given on page xiii.

Organization of entries continued

Entries dealing with the use of language to perform certain functions are presented in boxes like this. They give clear and comprehensive coverage of the use of English in many different situations, ranging from formal to informal.

ADDRESSING PEOPLE

You sometimes call people by their names when you are talking to them, or use some other form of address:

*I think I know what you mean, **Paddy**.*
*Thank you, **Mrs Presswood**.*
*Come on, **darling**, hurry up.*
*It's a pleasure, **madam**.*
*Thank you, **Doctor**.*
*Switch off the light, **someone**.*

Words or expressions appear in bold in examples, where appropriate (here, for example, to show which part of the sentence is the form of address).

POSITION OF FORMS OF ADDRESS

1 If you address someone by their name or some other form of address, you usually put it at the end of what you are saying to them:

*It's too late, **Tricia**.*
*Cheer up, **love**.*
*Follow me, **sir**.*
*What's the matter, **Mum**?*

2 If you want to get someone's attention, or make sure they are listening to you, you can use a form of address at the beginning of what you are saying:

***Ann**, can you remember Alison's surname?*

➤ See also **names and titles**.

Extensive cross-referencing enables users to extend their knowledge in related areas.

Pronunciation guide

Key to the phonetic symbols used in
Chambers Essential English Grammar and Usage

CONSONANTS

p	/piː/	pea
t	/tiː/	tea
k	/kiː/	key
b	/biː/	be
d	/daɪ/	dye
g	/gaɪ/	guy
m	/miː/	me
n	/njuː/	new
ŋ	/sɒŋ/	song
θ	/θɪn/	thin
ð	/ðɛn/	then
f	/fan/	fan
v	/van/	van
s	/siː/	see
z	/zuːm/	zoom
ʃ	/ʃiː/	she
ʒ	/beɪʒ/	beige
tʃ	/iːtʃ/	each
dʒ	/ɛdʒ/	edge
h	/hat/	hat
l	/leɪ/	lay
r	/reɪ/	ray
j	/jɛs/	yes
w	/weɪ/	way

VOWELS

Short vowels

ɪ	/bɪd/	bid
ɛ	/bɛd/	bed
a	/bad/	bad
ʌ	/bʌd/	bud
ɒ	/pɒt/	pot
ʊ	/pʊt/	put
ə	/əˈbaʊt/	about

Long vowels

iː	/biːd/	bead
ɑː	/hɑːm/	harm
ɔː	/ɔːl/	all
uː	/buːt/	boot
ɜː	/bɜːd/	bird

Diphthongs

eɪ	/beɪ/	bay
aɪ	/baɪ/	buy
ɔɪ	/bɔɪ/	boy
ɑʊ	/hɑʊ/	how
oʊ	/goʊ/	go
ɪə	/bɪə(r)/	beer
ɛə	/bɛə(r)/	bare
ʊə	/pʊə(r)/	poor

Notes

(1) The stress mark (ˈ) is placed before the stressed syllable (*eg* **invent** /ɪnˈvɛnt/).

(2) The symbol '(r)' is used to represent *r* when it comes at the end of a word, to indicate that it is pronounced when followed by a vowel (as it is in 'four' in the phrase *four or five* /fɔːr ɔː ˈfaɪv/).

Aa

a, an

1 **A** and **an** belong to the group of words called 'determiners' (see the entry on **determiners**). They are used before nouns or noun groups. You use **a** before words beginning with a consonant or a consonant sound (*eg* the /j/ sound at the beginning of the word 'European'), and **an** before words beginning with a vowel or vowel sound (*eg* the /ɔ/ sound at the beginning of the word 'honour'):

a hotel
a television set
a European
a yacht
an answer
an honour
an MP /ɛm 'piː/

2 **A** and **an** refer to people or things without specifying any one in particular:

We need a new car.
I'm going to a concert tonight.
She's having lunch with an old boyfriend.

3 **A** and **an** are often used when referring to a person or thing for the first time, as in the two examples above. When that person or thing is referred to again, a pronoun, or the definite article, **the** is used:

'I'm going to a concert tonight.' 'Where is the concert?'
She's having lunch with an old boyfriend. He was in her class at university.

4 You also use **a** and **an** to refer to classes of people or things, without meaning any particular one:

I'd like a drink
Why don't you discuss it with a friend?
A concert is a musical performance.

5 You use **a** and **an** when you are describing people or things, *eg* after linking verbs such as **be, become**, and **seem**, or after **as** and **like**:

He wants to become a politician.
On the surface, Anna seemed a normal happy girl.
In summer we used the conservatory as a dining room.

> ⓘ Note that **a** and **an** are used with singular count nouns. With plurals and uncount nouns you show indefinite meaning by using no article, or by using **some** or **any**:
> *He's mad about trains.*
> *She lacks patience.*
> *I've brought some wine.*
> *We haven't got any sugar left.*
> *I took her some magazines to look at.*
> *There weren't any volunteers.*

6 **A** or **an** is sometimes used with an uncountable noun when it is used like a countable noun:

She chose a red wine (= a type of red wine) *to drink with the meal.*
They had a natural love of language.
Can I get you a coffee?

➤ For more information about this topic see the entries on **articles** and **countable and uncountable nouns**.

7 You can omit **a** or **an** before the second and following count noun in a pair or list:

He passed me a knife and fork.
She quickly packed a swimsuit, swimming hat and towel.

8 You use **a** or **an** to mean 'one' in expressing number or quantity:

a year
an hour
a million dollars

9 You also use **a** or **an** in certain expressions of quantity:

a few books
a lot of paper
a little milk

10 You use **a** or **an** to denote frequency, rate or cost:

I clean the house once a week.
Petrol is 54 pence a litre here.

abbreviations

1 There are four kinds of abbreviation:

- The initial letters of a group of words are pronounced as separate letters. There is usually a stress on the last letter. This kind of abbreviation is called an **initialism**:

  BBC /biːbiːˈsiː/ = British Broadcasting Corporation
  USA /juːɛsˈeɪ/ = United States of America

- The initial letters of a group of words are pronounced as a word. This is called an **acronym**:

  Nato /ˈneɪtoʊ/ = North Atlantic Treaty Organization

- Letters are omitted from the middle of a word. This kind of abbreviation is called a **contraction**:

  Dr = Doctor

- Part of a word is cut off. This is called a **shortening**:

  Tues. = Tuesday
  kilo = kilogram

2 Plurals of initialisms and acronyms are formed by adding an **s**, usually without an apostrophe:
He knows how to repair TVs (or *TV's*).

3 Many shortenings (*eg* **kilo**) are treated as whole words. They have no full stop at the end, and form plurals like ordinary words:
We need 3 kilos of apples.

4 You use **a** or **an** according to the first sound you hear in the abbreviation:
She became an MEP. /ən ɛmiː'piː/
They have violated a UN resolution. /ə juː ɛn rɛzə'luːʃən/

•••• able ••••

be able to + infinitive = to have the knowledge, skill, strength, power, time, opportunity, resources to (do something):

1 You use **be able to** like **can** and **could**:
He was always able to (= he could always) *get what he wanted.*
I'm still able to (= I can still) *read without glasses.*

2 The opposite, or negative form, is **unable to**:
The children seem unable to concentrate.
She nodded, unable to speak.

> ⓘ Notice that you can use other words, like **feel** and **seem**, instead of **be** with **able** and **unable**.

3 When you are talking about single occasions in the past, you use **be able to** rather than **could**:
The rain stopped and I was able to cut the grass at last.

4 **Can** is more usual than **be able to** in the sense 'know how to':
Can you skate?

➤ See the entries **can** and **could**.

5 You use **be able to** with future and perfect tenses, and where an infinitive is required. In such cases, it would be impossible to use **can** and **could**:
I've been able to achieve one small thing.
The animal appeared to be able to think like a human.

•••• about ••••

1 You can use both **about** and **on** to refer to the subject of something spoken or written. **On** is more usual when you are referring to formal subjects like the subjects of academic articles and speeches:
She was the author of a study on language in the brain.
He was telling us about his experiences in Japan.

2 You **are about to** do something when you are just going to do it, or will be doing it soon:

I was about to serve dinner.
Claire looked as if she was about to cry.

3 In informal English, if you say that someone **isn't about to** do something, you mean that they are determined not to do it:

He wasn't about to leave without asking for her phone number.

•••• above, over ••••

Above is an adverb and a preposition. It is the opposite of **below**. **Above** often has the same meaning as **over** when it is used as a preposition:

We saw the sky above (adverb).
Above, we could see the sky (adverb).
We saw the sky above (or *over*) *the treetops* (preposition).

IN PHYSICAL RELATIONSHIPS

1 One thing is **above** another if it is higher than it:

We flew above the clouds.
We met them on the mountain path above Chamonix.
Loud noises were coming from the flat above.

2 **Above** and **over** as prepositions are both possible where there is a clear vertical relationship:

There was a sign above (or *over*) *the door.*
She had a cut above (or *over*) *one eye.*

3 Use **over** where the meaning is 'covering':

We put plastic sheets over the tables when it started raining.
She was wearing a raincoat over her summer dress.

4 Use **over** where one thing passes across the top of another:

We flew over Mont Blanc.
She looked at me sternly over the top of her glasses.

IN MEASUREMENTS

1 You use **above** in relation to a standard point on a scale of measurement:

The summit is 2556 feet above sea level.
The temperature is above average for March.

2 You normally use **over** (preposition and adverb) in relation to specific numbers or quantities:

The cost came to over £200.
The journey took us just over a week.
They were having temperatures of 80 degrees and over.

IN EXPRESSIONS ABOUT RANK

1 Use **above** when you are talking about one person being senior to another:

There were three people above him in his department, and he had little hope of promotion.
She made friends with a student in the year above.

2 Use **over** when the meaning is 'in charge of' or 'supervising':

We had an assistant manager and a department manager over us.

•••• absent ••••

1 Someone is **absent from** a place or event when they are not there, although they are expected to be there:

She's been absent from school for three weeks.
One million employees are absent from work every day.

> ⓘ Notice that **absent** is a rather formal word. In informal English you would say that someone **was not at** a particular place or event, or **was not there**:
> *His parents weren't at the school concert.*
> *'Did you see George at the funeral?' 'No, he wasn't there.'*

2 A quality or element is **absent from** something when it is missing from it:

Fairness and honesty were absent from his report.

•••• accept, agree to ••••

Use **agree** rather than **accept** before a **to**-infinitive:

Paul Spence has kindly agreed to (not *accepted to*) *give a talk on seventeenth-century architecture.*

•••• acceptable, agreeable, willing ••••

1 Something that is **acceptable** is satisfactory, or can be justified:

Try not to make drug-taking seem acceptable.
Fortunately my suggestion was acceptable to most people.

2 You say that people are **willing** to do something if they agree to do it, or are happy to do it:

Are you willing (not *acceptable*) *to work at the weekend if necessary?*

3 You can say that people are **agreeable** if they accept something that has been proposed:

We finally arrived at a figure of £250, and he was agreeable.

•••• accommodation ••••

In BrE this is an uncountable noun; **accommodation** is a room, or a set of rooms that you can stay in, live in, or work in:

Modern, desirable office accommodation could be provided in existing buildings.

In AmE, people use **accommodation** as a countable noun:

This lovely country house has accommodations for up to 104.

•••• accompany ••••

ACCOMPANY

You **accompany** someone somewhere when you go there with them:

Mr Bagshot accompanied Brian to the car.

> ⓘ **Accompany** is a rather formal word. In everyday informal English you would use **go with** or **come with**:
> *Would you like to come with me?*
> *Alison was driving into town so I went with her.*

> ⓘ Notice that you do not use **follow** to mean 'come with', 'go with' or 'accompany':
> *I'll come with you* (not *follow you*) *as far as the bus stop.*

ACCOMPANIED BY

1 The passive form of **accompany** is more frequently used than the active because there is no passive form of **go with** or **come with**:

She was accompanied by her husband.
He came to the house accompanied by a young girl.

2 **Accompanied by** is often used with the meaning 'together with', in reference to things rather than people:

The tennis player's photo was in the German newspapers today, accompanied by news of his physical condition.

•••• accord: of your own accord ••••

1 You do something **of your own accord** if you do it without being asked, or forced, to do it:

If the employee is leaving of his or her own accord, please inform the personnel department.

2 Something moves **of its own accord** if it moves by itself, or automatically:

The door seemed to open of its own accord.

•••• according to ••••

1 You use **according to** when you are quoting someone else's opinion, or a source of information. When you are expressing your own opinion, you use a phrase such as **in my opinion**:

According to this book we should be educating our children at home.
So according to Peter we don't need to keep a separate list.

But:

In my view (not *according to me*) *he's making a serious mistake.*

2 You also use **according to** to mean 'on the basis of' or 'in relation to':

The words are divided up according to their meaning, not according to word class.
The bank will act according to its clients' instructions.
Everything proceeded according to plan.

•••• account ••••

1 **On account of** means 'because of':

The match was postponed on account of heavy rain.

➤ See the entry for **due to, owing to**.

2 You do something **on someone else's account** if you do it for them or for their benefit; it is often used with a negative:

Please don't change your plans on my account.

3 You use **on no account** or **not on any account** as a strong negative statement or order:

On no account should you leave your car.
The cheese should be cut into chunks, and not on any account grated.

•••• accustomed to ••••

➤ See **used to**.

•••• acronyms ••••

➤ See **abbreviations**.

•••• across, over, through ••••

ACROSS, OVER

1 You go **across** or **over** something such as a road, river, bridge or frontier when you go from one side of it to the other:

How are we going to get across (or *over*) *this river?*
They were arrested for carrying whisky across (or *over*) *the border.*
How much does it cost to go across (or *over*) *the bridge by car?*

2 You use **over** rather than **across** with objects that are seen as obstacles:

I had to carry her over the wall.
We walked over the mountain, and into the valley.
They ran along, jumping over the puddles.

3 You normally use **across** with areas, or flat surfaces:

The couple danced across the floor.
He walked across the lawn.
We rowed across (or *over*) *the river.*
She wants to swim across (but not *over*) *the Channel.* [= the sea between England and France]

> ⓘ The preposition **over** can be used where there is no idea of getting to the other side:
> *We spent a day walking over the moors.*

> ⓘ Notice that the adverb **over**, as distinct from the preposition, can be used like **across** in relation to flat surfaces:
> *I saw him standing by the window and went over* (or *across*) *to join him.*
> *She will make another attempt to swim over* (or *across*) *to France.*

4 When something spreads, passes or extends from one side of an area to the other, you usually use **across**:

Later, rain is expected to spread across the whole country.
The earth's shadow passes across the moon.
He stepped over a branch that lay across the path.

5 People or things **across**, **right across**, or **all over** an area, are people or things everywhere in it:

Companies across the country will pay the same amount.
People right across (or *all over*) *the world will take part in the event.*

6 Something that is **across** or **over** a road or river is on the other side of it:

They moved into a flat just over (or *across*) *the road from us.*
My car's parked across (or *over*) *the road.*

ACROSS, THROUGH

You use **through** if you are thinking of a space or area in three dimensions:

We wandered through the forest.
Jack pushed his way through the crowd.

•••• act, action, activity ••••

ACT, ACTION

You can refer to something that someone does as *eg* **a brave act** or **a brave action**, but you can only say **an act** (not **an action**) **of bravery**:

It was clearly a desperate act (or *action*).

But:

It was a final act (not *action*) *of desperation.*

> ⓘ Notice that this language is rather formal; more informally, you would say:
> *It was a desperate thing to do.*

ACT, ACTION, ACTIVITY

1 The **action** of doing something such as walking refers to simple physical movement:

They were studying the action of opening and closing the gate.

2 The **activity** of doing something refers to the physical and mental processes that are

involved in doing it, or to the pastime or business of doing it:

They enjoyed the activities of reading and studying literature.
It was the activity of hunting that provided the real challenge.

3 You can use **act** in a similar way to **activity**:

the act of thinking
the act of eating

—— active sentences ——

The **active** forms of verbs are the forms you use when the person or thing that is the subject of the sentence performs the action of the verb, as in:

He drove the car into a wall.
She writes well.
Where will you be tomorrow?
The children were not doing their homework.

➢ See also the entry for **the passive**.

•••• actual ••••

You can use **actual** with the following meanings:

1 existing, not imaginary:

You'd never get actual people behaving like the characters in his plays.
People don't realize that the town in this novel is an actual place.

2 the particular one and no other:

Is this the actual pistol that killed Lincoln?

3 true, as distinct from supposed or guessed:

Early estimates suggested that about 100 had died, but the actual total was nearer 250.

4 the main item, as distinct from incidental ones:

Where's the actual demonstration taking place?

> ⓘ Notice that you do not use **actual** to describe things happening now:
> *In the present* (not *actual*) *circumstances all we can do is try to keep calm.*
> *The current* (not *actual*) *financial climate does not encourage investment.*

•••• actually ••••

1 You say that something **actually** happens or is so if you want to make it clear that this is the case:

Could you actually hear what they were saying?
Is this book actually useful to you?

2 You use **actually** to mean 'in fact', or 'in truth' as distinct from what people suppose, or are told:

He says he was born in 1910, but he's actually older, isn't he?

ADDRESSING PEOPLE

You sometimes call people by their names when you are talking to them, or use some other form of address:

I think I know what you mean, ***Paddy****.*
Thank you, ***Mrs Presswood****.*
Come on, ***darling****, hurry up.*
It's a pleasure, ***madam****.*
Thank you, ***Doctor****.*
Switch off the light, ***someone****.*

POSITION OF FORMS OF ADDRESS

1 If you address someone by their name or some other form of address, you usually put it at the end of what you are saying to them:

It's too late, ***Tricia****.*
Cheer up, ***love****.*
Follow me, ***sir****.*
What's the matter, ***Mum****?*

2 If you want to get someone's attention, or make sure they are listening to you, you can use a form of address at the beginning of what you are saying:

Ann*, can you remember Alison's surname?*

➤ See also **names and titles**.

3 A form of address placed between clauses, or after an initial sentence adverb, emphasizes that what you are saying is important:

Don't imagine, ***Brian****, that I think this is going to be easy.*
Clearly, ***Mrs Fletcher****, you have not understood what I said.*

...actually continued

3 **Actually** emphasizes the surprising part of what you are saying:

She took the exam eventually and actually passed.
He actually admitted that he was wrong.

4 **Actually** can mean 'in the true sense of the word':

I was never actually dishonest.

5 You use **actually** as a sentence adverb:

- to sound polite when you are disagreeing with someone or correcting them:

Actually, I think you've misunderstood what I was saying.
You won't get a better bargain than this, actually.

- when you are announcing something surprising or unexpected:

Actually, it was easy!
Actually, I'm afraid things haven't turned out as we were hoping.

ⓘ Notice that when you write forms of address, you separate them with a comma:
*That's very kind of you, **David**.*
***Hilary**, have you got the time?*

ADDRESSING A GROUP

In informal situations you can use **everybody** or **everyone** to address a group of people. Notice the possible uses also of **anybody** or **anyone**, *eg* after a negative command, and of **somebody** and **someone**:

Don't move, anyone!
Coming for a drink, anybody?
Help me, someone!
Come on, everybody!

OTHER FORMS OF ADDRESS

1 You can use some nouns and adjectives to address people if you want to show affection or some other feeling about them:

*You look lovely, **sweetheart**.*
*I know that, **stupid**.*

2 Sometimes an adjective is used ironically (= with the opposite meaning intended):

*You're wrong, **clever**.*

3 Words or phrases that people use to express impatience with the person they are addressing, are often preceded by **you**:

*Nobody hates you, **you silly thing**.*
*I didn't mean that, **you idiot**.*

...actually continued

ⓘ Notice that you do not use **actually** to mean 'at the moment', 'at present' or 'now':
Children used to know far more grammar than they do now (not *than they actually do*).

•••• addressing people ••••

➤ See above.

—— adjectives ——

Adjectives are used to describe the people or things referred to by nouns, and to tell you such things as:

- their size:

*a **large** table*
*a **thick** book*
***short** hair*

- their colour:
  *a **green** carpet*
  ***blue** eyes*

- the speaker's opinion of them:
  *a **good** example*
  ***nice** people*

- their type or class:
  *a **plastic** stool*
  *a **plastic** stool*
  ***Malaysian** cuisine*
  ***political** refugees*

TYPES OF ADJECTIVE

Adjectives can be divided into several types:

1 **qualitative adjectives** (*eg* **old**, **straight**, **tall**, **ugly**, describing what people or things are like, or what the speaker thinks of them):
__tall__ buildings
*a **horrible** old man*
*a **straight** road*
***old** methods*

- You can use two or more qualitative adjectives one after the other to describe something. The usual order is *personal opinion*, followed by *size*, *shape or character*, and *age*:

  *a **pretty little** girl*
  ***long sensitive** fingers*

- Qualitative adjectives are *gradable*. This means that there can be more or less of the quality specified. You can use 'intensifying' or 'moderating' adverbs with them, and also use them in comparative and superlative forms:

  *He was looking **very pale**.*
  *an **extremely nice** person*
  *It was a **rather dull** day.*
  *I was given the **smaller** bedroom.*
  *He's the **kindest** man I know.*

➤ See the entry **adverbs** for more information about these kinds of adverbs.

2 **classifying adjectives** (*eg* **wooden**, **oval**, **daily**, describing the class or category people or things are, *eg* what they are made of, their shape, their age):
***wooden** beads*
*a **Swedish** vase*
*an **oval** table*
***daily** papers*
*their **emotional** needs*

You can use two or more classifying adjectives one after the other to describe something. The usual order is, roughly: *time* (that is, *period* or *frequency*), *shape*, *origin or nationality* and *material*, and lastly *type*:

*an **ancient round** stone*
***long German** trousers*
*the **American electoral** system*
*the **annual financial** report*

3 **colour adjectives** (*eg* **grey**, **brown**, **pale blue**, specifying the colour of something):

***grey** skies*
*Already the leaves are turning **brown**.*
*The grass is **bright green**.*
*He was wearing a **pale blue** shirt and **dark blue** corduroy trousers.*

- You can use forms of the colour adjectives ending in **-ish** and **-y** to indicate a slight degree of a colour, or a mixture of two colours:

***yellowish-brown** walls*
*Her eyes are **greeny blue** and her hair is **reddish**.*

- The commoner colour adjectives have comparative and superlative forms:

*The grass is always **greener** on the other side.*
*He had the **bluest** eyes she'd ever seen.*

➤ See also the entry **colour.**

ⓘ The usual order, where two or more of the above three classes of adjective occur together, is *qualitative, colour, classifying*:
a large striped rubber ball
unsatisfactory academic standards

4 **emphasizing adjectives** (*eg* **complete**, **perfect**, **whole**) giving emphasis to the nouns they qualify:

*I was ill in bed for a **whole** month.*
*I've been a **perfect** fool.*
*I haven't a **single** thing to wear.*

ⓘ Notice that swear-words often function as emphasizing adjectives:
*It's a **bloody** nuisance.*

5 **specifying adjectives** (*eg* **additional**, **entire**, **principal**, **sole**) that go after a determiner and before a noun:

*Is there any **further** business?*
*We divided up the **remaining** bottles.*
*We've got three **extra** glasses.*

6 **nouns used as adjectives**:

*a pair of **gym** shorts*
*a **shopping** expedition*

> ⓘ A noun used in this way usually comes after all other adjectives and immediately before the noun it qualifies:
> *thick woollen **winter** clothes*
> *at one of their animated weekly **group** discussions*

INFLECTION OF ADJECTIVES

1 Adjectives keep the same form, whether they are qualifying a *singular* or *plural* noun:

*There was a **fine view** from the summit.*
*The walk to the summit offers a series of **fine views**.*

2 Certain one-syllable and two-syllable adjectives have an inflected *comparative* form ending in **-er**, and a *superlative* form ending in **-est**:

*thick - thick**er** - thick**est***
*narrow - narrow**er** - narrow**est***

> ⓘ It is chiefly **qualitative** or **gradable** adjectives (see above) that have inflected comparative and superlative forms.

> ⓘ Comparative and superlative adjectives usually come before any other adjectives:
> ***lower** annual profits*
> *the **finest** Indian teas*

➤ See the entry **comparatives and superlatives** for the formation of comparative and superlative adjectives.

MORE THAN ONE ADJECTIVE

1 When you are using two or more adjectives before a noun, you do not need commas between them if they are different types of adjective:

*a **long red cotton** skirt*
***dreary weekly grammar** classes*

2 A series of **classifying** adjectives before a noun should have no commas between them:

***postwar German political** thought*

3 Commas are often inserted between **qualitative** adjectives where there is an accumulation of similar qualities or where the individual qualities are being emphasized equally:

*She had a **loud, irritating** laugh.*
*It was a **grey, cold, windy** day.*

4 You can omit commas between two adjectives if you want one adjective to lead smoothly on to the next without a pause:

*She had **long slim** legs.*
*Before us lay a **vast empty** landscape.*

5 Commas are usual between a longer series of adjectives:

*She had **long, slim, nimble** fingers.*

> ⓘ In combinations of adjectives which follow the noun to which they refer, you put **and** between the last two:
> *She felt **calm and relaxed**.*
> *Our recipes are **simple, speedy, practical and delicious**.*

6 It is possible to use **and** between two adjectives coming before a noun if they represent related qualities. Notice that **but** is also possible, to convey a contrast:

*a **simple and inexpensive** method*
*a **simple but effective** remedy*

7 Before a noun, you need **and** between adjectives that refer to different parts or areas of something:

*an insect with a **yellow and black** abdomen*
*the **steel and concrete** structure*

COMPOUND ADJECTIVES

Compound adjectives are adjectives consisting of two or more words. They usually need to be written with hyphens:

*a **lemon-yellow** ceiling*
*an **odd-sounding** name*
*a **four-year-old** child*
*a **well-written** letter*

➤ See also the section on the **hyphen** in the entry **punctuation**.

OMITTING THE NOUN AFTER AN ADJECTIVE

1 In English you don't normally omit the noun after an adjective:

*Fritz has broken his arm, the **poor thing*** (or *the poor boy*, but not *the poor*).
*The **hardest part** is knowing* (not *the hardest is knowing*) *when to give up.*

2 There are some exceptions to this rule

- A noun that has already been mentioned can sometimes be omitted after an adjective that refers to it, especially a colour adjective. The typical situation is where a choice is being made:

  *'Which material do you prefer?' 'The **red**, definitely.'*
  *'I'll have coffee, please.' '**Black** or **white**?'*

  This happens particularly with *uncountable nouns*. *Countable nouns* are usually replaced by the pronouns **one** or **ones**, but these can be omitted in certain contexts:

  *I tried on several swimsuits but in the end I bought a **plain black one**.*
  *I'm looking for a pair of boots; **ordinary brown leather ones** will do.*

➤ See also the entry for **one**.

- You can often omit the noun after a *superlative* adjective, for example if it is easily understood, or has just been mentioned:

  *I was always **the youngest** in the class.*

➤ See also the entry for **comparatives and superlatives** for more information on their use.

USED WITH 'THE'

1 Certain identifiable groups of people, including whole nationalities, can be referred to by an adjective with **the**:

the blind *the brave* *the dead* *the deaf*
the elderly *the handicapped* *the homeless* *the living*
the old *the rich* *the sick* *the unemployed*
the young *the poor*
the British *the Chinese* *the Dutch* *the English*
the French *the Irish* *the Japanese* *the Manx*
the Portuguese *the Spanish* *the Swiss* *the Welsh*

Each summer more school-leavers swell the ranks of ***the unemployed****.*
The rich *just get richer and* ***the poor*** *get poorer.*
The Welsh *call this piece of furniture a 'deuddarn'.*
The Dutch *are surely the tallest race in the world.*

2 There are a few expressions of the form **the** + adjective that can be either singular or plural. They are rather formal:

He knew nothing about his father or mother, except that ***the former*** [= the first-mentioned = his father] *was Irish and* ***the latter*** [= the second-mentioned = his mother] *English.*
The Clyde Group and Forth Software both made an offer for the work and ***the latter*** *were successful.*
Was ***the deceased*** [= the dead person] *the legal owner?*

The following expressions can be singular or plural:

the accused
the deceased
the former
the latter
the undersigned

3 You can use **the** with certain adjectives to represent an abstract concept:

a natural fear of ***the unknown***

POSITION OF ADJECTIVES

An adjective may be used in any of three positions:

- before the noun (the *attributive* position):
  We came to a ***high*** *wall.*
  He was wearing ***dirty*** *overalls.*
- after a linking verb such as **be**, **become**, or **seem**, or a verb like **smell** or **feel** (the *predicative* position):
  He seemed ***uneasy****.*
  The situation was becoming ***desperate****.*
  It smells ***horrible****.*
  They all feel ***guilty****.*
- immediately after the noun (the *post-positive* position):
  We can only condemn the people ***responsible****.*

➤ See below for information about adjectives that come after the noun they qualify.

1 Most **qualitative** adjectives and all **colour** adjectives can be used both before the noun and after it preceded by a linking verb such as **be**:

*a **cloudless blue** sky*
*The sky **was blue and cloudless**.*

2 Certain **qualitative** adjectives, especially those formed from verbs, are nearly always used before the noun:

***adoring** parents*
*a **belated** thank-you*
*a **commanding** presence*
*a **thankless** task*

3 Many **classifying** adjectives can only be used before the noun. For example, you can say *my elder sister*, but not *My sister is elder.*

A list of classifying adjectives that are only used before the noun is given below:

atomic	*bridal*	*cardiac*	*countless*
cubic	*digital*	*east*	*eastern*
elder	*eventual*	*existing*	*federal*
forensic	*indoor*	*introductory*	*judicial*
live [= alive]	*lone*	*maximum*	*minimum*
nationwide	*neighbouring*	*north*	*northern*
occasional	*outdoor*	*preconceived*	*remedial*
reproductive	*smokeless*	*south*	*southern*
subterranean	*underlying*	*west*	*western*

4 Certain adjectives beginning with **a-**, and several other adjectives, listed below, are usually only used with a linking verb like **be** after the noun. For example, you can say *The baby is awake*, but you can't say *The awake baby.*

A list of these adjectives is given below:

afloat	*afraid*	*aghast*	*alert*
alight	*alike*	*alive*	*alone*
aloof	*amiss*	*ashamed*	*asleep*
awake	*content*	*due*	*glad*
ill	*ready*	*sorry*	*sure*
unwell	*upset*	*well*	

5 Some adjectives have different meanings, depending on whether they appear before the noun, or after it preceded by a linking verb:

*We came to a **dead*** [= complete] *stop.*
*Her parents are both **dead**.*
*He was driving without **due*** [= the necessary] *care.*
*The bus is **due*** [= expected] *soon.*

*We had **fine*** [= dry and sunny] *weather.*
*I feel **fine*** [= well].

*the **late*** [= recently dead] *owner of the property*
*I'm sorry I'm **late**.*

*the **present*** [= current] *Prime Minister*
*Many people were **present*** [= there].

a rather ***involved*** [= complicated] *system*
They are ***involved*** [= taking part] *in the project.*

6 When you are saying how **wide**, **deep**, **long**, or **high** something is, you put the adjective after the measurement:

The mine is seventy feet ***deep****.*
He's six years ***younger*** *than me.*
The road is at least a mile ***long****.*

➤ See the entry for **measurement** for more information on this.

WITH A PREPOSITION

Many adjectives, when used after the noun and preceded by a linking verb, are followed by a preposition + object:

Our room is ***adjacent to*** *yours.*
She is ***fond of*** *him.*
He was ***amazed at*** *their lack of knowledge.*
They were ***preoccupied with*** *their problems.*
He seems ***intent on*** *spoiling our plans.*
I'm ***interested in*** *old vases.*

A good dictionary will explain the use of prepositions with many adjectives.

FOLLOWED BY 'TO' + INFINITIVE

1 Some adjectives can be followed by **to** and a verb of *doing* or *happening*:

Naturally I'm ***reluctant to*** sign until I have more details.
This was ***bound to*** happen one day.

2 Certain adjectives expressing *reactions* can be followed by **to** and a verb of *finding* or *realizing*:

I was ***surprised*** *to see him back so early.*
I was ***relieved*** *to hear her voice.*

3 Certain adjectives, relating especially to the difficulty or advisability of an action, can be followed by **to** and a verb of *doing* or *saying*:

That was an ***idiotic*** *remark to make.*
What would be the ***proper*** *thing to do?*
The damage is ***difficult*** *to assess.*

FOLLOWED BY A CLAUSE

Certain adjectives expressing *reaction* or *feeling* can be followed by a clause, which may or may not be introduced by **that**:

I'm ***sorry*** *you're not well.*
I'm ***amazed*** *no-one was killed.*
I was ***unaware*** *that he was interested.*

ADJECTIVES PLACED IMMEDIATELY AFTER THE NOUN

There are a few fixed, mostly formal, expressions in which an adjective is used after the noun, for example the titles of certain office-bearers:

Secretary ***General***
President ***elect***

adjuncts

➢ See **adverbs**.

admit

1 If you **admit** someone you allow them into a place:
Season tickets admit visitors to all the city's museums.

2 If you **admit** something unpleasant, you agree that it is true. Here, the object can be a noun, a **that-**clause or a verb ending in **-ing**. **That** is sometimes omitted:
It would be better to admit the mistake.
He admitted having the drug in his possession.
She admits that she trusted him totally.
I have to admit you're good at your job.

adverbial clauses

An **adverbial clause** is a clause that has the same function as an adverb:

*I'll call you **when I'm ready**.*
*I got home **before it started raining**.*

Adverbial clauses express the following concepts, corresponding to functions of adverbs (see **adverbs**):

- manner:
  *It is important to do **as you are instructed**.*
- time:
  *We will see you **as soon as we get back from our holidays**.*
- place:
  *They were allowed to sit **where they liked**.*
- distance:
  *There were trees **as far as the eye could see**.*
  *The family history could be traced back **as far as 1066**.*

There are also adverbial clauses not corresponding to the main functions of adverbs. These express the following concepts:

- reason:
  *They went home **because it was getting dark**.*
  ***Since they are not here**, we cannot ask them.*

➢ See the entries for **because** and **since**.

- purpose:
  *We left early **in order to catch the last train**.*
- result:
  *They were going so fast **that they were in danger of tipping over**.*

➢ See also the entry for **so**.

- comparison:
  *His brother is older **than he is**.*
  *You're not **as** heavy **as I am**.*
- concession:
  ***Although we were tired**, we decided to keep on walking.*
- condition:
  ***If you want to**, we can go by car.*

> ⓘ Notice that the adverbial clause is often shortened by the omission of the verb:
> ***While** [**he was**] **writing**, he asked his mother for more money.*
> ***Though** [**they were**] **hungry**, they decided to walk on without stopping.*
> ***If you come**, we will take you with us. **If** [**you do**] **not**, we will meet you there.*

—— adverbs ——

The term **adverb** covers a wide range of words in English, and they have a wide range of functions. Adverbs are thought of chiefly as modifying verbs:

*They played the music **beautifully**.*

But they also modify other words:

- adjectives:
  *It is **rather** cold.*
- adverbs:
  *She arrived **very quickly**.*
- nouns:
  *You can use the bathroom **downstairs**.*
- phrases:
  *The situation was getting **completely** out of hand.*

Adverbs are also used as particles with verbs, often forming phrasal verbs:

*He came **in** and she looked **up**.*
*The plane was about to take **off**.*

TYPES

- adverbs ending in **-ly** formed from adjectives (*eg* **carefully**, **normally**, **frequently**, **suddenly**, **hopefully**)
- adverbs formed with other suffixes (*eg* **backwards**, **sideways**, **clockwise**)
- adverbs that are identical to adjectives (*eg* **fast**, **hard**, **straight**, **wrong**)
- other adverbs (*eg* **just**, **often**, **then**, **there**, **up**)
- adverbs or 'adverbials' consisting of more than one word (*eg* **all too clearly**, **little by little**)
- adverbs or 'adverbials' consisting of a prepositional phrase (*eg* **by car**, **in a dream**)

FUNCTIONS

- adverbs of manner (*eg* **gladly, quietly, separately, with a big grin**), answering the question 'how?'

  She closed the door ***quietly****.*
  The results were published ***separately****.*

- adverbs of time (*eg* **ago, for six years, soon, on Friday, yesterday**), answering the question 'when?' or 'for how long?':

  I'll see you again ***soon****.*
  He set off ***yesterday****.*
  The two sides should go on struggling ***indefinitely****.*

- adverbs of place (*eg* **abroad, aside, downstairs, on the roof, over there**), answering the question 'where?' or 'where to?':

  They live ***abroad****.*
  She walked ***downstairs****.*

- adverbs of distance (*eg* **a long way, to the station**), answering the question 'how far?'

  You've come ***a long way****.*
  There are roadworks ***all the way to the bypass****.*

- adverbs of degree or extent, answering the question 'to what extent?'

  These divide into intensifying adverbs (*eg* **very, extremely, greatly, much, badly, deeply, seriously, profoundly**), moderating adverbs (**fairly, rather, quite, slightly, pretty**), and adverbs of extent (**absolutely, completely, quite, utterly, barely, hardly, partly, almost, nearly, up to a point**):

  The new measures have ***greatly*** *improved traffic flow.*
  I was ***slightly*** *suprised.*
  We were ***utterly*** *exhausted.*

- emphasizing adverbs (**certainly, definitely, literally, really, simply**), which add force to your statement:

  I ***definitely*** *posted it.*
  You ***really*** *ought to see it.*

- focusing adverbs (*eg* **even, just, merely, only, purely, really**) which focus attention on particular words in a sentence:

  There was ***even*** *a nursery for the children.*
  I was ***only*** *trying to be friendly.*

- adverbs of frequency (*eg* **often, usually, sometimes, never, twice a week, rarely, yearly**), answering the question 'how often?':

  The rubbish was collected ***twice a week****.*
  Doctors ***rarely*** *agree on the best form of treatment.*
  I ought ***never*** *to have encouraged him.*

- sentence adverbs (*eg* **clearly, frankly, hopefully, thankfully**), used to modify a whole sentence. The adverb in these uses is like a comment on the whole statement:

***Frankly**, I'd rather not go.*
***Astonishingly**, the work was completed ahead of schedule.*

- linking adverbs (*eg* **consequently**, **furthermore**, **however**), which link one clause to the next:

  ***Consequently**, we must refuse your offer.*
  *There is, **however**, another problem.*

- adverbs specifying aspect (*eg* **financially**, **outwardly**, **technically**, **visually**), answering the question 'with respect to what?':

  *Things remain **outwardly** calm.*
  ***Financially**, we've had a successful year.*

- Adverbs used as replies (*eg* **absolutely**, **certainly**, **exactly**, **not in the least**):

  *'You do see my point?' '**Absolutely**.'*
  *'Am I disturbing you?' '**Not in the least**.'*

- Some adverbs have more than one function, for example **simply** can be an adverb of manner, an emphasizing adverb, or a focusing adverb:

  *She tried to describe it as **simply** as she could.*
  *It is **simply** impossible to tell the difference.*
  *It's **simply** a question of money.*

FORMATION

Adverbs ending in **-ly** are the commonest type.

➤ For information on spelling adverbs ending in **-ly** see **spelling rules**.

1 Some adjectives already end in **-ly** (*eg* **friendly**, **lovely**). You cannot form adverbs from these. Instead you use a phrase:
  in a friendly manner
  in a lovely way

2 Some adjectives of frequency already end in **-ly**. These adjectives also act as adverbs (*eg* **daily**, **hourly**, **monthly**):
  *There is an **hourly** bus service during the day.* (= adjective)
  *Buses leave **hourly** during the day.* (= adverb)

3 Some adjectives have two forms of adverb: one the same as the adjective, the other ending in **-ly** (*eg* **hard - hardly**, **right - rightly**). In each pair, the two adverbs have different meanings:
  *I don't think I've done it **right*** (= correctly).
  *They **rightly*** (= with justification) *deserve the publicity they are getting.*

The following adjectives have adverbs with the same form:

big	*cheap*	*clean*	*clear*
close	*dead*	*dear*	*deep*
direct	*early*	*easy*	*fair*
far	*fast*	*fine*	*firm*
first	*flat*	*free*	*full*
hard	*high*	*jolly*	*just*
last	*late*	*long*	*low*
most	*near*	*pretty*	*quick*

real	*right*	*rough*	*sharp*
short	*slow*	*sound*	*straight*
sure	*tight*	*well*	*wrong*

POSITION

1 Adverbs can be placed in the following positions in a sentence:

- at the beginning of a sentence (*initial* position):

Then we sat down again.
As a rule, candidates need to give three references.

- between the subject and the verb, or after an auxiliary or modal verb if there is one (*mid* position):

The significance ***gradually*** *dawned on him.*
He would ***surely*** *have let us know.*
Chris was ***normally*** *a pretty clear thinker.*
Did you ***ever*** *suspect him?*
We don't ***often*** *get the chance.*

- after the verb and after the object of the verb if there is one (*end* position):

The market is not operating ***smoothly****.*
Sophie welcomed her ***warmly****.*

2 Adverbs of manner, place and distance normally go in end position:

- manner:

The tendency is always to try ***harder****.*
She closed the door ***quietly****.*

One-word adverbs of manner can go in mid position when there is an object or other complement following the verb:

She ***quietly*** *closed the door.*
They ***slowly*** *walked out.*

Adverbs of manner can also go in initial position, especially in descriptive or narrative writing and usually for emphasis:

Gradually*, they began to see the answer.*

- place:

Could you bring it ***here****?*
It was time to take the children ***home****.*

> ⓘ Notice that adverbs of place never go in mid position.

3 Adverbs of time and frequency usually go in end position:

He set off ***yesterday****.*
It had happened to her ***before****.*
They try to meet ***three times a month****.*

- They can go in initial or mid position, especially for emphasis:

Yesterday *we met the Prime Minister.*
Very often *they refuse to come at all.*

- Some one-word adverbs (*eg* **already**, **eventually**, **finally**, **last**, **often**, **recently**, **soon** = quickly) also go in mid position:

  *I've **already** told him that.*
  *She **finally** agreed.*
  *When did you **last** see her?*
  *You'll **soon** make new friends.*

  ➤ See the entries for **already**, **yet**, **still** and **just**.

4 Adverbs of 'indefinite frequency' (*eg* **often**, **never**, **usually**) go in mid position, or after a negative if there is one:

*I can **never** remember her name.*
*They **usually** meet on Thursdays.*
*The boys aren't **often** very punctual.*

➤ See the entries for **always**, **often**, **quite**, **rather**, **sometimes**, **ever** and **never**.

5 Adverbs of degree and extent usually precede the word they modify. Adverbial clauses usually go in end position:

*We were **reasonably** satisfied.*
*You could have been **seriously** injured.*
*I enjoyed it **up to a point**.*
*We **strongly** disapprove.*
*This is **altogether** different.*
*They've **entirely** changed their policy.*

6 Focusing adverbs can go in many positions. They are usually close to the word or words they are focusing on:

*He called on other nuclear powers, **notably** China and the UK, to follow suit.*
*I was **especially** pleased to see my brother there.*

7 Sentence adverbs usually go in initial position, often followed by a comma:

***Sadly**, the weather wasn't good enough.*
***Apparently** the sales are better than expected.*

Sometimes they go in mid position:

*I had **unfortunately** missed her telephone call.*
*She **evidently** thought I was wrong.*

8 Some adverbs placed in initial position cause inversion of the following verb and its subject:

***Here** comes the bus.* (not *Here the bus comes.*)
***Little** do they realize how difficult it is.*

•••• advice, advise ••••

ADVICE

Advice is an uncountable noun:

I asked her advice about suitable schools for the children.
I need some advice.

ⓘ You refer to a useful suggestion or warning as **a piece of advice** or **a bit of advice**:
The most valuable piece of advice is undoubtedly to start planning early.

ADVISE

Advise is a verb. If the object is in the form of the person receiving advice, it is followed by a **to**-infinitive:

I advise you to tell the police immediately.
She advised me not to say anything.

If you do not mention the person who receives the advice, you can use a noun or an **-ing** form after **advise**:

I wouldn't advise flying in such bad weather.
We advise caution at this stage.

➤ See pages 26 and 27 for **giving advice**.

•••• affect, effect ••••

AFFECT

Affect is a transitive verb; something that **affects** you changes something in your life or in your behaviour:

How will the new tax arrangements affect you?
The century has been full of inventions that have affected the way we live.

EFFECT

Effect is most often used as a *noun*. Something that has an **effect** on you influences you:

His speech had the effect of turning the party against the Prime Minister.
She wondered what effect her decision would have on him.

You can also use **effect**, rather formally, as a verb: you **effect** something when you make it happen or carry it out:

The required changes will be effected without delay.

•••• affirmative, positive, negative ••••

1 An **affirmative** or **positive** statement is one that says that something is so:
Lions are dangerous.
The baby's asleep.

2 A **negative** statement states that something is not so, or denies something:
There are no easy answers.
He never saw her again.

3 An **affirmative** or **positive** reply is one that means 'yes'; a **negative** reply means 'no'.

4 You answer **in the affirmative** when you say 'yes'; you answer **in the negative** when you say 'no'.

5 The word **yes**, or any word that means 'yes', is an **affirmative**; the word **no**, and words such as **never, not, no-one** and **nowhere** are **negatives**.

GIVING ADVICE

You can give people advice in a variety of ways, depending on the circumstances, and on how well you know them.

INFORMAL SITUATIONS

1 I'd, I would..., I should... and **if I were you...**

A common way of offering advice to people is to say what you would do in their circumstances, using **I would**, **I should**, or the contraction **I'd**:

I should book early to make sure.

You often often add **if I were you**, or **myself**, to increase the impression of putting yourself in their place:

If I were you, I'd ask him to give you another day to think about it.
I would take the train myself.

2 you ought to and **you should**

You sound more forceful and direct if you begin your advice with **you ought to** or **you should**:

You should relax more.
You ought to save more money.

You can add **I think** to sound less assertive; or you can put your advice in the form of a negative question:

I think you ought to get a doctor to look at that cut.
I don't think you should take the dog.
Shouldn't you write and apologize?

➤ See also the use of **you could** and **why don't you?** in the entry **suggesting**.

3 you'd better

Another firm and direct way of giving advice, especially about things you think people should do for their own good, is to use the phrase **you'd better...**. Again, it's possible to sound less forceful by using the negative question form, or by adding **I think**, or a word such as **perhaps**, **maybe**, or **possibly**:

You'd better tell me the whole story from the beginning.
Perhaps you'd better take notes.
You'd better not tell them yet.

4 the informal imperative

- You can use the imperative form to give advice to someone you know well:

  Mind that nail.
  Ignore him.
  Don't lose the receipt.

- After giving advice people sometimes continue with **and** or **or**, to indicate the reason for it, or the possible consequence of not following it:

  Hold on to the rail and [= because if you do] *you'll be quite safe.*
  Keep an eye on that milk or [= because if you don't] *it'll boil over.*

FORMAL SITUATIONS

1 you must

When giving serious advice in more formal situations you can use **you must**:

You must make sure every class member signs the register before they leave.
You must write clearly or you may lose marks.

2 I advise you

You can introduce serious advice with **I advise you**; you can make it sound less forceful by using **I would** or **I'd**:

I'd advise you to give them half an hour's practice a day.
I advise you to give your description to the police as soon as possible.

ⓘ Notice these negative constructions, warning people not to do something:
I would advise against buying a flat in this part of town.
I wouldn't advise you to apply for the job.
I advise you not to sign anything yet.

➤ See also the entry **warning**.

PROFESSIONAL OR EXPERT ADVICE

1 the formal imperative

Professional or expert advice, *eg* in a broadcast or in written material, is often given in the imperative:

Keep all medicines out of the reach of children.
Do not attempt to remove pieces of glass from the wound.
Make sure the oil is very hot before cooking the omelette.

2 my advice is

Someone who is an authority on something may introduce their opinion with **my advice is**:

My advice is to avoid telling anyone about the project we're working on.

3 it's a good idea to

Experts also use the expression **it's a good idea to**:

It's a good idea to put a bit of money away every month.
It's a good idea to practise a little every day.

4 a word of advice, a piece of advice

You can introduce an important or useful reminder or tip with **a word of advice** or **a piece of advice**:

Two pieces of advice: answer all letters immediately.
One word of advice: try to get as much rest as you can.

—— affix, prefix, suffix ——

An **affix** is an element that is added to a word to form another word with a related meaning. Affixes such as **re-** and **un-**, which are added to the beginning of a word, are **prefixes**. Affixes such as **-ly** and **-ness**, which are added to the end of a word, are **suffixes**.

•••• afraid, frightened ••••

FEAR

1 **Afraid** is never used before a noun. You can say *a frightened child*, but not *an afraid child*:

He shut himself up in his flat like a frightened animal.

2 **Afraid** and **frightened** can both be used after linking verbs such as **be** and **become**, and can be followed, with various meanings, by **of** + noun or **to** + infinitive:

- You are **afraid of** or **frightened of** someone or something if you think they may harm you or make you suffer:

  Rachel had become rather afraid of dogs.
  I told him I was frightened of growing old.

- You are **afraid to**, or **frightened to**, do something, or **afraid of** or **frightened of**, doing something, if you do not have the courage to do it:

  Old people are frightened to open their doors.
  He isn't afraid of getting his hands dirty.

- You are **afraid of**, or **frightened of**, doing something bad if you are worried that you might do it:

  They were still very nervous and afraid of making mistakes.
  I was always frightened of causing offence.

- You can also be **afraid of** or **frightened of** something happening, or **that** it may happen, or may have happened:

  Cathy was afraid that she had really hurt him.
  I was frightened that my sister would discover the truth.
  She broke off, afraid of being overheard.

REGRET

1 You say you are **afraid that** something is the case to introduce a negative piece of information in a polite way. You don't use **frightened** in this way:

I'm afraid it has not been a success.
I'm afraid Mr Thomas is engaged at present.
I'm afraid I disagree.

2 You can use **I'm afraid so** and **I'm afraid not** as ways of saying *yes* and *no* regretfully:

'Is it still raining?' 'I'm afraid so.'
'Have you written to her yet?' 'I'm afraid not.'

after, afterwards

After is a preposition, conjunction, and adverb.

AS A PREPOSITION

1 Something that happens **after** a certain event or time happens in the period following it:

Are you free after lunch?
I don't like going out alone after dark.
He died on or sometime after 10th August.

2 **After** can be followed by an **-ing** form:

What are you going to do after taking [= when you have taken] *your degree?*
I'd planned to sit down with a book after putting [= when I had put] *the children to bed.*

AS A CONJUNCTION

1 **After** and its clause can come before the main clause, or it can follow it:

After she changed schools, she began to make much better progress.
Things started going wrong after he returned from the States.

2 When talking in a future context, you use the present tense in the **after** clause:

There'll be no-one to take over after she leaves (not *after she will leave*).

3 When talking in a future or present context, you can use a perfect tense in the **after** clause to make it clear that one action is finished before another begins. In a past context you can use a past perfect tense:

Please would you answer these letters after you've done that checking?
After we'd had a couple of drinks we went and did some late-night shopping.

ⓘ Notice how an **-ing** form can replace a clause if the subject of the main clause and the **after** clause are the same:
After she changed schools (or *after changing schools*) *she began to make progress.*
He actually went into publishing after he had trained (or *after having trained*) *as a teacher.*

AS AN ADVERB: AFTER, AFTERWARDS

1 **After** can be used as an adverb to mean 'later'. An expression such as **soon, shortly, some time** or **not long** always comes before it:

He was found at a friend's house not long after.

2 **Afterwards**, or AmE **afterward**, is used rather than **after** at the end of the clause, or immediately before the subject:

Let's have lunch now; and perhaps we could go for a walk afterwards.
I was rude to her at the meeting, and afterwards I apologized.

after all

1 **After all** is used at the end of a clause. It means 'in spite of what was expected':

She didn't get the job after all.
I needn't have got up early after all.

2 **After all** also means 'because it must be remembered that'; in this sense it can come at the beginning, in the middle or at the end of a sentence:

You can't expect to learn English in a few days; after all, it's a difficult language.
He's only a child, after all.

> ⓘ Notice that **after all** does not mean 'finally' or 'lastly':
> *I put the cat out, left a note for the milkman, and* ***finally*** (not *after all*) *locked up and went to bed.*

afternoon

The **afternoon** is the part of the day that starts at midday or lunchtime and finishes at about 6.00 pm, when normal working hours finish and the evening begins.

➤ For information about how **afternoon** is used, see **morning**.

again

Again means 'another time', or 'once more'. It is used in the following ways:

1 As part of a simple statement or question, usually at the end of the sentence but sometimes between the subject and the verb:

Please don't do that again.
We again succeeded in finding them.

2 At the end of a sentence, to ask someone to repeat something:

What's your name again?

3 At the beginning of a sentence, followed by a comma, to introduce another fact or piece of information:

Pollution is a big problem here. Again, industrial development in the area has contributed.

> ⓘ Notice that **again** can be used at the beginning of a sentence with the meaning 'another time'. To be quite clear what you mean, you can say **once again**:
> *Again she shook her head.*
> *Once again they played with enthusiasm.*

age

➤ See pages 32 and 33.

•••• aged ••••

Aged has two pronunciations, with different meanings:

1 You use **aged** /eɪdʒd/ in stating someone's age:
We have two sons, aged 12 and 14.

2 **Aged** /'eɪdʒɪd/ people are elderly:
He looks after his aged mother.

•••• ago ••••

You use **ago** to say how long it is since something happened. **Ago** follows the expression of time and is normally used with a past tense.

1 Something that happened a certain length of time **ago** happened that amount of time before the present:
*I saw her **only a week ago**.*
*It all happened **a long time ago**.*
***How long ago** did you buy this house?*
*We must have moved in **twenty-three years ago**.*

2 Something that happened **a year ago today** happened last year on the same day of the year as today:
He died twenty years ago today.

> ⓘ You only use **ago** for counting back from the present. When you are speaking in a *past* context, and want to count back from the time in the past that you are talking about, use **before**, **earlier** or **previously**:
> *He was looking for work, as he had lost his job **three months earlier**.*
> *We eventually found the restaurant we'd eaten at **many years before**.*
> *I'd seen the notice on the board **a few days previously**.*

AGO, FOR, SINCE

1 You use **ago** to say how long before the present something happened.

2 You use **for** to say how long a situation lasted, has lasted, or is going to last.

3 You use **since** with a date, to say how long a situation has lasted.

So, if it is now 1999, and you started your present job in 1994, you can say any of the following things about it. Note where simple past, present perfect, and perfect continuous forms are used:
*I **started** this job **five years ago**.*
*I **have been doing** this job **for five years**.*
*I **have been doing** this job **since 1994**.*
*I **have had** this job **since 1994**.*

> ⓘ Note that with **for** and **since**, you usually use the continuous form of the present perfect. Only use the simple form with the verbs **have** and **be**.

AGE

You can ask about, and state, the age of people and things in a variety of ways:

ASKING SOMEONE THEIR AGE

You ask the age of a person or thing by using **how old** with the verb **be**:

How old is your baby?
How old are these rocks?
How old are you?

STATING AND REFERRING TO AGE

1 He's twenty-one

- The commonest way of stating a person's age is by using the verb **be** and a number:
  'How old is your mother?' 'She's ninety-eight.'
  I'll be fifty this year.
  Her father died when she was only fourteen.
- A person **over** or **under** a certain age is more than, or less than, that age:
  The illness is commonest in women over forty.
  Children under two travel free.

2 She's two years old

- In fairly formal contexts, you can add **years old** after the number; note also that **years old** is needed in stating the age of *things*:
  Amy is two and a half years old.
  The car is two years old (not *is two*).
- People and things can also be so many **days**, **weeks** or **months old**:
  He's eighteen months old now, and talking all the time.
  The kittens were only a few days old.
- You can use **-old** to form compound adjectives referring to the age of someone or something, or to how long something has lasted:
  sixteen-year-old school-leavers
  an eight-month-old strike
- You can also use **year-old** to form hyphenated compound nouns referring to people:
  She teaches a class of five-year-olds.
  Jake is a lively four-year-old.

agreeing and disagreeing

➤ See pages 34 and 35.

agreement (grammatical)

➤ See **concord**.

3 He's twelve years of age

Instead of saying **years old** after someone's age you can say, even more formally, **years of age**:

He's twelve years of age and should know the difference between right and wrong.

4 a child aged three

You can refer to someone as a person **aged** a certain amount:

She had two sons, Joe, aged twelve, and Simon, aged seven.
She died aged only forty-three.

➤ See also the entry for **aged**.

5 the age of eight

■ You use prepositions such as **at**, **by**, **before** and **after** with **the age of**, to say how old someone is when they do something:

At the age of eight he was sent to boarding school.
She was already an accomplished pianist by the age of nine.
people who retire before the age of sixty
After the age of twenty-one you're free to do as you like.

6 She's my age

Someone who is **your age** is the same age as you are:

Their daughter must be about Jean's age.
At your age [= when I was the same age as you are now], *I was already in a job.*

7 in his seventies

Someone who is **in their seventies** is aged between seventy and seventy-nine:

In those days it was common for people to die in their thirties.
Mrs. Dale must be in her nineties by now.

8 a sixteenth-century building

You can date things to a certain century using an adjective formed with **-century**:

a tenth-century tombstone
life in sixteenth-century London

•••• alike ••••

If one thing is similar to another, you can say that the two things are **alike**.

1 You do not use **alike** before a noun. The adjectives **similar** and **identical** can be used before a noun instead:

The two plays are very alike.
In many ways these are very similar (not *alike*) *plays.*
We were always dressed in identical (not *alike*) *clothes.*

AGREEING AND DISAGREEING

As well as agreeing and disagreeing with the people you are talking to, you can ask them whether they agree with you.

AGREEING

1 yes and mm

You can show someone that you agree with them by saying **yes** or making the sound **mm**, or simply by nodding. You often add something after **yes**:

'I thought the evening went well.' 'Mm.'
'Horrible weather.' 'Yes, awful.'

2 tags

You often add a tag such as **I am** or **it is** after **yes**, and sometimes follow it with a question tag:

'You're on the staff council, aren't you, Stewart?' 'Yes, I am.'
'The new arrangement works fine.' 'Yes, it does, doesn't it?'

3 agreeing with a negative statement

You say **no** rather than **yes** when you are agreeing with a negative statement:

'It isn't fair.' 'No, it isn't.'
'It's not too bad.' 'No, it could be a lot worse.'

4 other expressions of agreement

- There are several answers that express agreement other than those shown above. Some common ones are **that's right**, **that's true**, **I agree** and **sure**:

  'She isn't usually late.' 'No, that's true.'
  'It's worth a try.' 'I agree.'
  'We can discuss it again tomorrow.' 'Sure.'

- You can agree with someone who has just said they like something, or they think something, by saying **So do I** or **I do too**:

  'I love it when it's still light at night.' 'Yes, so do I.'
  'Anyway, I think Geoffrey's a nice name.' 'I do too.'

ⓘ Notice that you agree with someone who says they don't like something, or don't think something, by saying **Nor do I**, **Neither do I** or **I don't either**:
'I don't approve.' 'Neither (or *nor) do I.'*
'I don't think it's necessary.' 'I don't either.'

5 more emphatic ways of agreeing

You can show strong agreement by using **absolutely**, **quite** or **exactly**:

'The police should try harder.' 'Yes, absolutely.'
'She's over-reacting a bit.' 'You're absolutely right.'

6 incomplete agreement

You indicate slight reluctance to agree with what someone has said by using the expression **I suppose so**, or **I suppose not**:

'It's the only way.' 'I suppose so.'

'It's not a very nice thing to say, is it?' 'No, I suppose not.'

You can agree tentatively by saying **I think so**, or **you're probably right**:

'She's German isn't she?' 'I think so.'

EXPRESSING DISAGREEMENT

1 disagreeing politely

You use words like **actually** and **not really** to sound polite, and you normally say **I don't think so** instead of **no**. You can also say you **don't know** or are **not sure**:

*'It's too detailed. Is that what you mean?' '**Not really, no**.'*
*'The meeting's on Wednesday.' '**I think it's on Tuesday, actually**.'*
*'Wouldn't Angela be a good choice?' '**I'm not sure if she would**.'*
*'We met last year, didn't we?' '**Actually, I don't think so, no**.'*

ⓘ Notice that you say **yes** rather than **no** to disagree with a negative statement:
'It doesn't matter very much, does it?' 'Well, yes, I think it does, actually.'
People often use **no, but ...** and **yes, but** ... before expressing an objection:
'There's a lot of evidence.' 'Yes, but it's not reliable.'
'This list isn't up to date, you know.' 'No, but it's still useful.'

2 disagreeing directly

You can disagree more directly with someone when you know them well, or when there is no particular need to be polite:

'You'll never manage that.' 'Yes, I will.'
'It takes about three hours, doesn't it?' 'No, two and a half.'

3 disagreeing strongly

Some ways of disagreeing strongly are shown in the following examples:

*'I'm not trying to avoid the issue.' '**Yes, you are**.'*
*'But that was never mentioned.' '**I'm sorry, but it was**.'*
*'We should sell everything now.' '**I disagree entirely**.'*

ⓘ Notice that when you apologize for disagreeing with someone, using such expressions as **I'm afraid** or **I'm sorry, but** ..., the impression is forceful rather than polite.

4 disagreeing angrily or impatiently

Below are some common expressions people use to express disagreement when they are angry or impatient, or are in a very informal situation:

*'They didn't deserve to win.' '**Nonsense**.'*
*'It's true.' '**Don't talk rubbish**.'*
*'She wouldn't even notice.' '**Don't be silly**, of course she'd notice.'*
*'You clearly don't care about this.' '**That's ridiculous**, of course I do.'*

...alike continued

2 You can make **alike** stronger with **very** or **very much**:

The two boys grew up together and were very alike (or *very much alike*) *in personality.*

•••• alive, live, living, lively ••••

1 Do not use **alive** before a noun. **Living**, used to talk about people, and **live** /laɪv/, used to talk about animals, can be used before a noun. They are useful alternatives to **alive**:

The animal was still breathing, but looked barely alive.
Her only living relations were somewhere in the States.
It's such a shame to keep live animals in a cage.

2 You describe someone who is cheerful, active, energetic and sociable as **lively**:

They had five lively, humorous sons.

3 When you use words like **very** or **more** with **alive**, it means 'lively and full of energy':

These eighty-year-olds are very alive, very active.
Now that he's retired, her dad's more alive than ever before.

•••• all ••••

All can be used as a predeterminer, determiner, pronoun or adverb.

AS A PREDETERMINER

1 You use **all** before predeterminers like **this, these**, and **my** when you are referring to a known group or amount. (For the use of **all of** in this way, see below.)

All the senior staff have been told.
Who's eaten all the ice cream?
All this publicity is upsetting him.
Are all these children staying with you?

2 You use **all** with demonstrative pronouns such as **this** and **those**, and possessive pronouns such as **yours** or **mine**:

Have you any children? All mine are grown up.
All those are out of date.
You know all that already.

AS A DETERMINER

1 **All** people, or **all** things, or **all** something, means 'any in existence':

All people are equal.
All paper yellows in time.
Not all mountains are dangerous.

Not all means 'some but not all':

Not all the books were lost. [= some were lost but others weren't] is the same as *Some of the books were not lost.* or *The books weren't all lost.*

ⓘ Like **all**, the determiner **every** is used with countable nouns, but notice that **every** is followed by a singular noun and verb:
All possible precautions are being taken.
But:
Every possible precaution is being taken.

2 Followed by a word such as **day**, **week** or **year**, **all** means 'for the whole of':
I had to stay up all night to finish the work.

➤ See the entry **whole** for more information about uses of **the whole**.

AS A PRONOUN

1 Speakers of American English, and some speakers of British English, regularly use the form **all of** + determiner or pronoun in preference to **all** + determiner or pronoun (see above):
All of these points are important.
I've got plenty of paint, if you've used up all of yours.

2 **All of** is the form that *must* be used before personal pronouns. You use the object form of the pronouns, **him**, **them**, **us** and so on:
We'd better remind all of them (not *all them*).
'How many of you want to come?' 'All of us (not *all we*).'

You can also say **them all** and **us all**, with **all** following the pronoun:
He loved us all equally.

3 **All** is used for clarity or emphasis. It comes in mid position like an adverb when it refers to the subject of the sentence:
Our relations were all delighted at the news.
You've all met this problem before.
These all need to be sorted out.

When it refers to the object of the sentence, **all** follows the pronoun:
She receives lots of invitations but refuses them all.
There was a fall of snow this morning, but the sun has melted it all.

4 **All** is sometimes used as a pronoun on its own followed by a relative clause; in this use it is rather formal and dated:
Have you told me all you know?
She used to charm all who met her.

ⓘ Instead of using **all** as shown above you can use the pronouns **everything**, **everybody** and **everyone**; you *must* use these when no relative clause follows. Notice that unlike **all** they take a singular verb:
Have you told me everything (or *all*) *you know?*
I think you've met everyone (not *all*) *before.*
Is everything (not *all*) *OK?*

There are a few special uses of **all** as an independent pronoun, some of which are common in newspaper reports and headlines:
I hope all is well with you.

An enjoyable time was had by all.
Shock report: schoolboy reveals all.

5 **All** is often used with a relative clause to mean 'the only thing, or things':
All I need is a bit of rest.
All he had was a small rucksack.
I'm afraid that's all I know.

6 Notice two distinct uses of **that's all**:
That's all [= there's no more] *for now.*
I wanted to warn you, that's all. [= I merely wanted to warn you.]

AS AN ADVERB

All is often used for emphasis with certain prepositions, adverbs, adjectives and conjunctions:
You've got jam all over your face.
Tell me all about it.
My hands are all sticky.
She was all alone in the house.
He's sulking, all because I forgot his birthday.

•••• all right ••••

1 Something that is **all right** is satisfactory or acceptable, or 'OK':
You look a bit worried. Is everything all right?

2 You can say that something is **all right by** someone when it is acceptable to them:
If you want to stay, that's all right by us.

> ⓘ The spelling **alright** is sometimes used, but **all right** is generally regarded as the standard spelling.

•••• allow, permit, let ••••

ALLOW, PERMIT

Allow and **permit** have similar meanings, but **permit** is more formal than **allow** and is more often used in written English, or in official notices and announcements.

1 Both verbs are used in the construction verb + object + **to**-infinitive, and both are frequently used in the passive; you **are allowed** or **permitted to** do something if you are not forbidden to do it, or if it is all right to do it:
You're not allowed to park here.
College members are permitted to borrow up to five books from the library.

2 You can also say that someone **allows** or **permits** a certain *thing* such as an activity, or that a certain thing **is allowed** or **permitted**:
The landlady didn't allow pets.
Smoking is permitted in the foyer.
Fighting isn't allowed in the playground.

3 **Allow** can have an indirect object as well as a direct one. So you can say that someone **allows** you something, or, in the passive, that you **are allowed** something:

Prisoners were allowed one letter and one visit per week.

4 You can also say that you **are allowed** *somewhere*; **permit** is not used like this:

We weren't allowed into her hospital room.
They allowed us in later.

ALLOW, LET

1 **Let** is a less formal word than **allow** and **permit** and is used with an infinitive without **to**. You say that someone **lets** you **do** (*not* to do) something:

She let me leave early.
Let me help you with those bags.

2 Passive constructions are not possible with **let**:

We were allowed to use (not *we were let use*) *the main hall.*

> ⓘ Although passive constructions are not possible with **let** by itself, they are possible with phrasal verbs formed with **let**:
> *I rang the bell and was let in by the housekeeper.*

➤ See also the entry **let**.

• • • • almost, nearly • • • •

Both **almost** and **nearly** take the mid position.

1 Both **almost** and **nearly** are used to express the idea of being close to a particular state, *eg* the achievement of a goal:

She's nearly finished.
We're almost ready.
We were nearly at the summit.

2 Both **almost** and **nearly** can express closeness to a certain amount:

The twins are nearly ten.
It was almost two-thirty by my watch when I left the office.
She's almost six feet tall.
My son-in-law calls nearly every day to make sure we're OK.

3 Both **almost** and **nearly** are used with verbs in the simple past tense to convey the ideas of:

- only just avoiding some usually undesirable circumstance:

  I nearly hit him, I was so angry.
  I almost gave up.

- not quite succeeding in achieving something:

  She tried to steal Maggie's husband, and very nearly succeeded.
  I got there almost in time to catch the earlier train.

ⓘ Notice that you can use **very** and **so**, and, informally, **pretty**, before **nearly**, but you cannot moderate **almost** in this way:
It was very nearly time to go.
He was a member of the team that so nearly succeeded in climbing the south face.

4 You can use **almost** (but not **nearly**) to convey the idea of approaching close to something in terms of qualities:
Horses are almost human; they understand everything you say.
I almost wished I hadn't won.

5 **Almost** and **nearly** are used with negatives in their own special ways:

■ **Almost** can be used with negatives such as **nobody**, **nowhere**, **never** and **none**:

There are almost no [= hardly any] *quiet pubs nowadays.*

ⓘ Notice also that you use **almost** rather than **nearly** with **any-** words:
She can wear almost anything and look good.
Almost any colour would do.

ⓘ **Nearly** is used in the combination **not nearly** as an emphatic form of 'not', usually in comparisons, especially between what is needed and what is actually the case:
Sports facilities here aren't nearly as good as in American universities.

•••• alone, lone, lonely, lonesome, only, sole ••••

ALONE, LONE

1 Someone is **alone** when they are not with anyone else:
She was standing alone in the middle of the lawn.
People may feel unsafe alone in their homes at night.

2 **Alone** is not used before a noun. You cannot say '*an alone person*'. Instead you can use **lone**:
We met a lone walker, a German lad.

SINGLE, LONE

1 A **single** man or woman is someone who is not married, or does not live with a sexual partner:
Next year I join the ranks of single career women in their thirties.

2 A **single** parent or **lone** parent is someone bringing up a family on their own:
Sheila is a lone parent with two children.
If you are a single father you have no automatic right to appoint a guardian.

LONELY, LONESOME

If you are **lonely** you are unhappy because you are alone. In AmE **lonesome** is used in this sense:

What a lonely man he is, she thought.
Hungry and lonely, they would meet in the park for the company.
He was as unhappy and lonesome as myself.

ⓘ You can use **sole** before a noun, and **alone** after a noun, with the same meaning as **only**:
Clearly television is not the only reason for falling attendances at cinemas.
Madeleine was his sole reason for wanting to return to England.
For this reason alone the patient's heart rate should be monitored.

•••• along, through ••••

ALONG

You use **along** to express movement and position on or in long narrow things such as roads, paths and rivers:

He saw a coach coming along the road.
Tall trees used to grow along these lanes.

ALONG OR THROUGH

With long narrow three-dimensional spaces such as tunnels, **along** and **through** are both possible, but **through** is preferred when the movement is not horizontal:

She turned and walked back along (or *through*) *the tunnel.*
It can take 72 hours for food to pass through the body.

THROUGH

You use **through** with periods of time, and you use **all through** or **throughout** to show that you mean from the beginning to the end of the period:

Traditions change and adapt through the ages.
Halfway through the journey he wrote the following words to a friend.
He avoided her glance all through (or *throughout*) *the meal.*

•••• aloud, loudly, out loud ••••

ALOUD, OUT LOUD

You say something **aloud** or **out loud** when you say it so that it can be heard, rather than just thinking it. **Aloud** is slightly more formal:

'If only it was that simple,' said Jay aloud to herself.
I was just thinking out loud.

LOUDLY

1 You do something **loudly** when you make a lot of noise doing it:
She was laughing loudly and helplessly.

2 **Loudly** is also often used in a comparative way:

He coughed and spoke a little more loudly.

•••• already, yet, still ••••

These three words all refer in different ways to the *present* state of things, and all three can be used to express surprise.

- You use **already** when something *has happened*. **Already** usually takes mid position:

  She's already gone.

- You use **still** when something *is continuing to happen*, or *has not stopped*. **Still** usually goes in mid position:

  She's still here.

- You use **yet** when something *has not happened* up to the present time. **Yet** often goes in end position in a present context, and in mid position, after **not**, in a past context:

  Is she here yet?
  He's back but I haven't seen him yet.
  She wasn't yet eighteen.

ALREADY

1 When using **already** to refer to things that have happened at an earlier time, you use the perfect form of verbs:

He's already told me the whole story.

> ⓘ Notice that in AmE people use the simple past where BrE uses the perfect:
> BrE: *I've already told you.*
> AmE: *I already told you.*

2 You use the present or past tense of verbs representing states and activities that exist now, or that existed in the past, earlier than expected:

You know that already don't you?
Similar techniques are already being used elsewhere.
The tanks ahead were already moving again.

> ⓘ Notice the difference between **all ready** and **already**:
> *Are those parcels all ready for posting?*
> *They've already been posted.*

YET

1 **Yet** is used with **not** or other negatives, in questions, and with words like **hardly**. When using **yet** to refer to the present you use the perfect form of verbs:

He hasn't finished his homework yet.

> ⓘ Notice that in AmE people use the simple past tense where BrE uses the perfect:
> AmE: *Did you call Irene yet?*
> BrE: *Have you rung Irene yet?*

2 You use the present tense tense of verbs which represent states or continuous activities that have not so far begun:
I'll probably be able to come, but I'm not sure yet.
We're not using the new software yet.

3 You use the past tense of verbs representing states in the past:
I had to confess that I did not yet have an e-mail address.

> ⓘ **Yet** is sometimes used rather like **still**, with **be** or **have** and a **to**-infinitive:
> *She's doing brilliantly, but her best is yet* [= still] *to come.*
> *We have yet to receive confirmation* [= we are still waiting to receive confirmation].

STILL

1 You use **still** to say that something continues to happen now, or continued to happen in the past:
Talks are still in progress.
The place was still busy at eight in the evening.

2 You use **not** before **still** when expressing surprise that something is continuing, or was continuing at some point in the past:
You're not still worrying about that, are you?
She wasn't still working in the office at eleven o'clock last night, was she?

4 You use **not** after **still** with the same meaning, and the same tense patterns, as **not yet**:
I still haven't sent in [= I haven't yet sent in] *my application form.*
I am still not convinced.
By seven o'clock the climbing party had still not returned.

➤ See also the entry **no more, any more, no longer, any longer**.

• • • • also, as well, too • • • •

POSITION

Also, **as well** and **too** have more or less the same meaning, but do not come in the same position in a sentence. **Also** goes with the verb in mid position, but **as well** and **too** come in end position:
The disease is common in cattle; it also occurs in horses.
or: *...it occurs in horses as well.*
or: *...it occurs in horses too.*

> ⓘ In AmE, **also** can be used in end position:
> *Do you have this problem also?*

INFORMAL SITUATIONS

Also is more formal than **as well** and **too**, and is therefore less common in everyday conversation:

Bring some spare disks as well. (not *'Also bring some spare disks'*)
He likes music. Books too. He's got lots of books.

AS A SENTENCE ADVERB

You can use **also** as a sentence adverb, to refer to a whole clause:

The doctor told him he should diet. Also, he needed more exercise.

In more formal English, **too**, where it refers to the subject of a clause, can come immediately after it, separated by commas:

Darwin, too, as we have seen, accepted this possibility.

ADDING A NEGATIVE IDEA TO A POSITIVE ONE

If you add a negative item after a positive one, you can use **as well** or **too** with it:

They allowed me to take the Russian exam, but they wouldn't let me take art as well.

> ⓘ Notice that **also** does not mean the same as **even**:
> *Even* (not *also*) *in old age she was beautiful.*

••• alternate, alternative •••

Alternate is an adjective (with stress on -**tern**-), and a verb (with stress on **alt**-); **alternative** is an adjective and noun (with stress on -**tern**-).

ALTERNATE

1 adjective

Alternate processes, happenings or objects are repeated several times in turn, first the one and then the other:

Add the cocoa and egg yolks in alternate spoonfuls, mixing well.
The floor is patterned in alternate strips of oak and walnut.

Something that happens on **alternate** days, or in **alternate** years, happens every two days, or every two years:

The game will be played in alternate years in Manchester and Sydney.

> ⓘ The adverb **alternately** referring to two people or things means 'first one then the other':
> *The works will be displayed alternately in Barcelona and Figueras.*
> *One house had US and Czech flags arranged alternately across its windows.*

2 verb

One thing **alternates** with another when each keeps following the other in turn:

Blazing hot days alternated with freezing cold nights.

People **alternate** between states or activities when they keep changing from one to the other:

Typically, they alternate between dieting and overeating.

ALTERNATIVE

1 adjective

An **alternative** possibility or choice is one that is available *instead of* something else:

We tried to find alternative jobs for those who were being made redundant.

2 noun

An **alternative** to something is another possibility that you can use instead:

Try grilling as an alternative to frying.
Let's see what the available alternatives are.

> ⓘ The adverb **alternatively** means 'as an alternative' or 'as another choice or possibility':
> *We could meet at lunchtime or, alternatively, we could get up early and go for a swim before work.*

•••• although, though ••••

IN SPITE OF THE FACT THAT ...

You use both **although** and **though** to mean 'in spite of the fact that', to introduce an idea that contrasts with the main statement. The **although-** clause and the **though-** clause can come before or after the main clause:

Although the subject of the novel is death, it does not feel gloomy.
The cat was only kitten-sized, though it was full grown.

> ⓘ You can use **even** before **though** to give force to the contrasting ideas, but you cannot use it before **although**:
> *Even though* (but not *even although*) *he is 24, he is still like a little child.*

BUT IT IS TRUE THAT ...

You can use both **although** and **though** to mean 'but it is true that ...', to modify the impression you have just given:

He now reads quite well, although he is still behind in maths.
The overall standard is high, though it varies from area to area.

HOWEVER ...

Though is frequently used as an adverb with the meaning 'however'. It usually comes at the end of a statement that contrasts with something already said:

I could have asked him to take the books with him; it's too late now, though.

> ⓘ Note that **though** can be used in a special word order (adjective + **though** + clause) if the verb is a linking verb such as **be**:
> *The belief that the human mind is essentially good, false though it is* [= though it is false], *forms the basis of many of our ideas.*

•••• altogether, all together ••••

ALTOGETHER

The adverb **altogether** has two main uses: it can be an adverb of extent, meaning 'completely', or it can be a word that sums up, meaning 'in total'.

1 completely

Altogether means 'completely', and is used for emphasis, *eg* with the verbs **stop** or **avoid**:

Stop drinking alcohol altogether until the baby is born.

You can also use **altogether**, *eg* with comparatives, to emphasize a contrast:

The second film was altogether [= very much] *more interesting.*

Not altogether is used as a weak form of **not**:

There were rumours of something not altogether pleasant [= something not very pleasant] *going on.*

2 in total

You use **altogether** to mean 'in total' when giving the full amount of something:

Altogether the sale raised £86 000.
There were about 40 of us altogether.

Altogether is used as a sentence adverb, meaning 'considering everything':

Altogether, Jim's career presents an amazing catalogue of successes.

ALL TOGETHER

People or things that are **all together** are all in one place; people do something **all together** when they all do it at the same time:

Someone had put my books and papers all together in one corner.
We try to do lots of things all together as a family at the weekend.

•••• always ••••

TENSES

1 You use **always** with the simple present, simple past and future tenses, and with perfect forms, when talking about regular happenings, habits and permanent states or situations:

There are always practical difficulties in getting planning permission.
He always helped her when she had problems.
I won't always be around to stop you making a fool of yourself.
He has always found Chang a difficult opponent.

2 You use **always** with progressive forms to mean 'continually', often as an expression

of annoyance:

She's always trying to make trouble for me.
He was always criticizing me.

3 You use **always** after **can** and **could** to mention or suggest an alternative course of action:

You can always have fish and chips if you don't like the food.
I could always ask Pete upstairs to help me if I have any trouble.

POSITION

1 Like other adverbs of indefinite frequency, **always** comes with the verb in mid position:

I always choose a window seat when travelling by plane.

2 In instructions, **always** comes before the verb:

Always make sure you can be seen easily at night.

ⓘ In comparisons and negative sentences where the meaning is 'at any time', you use **ever**, not **always**:
This is going to be the best film ever made in America.
No machine has ever beaten me.

•••• am ••••

➤ See the entry for **be**.

American and British English

The variety of English described in this book is mostly standard British English (BrE) but there are many references to American English (AmE) too.

Standard American English differs from British English in various ways – in pronunciation, in grammar, in vocabulary, in spelling, even in punctuation. This entry covers some of the most important differences between the two standard languages.

PRONUNCIATION

1 **general differences**

- BrE /ɑː/ + /f/, /s/, /θ/, /n/ or /m/ = AmE /a/:
  after, ask, banana, can't, dance, half, laugh, pass, path, rather

- BrE /ɒ/ = AmE /ɑː/:
  block, got, pond, probable, top

- BrE /juː/ before /t/, d/, /n/, /l/, /s/ and /θ/ = AmE /uː/
  This difference is common if the vowel is stressed:
  duty, new, tune
  However, the /j/ sound is retained in AmE in unstressed syllables:
  menu, value

- BrE final syllable /aɪl/ (spelt *-ile*) = AmE /əl/:
  futile, fragile
- In words such as **latter**, **metal** and **writing**, BrE /t/ is pronounced in AmE with the same sound as that of the /d/ of **ladder**, **medal** and **riding**.
- In most accents of AmE (but not, for example, in New York and the Southern States), /r/ is pronounced at the end of words and before consonants.
- AmE tends to give greater importance to the suffixes **-ary**, **-ory** and often **-ery:**
  monetary (BrE /-tərɪ/ or /-trɪ/, AmE /-tɛrɪ/)
  confectionary (BrE /-nərɪ/, AmE /-nɛri/)
  obligatory (BrE/-tərɪ/, AmE /-tɔːrɪ/).
- In AmE, /t/ is often not pronounced after /n/ when what follows is an unstressed vowel, as for example in *Atlantic, gentleman, international, plenty* and *winter.*

2 differences in individual words

In addition to the general differences listed above, there are many differences between BrE and AmE in the pronunciation of individual words. This is a list of some of them:

	BrE	**AmE**
anti-	/ˈantɪ-/	often /ˈantaɪ-/
depot	/ˈdɛpoʊ/	/ˈdiːpoʊ/
epoch	/ˈiːpɒk/	/ˈɛpək/
lever	/ˈliːˈvə/	usually /ˈlɛvə/
leisure	/ˈlɛʒə/	usually /ˈliːʒə/
lieutenant	/lɛfˈtɛnənt/	/luːˈtɛnənt/
moustache	/məˈstɑːʃ/	/ˈmʌstaʃ/
schedule	/ˈʃɛdjuːl/	/ˈskɛdjuːl/
simultaneous	/sɪməl-/	usually /saɪməl-/
suggest	/səˈdʒɛst/	usually /səgˈdʒɛst/
tomato	/təˈmɑːtoʊ/	/təˈmeɪtoʊ/
vase	/vɑːz/	usually /veɪs/
vitamin	/ˈvɪtəmɪn/	/ˈvaɪtəmɪn/
z	/zɛd/	/ziː/

GRAMMAR

1 gotten

In AmE, the past participle of the verb **get**, when it is used to describe a process of some kind, is **gotten**:

The situation has gotten much worse, I'm afraid.
I could see she hadn't gotten the joke yet.

2 have

The question form *Has she enough money?* is not used in AmE, which uses the forms, also used in BrE, *Does she have enough money?* and *Has she got enough money?* Similarly, instead of the negative statement form *She hasn't enough money,* AmE uses *She doesn't have enough money* and *She hasn't got enough money.*

3 past tense

The simple past tense form of a verb is often used in AmE where BrE would use a perfect tense:

Did she leave yet?
I already did my homework.

4 will/shall

Will is used rather than **shall** to form the simple future tense with first person pronouns:

We will come back again soon.

VOCABULARY

There are many differences in vocabulary between BrE and AmE, some of which are given in the following list:

British	American	British	American
aubergine	*eggplant*	*autumn*	*fall*
biscuit	*cookie*	*bonnet (of car)*	*hood*
boot (of car)	*trunk*	*caravan*	*trailer*
car park	*parking lot*	*chips*	*French fries*
condom	*rubber*	*courgettes*	*zucchini*
crisps	*chips*	*cupboard*	*closet*
drawing-pin	*thumb tack*	*first floor*	*second floor*
garden	*yard*	*ground floor*	*first floor*
handbag	*purse*	*holiday*	*vacation*
lift	*elevator*	*pavement*	*sidewalk*
petrol	*gas*	*suppose*	*guess*
sweets	*candy*	*tights*	*pantyhose*
trousers	*pants*	*vest*	*undershirt*
waistcoat	*vest*		

SPELLING

1 general differences

- BrE **-our** = AmE **-or**

  AmE: *armor, color, flavor, humor.*

- BrE **-re** = AmE **-er**

  AmE: *center, fiber, meter, theater.*

- BrE **-ll-**, **-pp-**, **-tt-** = **AmE -l-**, **-p-**, **-t-**
  In verb endings and derivatives of words ending in **-l**, **-p**, or **-t** without a single stressed vowel immediately before them, AmE generally does not double the final letter as BrE does:

  BrE: *cancelled, counsellor, equalled, traveller*
  AmE: *canceled, counselor, equaled, traveler*
  (but AmE *formatting* and *controlled* as BrE)

- BrE **-l** = AmE **-ll**
  AmE may have a double **l** where BrE has a single **l**, at the end of certain two-syllable words:

  BrE: *appal, enrol, fulfil, skilful, wilful*
  AmE: *appall, enroll, fulfill, skillful, willful*

- BrE **ae/oe** = AmE **e**

  The tendency to replace **ae** and **oe** by **e** in words derived from Latin and Greek is more strongly developed in AmE than in BrE:

  BrE: *aesthetic, amoeba, foetus, haemoglobin*
  AmE (more often): *esthetic, ameba, fetus, hemoglobin*
  (but *aerobics* and *aerosol* in AmE also)

- BrE **-ize** or **-ise** = AmE **-ize**

In verbs that can be spelt either **-ise** or **-ize**, the use of **-ize** is now standard in AmE.

As a rule, hyphens are used less frequently in AmE than in BrE, for example **dining room** rather than **dining-room**.

2 differences in individual words

BrE: *axe, catalogue, cheque, cosy, defence, grey, jewellery, licence, manoeuvre, moustache, offence, pyjamas, practice/practise, pretence, programme, sceptic, sulphur, storey, tyre*

AmE: *ax, catalog, check, cozy, defense, gray, jewelry, license, maneuver, mustache, offense, pajamas, practice, pretense, program, skeptic, sulfur, story, tire*

DATES

➤ See the entry **dates**.

•••• among, amongst ••••

➤ See the entry for **between**.

•••• amount, quantity, number ••••

AMOUNT

1 You use **amount** with uncountable nouns:

A considerable amount of research is presently going on.
I hoped I'd given her the right amount of money.

2 **Amount** is used by itself to mean a sum of money:

If the full amount is not spent, the employee pays back the difference.

QUANTITY

You can use **quantity** with both countable and uncountable nouns:

She had collected a vast quantity of shells.
Make sure you use just the right quantity of sugar.

> ⓘ Notice that **a quantity of things** can be followed by a singular or plural verb (a singular verb is more usual):
> *A small quantity of substances was sent for analysis.*
> *When we carried out the raid, a quantity of drugs were discovered.*

ⓘ **The quantity of things** refers to a precise number, and is always followed by a singular verb:
The quantity of cassettes to be manufactured is decided by the marketing department.

NUMBER

You use **number** with countable nouns:

Surely the job must have attracted a large number of people?
A small number of large firms dominate the market.

ⓘ Notice that **a number of things** is followed by a plural verb:
A number of changes are needed.

ⓘ **The number of things** refers to a precise number, and is always followed by a singular verb:
The number of cases has reached 5000.

A LARGE AMOUNT

Amount, **quantity** and **number** can be qualified by **large**, **small**, and some other adjectives of size, *eg* **vast**, **immense**, **huge**, **tiny**. The adjectives **big** and **little** are never used with them:

Parents arrive at these meetings with a large (not *big*) *number of complaints about their child's education.*
Police discovered a small (not *little*) *quantity of explosives.*

•••• an ••••

➤ See the entry for **a**, **an**.

•••• and ••••

LINKING WORDS OF THE SAME GRAMMATICAL CLASS

You use the conjunction **and** to link word groups of the same grammatical class:

I'm planning to visit Fritz and Ulrike.
They have a flat in town and a house in the country.
The weather was sunny and warm.
Samples can be quickly and accurately analysed.
She lives and works in Newcastle.

A comma usually replaces **and** before all but the last item in a list of more than two nouns:

Add the sugar, margarine, eggs and milk.
The conversation left me uneasy, suspicious and depressed.

LINKING NOUNS AND PRONOUNS

You can link personal pronouns, or combinations of nouns, proper nouns and personal pronouns, with **and**:

We seem to agree about most things, you and I.
Is something going on between you and him?
Jack and he have still got to discuss it.
He and my cousin met at university.

USED WITH COMPARATIVES

1 You can use **and** with a repeated comparative adjective to express continued increase in some quality:

I was becoming thinner and thinner.
It's a sight that is getting rarer and rarer.

2 You can use **and** before a repeated comparative adverb to express continued increase or decrease:

It rained harder and harder.
As the war drew on he spoke in public less and less frequently.
She was behaving more and more unpredictably.

ⓘ Notice that you do not repeat an auxiliary or modal verb after **and**:
Then they would sit and chat (not *they would sit and would chat*) *for ages.*
People were talking and laughing in groups.

ⓘ You can use **and** with a repeated verb to express continuous or repeated activity
I just cried and cried.
He pulled and pulled but couldn't shift it.

INFORMAL ENGLISH

Many expressions in informal English use **and**:

Try and imagine [= try to imagine] *what it must be like.*
*I'd better **go and see*** [= go to find out] *who's at the door.*
'What's for dinner?' ***'Wait and see.'***
*You should **go and see** the doctor.*
***Go and play**, there's a good girl.*
***Come and have** a drink.*
*Could you **stay and have** dinner with me?*
*I wish they'd **hurry up and do** something.*

LINKING CLAUSES

You link clauses with **and** to express a variety of meanings:

He put the children to bed and [= while] *I made supper.*
I washed the clothes and [= then] *ironed them.*
Then at the age of 60 she got married and [= which] *amazed her friends and relations.*
Tell me the truth and [= because if you do] *I'll buy you a drink.*
Say that again and you'll be sorry [= if you say that again I'll do something to make you sorry].

•••• another ••••

Another can be used as a determiner or a pronoun.

AS A DETERMINER

1 one more

Another is used with singular countable nouns to mean 'one more' of the thing mentioned:

I can get you another copy of the instruction booklet.
Another woman was attacked last night.

> ⓘ With plural nouns and uncountable nouns you use **more**, especially with **some**:
> *Have some more pudding.*
> *We'll be needing some more light bulbs shortly.*

Another can also be used, with the meaning 'more' with a particular number:

We'll wait another few [= a few more] *minutes.*
I need another three [= three more] *volunteers.*

2 different

Another is used with singular countable nouns with the meaning 'different':

We had to find another school for him.
This is another man I'm talking about, not Edward.

> ⓘ With plural nouns and uncountable nouns you use **other** if you want the meaning 'different' or 'alternative':
> *guavas, pawpaws, mangoes and other exotic fruit*

PRONOUN

1 another of

You use the form **another of** before a determiner or pronoun:

Another of his plans is to retire at 50 and see the world..
You know those funny insects we saw? There's another of them.

2 as an independent pronoun

Another can be used independently, but is quite often followed by **one**:

You just get all your problems solved when along comes another (or *another one*).
Our secretary has resigned so we're looking for another (or *another one*).

➤ For information about **one another** see the entry **each other**.

•••• any ••••

Any can be used as a determiner, a pronoun, or an adverb. As a determiner it has two distinct uses.

AS A DETERMINER

1 there aren't any seats left

You use **any** instead of **some** before plural and uncountable nouns in negative sentences, questions, after **if**, and after words like **hardly**. You also use **any** after other words which have a negative effect:

There aren't any seats left for tonight's performance.
Did they get any extra lessons in the language?
Are there any more questions on this particular issue?
If you have any problems, please ring our Customer Care unit.
They charge hardly any rent.
They do more work without any increase in pay.

> ⓘ Use **no** rather than **not any** when you want to be more emphatic, or at the beginning of a sentence:
> *I have no faith in diets.*
> *No records of the incident survive.*

2 no matter what

Any can be used in positive statements, with both singular and plural, as well as uncountable nouns. It refers to groups of people or things that actually exist:

The bank's financial adviser can deal with any aspect of personal finance. [= every aspect, no matter how difficult]
Any map would be better than none. [= whatever map exists, no matter how bad]
'When would it be convenient to call back?' 'Any time.' [= it doesn't matter when]

Any can be followed by a number:

Take any three cards from the pack. [= whichever three you like]

> ⓘ Notice the difference between **any** and **every**:
> Use **any** when you are thinking of the members of the class individually, and meaning 'it doesn't matter which':
> *Any* (not *every*) *corner of the floor will do for me to sleep on.*
> Use **every** when you are thinking of the members of the class all together:
> *Children of every* (not *any*) *race are participating in the peace festival.*

AS A PRONOUN

1 any of

Use the form **any of** before another determiner such as **the, this** or **those, my** or **your** or before a pronoun:

- **questions and negatives**

  I didn't get to any of the lectures.
  Is any of that honey left?

- **no matter which**

  She's a good teacher; ask any of her students.
  All this equipment is spare; you can help yourself to any of it.
  She has a lot of relations, any of whom could give her a home.

2 as an independent pronoun

- **questions and negatives**

  If they ask you for money, just tell them you haven't got any.
  'Could we borrow some chairs from you?' 'I'm afraid I don't have any.'
  We need some fresh milk. Is there any in the fridge?

- **no matter which**

  We specialize in antique furniture, but we'll buy any that's in good condition.
  'Which mug do you use?' 'It doesn't matter. Any'.

> ⓘ **None** has the same meaning as **not any**, but is stronger:
> *I tried to think of solutions, but there were none.*

> ⓘ **Any** refers to a possible group of three or more. When you are referring to two only, you use **either**:
> *Any child could tell you that.*
> *You can look through a telescope with either eye.*

AS AN ADVERB

Before comparative adjectives and adverbs, and before the word **different**, **any** can be used for emphasis to mean 'at all':

Can't you work any more quickly than that?
I don't suppose my case is any different from other people's.

> ⓘ Notice that **no** can be used in this way, but is more emphatic:
> *We are no different from people like Mozart and Shakespeare.*

AT ALL

The phrase **at all** is used to emphasize **any** as a determiner, pronoun or adverb:

They didn't give me any warning at all.
I'm willing to consider any work at all.
He said it was an improvement, but it really wasn't any better at all.

•••• any longer, any more ••••

➤ See **no more, any more, no longer, any longer**.

•••• anybody, anyone ••••

There is no difference in meaning between **anybody** and **anyone**. They both represent an indefinite person. Their uses correspond to the uses of **any**.

QUESTIONS AND NEGATIVES

Anybody and **anyone** are commonly used instead of **somebody** and **someone** in negative sentences, in questions, after **if**, after words like **hardly** and **scarcely**, and after other words that have a negative effect:

I never told anybody about it.
Is anyone there?
If there's anyone you'd like to recommend, let me know.
I can remember hardly anyone's name.
You clearly have more information than anybody else.

> ⓘ You never use **anyone** and **anybody** as the subject of a negative sentence:
> *Nobody saw me.* (not *Anyone didn't see me,* and not *Not anyone saw me.*)

> ⓘ Certain adjectives, such as **special**, **unusual**, **interesting**, **nice**, can be used with **anybody** and **anyone** and always follow them:
> *I don't have anyone special in my life just now.*

NO MATTER WHO

Anybody and **anyone** can mean 'any person, no matter who', and can be used in positive sentences in this sense:

It could happen to anyone.
Anyone who chooses to be a teacher deserves a medal.

- Although **anybody** and **anyone** are singular, they are both often followed by the pronoun **they**, which takes a plural verb:
  If anyone calls for him, could you let them know where he'll be?

➤ For more information see the entry **he, he or she, or they?**

•••• anything ••••

The uses of **anything** correspond to the uses of **any**.

QUESTIONS AND NEGATIVES

Anything is mainly used in negative sentences, in questions, after **if**, after words like **hardly**, and after other words such as **refuse** that have a negative effect:

I don't have anything to say.
They refused to have anything to do with it.
Is anything wrong?
There isn't anything the matter, is there?

> ⓘ You never use **anything** as the subject of a negative sentence:
> *Nothing's wrong.* (not *Anything isn't wrong*, and not *Not anything is wrong.*)

> ⓘ Notice that adjectives describing **anything** come after it:
> *I didn't notice anything unusual.*

NO MATTER WHAT

Anything can mean 'any thing, no matter what', and in this sense it can be used in positive sentences:

Anything could happen before then.
'What shall I give?' 'Anything.'

AS AN ADVERB

Notice the following adverbial uses of **anything** before **like**:

It wasn't anything like [= not nearly] *as bad as he feared.*
He doesn't look anything like [= in the least like] *my idea of a soldier.*

➤ See the entry **like** for more information about **anything like** and **nothing like**.

•••• anyway ••••

Anyway is used in several different ways.

IN FINAL POSITION

1 You use **anyway** to reinforce an argument:
Don't blame yourself. She would have died anyway [= however you had acted].

2 **Anyway** can mean 'in spite of that':
Experts said their ship would sink, but they went ahead anyway.

3 You can use **anyway** when correcting, or adjusting, a statement:
I was there three years, or two and a half years, anyway [= at least, to be more exact].

AS A DISCOURSE MARKER

You use **anyway** as a discourse marker, usually in initial position, to resume a story, refer back to a previous point, or come to a conclusion:

Anyway, do you know what he said?
Anyway, you were saying?
Think about it, anyway.
So, anyway, we'll see you on Tuesday.

•••• anywhere ••••

The uses of **anywhere** correspond to the uses of **any**.

QUESTIONS AND NEGATIVES

1 **Anywhere** is mainly used in negative sentences, in questions, after **if**, after words like **hardly**, and after other words, such as **than**, which have a negative effect:
I went to the shops, but I didn't go anywhere else.
Have you seen Luke anywhere?
Volcanoes have killed more people there than anywhere else on earth.

2 You can use **anywhere** rather like a noun, and you can use an adjective after it:
They haven't got anywhere to live.
Did you go anywhere interesting?

3 You can use **anywhere** with a negative and **near** to mean 'not nearly':
He was never anywhere near achieving his intention.

NO MATTER WHERE

You can use **anywhere** to mean 'any place, no matter where':
Click the mouse button anywhere in the menu box.

AT NO MATTER WHAT POINT

You can use **anywhere** to mean any point within a range or period:
A therapy session could cost anywhere between £20 and £35.
The woman could have been aged anywhere between 45 and 60.

ⓘ In AmE **anyplace** is often used instead of **anywhere**:
Do you have anyplace to stay?
'Where shall I put the shopping?' 'Anyplace. Here will be just fine.'

•••• apart from ••••

➤ See the entry for **besides**.

—— apologizing ——

➤ See pages 60 and 61.

—— apostrophe ——

➤ See the entry **punctuation**.

•••• appear ••••

AS A LINKING VERB

1 **Appear** is used as a linking verb like **seem** and **look**. The three verbs are not completely interchangeable, however. You can use all three before an adjective, but only **seem** and **appear** before a **to**-infinitive or **that**-clause:
They all appeared (or *seemed* or *looked*) *cheerful as they rushed away.*
She appeared (or *seemed*) *to be nervous.*
He appears (or *seems*) *not to notice insults.*
It appears (or *seems*) *that no treatment will be needed.*

ⓘ You use **seem** rather than **appear** when you are giving your own personal opinion:
He's working in a pub at present; it seems (not *appears*) *rather a waste of his talents.*

2 **Seem** and **look** can be followed by **like**, but this construction is not usual with **appear**:

That seems like (but not *appears like*) *a good idea.*

'COME INTO VIEW'

When someone or something **appears** somewhere they come into view, arrive, or can be seen there:

A figure wearing a backpack appeared in the distance.
She has appeared on television several times.
He is due to appear in court tomorrow on a charge of robbery.

'COME INTO BEING' OR 'COME INTO USE'

Something new **appears** when it comes into existence, or becomes available:

The cheese called Port Salut appeared in 1873.

.... appreciate ....

1 You say you **appreciate** something if you value it or are grateful for it. If you say you **would appreciate** something, you mean you would like to get it:

I appreciate your help.
We would appreciate your suggestions.

2 **I'd appreciate it if ...**

Notice that when asking someone to do something you say, *eg*:

I'd appreciate it if (not *I'd appreciate if*) *you came along tonight.*

.... arise, rise ....

Arise and **rise** are both irregular verbs:

arise, arises, arising, arose, arisen
rise, rises, rising, rose, risen

ARISE

Something such as a situation, possibility or difficulty or question **arises** when it begins to exist:

A legal problem has arisen concerning the defendants.
We can lend you the money should the need arise.
There are certain questions arising from the report.

RISE

1 To **rise** is to go higher or go upwards:

The figure has risen to over 100 000.
The cliffs rise steeply out of the calm sea.

2 You **rise** when you get up in the morning. You also **rise** when you get up from sitting:

Graham and I had risen early.
She rose to her feet.

.... around, round, about ....

Around, **about** and **round** can all be prepositions or adverbs, and they have a lot of the

APOLOGIZING

You apologize to someone when you have upset them or caused them trouble or inconvenience. People also apologize sometimes when they say something wrong or inaccurate and have to correct themselves. There are a number of informal and formal ways of apologizing.

WHEN YOU UPSET SOMEONE

1 informally

The usual way to apologize to someone when you have upset them, or cannot do what they ask you, is to say **sorry** or **I'm sorry**. You can use words like **so**, **very**, **really**, **extremely**, and also **terribly** and **awfully** before **sorry** to sound more apologetic:

Sorry I'm late.
I'm sorry I was rude to you.
I'm so sorry, I meant to be at the station to meet you.
Sorry to disappoint you.
'Have you got change for a pound coin?' 'No, sorry.'

2 more formally

- In more formal circumstances you can say **I apologize**:

I apologize for taking so long to reply.
I must apologize to you for my unintentional rudeness.
I apologize if I seemed uncooperative.

- More formally still, you can say **please accept my apologies** or **I owe you an apology**, or **forgive me**:

Please accept my apologies. This has never happened before.
I owe you an apology for disbelieving you.
Forgive me for telephoning you so late.

- People making official apologies often use the verb **regret**:

The Institution regrets any misunderstanding that may have arisen.
We regret that we cannot provide data or answer queries.

WHEN YOU INTERRUPT OR DISTURB SOMEONE

You usually say **excuse me**, or **sorry to interrupt** (or **bother**, **disturb** or **trouble**) **you**, when interrupting or disturbing someone:

I'm so sorry to disturb you, but could you sign this piece of paper?
Excuse me, sir, I've brought your coffee.

WHEN ASKING A STRANGER SOMETHING

You use **excuse me** when you want to ask strangers something, or when you need to pass them:

Excuse me, is that a spare chair?
Excuse me, please, could I get past?
Excuse me, could you tell me how to get to Circus Place?

WHEN YOU ACCIDENTALLY DO SOMETHING UNDESIRABLE

1 If you bump into someone accidentally, or stand on their toe, you say **I'm sorry** or **I beg your pardon**:

Was that your arm? I'm so sorry.

2 If you do something a bit embarrassing, such as burp or sneeze or hiccup, you can say **excuse me** or **I beg your pardon**.

WHEN YOU HAVE TO LEAVE SOMEONE

If you have to leave someone, or have to interrupt a conversation with them, you say **excuse me**:

Excuse me while I answer the telephone.
If you'll excuse me, I have a train to catch.
Would you excuse me for a few moments while I attend to the meal?

WHEN YOU MAKE A MISTAKE

People often say **sorry** or **I beg your pardon** when they have said something wrong and have to correct themselves:

That means 'x' is seven, sorry, 'x' is three and 'y' is seven.
That equals 26, I beg your pardon, no it doesn't.

WHEN YOU HAVEN'T HEARD WHAT SOMEONE HAS SAID

When you haven't heard what someone has said properly, and want them to repeat it, you can say **sorry?** or **I'm sorry?** or more formally, **I beg your pardon?**:

I beg your pardon, what was that figure?
'This is a good example of a skeuomorph.' 'Sorry?'

AmE speakers say **excuse me?** and sometimes **pardon me?** when they haven't heard properly:

'You're on.' 'Excuse me?'

ACCEPTING AN APOLOGY

1 When you accept someone's apology in informal circumstances, you can say **it's OK** or **that's OK** or **it's all right** or **it doesn't matter**, or **don't worry about it** or, very informally, **'forget it'**:

'Sorry I can't take you for a drink.' 'That's OK.'
'I'm sorry for not coming to see you.' 'It's perfectly all right.'
'Sorry I'm late, sir.' 'That's all right.'
'Sorry I got angry.' 'Forget it.'
'I'm so sorry I forgot the paper.' 'It doesn't matter.'

2 **more formally**

You can say **don't mention it** or **think nothing of it** when accepting an apology in more formal circumstances:

'I apologize for getting carried away.' 'Think nothing of it.'

same meanings and uses.

> ⓘ In any use where **around** and **round** are both possible, AmE prefers **around**. Generally speaking, AmE speakers do not use **about** except in the sense 'approximately'.

ROUND AND AROUND

1 moving in a circle, or surrounding

Round and **around** both convey the idea of moving, or being, in a circle surrounding something:

The moon moves in its orbit round (or *around*) *the earth.*
Gather round (or *around*) *and watch.*
Our office is just round (or *around*) [= beyond or after] *the corner.*

2 wrapping

One thing has another **round** or **around** it when it is wrapped in it:

All his books had brown paper wrapped round (or *around*) *them.*

3 turning and revolving

Things go **round** or **around** when they revolve or rotate. People turn **round** or **around** when they turn to face in the opposite direction:

The wheels go round and round (or *around and around*).
He swung round (or *around*) *to face me.*

4 focusing

Things revolve or centre **round** or **around** someone or something when they have them as a focus:

Ken's whole life revolved around surfing.

AROUND, ROUND AND ABOUT

1 in various places and directions

Things that are placed, or move, **round**, **around** or **about** an area are in various places, or move in various directions, within it:

Clothes were strewn about (or *round* or *around*) *the room.*
The director will show the Queen round (or *around*) *the exhibition.*
Stop waving your fork about (or *around*) *like that.*

2 People are **around** or **about** when they are somewhere close by:

I called at your house but there was no-one around (or *about*).
Stay around. I might have a job for you.

3 There is a lot of something **around** or **about** if it is common:

There are plenty of new travel books around (or *about*).
There's a lot of flu about (or *around*).

LACK OF PURPOSE

About and **around** are both used to suggest a lack of serious purpose:

I hate fiddling around (or *about*) *doing nothing.*
Well we can't sit around (or *about*) *here all day.*

ⓘ Phrasal verbs formed with **about** and **around** in this sense are quite common, and most of them can use either particle. Examples are **wait about** or **around**, **fool about** or **around**, **mess about** or **around**.

APPROXIMATELY

About, and **around**, and the phrase **round about** are all used to mean 'approximately':

I'll see you about (or *around* or *round about*) *ten, then.*
Most banks still charge around (or *about* or *round about*) *19%.*
She died round about (or *around* or *about*) *1970.*

PHRASAL VERBS

Some additional senses of **around** and **round** are found in phrasal verbs, for example:

1 People **come round, call round** or **drop round** to see you, or you **go round** or **pop round** to see them, when you visit each other:
Maureen popped round to see what we were doing.

2 You **talk** someone **round**, or **win** them **round** when you get them to agree with your point of view.
She hasn't agreed yet, but I think I can talk her round.

3 People **come round** or **are brought round** when they recover from unconsciousness.
Some fresh air might help to bring him round.

4 Things **are passed round** or **handed round** when they are distributed or passed from one person to another.
The jury was asked to pass the letter round.

5 Things **are changed round** or **around** when they exchange places or positions, or are put in different positions:
The office-bearers are changed round (or *around*) *every year.*

6 You **shop round** or **around** when you find the best place to buy something, and you **phone round** or **around** when you make similar enquiries by telephone.
I'm sure we can get a cheaper one if we shop around.

7 You **skirt round** or **talk round** an issue when you avoid talking about it. You **get round** a difficulty when you find a way of avoiding it.
Transport might be a problem but we'll get round it somehow.

•••• arrive, reach ••••

Arrive is used without an object. **Reach** takes a direct object. The following sections show how the two verbs are used in various senses.

GET TO A PLACE OR POINT

1 **Arrive** is regularly used with the preposition **at**. You **reach** a place or point or you **arrive at** it:
When she arrived at (or *reached*) *the station she bought herself a coffee.*
I arrived at (or *reached*) *the theatre early.*
We've reached a critical stage in this delicate process.

2 But you **arrive in** a country or city:
Gorbachev arrived in Berlin yesterday.
Some 7000 people arrived in special trains.

3 **Arrive** can also be used independently or with the preposition **from**:
He will hear about it before he arrives (but not *before he reaches*).
They had just arrived from Paris.

4 **Arrive** can be followed by the words **home**, **here**, **there**, **somewhere** and **anywhere** without any preposition:
When he arrived home the pain in his head was getting worse.
They'll be arriving here about midnight.
I hate arriving anywhere late.

DECISIONS AND CONCLUSIONS

You **arrive at**, or **reach**, or **come to**, a decision or conclusion when you make it or form it:
I had arrived at (or *reached*, or *come to*) *a surprising conclusion.*
As she sipped her tea, Elizabeth reached (or *arrived at*, or *came to*) *a decision.*
The agreement was reached (or *arrived at*) *at a meeting of foreign ministers in Luxembourg.*

articles

In English there are two articles, **the definite article** and **the indefinite article**.

WHAT ARE ARTICLES?

Articles indicate whether you expect the hearer to know which things or people you are referring to. You can indicate, by using an article, or by leaving it out, whether you are talking about *particular* things or people, or about things or people *in general.*

WHEN DO YOU NEED TO USE ARTICLES?

Singular countable nouns normally need a determiner of some kind, whether you are talking in general, or in particular:
the cup, a cup, this cup, each cup, every cup

Plural nouns and *uncountable nouns* can be used without an article or other determiner:
cups and teaspoons
crockery and cutlery

THE DEFINITE ARTICLE 'THE'

You use the definite article **the** to refer to things or people when you expect your hearer or reader to know which ones you mean:
I'm afraid I'll have to go back to the office tonight [= where you know I work].
I'd better go and cut the grass [= which grows in my garden].
I've got an appointment with the dentist [= my dentist].

➤ See the entry **the** for more details about its use.

THE INDEFINITE ARTICLE 'A' OR 'AN'

You use the indefinite article **a** or **an** with singular countable nouns, chiefly in the following three situations:

1 **a thing or person not known to your hearer**:
I'll be staying with a friend in Heidelberg.
I've just been reading a book about whales.

You use **a** and **an** typically when you are mentioning a person or thing for the first time. When that person or thing is referred to again, the definite article **the** can be used:
'I'm going to a film tonight.' 'What's the film called?'

2 **any member of a class:**
A computer is indispensable these days.

3 **after a linking verb**:
She's a teacher.

ⓘ You cannot omit the indefinite article when saying what job a person does:
She's a lecturer (not *she's lecturer*).
With a unique post or position, no article is necessary:
He's been managing director since 1989.

➤ See the entry **a, an** for full details about the use of the indefinite article.

SOME AND ANY

You use the indefinite article **a** or **an** with *singular countable nouns*. **Some** and **any** can be used with *plural countable nouns*. They function as plural forms of **a** or **an**.

➤ See the entries **some** and **any** for more information about their use.

NO ARTICLE

1 **with uncountable nouns and plurals**

When using plurals and uncountable nouns to refer to things and people *in a general way*, you do not need any article:
He's always been afraid of cows.
They're increasing the tax on wine.

2 **with proper names**

In general, you do not use an article with proper names, such as the names of people, companies, countries, continents, states, counties, towns, streets, lakes and mountains:
Jamie starts a job in London next week with Reuters.
He was planning to go sailing on Lake Geneva and climb Mont Blanc.
Where is Professor Donaldson lecturing today?

- But you can refer to *families*, or to *married couples*, by a plural form of their surname, with **the**:
  Should we invite the Kellys?
- You also use **the** with the following classes of *place names*:
  rivers: *the Amazon*
  seas and oceans: *the Pacific, the Irish Sea*
  islands: *the Isle of Man, the Scillies, the Canary Islands, the British Isles*
  mountain ranges: *the Alps, the Cairngorms*
  deserts: *the Sahara*

certain countries if they have a plural form, or include a term such as **kingdom**, **union** or **republic**: *The Netherlands, The United States, The Czech Republic, The United Kingdom*
hotels: *The Adelphi, The Great Northern Hotel*
cinemas and theatres: *The Lyceum, The Playhouse*
art galleries and museums: *The Serpentine Gallery, The National Museum*

- Newspapers usually include **the** in their name, or are referred to by **the**: *The Times, the Independent*

3 off to school, still in bed

Some countable nouns can be used without an article. This usually happens in certain expressions concerning places and movement beween them. The commonest expressions of this kind are shown in the examples below:

She's gone to school.
He was taken to hospital with pneumonia.
They go to church regularly.
I got to work late.
I was at home yesterday but I'll be in town today.
Is he still in bed?
A lot of students are shy about asking questions in class.
Some animals are active by day and some at night.
Do you prefer to travel by plane (or *by air*) *or by boat* (or *by sea*)?
He never writes but he sometimes gets in touch by phone.
You'll have a reply from us by post tomorrow.

> ⓘ Notice the difference between *'She wasn't at school* [= she didn't attend school] *today'* and *'She wasn't at the school* [= I couldn't find her in the school building] *when I went to collect her.'*

4 with the possessive 's

You do not use an article with possessive **'s** forms:

I discovered James's letter in my drawer.
Bulgaria's rail network
I'm concerned about Dorothy's reputation.

5 after 'and' or 'or' between nouns

You do not need to repeat **the** or **a** before the second of two nouns linked by **and** or **or**:

I realized I'd left the towels and swimming costumes at home.
I was furious with myself for not bringing a notepad or pencil with me.

6 after 'kind of', 'sort of' and 'type of'

You can omit **a** or **an** after expressions such as **sort of** and **type of** when they are used before singular countable nouns:

What kind of house have they got?
A new variety of banana has been developed.
Some people like that type of bed.

7 seasons, festivals, months and days of the week

- You don't use an article with months, days of the week, or festivals, when you are referring to the one coming next, or the one just past:

  They're moving in August.
  We're hoping to publish her book next April.
  Last Easter we went climbing in Austria.

- You can refer to seasons in general with or without **the**:

  The Botanic Gardens are at their best in autumn.
  You tend to fall in love in the spring.

- You can treat seasons, festivals, months and days like countable nouns and use articles with them when you are referring to particular ones:

  We visited Zambia in the autumn of 1993 (or *in autumn 1993*).
  He resigned in the January of 1989 (or *in January 1989*).
  I haven't seen my brother since the Christmas before last.

➤ See the entries **days**, **months** and **seasons** for more information.

8 illnesses

Most illnesses are uncountable nouns and are therefore used without an article:

She had pneumonia twice last year.
I think I've got flu again.

> ⓘ But notice that **cold** is a countable noun and takes an article:
> *Have you got a cold?*

9 entertainments and the media

- **television**

  You use **television** without an article unless you are talking about the television set itself:

  It's ages since I saw a good film on television.
  I'll just stay at home and watch television.
  Shall I turn the television on?

- **the radio**

  You usually use an article with **radio** whether you are talking about the programmes on it, or about the actual set:

  There was a good programme about genes on the radio last night.
  I listen to the radio a lot.

- **the cinema** and **the theatre**

  Cinema and **theatre** are normally used with an article:

  We go to the theatre a lot, but I don't know when we last went to the cinema.

USING ARTICLES WITH OTHER DETERMINERS

1 with 'both' and 'all'

- You can omit **the** after **both**, and after **all** when it is followed by a number:

  Morals play an important part in both novels (or *both the novels*).
  He paid for all five brothers.

- You do not need an article in expressions like **all night** and **all day**:

  The medical registrar had been working all night.

2 in referring to parts of the body

- **I've broken my wrist**

  You use a possessive determiner, rather than **the**, when saying what someone does to part of their body:

  Mario has hurt his leg.
  She wound a long scarf round her neck.

- **shot through the heart**

  However, in prepositional phrases when a part of the body is the object of a verb, or the subject of a passive verb, or of a linking verb such as **be,** you use **the**:

  The 29-year-old Catholic had been shot through the heart.
  He looked her straight in the eye.

3 no article with demonstrative or possessive determiners

You do not use articles with possessive or demonstrative determiners:

Robert Chambers once lived in this house (not *the this house*).
Here's your bedroom (not *the your bedroom*)

➤ For more information see the entry **possessive determiners and pronouns**.

•••• as ••••

As can be a conjunction or a preposition.

THE CONJUNCTION

1 of time

As is a conjunction of time, meaning 'at the moment that' (often used with **just**) or 'during the time that':

She reached the gate just as the van was disappearing down the road.
The weather was dull as I stepped off the train.
These thoughts occupied my mind as I tried to sleep.

> ⓘ **As** is not used quite like **when** or **while**. **As** often conveys an idea of continuous progress, especially of one thing in combination with another.

2 of reason

As is used like **seeing, since** or **because**:

They allowed him to stay the night, as he was obviously homeless.
As I was the oldest, I had to look after the others.

3 conjunction of manner

As is a conjunction of manner, meaning 'in the way that':

We'll keep things as they are for the moment.

ⓘ Although **as** in this sense often introduces a clause, it can be followed by other grammatical forms, *eg* an adverb, a past participle, or an adjective (which all imply a clause) or by a reduced clause in which **as** has the function of subject:
■ (reduced clause:) *If, as **frequently happens**, the program crashes, restart your computer.*
■ (adverb:) *The truth, as **always*** [= as it always is], *is more complex.*
■ (past participle:) *I'm enclosing a copy of the report, as **requested*** [= as was requested].
■ (adjective:) *Children were arriving for school as **usual*** [= as was usual].

3 conjunction of concession

As a conjunction of concession, **as** means 'though' or 'although'. In this sense it uses the inverted word order adjective or adverb + **as** + clause:

Improbable as it seems, he must have been in love with her.
Try as we may [= however hard we try] *we cannot win every time.*

THE PREPOSITION

1 You use **as** in describing, or referring to, the roles, jobs or functions of people or things:

She worked as a taxi-driver for four months.
As her sister, I was closer to her than anyone.
I wish you wouldn't use my saucers as ashtrays.
Her resignation came as a complete surprise.

ⓘ Notice the difference between **like** and **as**. **Like** is used in comparisons, but **as** on its own is not used in this way:
As his mother [she was his mother], *she couldn't help loving him.*
She loved him like a mother [although she wasn't his mother].

ⓘ Notice also that you can use phrases like **as a boy** and **as a young man** to mean 'when he was a child, or a young man':
As a young doctor he had met similar cases.

2 Some verbs of *regarding* and *describing* take **as** in a variety of constructions after their object:

Fortunately she viewed the whole incident as a joke.
He sees everyone as a potential customer.

➤ See the entries **same** and **so** for more information about the constructions **same … as** and **so … as**.

.... as ... as ....

IN COMPARISONS, TO EXPRESS EQUALITY

You use the construction '**as** something **as** something else' to express equality in comparisons:

They worked as hard as I did to get the project going.
He's tall, though not as tall as your brother.

As ... as can be followed by:

- a *clause* with subject and verb:
  *She feels as strongly about it as **I do**.*
- a *personal pronoun*, usually in the objective case:
  *They're as eager as **me*** (or, in very formal English, *as **I***).
- a *noun, noun phrase* or *proper noun*:
  *I'm not as optimistic as **Michael**.*
- an *adverb representing a clause*:
  *He was as helpful as **ever*** [= as he always is].
- an *adjective representing a clause*:
  *Jack's voice was as loud as **usual*** [= as it usually is].
- a *past participle representing a clause*:
  *Policies have not worked as smoothly as **expected*** [= as was expected].

USE OF AUXILIARY VERBS

1 After **as ... as**, if you are referring back to the verb in the main clause, you usually use an auxiliary verb or modal verb on its own:

*You **look** as fit as you **did*** (rather than *as you **looked***) *20 years ago.*
***Stretch** your arms out as wide as you **can**.*

2 You may need to add an auxiliary verb to avoid ambiguity:

*I **don't punish** you as often as your mother **does*** (rather than *as often as your mother*, which could mean 'as often as I punish your mother').

AS MANY AS, AS MUCH AS

The phrases **as many as** and **as much as** occur frequently in discussions of amount and extent:

We ought to get as much done as we can by Thursday.
He drank several pints, though not as many as usual.
Try to relax as much as possible.

> ⓘ **As many as** and **as much as** are often used to emphasize an amount:
> *Seats for the opera could cost as much as £100 each.*

FIXED COMPARISONS

The construction **as ... as** provides the framework for a lot of fixed comparisons:

She turned as red as a beetroot.

ⓘ In AmE, the first **as** is sometimes omitted:
She's slim as a board.

ADDITIONAL NOTES

1 You can use a number of modifying words and phrases with **as ... as**. They include **almost**, **every bit**, **just**, **nearly**, **not nearly**, **not quite**, **nothing like**:

You're nearly as old as I was when I had my first child.
I don't think it's quite as cold as it was yesterday.

2 You can omit the second **as** and what follows it if the meaning is already clear from the main clause:

Last year was the best ever for sales, so it's not surprising that this year hasn't been as successful [= as successful as last year].

2 After a negative, the first **as** is sometimes replaced by **so**:

He's not quite so confident of success as he used to be.

•••• as for, as to ••••

As for and **as to** are both used to mean 'regarding' or 'with regard to'. **As for** can be used to refer to people or things. **As to** is mostly used to refer to things:

There is a lot of uncertainty as to the possible cost.
As for Jim, he's respected because he can box a little.
As for the other movements of the symphony, they are very exciting.

•••• as if, as though ••••

As if and **as though** mean the same. You use them to talk about the way things look or seem.

PROBABILITY

You use **as if** and **as though** with verbs like **look**, **feel**, **sound** and **seem** to express **probability** in the present or the past:

It sounds as if (or *as though*) *there's more than one of them.*
He looked as if (or *as though*) *he hadn't shaved.*

UNREAL COMPARISONS

1 You use **as if** and **as though**, to say how something seems, or seemed, even though it is not, or was not, the case:

I feel torn apart; it's as though (or *as if*) *I'm bleeding inside.*
It's as though (or *as if*) *you've stopped living; your mind goes dead.*

2 You use the construction **it's not as if**, or **it's not as though**, as an emphatic way of saying that something is not the case:

It's not as though (or *as if*) *I were writing a completely new book.*

•••• ask ••••

You use the verb **ask** in a large variety of constructions, in relation to three broad functions: *finding things out, making requests, and inviting.*

FINDING THINGS OUT

You **ask** someone something when you address a question to them in order to get information from them, or find something out.

1 followed by a clause

- **Ask** is followed by a clause introduced by **if** or **whether** when the answer to the question is 'yes' or 'no':
  Ask them if they are having the same problem.
  He asked me whether I had taken the cat to the vet.

ⓘ Notice that you never put **to** before the person to whom the question is addressed.

- When the question does not expect the answer 'yes' or 'no', you follow **ask** with a clause beginning with a **wh-**word like **what**, **how**, **when**, **where** or **why**:
  I asked what would happen if I didn't pay.
  The children were asked what colour the card was.

ⓘ Notice that you do not use the inverted construction *auxiliary verb* (or **be**) + *subject* in the clause that follows **ask**, as you do in a direct question:
I asked where her suitcase was (not *where was her suitcase*).

- **Ask** is also used in reporting direct questions:
  'What do you find to do all day?' asked my mother.

2 with a direct object

You often use **question** as the direct object of **ask** (*Stop asking questions*), but there are a number of other words, referring to things that that people want to find out, that are also used as the direct object of **ask**:

*The porter asked **my name**.*
*Nobody asked **my opinion**.*
*She stopped to ask **the way**.*

3 used intransitively

You can use **ask** without an object, independently or followed by **about**:

The police were asking about Boris.
They offer credit; just ask at the counter.

MAKING REQUESTS

1 ask for ...

- You **ask** someone **for** something when you want them to give it to you:
  He never asked for money.
- You can **ask for** something **to be done**:
  She wrote to the school and asked for him to be excused.

- You **ask for** someone when you say you want to speak to them:
  A man came in, asking for you.
  Go straight to reception and ask for Mrs Thompson.

2 getting people to do things

If you want someone to do something you **ask** them **to do** it, or **ask** them **if** they **would do** it:

A Japanese couple asked me to take a photo of them.
She asked me if I would chair the meeting.

3 getting permission, or arranging to do something

When you want to do something you **ask to do** it, or **ask if** you **may** or **can, do** it:

She asked to make one final phone call.
He asked me if he could borrow my dictionary.

4 inviting and summoning

You **ask** someone somewhere when you invite them, or summon them, there:

They've asked us to their New Year's Eve party.
The boss asked me into his office.

➤ See the entry **requests** for ways of asking people to do do things, or give you things.

•••• as long as, so long as ••••

IN COMPARISONS

As long as occurs frequently in comparisons about length. **So long as** is sometimes used after a negative:

The book is about four times as long as it needs to be.
The journey home never seems quite so long as the outward journey

WITH 'POSSIBLE' AND 'CAN'

As long as is often used with the adjective **possible** or the verb **can** to mean the maximum period of time that can be managed:

He resolved to lead a normal life for as long as possible.
I resisted as long as I could.

USED FOR EMPHASIS

As long as can be used to emphasize the length of something, *eg* a period of time:

The life cycle of the adult worm can be as long as six weeks.
This surface may stay in good condition for as long as five years.

IN CONDITIONAL SENTENCES

1 **As long as** and **so long as** are both used as conjunctions of condition, with a meaning roughly similar to 'if':

The patient's blood pressure remains stable as long as (or *so long as*) *he or she is lying down.*

2 You also use **as long as** and **so long as** to mean 'on condition that', or 'provided that':

He doesn't care what I do, as long as I let him know where I am.

ⓘ Notice that in referring to the future, a present tense rather than a future tense is used after **as long as** or **so long as**:
So long as you set a time limit, you will have confidence and control.
I shall resist for as long as I can.

assertive and non-assertive

Certain words and phrases, such as **some**, **a few** and **a lot**, are used mainly in affirmative, or positive, statements. Grammarians call these words *assertive.* Other words and phrases, such as **any**, **at all** and **yet**, are used mainly after a negative (such as **not** or **never**), or a broad negative (such as **hardly** or **scarcely**), or in questions, or after **if**, and are called *non-assertive.*

as soon as

THE CONJUNCTION

1 Something happens **as soon as** something else happens, when it happens immediately after it, or at the same time:

As soon as I heard her voice I knew that something was wrong.

2 Notice that **as soon as** can refer to repeated action, with much the same meaning as **whenever**:

As soon as she expressed any opinion he felt sympathy for the opposite view.

ⓘ In references to the future, a simple present tense is usual after **as soon as**, but a perfect tense can be used to indicate completed action. In references to the past, a simple past tense is usual after **as soon as**, but the past perfect is sometimes used to indicate completed action:
As soon as you reach the road you'll see the signpost for Brighton.
Insurance cover will begin as soon as you have paid the deposit.
He got up as soon as the alarm went off.
As soon as I'd said it, I realized my mistake.

AS SOON AS POSSIBLE

As soon as is frequently used with **possible**, meaning the earliest time that can be managed:

I will get a job and pay you back as soon as possible.
I had to find shelter as soon as possible.

as well

➤ See the entry **also, as well, too**.

•••• as well as ••••

As well as is used to link pairs of words or phrases of the same grammatical class or part of speech. When you refer to one thing **as well as** another you are emphasizing that you mean the first *in addition to* the second. You are implying that the second thing is probably known about already:

- nouns or noun phrases:

  ***Locals** as well as **tourists** left the state to escape violence.*

- adjectives and adjectival phrases:

  *Behaviour of this sort can be **frightening** as well as **disruptive**.*

- adverbs and abverbial phrases:

  *It would be **economically** as well as **politically** disastrous.*
  *She misbehaved **at school**, as well as **at home**.*

- verbs:

  When **as well as** links verbs, the verb that comes after **as well as** is in the form of a verbal noun ending in **-ing**:

  *The waste **threatens** resources as well as **polluting** the land.*

- infinitives:

  The word **to** is usually omitted before the infinitive that follows **as well as**:
  *She likes **to consult her staff** as well as **delegate** responsibilities to us.*

•••• at ••••

At has two main functions: as a *preposition of place*, and as a *preposition of time*, but it has a number of other important uses too.

AS A PREPOSITION OF PLACE

1 position or location

You use **at** to refer to an exact location:

I promised to be at the station to meet him.
Mark stood at the corner of the street.
Jean gave Teresa a hug at the street door.

2 places of activity

When you are thinking of a place in terms of the activity that goes on there, you usually use **at**:

Enjoy a drink at the King's Bar.
He asked her if she'd like to go to the dance at the hotel.
He worked at Sothebys for a year.
She's reading chemistry at Hull University.

3 gatherings

You use **at** with gatherings such as meetings and parties:

We don't yet know precisely what happened at the meeting.
How many people were at the party?

AS A PREPOSITION OF TIME

1 **At** is used in certain expressions of time:
All seems well at the moment.
The item is not in stock at present.
At that point I began to get worried.
I'll call again at a more convenient time.

2 You use **at** before a specific time of day:
The coach leaves at 8.45 am and returns at 5 pm.
Where can we get a drink at this time of the morning?
The money is counted at the end of the day.
She carried his lunch out to him at midday.

ⓘ Although you use **at** in referring to a *specific time of day*, you use **in** to refer to *part of the day* such as the morning or afternoon:
I work better in the evenings.
I visited the museum in the afternoon.
But notice the way **at night** and **in the night** are used:
It isn't safe walking home by yourself at night [= any night].
I got up twice in the night [= last night, or during some other particular night].

3 You say **on Saturday** and **on Sunday**, and AmE speakers also say **on the weekend**. BrE prefers **at the weekend**. You also use **at** with annual festivals and holidays:
I'll see you at the weekend.
He's coming back at Easter.

ⓘ Notice that if a determiner is used with expressions of time, the preposition is usually omitted:
He was here at Christmas. But: *He was here last Christmas.*
I play golf at the weekends. But: *I play golf most weekends.*
We let the cat out at night. But: *We let the cat out every night.*

4 You say that something happens **at** a certain age:
At the age of 11, David went to Bromley High School.
Is it sensible to employ a man at 73?

5 You say that something happens **at** dinner, or **at** breakfast:
I'll see you at lunchtime.
I hate people who smoke at mealtimes.

OTHER USES

1 **in front of something**

You use **at** to describe the position of someone standing, or especially sitting, and facing something:
Danielle could listen to a tune, then sit at the piano and play it.
Workers now sit at computer terminals all day.

2 direction of attention

You use **at** to express the action of turning your eyes or attention towards someone or something, or making a gesture towards them:

Elinor was still looking at him.
He pointed at the man in the front row.
The police were shooting at anything that moved.
Jinny thought he was laughing at her.

ⓘ Notice that **to**, in contrast to **at**, tends to express co-operation or friendliness:
The fans invaded the pitch, throwing stones at the referee.
I found a rope and threw it to Pete.

3 reaction or response

You use **at** when talking about how people react or respond to something:

We smiled at this accurate description of the President.
Yvonne was amazed at my answer.

4 measurement of speed, rate, price etc.

A measurement is a place **at** a particular point on a scale:

We are flying at a height of 11 000 metres.
He was fined £150 after admitting driving at 103 miles per hour.
The updated First-Aid Manual is published at £5.95.

5 state and status

At is used in describing the state or status of people or things:

England and France were continually at war.
The owner of the car had been taken hostage at gun point.
He remained at a distance, watching the dancing.
Most of the tourists were at lunch.

6 skill

You use **at** in indicating someone's level of skill in doing something:

Charles was pretty good at changing nappies.

•••• at all ••••

WITH A NEGATIVE

You use **at all** to emphasize a negative, or words such as **scarcely** or **hardly**:

That doesn't surprise me at all.
I'd hardly seen her at all that summer.

IN QUESTIONS AND NON-ASSERTIVE CONTEXTS

At all also occurs in questions, after **if**, and after non-assertive words such as **any** and **ever**:

Did he seem at all anxious?
He'd have got in touch by now if he cared about me at all.
Just give what you can afford; anything at all will be appreciated.

MEANING 'NOT AT ALL'

You use **not at all** as a polite response when somebody thanks you:

'Thanks so much for your help.' 'Not at all.'

•••• at first, first, firstly ••••

AT FIRST

You use **at first** with reference to what happened early in a situation, in order to contrast it with what happened later. The conjunction **but** often follows **at first**:

At first I was grateful for her company, but later it began to irritate me.

FIRST

1 You do something **first** if you do it before anyone else does it:

Judy arrived first.

2 You do something **first** when you do it before you do anything else:

First make sure that she's actually free that evening.

3 When you **first** do something, you have never done it before:

I first took an interest in archaeology at the age of ten.
When I first came to London I worked in a restaurant in the East End.

FIRST, FIRSTLY, FIRST OF ALL

You can use **first** and **firstly** to introduce the first of a series of points:

First, (or *firstly* or, emphatically, *first of all*) *let me remind you that we don't have much time. Secondly, ...*

•••• at last, last, lastly ••••

AT LAST

Something that happens **at last** or, more emphatically, **at long last**, happens after a long period of waiting for it to happen:

At last I can relax.
At long last everyone went home.

LAST

1 Something that happens **last** happens after everything else, or comes at the end:

Jane spoke last.
Unfortunately my horse came last.

2 Something that **last** happened on a particular occasion has not happened since then:

I last visited Venice in 1965.
When did you last see her?

LAST, LASTLY

1 You use **last** and **lastly** to introduce a final point:

Last (or *lastly*) *I'd like to thank my parents.*

2 You also use **lastly** to introduce the last action, event or item in a series:

First came Joseph, clearly shocked, next myself, rather surprised, and lastly Philip, who seemed quite normal.

•••• at once, all at once •••

AT ONCE

1 Something that happens **at once** happens immediately:

Stop this noise at once!
I realized at once that I'd said the wrong thing.

2 You do several things **at once** when you do them all at the same time, or all on one occasion:

I'll help you as soon as I can, but I can't do six things at once.
You can either sing or whistle, but it's difficult to do both at once.
I can't hear you if you all talk at once.

ALL AT ONCE

Something that happens **all at once** happens suddenly:

We were just standing there when all at once David collapsed.

•••• autumn •••

➤ See the entry **seasons**.

—— auxiliary verbs ——

The **auxiliary verbs** are **be**, **have** and **do**. Their parts and contractions are shown below:

be

am or *'m*	*[aren't]*
are or *'re*	*aren't*
is or *'s*	*isn't*
was	*wasn't*
were	*weren't*

have

have or *'ve*	*haven't*
has or *'s*	*hasn't*
had or *'d*	*hadn't*

do

do	*don't*
does	*doesn't*
did	*didn't*

➤ These verbs all have their own entries in this book, which can be referred to for more detailed information.

Related to the auxiliary verbs are the **modal verbs**, also called **modal auxiliary verbs**. They are the verbs **can, could, dare, may, might, must, need, ought to, shall, should, used to, will** and **would**.

➤ These are dealt with at the entry **modal verbs** and they also have their own individual entries.

Auxiliary verbs have the following functions:

- They help form parts of other verbs, namely the progressive or continuous tenses, the perfect tenses, and the passive voice.
- They are used with **not** to form the negative of other verbs.
- They are used to form the interrogative of other verbs.
- They are used with **n't** to form the negative interrogative of other verbs.
- They act as the main verb in question tags.
- They are used to provide an emphatic form of other verbs.
- They act as a substitute for another verb wherever the speaker wants to avoid repeating it.

Do has an extra function as an imperative.

> ➤ See FORMING IMPERATIVES WITH 'DO' below.

The contractions, which either join the personal pronouns to the auxiliary (**I've, he'd**), or join the auxiliary to **not** (**haven't, weren't**) are shown in some of the examples below as alternatives. They are used mainly in speech and informal writing.

HELPING TO FORM VERB PARTS

1 be

You use parts of the verb **be** with **-ing** to form the continuous or progressive tenses of other verbs:

*I **am** (or **I'm**) thinking.*
*They **were** talking.*

You use parts of the verb **be** with **-ed** to form the passive of other verbs:

*She **was** supplied with a uniform.*
*We **are** (or **we're**) placed at a disadvantage.*

2 have

You use parts of the verb **have** to form the perfect tenses and the past perfect tenses of other verbs:

*She **has** (or **she's**) left him.*
*I **have** (or **I've**) been seeing someone new.*
*We **had** (or **we'd**) lost a lot of time.*

> ⓘ **Will** and **shall** are used to form the future tenses of verbs, and you combine **used to** with other verbs to talk about a past state of things that no longer exists.
> ➤ See the entries **will**, **shall** and **used to**, and the entry **modal verbs** for details.

FORMING NEGATIVES

1 Auxiliary verbs, followed immediately by **not**, make verbs negative:

*You **have not** (or you **haven't** or **you've not**) completed the form.*
*They **are not** (or they **aren't** or **they're not**) deceived.*

> ⓘ Notice that the only possible contracted form for **I am not** is **I'm not**:
> *I'm not leaving yet.*

2 Parts of the auxiliary verb **do** are used to form the negative of the simple present and the simple past tense of other verbs:

*We **do not** (or we **don't**) know.*
*I **did not** (or I **didn't**) understand.*

FORMING QUESTIONS

Auxiliary verbs combine with other verbs, in the order auxiliary + subject + verb, to provide a question form. Parts of the auxiliary verb **do** are used to provide a question form for the simple present tense and the simple past tense:

***Is** she going to the meeting?*
***Have** you written to Granny?*
***Does** she agree with you?*
*What **did** you think of the lecture?*

> ⓘ Notice that in indirect speech, there is no inversion of subject and auxiliary, and that the auxiliary verb **do** is therefore not needed in the simple present and past tenses:
> *I asked if she was going to the meeting.*
> *I asked him what he thought* (not *what did he think*) *of the lecture.*

FORMING NEGATIVE QUESTIONS

Auxiliary verbs combine with **n't**, in the order auxiliary + **n't** + subject + verb, to provide a negative question form:

Hasn't Cynthia found a job yet?
Doesn't it seem strange to you?
Aren't you coming to the party?

> ⓘ Although in negative statements the only possible contraction for **I am not** is **I'm not** (see note above), the negative question form **aren't I?** is possible:
> *Aren't I included?*

FORMING IMPERATIVES WITH 'DO'

1 **Do** is used to form the negative imperative or command form:

*Please **do not** feed the animals.*
***Don't** listen to him.*

2 **Do** is also used to emphasize the imperative:

***Do** stop making such a noise.*
***Do** be sensible.*

ACTING AS THE VERB IN QUESTION TAGS

Auxiliary verbs act as the verb in question tags. The subject is always a pronoun:

*Bill and Sheila were going to emigrate, **weren't** they?*
*You two haven't met before, **have** you?*

Your parents look well, ***don't*** *they?*
We didn't stand a chance, ***did*** *we?*

ⓘ Notice that the auxiliary must be in the *same tense* as the verb in the main part of the sentence, and must be the *same auxiliary* as the one in the main sentence, if there is one there, and must have the *same subject* as the verb in the main sentence has:
You know that already, ***don't*** *you?*
Carol and Jean ***aren't*** *living in the hostel this term,* ***are*** *they?*
The computer ***had*** *already completed that operation,* ***hadn't*** *it?*

USED FOR EMPHASIS

The auxiliary verbs combine with other verbs to emphasize an affirmative structure. The auxiliary verb is stressed:

'Oh, sorry, you haven't met Peter yet.' 'I ***have*** *met him, actually.'*
I ***do*** *go and see her occasionally, but she's so bad-tempered.*

AVOIDING REPETITION OF THE VERB

Auxiliaries are very often used to replace, or refer back to, a previously used verb, and so avoid repetition. You use them both in your own continuous speech or writing, and in conversation, to 'pick up' a verb that the other speaker has used.

1 Here are some examples of speakers referring back to their own verb with an auxiliary:

Lindsay ***has*** *put her name down, and I* ***have*** *too.*
*They****'re*** *taking lunch in college, but* ***I'm not****.*
*She tells everyone she****'s been*** *badly-treated, but she* ***hasn't been*** *really.*
He suspected that she ***liked*** *him, which of course she* ***did****.*
We still ***meet*** *sometimes, but we quarrel whenever we* ***do****.*
He hasn't ***contacted*** *me so far; if he* ***does*** *I'll let you know.*

2 Here are some examples of a second speaker referring back to the first speaker's verb with an auxiliary:

*'****Have*** *you* ***phoned*** *Irene?' 'Yes, I* ***have*** (or *I* ***did***) *but she was out.*
'I ***think*** *that's probably unnecessary.' 'So* ***do*** *I.'*
*'It****'s*** *raining.' 'Oh, no,* ***is*** *it?'*
*'Alistair****'s*** [= has] *left already.' 'Yes, I thought he* ***had****.'*

ⓘ Notice that, in contrast to the situation with question tags, where there must be complete agreement between the auxiliary in the question tag and the verb in the main sentence, here the 'picking-up' clause may use a different auxiliary, or an auxiliary in a different tense:
Howard ***was*** *going to* ***apply*** *but I don't think he* ***has*** [= has applied] *yet.*
'As a child I ***hated*** *cheese.' 'But you* ***don't*** *any more?'*

ⓘ Notice that the contractions (**I'm**, **you're**, **he's**, **I've**, **it's**, **I'd** and so on) are not used at the end of a sentence:
*I thought she **hadn't** heard but she **had*** (not ***she'd***).

•••• awake, awaken, wake, waken ••••

The verbs **waken** and **awaken** are regular verbs, but **wake** and **awake** are irregular:

wakes	*awakes*
waking	*awaking*
woke	*awoke*
woken	*awoken*

In AmE the past tenses and past participles **waked** and **awaked** are also used.

WAKE

Wake is the most commonly used verb of these four.

You **wake**, or **wake up**, when you stop sleeping and become conscious; someone or something **wakes** you, or **wakes** you **up** when they make you stop sleeping:

It's great when you wake up and find it's only a dream.
Sorry to wake you at this early hour.
Something woke him up at two in the morning.
That night she was woken by planes.

AWAKE, AWAKEN, WAKEN

1 These three verbs can be used in the same way as **wake**, to mean 'stop sleeping', or 'stop someone sleeping', but they are slightly more literary than **wake**:

When he awoke again it was seven.
What had wakened her, she lazily wondered.

2 Something **awakes** or **awakens** memories or feelings when it brings them back to you:

The trip awakened many boyhood memories.
The words of the hymn awoke memories of school.

SHARED USES

1 You **awake**, **wake**, or **wake up**, **to** something, or to experience something, if that is what you find when you wake up:

We awoke to sunshine and a cloudless sky.
One day he woke to find himself famous.
I woke up to the sound of shouting in the street.

2 You **awaken**, **awake** or **wake up** to a fact or situation, especially one that is unpleasant or difficult to accept, when you become aware of it:

The authorities finally awoke to the extent of the problem.
You must wake up to the fact you'll have to work hard to pass this exam.

AWAKE AND WAKING

1 You use the adjective **awake** rather than the present participle **waking** to describe someone who is not asleep. Similarly, it is more usual to say someone is **asleep** than that they are **sleeping**. **Awake** and **asleep** are never used before a noun:

Is he awake yet?
I couldn't stay awake any longer.
Why aren't you in bed and asleep?

Sleeping is often used in the attributive position:

They looked down at the sleeping child.

2 Your **waking hours** are the time you spend awake and not sleeping:

He spends all his waking hours at his computer.

3 Notice that you describe someone as **wide awake** or **fully awake**, not **very awake**. And you say that someone is **sound asleep**, **fast asleep** or **deeply asleep**. You are only **half awake** when you are not yet fully awake, and **half asleep** when you are almost asleep.

Bb

.... back ....

Back is an adverb and a noun.

AWAY FROM THE FRONT

1 You use **back** to mean the opposite of **forwards**:

Stand back and let the ambulance pass.
Her long hair was tied back from her face.
One house was set back from the rest.
He looked back over his shoulder.

2 You keep **back** laughter or tears when you manage not to laugh or cry:

The child turned his head away, fighting back the tears.

3 Something **back** in time is in the past:

Her career in show business stretches back 50 years.
The clocks go back [= are adjusted to an earlier time] *on the third Sunday in October.*

RETURNING

1 You go **back** when you return to a place:

She dashed off, shouting 'Back in a minute!'
I've got to be back here at seven.
It seems that no-one can tempt her back from Hollywood.

> ⓘ Notice that you do not use **back** after the verb **return**:
> *I returned* (not *I returned back*) *to the flat on Monday.*

2 A feeling or condition comes **back** when it starts again:

Memories of that painful evening came flooding back.
If the headache comes back take another painkiller.

3 You take, send, put, or give, something **back** when you return it:

We have sent the report back and asked for a translation.
She clipped the letters together and put them back in the drawer.
I must give you back your map.

4 You get something **back** when it is returned to you:

Customers are asking for their money back.
The company will buy back about 10 per cent of the shares.

> ⓘ **Back** can come between a verb and its object, if the object is *not a pronoun*:
> *Do they **get back** from Brussels **more than they put in**?*
> *Here's your book; could you **put it back** when you've finished with it?*

5 Someone or something is **back** in a particular state or situation when they are in it again:

I went back to bed.
Go back to sleep.
He cleaned his glasses and put them back on.
The mill could be put back into full working order.

REPEATING OR RESPONDING

1 You do something **back** to someone when you do the same to them as they did to you:

He hit me and I hit him back.
Huge blue eyes stared back at him from the white face.

2 You also use **back** when something is repeated by reproduction:

Let's record the first scene and play it back before we go on.

> ⓘ Notice the difference in use between **back** and **again**. You use **again** when you simply repeat an action:
> *I played the message back but I had to play it again several times before I understood it properly.*
> *I wrote back as soon as I received the invitation.*
> *I sent her a form in May, but heard nothing, so wrote again in June.*

3 When talking about telephone calls, you can use **back** to refer both to calling a second time, and to responding to someone else's call:

Can I give her a message or will you ring back?
Take her name and number and tell her I'll call her back.

AS A NOUN

Use **back** as a noun to mean:

1 the part of your body around your spine, opposite your chest and stomach:

He has a back injury.

2 the side of an object that is opposite to the front:

There's a garden at the back of the hotel.

3 the rear area of a space, such as a room or the inside of a vehicle:

We used to sit at the back of the cinema holding hands.
Get in the back of the car.

4 the blank, or less important, side of something thin and flat, such as a piece of paper:

Sign the cheque on the back.

ⓘ You talk about the **back** of an object, not its **back side** (your **backside**, in informal English, is your bottom):
When she took the picture down she found a name scribbled on the back.

•••• badly ••••

1 Use **badly** as an adverb from **bad**, to mean 'not well':

He thought the book was dull and badly written.
The troops were badly equipped.
The Democrats had done very badly in the election.
She knocked me around and treated me badly.

The comparative and superlative for this usage are normally **worse** and **worst**:

These must be the worst-behaved children in the county.

ⓘ People often prefer the less strong **not very well** to **badly**:
I didn't do very well in my exams.

2 **Badly** also has two more meanings as an intensifier:

- emphasizing the *seriousness* of a bad situation:

  The financial markets were badly depressed.
  Poorer families will be badly hit by this tax.

  In this case, the comparative and superlative can be **worse** and **worst**, or **more badly** and **most badly**:

  Try to identify the worst-affected areas.
  The ship proved to be more badly damaged than had been thought.

- stressing how much someone *needs* or *wants* something:

  He badly wants to pass this time.
  These people are badly in need of help and advice.

  The comparative and superlative for this sense are **more badly** and **most badly**:

  Because of this she needs your love and attention more badly than ever.

•••• barely ••••

➤ See **hardly**.

•••• bath, bathe ••••

Bath is pronounced /bɑːθ/ and is used mainly in British English. **Bathe** is pronounced /beɪð/ and is used in British and American English, but in different ways. Note that the verbs **bath** and **bathe** have the same present participle (**bathing**) and the same past tense and past participle (**bathed**).

BATH

1 In BrE a **bath** is a long deep container that you fill with water and lie in to wash your body:

The hotel offers 140 bedrooms, all with a bath or shower.

In AmE this container is usually referred to as a **bathtub** or **tub**:

A long soak in the tub is relaxing and enjoyable.

2 You **have** a **bath** or, especially in AmE, **take** a **bath** when you wash yourself in a bath:

All she wanted was a hot bath.

BATH AND BATHE

1 In BrE, you **bath** someone when you wash them in a bath and **bath** when you wash yourself in the bath. In AmE, **bathe** is used in the same way:

He could vaguely remember his mother bathing (BrE /ˈbɑːθɪŋ/, AmE /ˈbeɪðɪŋ/) *him when he was a child.*

He shaved and bathed (BrE /bɑːθt/, AmE /beɪðd/) *and went out.*

2 In BrE, **bathe** is a formal word meaning 'swim for pleasure':

The sign said 'Bathing (/ˈbeɪðɪŋ/) *and fishing prohibited'.*

In the 1930s sunbathing (/-beɪðɪŋ/) *became more popular.*

> ⓘ **Go for a swim** or **go swimming** are more informal than **bathe** in BrE. In AmE you **take a swim**.

3 In both BrE and AmE you **bathe** a part of the body when you wash it gently:

She returned with a bowl of water to bathe his injured arm.

4 To be **bathed in** something means to be covered in it:

The horse was bathed (/beɪðd/) *in sweat.*

The little garden was bathed in sunlight.

•••• be ••••

The verb **be** has two main functions – as an ordinary verb, and as an *auxiliary* verb. The parts of **be** with their shortened forms (affirmative and negative), are:

present tense

I am or *I'm*	*I'm not* [question tag: *aren't I*]
you are or *you're*	*you aren't* or *you're not*
he is or *he's*	*he isn't* or *he's not*
she is or *she's*	*she isn't* or *she's not*
it is or *it's*	*it isn't* or *it's not*
we are or *we're*	*we aren't* or *we're not*
they are or *they're*	*they aren't* or *they're not*

past tense

I, he, she, it, was	*I, he, she, it, wasn't*
you, we, they, were	*you, we, they, weren't*

present participle

being

past participle

been

infinitive

be

subjunctive

be, were

ⓘ The contraction **'s** for **is** can be used after nouns, names, and pronouns, and after **there**, **here**, **where**, **what** and **who**. The contraction **'re** is only used after a personal pronoun:
*It'**s** not fair.*
*His wife'**s** a dentist.*
*Edinburgh'**s** a lovely city.*
*Here'**s** Paula.*
*You'**re** mistaken.*
*People **are*** (not *People'**re***) *different.*

ORDINARY VERB

1 Use **be** to link a subject and what you want to say about it:

Jennifer's ill.
I'm glad to have been useful.
His novel has been a best-seller for over a year.
He's a doctor.
That book wasn't mine.
The theatre was only half full.

2 You use **be** rather than **have** to describe people's physical or mental condition:

Are you thirsty (not *have you thirst*)*?*
I'm too hot.
She was afraid.

Notice also the use of **be** in the following situations:

I was lucky.
You're right.
I was wrong.

3 Don't use the progressive tenses of **be** to describe the *state* that people or things are in, or how people *feel*:

At that stage I was very unhappy. (not *I was being very unhappy.*)

However, you can use **be** to talk about *behaviour* and can use the progressive tenses to say how people are *acting* or *behaving*:

Be brave.
Just be yourself.
He was just being obstinate.
I'm being as understanding as possible over it.

4 Only use the auxiliary **do** with **be** if you are *instructing* or *advising* people about how to *behave*:

Do be quiet.

Don't be so unhelpful.
Don't you be too sure.

5 **Be** is used to talk about *jobs* and about *choosing careers*:
'What do you do?' 'I'm a systems analyst.'
She'd always wanted to be a dancer.

> ⓘ You can omit **the** before a unique job or position:
> *She was Prime Minister from 1979 till 1990.*

6 You use **be** to specify such things as *age, size, cost*:
He is (not *has*) *about 70 now.*
She's six feet tall already.
What weight are you?
How much are those plums?
They're 75 pence a pound.
What colour were his eyes?

7 You use **be** with **it** to talk about such things as the *time, weather, environment* or a particular situation:
It's nearly two o'clock.
It was a bright sunny day.
It's warm in here.
Isn't it quiet?
It's a shame you can't come.

8 You can use **be** with **it** to emphasize a particular part of a sentence:
It's the Department of Employment you should contact.
(instead of *You should contact the Department of Employment.*)

9 You use **be** with **there** to say that things or people exist or are present:
There's food in the fridge.
There was a crowd at the gate.
Are there any paper clips?

10 You use **be** with **this, that, it** and personal pronouns to identify people and things:
Jenny, this is Dr Wilson.
Is that the Post Office tower?
Hallo, it's Meg here.
Hi, I'm Jack.

➤ See also the entry **been**.

AUXILIARY VERB

1 You use **be** with the *present participle* of another verb to form its progressive tenses:

the present progressive: *The children are playing in the garden.*
the past progressive: *I was peeling the potatoes.*
the present perfect progressive: *We have been watching too much television recently.*
the past perfect progressive: *I heard they had been making enquiries.*

2 The progressive can be used to refer to future plans and intentions:

I'm meeting him for lunch tomorrow.
We're leaving at seven in the morning.
We were setting off very early, so we packed the night before.

3 **Be** is used with the *past participle* of another verb to construct its passive forms:

the present passive:	*Hot meals are served at all times of the day.* *I'm being trained as a designer.*
the past passive:	*The interview with the Princess was broadcast last night.* *We were being treated with special respect.*
the present perfect passive:	*He's been injured.*
the past perfect passive:	*They had been warned not to mention it.*
the future passive:	*When will it be delivered?* *I'll be being entertained at the Sheraton that evening.*
the future perfect passive:	*Surely the clock will have been repaired by then?*

QUESTIONS

1 **Be** comes before its subject in direct questions:

Are the others coming?
Is she on the list?

But if the subject is a **wh**-question word, the subject and **be** are not reversed:

Who's there?
What's in this box?

2 In reported questions **be** comes after its subject as in a statement:

I asked if the others were coming.
I enquired whether she was on the list.
I wondered who her husband was.

ELLIPTICAL USE

You can use **be** to stand for a whole clause:

1 in question tags:

You're Michael, aren't you?
They weren't very helpful, were they?
The days are getting longer, aren't they?
It isn't 6 o'clock already, is it?

2 to avoid repetition:

Phyllis was in time, but Peter wasn't [= wasn't in time].
I'm not a smoker. Are you? [= are you a smoker?]
'Are they ready?' 'No, they aren't (or *they're not*).*'*
The children are playing in the garden, or they were [= they were playing in the garden] *when I last looked.*
'The interview was broadcast last night.' 'I knew it was going to be [= was going to be broadcast] *but I forgot to watch.'*

ⓘ The short forms **I'm**, **you're**, **he's**, **we're** and so on are never used alone at the end of a clause, unless followed by **not**:
'Am I late?' 'Yes, you are (not *you're*).'
I thought he was coming but he's not (or *he isn't*).

ⓘ The only possible short form of **I am not** is **I'm not**. BrE uses **aren't I** as the negative question form:
Wanda's quite enthusiastic but I'm not.
Sorry, I'm boring you, aren't I?

BE TO

You use **be** before **to** and an infinitive to refer to the future in various ways, *eg* to indicate:

1 what is expected to happen:
She is to arrive in Argentina today.
She was to have joined us for dinner, but she was too ill.

2 what you intend to happen:
This food is to last until Friday.
You'd better hurry if you're to catch that bus.

3 what might happen:
If they were to increase my salary I might stay on.

4 what fate decides:
The expedition was to end in disaster.
They were never to meet again.

5 uncertainty about what to do:
What am I to tell her parents?

6 orders and commands:
You're to do as I say!
You're not to tell anyone.
Hospital property. Not to be Removed.

SUBJUNCTIVE

In formal English, **were** can be used not only with **you**, **we** and **they**, but also with **I**, **he**, **she** and **it**, to express very unlikely events in the present or future, most commonly in **if**-clauses such as the one for giving advice, **if I were you**, and in clauses that begin with **I wish**:

I'd forget the whole thing if I were you.
I wish he were (or *was*) *just a few years older.*

The present subjunctive **be** is often used in AmE, and increasingly in BrE, with words expressing advice, wishes, or orders (BrE formerly preferred **should be**):

We recommend that he be (or *should be*) *transferred to a secure prison.*

• • • • bear: can't bear • • • •

➤ See **can** and **like**.

•••• beat, win ••••

Beat and **win** are both irregular verbs:

beats	*wins*
beating	*winning*
beat	*won*
beaten	*won*

BEAT

Beat must have an object. You **beat** someone in a competition when you defeat them:

Last year Andres Gomez beat him in the final.
He usually beats me at chess.

WIN

1 You can use **win** without an object:

We didn't play often, but he always won.
I really enjoy winning!

2 You can **win** a prize, and you can **win** a competition, but you **beat**, not **win**, another person:

You could win the holiday of a lifetime.
I won the 200 metres easily.
Politics is about communicating, not winning an argument.

ⓘ You **beat** someone, or **win**, **at** a certain kind of game or activity, but **in** a particular contest:
William invariably wins at table tennis.
The San Francisco Giants beat the Chicago Cubs in the National League.

•••• because ••••

BECAUSE

Because is a *conjunction* and is used to introduce a *clause.*

1 You use **because** to introduce the reason for something, before or after the main clause:

She forgave him because she loved him.
Because I'm short, I like to sit at the front.

2 A **because**-clause by itself can be an answer to the question 'why?':

'I can't come out tonight.' 'Why not?' 'Because I'm too tired.'

➤ See entries for other conjunctions of reason: **as**, **since**, **seeing** and **for**.

BECAUSE OF

Because of is used like a *preposition*, before a noun or pronoun.

One thing happens **because of** another if the second is the cause of the first:

The world has changed a lot because of feminism.
Because of high interest rates, we can't borrow any more money.

•••• become ••••

Become is irregular:

becomes, becoming, became, become

Become is one of the verbs like **get**, **grow**, **go**, **turn** and **come**, that expresses change in the state of a person or thing.

➤ See the entry **change** for more information about these verbs.

A person or thing **becomes** something when they start being that thing:

Peter and Jeremy had become friends the previous year.
Since I became involved in politics, I've met a lot of interesting people.
Things are changing as women become more self-confident.

•••• been ••••

Been is the past participle of the verb **be** (see the entry **be**), but it can mean 'come' or 'gone' when it is used with **have**, **has** or **had**:

1 You **have been** to a place if you have visited it:
I'd been to Rome before, of course.
Have you been to the library yet?
She'd just been to see her mother in Ireland.
We had been to the pub and were walking home.

2 You **have been** somewhere such as school, church, or a performance, if you have attended it:
Their children have been to three different schools.
We haven't been to a film for months.
She's been to (or *She's been to see*) *the doctor twice.*

3 Someone **has been** when they have called and gone away again:
Has the telephone engineer been yet?

> ⓘ You use **been** when referring to completed visits:
> *Rita has gone to the dentist* [and has not come back yet].
> *Where have you been?* [said to someone who has just returned from somewhere]
> *I've been to the supermarket* [and here I am back again].
> *The doctor has come* [and has not left yet].
> *Look in the mailbox and see if the postman's been* [= has called, delivered the mail, and gone away again].

•••• before ••••

Before is used as a *conjunction*, a *preposition* and an *adverb* and can refer both to time and, in a few special cases, to place.

AS A CONJUNCTION OR PREPOSITION

1 One thing happening **before** another, happens *earlier* than it:
The letter was written a year before we met.

2 Something that is so **before** another thing happens is already so when it happens, or is no longer so after it happens:

She was always up and dressed before her husband left for work.
We were always worried about money before I got this job.

3 You can modify **before** by using **long**, **not long** or **shortly**:

She held those views long before they became fashionable.
Someone said the same thing not long before (or *shortly before*) *you joined us.*

4 If the subject of the main clause and the subordinate clause are the same person or thing, you can use **before** with an **-ing** form of a verb, as a rather formal alternative to the subordinate clause:

The price went up 30 cents a barrel before coming (or *before it came*) *back to $19.45.*
Think carefully before answering (or *before you answer*).

5 **Before** can be used before or after the main clause. If it comes first, it is usually followed by a comma:

I normally have a small whisky before going (or *before I go*) *to bed.*
Before turning (or *before you turn*) *the machine on, make sure you understand the instructions.*

6 In referring to the future, you use a present tense in the **before** clause:

Warm the pot before you put (or *before putting*, but not *will put*) *the tea bags in.*

7 When one person does the *same* thing more quickly than another, you can use **before** as a preposition instead of using a subordinate clause:

Mary normally finishes work before me.

If you do use a subordinate clause, you usually use an auxiliary or modal verb in it, instead of repeating the verb used in the main clause:

In the end, we finished the job before they did.

8 Use **before** when you do one thing to stop another thing happening:

I must finish this list before I forget all your names.

9 **Before** is often followed by **any-** words:

Before you tell me anything more, please explain why you're here.
I arrived before anyone else.
I think you ought to explain now, before there's any more confusion.

10 One thing happens **before** another can happen if it happens too quickly or too soon for the other to happen, or finish happening:

Before I could reply, a bomb fell a short distance away.
'I've got to go.' 'OK, but not before I've told you my big news.'
He hung up before I'd finished speaking.

11 Things that happen **before long**, happen soon or quickly:

You'll find, before too long, that the new software is much easier to use.

AS A PREPOSITION

1 of time

Before is used mainly as a preposition of *time*, meaning 'earlier than':

The move took place just before Christmas.
I had to be back before dark.
I could see you just before nine o'clock.
I ought to have written long before now.

2 of order

When talking about *order*, you can say that one thing comes **before** another in *time* or in *position*:

I only arrived the day before yeserday.
I was ill the Monday before last.
The apostrophe should come before the 's'.
Do go first. I think you're before me (or *in front of me*) *in the queue.*

3 meaning 'in the presence of'

You do something **before** someone important when you do it in their presence:

I performed before (or *in front of*) *Her Majesty The Queen.*
When the case comes up before the judge, he can make a decision.

4 You can say that something happens **before your very eyes** if it happens right in front of you:

What do you do if someone steals something before your very eyes?

AS AN ADVERB

1 Use **before** as an adverb to mean 'at an earlier time than now', or 'on a previous occasion':

Haven't we met before?
I ought to have written before, but I've been so busy.

2 The *perfect tense* is used with **before** when it means 'earlier than *now*'. When it means 'earlier than *then*', that is, a point in the past, the *past perfect tense* is used:

I've heard that several times before.
I'd never been skiing before.

3 You use **before** instead of **ago** when you want to refer to a time earlier than a point in the past:

I remember it was May when we met, because we'd moved house not long before.
We had seen her only two months before (or *earlier, or previously*).

4 The **day**, **week** or **month before** is the one earlier than the one in the past just mentioned:

It had rained the night before (or *the previous night*).
They'd had that earthquake the year before (or *the previous year*).

•••• begin, start, commence ••••

These three verbs mean the same, but **commence** is much more formal than **begin** or **start**, so is not used much in conversation.

Begin is irregular:

begins, beginning, began, begun

CONSTRUCTIONS

1 After **begin** and **start**, you can use a **to-**infinitive or an **-ing** form:
I'm beginning to wonder if I was wrong.
The eggs all begin developing at the same time.
We're starting to think about expansion now.
She went upstairs to start packing.

2 After **commence** you can only use the **-ing** form:
The BBC commenced transmitting (not *to transmit*) *regular programmes to the public in 1926.*

3 You cannot use an **-ing** form after a progressive tense:
I was just beginning to feel (not *beginning feeling*) *at home.*
It's all starting to make (not *starting making*) *sense.*

4 You can use a direct object after all three verbs:
How do you feel when you start each day?
Begin each question at the top of a new page.
Mr Ahmed commenced work in Bangladesh in 1972.

5 All three verbs can be used intransitively, that is, without any object:
The fun was only just beginning.
That's how rumours start.
Work commenced in January 1981.

SPECIAL USES

1 **start**

- **get a machine to go**

Start is used for engines, machines or processes:
My car wouldn't start this morning.
How do you start the tumble-dryer?
He seemed to start the argument deliberately.

- **set off**

Start can mean 'set off somewhere', *eg* on a journey:
We must be there by 6.30, so that means starting at 3.30.
I closed the front door and started along the road.

- **found**

You **start** a business or organization:
She saved up enough money to start her own hairdressing business.

2 **begin**

- come into existence

Generally, **begin** is used to refer to the origin of things:
Did the universe actually begin with a Big Bang?

- You say someone **doesn't begin to** do something if they cannot do it at all:
You don't even begin to see the point, do you?

•••• behind ••••

Behind can be used as a *preposition* or *adverb.*

1 at the back of

Use **behind** when one thing is at the back, or facing the back of another:

I was sitting behind (not *behind of*) *a woman with a large hat.*
She hid behind a bush.
I heard footsteps behind me.
It's an old house with a big garden behind.
I walked along with Jim following a few paces behind.

2 responsible for

One thing is **behind** another if it is the cause of it:

What were the reasons behind the change of policy?
We need to find out who's behind these attacks.

3 supporting

You are **behind** someone when you support them:

We're all behind you in your fight for justice.

4 when you depart

- You leave a state of things **behind** you when you go away:
  Remember to lock the door behind you.
  The workmen always leave such a mess behind them.

- You leave something **behind** when you don't take it with you:
  I'm amazed at the things people leave behind on the bus.
  Unfortunately we had to leave the dog behind.

5 not as far ahead as

- One place is **behind** another when it is earlier there:
  We're eight hours behind Singapore.

- You are **behind** when you have not progressed as fast as you should have:
  The train is thirty minutes behind schedule.
  I've been falling behind with my work this week.
  He finished several seconds behind the leaders.

•••• believe ••••

Believe is mostly used in three ways:

- you can **believe** *that something is the case*
- you can **believe** *a story* or *something you are told*
- you can **believe** *a person*

You can also **believe in** things.

BELIEVE (THAT) ...

1 You use **believe** to explain what you know:

I believe (that) he's an inspector of mines.
She's abroad just now, I believe.

2 You **believe** something is the case if it's your opinion:
We believe higher standards are required.
These incidents happen more often than most people believe.

3 When it's difficult to accept that something is true or possible, you use **believe** with a negative, or in a question:
I could hardly believe how lucky I'd been.
You won't believe what's happened.
I don't believe it was a coincidence.
Can she really believe she's in love with a man like that?

ⓘ You say you **don't believe something is so** rather than you **believe something is not so**:
Peter, I don't believe you've met my mother? (Rather than *I believe you haven't met my mother.*)
'Did you tell her?' 'I don't believe I did, no.'

ⓘ In conversation, **I believe so** is an affirmative answer, and **I believe not** is a negative one:
'Is he applying?' 'I believe so (not *I believe it*).'
'Has she any experience?' 'I believe not (or *I don't believe so*).'

4 Instead of using **believe (that)** + subject + verb *etc*, you can use the construction **believe** + object + **to** + infinitive:
At the time, she believed him to be mad.

In the case of the verb **be** the infinitive may sometimes be omitted:
His followers believed him capable of performing miracles.

5 Impersonal uses of **believe** are common: **it is believed** that something is so, and something **is believed** to be so:
It is believed that she slipped and fell down the hillside.
The last inhabitant of the island is believed to have died in 1874.

BELIEVE SOMETHING OR SOMEONE

1 You **believe** a story, or something you are told, if you think it's true:
We believed the explanation the adults gave us.
That's what she said, but I didn't believe a word of it.
'It's true!' 'I don't believe it!'

2 You say you couldn't **believe your eyes** or **your ears** when you report something astonishing:
I could hardly believe my eyes when I opened the door and saw a bear!

3 You **believe** *a person* when you accept what they say as the truth:
Why was I stupid enough to believe him?
If you don't believe me go and see for yourself.

BELIEVE IN

1 You **believe in** something or someone if you are sure they exist:
Do you believe in heaven and hell?

2 You **believe in** something if you think it's a good thing:
We believe in equal pay for women.

•••• belong ••••

BELONG TO

1 Something **belongs to** you if you own it:
Who (or *whom*) *does the house belong to?*
Melanie thought the gloves belonged to Philip.
Would you take what doesn't belong to you?

2 One thing **belongs to** another if it is a part or piece of it:
This lid obviously belongs to another pan.
His lips were pretty enough to belong to a girl.

3 People or things can **belong to** a group or class of similar things or people:
You get a feeling of belonging to a community.
Employees have the right to belong to a trade union.
He wasn't older than me, but seemed to belong to a different age group.

BELONG TOGETHER

You can say that things or people that should not be separated **belong together**:
You two belong together, I can see that.

BELONG SOMEWHERE

The place where a thing or person should be is the place where they **belong**:
Coffee cups belong in the top cupboard.
I didn't belong in her world of babies and housework.
It's good to be back where I belong.

•••• beneath, underneath ••••

Beneath and **underneath** have many of the same uses as **below** and **under** (see the entry **above**, **over**) but there are some special points to notice about each of them.

BENEATH

1 like **below** and **under**

Beneath is a *preposition* or *adverb*, and can usually be used instead of **below** or **under**:
The grass felt wet beneath her feet.
We climbed up and watched the waves crashing on the rocks beneath.
Fish swam just beneath the surface.

2 not like **below** and **under**

You can't use **beneath** like **below** and **under** to mean 'less than', in talking about measurements or age:
below-average (not *beneath-average*) *temperatures.*
children under (not *beneath*) *twelve.*
We do the journey in under (not *beneath*) *an hour.*

UNDERNEATH

1 as a preposition
As a preposition **underneath** is like **under**:

Many people were actually smoking underneath the 'no-smoking' signs.
She signed her name underneath my signature.
Trevino still had his pyjamas on underneath his golf trousers.

2 as an adverb
Underneath is much more common than **under** as an adverb:

There was a photo of each member of staff, with their names written underneath.
She wore a blue suit and had a white shirt on underneath
He's so bad; underneath he's a very sensitive man.

3 not like **below** and **under**
Underneath cannot mean 'less than' in age or amount, or 'junior to' in rank:

people under (not *underneath*) *the age of 45*
people with incomes of £5000 and under (not *underneath*)
As a manager he was kind to the staff under (not *underneath*) *him.*

•••• beside, besides ••••

BESIDE

One thing is **beside** another if it is next to it:

She sat down beside her son.
He was sitting at the desk with the dictionary beside him.
My wife has been right beside me [= has helped me] *during this difficult time.*

BESIDES

1 **Besides** is a preposition or adverb meaning 'as well (as)', 'apart from' or 'in addition (to)':

What other subjects are you taking besides English?
Who else is coming besides me?
I bought bread, cheese, crisps, wine, and loads of other things besides.

2 Like **as well as, besides** can be followed by an **-ing** form:

Besides collecting the question papers you will have to answer any queries.

3 **Besides** can also be used as a sentence adverb, introducing an additional point:

I'm sorry, I don't want to go out this evening; and besides, I've seen the film before.

•••• best ••••

1 **Best** is the superlative of **good**:

Which method is best?
I want to get the best possible price.
It's best not to [= I advise you not to] *feed your fish for the first few days.*
English was my best subject; what were you best at?
Best wishes for your future.

2 **Best** is also the superlative of **well**:

I can demonstrate this best using a model.
She's best known for her novels.
They enjoy showing off; that's what actors do best.

> ⓘ You like someone or something **best**, or **the best**, if you like them more than anyone or anything else; the opposite is **least**:
> *She loved my brother best of all.*

> ⓘ Your **best friend** is your closest friend.

3 **useful idioms**:

*The situation isn't ideal, but we'll have to cope **as best we can*** [= as well as we can].
*This symphony shows Beethoven **at his best*** [= doing what he is most skilful at doing].
*He **does*** (or ***tries***) ***his best*** [= tries as hard as he can].
*People are finding it hard to accept, but it's **for the best*** [= brings more good than bad].
*We slept four to a bed and had to **make the best of it*** [= bear it cheerfully].
*He's **not in the best of health*** [= he's ill].

➤ See also the entry **comparatives and superlatives**.

•••• bet ••••

The verb **bet** is irregular:

bets, betting, bet, bet

1 When people **bet** each other, the person who is right wins money from the person who is wrong:

Did you bet her five pounds that she'd pass her driving test first time?

2 In informal English **I bet**, or **I bet you** at the beginning of a sentence shows that the speaker is very sure that something is true:

I bet you he's forgotten to buy milk.
I bet I know who's responsible for this.

> ⓘ Note that you can use a present tense after **bet** to refer to the future:
> *I bet you anything she **forgets*** (or ***she'll forget***) *to bring my book back.*
> *I bet he **doesn't*** (or ***won't***) ***win***.

•••• better ••••

➤ See also the entry **comparatives and superlatives**.

1 **Better** is the comparative of **good**:

We now have a better idea of how much it will cost.

Better and better telescopes are available.
Some systems are obviously better than others.
Maybe it would be better if we sat opposite each other.
Is wholemeal bread really better for you than white bread?
I was much better at parking the car than he was.
The more you practise, the better you play it.
She got better-looking as she got older.

2 **Better** is the comparative of **well**:

Some children behave better than others.
He couldn't have expressed it better [= he expressed it in the best way possible].
She's a lot better known in her own country.
I'm looking for a better-paid job.

3 You are **better** after being ill

- if you are less ill than you were:

I'm feeling much better today, thanks.
She's getting better.

- if you have fully recovered:

I'm quite better, thanks.
I do hope your cold's better now.

> ⓘ Notice the difference between **better** and **rather**:
> - **Better still** or **even better** introduce a better idea:
> *Why don't you spend the day with us, or better still, the whole weekend?*
> *Could you get me a copy of the music, or even better, a tape?*
> - When you are correcting something you have just said, you use **or rather**:
> *It's money, or rather* (not *or better*) *not having any money, that's the problem.*

4 **had better**

Had better is similar in meaning to **should** or **ought to**, but its use shows that the action is more likely.

Compare:

We should/ought to hurry [but we're not going to hurry].

and:

We'd better hurry [let's hurry].
She'd better be here soon, or she'll be too late.
'I suppose I'd better tell her it was my fault.' 'Yes, you'd better, or I will.'

Notice the placing of **not** in statements and questions using **had better**:

We'd better not (not *we hadn't better*) *disturb her.*
Hadn't you better phone her?
I'd better speak to her, hadn't I?

5 **useful idioms**:

We're ***better off*** [= have more money] *now than we used to be.*

She'd be ***better off*** [= happier, more comfortable] *in hospital.*
For better or worse [= whether we like it or not] *computers have taken over our lives.*
On the whole the changes are ***for the better.*** [= are an improvement]
I usually ***get the better of*** [= defeat] *my brothers in any argument.*
Curiosity eventually ***got the better of*** *him, and he* [= he became so curious that he] *went to see what was happening.*
She ought to ***know better than to*** [= she ought to have learnt not to] *chase men at her age.*
I was feeling ***the better for*** [= I had benefited from] *a good night's sleep.*

•••• between, among, amongst •••

There are some senses in which these prepositions are interchangeable, and some in which only one or the other can be used.

BETWEEN

1 A thing is **between** two other things when they are on either side of it:

I was sitting between Lorna and her husband.
The book lay between us on the table.
the wall between our garden and the next one
Slough is halfway between London and Reading.
The town hall was built between 1900 and 1910.
children aged between 7 and 9 [= aged from 7 to 9]
a daytime temperature of between 25°C and 30°C.

> ⓘ A thing is **among** (rather than **between**) many or several other things when they are all around it:
> *a little village high among the hills*
> But:
> *The stream runs between two hills.*

2 You travel **between** two places when you regularly go from one to the other and back again:

a regular train service between Leeds and Bradford
commuting between home and work

3 Two or more people do something, or possess something, **between** them when they do or possess it together:

Between us we managed to fix the lock.
Between them they had a total of six children.
We had eight identical black bags between the four of us.

4 You *choose* or *distinguish* **between** two or more things:

the choice between good and evil
I can't decide between the red ones and the green ones.
There's one major difference between these styles.

BETWEEN OR AMONG?

1 A group of two or very few specified individuals share something **between** them:

The fees are divided between the writer and the publisher.
the love between man and wife
Duties are shared between Geoffrey, Isobel and myself.
Agreement has been reached between management, trade union officials and workers.

Among is not used if the group only consists of two:

After the divorce, she divided her time equally between her parents.

2 Use **between** or **among**:

- with a specified *number* of people or things:

  a prize of $2 million, to be divided between (or *among*) *the top eight players*

- with a group of people or things that are not individually specified:

  The profits are shared out between (or *among*) *the employees.*
  Divide the sweets between (or *among*) *yourselves.*

> ⓘ You say that something is **between** you and one or more others if you want it to be a secret:
> *Charlie, this is just between you and me.*
> *Between ourselves, I can't stand the man.*

AMONG AND AMONGST

1 You can use **amongst** instead of **among** when referring to something within a certain group:

Divorce is common amongst young people who marry as soon as they leave school.
We have reports of sexist attitudes amongst ordinary policemen.

2 You use **among** or **amongst** to mean 'included in':

Amongst the works on view was a portrait of the artist's wife.
I was delighted to be amongst those chosen to compete in the final.

•••• big, large, great ••••

SIZE

1 **Big** and **large** are both used to express *physical size*. **Large** is slightly more formal than **big**:

The housing problems in the big cities would not go away.
She had big (or *large*) *blue eyes.*
He was wearing a jacket that was much too big (or *large*) *for him.*
A big smile for the camera, please!

- If you describe a person as **big** or **large** you mean that they are rather heavy as well as tall:

  I sat next to a big (or *large*) *dark bearded man.*

- **Great** is a literary alternative to **big** and **large**:
  the great dome of St Paul's
  great rivers of the world

2 **Large** is often used with amounts:
You'll need a large supply of paper towels.
Production was continuing on a large scale.
He'd made a large profit on every deal.

> ⓘ With an uncountable noun, like **equipment**, **furniture** or **luggage**, you use **big** or **large pieces** (of luggage etc) to express physical size, or **a large amount** (of furniture etc) to express quantity.

Informally however, there are a few uncount nouns that **big** can be used with:

- **Big business** is business done on a large scale:
  Building societies soon became big business.
- **Big money** means a large profit:
  There's still big money to be made in software.

3 Your **big brother** or **big sister** is one that is older than you are. The opposite is **little**:
The new baby loves her big brother.

INTENSIFYING

1 You can use **big** and **great** to intensify *abstract count nouns*. **Great** is more formal than **big**:
You're making a big (or *great*) *mistake.*
He's a bigger (or *greater*) *fool than I thought he was.*
There's been a big (or *great*) *improvement.*
It's a big (or *great*) *responsibility for us.*
Electronic mail was proving a big (or *great*) *success in the UK.*
That must have been a great (or *big*) *disappointment.*

2 **Great** is used to intensify *abstract uncount nouns*:
He felt great pride when he looked at his two sons.
Great care should be taken.

3 Use **great** to describe someone who does something keenly:
The children are great readers.
I'm a great believer in exercise.
I was never a great opera fan.

4 **Great** and **big** can be used together, to emphasize the idea of size:
They had this great big hairy dog called Sam.
She was delighted, and gave me a great big hug.

5 Informally, **great** expresses approval or pleasure:
This hair gel is great.
OK, that sounds great.
It's a great feeling to win.
It was great to see you.

6 **Great** (or informally, **big**) people and achievements are famous or important:
Reaumur was one of the great naturalists of his time.
Why is Shakespeare great?
great scientific discoveries of the century
She never expected to become a big name in the fashion world.
directors like Oliver Stone, who are big in the American film industry

• • • • billion • • • •

In Britain and Europe, a **billion** is traditionally a million millions, but in the US, and nowadays increasingly in Britain and Europe, it is a thousand millions.

➤ See also the entry **hundred, thousand, million**.

• • • • bit: a bit • • • •

1 **rather**

- **A bit** is a moderating adverb which means 'to some extent' or 'rather':
Can't you speed up a bit?
It's a bit like being colour-blind.
I've been a bit depressed.
It's a bit warmer today.
Could you speak a bit more slowly?

- You use **a bit of a** before a noun, to mean the same as **rather a**:
This letter-writing is a bit of a bore.
Now I feel a bit of a fool.

ⓘ Notice that **a bit** usually implies disapproval or negativity (except in combination with comparative expressions):
It's a bit cold in here.
I'm a bit shortsighted.
Sorry I was a bit late.
You never say, for example, *It's a bit cosy in here* or *I'm a bit happy.*

2 **rather too**

A bit often has the meaning 'rather too':
Isn't she a bit old to be playing the romantic heroine?
It's a bit late to change your mind now.
I thought you were being a bit optimistic.

3 **at all** or **in the least**

- **A bit**, and also **one bit** are used like **at all**, and **in the least** to emphasise negative expressions:
This isn't a bit like the old days.
I'm not a bit surprised.
I don't blame you one bit.

- The expression **not a bit** can stand by itself as an answer, like **not at all**:
'Would you mind if I opened a window?' 'Not a bit. Go ahead.'

•••• blame, fault, guilty ••••

You use **blame**, **fault** and **guilty** to talk about who is responsible for things that have gone wrong. They are, however, used in different ways.

BLAME

Blame is used as both a noun and a verb.

1 You **blame** a person or thing for something bad if you think, or say, that they are responsible for it:
He did not blame the police for the crime wave.

2 You **blame** something bad that has happened **on** a person or thing, when you think or say that they are responsible for it:
It is all too easy to blame everything on capitalism.

3 The **blame** for is the responsibility for letting it happen or causing it:
The management refused to accept the blame for the falling profits.

4 You **are to blame** for something bad that has happened if you caused it, or let it happen:
The official report says no one was to blame for the fire.
The court heard that the worker wasn't to blame.

FAULT

Fault can be used as a noun.

1 You say that something that has gone wrong is someone's **fault** if you think they are responsible for it, or that they should be blamed for it:
It was the driver's fault; he hadn't noticed the pedestrian crossing.
I'm sorry; it was all my fault.

2 You are **at fault** when you deserve the blame for something, or when you are mistaken:
The Government is at fault in the present crisis.
I think the owners are at fault for not acting responsibly.

GUILTY

1 You are **guilty** of doing something bad or wrong or illegal if you are the person who caused it, or let it happen:
The jury found him guilty of murder.

2 You **feel guilty** about something you have done when you feel unhappy because you think you should not have done it:
Have you ever felt guilty about your drinking?
Jake felt guilty that he had not spoken to Kathleen.

•••• born, borne ••••

BORN

When you are referring to someone's *birth* you use the passive verb **to be born**:
David was born (not *is born* or *has been born*) *on 8 March 1947.*
Alfred was born in 1830, the first of six children.
She was born in Uganda, and brought up and educated there.

Many babies are being born with breathing difficulties.
The cubs are born blind and helpless.

BORNE

Borne is the past participle of the verb **bear**:

bears, bearing, bore, borne

Most of its uses are rather formal:

In this case the repair costs will be borne [= paid] *by the company.*
We were borne [= carried] *along by the crowd as it moved forward.*
Their suspicions were borne out [= proved right] *by a second investigation.*
Two further points must be borne [= kept] *in mind.*

•••• borrow, lend, loan ••••

If you've got something, you can **lend** it to someone else. You **borrow** something that belongs to someone else.

BORROW

You **borrow** something **from** someone when you take something belonging to them, with or without their knowledge or permission, intending to return it to them:

He said I could borrow his horse.
I borrowed the fare from my sister, and here I am.
The glasses were borrowed from a local hotel.
He had a borrowed car for a week after the crash.

LEND

The past tense and past participle of **lend** is **lent**.

You **lend** someone something, or **lend** something **to** someone, when you temporarily let them have something that belongs to you:

I didn't have a book, but the teacher lent me one.
Someone had lent Robert a car.
Public money will be used to lend up to £420 a year to each student.

As with **give**, a passive construction is possible:

I'd no idea where we were, until I was lent a map.

LOAN

The verb **loan** is often used instead of **lend** in AmE:

Moran had loaned McQuaid money when he started in the cattle business.

In BrE, **loan** is often used as a verb to refer to items in an exhibition:

Reynolds' self-portrait is a painting loaned from the Royal Collection.

•••• both ••••

Grammatically, **both** is used in the same way as **all**. It is always used with a plural noun or pronoun, and a plural verb, but, unlike **all**, it refers to only two people or things.

1 **Both** can be used directly before a noun:

Both sons are doing well in their careers.
She's had both hips replaced.

2 Before **the**, **these**, **those**, **this** or **that** or a possessive adjective (**his**, **her** etc), you can used **both** or **both of**:

Both (of) the twins chose to study medicine.
Both (of) my parents smoke.
She broke both (of) her legs in a skiing accident.
Both (of) these tables will be needed.

3 **Both of** is the form that is nearly always used before pronouns:

I want to see both of you after school today.
You'll probably need to remind both of them (not *both them*).
Both of us (not *both we*) *know what it is like to lose a close friend.*

4 Where a negative applies to each one of two, you use **neither of**, or **not either of**, rather than **both ... not** or **not ... both**:

Neither of her current boyfriends looks very interesting.
I haven't seen either of them (not *I haven't seen both of them*) *for ages.*

5 You use **both** after a noun or pronoun to emphasize that you mean each one of the two:

My parents were both relieved when I married Steven.
Their twins are a boy and a girl, but ours are both girls.
You both did a lot of work; sincere thanks to you both.
We're both hoping to come.
We can't both refuse.
How are you both?
with best wishes from us both

> ⓘ Notice that the use of **both** in paragraph **5** is an alternative to the construction with **both of** shown in paragraph **3** above:
> *I'd like to thank you both* (or *both of you*).
> *'I was wondering if either or both of you would be interested?' 'We both would* (or *Both of us would*).*'*
> You can use, *eg* **Both of us** or **Both of them** as a short, verbless reply, but you can't use **We both** or **Them both** in this way:
> *Which file did you want: the old one or the new one?' 'Both of them* (not *them both*)*, please.'*
> *Who's going to speak, you or Sheila? Or both of you?* (not *you both*)

6 You can use **both** on its own as a pronoun:

He suggested two dates but both were impossible.
You'll need a dictionary or phrase book; I usually take both.

7 If you are making one comment about two different things, you can join them with **both ... and**:

Both my mother and my aunt have red hair.
Both you and she have a good chance of getting the job.
Please sign both Section I and Section II.
It's wonderful news, both from my point of view and from his.

ⓘ Notice that the word or phrase that follows **and** matches the word or phrase that follows **both**, that is, it belongs to the same grammatical class (noun, verb, adverb, clause, and so on):
*She's famous for being both **witty** and **entertaining**.*
*He both **adored** and **admired** her.*
*I both **liked him as a colleague** and **depended on him as a friend**.*
The corresponding negative situation, that is, a situation where you want to apply a negative to both of two alternatives, is expressed using **neither ... nor**:
*I neither **knew** nor **cared** what had happened to him.*

•••• brackets ••••

➤ See the entry **punctuation**.

•••• breakfast ••••

➤ See the entry **meals**.

•••• breath, breathe ••••

1 **breathe** (/briːð/) is a verb:

breathes, breathing, breathed

You **breathe** when you take air into your lungs and let it out again:

The baby was sleeping at last and breathing peacefully.
He wanted to breathe the fresh sea air again.

2 **breath**

Breath (/brɛθ/) is a count or uncount noun.

- a **breath** is an act of breathing:

  Take a big breath.

- **Breath** is the air you take into your lungs and let out again when you breathe:

  Her breath smelt of alcohol.
  You can't be out of breath already!

•••• bring, take, fetch ••••

There are variations in the way these three words are used by English speakers throughout the world. Standard English uses them in the following way:

TAKE

You use **take**, like **go**, to express a direction away from you. It is often used with **there**:

Do we need to take sandwiches with us?
If you're going to Kay's, could you take her this book?
She asked about the castle, so I took her there.

BRING

Someone **brings** something towards you, and you **bring** something to your hearer:

Do bring the children when you come next time.
Shall I bring my photos to your house tomorrow?
If they don't find anywhere to stay you can bring them here.

> ⓘ In telling a story, you use **bring** from the point of view of the person you are identifying with:
> *He brought her flowers* [the speaker is identifying with the woman].

FETCH

You **fetch** something when you go and get it, and return with it:

I'm going to fetch Peter from the swimming pool.
Could you fetch me a few more nails?

•••• bring up, raise, educate ••••

1 To **bring** children **up** is to care for them until they are grown up:

Mike walked out in '85, and I had to bring up the girls on my own.
I thought I'd brought my sons up to be polite.
I was brought up in the country.
The children were all brought up as Protestants.

> ⓘ **Upbringing**, as distinct from **education**, trains children how to behave *morally* and *socially*, and teaches them particular attitudes, principles and beliefs:
> *I'd had a strict upbringing and was amazed at the stories these boys told.*

2 AmE uses **raise** rather than **bring up**:

He moved to California, where he settled and raised a family.
I know all about that sort of thing; I was raised on a farm.
Raised as a Roman Catholic, he disapproves of divorce.

3 People **are educated** when they are taught academic or school subjects:

Edith was born, brought up and educated on the Isle of Lewis.
This teacher said he was impossible to educate and refused to teach him

•••• Britain, Great Britain, the United Kingdom, The British Isles ••••

TERRITORIES

Great Britain or **Britain** = England, Scotland and Wales
the United Kingdom = England, Scotland, Wales and Northern Ireland
The British Isles = Britain, Ireland and the smaller islands off their coasts

NATIONALITIES

1 People from the United Kingdom are all officially **British**.

2 People from England can call themselves **English**; similarly, people from Scotland, Wales and Northern Ireland can call themselves **Scottish**, **Welsh**, or **Northern Irish** respectively, and not **English**.

3 The noun **Briton** is used, especially in newspaper reporting, to refer to a British person:

The 5 hostages (two Britons and three Germans) are being held by the kidnappers.
Hotel roof collapses and kills Briton.

4 People from Britain, and any group of people representing Britain, can be referred to as **the British**:

The British don't like direct forms of criticism.
The British have only won one silver medal so far.

•••• broad, wide ••••

Broad and **wide** mean the same in some senses, but there are areas where one is used rather than the other.

1 People usually use **wide** rather than **broad** when talking about features of the landscape, or physical objects, especially if a measurement is being given:

The river is 2 miles wide.
The stage was about six metres wide.
The island is 50 miles long and 25 miles across at its widest point.
Gerard came through the wide entrance at the back of the hall.
I drove through the wide streets of New Delhi.

2 **Broad** is preferred for describing people's physical features:

These monkeys have broad noses.
He shrugged his broad shoulders.
She grinned all over her broad features.
His broad forehead and narrow jaw reminded her of Fred Astaire.

ⓘ Notice that in describing clothes, you would use **wide** rather than **broad** for shoulders, sleeves, legs etc:
a suit with wide, baggy trousers

FIGURATIVE MEANINGS

The figurative senses of **broad** and **wide** are closely connected.

1 You can use **broad** to mean 'general', when referring to things like issues or principles:

We've been trying to take a broad view and not concentrate on details.
These people can, broadly speaking, be described as 'working class'.

2 The figurative sense of **wide** expresses *distribution* or *spreading outwards*:

Since retiring, he's developed a wide range of interests.
Her books are widely read in this country.

• • • • business • • • •

Business has various count and uncount uses, and it is important to distinguish between them.

1 (*uncount*) **trading and commerce**

Business is the work of producing and buying and selling:

I went into business with my two brothers, selling our design ideas.
I've been abroad on business.
Hollywood became big business as cinema audiences grew.
Here's my business address.

2 (*count*) **a commercial organization**

A **business** is a commercial organization such as a company or shop:

He ran a printing business.
The local grocery was one of those old established family businesses.

3 (*uncount*) **important matters**

You can use **business** to describe important matters that you must deal with:

He had some urgent business to attend to.
Further diplomatic business will be handled by Freda.
Since there is no further business, I declare this meeting closed.

4 (*count, usually in the singular*) **a situation**

Informally, any situation, or series of events, can be referred to as a **business** of some sort:

That accident was a rotten business.
Life's a funny business anyway.
the time-consuming business of interviewing witnesses

5 (*used in the singular*) **That's my business**

- A private matter, that concerns or affects you personally, is **your business**:

I think that's my business, not theirs.
She told me to mind my own business [= to stop being nosy].
Her private life is none of our business (or *no business of ours*).

- Your duty or your role is your **business**:

Discipline should be the parents' business, not the teacher's.

• • • • busy • • • •

You say you are **busy doing** something at a particular moment if you happen to be doing it then:

We were busy looking at our holiday pictures when you rang.
We've been busy painting the hall for the last few days.

➤ For a similar use of **in the middle of** see **middle**.

.... but ....

But has two main uses: as a *conjunction* introducing a contrast to something just mentioned, and as a *preposition* meaning 'except'.

AS A CONJUNCTION

1 The most usual use of **but** is as a link between *contrasting clauses*:

I'd hoped to see the cathedral too, but there wasn't time.

The subject of the **but** clause is often omitted if it is the same as that of the main clause:

The picture may look like a model of the hotel, but is (or *but it is*) *in fact the real thing.*
Francis didn't knock at the door, but walked (not *but he walked*) *straight in.*

The main verb can often be replaced by an auxiliary or modal verb in a **but** clause:

I hoped Liz would phone, but she ***didn't****.*
'You must tell your parents.' 'But I ***daren't****'.*

2 **But** can also be used to link phrases, and parts of speech such as adjectives, adverbs and nouns:

Our technicians have discovered a ***simple*** *but* ***effective*** *solution to the problem.*
She lead him ***gently*** *but* ***firmly*** *towards the door.*
It's not ***the clever children****, but* ***the interested ones****, that I enjoy teaching.*
I'd call myself ***a historian*** *but not* ***an archaeologist****.*

3 You use **but** to raise objections:

'Let's pretend you got a six.' 'But that's cheating!'

4 You can use **but** to change the direction of a conversation or discussion:

I'll tell you all about that in a minute, but first, let's hear about your holiday.

AS A PREPOSITION

1 After words such as **all**, **everything**, and **anything**, negative words such as **no**, **no-one**, **nothing**, and **nowhere**, and question words such as **who**, **what** and **where**, **but** is used to mean 'except':

You've discussed everything but the most important point.
All but two of them were women.
'Are you an expert?' 'Anything but!' [= not at all!]
I had no choice but to accept their decision.
No-one but a fool would believe that nonsense.
There seems to be nothing but beer in the fridge.
They do nothing but quarrel, those two.
Who but Purcell [= only Purcell] *could have written that?*
What could I do but thank him?

2 The verb form that most often follows **but** is the infinitive, usually without **to**:

She believed the bird was saying real words, when in fact it did nothing but whistle.
Frank does nothing but sit in the house all day.
The bank will have no choice but to raise interest rates.

3 **But for** can have a similar meaning to 'without':

But for your help, I could have died.
But for her, the whole performance might have collapsed.

4 The **last** thing **but one** in a series is the one just before the last one.

The **next** thing **but one** is the one just after the next one:

Alison lived next door but one to me in Oxford.

> ⓘ **not only** ... , **but also** ...
> You use **but also** after **not only** to add a second statement that supports the first one:
> *I was impressed, not only by his good looks, but also by his charm.*
> *The conference attracted not only authors, but also several publishers.*

•••• by ••••

AS A PREPOSITION

1 **By** is used after a passive, before the agent, that is the doer or cause. **With**, rather than **by**, is used to refer to the instrument used by the agent:

The letter was evidently written by a foreigner.
He was met at the airport by the manager herself.
She was blinded by the bright lights.
The village was destroyed by an avalanche.

But:

His skull had been crushed with a heavy object.

2 You achieve something **by** doing a certain thing, or by a certain means if that is *how* you achieve it:

She made a bit of money by selling her paintings.
You can cook an egg by boiling it in water.
May I pay by credit card?
She's arriving in London by air this afternoon.

3 Notice some other related uses of **by**:

Grandfather took Peter firmly by the hand [= he took Peter's hand].
Purely by chance, I met him again that weekend, in the wine shop.
I called John 'David' by mistake.
What do you mean by [= when you say] *'off-hand'?*
'Cats' is the most recent novel by this remarkable young writer.

4 **By** can be used as a preposition of place:

- one thing is **by** another if it is beside it, or next to it:

  There was a low table by her chair.
  The dog lay by (or *at*) *her side.*

- To go **by** someone or something is to pass them, or go past them:

  The bus flew by me before I could stop it.

5 **By** can be a preposition of time:

- Something that happens **by** a certain time happens at that time, or before it:
  By five thirty she was feeling pretty hungry.
  Library books must be returned by Friday at the latest.
- You do something **by day** or **night**, if you do it during the day or night:
  Owls sleep by day and hunt by night.

6 You are a certain person **by nature** if that is your character:
He was quite a shy person by nature.

7 You are something **by trade**, or **by profession**, if that is your job:
Her next boyfriend was Jack, who was a psychologist by profession.

8 Things happen **by law** if they happen according to law:
Employers must by law employ workers from minority groups.

EXPRESSING MULTIPLICATION, DIVISION, MEASUREMENT AND RATE

Notice the following uses of **by**:

Divide twenty-seven by three.
Four multiplied by three is twelve.
The bedroom was about ten metres by six [=10m long and 6m wide].
The situation was worsening by the hour [= very quickly].
Prices have risen by an average of 4% this year.
Interest rates are to be cut by 1%.
Her sister was taller by at least two inches.
I only missed my train by a couple of minutes.

> ⓘ You use expressions such as **little by little** and **day by day** to express the idea of gradual but steady progress:
> *Add the milk bit by bit.*
> *Month by month his strength returned.*
> *One by one the musicians left the stage.*

• • • • by far • • • •

➤ See entry for **far**.

Cc

call

The verb **call** has four main divisions of meaning: to *shout*, to *telephone*, to *visit*, and to *name*.

SHOUT

- You **call** when you shout or speak loudly, *eg* to attract attention:
  'This way!' called Alan, raising his voice.
  Call me when you're ready.
  He ran after her calling her name.
- You **call for** something, or **call on** someone **for** something, or **to do** something, when you request it:
  He called for a single European currency.
  The party called on the minister to resign.
- Circumstances **call for** certain actions, measures or qualities if they require them:
  This calls for a celebration.
  A bit of diplomacy is called for here.

TELEPHONE

You **call** someone when you contact them by phone:
David called from New York a couple of times.
He called the number in the newspaper ad.
She stayed with him while the others called an ambulance.

> ⓘ Notice that **call** takes a direct object without **to**:
> *I tried to call you* (not *call to you*) *this morning.*

VISIT

1 You **call on** people, **call at** places, and **call at**, or **in at**, buildings, when you visit them:
While in town they called on David but he was out.
This is the eleven-forty train for Edinburgh, calling at Newcastle and Durham.
Call in at your local bank and get a form.
I just called in for a chat.
They sent a card saying that the inspector was going to call.

2 You **call for** someone or something when you collect them from somewhere:
I'll call for you at seven.

NAME

1 People or things are **called** something if they have, or are given, that name or title:

I remember a little girl called Lucy.
And I hate being called 'dear' or 'darling', as if I were a child.
He played an instrument called a 'theorbo'.

2 You **call** a person or thing something when you describe them in that way, or use that word about them:

Charles called Harry a liar.
They call it brainwashing. I call it common sense.
Dr Steel called Jackson's work 'crucial'.

•••• can ••••

Can is one of the *modal* verbs, which are used with the infinitives of other verbs to express such ideas as possibility, probability and necessity. They always keep the same form.

The modal verb **could** is used as the past tense of **can** and shares many of its senses.

➤ See also the entries for **could** and for **modal verbs**.

The formal negative form of **can** is **cannot** and the contracted negative form is **can't**.

The chief uses of **can** are to express the ideas of *ability* and *possibility*, to ask for and give *permission*, and to make *requests*, *offers* and *suggestions*.

ⓘ **Can** has two pronunciations, the unemphatic /kən/, which is the usual one, and /kan/, which is used for special emphasis, and is the pronunciation regularly used in question tags.
Can't is pronounced /kɑːnt/ in BrE, and /kant/ in AmE.

ABILITY

1 You **can** do something if you are able to do it, if you have the skill to do it, or if it is possible to do it:

Now his leg is better, he can ride a bike again and play football.
Can she read yet?
How many languages can you speak?
But can we afford this?
We cannot change the past.
Speak up, I can't hear you.

2 In BrE **can** is often used, without any real addition of meaning, in combination with:

- verbs of sensing, such as **hear**, **see**, **feel**. This is not common in AmE:

  I can hear (or AmE, *I hear*) *music coming from upstairs.*
  You can feel the warmth coming up through the floor.
  Can you see (or AmE, *do you see*) *the hut down there?*

- certain verbs representing the mental processes of remembering and comprehending, *eg* **remember**, **understand**, **guess**, **tell**, **follow**:

  I can remember the first time it happened.
  I can understand that people want to know.

You can guess what happened next.
Something's wrong, I can tell.

ⓘ Verbs that imply the acquisition of a skill, such as playing a game, or speaking a language, are sometimes used without **can**:
Do you (or *can you*) *play croquet?*
I don't think she speaks (or *can speak*) *German.*

3 Normally, **can** becomes **could** in reported speech:

He said we couldn't change the past.

4 Since **can** has no infinitive sense, or **-ing** form, it is grammatically impossible to use it after other auxiliary or modal verbs, or after verbs and phrases that are followed by an infinitive or **-ing** form. You use **be able to** instead:

I'll be able to get to work more quickly if I get a flat in the city.
That's one thing I've been able to do.
I might be able to move the sofa into the bedroom.
The animal seemed to be able to understand what we wanted.
It's great being able to send files by e-mail.

5 When you are talking about plans for the future, as distinct from future skills or physical abilities, **can** is possible:

I can see her at twelve, if she wants to come then.
Sorry I can't be with you on Friday; I'll think about you though!

➤ See also the entry **able**.

PERMISSION

1 You use **can** to ask for and give permission. You **can** do something if you are allowed to do it. **Can** is a less formal alternative to **may**:

Can I speak to Mrs Travers, please?
Can I have the key?
You can (or, more formally, *may*) *have my room if you like.*
I'm afraid you can't smoke in here.

ⓘ People often *ask* permission using **could** rather than **can**, so as to sound more polite. Notice that in the reply *giving* permission, you usually use **can**:
'Could I have a look at your paper?' 'Yes, of course you can.'

OFFERS, REQUESTS, SUGGESTIONS AND ORDERS

1 You use **can** to offer to do something, or to ask someone, or invite them, to do something, or make a suggestion about doing something:

Can I get you a drink?
Can you post those letters on your way home?
Can we meet for a drink sometime?

ⓘ People sometimes use the negative question form to make rather impatient suggestions, or to express impatience at the way someone is acting or behaving:
Can't you see I'm busy?
Just listen to me, can't you?
Why can't they think of other people for a change?

POSSIBILITY

1 You use **can** when asking or wondering what to do, *eg* to achieve something:
How can I help you?
What can I do to avoid catching flu?
Who can she ask?

2 You use **can** when saying what is possible or appropriate, or when presenting a choice of courses of action:
You can ask our expert to call or you can visit our showroom.
You were a teacher once; can't you go back to that?

3 **Can** expresses what is theoretically possible:
Can people really live in conditions like that?
I doubt if the relationship can be saved now.
Some dreams can't ever come true.

4 **Can** also expresses what sometimes happens or what typically happens:
The town can get very crowded, especially in the summer.
You can get very dirty mending a car.
A week can seem a very long time to a child.

5 You use **can** in the negative, or in questions, or with words like **scarcely**, to express doubt about the possibility of something, or to wonder or speculate about possibilities:
How can you be so sure?
A change of plan now can only lead to disaster.
He can scarcely expect us to go on supporting him after this.

6 You use **can have** in the negative, or in questions, to speculate about something that has happened, to wonder what has happened, or wonder whether something has happened:
Where can I have put that letter?
There is only one witness; can he have been mistaken?

7 You say that people **can't** do something as a way of saying they mustn't do it:
Well, we can't sit around here all day talking.
But you can't tell them a lie.

FIXED COMBINATIONS

Some verbs are used regularly with **can't** to express strong feelings of various kinds.

1 If you say you **can't bear**, **can't stand** or **can't abide** something, you mean you dislike it or hate it:
I can't bear the thought of going back to the empty flat alone.
She can't stand the sight of him.

2 You use **can't think** and **can't imagine** with a **wh-**clause to wonder in amazement about something:

I can't imagine why you like this music.

3 You say you **can't believe** something to express amazement or dismay at it.

I can't believe what I'm hearing.

4 Something that you **can't wait** for, or **can't wait** to do, is something you are eager for, or eager to do:

Most girls can't wait to leave home.

AS A PHRASE SUBSTITUTE

1 You use **can** to stand for the whole of a clause:

- to avoid repetition, for example when answering someone:

  'Are you joining us later?' 'No, sorry, I can't.'
  'Leave a seat for me.' 'I don't see how I can.' [= can leave a seat for you]

- to refer back, *eg* in a subordinate clause, to something you have said:

  I'll see to it as soon as I can.
  He can't see the point of it. I can [= can see the point of it].
  Either you can paint or you can't.

- in question tags:

  I can't win, really, can I?
  You can't prove it isn't, can you?
  You can see that, can't you?
  Johnny can give us a hand, can't he?

2 In short answers and other elliptical structures, **can** is often followed by **be**, **do**, or **have**, and **can have** by **been** or **done** in referring back to verbs that use these auxiliaries:

'The shop's closed.' 'It can't be!'
'Does the static electricity cause problems?' 'It can do (or *it can*).*'*
'You obviously weren't concentrating.' 'I can't have been.'
'He's written his report already.' 'He can't have done (or *he can't have*)*!'*

— can't help —

➤ See **help**.

— capital letters —

➤ See **punctuation**.

• • • • care • • • •

BE CONCERNED

1 You **care about** something, or **care**, *eg* **whether** something happens, if it concerns or worries you. In this sense **care** is frequently used in the negative or in questions:

60% of customers did not care about calories.
He really didn't care whether he got his bike back or not.
If the result's good, who cares how you achieve it?

2 You say you **couldn't care less** about something if it doesn't worry or concern you at all:

I couldn't care less what happens to her.

3 You are **past caring** about something if you are in such an extreme emotional state that it doesn't matter to you any more:

I was past caring about my luggage; I just wanted to get home safely.

4 You say you **care for** someone if you love them:

I did care for him, although maybe not in the way a wife should care for her husband.

5 Something that you **don't care for** is something you dislike:

He doesn't care for alcoholic drink.
I don't care much for housework.

6 If someone asks you if you **would care to** do something, or **would care for** something, they are inviting you to do it, or offering it to you, in a rather formal or old-fashioned way:

Would you care to join me for dinner?
Would you care for a drink?

LOOK AFTER

1 To **care for** someone or something, or **take care of** them, is to look after them:

She took time off to care for her dying father.
Some hand creams also care for your nails.

2 You **take care of** a matter when you deal with it:

The hotel staff will take care of all your needs.
Tell me the general idea and I'll take care of the details.

• • • • case • • • •

➤ For information about **in case** and **in case of**, see the entry **in case**.

SITUATIONS AND INSTANCES

1 The following examples show the range of uses that **case** has when referring to situation or instances:

We don't normally take cash, but in your case we can.
In many cases, children chose their own themes.
It was a case of mistaken identity.

2 A crime, mystery or the investigation into it is referred to as a **case**. A legal **case** is a matter that is tried or examined in a court of law. In medical terms, a **case** is the occurrence of a particular illness in, or injury to, some person; doctors often refer to their patients as **cases**:

We deal with about a hundred cases of physical assault every year.
Of the cases reported, less than half will go to court.
We had a severe case of bleeding in the emergency ward last night.

3 The **case for** or **against** a proposal or theory is the evidence and reasoning that is used to support it or oppose it:

The management will have to present a convincing case.
In fact the reverse case can be argued.

IDIOMS AND OTHER USES

1 Something **is the case** if it is so, or is true:

That's what I thought, but it was in fact not the case.
If that were the case we'd have heard.
If, as is sometimes the case, the child is lying, the problem is a different one.

2 Something that is so **in any case** remains true whichever possible situation turns out to be the actual one; you also use **in any case** to add a comment that supports something you have just said:

We had no telephone, and in any case there was no time to call a doctor.

3 You can use **in that case** and **in which case** to mean 'if that is so':

This pill may not work, in which case I'll give you a different kind.
'I need a rest.' 'In that case you had better sit here a while.'

• • • • cause • • • •

AS A NOUN

1 The **cause of** something is what makes it happen:

Investigations are continuing into the cause of the fire.
Doctors deny that natural sugars are a significant cause of tooth decay.

2 **Cause** is used, often as an uncountable noun, with **for**, to mean 'grounds or justification':

We checked the kitchens and found no cause for complaint.
The most obvious cause for alarm was the state of the economy.

AS A VERB

1 One thing **causes** another when it makes it happen. Notice that **cause** can take a second object, in the form of the person affected:

The illness can cause severe mental and physical damage.
Our middle child caused us more worry than the other two.

2 Something **causes** you to do something if it makes you do it:

What caused him to think that?
Her behaviour caused us to begin to worry about her mental health.

•••• certain, sure, uncertain, unsure ••••

CERTAIN

1 You use **certain** as a determiner to refer to a particular person or thing, or to particular people or things, without stating which. You also use it to refer to particular amounts, without saying how much:

A certain scientist refused to believe that the results were genuine.
There are a number of rooms that we may only enter at certain times.
The similarity of the two names caused a certain amount of confusion.

2 **Certain** is used with uncountable nouns to describe a quality that is noticeable but difficult to analyse. In such cases, the article **a** is used:

There was a certain tenderness in the way he looked at her.

3 **Certain of** a number or group of things are particular, but unspecified, ones:

She returned certain of the gifts, but kept the others.
The children crowded around and certain of them reached out to touch him.

CERTAIN OR SURE

1 You are **certain** or **sure that** something is so if you have no doubts about it:

Mary was certain (or *sure*) *that it was the same car.*
He felt certain (or *sure*) *she wouldn't mind.*
I was never sure (or *certain*) *that he was telling the truth.*

2 You say you are **not certain** or **not sure** if you do not know about something; **not certain** and **not sure** in this use are followed by question words such as **whether**, **if**, **what**, and **how**:

He was not certain (or *not sure*) *which door to open first.*
He's got a new job; I'm not certain (or *not sure*) *what it is.*
Doctors themselves are not certain (or *not sure*) *how the drug works.*

> ⓘ Notice that **uncertain** and **unsure** can be used in the same way as **not certain** and **not sure**:
> *He looked up, uncertain* (or *unsure*) *where he was.*
> *She was uncertain* (or *unsure*) *what to do next.*

3 You can also **be**, or **feel**, or **seem** (to someone else) **certain** or **uncertain**, or **sure** or **unsure**, **about** or **of** something:

He was not certain (or *sure*) *of the exact meaning of the word.*
They were talking about him, he was sure (or *certain*) *of that.*
Some parents are unsure (or *uncertain*) *about how to deal with this.*
He seemed uncertain (or *unsure*) *of his facts.*

4 Something is **certain**, or it is **certain** that something is, or will be, the case, if there is no doubt about it. Something that is **not certain** is not known definitely:

It now looks certain that the offer will be refused.
It is not yet certain where the British forces will go.

> ⓘ Notice that the impersonal use is possible only with **certain**:
> *It is possible but not yet certain* (not *sure*) *that talks will be held.*
> *Success seems certain* (rather than *sure*).

5 Something is **certain** or **sure to** happen or be so if it is very likely to happen or be so:
The boys were sure (or *certain*) *to laugh at him behind his back.*
He's sure (or *certain*) *to have a wife and kids back home.*

6 You are **certain** or **sure of** achieving something if there is no risk of your failing:
We need to be sure of raising £300.
He wanted to be quite sure of finding her at home.
Even graduates can't be certain (or *sure*) *of getting a job.*

7 You are **sure of** something when you can definitely expect it:
You can be sure of a warm welcome in this hotel.

> ⓘ Notice that you emphasize the adjectives **certain** and **sure** with adverbs of extent, such as **completely**, **absolutely** or **entirely** rather than intensifying adverbs such as **very** or **extremely**:
> *You can never be absolutely certain how you'd react to an attack.*
> *The doctor wanted to give her another check-up, to be completely sure.*

8 You **make certain** or **sure of** something, or **that** something happens, when you act so that there is no risk of it not happening; you **make sure** or **certain that** something is the case when you check that it is:
Make sure (or *certain*) *that the whole shoulder area is supported.*
Make (or *Be*) *sure you know where to leave the keys.*

9 If you tell someone to **be sure to** do something, you are reminding them, in a slightly old-fashioned way, to do it:
Be sure to leave some time for shopping.

10 You know something **for certain** or **for sure** if you have no doubts about it:
I knew for sure that he was lying.
Exactly what happened is not known for certain.

•••• certainly ••••

1 **Certainly** means 'definitely' or 'without doubt', and can be used:

- to give confirmation about what you are saying:
  Saint Peter was certainly married.
- as an *emphasizing adverb*, to give extra force to your statement:
  He certainly seems keen.

2 Like other emphasizing adverbs, **certainly** usually occurs in mid position, that is, before a main verb, after an auxiliary verb, after the first auxiliary verb if there are more than one, and usually after the verb **be**:
His humour certainly adds to my enjoyment of office life.
I would certainly know if he'd died.
That's certainly one way of looking at things.

3 You often use **certainly** with an auxiliary or modal verb, or the verb **be**, in constructions where the main verb or the adjective is omitted. **Certainly** comes before the auxiliary verb:

'Think of me on the day of my test.' 'I certainly shall'.
'You were so lucky with the weather.' 'I certainly was.'

4 **Certainly** is often used as a reply, expressing agreement with something said, or agreement to a request, proposal or suggestion. **Certainly not** is an emphatic way of saying 'no':

'I take it you agree so far?' 'Certainly.'
'Vic, can I have a word?' 'Certainly.'
'You won't tell anyone?' 'Certainly not!'

5 You can say that something is **almost certainly** so when you think it is so, but do not know definitely that it is:

He will almost certainly get paid less.
They would almost certainly support Europe's action.

6 **Certainly** can be used as a sentence adverb:

She's better, certainly, but still very weak.

•••• chance ••••

POSSIBILITY

1 If it is possible that something will happen, you can say that there is **a chance of its happening** or that there is **a chance that it will happen**:

She had a one-in-180 chance of catching the disease.
If you get his agreement in writing now, you'll reduce the chance of him changing his mind.
There is a chance that her father will refuse to co-operate.

2 You say there is **a good**, **fair** or **real**, **chance** of something happening if it is quite likely to happen, and **little**, or **no**, **chance** if it is unlikely to happen:

There's a good chance that the thief is still in the building.
There's a real chance that it might all happen again.
There was little or no chance that the Government would win.

3 Your **chances of doing something**, or the **chances of something happening**, are your prospects of doing it, or the likelihood of it happening:

This course should increase your chances of passing the exam.
What are the chances of finding her now?

4 You have **a chance to do something** when you have an opportunity to do it:

Will he get a chance to explain exactly what he means?

➤ See also **possibility** and **opportunity**.

FATE

The uncountable noun **chance** means much the same as **fate**. You **leave things to chance** when you leave them to fate, that is, fail to organize them in a particular way. Something that happens **by chance** is not planned or expected:

By chance, these two articles appeared side by side in the newspaper.
It was not entirely by chance that we both went to the same restaurant.

> ⓘ Notice that **chance** does not indicate whether what happens is lucky or unlucky. You can refer to lucky happenings as **luck** or **good luck**, and unlucky ones as **bad luck**. But **luck** can, like **chance**, also refer to both lucky and unlucky happenings: *I went sliding over the ice, only by luck managing to stay upright.*

change: ways of expressing it

The verbs **alter**, **become**, **change**, **come**, **get**, **go**, and **turn** are all used in various ways to express change. The verb **fall** has a few fixed uses expressing change. All these verbs, apart from **alter** and **change**, can be used as linking verbs, that is, they belong to the group of verbs that includes **be** and **seem**.

➤ See the entry for the verb **change** for its other particular uses.

BECOME

You can use an adjective, a noun or a past participle after **become**:

I've been feeling great since I became pregnant.
She's becoming more assertive every day.
I'm so glad we've become friends.

➤ See also the entry **become**.

COME

Dreams and wishes **come true** when they are fulfilled:

It was like a dream come true when they finally arrived.

GET

1 You can use **get** with adjectives or past participles as an informal and natural-sounding alternative to **become**:

It's getting cold; let's go in.
I must be getting old.
I realized I was getting weaker by the minute.

2 You use **get**, especially with a past participle, to express the process of something happening to someone or something:

You should be more careful; you'll get run over one day.
It was a lovely jug, but unfortunately it got broken.

3 You use **get** especially with a past participle to express deliberate actions:

Anyway, he's thinking about getting divorced.
I'd better get ready to go out.
He got shaved and changed.

GO

Go is used with adjectives to express two sorts of change:

1 **deterioration**

The following list shows how **go** expresses the process of passing into a worse state:

people	**things**
go mad	*food goes bad*
go crazy	*cheese goes mouldy*
go deaf	*bread goes stale*

go blind *milk goes sour*
go bald *iron goes rusty*
go grey *beer goes flat*

You also frequently hear about things such as relationships, or machines, **going wrong**.

2 change of colour

Go, like **turn**, is used to express the process of changing colour:

He went pale and then red.
The leaves were already going brown or yellow.
Everything went black and I must have fainted.

GROW

Like **get** and **come, grow** can be used both with an adjective and with a **to-**infinitive, but is rather more formal and literary-sounding.

1 grow + adjective

Grow expresses slow or gradual change from one state to another:

He felt his cheeks growing hot.
Spring approached and the evenings grew longer.
The sky was growing pink in the east.

2 grow + to-infinitive

You **grow to** do something, especially develop a particular attitude, when you begin to do it gradually:

We grew to love the strange flatness of the island.

TURN

1 **Turn** is often used with an adjective to talk about obvious changes, *eg* of colour or behaviour, that are immediately noticeable:

The way he drives would turn your hair white.
Then the weather turned cold and wet.

2 One thing **turns** or **changes**, or **is turned** or **changed**, **into**, or **to**, another when it is transformed into the other:

I'm going to change into a whole new person.
We'll help you turn your dream into reality.

FALL

The verb **fall** has a similar meaning to **become** in the following uses:

People can:

fall asleep *fall ill*
fall in love

SUFFIXES AND PREFIXES EXPRESSING CHANGE

1 There are certain verb prefixes and suffixes that express an increase, or reduction, in the quality indicated: when you **enlarge** something or **enrich** someone, you make them larger or richer; when you **simplify**, **glorify**, **purify**, **solidify**, or **beautify** things, you make them simpler, more glorious, purer, solid, or more beautiful; when you **equalize, legalize**, **anglicize**, or **idealize** things, you make them equal, legal, more English, or turn them into an ideal.

2 One of the commonest suffixes indicating increase or reduction in a quality is **-en**:

The days are already beginning to lengthen.
Her face brightened as soon as he appeared.

Below is a list of **-en** verbs:

blacken	*brighten*	*broaden*	*coarsen*
dampen	*darken*	*deaden*	*deafen*
deepen	*fatten*	*flatten*	*gladden*
lessen	*loosen*	*madden*	*moisten*
neaten	*quicken*	*quieten*	*redden*
ripen	*sadden*	*shorten*	*sicken*
smarten	*soften*	*straighten*	*strengthen*
sweeten	*thicken*	*tighten*	*toughen*
weaken	*whiten*	*widen*	*worsen*

You should consult a dictionary to make sure of the uses of the above verbs. Some, for instance, are only used transitively.

■ Notice also the pronunciation of **moisten** is /ˈmɔɪsən/ and the pronunciation of **soften** is /ˈsɒfən/.

ⓘ Certain verbs indicate a change in quality without the help of a prefix or suffix:
Many climbers cope with thinning air without the aid of oxygen.
The road narrows and goes over a bridge.

CHANGE AND ALTER

You use the verbs **change** and **alter** to talk about things becoming, or being made, different, without mentioning what the effect is:

You've changed so much in the last year!
The earthquake changed everything.
We can't alter the past.

NO CHANGE

You express the absence of change with verbs such as **remain**, **stay** and **keep**, followed by an adjective or participle:

I don't know how he manages to keep smiling and cheerful.
Passengers are asked to remain calm and to stay seated.

•••• change (verb) ••••

1 You **change**, **get changed**, or **change your clothes**, when you put on different ones. You can also **change out of** one set of clothes and **into** another:

We're expected to change for dinner, by the way.
I'll just go and get changed.
They all changed their muddy boots and went home.
You should change into dry clothes.

2 You **change** a particular thing when you replace it with a new or different one:

He was up a ladder changing a light bulb.
Let's change the subject [= talk about something else].

3 When travelling, you **change**, or **change buses** or **trains**, when you get off one and on to another, to continue your journey towards your destination:

At Madrid I had to change trains for Salamanca.
Change at Perth for Glasgow.

4 You can talk about **changing** such things as **jobs** or **rooms** when you move from one to the other:

You should think about changing jobs.
The street below was noisy; next morning she asked to change bedrooms.

5 You **change** money when you exchange it for different notes or coins of the same value:

Can anyone change a twenty-pound note for two tens?
They'll change travellers' cheques for you at the hotel.

6 Money or property **changes hands** when a transaction takes place:

A lot of money changed hands.

clauses

A **clause** is a series of words that includes a verb and its subject:

One day our hamster disappeared.

ONE-CLAUSE SENTENCES

A *simple sentence* contains only one clause:

The animal had escaped from its cage.

MORE THAN ONE CLAUSE IN A SENTENCE

1 A compound sentence contains two or more clauses, both called main clauses, because they have equal grammatical importance. The second clause is independent of the first clause. These main clauses are linked by a conjunction such as **and**, **but** or **or**:

There was a hole in the cage and the hamster had gone.
We looked all over the house, but we couldn't find him.
He had run away, or perhaps the cat had eaten him.

> ⓘ Notice that after **and**, **but** and **or** you can avoid repetition by omitting the subject and any other parts of the second main clause, *eg* the auxiliary verb, that are the same as in the first main clause:
> *He had managed to escape from his cage and* [= and he had] *disappeared.*
> *The cage was a strong one, but* [= but it was] *not strong enough for our hamster.*

2 A *complex sentence* contains at least one *main clause* and a *subordinate clause*. A *subordinate clause* is a clause that adds information about some part of the *main clause*, and so is *dependent* on it. Subordinate clauses fall broadly into three classes:

- An **adverbial clause** tells you more about the *action* of the main clause, represented by the *verb*, for instance, its time or place, or the reason for it, and is introduced by a subordinating conjunction such as **when, where** or **because**:

  When we woke up that morning the hamster was gone.

There was a big hole where he had escaped from his cage.
The whole family was upset because the hamster had disappeared.

- An *adjectival* or *relative clause* qualifies one of the nouns in the main clause, and is introduced by a relative pronoun such as **that**, **which** or **who**:
  Is a hamster one of those creatures that sleep through the winter?
  We heard from other people who had lost their pets.
- A *noun clause* is typically a clause containing a reported statement or question, acting as the object of a saying, knowing, thinking or asking verb, so it is likely to be introduced by **that** or by a question word, such as **how**, **why** or **who**:
  Everyone in the office knew that we'd lost our hamster.
  People kept asking how it had managed to escape.

➤ For more information on clause types, see the entries **conjunctions**, **subordinate clauses**, **relative clauses**, and **ellipsis**.

—— cleft sentences ——

➤ See the section SENTENCE STRUCTURE at the entry **emphasis**.

•••• close, closed, shut ••••

The verb **shut** is irregular:
shuts, shutting, shut

CLOSE AND SHUT (VERBS)

1 The verbs **close** /kloʊz/ and **shut** share many of the same transitive and intransitive uses:

- *The old man carefully closed* (or *shut*) *the door behind him.*
  The old-fashioned windows opened and shut perfectly.
- *The cafe closes at 6.30 pm.*
  At midday we close (or *shut*) *the shop for lunch.*

2 Communication or transport routes are **closed**, not **shut**:
The fog closed airports across the country.
Police closed 57th Street and all traffic was stopped.
The authorities closed the border to refugees on 22 August.

3 Things such as meetings, letters or conversations **close**, not **shut**, when they come, or are brought, to an end:
The meeting closed at 4.03 pm.
The offer closes on 1 December.
The report closes with suggestions for the future.

CLOSED AND SHUT (ADJECTIVES)

The past participles **shut** and **closed** are both used as adjectives, but only **closed** can be used before a noun:
The door's shut.
Evelyn Street is closed.
She sensed his movements through closed eyelids.

CLOSE (NOUN)

The **close** /kloʊz/ of a period or an event is the end of it:

Towards the close of the century the mill was sold again.
By the close the score was 4 all.

•••• close (adjective), close to ••••

➤ See **near**.

•••• cloth, clothing, clothes ••••

CLOTH

Cloth (/klɒθ/) has an uncountable and a countable meaning:

1 **Cloth** is woollen, cotton or other material, especially a woven fabric, for making clothes or furnishings such as curtains:

The suits were made of striped cloth.
She gave me a piece of cloth with some coins in it.

2 **A cloth** is a piece of fabric usually with a particular household or cleaning purpose:

Use a cloth to apply the paint.
The waitress wiped their table with a cloth.
They lay the white tablecloth over the long table.

CLOTHING

Clothing (/ˈkloʊðɪŋ/) is an uncountable noun referring collectively to clothes of various kinds:

Please wear suitable warm clothing.
The police searched his flat and took away a bag of clothing.
We had to cut the clothing away from the wound.

> ⓘ You can refer to an individual garment such as a sweater or a sock as **a piece**, **item**, **article**, or **bit**, **of clothing**:
> *He took each piece of clothing off slowly.*
> *She looked through the items of clothing hanging in the wardrobe.*

CLOTHES

1 **Clothes** (kloʊðz/) are shirts, sweaters, dresses, trousers, skirts, coats, hats and gloves, and other things that you wear:

Maggie undressed, folding her clothes neatly.
He pulled his clothes on quickly.
She had slept in her clothes as usual.

2 There is no singular form for **clothes**. A single item is a **garment**, or a **piece**, **article**, **item**, or **bit**, **of clothing**, as shown in the note above at **clothing**:

Sometimes he liked to wear a garment inside out.

3 Notice that you cannot use the expressions **a number of**, or **several** before **clothes**, or talk about any specific number of **clothes**:

Take plenty of warm clothes.
Aren't there any clean clothes?
I bought lots of clothes in the States.
I won't need many clothes just for ten days.

But:

A number of (or *several* or *one or two*) *items of clothing have been withdrawn.*

collective nouns

There are three classes of **collective noun**.

GROUPS

Some examples of units consisting of a number of individuals are:

audience	*band*	*bank*	*board*
body	*cast*	*choir*	*class*
club	*committee*	*company*	*crew*
crowd	*family*	*firm*	*gang*
government	*group*	*herd*	*jury*
ministry	*orchestra*	*party*	*staff*
team	*tribe*	*troop*	*union*

■ Note that the noun **staff** also refers to a plural group (see below).

In addition to these are the names for armed forces:

air force	*army*	*fleet*	*navy*

and names for classes or groups within society:

aristocracy	*bourgeoisie*
élite	*intelligentsia*
nobility	*press*
proletariat	*public*

BrE speakers do not always agree about whether collective nouns like these should take a plural verb or a singular verb.

AmE speakers rarely treat these nouns as plural, though they sometimes make an exception in the case of **family**.

The following points may help you in deciding which form to use:

1 The determiner you use may guide your choice of singular or plural agreement.

■ If you use a singular determiner, such as **a** or **an**, **another**, **this**, **that**, or **each**, a singular verb usually follows naturally:

An audience helps singers to communicate.
Another group of researchers is working on the same project.
This party now has a programme.

■ You also use the singular after the determiners **any, no**, and **which**:

The rules on how any government spends money are strictly controlled.
No group of women is more famous.
The only question is, which team comes with us?

- After the determiner **the**, or any of the possessive determiners (*eg* **my**, **your**, **their**), singular and plural agreement are both possible, and the plural is often selected.

  The use of a unifying expression such as **whole** may guide you towards the singular, and words like **all** or **most of** will guide you towards a plural:

  The audience was asked to be silent.
  No wonder the audience go wild at the end.
  The crowd were shouting for him to speak.
  The whole crowd was shouting.
  Her family is smaller than mine.
  I'm not sure if my family know where I am.
  All my family were priests.

2 Another consideration that may guide your choice of singular or plural agreement is whether you are thinking of the group as a single body (singular), or as a collection of thinking individuals (plural):

Our club was founded in 1905.
The club are optimistic that he will play for them again.
The Press has a duty to investigate.

3 If you choose a singular verb, the appropriate pronoun to use it with is the singular **it**, and if you choose a plural verb, the appropriate pronoun to use with it is the plural **they**:

My family never know what they will find in the oven.
The club itself was mainly art students and hippies.

4 The singular **there is** is preferred to the plural **there are** for introducing a group noun:

There is another group who may need support: the parents.

> ⓘ Notice that all the collective nouns in the *group* class have plural forms -**s**, and naturally take a plural verb when they are used in the plural:
> *In the American courts, juries are able to award even higher damages.*

5 The names of firms, companies and organizations are group nouns. These can be followed by a plural or singular verb:

When British Telecom was privatized, shares were issued both in the US and in the UK.
British Telecom have donated £100 000 to the appeal.

CLASSES OF ARTICLES

Nouns such as **furniture** (chairs, tables, etc) and **clothing** (sweaters, trousers, etc) represent a variety of objects classed under one heading, and are therefore thought of as collective nouns. Examples are:

baggage	*clothing*	*crockery*
cutlery	*equipment*	*fruit*
furniture	*luggage*	*stationery*

1 These nouns are *singular* and *uncountable*:

Next morning our baggage was unloaded.
Fresh fruit is good for you.
I buy clothing that is inexpensive and fun.

2 Notice that nouns of this class are not used in the plural. You use the form **pieces**, **articles**, or **items of** *eg* **furniture**, **clothing**, or **luggage** to refer to a number of individual items:

I kept counting my six pieces of luggage (not *six luggages*).

> ⓘ **Fruit** has a countable use:
> - **a fruit** is a kind of fruit:
>   *mangoes and other exotic fruits*
> - **A piece of fruit** is a single apple, pear, orange or banana, and so on.

➤ See also the entry **cloth, clothing and clothes**.

PLURAL GROUPS

Plural words like the following are sometimes classed as *collective nouns*:

cattle	*folk*	*people*
police	*staff*	

These nouns take a plural verb, and have no singular form. **Person** is used as the singular of **people**, and as singular forms of *eg* **police** and **staff** you can use **policeman**, **policewoman** or **police officer**, and **member of staff**. Notice that these plural words can be used without determiners:

How effective are the police?
Police are regarded as enemies.
A senior police officer has been appointed for the task.
People who do that should be fined.
No two people are the same.
I was a lonely person in those days.

—— colon ——

➤ See **punctuation**.

—— colour ——

COLOUR WORDS

1 Colour words are most commonly used as adjectives:

The waitresses wore red dresses and pale green aprons.
Our uniform was purple.
Ginny went bright red.

2 You can also use colours in several ways as nouns:

■ uncountable nouns

The following examples show typical uncountable uses of colour nouns:

The flowers were embroidered in shades of cream, pale green, and silver.
She chose white for the snow and deep green for the leaves.
Picasso understood colour. He used a lot of black.

■ countable nouns

You can refer to different shades of a colour as *eg* **yellows** or **reds**:

I remember the soft greens and browns of the grass and heather.

THE WORD 'COLOUR'

1 You can use the word **colour** in descriptions and questions using the verb **be** or another linking verb:

What colour are the seats in the office?
Did you notice the colour of the water?
What colour does litmus paper go in acid?

2 Notice the following rather informal but quite common construction:

She was wondering what colour shoes to buy.

3 Notice that you don't use the word **colour** with common, everyday colour adjectives:

She was wearing a red (not *red-colour*) *blouse.*

4 You can add **-coloured** after a colour word, usually one consisting of the name of a material or object:

She was still wearing her plum-coloured anorak.
Her hair was blonde and her eyes were slate-coloured.

• • • • come, go • • • •

The verbs **come** and **go** are irregular:

comes	*coming*	*came*	*come*
goes	*going*	*went*	*gone*

COME OR GO?

1 Someone **comes** to the place where you are, and you **come** to the place where your hearer is; you **go** to a place where neither you nor your hearer are; you use **here** with **come**, and **there** with **go**:

Come here a minute and I'll comb your hair.
Where shall we go for lunch?
They've gone shopping.

2 In reference to the past or future, you use **come** when thinking of the place where your hearer or you were or will be at the time of the movement towards it:

Which year did I come and visit you in Singapore?
I went to the pub at 12.45, but you weren't there.
I won't be able to come to your reception on the 13th, as I have to go to a meeting in London.

3 In telling a story, you use **come** from the point of view of the person you are identifying with:

He came to see her that same evening [the teller is identifying with the woman].

4 You use **come** when talking about joining your hearer, or your hearer joining you, to go somewhere:

I thought I'd go across to the club; do you want to come?

COME TO

You use **come to** to mean *arrive at* or *reach*:

Go straight on till you come to another set of traffic lights.
We came to a village called Waterloo.

COME FROM

You use **come from** when talking about places or directions of origin. If someone asks you where you **come from** they want to know about your home town or home country:

The sound was coming from our right.
Do you come from (not *are you coming from*) *Latvia too?*

➤ See the entries **change**, **complements** and **linking verbs** for information about **go** as a linking verb expressing change.

comparatives and superlatives

This entry first explains the rules for the *formation* of comparative and superlative adjectives and adverbs, and then provides information on the *use* of comparatives and superlatives.

FORMATION – ADJECTIVES

Adjectives that form comparatives and superlatives are usually the *qualitative* or *gradable* kind (see **adjectives**), but the common colour adjectives also have comparatives and superlatives (*He had bluer eyes than his brother.*).

1 one-syllable adjectives

- the general rule:

  one-syllable adjectives form their comparative by adding **-er** and their superlative by adding **-est**:

bright	*bright**er***	*bright**est***
great	*great**er***	*great**est***
dark	*dark**er***	*dark**est***
long	*long**er*** /ˈlɒŋgə(r)/	*long**est*** /ˈlɒŋgɪst/
sly	*sly**er***	*sly**est***
thick	*thick**er***	*thick**est***

- adjectives ending in **-e**: add **-r** for the comparative, and **-st** for the superlative:

pale	*pale**r***	*pale**st***
ripe	*ripe**r***	*ripe**st***
true	*true**r***	*true**st***

- adjectives with a single short vowel, ending in a single consonant: double the consonant:

big	*big**ger***	*big**gest***
fat	*fat**ter***	*fat**test***
red	*red**der***	*red**dest***

- irregular adjectives: the following adjectives and determiners have irregular comparatives and superlatives:

adjective	**comparative**	**superlative**
bad	*worse*	*worst*
good	*better*	*best*
far	*farther, further*	*farthest, furthest* (see entry **far**)
old	*older, elder*	*oldest, eldest*
determiners		
little	*less*	*least*
many	*more*	*most*
much	*more*	*most*
some	*more*	*most*

Notice also:

dry	*dr**ier***	*dr**iest***

but:

shy	*shy**er***	*shy**est***
sly	*sly**er***	*sly**est***

> ⓘ The rule is sometimes given that the comparative of ***ill*** is ***worse***, but ***iller*** is also possible:
> *It isn't serious, whatever it is; you'd be much iller* (or *worse*) *if it were.*

➤ See **elder** for more information about the difference between **elder**, **eldest** and **older**, **oldest**.

2 two-syllable adjectives

- ending in **-y** : change **y** to **i** and add **-er**, **-est**:

easy	*eas**ier***	*eas**iest***
funny	*funn**ier***	*funn**iest***
happy	*happ**ier***	*happ**iest***
lovely	*lovel**ier***	*lovel**iest***
naughty	*naught**ier***	*naught**iest***

- some two-syllable adjectives, especially if they have an unstressed second syllable, have **-er** and **-est** comparative and superlative forms, *eg:*

clever	*clever**er***	*clever**est***
common	*common**er***	*common**est***
cruel	*cruel**ler***	*cruel**lest***
gentle	*gentl**er***	*gentl**est***
mature	*matur**er***	*matur**est***
narrow	*narrow**er***	*narrow**est***
obscure	*obscur**er***	*obscur**est***
remote	*remot**er***	*remot**est***
quiet	*quiet**er***	*quiet**est***
shallow	*shallow**er***	*shallow**est***
simple	*simpl**er***	*simpl**est***
subtle	*subtl**er***	*subtl**est***
stupid	*stupid**er***	*stupid**est***

3 other two-syllable adjectives, adjectives with three or more syllables, and compound adjectives: use **more** before the adjective for the comparative, and **most** for the superlative:

correct	***more*** *correct*	***most*** *correct*
foolish	***more*** *foolish*	***most*** *foolish*
hopeful	***more*** *hopeful*	***most*** *hopeful*
hopeless	***more*** *hopeless*	***most*** *hopeless*
spacious	***more*** *spacious*	***most*** *spacious*
thrilling	***more*** *thrilling*	***most*** *thrilling*
active	***more*** *active*	***most*** *active*
frantic	***more*** *frantic*	***most*** *frantic*
careless	***more*** *careless*	***most*** *careless*
rural	***more*** *rural*	***most*** *rural*
decent	***more*** *decent*	***most*** *decent*
similar	***more*** *similar*	***most*** *similar*
obstinate	***more*** *obstinate*	***most*** *obstinate*
legible	***more*** *legible*	***most*** *legible*
oldfashioned	***more*** *oldfashioned*	***most*** *oldfashioned*
longwinded	***more*** *longwinded*	***most*** *longwinded*

4 A number of two-syllable adjectives, *eg* **pleasant**, **handsome**, **common**, **polite**, **mature**, **obscure**, can have both forms of comparative and superlative:

He's even handsomer (or *even more handsome*) *than his brother.*

The adjective **likely** also has both forms, and its **more** and **most** forms are very common:

They're likelier to lead a healthy life if they eat natural foods.
Happy children are more likely to succeed.

5 Notice that nearly all adjectives ending in **-ed**, including one-syllable ones, use the **more** and **most** forms:

That's one of the most used expressions I can think of.
David was the most inclined to take that view.

6 The negative **un-** versions, or 'opposites', of two-syllable adjectives ending in **-y** behave like the positive form, even though they have three syllables (**unhappier**, **unhappiest**; **unluckier**, **unluckiest**).

7 Compound adjectives sometimes change the first element, which may be an adjective or an adverb, rather than use **more** and **most**:

faster acting painkillers
longer-lasting batteries
the nicest-looking man I know

8 The adjectives **real**, **right** and **wrong**, and the preposition or adjective **like** always use the **more** and **most** forms:

I think I'm more like my brother than my sister.

FORMATION – ADVERBS

1 **the general rule**
With adverbs ending in **-ly**, you form the comparative and superlative by putting **more** and **most** before the adverb:

We communicated more successfully at our second attempt.
We're looking for the workers who can work most efficiently in a team.

2 Some adverbs have the same form as the adjective (see **adverbs**), for instance, **early**, **fast**, **hard**, **high**, **late**, **long**, **near**, **low** and, in informal English, **easy**, **loud**, **quick**, **slow**, and these, along with a few other adverbs (*eg* **soon**), have **-er** and **-est** forms:

It was finished sooner than we'd expected.
Nick's version comes nearest to the truth.
You should take things easier.

3 The following adverbs have irregular comparative and superlative forms:

adverb	**comparative**	**superlative**
badly	*worse*	*worst*
far	*farther* or *further*	*farthest* or *furthest*
little	*less*	*least*
much	*more*	*most*
well	*better*	*best*

➤ For more information on **farther**, **farthest** and **further**, **furthest** see the entry **farther, further, farthest, furthest**.

LESS AND LEAST

You use **less** and **least**, like **more** and **most**, but with the opposite meaning:

Businessmen are feeling less confident than [= not as confident as] *they were.*
Her complexion was rather pale, less rosy than [= not as rosy as] *her sister's.*
This is the least complicated [= the simplest] *method.*

USING COMPARATIVES

1 When you use comparatives, you are talking about inequality between *two* things. You are comparing, for instance, one thing or person with another, or one group with another, or one thing or person with a group:

Your name's longer than mine.
Do women marry earlier than men?
They're better educated than I was at their age.

2 You can also compare the state of something with its state at another time, or in another situation:

Things are better than they were.
She seemed happier than usual.

3 After a comparative you often use **than** followed by the words that provide the contrast. **Than** can be followed by:

■ a noun:

The article says that dogs are more intelligent than cats.

- a noun phrase:

  A filofax can be more useful than a conventional diary.

- a pronoun:

  Wendy was luckier than most.

- a personal pronoun, usually in the objective case:

  Some of our relatives are better off than us.

- a clause:

  I know 'Othello' better than I know 'Hamlet'.

4 The conjunction or preposition **as** behaves in a similar way to **than**. For more information, see the entries **as** and **than**. Notice how an expression with **than** can be replaced by an expression with **as** in comparative sentences:

He was less talkative than (or, more naturally, *not as talkative as*) *his sister.*

5 In phrases and clauses after **than** you usually try to avoid repetition, *eg*:

- by replacing previous nouns with pronouns:

  Their project is likely to finish earlier than ours [= our project].
  Any bed has to be more comfortable than this (or *this one*).

- by substituting auxiliary verbs for the previous main verb:

  Other European countries manage their health services better than we do [= than we manage them].

- by making an adjective stand for the noun it qualifies:

  For some reason we found three times more male toads than female.

6 The following examples show some of the adverbs that are used to identify or moderate comparatives:

She finds it very much easier to read now.
The soup tasted a lot better with salt and pepper in it.
'Are you hurt?' asked Guy, his voice even softer than before.
Most of us need to spend much more time with our children.
At 39 he's a bit older than my other boyfriends.

7 You can use a double comparative with **and** to express the idea of progress:

The sky was getting darker and darker.
I was putting on more and more weight.
It became more and more obvious that a crisis was coming.

8 You use two comparatives, each normally introduced by **the**, to express the idea of one circumstance increasing at the same rate as, and because of, another:

The more you try to understand it, the more confusing it becomes.
The deeper I investigated, the more concerned I got.
We need to take a holiday, and the sooner the better.

> ⓘ Notice the adverbial expression **more or less**, which has a meaning close to 'almost' or 'virtually':
> *The portrait was more or less finished.*
> *The gold medal is now more or less a certainty.*

USING SUPERLATIVES

When you use superlatives, you are talking about an outstanding member of a group:

She called me her dearest friend.
This week the judges announce their choice for Most Beautiful Village.

1 As a general rule, you use **the** or a *possessive adjective* before a superlative:
It was the best holiday we'd had for years.
The children will be wearing their newest clothes at the party.

2 The noun qualified by a superlative can be omitted if it has already been given in the earlier context:
Which of these colours is the prettiest?

But note that the noun cannot be omitted if it is not given in the earlier context:
The most important thing (not *the most important*) *is to get the message across.*

3 Where the group consists of only two, people feel it is more logical to use **the** with the comparative, rather than the superlative:
They cut the the cake into two pieces, and argued about which was the bigger.

4 After a superlative you can use:

- **in** to refer to the place concerned, or the group concerned if it is represented by a singular noun:
  He is the most famous footballer in the history of the team.
  She's the best violinist in the orchestra.
- **of** to refer to the group concerned if it is a plural noun; notice that **of all** can be used simply to emphasize a superlative:
  This is the stupidest of his theories.
  It was the finest adventure of all.

5 Before a superlative you can use:

- a noun in the possessive form, that is, ending with **-'s**:
  It was a buffalo, one of Africa's most dangerous animals.
  The greenhouse effect is now the world's biggest environmental problem.
  It is possibly Britain's most boring city.
  They had advice from the century's finest archaeologists.

6 Typical grammatical forms after a superlative are:

- a relative clause:
  It was the best film I had seen for years.
  He is the stupidest person I know.
  That's the strangest incident I've ever heard of.

- a reduced relative clause:

  One of the most stylish musicals ever made [= that was ever made] *was 'Funny Face'.*

- an infinitive with **to**:

  He was the most famous person to wear false teeth.
  At 63, she was the first woman ever to lead a major US agency.

- an adjective ending in **-able** or **-ible**:

  The latest possible date for the meeting was Tuesday 5 March.
  This is one of the finest available recordings of the Sixth Symphony.

7 You can use ordinal numbers with superlatives:

Virginia Falls, possibly the second best known falls in Canada.
I was the fourth last on the waiting list.

8 Superlatives are followed by words like **ever** and **yet**:

Surely this is the strangest family you've ever known?
This was the oddest coincidence yet.

9 The following examples show some of the adverbs that are used to intensify superlatives:

She's ***by far*** *the biggest influence on my writing.*
This was ***quite*** *the most sensible arrangement.*
The budget reached £20 billion, ***easily*** *the largest figure on record.*
Such orchestras only employ the ***very*** *best musicians.*

10 **The** is normally used with superlatives, but you do not use **the** before a superlative when you are talking about the state of a person or thing at certain times:

In the primary school, drama is most successful when it is a natural development of children's play.
Ed knew she was most unsure of herself when she seemed most confident.

• • • • compare with, compare to • • • •

A lot of English speakers use these two forms interchangeably, but a useful distinction can be made:

1 When you **compare** things, or **compare** one thing **with** another, you are typically comparing things *of the same class*, and considering in what ways they are similar or different, or how one is better or worse than the other:

The weather's been reasonably OK, compared with last week, anyway.
We compared prices of vegetables at a number of supermarkets.

2 When you **compare** one thing **to** another, you are usually saying that the first is *like* the second:

Our style of management is often compared to the Japanese approach, although I think the styles are very different.

comparison

THE SAME

1 When you describe two or more things as being the same or equal, you use **like** or **as**, or the expression **as ... as**:

He tries as hard as I do to save money.
She's already as tall as me.
She makes soup just like my mother's.
He's sorry about the mistake, as we all are.

2 You can also say that two things are **the same**, or that something is the case **too**, **as well**, or **also**.

3 Note that when comparing people or things in the negative, you can use **not as ... as** or **not so ... as**:

She's not as intelligent as her sister.
He's not so excitable as he used to be.

ⓘ Some people find the form **not so ... as** less acceptable in formal English.

DIFFERENT

When you describe people or things as being different, or acting differently, you can say that they are **not like** each other, or that they are **not the same as** each other. You can also use **more ... than** or **less ... than**:

There was more money in the account than we thought.
She spends less time on her homework than her brother (*does*).
He's less interested in football than I am.

➤ See also entry on **comparatives and superlatives**.

complements

A **complement** is the part of a sentence that follows a 'linking' verb, such as **be** or **become**, and usually consists of a noun, noun phrase, adjective or adjectival phrase. A complement *completes* the meaning of the verb:

Her son's ***a doctor****.*
She became ***manager*** *in 1987.*
After a while I started to get ***tired****.*
Most young girls would turn ***pale*** *at the idea.*
It began to grow ***dark*** *at about six o'clock.*

➤ See the entry **change** for more information on the use of the verbs **come**, **get**, **grow**, and **turn**.

compliments

➤ See pages 146 and 147.

COMPLIMENTS

PAYING COMPLIMENTS

1 For many speakers of English, it is not common to compliment someone on their appearance in a very formal situation. Similarly, men, especially older men, do not often compliment each other on their appearance.

- If you know someone quite well, you might say how much you like something they are wearing. The most common phrases are **I like your ...** and **I love your ...** or **What** (a) **lovely/sweet/nice**, etc... :

  I love your dress!
  I like your hair that way.
  I do like your tie.
  What a lovely bag!

- You can also comment on the way someone looks, using such phrases as **You look ...**, **You're looking ...** or **That really suits you**:

  You look great, Susanna.
  You're looking fantastic!
  You've had your hair cut differently. It suits you.

- If men comment approvingly on each other's appearance, they are likely to use briefer, and less personal expressions:

  Nice hat!
  Good tie!
  Hey, where did you get your boots?

2 To tell people that you think they do something well, you can use **You're so good at ...**, **You're such a good ...**:

You're so good at describing things.
You're such a good story-teller!
You're a great cook, Mike.

3 When complimenting someone on a meal they have cooked for you, you usually comment on how good the food looks, tastes or smells:

.... comprise, compose, composed of, consist of, constitute, include ....

The above verbs can be easily confused because they have fairly similar meanings. There are some important differences, however, not only in usage, but also in the way they behave grammatically.

COMPRISE

Something **comprises** certain things when they are the elements that it contains:

The living accommodation comprises a bedroom, a kitchen, a bathroom and a living room.
The course comprises coursework followed by two extended essays.

- before the meal:

  Mmm. Something smells good!
  This looks delicious!

- during the meal:

  This is delicious!
  This is lovely!
  Mmm. You must let me have the recipe for this.

- after the meal:

  That was excellent.
  Thank you so much. That was absolutely delicious.

ACCEPTING AND RESPONDING TO COMPLIMENTS

1 If someone compliments you on your appearance, it is normal to thank them and to make a comment. For example, if they have complimented you on something you are wearing, you might say where you got it, or something about how long you have had it:

'That's a nice blouse, Louise.' 'Thanks – I got it in the sale.'
'What a lovely dress!' 'Oh thanks. I've actually had it for years.'
'I like your hair like that.' 'Thank you. I had it done yesterday.'

2 If someone comments on how good you are at something, the most common way is either to thank them or to modestly disagree with them:

'The flat looks great!' 'Oh thanks. We've made a few small changes.'

3 If someone compliments you on something you have done for them, you can say that you are happy that they like it:

'That was delicious.' 'I'm glad you enjoyed it.'
'Thanks. That was great.' 'I'm really pleased you liked it.'

ⓘ Note that it is not usual to agree with someone when they compliment you: *'You look great in that dress.' 'Oh, thanks!'* (not *'Yes, thanks.'*)

... comprise, compose, composed of ... continued

ⓘ Some people say that something **comprises of**, or **is comprised of**, certain things or activities. This is not generally accepted in standard English.

COMPOSED OF, CONSIST OF, COMPOSE

1 Something **is composed of** or **consists of** the different things that make it up when they are the things that it contains:

The House of Assembly is composed of (or *consists of*) *21 elected members.*
Our society is composed of (or *consists of*) *a variety of religious groups.*
At present the Board consists of (or *is composed of*) *28 directors.*

... comprise, compose, composed of... continued

2 The people or things that **compose** something are all the people or things that are in it:

Citizens can be witnesses in the courts and also compose the jury.

CONSTITUTE

The things or people that **constitute** something are the things or people that make it up:

The symptoms which constitute jet-lag have already been mentioned.
When asked, they had no idea of what constituted job satisfaction.

INCLUDE

1 One thing **includes** certain people or features when they form part of it:

The library includes a large section for Asian members.
The staff included a cook and a private nurse.
The course includes video sessions and project work.

2 The services that **are included** in a price are those which the price covers; a price **includes** certain services when these are covered by the price:

Package and posting are included in the price.
The price includes dinner, lunch and bed and breakfast.

> ⓘ None of these verbs can be used in the progressive form.
> Notice, however, the preposition **including:**
> *There were six full-time staff, including a cook and a private nurse.*

concord: grammatical agreement

Concord is the grammatical name given to the way you make a verb match its subject with regard to *person*, and with regard to *number*, and to the way you make pronouns and possessive determiners match the nouns they refer to.

1 People worry about whether to use a plural or singular verb and pronoun after singular nouns like **audience** and **team**, which represent a number of individuals:

The team is (or *are?*) *delighted with its* (or *their?*) *performance.*

➤ The question of singular or plural agreement with collective nouns like these is fully dealt with in the entry **collective nouns**.

2 Below are shown some *singular quantifying expressions* that can be followed by plural nouns, plural pronouns, and plural verbs:

A number of *changes are needed.*
A lot of *ladies carry this sort of gun in their handbags.*
The majority of *the 440 workers were Asians.*
A couple of *people have made comments.*
The rest of us *were bored.*
A group of *editors are looking at the text.*

➤ For more information about using the word **number** see the entry **amount, quantity** and **number**.

3 expressions using 'one'

- **More than one** is followed by a singular noun and verb:

  More than one visit was made to the client.
  More than one of these people has no right to be here.

- After a phrase such as **one of their employees**, a singular verb follows naturally:

  One of their employees has decided to leave.

  The difficulty arises when **one of** is followed by a relative clause (*One of the things that …*). Frequently, a singular verb follows more naturally, even though it refers back to plural things:

  One of the things that is absolutely necessary is strong central control.

  To avoid difficulty the phrase **one thing that** could be substituted for **one of the things that**, without much change of sense:

  One thing that makes me angry is their lack of concern for the patient.

- A structure like **one in ten** should be followed by a singular verb referring back to **one**, but in practice, a plural verb may follow naturally:

  Only about one in ten of their ideas are likely to be useful.
  Just over one in ten fall into this category.
  Fewer than one in ten of the country's children were immunized.

4 nouns linked by 'and'

Two singular subjects linked by **and** take a plural verb, unless the combination is being thought of as a single idea. Compare the following few examples:

Peter and Carina have invited us to their wedding
Food and water were running out.

But:

Law and order is seen as a key issue.
Your board and lodging is going to cost more in future.

5 amounts, quantities and calculations

- You usually use singular verbs, pronouns and determiners to refer to amounts, even if the amount is represented by a plural noun:

  Two million pounds is my price.
  I started with fifty pounds; I wonder where it's all gone?

- People often use a singular verb when giving the result of a calculation they are making aloud:

  Two and five is seven.
  Yes, that's right, three times nine is twenty-seven (but *three nines are twenty-seven*).

6 using 'they' to refer to a singular pronoun or noun:

Everyone's welcome, aren't they?

When **they** is used to refer back to the singular pronouns **someone** (or **somebody**), **anyone** (or **anybody**), **no-one** (or **nobody**), objections are often raised.

However, the use of **they** to refer back to these indefinite pronouns and the determiners **every**, **each**, **either**, **neither**, **any** and **no**, is well established, and has the advantage of referring to a male or female person. The alternative **he or she** is very formal-sounding, and **he** on its own is now regarded as politically incorrect.

Below are some examples where **they** is used naturally after some of the words listed above:

Nobody's allowed in yet, are they?
Has anybody got a knife on them?
Each patient has their own room.

> ⓘ It is quite usual for common-gender nouns, such as **doctor**, **lawyer**, **teacher**, **participant**, to be followed by **they**:
> *Any delegate who has not yet collected their conference folder ...*
> But speakers can usually avoid this, if they wish to, by pluralizing:
> *Delegates who have not yet collected their conference folders ...*
> **He or she** can always be used where pluralization is impossible:
> *You should tell your child's teacher so that he or she can take the appropriate action.*

7 The linking verb **be** usually agrees with its subject rather than its complement, so that a singular subject regularly has a singular verb even when the complement is plural, and a plural subject has a plural verb even when the complement is singular:

One drawback is the higher transport costs.
The last thing we want is pictures of him in a fight.
Single parents are another important group.

conditional clauses

➤ For more detailed information about the uses and structures of conditional clauses see the entry **if**.

1 Clauses beginning with **if** are generally termed *conditional*. Notice however that **if** also has a function like that of **whether** in reported questions or requests (*He asked me if* (or *whether*) *he could borrow my pen*).

A conditional clause is a subordinate clause containing a *condition*, that is, a circumstance that must exist before the possibility in the main clause can happen:

If you miss the appointment, a fee will still be charged.

➤ For the use of **unless** in conditional clauses see the entry **unless**.

2 More details of verb tenses that should be used in conditional clauses will be found at the entry **if**, but a rough and simple guide is:

- **future**

A conditional sentence referring to the future, which has a future tense in its main clause, has a present tense in its **if**-clause:

If this goes well, your next attempt will be easier.

- **present**

  A conditional sentence referring to the present, which has a modal verb such as **would** or **should** in its main clause, has the simple past tense in its **if**-clause:

  I wonder how she'd [= she would] *react if I told her the truth.*

- **past**

  A conditional sentence referring to the past, which has a modal-auxiliary combination such as **would have** or **could have** in its main clause, has the past perfect in its **if**-clause:

  If we had known of the risk of infection, we would have kept her away from school.

3 In a rather formal style, it is possible to invert the subject and the auxiliary verb in the conditional clause, as an alternative to using **if**. This kind of inversion is found with **had**, **should** and the present subjunctive **were**, which regularly takes the place of **was** in present conditional sentences. It is only rarely used with **did** and the remaining modal verbs:

The policy will cover you, should you need [= if you need] *to cancel your holiday.*
Had I realized, I'd have warned you.

— conjunctions —

Conjunctions are words that link clauses together in different ways to form sentences. In the sentence *'His girlfriend drove while he slept on the back seat.'*, **while** is a conjunction of time, and tells you that two things were going on at the same time. The conjunction **and** simply adds another circumstance:

My wife cooks the food and I run the shop.

The conjunction **because** introduces a reason:

She understood his need for sport, because she too enjoyed exercise.

Different types of conjunctions, along with their functions and typical behaviour, are set out in a general way below, but each conjunction has its own entry, where you will be able to find more details about it.

➤ See also the entry **clauses**, and the entries **adverbial clauses** and **relative clauses**.

CO-ORDINATING CONJUNCTIONS

1 The following conjunctions link clauses that are grammatically independent of each other:

and *but* *or*

The conjunction **and** introduces an addition, **but** a contrast, and **or** an alternative. Notice that after any of these conjunctions, speakers tend to avoid repetition by omitting the subject, and any other parts of the second clause, for instance the auxiliary verb, that are the same as in the first clause:

The child had unlocked the front door and gone off [= and she had gone off] *by herself into the street.*
She might be shopping or collecting [= or she might be collecting] *the children from school.*

2 Notice that conjunctions that come in pairs, *eg* **both ... and**, **not only ... but also**, **either ... or**, and **neither ... nor**, are also co-ordinating conjunctions of a kind, and introduce grammatically independent clauses. More details about them will be found at their individual entries.

3 **So** and **yet** can be classified as co-ordinating conjunctions; they can be used on their own, or after **and**:

The new engine has more power, yet (or *and yet*) *uses no more fuel than the old model.*

SUBORDINATING CONJUNCTIONS

Conjunctions that introduce *subordinate clauses*, that is, *adverbial, relative* (or *adjectival*) and *noun* clauses, are called *subordinating conjunctions*:

I went to see my tutor when I arrived.	(adverbial clause introduced by **when**)
This is a task which cannot be done.	(relative clause introduced by **which**)
Has she told you that she's engaged?	(noun clause introduced by **that**)

1 conjunctions introducing adverbial clauses

- **time**

The following conjunctions introduce clauses of *time*; they answer the question *when?* in relation to the main clause:

when	*before*	*after*	*since*
while	*as*	*till/until*	*once*
as soon as	*next time/last time*		
the moment/minute/instant that			

Next time you say something like that, think what the words actually mean.

- **place**

The following two conjunctions introduce clauses of *place*; they answer the question *where?* in relation to the main clause:

where	*wherever*

Wherever conditions are difficult, the number of animals is low.

- **manner**

The following conjunctions introduce clauses of *manner*; they answer the question *how? in what way?* in relation to the main clause:

as	*as if*	*as though*	*like*
just as	*much as*	*the way*	

She went racing down the stairs to her room the way she always did.

- **reason**

The following conjunctions introduce clauses of *reason*; they answer the question *why?* (or *why not?*) in relation to the main clause:

as	*because*	*in case*	*just in case*
since	*seeing*	*considering*	*for*
inasmuch as	*insofar as*	*in that*	*to the extent that*

Take your umbrella, just in case it rains.
The match was unfair in that they had more men in their team.

■ **concession**

The following conjunctions introduce clauses of *concession*. Clauses of concession grant or allow a point that contrasts with what is being said in the main clause, and most of the conjunctions have meanings similar to **although**:

though	*although*	*even though*	*even if*
much as	*whereas*	*not that*	*while/ whilst*

Much as I like men, I like spending time in the company of my girlfriends.

■ **purpose**

The following conjunctions introduce clauses of *purpose*; they answer the question *why? for what reason or purpose?* in relation to the main clause:

so	*so that*	*in order that*

They attached pens to the counter, so they wouldn't be stolen.

■ **result**

The following conjunction introduces clauses of *result*; they tell you the result of what happens in the main clause:

so that

They were wearing jeans like everyone else so that no-one recognized them.

■ **condition**

The following conjunctions introduce clauses of *condition*; they say what must happen before the possibility mentioned in the main clause can become reality (see also **if**, **unless** and **conditional clauses**):

if	*unless*

Unless we talk to these people, we're never going to find a solution.

2 The following relative pronouns introduce *relative* or *adjectival* clauses; they *identify* or *define* a noun in the main clause, or *add information* about it:

who	*whom*	*whose*	*which*
that	*when*	*why*	*where*

I was joined by a lady whose face looked familiar.
The première, which took place in Prague, was a huge success.

3 The word **that** and the range of **wh-**question words act as conjunctions for introducing noun clauses. These clauses explain *what* someone is *saying*, *knowing*, *thinking*, *wondering* or *asking*, etc:

that	*how*	*what*	*when*	*where*	*why*
who	*whom*	*whose*	*which*	*whether*	

I couldn't work out how you got there so quickly.
Have you decided which of the lectures you want to attend?

FURTHER POINTS

1 order

Most kinds of *adverbial clauses* can come before or after the main clause:

We couldn't visit the cathedral because it was late.
or
Because it was late, we couldn't visit the cathedral.

2 omitting words

The possibility of omitting words after the co-ordinating conjunctions **and, but** and **or** has been mentioned above. It is not usually possible to leave words out in the same way after a *subordinating* conjunction:

I'll call you as soon as I get home (not *I'll call you as soon as get home*).

However, you can omit the pronoun acting as subject, and the verb **be**, after the following conjunctions: **when**, **whenever**, **while**, **once**, **until**, **if**, **unless**, **though** and **although**:

I hope to make quite a few useful contacts while in the States [= while I am in the States].
We can make a special delivery if necessary [= if it is necessary].

After **than** and **as** the verb **be** can be omitted:

I won't keep you any longer than necessary.
Keep telephone conversations as brief as possible.

3 conjunction + clause used independently

A conjunction is normally used to join two clauses into a single sentence, but especially in conversation the combination conjunction + clause can stand independently. This can also happen when speakers answer their own question, or separate the subordinate clause in order to emphasize it, or add an afterthought in the form of a subordinate clause:

'Could you ring Bridget to remind her?' 'When I have a moment.'
'Can I turn on the television news?' 'If you must.'

4 when to use a comma

- As a comma represents a pause, writers usually insert one between clauses that are long or complicated, but don't bother with one between short simple clauses:

  I wanted to go and see the exhibition of Matisse's later paintings at the museum, but the others wanted to take a boat trip through the canals.
  Mary won't be in today because she's got flu.

- An adverbial clause that comes before the main clause is often followed by a comma:

  As soon as I hear anything from the hospital, I'll give you a call.

- With relative clauses there is a distinction between the *defining* or *identifying* kind of clause, which needs no commas round it, and the *non-defining information-adding* kind of clause, which does need commas before and after it (see **relative clauses**):

  People who feed their children on this kind of food rarely enjoy cooking.
  My mother, who didn't like cooking, always fed us well.

—— continuous tenses ——

➤ See the entry **progressive forms**.

contractions

CONTRACTED FORMS

Contractions are acceptable in any informal piece of writing, as they represent the way people naturally talk to each other, but they are usually out of place in formal reports or other formal documents.

1 pronoun + auxiliary verb

contraction	pronunciation	full version
I'm	/aɪm/	*I am*
I've	/aɪv/	*I have*
I'll	/aɪl/	*I will*
I'd	/aɪd/	*I had* or *would*
you're	/jɔː(r)/	*you are*
you've	/juːv/	*you have*
you'll	/juːl/	*you will*
you'd	/juːd/	*you had* or *would*
he's	/hiːz/	*he is* or *has*
he'll	/hiːl/	*he will*
he'd	/hiːd/	*he had* or *would*
she's	/ʃiːz/	*she is* or *has*
she'll	/ʃiːl/	*she will*
she'd	/ʃiːd/	*she had* or *would*
it's	/ɪts/	*it is* or *has*
it'll	/ɪtəl/	*it will*
it'd	/ɪtəd/	*it had* or *would*
we're	/wɪə(r)/	*we are*
we've	/wiːv/	*we have*
we'll	/wiːl/	*we will*
we'd	/wiːd/	*we had* or *would*
they're	/ðeə(r)/	*they are*
they've	/ðeɪv/	*they have*
they'll	/ðeɪl/	*they'll*
they'd	/ðeɪd/	*they had* or *would*
there's	/ðeəz/	*there is*
there'll	/ðeəl/	*there will*
there'd	/ðeəd/	*there had* or *would*

2 negative contractions: auxiliary verb + **not**

contraction	pronunciation	full version
aren't	/ɑːnt/	*are not*
isn't	/ˈɪzənt/	*is not*
wasn't	/ˈwɒzənt/	*was not*
weren't	/wɜːnt/	*were not*
haven't	/ˈhavənt/	*have not*
hasn't	/ˈhazənt/	*has not*
hadn't	/ˈhadənt/	*had not*
don't	/doʊnt/	*do not*
doesn't	/ˈdʌzənt/	*does not*
didn't	/ˈdɪdənt/	*did not*
won't	/woʊnt/	*will not*

wouldn't	/ˈwʊdənt/	*would not*
shan't	/ʃɑːnt/	*shall not*
shouldn't	/ˈʃʊdənt/	*should not*
can't	/kɑːnt/ or AmE /kant/	*cannot*
couldn't	/ˈkʊdənt/	*could not*
daren't	/deənt/	*dare not*
mayn't (rare)	/meɪnt/	*may not*
mightn't	/ˈmaɪtənt/	*might not*
mustn't	/ˈmʌsənt/	*must not*
needn't	/ˈniːdənt/	*need not*
oughtn't	/ˈɔːtənt/	*ought not*
usedn't	/ˈjuːsənt/	*used not*

POINTS TO REMEMBER

1 Contractions using the verbs **be** and **have** can be used when **be** and **have** are functioning as ordinary verbs as well as when they are functioning as auxiliary verbs:
There aren't enough chairs.
Sorry, I haven't (or, less formally, *I haven't got* or *I don't have*) *a clue.*

2 In written English the contraction **'s**, representing **is** or **has**, can also be used after nouns, proper names, pronouns other than those shown above, the **wh-** question words, and **here** and **now**:
The mail's come.
Martin's on the phone for you.
So that's the answer.
Who's calling?
How's the baby?
Now's our chance.

> ⓘ In spoken English you will hear the contractions **'ll**, **'d** and **'re** in positions similar to those listed above, but they are rarely used in written English:
> *Dad will* (/ˈdadəl/) *be ever so pleased.*
> *What are* (/ˈwɒtər/) *astrocytes?*

3 **Aren't** is used in BrE as a contraction for **am not**, but only in the inverted question form **aren't I?**

4 Notice that the contracted forms listed in section **1** above can be followed by **not**, as an alternative to the combination of pronoun + negative contraction:
She'll not (or *she won't*) *be back before eight.*
You're not (or *you aren't*) *concentrating.*
He's not (or *he isn't*) *completely opposed to the idea.*

> ⓘ Notice that there is no **-n't** alternative to **I'm not**.

5 You put the apostrophe (') in the place of the letters that are omitted:
we've, she's, they'll, haven't, aren't, didn't

Letters are omitted in two places in **shan't** [= shall not] and **won't** [= will not], but you only insert a single apostrophe, to represent the missing **o** in **not**.

ⓘ The contraction **it's** for **it is** or **it has** must not be confused with **its**, the possessive pronoun, which has no apostrophe.

6 You normally use the full form rather than the contracted form when you have a double subject:

You and I have (not *you and I've*) *got to talk.*
The boys and I will (not *the boys and I'll*) *travel by train.*

7 The contracted forms in section **1** above are not used by themselves at the end of a clause, unless they are followed by **not**. The negative contractions (**haven't**, **wasn't** and so on), however, are possible in final position:

I'm not taking chemistry, but he is (not *he's*).
I'm taking chemistry but he isn't (or *he's not*).

➤ For the contraction **let's**, see **let**.

•••• contrary ••••

Contrary and **on the contrary** can easily be confused with other words and expressions that are similar to them, but not the same, in meaning.

'ON THE CONTRARY' AND 'ON THE OTHER HAND'

1 **On the contrary** has two main uses:

- You introduce a reply to someone with **on the contrary**, either when you are about to contradict something they have just said, or as a way of doing so:

  'I thought she didn't want me to come.' 'On the contrary, I think she missed you.'
  'I could move out if you want.' 'No, no, on the contrary! It's easier with you here.'

ⓘ **On the contrary** is often enough by itself to indicate that you disagree with someone.

- You also use **on the contrary** when you are about to support a negative statement you have just made with a positive, often emphatic, one:

  She had not forgotten him. On the contrary, she often found herself thinking about him.
  Nothing is wrong; on the contrary, everything is absolutely perfect.

2 **On the other hand** is used to show contrast between two statements:

He could be very kind to other performers. On the other hand, he could be very irritable with us.

CONTRARY AND OPPOSITE

1 **contrary**

- **Contrary** pieces of advice, views or intentions are pieces of advice, views or intentions that don't agree with each other:

  Some people believe that children can learn to be good or bad. The contrary view is that they are born good or bad.

- Something such as evidence **to the contrary** is evidence stating or suggesting that the opposite is true:
  In spite of everything he's said to the contrary, I know that he still loves his wife.

2 **opposite**

- Opposite things are as different as possible from each other:
  I asked everyone to keep calm and most of them did exactly the opposite.

> ⓘ You use **opposite**, rather than **contrary** to talk about meanings of words:
> *'What's the opposite of cheerful?' 'Well, what about bad-tempered?'*

> ⓘ **Opposite** also refers to things and people that face each other:
> *These are the people who live on the opposite side of the square to us.*

• • • • control, check • • • •

Control is a false friend for many speakers of languages of European origin. These languages have words that resemble **control**, meaning 'to inspect', 'examine', or 'look over', in order to allow to pass a test, for example. In English, **control** can be a verb or a noun.

THE VERB

1 You **control** a vehicle or other device when you operate it or guide its operation:
He relies on a pilot to control the plane while he takes the photos.

2 To **control** something such as a country or a commercial company is to be in complete charge of it:
Enemy forces control all the hills surrounding the town.
Central government attempts to control local authorities.

THE NOUN

1 **Control** is authority, or the power to influence or guide something:
In May 1976, the Democrats won control of the region.
The car was obviously out of control, swerving from left to right on the wet road.
I dislike flying because I don't feel that I'm in control of what's happening to me.

2 **Passport control** and **customs control** are parts of an airport or sea port where you have your documents checked and your baggage inspected:
When you arrive at the airport you will have to pass through passport control before claiming your baggage.

WHEN NOT TO USE 'CONTROL'

1 You should not use the verb **control** when you want to say that someone checks, monitors or examines something:
They'll want to check (not *control*) *your passport again at the other end.*
He's going to service (not *control*) *the car before we drive to Germany.*

2 You should not use the noun **control** when you want to talk about having a check-up or having your car serviced:

'I'm off to the dentist's.' 'Anything serious?' 'Hope not. Just a check-up.' (not *control*)

—— copular verbs ——

➤ See **linking verbs**.

•••• could ••••

The modal auxiliary verb **could** has a range of uses. It can be the past tense of **can** (compare this entry with **can**) and it has a variety of uses of its own, some of which are important for politeness. This entry deals separately with these two sets of uses. The negative contraction of **could** is **couldn't**.

IN A PAST CONTEXT

1 **ability in the past**:

He was good at telling jokes and could be very funny indeed.
Someone who could speak English was always there to translate.
She kept wondering where he was, and could not sleep.
She rang the police because she couldn't contact her parents.

- **Could** is used to express general, or ongoing, ability (*She could speak Swedish. He could be very funny*), and is also used with a negative, or a word like **hardly**, to say what was not achieved. To express achievement in the past you can use **was able to** or **managed to**:

All three of us managed to get on the bike.
They were busy arguing and I was able to leave unnoticed.

- **Could** is also used with verbs of sensing (such as **hear**, **see** or **feel**) and of remembering and comprehending, with reference to the past:

She could hear shouts coming from inside.
I could understand how she felt.
He could remember calling out.

2 **permission or freedom in the past**:

He could say what he liked because they never listened anyway.
I could spend half my money each week, but had to save the rest.

- Notice again that **could** is only used to refer to a general or ongoing freedom to do or have something. You can use **was allowed to** where permission was given, on a specific occasion:

The passengers were allowed to leave the plane one by one.

3 **possibility and likelihood in the past**

Could replaces the present of **can** in contexts dealing with various types of possibility or likelihood, or with speculation about them:

They were her relations; how could she refuse to invite them?
The crowds could be [= were often] *dangerous on occasions like that.*

4 could have

You use **could have** with negatives or in questions, to wonder, speculate, or exclaim about situations in the past:

The contrast could not have been more obvious.
Now how could we ever have forgotten it?

- **Could have** is used to talk about *unreal possibilities* in the past:

Things could have been much worse.
She could have been a top model.
There could have been a commuter rebellion last week.

- You also use **could have** to talk about *real possibilities* in the past, that is, things that possibly happened if the facts are interpreted a certain way:

I could have jumped to the wrong conclusion, I suppose.
The bruises could have been caused in other ways.

IN A PRESENT CONTEXT

1 You use **could** to ask permission politely, or make polite requests:

Could I leave early today?
Please could I speak to Sue?
Could you tell me the way to Leicester Square?

> ⓘ Notice that when somebody asks your permission to do something, using **could** (*eg Could I borrow your bike?*), you usually give your permission using **can** (*eg Yes, of course you can*).

2 You use **could** to make polite offers, invitations and suggestions; use of the negative question form makes a suggestion even more tentative and formal:

I could drive you down to the station.
Could you possibly meet me for lunch?
We could have a meal later; I'm sure you like Chinese food.
Couldn't we find that out?

3 You use **could** to express possibilities in a tentative or unassertive way:

If the ban is disobeyed, there could be big trouble.
We could build a garden room.

4 You use **could**, rather like **can**, with a negative or in questions, to wonder, speculate or exclaim about situations in the present or past:

How could I be so clumsy?
I couldn't agree with you more [= I agree with you absolutely].
The hotel has everything you could need; what more could you want?

COMPLAINTS

You use **could** and **could have** to express complaints about what you think *should* happen, but doesn't, or *should have* happened, but didn't:

You could do the washing yourself sometimes.
You could have warned me.

AS A PHRASE SUBSTITUTE

1 Being a modal auxiliary verb, **could** can stand by itself in place of the main verb, to avoid repetition, *eg* in subordinate clauses or in short answers, or in question tags:

He was trying to get a divorce, but he couldn't.
They asked us to support them, but how could we? (or *how could we have?*)
As soon as she could, she had a serious talk with her mother.
I could drive you to the airport, couldn't I?

2 In short answers and other elliptical structures, **could** is often followed by **be**, **do** or **have**, and **could have** by **been** and **done** in referring back to verbs that use these auxiliaries:

'Are they trying to cheat us?' 'They could be.'
I wasn't going to phone her today, but I could (or *I could do*).
I thought I'd told you, but I couldn't have (or *I couldn't have done*).
'Was he lying to us?' 'No, he couldn't have been.'

countable and uncountable nouns

Most nouns are countable. **Countable nouns** are the names of things that can be seen as separate and individual, such as people, animals, objects, certain abstract ideas such as thoughts and reasons, and that can be counted; that is, they have plurals, and you can use numbers, or the determiners **a** or **an**, **many**, or **few** (and others, such as **several**, **various**) with them. Here are four examples of countable nouns:

a cup	*two cups*	*not many cups*
a goat	*five goats*	*several goats*
a doctor	*a team of ten doctors*	*very few doctors*
a problem	*three major problems*	*various problems*

Uncountable nouns, sometimes called **mass nouns**, are the names of things such as materials and liquids, things that occur in masses, such as **butter** and **sand**, qualities of people or things, such as **beauty** and **thickness**, emotions, such as **love** and **horror**, and abstract concepts such as **truth** and **destruction**.

The typical uncountable noun is singular, without a plural, and cannot be used with numbers or the determiner **a** or **an**. Instead of the determiners **many** and **few**, you use **much** and **little**; otherwise, determiners such as **some**, **more** and **a lot of** occur most frequently. You can usually talk about a certain amount **of** an uncountable noun. Here are four examples of uncountable nouns:

sheets of steel	*It contains some steel.*
Milk is good for you.	*Drink more milk.*
Cats hate snow.	*A lot of snow has fallen.*
Power corrupts.	*not enough power*

The purpose of this entry is to deal with some of the more difficult aspects of countability and uncountability, and a few unusual cases.

NOUNS WITH COUNTABLE AND UNCOUNTABLE USES

A lot of nouns can be used countably and uncountably in different senses.

countable and uncountable nouns

1 Some typical uncountable nouns have countable senses:

uncountable	**countable**
I rarely drink beer	*Shall I get us three beers?*
a pile of broken glass	*a glass of wine*
Are you afraid of death?	*It caused 2000 deaths.*
a lot of activity	*enjoyable activities*

ⓘ Notice that words such as **meat**, **wine**, **bread**, **margarine** and **cheese**, which are usually uncountable, are countable when different varieties of them are being considered:
I was offered a plate of cold meats and cheeses.
We stock the finest French wines.

2 Several countable abstract nouns can be used uncountably after quantifiers like **much**, **some**, **little**, **no** and **any**:

countable	**uncountable**
He's had a great idea.	*I've got no idea what to do.*
by a lucky chance	*We had little chance of success.*
the first question	*There was never any question of giving up.*
many important differences	*This makes no difference to our relationship.*

3 You can use **a** or **an** before some uncountable nouns, *eg* qualities or emotions, if they are qualified by an adjective:
*As a child I had **a terrible fear** of spiders.*

HOW TO REFER TO THE UNIT

You often want to refer to a single item of some uncountable-only nouns, such as **baggage**, **furniture** and **information**. In many such cases, English uses **a piece of**. However, there are possible alternative countable 'unit' words; some useful ones are given in the list below:

uncountable noun	**countable alternative**
accommodation	*a place to stay* or *live*
advice	*a piece*, or *word*, *of advice*
apparatus	*a piece of apparatus*
baggage	*a piece*, or *item*, *of baggage* *a case; a bag*
bread	*a piece*, or *slice*, *of bread* *a loaf; a roll*
chewing gum	*a piece*, or *stick*, *of chewing gum*
equipment	*a piece of equipment; a tool*
furniture	*a piece*, *bit*, *item*, or *article*, *of furniture*
grass	*a blade of grass*
information	*a piece*, or *item*, *of information; a fact*
knowledge	*a fact*
lightning	*a flash*, or *streak*, *of lightning*
luck	*a piece*, *bit*, or *stroke*, *of luck*
luggage	*a piece*, *bit*, or *item*, *of luggage*

money	*a sum,* or *amount, of money; a coin; a note; a sum*
news	*a piece,* or *item, of news*
permission	[*a permit; a licence; an authorization*; these refer only to documents]
poetry	*a poem*
progress	*a step forward; an advance*
publicity	*an advertisement*
research	*a piece,* or *bit, of research; an investigation; an enquiry*
rubbish	*a piece,* or *a bit, of rubbish*
spaghetti	*a piece of spaghetti*
thunder	*a clap of thunder*
traffic	*a vehicle*
travel	*a trip; a journey; a voyage*
work	*a piece of work; a job; a task; a project*

PLURAL UNCOUNTABLE NOUNS

1 A number of nouns, especially nouns concerning human matters, movements, transactions, and other activities, only have a plural form; there is no singular countable equivalent. Some typical examples are given below:

arms	*bearings*	*belongings*
clothes	*congratulations*	*customs* [at a frontier]
dealings	*earnings*	*goods*
groceries	*premises* [= a building]	*provisions*
remains	*surroundings*	*thanks*
travels	*whereabouts*	*wits*

- You cannot normally use numbers with these plural 'uncountable' nouns, but quantifiers such as **many** and **few** are possible in a lot of cases:

  Many of their belongings were destroyed by the bomb.
  They had had few previous dealings with the police.
  Many thanks for your letter.

- Some of these plural nouns are a particular use of a noun. You can refer to a journey or a foreign holiday as your **travels**. Although there is no countable noun **a travel**, there is an uncountable noun **travel**, representing the abstract concept of travelling.

  Good to see you back from your travels!

2 Another class of plural 'uncountable' nouns are articles such as **trousers**, **tights**, **spectacles** and **scissors**, which consist of two identical joined parts. The words for these are not used in the singular. You can refer to the individual article as, *eg* **a pair of tights**, or as **some tights**:

I've got some binoculars you can borrow.
I meant to bring a spare pair of tights with me.

ⓘ You do not use **many** or **few** with these 'pair' words:
How many pairs of trousers (not *how many trousers) have you got?*

➤ See also the entry **pair**.

3 There are some plural nouns not ending in -**s** that are normally uncountable, for example **police** and **cattle**. It is possible, however, to use quantifiers such as **many** and **few** with these, and even the higher numbers:
There were a few police around.
Several thousand police were on duty.
She owned three hundred cattle.

ILLNESSES

1 Illnesses are generally uncountable, even if, like **measles** or **mumps**, they end in -**s**:
I'm probably getting flu.
As a result of immunization, measles is now quite rare.

2 Other health problems are countable, however:
I think I've got another cold starting.
He's got a really bad sore throat.

3 Some **-ache** words are countable and some are uncountable:
I've got a headache and a stomachache.
But:
I've got earache, toothache, and backache.

■ In AmE all these **-ache** words are countable.

➤ See also **articles**.

•••• country ••••

THE COUNTABLE NOUN

A **country** is a division of the world ruled by a particular government or monarch, often with its own language and culture:
The drugs had been smuggled into the country.
The law in this country tries to protect children from such abuse.
This will be an important debate between EC member countries.

THE UNCOUNTABLE NOUN

1 **Country**, like **countryside**, is open land away from towns and cities:
It's good to breathe in some fresh country air
And you'll be travelling across country, so make sure you've got plenty of food.

2 **The country** is open land without many buildings or public facilities, as opposed to **the town** or **the city**:
Why don't you go and live in the country again?

—— criticizing ——

➤ See facing page.

You need to be very careful about criticizing people, or their work, since any direct criticism is likely to sound offensive. Instead, speakers of English tend to use more indirect methods, such as suggestions in the form of negative questions. Of course, when people are angry, especially when they are talking to people they know well, direct forms are used.

1 tentative criticism

In a formal, or work situation, or if you are being very careful not to offend someone, phrases like **I'm not sure ...**, **Don't you think ...** and **I've got a bit of a problem with ...** are appropriate:

I'm not sure that your argument is quite right.
I wonder if you might have missed something.
Don't you think this paragraph should come later?
I've got a bit of a problem with this sentence you've written here.

2 stronger criticism

The following forms might be used in a formal situation by someone who is particularly angry, or, between people who know each other well, when the speaker is fairly annoyed:

Why on earth did you do this?
How could you say such a thing?

3 more direct criticism

If you tell someone directly that you do not approve of, or like, what they have done, they may be offended. This sort of criticism is often used, and considered acceptable, by people in authority (*eg* teachers, parents):

This work isn't really good enough.
You should have thought about this more carefully.

4 very strong criticism

The following examples of strong criticism are likely to offend anyone in any situation, if said directly to them:

This is awful.
You're hopeless at this.
You've done this all wrong.
That's rubbish!

Dd

dare

The verb **dare** behaves as a modal verb, as an ordinary verb, and sometimes as a mixture of the two. It is used mostly with negatives, in questions and in **if**-clauses.

PRESENT TENSE USES

In the present tense the forms without the auxiliary **do** are more frequently used than those with **do**:

Dare I ask what's been happening here?
If he dares come here again I'll make him sorry he did.
I daren't go out in case I meet somebody.
The children don't dare to argue with her.

PAST TENSE USES

In the past tense, the forms using the auxiliary verb **do** are more usual than the forms without it:

He did not dare let go of her hand.
Did she dare go back and look for it?
She dared not interrupt.

> ⓘ Notice that the forms **dare not** (or **daren't**) and **dared not** never take **to** before a following infinitive:
> *I dared not move* (not *dared not to move*).

Notice also that a **to**-infinitive after **dare** often gives the idea of taking up a challenge:

Dare to be different.

ELLIPTICAL USE

Like other modal verbs, **dare** can stand by itself for the main verb, to avoid repetition:

He could have asked for a copy of the report, but did not dare.

IDIOMS

1 I daresay

I daresay (also written **I dare say**) means much the same as **probably**:

I daresay we would have managed.

2 how dare you! and don't you dare!

People say **how dare you!** to express anger at someone's behaviour; **Don't you dare!** is used as a strong prohibition:

How dare you patronize me!
Don't you dare give up yet!

3 I dare you to

If you say to someone **I dare you to** do something dangerous or shocking, you are challenging them to do it:

I dare you to dive into the sea from this cliff.

dates

There are several ways of writing dates. British and American styles differ.

WRITING DATES

1 In Britain the usual way of writing the day's date is (number of) day, followed by month, followed by year, *eg*:

31 May 1995 *22 June 1996* *23 March 1997* *14 July 1998*

> ⓘ Notice that the month has a capital letter and comes after the date.

It is not very common now to write -**st** (as in *1st*), -**nd** (as in *2nd*), -**rd** (as in *3rd*) and -**th** (as in *4th*) after the number of the day.

Note the following abbreviated forms of the longer month names:

Jan, Feb, Mar, Apr, Aug, Sept, Oct, Nov, Dec

2 The usual American style is to give the month before the date, and to insert a comma before the year, *eg*:

May 31, 1995

3 Dates can also be written using **figures only**, *eg 22/6/96* or *22.6.96*, but because of the different order in which the British and the Americans write the full form of the date, the order differs in the all-figure version too:

British	American
12.5.99 (= 12 May 1999)	*5.12.99* (= May 12 1999)

> ⓘ Using the full form of the date avoids confusion.

SAYING DATES

Someone asking about the day's date asks:

What's the date today? or *What date is it today?*

British and American styles can differ in speech too:

	written	spoken
British	*21 July 1996*	*the twenty-first of July* (or *July the twenty-first*), *nineteen ninety-six*
American	*July 21 1996*	*July twenty-first* (or *twenty-one*), *nineteen ninety-six.*

OTHER USEFUL DATE EXPRESSIONS

written	said
1500	*fifteen hundred*
1604	*sixteen oh four* (or *sixteen hundred and four*)

1711	*seventeen eleven* (or *seventeen hundred and eleven*)
1951	*nineteen fifty-one*
2000	*two thousand* (or *the year two thousand*)
2003	*two thousand and three* (but not, so far, *twenty oh three*)
the 1900s	*the nineteen hundreds*

FURTHER POINTS

1 You can write 'the nineteen seventies' as **the 1970s**, and 'the seventies' as **the '70s**, without an apostrophe between the **0** and the **s**.

2 Write **AD** ('after Christ's birth') before the date, and **BC** ('before Christ') after it:
in 490 BC
in AD 23

3 When giving a period you can write, eg ***from 1992 to 1996***, or ***1992–1996***:
The partnership lasted from 1986 to 1990.
British Fashions, 1880–1914.

•••• day ••••

TWO MAIN MEANINGS

1 A **day** is a 24-hour period from one midnight to the next:
My next mission is in four days' time.
Forty thousand children are dying every day.
Any day would suit me for the interview.

2 A **day** is also the period between dawn and nightfall, as distinct from **night**:
Sunday is seen more and more as a normal working day.
I work with them all day.
He walked by night and slept by [= during the] *day.*
She no longer knew which was day and which was night.
What time of day would suit you best?

REFERRING TO PARTICULAR DAYS

1 The preposition **on** is needed where a day has a proper name, or where you are using a determiner that is different from **the**:
Everyone had to meet at the cottage ***on Christmas Day****.*
On my first day *at university I went straight to the library.*

2 **The day after tomorrow** means 'two days from now', and **the day before yesterday** means 'two days ago':
The day after tomorrow you'll receive a visitor.
The day before yesterday we were thinking of giving up.

3 You can refer to a particular day in the past or future as **that day**:
Later that day a letter was delivered by hand.
I think I'm due to be in Manchester that day.

4 When talking about a day in the past or future, use **the following day, the next day**, or **the day after** instead of tomorrow, and **the previous day** or **the day**

before instead of **yesterday**:

The day after that they hired their own helicopter.
We were told to leave the area, but we returned the following day.
She touched his shoulder, as she had done the day before.
He'll be arriving in Liverpool the following day.

IDIOMS

1 **One day** is an unspecified day in the past, or an unknown time in the future:
One day I was in the library and came across this book.
One day I hope to spend several weeks exploring County Galway.

2 **The other day** is some time in the recent past:
Marie read me one of her poems the other day.

3 You can refer to the present as **the present day**:
This play has remained popular right up to the present day.

4 People use **these days** and **nowadays** to mean 'now', 'at present' or 'as things are':
Children have much more freedom these days, don't they?

the days of the week

The days of the week are:

Sunday	*Monday*	*Tuesday*	*Wednesday*
Thursday	*Friday*	*Saturday*	

The days from Monday to Friday are called **weekdays** and Saturday and Sunday make up **the weekend**.

TALKING ABOUT A PARTICULAR DAY OF THE WEEK

You usually use **on** to refer to a particular day of the week when something happens:

Twenty-two people were arrested on Thursday.
It's my birthday on Friday.

REGULAR ARRANGEMENTS

You can use, *eg* **on Mondays** or **on a Monday** to talk about regular happenings. **On** is sometimes omitted before the plural form, especially in AmE:

On Fridays she has a day at home.
The animals are fed at 11.00 am and 4.00 pm, except on a Friday.
They'd rather work Saturdays than during the week.

MORNING, AFTERNOON AND EVENING

The names of the days are often used before a particular part of the day:

I'll see you on Wednesday afternoon, then.
A meeting has been planned for Tuesday morning.
It was a Friday evening and I was in London.

PAST AND FUTURE

This Friday is the Friday of this week, **next Friday** is the Friday of next week, and **last Friday** is the Friday of last week:

The competition starts this Sunday.
The book will be published next Thursday.
We made the reservation last Monday.

dead, died

These two words are often confused.

DEAD

Dead is an adjective. It can come before or after the noun:

The dead body was found by a couple out walking in the woods.
Beckett? But he's dead, isn't he?

DIED

Died is the past tense and past participle of the verb **die**:

She died peacefully in the summer of 1985.
So far, we know that 30 people have died.

demonstratives

Demonstratives are 'showing' words. You use them to refer to things or people within your view or surroundings, and also to refer to things or people just mentioned. The demonstratives in English are the determiners and pronouns **this** and **that**, their plurals **these** and **those**, and the two adverbs **here** and **there**. For the use of the determiners and pronouns see the entry **this, that, these** and **those**. **Here** and **there** have their own entries.

determiners

Determiners are words like **this, some, every, many, both**, which you use before nouns to indicate which, or how many, people or things you mean. Individual entries in this book deal with each particular determiner. Determiners fall roughly into two classes:

SPECIFIERS AND IDENTIFIERS

The following determiners belong to this group:

articles:

a, an	*the*		

demonstratives:

this	*these*	*that*	*those*

possessives:

my	*your*	*his*	*her*
its	*our*	*your*	*their*
one's	*whose*		

1 function

You use these determiners to indicate whether or not you expect your hearer to know which people or things you are talking about.

If you use the indefinite article **a** or **an** (*She needs a doctor*), you do not expect your hearer to identify any particular person or thing.

If you use the definite article **the** (*I've just been to the doctor*), your hearer will presume you mean a particular one.

2 characteristics

It is typical of this group of determiners that you cannot use them in combination with each other.

Notice that the possessive form with **'s** has an identifying function, and belongs to this group of determiners:
Shakespeare's plays

QUANTIFIERS AND OTHERS

1 function

These include:

quantifiers:

some	*any*	*no*	
each	*every*	*either*	*neither*
many	*much*	*more*	*most*
(a) little	*less*	*least*	
(a) few	*fewer*	*fewest*	
enough	*several*	*other*	
all	*both*	*half*	

wh-words:

what	*which*	*whatever*	*whichever*

numbers:

one	*two*	*three*, and so on

This group of determiners can be described very generally as having a *quantifying* function. You use the majority of them to indicate *how many* people or things, or *how much* of something, you mean.

2 characteristics

These determiners can be used in combination with each other, where appropriate:

*He stopped the tractor **every few** yards.*
*It displays **a little more** originality.*
*They've lost **all five** matches so far.*

COMBINING DETERMINERS

1 You can use quantifying determiners immediately before nouns:

*Was **much** time lost?*
***Several** pupils fell ill.*
***Each** copy was personally autographed.*

But when you want to put a quantifying determiner before a specifying determiner, you require **of** beween them:

any example	*any **of** these examples*
less food	*less **of** the food*
either alternative	*either **of** those alternatives*
most products	*most **of** our products*
enough complaints	*enough **of** my complaints*
which maps?	*which **of** these maps?*
twelve red roses	*twelve **of** the red roses*

> ⓘ The three determiners **all**, **both** and **half** can be used with or without **of** before a following determiner:
> *all my* (or *all **of** my*) *children*
> *both these* (or *both **of** these*) *wines*
> *half the* (or *half **of** the*) *population*

The two determiners **no** and **every** cannot be used before **of**:

2 You can use the specifying determiners before the quantifying determiners **many**, **most**, **little**, **least**, and **a few**:

her many films — *the most benefit*
a little tact — *the least effort*
her few relatives — *a few problems*

QUANTIFYING DETERMINERS + OF + PRONOUNS

Quantifying determiners can be followed by a pronoun after **of**. Notice that you use the object pronouns **us** and **them**:

*several **of** us* — *whichever **of** them*
*most **of** it* — *any **of** you*

USED WITHOUT A FOLLOWING NOUN

Determiners can act as pronouns:

1 You can omit the noun after a determiner if it has already been mentioned:
'Will the new arrangements make much difference?' 'Very little, actually.'
Most of the eggs were cracked but these are OK.

2 In a style that is becoming rather old-fashioned, you can use plural determiners to refer generally to people:
I think your plan is acceptable there, though some would disagree.

•••• different ••••

DIFFERENT FROM

A person or thing that is **different from** another is not like them in some way:

Modigliani's style was entirely different from Picasso's.
The grammar of spoken English is different from that of written English.

DIFFERENT THAN

Traditionally, **different than** is typical of AmE, but it is becoming common in informal BrE too. It acts in the same way as **different to/from**:

He is no different than any other pop star.
That's the security people. They're different than the other policemen. Sure it was different than what they had been expecting.

—— direct speech ——

➤ See **reporting**.

—— disagreeing ——

➤ See **agreeing and disagreeing**.

•••• disinterested ••••

A **disinterested** person is someone who is not involved personally in a certain situation and can be expected to judge it fairly:

A solicitor's ability to give disinterested advice is essential.
Their concern with these matters was a disinterested academic one.

> ⓘ Some people use **disinterested** to mean 'uninterested':
> *His wife left him, he became increasingly disinterested in his work and he started drinking again.*
> This use of **disinterested** is often regarded as incorrect. **Uninterested** is considered the correct word to express this meaning.

•••• dislike ••••

➤ See **like**.

—— distance ——

➤ See **measurement**.

•••• distancing ••••

We use **distancing** in language when we want to make what we are saying seem more polite and less direct. In English direct requests or questions can seem rude or offensive.

PAST TENSES

The past tense is often used for distancing in questions, requests, invitations and suggestions:

I'm here. ***Did you want*** *something?*
And, how ***did you want*** *to pay?*
What kind of colour ***were you looking for****?*
I was wondering if anyone ***could*** *help me.*

FUTURE

You can also use the future continuous form to ask a question in an extremely polite way. This form is generally only used by people who are serving other people:

How ***will you be paying****, Madam?*
Will you be wanting *your usual after-dinner drink?*

WOULD, COULD, MIGHT AND THE CONDITIONAL

Modal verbs and conditional forms such as **what if** and **suppose** are commonly used in making polite suggestions and requests, or in asking questions:

It ***would*** *be nice if you could come.*
You ***could*** *try calling him at the office.*

Might *it be a good idea to get some sleep now?*
Would *it be at all possible to come and pick me up at the airport?*
What if *we just waited a bit before we tried again?*
Suppose *I went out to get us some lunch?*

> ⓘ A suggestion or request can be expressed in the negative. This has the effect of making the person being addressed feel less obliged to respond:
> *You* ***wouldn't be able to*** *give me a hand, would you?*
> ***I don't suppose*** *anyone's interested in going to see this play, are they?*

INDIRECT QUESTIONS

When you are asking for information, it is common to introduce your question with a phrase like **Could you tell me...** or **Would you mind telling me...** :

Could you tell me where you were born?
Would you mind telling me how old you are?

> ⓘ Notice that inversion does not take place in indirect questions.

SUGGESTIONS

You can make suggestions in an indirect way with the words **Wouldn't it be better...** and **Mightn't it be a good idea...** :

Mightn't it be better to rent it?
Wouldn't it be better if I came to see you?
Would it be better to warn him first?

.... do ....

Do is irregular:

do, does, did, done

negative contractions:

don't, doesn't, didn't

> ⓘ The negative contractions can only be used where **do** is acting as an *auxiliary* verb.

The verb **do** has two functions:

- It is used as an *auxiliary* verb, helping to form questions and negatives with the infinitive form of other verbs.
- It is used as an *ordinary* verb meaning 'deal with in the approprite way', and as a general verb of action.

USED AS AN AUXILIARY VERB

As an auxiliary verb, **do** has several roles:

- It forms the *negatives* of other verbs.
- It forms *questions* with other verbs.
- It plays an important part in *emphasis*, and in *substitution*.

1 negatives

You use **do** with **not** or **-n't** to form the negatives of ordinary verbs:

*She **doesn't feel** well.*
*I **don't want** him to be punished for something he **didn't do**.*

ⓘ
- Note that auxiliary **do** is not used to form the negative of the verb **be**, or the modal verbs:
  *You **can't*** (not *don't can*) *be in two places at the same time.*
- Note also that **do** as an auxiliary verb can occur with **do** as an ordinary verb:
  I don't do much work at home.

2 questions

You use **do** to form questions with other verbs. In questions, **do** usually changes places with the subject:

Why did he say that?
What do you do all day?
Does he have any money?

ⓘ
- Note that auxiliary **do** is not used to form questions with **be**, or with modal verbs:
  Can you (not *do you can*) *ski?*
- Note also that **do** as an auxiliary verb can occur with **do** as an ordinary verb:
  What do you do at the weekends?

3 used for emphasis

Do can be used in positive sentences to emphasize the main verb:

I haven't decided yet, but if I do go, would you like a lift?
It's only been a couple of weeks, but it does seem longer.
We do do things well, generally speaking.

4 in commands

You use **do** with other verbs to form negative commands, and to emphasize positive commands and invitations:

Don't hurt him.
Do take notes.
Do take a seat.

ⓘ Notice that in this use, **do** can be used with **be**:
Don't be silly.
Do be sensible.

5 elliptical use

You can use auxiliary **do** to stand for the main verb and its object:

We're not supposed to go out, but we do.
They like it. So do we.
He thinks it's too much of a risk, and I do too.
'I think it's OK.' 'Well I don't.'

You also use auxiliary **do** in *question tags*:

But you want to go home, don't you?
That seems to be the best thing, doesn't it?
Chris doesn't like it, does he?

➤ For **do** with **have**, see entry for **have**.

AS AN ORDINARY VERB

As an ordinary verb, **do** has a range of functions.

1 You **do** something such as your *hair* or *teeth* when you deal with them in the way they usually need to be dealt with:

I left the two youngest to do [= wash] *the dishes.*
You've done [= arranged] *your hair differently.*

2 You **do** something such as *a task* when you carry it out or complete it. You **do** something such as an *activity* when you take part in it:

I'll stay at home and do some homework.
She planned to do some cooking.

3 You use **do** to represent any kind of action:

What can I do today?
You'd better do something, quick.
Mansell has done the right thing.

4 You use **do** as a phrase substitute

- **Do** can be used after an auxiliary verb, or modal auxiliary verb, as a substitute for a verb phrase that has already been used:

  Will you hold my hand, the way you used to do (or *used to*)*?*
  I can't try any harder than I already am doing (or *am*).

- You can use **do so** to avoid repeating the verb phrase:

  If anyone can help, please do so [= help] *as soon as you can.*
  I asked her to move her car, but she refused to do so [= move her car].

DO OR MAKE?

Things that you **do** are concerned with action or work:

do *your duty*
do *some work*
do *the dusting*
do *the washing up*

You **make** things when you create or produce them:

make *a cake*
make *a meal*
make *a film*

With objects of a more abstract kind, it is difficult to know which verb to choose. The following list of common collocations with **do** and **make** may help:

do *damage, good or harm*
do *business with people*
do *someone a favour, or a service*
make *comments, remarks, suggestions, statements, jokes*
make *plans, decisions, claims, accusations, excuses*
make *attempts, efforts, mistakes*
make *preparations, contributions, improvements, alterations, amends*
make *enquiries, discoveries*
make *noises*
make *progress, an impact*

•••• doubt ••••

AS A VERB

1 The verb **doubt** usually behaves in a similar way to **not know** or **wonder**, so it is usually followed by **whether** or **if**:
Our financial adviser doubted whether we could sell the business at all.
I doubt if I could pass the exams.

2 People also sometimes use **that** after **doubt**, and, informally, no conjunction at all:
I doubt that these changes will alleviate the problem.
I doubt we'll hear from them before six o'clock.

3 If **doubt** is used with a negative, you follow it with **that**:
No-one could doubt that [= everyone could be certain that] *he was an expert in his field.*

4 If you **doubt** a *thing*, you distrust it, or don't believe in it:
I don't doubt your friend's sincerity.

AS A NOUN

The structures after the noun **doubt** reflect those used with the verb:
I don't know what happened, but there's no doubt that there was a fight.
There is some doubt as to whether they can help us at all.

•••• dress ••••

AS A NOUN

Dress has a countable and an uncountable meaning.

1 A **dress** is an article of women's or girl's clothing, with the lower part in the form of a skirt:
Alison planned to wear a white evening dress.

2 Uncountable **dress** has a similar meaning to 'clothes' or 'clothing', and is used in compound nouns:
At ten o'clock Mark put on full evening dress.
The soldiers were in national dress for the occasion.

AS A VERB

1 You **dress**, or **get dressed**, when you put clothes on yourself. You can also **dress** someone else:

There was no electric light and we dressed in the dark.
She got dressed after breakfast.
Peggy dressed the boy for the cold.

2 The way you **dress** is the typical style of clothing that you wear:

How should I dress for this kind of occasion?
I really like the way she dresses.

3 You can say that someone **is dressed in** something to mean that they are wearing it:

I saw three small children dressed in traditional silk tunics.
He was dressed in a T-shirt and jeans.

• • • • drink • • • •

Drink can be used either as a verb or a noun. Depending on the way you use it, you may give the impression that you are speaking about drinking alcoholic drinks only.

THE VERB

Drink is an irregular verb:
drinks, drinking, drank, drunk

1 **with or without an object**

You **drink** a liquid when you swallow it; you **drink** when you swallow a liquid:

Father McCormack drank his tea.
Can I get you something to drink?
She raised the cup and drank.

2 **without an object**

When people use **drink** without an object, they are often referring to the drinking of alcohol:

She drinks too much.
I could tell that they had been drinking.
I'm not drinking tonight. I'm on medication.

> ⓘ If you say that someone **drinks**, you probably mean that they drink too much alcohol:
> *Dylan Thomas was a real poet; he was Welsh, he drank, and he became Burton's friend.*
> Someone who **doesn't drink** never drinks alcohol:
> *No thanks, I don't drink.*

THE NOUN

1 **used as a countable noun**

- A **drink** is often an alcoholic drink:

Would you like a drink before you go to your table, sir?

If you don't mean an alcoholic drink, it helps to make this clear by saying what sort of drink you are talking about:

a drink of milk
She made him a hot drink and turned on the TV.
a soft drink

- You **have a drink** when you drink something, usually alcoholic:

  Have a drink.
  I'll pick you up at eight. Then we can have a drink in the bar first.

- You **get**, or **buy**, **someone a drink** when you pay for their drink:

  Let me get you a drink.
  He bought me a drink. That's all.

- You **go for a drink** when you go to a bar to drink something, usually alcoholic:

  We often went for a drink together after work.

2 used as an uncountable noun

Drink is alcohol:

They gave us money to buy drink.
He lost his job on the railway, through drink and bad conduct.

> ⓘ In AmE, **drink** in this sense is commonly referred to as **liquor**.

COMMON EXPRESSIONS USED IN SOCIAL DRINKING

Drink up! [= Finish your drink.]
What're you having? [= What would you like to drink?]
What can I get you? [= What would you like to drink?]
It's my round. [= It's my turn to buy drinks for everyone]
Thanks, but I'm driving. [= I can't accept your offer of an alcoholic drink because I'm driving]

People say **cheers** to each other when they raise their glasses before they start to drink an alcoholic drink. People also say **to your health**, or **here's to** … , as a way of wishing each other good health, success or happiness:

Here's to your new job!

•••• drown ••••

In British English, both active and passive forms are used to talk about drowning by accident:

He (was) drowned in a boating accident.

In American English, only the active form can be used to talk about accidental drowning:

He drowned at sea.

Drown is commonly found in the passive form in both British and American English when used figuratively to talk about loud noise overpowering a sound:

The music was drowned by the fire alarm.

•••• drunk, drunken ••••

Drunk and **drunken** are both adjectives that refer to a person who has drunk too much alcohol. But there are some differences in meaning and use between the two words.

DRUNK

1 **Drunk** is the past participle of the verb **drink**.
For more information about this verb, see the entry **drink**.

2 **Drunk** is an adjective that is used to refer to someone who has consumed too much alcohol. It usually comes after the noun with a linking verb like **be**:
Police announced that they would refuse entry to anyone who was obviously drunk.

3 You can talk about **getting drunk**, to describe the process of drinking too much alcohol:
He got drunk one night and fell downstairs.

DRUNKEN

1 **Drunken** has a very similar meaning to **drunk** , but it can only be used before the noun it describes:
Drunken patients dominate the emergency wards between 2 and 4am.
His drunken father physically abused him.

2 **Drunken** is often used to talk about things people do when they have drunk too much alcohol:
*She faces charges of **drunken driving** following a road accident.*
*The police were called to a **drunken fight** outside the club.*

•••• due to, owing to ••••

There are many cases where you can use either **due to** , **owing to**:
Due to (or *owing to*) *lack of resources there are only three planes in use.*
The charity had to reduce its activities due to (or *owing to*) *lack of money.*
Owing to (or *due to*) *space restrictions, suitcases are not allowed in the cabin.*

> ⓘ Some people think that **due to** should not be used at the beginning of a clause. This is because **due** is actually an adjective. However, it is commonly used at the beginning of a clause, even in formal English, and must therefore be accepted as standard. **Owing to** should not be used after the verb **be**:
> *The strike was due to* (not *owing to*) *unease about social changes.*
> *His change of attitude was due to* (not *owing to*) *concern for her feelings.*

•••• during ••••

There are several differences in use between **during** and **for**, and between **during** and **in**.

DURING OR FOR?

Something that happens **during** a period of time happens at some time while it is passing. Something that happens **for** a period lasts as long as that period:

Keep all the windows open for three weeks.
How many issues of the newsletter do you produce during the year?

DURING OR IN?

1 Something happens either **in** or **during** a period of time such as the night, or a certain month or year, if it happens while that period is passing:
There were a lot of job losses in (or *during*) *1995.*
Lucy rang her in (or *during*) *the evening.*

2 Something is the case **during** (not **in**) a period of time when it is the case *throughout* that period:
Theatres were closed during (not *in*) *the whole period.*

3 Something happens **during** (not **in**) an activity:
He was murdered during (not *in*) *an argument at his hotel.*
During (not *in*) *their stay they visited the British Museum.*

Ee

each

AS A DETERMINER

1 As a determiner, **each** is used before a *singular* noun:

Each water molecule contains two atoms of hydrogen.
Place a spoonful of beans at the bottom of each tin.
Look at the facts in each particular case.

> ⓘ **each** or **every**?
> You can use **each** where the group consists of two or more. You can use **every** only for groups of three or more:
> *Nick came in, a bottle of wine in each* (not *every*) *hand.*
> *Every* (or *each*) *student's style will be different.*

> ⓘ You tend to prefer **each** when you are thinking of the members of a group individually, and **every** if you are thinking of the group as a whole. In a lot of cases **each** and **every** are interchangeable:
> *We check carefully at each* (or *every*) *stage.*
> *Our monthly magazine is sent free to every member.*
> *She asked each member to sign the letter.*

AS A PRONOUN

1 The preposition **of** has to follow **each** before a *pronoun* or a *determiner*:

The house had two bedrooms on each of the upper floors.
Each of these proposals deserves careful examination.
They made three recordings, each of which I bought.

2 The traditional grammar rule is that a singular verb should be used with **each of**, but it is not followed very strictly by native speakers, and in some cases a plural verb sounds more natural:

Each of you has (or *have*) *different qualities and skills.*
What do each of you feel about it?
Each of us is unique.
Do you know what each of them is worth?

3 Where **each** refers to the *subject* of the clause, it can behave like the pronouns **both** and **all**, going in mid position. The verb is always plural:

The boy and girl each hold a corner of the same handkerchief.
We have each received a copy of the guarantee.

We were each given two slices of bread.
The prize-winners can each choose £1000 worth of items.

4 **Each** can follow the *object* of a verb or preposition. In cases where this happens, the object is usually a pronoun, and **each** is rarely the final word in the clause:
I will be speaking to you each individually.
They paid us each 100 roubles a month.
He made them each a cup of tea.

5 When talking about the distribution of something, you use **each** after a quantity to represent the individual people or groups that get or have that quantity:
She left £20 each to her cousins Mary and Sarah.
There are two houses, which care for up to nine children each.
The music is for five choirs of four voices each.

6 You use **each** when talking about prices:
The cottages were for sale at £1000 each.

7 You can use **each** when specifying an equal number from two or more varieties:
Red or white? We have a bottle of each.
I'd like boys and girls; two of each, ideally.

8 **Each one** can often be used as a more natural and conversational alternative to **each**, which sometimes sounds rather formal when it is used as an independent pronoun:
When the members meet, each (*one*) *describes his or her day.*
The thought came to each (*one*) *of the four as they ate.*
There are hundreds of varieties, each (*one*) *different from the others.*
Desire is a powerful force within each (*one*) *of us.*

ⓘ pronouns and possessives after **each**
In traditional grammar, **each** is followed by singular pronouns and possessives, but in practice, plurals often sound more natural, especially after an expression such as **each of you** or **each one of us**:
Each one of us must be responsible for our (more natural than *his or her*) *own actions.*
There is much that each of us can do to help ourselves (more natural than *himself or herself*).
Each of you, in your own way (more natural than *in his or her own way*), *needs* (or *need*) *help.*

• • • • each other, one another • • • •

1 Even where a group of more than two is involved, native speakers of English tend to use **each other** and **one another** interchangeably:
Friendships developed as we helped each other carry the luggage.
His parents did not love one another.

2 Both **each other, one another** can be used in the possessive form:
We all know each other's faces by now.
The soldiers fought together and then dressed one another's wounds.

3 Notice the distinction between the expressions **each other** (or **one another**), and **-selves**, as illustrated by the following examples:

His parents blamed each other for what happened to him (= she blamed him and he blamed her).
His parents blamed themselves for his problems (= they both thought they were both responsible).
The children were all quietly talking to one another.
Many children talk to themselves when they are alone.

4 There are certain verbs that represent reciprocal action, that is, people or things doing the same thing to each other, so that, *with a plural subject*, **each other** or **one another** is already implied by the verb, and need not be used.

Later that year we met at the Majestic Hotel.
Although we sat close together, we avoided touching.

A list of verbs that behave like this may be useful:

chat	*coincide*	*confer*	*converse*
fight	*marry*	*meet*	*quarrel*
touch			

•••• easily ••••

1 The adverb **easily** can be used with comparatives and superlatives, with an intensifying meaning:

Liverpool was easily the better side.
These photos are easily the best we've ever taken.

2 Notice that **easily** can also be used to intensify adjectives that are not strictly superlatives or comparatives, but represent a top or leading position:

Archie was easily the leading scorer in our first season.
In that marriage she was easily the dominant partner.

•••• east, eastern, easterly; words dealing with direction ••••

Style questions arise concerning the compass-direction words **north**, **south**, **east** and **west** (always said in this order), their derivatives **northern**, **southern**, **northerly**, **southerly** and so on, and the compound direction words **northeast**, **northwest**, **southeast**, **southwest**, **northwestern**, **northwesterly**, and so on. Here are a few points on the subject:

NORTH, SOUTH, EAST AND WEST

1 You give the *nouns* a capital letter only if you are using them as proper names representing particular geographical areas (as distinct from directions):

There is a white cheese which is very popular in the North of England.
Opinion in the South gradually changed.
Travellers from the west joined those coming from the east.
The star will rise in the east at 5.00 tomorrow.

2 As with the nouns, you give the *adjectives* capital letters only where they are part of a proper name or place name:

There was a big robbery in the East End last night.

The film was shot in South Central LA.
He underlined the costs for West Germany.

But:

There was a gallery on the west side of the house.

3 The *adverbs* don't need a capital letter:
This wine comes from south of the River Vienne.
The Leroghi hills are about 750 miles north of Nairobi.
His house faces east.

NORTHERN, SOUTHERN, EASTERN, WESTERN

1 The adjectives **northern**, **southern**, **eastern** and **western** have a less precise meaning than **north**, **south**, **east** and **west**, and are useful if you want to describe a more general idea of a direction, or refer to a wider area. For instance, you refer to the **western** part of a country, rather than the **west** part of it:
They are trying to develop better grapes for northern climates.
They didn't want a revolutionary state along their western frontier.
We flew over a town in southern Sudan.
There were huge losses among civilians in the eastern sector of the city.

2 If these **-ern** adjectives refer to the proper names **the North**, **the South**, or especially **the East** or **the West** in the cultural or political sense, they need capitals:
Arab oil became the focus of Western concern.

3 The **-ern** adjectives are frequent in place names and proper names, where they always have capitals:
The Northern People's Congress was founded at this time.
The area is served by Eastern Electricity.

NORTHERLY, NORTHWARDS, NORTHWARD, ETC

1 The adjectives **northerly**, **southerly**, **easterly** and **westerly** never have capitals, but their meanings need attention. An **easterly** wind blows *from* the east, but a wind that blows in an **easterly** direction is blowing towards the east. The furthest point in an **easterly** direction can be referred to as the **most easterly** point:
Vegetation changes were the result of stronger westerly gales.
an alternative southerly route from Malta to Kano in Nigeria
Eureka is Canada's most northerly permanent weather station.

2 The **-wards** forms (**northwards**, **westwards** and so on) are *adverbs*:
The army fired on northern rebels advancing southwards to the capital.

3 BrE uses the **-ward** forms chiefly as adjectives:
You'll get worse jet lag on eastward or westward journeys than on flights in a north-south or south-north direction.

In AmE, the **-ward** form is used as an adverb.

NORTHEAST, NORTHWEST, SOUTHEAST, SOUTHWEST AND THEIR DERIVATIVES

The principles outlined above for the usage and capitalization of **north**, **south**, **east** and **west**, and their derivatives in **-ern**, **-erly** and **-wards**, apply also to the 'compound' directions **northeast**, **northwest**, **southeast** and **southwest**. So that, for instance, the **Northwest**, with a capital letter, is the proper name for a part of a country, *eg*

England. Have a look at the following examples:

The problem is very common in the northeast of the continent.
Here's the weather outlook for the Bristol area and the Southwest.
a southwest-facing window
the northwest coast of the island
In China and Southeast Asia, milk and cheese are not part of the diet.
Edgecote House is situated about 8 miles northwest of Brackley.
the southeasterly trade winds

> ⓘ The 'compound' direction words can also be written as two words, but when they are, care must be taken over capitalization and hyphenation. It is therefore probably sensible to save yourself trouble by always writing these as one word.

-ed, -en adjectives

A lot of adjectives in English end in **-ed** or in other past-participle endings, such as **-en** or **-t**. These adjectives fall into a variety of categories, which it may be useful to note here.

1 Most adjectives that have the form of past participles have a passive sense, like a past participle (so *an exaggerated account* is an account that *has been exaggerated*):

We were delighted at the news.
a trail of broken promises
spoilt children

2 Some adjectives in the form of past participles come from intransitive verbs, and therefore have an *active* sense, rather than a passive one, so a **retired** colonel is a colonel who *has retired*. Here are some more adjectives like this, used in typical ways:

advanced cancer
dated slang
a swollen knee
recently arrived guests
an escaped prisoner
faded curtains

3 Some adjectives in the form of past participles have developed special meanings, no longer close to the verb they come from. For instance, to **reserve** a seat is to book it in advance, but a **reserved** person is someone who does not express their opinions or feelings freely. A list of adjectives with similarly 'developed' meanings follows:

I'm quite attached to him.
a distinguished scientist
a marked contrast
a noted expert
a determined chin
disturbed teenagers
The book had a mixed reception.
She drove like someone possessed.

4 A lot of adjectives are formed by the addition of **-ed** to a noun. These adjectives indicate *possession* of the noun in question. For instance, a **pointed** object is an object with a *point*, and a **wheeled** vehicle has *wheels*. The following adjectives are formed in a similar way:

armoured vehicles
barbed wire
detailed instructions
flowered material
gifted musicians
skilled workers
a bearded gentleman
disadvantaged children
freckled faces
a hooded jacket

a pointed knife | *salaried workers*
a spotted dog | *striped trousers*
a talented dancer | *waged staff*
a walled garden | *winged insects*

5 There is also a large range of compound adjectives that add information about the *quality* or *quantity* of the noun that a person or thing possesses. You can say, for instance, that a bicycle is a **two-wheeled** vehicle, and that a giraffe is a **long-necked** animal. Some more examples follow:

four-legged animals
two-winged insects
a double-breasted jacket
my multi-talented wife
a short-sleeved dress
a black-and-white-striped creature
a strongwilled child
a level-headed person

6 A number of adjectives have past-participle form, but are not related directly to a verb, or are related to a little-used verb. Some examples follow:

I'm so ashamed.
a belated reply
the deceased owner
a disjointed conversation
his estranged sister
I'm indebted to you.
rugged features
assorted nuts
a beloved friend
a dejected expression
Don't be downhearted.
an impassioned appeal
an opinionated man
a sophisticated device

.... effort, attempt ....

1 **Effort** is hard mental or physical work. If you **make an effort** to do something you try very hard to do it:

We had to make an effort to finish the job on time.

2 You **make an attempt** to do something when you try, on a particular occasion, to do it:

She made an attempt to stand up, but fell over again.

.... either ....

AS A DETERMINER

As a determiner **either** is used before a singular noun, and has four different senses:

1 **one or the other of two, but not both**

In this sense, a choice is usually being presented between alternatives:

You can use either method; you can also try a mixture of both.

2 **whichever of two, it doesn't matter which**

The sense here is that the same holds, whichever alternative is the case:

With either system, this is the easiest point for adding extensions.
Either way, devaluation would not solve the real problem.

3 **(not) the one or the other**

Either is always in a non-assertive context in this sense; there is always a negative, a broad negative (such as **hardly** or **scarcely**), a doubt, or a question, that applies to both alternatives:

There was not enough skill on either side for an interesting match.
We wondered whether either government was making the right choice.

4 each of two

Either can be used in the sense of 'each', especially in expressions like **on either side** or **at either end**:

Cattle were grazing on either side of the path.

AS A PRONOUN

As a pronoun, **either** reflects the first three senses of the determiner shown above.

1 **Either** can be used as an independent pronoun:

The 27 bus and the 23 bus both go in that direction; you can take either.
If either considers it necessary, the manager or the supervisor may send an employee home.
Which of the two horses, if either, was responsible for the accident?

2 The preposition **of** has to follow **either** before a *pronoun* or a *determiner*:

Can I offer either of you a drink?
It was doubtful whether either of them had committed a crime before.
An independent inquiry would not have helped in either of these cases (or *in either case*).

> ⓘ **Either of** is used before plural nouns and pronouns, and usually takes a singular verb, but can have a plural verb, especially after a negative:
> *All the clothes that either of us has are in the bag or on our backs.*
> *She does care for him; probably more than either of us realize.*
> *I had my first child when I was younger than either of you are now.*
> *Do either of you smoke?*

AS AN ADVERB

1 **Either** is used at the end of a sentence when negative statements are being made about two similar or related people or things, or about two circumstances concerning the same person or thing:

She hated sailing and didn't much like fishing either.
I know nothing about that and she doesn't either.
'I didn't hear the programme unfortunately.' 'I didn't either.'

Notice that alternatives to the endings in the last two examples are *'Neither does she'* and *'Neither did I.'*

2 You can use **either** at the end of an additional, negatively phrased, comment, to emphasize that what you are saying is rather impressive:

Yes, I can play bridge; and I'm not bad at it, either. [= I'm quite good at it too.]

AS A CONJUNCTION: EITHER ... OR

1 You use **either** before the first of two alternatives, only one of which is possible or true, with the second alternative introduced by **or**:

He will either come forward to meet you, or back off.
Either you apologize, or you leave immediately.

> ⓘ Notice that the subject of the **or**-clause can be omitted if it is the same as in the **either**-clause:
> *You can either come with me, or stay* (or *or you can stay*) *here by yourself.*

The second alternative can be highlighted by adding **else** after **or**:

Either he was drunk, or else he was seriously ill.

2 The framework **either ... or** is used more generally to present alternatives and possibilities:

This variety of plum can be enjoyed either fresh or cooked.
There's either porridge or cornflakes for breakfast.

3 Even where **either ... or** is used with singular nouns or pronouns, people sometimes use a plural verb:

Do either your mother or your father smoke?

•••• elder, eldest; older, oldest ••••

Elder and **eldest** are rather formal and are used mainly for comparing ages within a family. It is normal to use **older** and **oldest** for comparing the ages of people generally.

ELDER

1 **Elder** has a limited range of usage. As an adjective it is only used attributively, that is, before a noun. You can refer to *my elder sister*, but you have to say *My sister is older than* (not *elder than*) *me.*:

Her elder sister died abroad.
Mr McNab and his elder son called at my home.
When he was born his two elder brothers were already 12 and 13.

2 You can use **elder** with **the** or a possessive determiner in a variety of constructions, without a following noun:

The king asked the elder of the brothers to accompany him.
Jane was 21 and Billie her elder [= older than her] *by three years.*

3 **Your elders** are people who are older than you, especially people who deserve your respect because of their greater age, such as your parents:

Take some advice from your elders.

ELDEST

Eldest, like other superlative adjectives, is used with **the** or a possessive determiner, and can be used without a following noun:

The couple have five kids and their eldest daughter is seventeen.
My eldest brother was called Ralph.
Patty, our eldest, is nine.
He was the eldest of four brothers.

—— ellipsis ——

Ellipsis is the leaving out of words that do not need to be repeated, because the meaning of what is said next is clear without them:

'What time do you want to leave?' 'About ten-thirty. [= I want to leave at about ten-thirty]*'*

'I was planning to go to the conference.' 'And do you still want to? [= And do you still want to go to the conference?]*'*

ⓘ **Ellipsis** is closely connected with *substitution*, the practice of using a short substitute word for a previously used longer expression. You will find **substitution** as a separate entry in this book.

AFTER AUXILIARY AND MODAL VERBS

1 You can cut a clause off after an auxiliary verb, and your hearer or reader will understand the rest of the clause from what has been said previously:

I was doing my best, truly I was [doing my best].
Don't panic when things go wrong, as they inevitably will [= they inevitably will go wrong].
'Do you mind?' 'No, of course I don't [mind].*'*
'Can you hear the dove out there?' 'Just a second... Yes, I can.'

The elliptical clause can precede the clause that provides the context:

As soon as she could, she had a serious talk with her mother.

ⓘ Notice that you stress the auxiliary verb when you are using it elliptically, and you do not use its contracted forms:
'You haven't dealt with section B yet.' 'Yes, I have (not *I've*).*'*

2 Where two or more auxiliaries have already been used, the elliptical clause need contain only the first of them. A second and third auxiliary can be added, but they are not necessary:

'Do you think he'll have got home by now?' 'I expect he will (or *will have*).*'*
'I could have looked it up in a dictionary, I suppose.' 'Yes you could (or *could have*).*'*
'I would have been punished for cheating.' 'I suppose you would (or *would have*, or *would have been*).*'*

3 If new auxiliaries, or new forms of them, are introduced in the elliptical clause, the new forms are normally included:

'Do you think he was warned?' 'He could have been.'
'Did you read the article?' 'I'm not sure. I might have (or *might have done*).*'*

➤ See also **do** and **substitution**.

4 Question tags are a common form of ellipsis. In the regular type of question tag, where a negative statement is followed by a positive tag, and a positive statement by a negative tag, the auxiliary used in the main clause is always repeated in the same form in the tag; this happens also with **have** and **be** when they are behaving as 'ordinary' verbs:

Now I'd better be going, hadn't I?
But they don't have a video, do they?
He won't have seen it yet, will he?

5 Question tags use the auxiliary **do** to refer back to a lexical verb used without auxiliaries:

You want me to say 'No, stay', don't you?

➤ See also **question tags**.

6 Ellipsis often occurs with **neither**, **nor**, **so**, and **too**:

In fact I don't care at all; and neither do you.
If you're not going to tell him, nor am I.
'Are you hungry, Carrie?' 'No.' 'I'm not either.'
'I'm looking forward to this evening.' 'So am I.'
She thought it was very funny. I did too.

➤ See **conjunctions** for more information about omitting words after conjunctions.

➤ See **substitution** for information about the substitution of **not** and **so** for whole clauses (*I hope not*, *I expect so*).

AFTER WH- QUESTION WORDS

Ellipsis can be seen where the whole of a noun clause is omitted after a **wh-**question word:

I knew something was worrying him, but he wouldn't tell me what.
Well, we won, but it's a mystery how.
They're paying us a visit in April. I'll let you know when.
She's very upset, and I'll tell you why.

WITH INFINITIVES

1 A lot of verbs, adjectives and nouns can be followed by **to-**infinitives:

I didn't mean to hurt your feelings.
He's bound to forget.
There's no need to rush.
I decided not to go swimming.

You can usually 'cut off' the infinitive after **to**; the infinitive form of the previously mentioned verb, and anything that follows it, will be understood from the previous context:

I'm sorry if I hurt your feelings. I didn't mean to [hurt your feelings].
'Do you think he'll forget?' 'He's sure to.'
Why are you running? There's no need to.

2 You make a negative infinitive by inserting **not** before **to**:

'I thought you were going swimming this morning?' 'I know, but I decided not to'.

➤ See **infinitive** for lists of words that are followed by a **to-**infinitive.

3 An object may follow the verb before **to**:

He still refuses to sign, but I think we can probably persuade him to.
He phoned again, though Julie asked him not to.

4 A passive form is also possible:

At first your body won't cope with the exercise, but it can be trained to.

ⓘ The verb **be**, whether auxiliary or 'linking', and 'possessive' **have**, are not normally omitted after **to**:
I'm not a friend of hers, and I don't want to be.
He hasn't been invited but I think he'd like to be.
She didn't have all the qualifications she claimed to have.

5 Ellipsis with infinitive forms often follows structures containing **enough** or **too**:
They could contribute some money; they're just too selfish to.
I thought you were one of the actresses; you're pretty enough to be.

6 Ellipsis implying an infinitive can also follow the question word **how**:
I would have started the washing machine, but I didn't know how to.

7 **To** can be omitted after **try**, but not after **try not**:
I always fall asleep, even when I try hard not to.

8 **To** is not essential after the verbs **want** and **wish**, and is rarely used after **like**, when they are used after the conjunctions **when**, **whenever**, **as**, **what** and **if**:
You may take breakfast in your own room, if you wish (or *wish to*).
I can do what I like with my free time.
I could stay with them whenever I wanted (or *wanted to*).

•••• else ••••

INDEFINITE WORDS AND WH-WORDS

1 With the following groups of words, **else** is used to mean 'other than the people, things, places, and so on, that have already been mentioned, or are known about':

some-words: *someone, somebody, something, somewhere*
any-words: *anyone, anybody, anything, anywhere*
no-words: *no-one, nobody, nothing, nowhere*
every-words: *everyone, everybody, everything, everywhere*
wh-words: *what, who, why, when, where, how; whatever, wherever*
quantifiers: *little, much*

Notice that **else** always follows the word it is modifying:
She moved aside to allow someone else [= whoever was next] *room at the counter.*
He confessed to Sarah that he had been seeing somebody else [= another person].
You won't get a better choice anywhere else [= in any other place].
Only you can do it; there's no-one else [= no other person].
After he had written the first sentence, he couldn't think what else [= what more] *to put.*
'Where did he get the money?' 'From his father. Where else? [= from what other source?]*'*
I want to make money. Why else [= for what other reason?] *should I be here?*
Well, I listened and sympathized; there wasn't much else I could do.
At Juara there's the wind, the sea, and very little else.

2 The possessive form **else's** is possible after **somebody** and the other indefinite pronouns referring to people:

She looked at the photos in amazement; had she picked up someone else's by mistake?
I wonder if you'd like to add your signature? I've got everybody else's.

> ⓘ Notice that phrases using **else** are singular. If you want to convert, *eg* **anyone else** or **something else** into a plural, you would say **any other people** or **other things**.

OR ELSE

Or else is really a strong form of **or**, and is used in three ways:

1 as an emphatic introduction to an alternative, *eg* after **either**:
Either try to get him to discuss the problem, or else send him for therapy.

2 as an alternative to **otherwise**, introducing the consequences of not doing what has just been mentioned:
Hurry up, or else we'll be late.

3 independently, *eg* after a command, as a vague threat about the consequences of not doing what is asked:
The President last night warned 'Stop the fighting or else.'
In those days people did what they were told, or else.

ELSEWHERE

Elsewhere means either 'somewhere else' or 'in other places':

Patients can get better service by going elsewhere [= somewhere else] *for treatment.*
See the notes on this topic elsewhere [= in other places] *in the book.*
Kerala has less crime than elsewhere [= other places] *in India.*

—— emphasis ——

➤ See pages 194 and 195.

.... end, finish ....

FINISH

1 You **finish** a task, or **finish doing** something when you complete it:
He had to finish his exams before he could get a job.
He realized that he could not finish the accounts before 31st December.
Have you finished making your holiday plans yet?
When she'd finished washing up she began to calm down.
When you've finished doing that, press the 'end' key.

2 You **finish** school or work when you stop lessons or work and go home:
What time do you finish school?

3 You **finish** something you have been eating or drinking when you eat or drink the last bit of it; someone **finishes** a cigarette when they smoke the last bit of it, and extinguish it:

EMPHASIS

There are various ways of emphasizing speech and writing in English.

STRESS

1 In speech, words which are louder and higher than others carry more emphasis. In writing, you might underline a stressed word, or write it in capitals:

I thought she was married to ANDREW!
I asked them to come before the match!

2 In printing, stressed words are shown by use of **bold** or *italics*.

3 Auxiliary verbs are commonly stressed as a way of showing emotions such as surprise, delight, frustration or anger:

*What **have** you done?*
*That **is** a lovely dress!*
*So how **should** I have done it?*

4 In some cases, you may insert an auxiliary verb where one would not normally be necessary:

*I **do** like your shoes.*
*I **did** phone him!*
*I **have** made my bed!*

INTENSIFYING WORDS

Intensifying words that are used with adjectives can be divided into two kinds: those which can be used with gradable adjectives, and those which can be used with non-gradable adjectives.

ⓘ Gradable adjectives are words like **nice** and **difficult**; you can say that something is **more** or **less** nice or difficult. Non-gradable adjectives are words like **dead** or **alive**; a person cannot be described as being more or less dead or alive – they are either one or the other.

... **end**, **finish** continued

He had time to finish his drink before his boss arrived.
Roberts finished his cigarette, crushing it in the ashtray.

END

1 You **end** something when you stop it, or break it off:

He knew an argument was starting and thought it would be better to end the conversation quickly.
He came to the White House with promises to end the Vietnam War.

2 You **end** something such as a speech in a certain way when you bring it to a close in that way:

He ended his talk with a quotation.
He ended his presentation with the words 'We aim to be the number one in Europe'.

1 Common intensifiers that are used with gradable adjectives are **so**, **too**, **very** and **extremely**:

Let's eat in the garden; it's too nice to stay indoors.
It was so cold that we had to go home early.
It's very kind of you to help us.

2 Common intensifiers that are used with non-gradable adjectives are **totally**, **completely** and **absolutely**:

He was totally exhausted by the end of the day.
The weather was absolutely perfect for sailing.
That's completely ridiculous.

ⓘ Some intensifiers and adjectives always come together. You can say that the weather is **absolutely perfect**, but not that it is *completely perfect*. If you are unsure which intensifier is correct, use **absolutely**, which works with nearly all non-gradable adjectives.

3 You can also use repetition of the intensifier to emphasize gradable adjectives. Use **very** with ordinary adjectives, and **much** with comparatives:

It's a very kind offer, but I think we'll manage by ourselves.
This flat is much, much nicer than the last one.

SENTENCE STRUCTURE

You can give emphasis to different parts of a sentence by changing the word order. A sentence like this is sometimes called a 'cleft sentence':

***That boy**, I've seen him before.* (instead of: *I've seen that boy before.*)
***It wasn't a ghost** that you saw, it was me!* (instead of: *You didn't see a ghost, you saw me.*)
***What I think**, is that these poorer areas should get more money.* (instead of: *I think these poorer areas should get more money.*)

... end, finish continued

ⓘ Note that you can't say that someone **ends doing** something. You have to use the verb **stop** in this case:
He stopped speaking (not *ended speaking*) *when the alarm went off.*

3 An object **ends in** something, or **ends at** a certain place, when it has that thing or place at its end or tip:

To their right, the road ended at a gate in a wall.
This section looks at words ending in -sion, -tion and -ture.

4 You **end up** in a particular place or doing a particular thing when you find yourself in that place or doing that thing, especially when it was not your intention; a situation **ends up** being a certain way when that is the way it goes, especially when it was not your intention for it to be so:

We had no cooking facilities so we ate in restaurants all the time. It ended up costing a fortune.
I wanted to be a scientist but I ended up as a doctor.

END OR FINISH

You can use either **end** or **finish** interchangeably when you want to say that something stops at a particular time or on a particular date:

What time does the lesson end (or *finish*)?
The holidays finish (or *end*) *on 8 September.*

•••• enjoy ••••

The main point about **enjoy** for learners to remember is that it needs an object. The object can be a noun (or pronoun), a reflexive pronoun, or the **-ing** form of another verb.

1 enjoy + noun or **pronoun:**

Young people meet here daily to enjoy each other's company.
He enjoyed the feeling of being on the winning side.
I've seen this films loads of times but I always enjoy it.

2 enjoy + -self

People sometimes say **enjoy!**, especially in AmE, but the regular formation is **enjoy yourself!**:
Come in and enjoy yourself!
We all went together and thoroughly enjoyed ourselves.
Johnson enjoyed himself when he was talking (not *enjoyed when he was talking*).

3 enjoy + -ing:

I don't enjoy watching (not *enjoy to watch*) *my own team.*
You must learn to enjoy eating without feeling guilty.
She enjoyed being photographed.

•••• enough ••••

Enough can be a *determiner*, a *pronoun* or an *adverb*.

AS A DETERMINER

1 Enough can be used before an uncountable noun or a plural noun:

We only had enough food for ourselves.
Are there enough books to go round?
I've had enough trouble [= as much as I can bear] *for one day.*

2 In a slightly old-fashioned, literary style, **enough** can follow the noun:

There would be time enough in the months ahead for such discussions.
They had courage enough for anything.

> ⓘ You will sometimes find **the** used like the determiner **enough**, especially in non-assertive contexts:
> *He hadn't the strength to argue.*
> You can use **time** and **room** by themselves with the sense 'enough room' and 'enough time':
> *There'll be room in our house for someone else.*
> *No-one has time to attend to you.*

AS A PRONOUN

1 As a pronoun, **enough** reflects the uses of the determiner:
She counted the plates; there were not enough.
I hadn't got enough to do so I helped the others with their work.
We all wanted some of the cake but there wasn't enough to go round.

2 **Enough** is used with **of** before a pronoun or a determiner:
There weren't enough of us to search the ship.
They can't start the scheme if enough of you object.
You're not getting enough of the right kind of food.

3 The form **enough of** can be used, often without a determiner, where the meaning is 'as much as can be tolerated':
We had had enough of his boring jokes.
I've had enough of being nice for one day.

AS AN ADVERB

Enough comes *after* both attributive and predicative adjectives:
There isn't a large enough supply to satisfy the present demand.
The program is simple enough for children to use.
At 27, he's still young enough to start a new career.
The product, though cheap enough [= quite cheap], *is difficult to find.*

WITH ADVERBS

1 **Enough** follows the adverb:
I'll take part next year, if I'm still playing well enough.
I didn't plan my answers carefully enough and then I ran out of time.
You will see us in London soon enough [= quite soon].

2 **Enough** is used to add weight to certain sentence adverbs:
Naturally enough, prisoners expect their families to visit them.
We met him on holiday, but funnily enough, he lives in the next street.

•••• especially, specially; especial, special ••••

ESPECIALLY OR SPECIALLY?

Both **especially** and **specially** mean 'in particular' or 'particularly'. In some cases, both **especially** and **specially** can be used. In other cases you must use either one or the other.

1 Before an adjective, you can use both **especially** and **specially**, without changing

the meaning:

She was not especially (or *specially*) *beautiful, but she had lovely eyes.*
She is especially (or *specially*) *sensitive to the effects of her comments.*
'That's true of many people,' I said. 'Yes, but especially (or *specially*) *true of you.'*

2 When **especially** has the meaning 'above all', it cannot be replaced by **specially**:

A lot of people, especially the unemployed, would appreciate this money.
This leaflet may be helpful, especially if you are setting up in business.
Life there was hard, especially in winter.

3 When **especially** refers to the subject of a sentence, it always comes after it:

Scots, especially, disliked the decision.
My mother, especially, is beginning to feel the stress of the situation.

4 You use **specially** when you want to say that something is done or prepared for a specific purpose:

Specially designed for women, the range comes in a choice of colours.
a specially modified bungalow for disabled holidaymakers
They are specially trained in these techniques.
He'd flown in with his daughter specially for the concert.

ESPECIAL OR SPECIAL?

1 The adjective **especial** is not used very commonly, but where it is used, it has the meaning of 'greater than usual', and is most commonly found before nouns such as **interest**, **significance** and **reference**. **Special** can also be used in this way:

Of especial (or *special*) *interest is the work on the north-facing façade.*
She described her trip with especial (or *special*) *reference to the people she had met and the important positions they occupied.*
The work of these two men was of especial (or *special*) *significance.*

2 **Special** describes a person or thing that is different from, better than, or more important than, others of the same class:

Mum said that as a special treat, my sisters and I could come too.
See page 112 for details of a special offer.
'Surely a man like you has someone special in his life.' 'Girlfriends, yes. But no one special.'

3 **Special** also means 'definite' or 'specific', particularly when it follows **no**, **nothing**, or **anything**:

'What are you doing here?' 'Nothing special.'
Is there anything special you'd like me to order for you?

4 Someone or something that is appointed, designed, intended or required for a specific purpose is described as a **special** person or thing:

A special school opened for pupils with problems in addition to blindness.
The high ceilings are necessary to house special machinery.

5 **Special** can also mean 'exceptional' or 'unusual':

... better education facilities for children with special needs
Only candidates with special permission may bring written material to their examination places.

6 **Special** is used to mean 'greater than usual':

Special care should be taken to follow manufacturers' instructions.
I want you all to make a special effort to be on time tomorrow.

7 People's own **special** things are the things which belong to, and are particular to, them:
The directors have their own special area for relaxing and meeting.
All this equipment should be stored in its own special packaging.
They are interested, but in their own special way.

•••• even ••••

POSITION

1 **Even** usually goes in mid position, that is, before the verb, after an auxiliary or modal verb, and after the verb **be**:
I had a fear of water, but I learnt to live with it, and even became a good swimmer.
I needed a fresh-air life; I even tried window-cleaning.
Look, you can even see the airport down there.

2 **Even** can also come immediately before the word or phrase it focuses on:
Every possible subject came into the curriculum, even gardening.
Even the most experienced managers cannot explain why it happens.
Even as a child he had not had many friends.

3 Occasionally you find **even** placed *after* the word or phrase it focuses on:
Mr Skinner was strange, dangerous, even, but he was fair.

MEANING

Even is one of the 'focusing' adverbs (see **adverbs**). You use it to 'focus' on some extreme or surprising aspect of what you are saying.

> ⓘ Distinguish between **even** and **also**: you use **also** merely to add something, not to introduce surprising or extreme facts:
> *Even* (not *Also*) *in old age she was beautiful.*

1 **Not even** focuses on the surprising non-happening of something you would expect to happen:
He ran off through the back yard, not even stopping to shut the door.
They didn't even share the same hobbies.

2 You can put **even** before a *comparative* to emphasize its striking aspect:
When children arrived, life became even more complicated.
The design is even better in the new models.
All this makes the evidence we already have even more important.
There will be even less money available for education after September.

3 You use **even if** and **even though** to introduce a clause that does not change the truth of what you say in the main clause:
Even if they haven't much money, students must buy these books.
Even though he is 24, he is still like a little child.

> ⓘ You can use **if** in a limited range of phrases to mean **even if**:
> *I'm going to track him down if it's the last thing I do.*

4 **Even so** introduces a statement that might seem surprising after what has just been said:

I suppose it was to be expected, but even so it came as a shock.

•••• evening ••••

The **evening** is the part of the day between the end of the afternoon, and the time when you go to bed.

➤ For information about how **evening** is used see **morning**.

•••• eventually, eventual ••••

1 **Eventually** means 'finally' or 'at last', or 'after all that', and is used when you are saying that something happened after a long wait:

Eventually this plan was abandoned in favour of a completely new one.
She eventually decided she didn't want the job anyway.

> ⓘ **Eventually** is not used as an exclamation; instead, use **finally** or **at last**:
> *At last* (not *eventually*) *you're here!*

> ⓘ **Eventually** is not used when giving news:
> *They've finally* (not *eventually*) *done it!*

2 **Eventual** means 'final':

The eventual winners were 4 boys from St Patrick's School.
This has resulted in the eventual closure of the establishment.

> ⓘ Note that some European languages have words that resemble **eventually** and **eventual**. These are 'false friends'.
> **Eventually** does not mean 'possibly' or 'if it comes to it', and **eventual** does not mean 'possible':
> *If it comes to it* (not *eventually*), *we could drive to the garage and see if they've got any milk.*
> *There's always someone to help you with any problems you might have* (not *with eventual problems*)

•••• ever ••••

The meaning of **ever** is 'at any time'. **Ever** is used in non-assertive contexts, especially in questions, after **if** and after words like **hardly** and **scarcely**. It is not so often used after **not**, because **never** is more natural than **not ever**. The role of **ever** is often to reinforce a sense rather than add anything to it, as in '*What have I ever done to deserve this?*', where **ever** could be omitted without changing the meaning very much.

IN QUESTIONS

1 The following examples show **ever** being used in questions relating to the present, past and future:

Have I ever broken a promise to you?
Had you ever met him before last weekend?
When will they ever learn?
Will he ever forgive me?
Does she ever talk about coming home?

2 Notice that **have** + **ever** refers to the time up to the present, and **had** + **ever** to the time up to a point in the past that has been mentioned or is understood:

When have nurses ever been given a reasonable pay deal?
Did you enjoy his lecture? Had you ever heard him speak before?

3 You can emphasize question words such as **who**, **what**, **why**, and **how** with **ever**:

Who ever told you that?
How ever did you work that out?
Why ever should you think that?

> ⓘ The use of **ever** here is parallel to less formal expressions like **on earth** and **the hell**, as in **why on earth... ?** and **what the hell... ?** To distinguish between this use of **ever** after a **wh**-word, and the indefinite words **whatever**, **however**, **whoever** and so on, it is a good idea to write **ever** as a separate word:
> *We'll help in whatever way we can.*
> But:
> *What ever do you think you're doing?*

OTHER NON-ASSERTIVE CONTEXTS

The following examples demonstrate the use of **ever** in non-assertive contexts other than questions:

At no point in the book does he ever mention the subject.
No-one ever calls me 'Mr'.
He scarcely ever turned up to practices.
He hardly ever spoke about his mother again.
I don't think we ever had a key to the front door.

IN COMPARISIONS

1 **Ever** is useful in making comparisons, whether they are expressed through comparatives, superlatives, words such as **first** and **only** that imply uniqueness, or through a construction with **as ... as**:

We could talk together; we were closer than we had ever been.
Jeff is one of the nicest people I have ever met.
He says Dickens is the greatest novelist ever to have written in the English language.
This is the first time I've ever flown.
I've only ever seen him in a suit.
That was as close as I've ever come to death.

2 Notice that **ever** can stand by itself after **than, as** and **if** to represent a whole clause:

The locked door made him less hopeful than ever [= than he had ever been before].
In such dances, physical contact between lovers rarely, if ever, [= if it ever does, perhaps never] *takes place.*
The island was looking as lovely as ever.

3 **Ever** can also stand by itself after superlatives, and form compound adjectives with them:
It was her best performance ever.
This is my first-ever flight.

EVER AND BEFORE

1 You use both **ever** and **before** to mean 'at any time in the past', but the difference between them is that when you use **before** you are referring to something that is happening in the present, and the question is whether the same thing has happened in the past. When you use **ever**, you are not referring to a present happening:
Haven't we met before? [we're meeting now]
My daughter's in dentistry too; have you ever met her? [the hearer is not meeting her now]

2 You can reinforce **before** with **ever** when referring to a present happening, or, when talking in a past context, to something happening at the time concerned:
I don't think we've ever met before, have we? [we're meeting now]
They need help now more than ever before.
That week we worked harder than we'd ever worked before.

FURTHER USES

1 In the fixed uses **for ever** (or **forever**), and **ever after**, **ever** means 'always':
I think her name will live for ever (or *forever*).
He took the gold ring from her finger and wore it ever after.

The combination **for ever** or **forever** can also mean 'always' or 'constantly':
My dog is forever chasing rabbits.

2 The following examples demonstrate further fixed or common uses of **ever**; explanations are given in brackets where necessary:
I've driven a Porsche ever since [giving emphasis to *since*] *I could afford one.*
The nightmares began then and I've had them ever since.
She's never ever [*ever* reinforcing *never*] *thanked me for all that extra work I did.*
It's ever so [*ever* informally emphasizing *so*] *kind of you to drop in.*
I had ever such [*ever* informally emphasizing *such*] *a long way to walk home.*
As ever [= as always], *the women were expected to do the cooking.*

•••• every ••••

EVERY, ALL, EACH

1 Grammatically, the main difference between the determiners **every**, **all** and **each** is that **all** is used with plural nouns, and **every** and **each** with singular ones:
All police officers are trained in the use of firearms.
Every candidate has the right to appeal against the examiners' decision.

Each copy has been signed by the author.

2 Another grammatical difference is that **all** and **each** share an ability to act as pronouns, whereas **every** can only be a determiner:

This applies to all of us.
There are two bedrooms on each of the (but not *every of the*) *upper floors.*

3 As far as *use* and *meaning* go, the three determiners tend to have slightly different focuses.

- **All** includes the whole group or class:

  All students have an examination in their first year.

- **Every** focuses on what is *common* to the *members* of a group or class:

  Every student knows the anxiety of waiting for exam results.

- **Each** focuses on the member as an individual:

  Each student is tested in fluency and comprehension.

4 Another point to notice is that **all** and **every** have the sense 'any, you name it', which is not shared by **each**:

Our attractive circular table suits every household (or *all households, but not each household*).

5 **Every** and **all** can be modified by **almost**, **nearly**, **practically** and **virtually**, but **each** cannot.

EVERY

1 The following examples demonstrate the use of **every** as a singular determiner qualifying a singular countable noun (and taking a singular verb when the noun is its subject):

The British Museum keeps one copy of every newspaper published.
Things are the same in this house as in every other house in the country.
Every time I go there I come back depressed.
Not every marriage is as successful as yours.
Every town in Iceland has its own swimming pool, usually geothermically heated.

> ⓘ Notice the use of **not every**. You say, for instance, *Not every bomb has reached its target* (rather than *Every bomb hasn't reached its target*), to mean 'Some bombs haven't reached their target'. Notice the difference between this and *Not one* (or *none*) *of the bombs has reached its target.*

2 **Every** can be emphasized by inserting **single** between it and its noun:

They can hardly understand what we're saying; we have to explain every single thing.

3 The last example in section **1**, *Every town in Iceland has its own swimming pool,* shows the possessive **its** referring back to an impersonal noun, **town**, qualified by **every**. When you have a *personal* noun qualified by **every**, you have to decide whether to use the more natural-sounding – but to some people unacceptable – plurals **they** and **their** to refer back to the singular noun group, or to go for the formal-sounding **he or she** and **his or her**, since many people find the use of **he** and **his** to cover both sexes unacceptable. *Every man took his turn at commanding his section* of course works satisfactorily, but *Every patient is an expert on himself*; seems unfairly to exclude female patients. You have the choice of *Every patient is an expert on themselves*, or the formal *Every patient is an expert on himself or herself*, or you can get out of the difficulty by pluralizing, and try *Patients are all experts on themselves*.

Notice, however, that where the action includes, simultaneously, the whole group referred to by **every**, you refer back with a plural:

The checkers double-check every piece of baggage and then collect them together for loading.

4 **Every** cannot stand on its own as a pronoun, but you can convert it into a pronoun by using the combination **every one**. You use **every one** + **of** before a pronoun or a determiner:

He made her lots of promises, and broke every one.
God bless us, every one.
Every one of us felt sad at having to part with our (or, very formally, *his or her*) *possessions.*
I've read every one of his books.

5 Notice the difference between **all** and **every** when applied to a period of time:

They had been out picking berries all day [= for the whole of the day].
Follow these exercises every day [= regularly, day after day, or 'daily'].
He decided to stay awake all night.
They would eat together every night at 7 o'clock.

> ⓘ Distinguish between **every day** and **everyday**. **Everyday** is an adjective meaning 'routine', 'regular', 'ordinary' or 'usual':
> *He opened the office every day at 7.45 am.*
> *Arguments between her parents were an everyday occurrence.*

6 **Every** has an important use in expressing the concept of regular intervals in time or in space. If you say, for instance, that something happens *eg* **every two days** or **every second day** you mean that it if it happens today, it doesn't happen tomorrow, but it does happen the day after tomorrow. **Every other day** means the same as **every two days**. You can use **every now and then** and **every so often** to mean 'from time to time' or 'occasionally':

Forty thousand children are dying daily; nearly one every two seconds.
Most animals are tested every three years.
Every now and then we slowed down as we touched a sandbank.
Every few yards there were holes in the road.
I wash my hair every other day.
After every third chapter there is a section of short tests.

7 In a use similar to that demonstrated in section **6**, you can use **every** to express ratio or proportion:

In 1981, only eleven individuals in every thousand were aged 85 or over.
For every one person who succeeds, there are likely to be dozens who fail.

8 Notice also this rather literary use of *possessive* + **every** + noun:

It felt as though someone was out there, watching our every move [= every move we made].

•••• everybody, everyone ••••

1 There is no difference in meaning between the two pronouns **everybody** and **everyone**. They both refer to all the people in a class or group, and they can both, more loosely, mean 'most people' or 'people in general'. Notice that they are *singular* pronouns:

Mairi sang the verses, and everybody else joined in the chorus.
I had a get-well card from the office, with everyone's signature on it.
Tennyson isn't everybody's favourite poet.
Doesn't everyone read a newspaper these days?
Everyone knows that.

2 Notice that although **everybody** and **everyone** are singular, they are both usually followed by the pronoun **they**, which takes a plural verb:

Everybody's invited this time, aren't they?
Everyone has a right to their own (or, very formally, *his or her) own opinion.*

3 Distinguish between **everyone** and **every one**. The pronoun **everyone** can refer only to people, and means 'every person'. **Every one** can refer to people or things, and means all the people or things just mentioned:

Will everyone please come to the hall for a meeting at four o'clock?
I interviewed about eighty passers-by, and every one was in favour of the Euro.
We viewed dozens of houses, but every one of them had some major disadvantage.

4 Notice how **not everybody** (or **not everyone**) is used. You say, for instance, *Not everybody was pleased* (rather than *Everybody was not pleased*) to mean some people were not pleased. Notice the difference between this and *Nobody was pleased.*

•••• everything ••••

1 Like **everybody** and **everyone**, **everything** is a singular pronoun. It can refer to all the things concerned in a particular situation, or, like **things**, to life in general. And something that **is everything** or **means everything**, is something that is considered very important:

Here are some scissors. Have you got everything else you need?
She kept everything valuable under the bed.
Are you sure you've told me everything?
They lost everything in the war.
I just wish everything was as simple as that.
Is everything OK?
Everything continued as if nothing had happened.
Money's not everything.

2 Notice the way **not everything** is used. You say, for instance, *Not everything is* (rather than *Everything isn't*) *predictable* to mean 'some things are not predictable'. Notice the difference between this and *Nothing is predictable.*

• • • everywhere • • •

1 **Everywhere** is an adverb, meaning in, or to, all places:

These gangs are operating everywhere in the world.
Environmentalists everywhere are deeply concerned.
It isn't everywhere you [= hardly anywhere do you] *find such kindness.*
I walk everywhere locally and take the bus for longer journeys.

2 As shown in the examples in section **1**, you use **everywhere** without the prepositions **in** or **to**. But you can use **from** with **everywhere**:

Visitors were arriving from everywhere.

3 The following examples show **everywhere** being used rather like a noun:

Everywhere was covered in snow.
I usually work in the kitchen. Everywhere else in the house is too cold.

• • • • except • • • •

Except is used in a variety of ways to introduce the only person or thing that a statement does not apply to. In certain cases it must be followed by **for**.

1 **Except** is typically used as a preposition before a noun or noun phrase, after a statement that includes a term such as **everyone**, **all**, **nothing**, or **any**:

The competition is open to all readers in the UK except employees of this company.
Everyone saw what was coming except perhaps the President himself.
The mill is open to visitors every day except Tuesday.
He said he didn't know anyone in the music business except me.

> ⓘ Notice that you use the object form of the personal pronouns after **except**:
> *No-one would understand them except Anne and me.*
> *Apparently everyone had been drowned except us.*
> *He has no thought for anyone except himself.*

2 **Except** is frequently followed by an adverbial phrase introduced by a preposition:

I don't usually have breakfast except at weekends.
You can buy this everywhere except in very small villages.
The public didn't visit much except over Christmas and New Year.

3 **That** is often used after **except** to introduce a circumstance that prevents the statement in the main clause from being completely true, or makes it less valid in some way. Notice that the introductory **that** is sometimes omitted:

The grass is great to walk on, except (that) you have to look out for rabbit holes.

4 **Except** can also be followed by a conjunction such as **when** or **where** introducing an adverbial clause, or the pronoun **what** introducing a relative clause:

He was friendly – except when he was in the boxing ring, or after a few whiskies.
I haven't got any clothes at all except what I've got on.

5 Where a verb is wanted after **except**, the form most often required is the infinitive, usually without **to**:

He did almost nothing, except raise the tax on petrol by ten per cent.
I'd done everything except back up the file on to the network.

6 A verbal noun in **-ing**, or the infinitive with **to**, sometimes fit more appropriately into the syntax:

They have no interest in anything except getting through the exam.
We don't need to discuss the results, except to note the following points.

EXCEPT FOR

Except for is used like a preposition before nouns and noun phrases, and has two uses:

1 You can use **except for** as an alternative to **except** in cases like those shown in section **1** above:

None of the Arab countries except for (or *except*) *Egypt is prepared to take its citizens back.*

2 Notice that you must use the form **except for** rather than **except** if the **except** phrase is placed at the beginning of the sentence:

Except for (not *except*) *my mother, no-one had ever laid their hands upon my head.*

3 You use **except for** to introduce something that prevents a statement from being absolutely true. Such statements do not usually include any of the 'generalizing' words such as **any**, **every** or **all**:

She was good-looking, except for the hard lines round her mouth.
He realized he was completely alone except for the dog.
Except for a sports day once a year, parents were not invited to visit.
Here you get a good view of the stage, except for one corner.

ⓘ Distinguish between **but for**, **without** and **except for**. When some event, especially an unpleasant one, is prevented, you say that it might have happened **without** or **but for** (rather than **except for**) a certain factor:
But for (not *except for*) *you, we might have been in a lot of trouble.*
Without (not *except for*) *you we could not have succeeded.*
As well as **but for**, you can say **if it had not been for**:
We would have failed if it had not been for you.

➤ See also the entry for **but**.

exclamation mark

➤ See **punctuation**.

exclamations

➤ See pages 208 and 209.

EXCLAMATIONS

An **exclamation** is a word or expression spoken suddenly and loudly. People use exclamations to express approval, disapproval, embarrassment or annoyance at something. Sometimes an exclamation consists of one word, such as **No!**, and sometimes it is expressed in a sentence. An exclamation in a sentence might be formed in one of four possible ways:

1 One of the most common ways of forming an exclamation is by turning a statement about someone or something into a negative question form:

Doesn't she work hard!
Wasn't it fun!
Haven't I been stupid!
Didn't we have a laugh!

Note that this sort of exclamation usually expects some kind of reply from the person being addressed:

'Isn't he cute!' 'Yeah, a real darling.'
'Haven't I been stupid!' 'No, of course not.'

Speakers of AmE and some speakers of BrE use ordinary question forms, rather than negative question forms:

Boy, was I tired!
Wow, was that good!
Man, have I got news for you!

2 In exclamations, **what** is always followed by a noun phrase:

- When the noun following **what** is a singular countable noun, it must always be preceded by **a** or **an**. The noun may or may not be preceded by an adjective:

  What a fool!
  What a joke!
  What a surprise!
  What an awful shock!
  What a gorgeous day!

- When the noun following **what** is an uncountable or plural noun, no article is necessary. The noun may or may not be preceded by an adjective:

  What awful wine!
  What luck!
  What idiots!
  What beautiful flowers!

- **What** can be followed by an object or complement + subject + verb construction:

  What a fool I've been!
  What interesting tastes you have!
  What ridiculous things he says!
  What a stupid idiot I am!

3 There are three types of exclamation that can be formed with **how**:

- **how** + adjective

  This form of exclamation can sound a little formal or old-fashioned, although the form **How lovely!** is common and fairly neutral:

  Oh daffodils. How lovely, they're my favourite flowers.
  Lulu, how lovely to see you!
  How nice to see a friendly face.
  'How nice he is,' thought Melanie.

- **how** + subject + verb

  This form is rather old-fashioned or formal, and is common only in the following idiomatic phrase:

  'He'll be two in August.' 'Really? How time flies!' [= time passes very fast]

- **how** + adverb + subject + verb:

This form rather literary and not very commonly used:

How beautifully that couple are dancing!

4 You can also form an exclamation by making a statement and adding **so** or **such a/an** for emphasis:

- You use **so** before an adjective or adverb on its own:

  He's so good to me!
  They're so happy together!
  That's so funny!
  They walk so slowly!

➤ See also entry for **so**.

- You use **such** and **such a** before nouns, adjectives that qualify nouns, or adverbs that modify these adjectives. **Such** is used with plural and uncountable nouns, and **such a/an** is used before singular uncountable nouns:

  She's such a good tennis player!
  They're such lovely flowers!
  We had such amazingly good weather.
  They're such good children.
  She's such a hypocrite!
  They're such fools!
  It's such nonsense!

➤ See also entry for **such**.

ⓘ Remember: **so** + adjective or adverb
such a/an (+ *adjective*) + *singular countable noun*
such (+ *adjective*)+ *plural* or *uncountable noun*

•••• experience ••••

AS A NOUN

When used as a noun, **experience** can be either countable or uncountable, depending on its meaning.

1 As an uncountable noun, **experience** is knowledge or skill gained through practice, or through having seen or done something before:

She has a lot of experience in this field.
I have no experience of this kind of behaviour.
This will be a chance to gain some valuable experience.

ⓘ Schoolchildren or school-leavers often do **work experience**, spending several weeks in the workplace, as a way of seeing what sort of work interests them.

2 As a countable noun, an **experience** is an event that affects or involves you:

Speaking in front of an audience can be a frightening experience.
Flying a small plane was a fantastic experience.

AS A VERB

You **experience** something when it happens to you, or when you feel it or are affected by it:

She had never before experienced war.
We've been experiencing a lot of difficulties with this project.

•••• explain ••••

1 **explain something**

You **explain** something when you supply information or details that make it clear or easy to understand:

She couldn't understand because he never explained anything.
We're asking parents to explain the facts clearly and simply.
She had not tried to contact him to explain the situation.

2 **explain something to someone**

If you want to specify a person as an indirect object to the verb **explain**, you say that you explain that thing **to** them:

He was trying to explain to us exactly how he felt.
She couldn't find the words to explain to him what she meant.
I tried to explain the new voting system to them.

ⓘ Notice that you never say *I'll explain you the problem.* The more common way of saying this would be: *I'll explain.*

3 explain that

You can use **explain** with a **that**-clause to give the reason for something:

I explained that he'd come to take a few photographs.
The minister has explained that the committee cannot agree about the report.
John explained that he had taken a wrong turning.
Suzy explained that the scheme was designed to help young people.

Ff

•••• fairly ••••

➤ See **quite**.

•••• far, a long way ••••

Far is an adverb and expresses physical distance, length of time, progress and extent. It can also act as an intensifying adverb. **Far** is also an adjective.

> ⓘ Notice that **far** is mainly used with negatives, in questions (especially with **how**) and in combination with words such as **so**, **as**, **too** and **enough**. In affirmative sentences, **a long way** usually sounds more natural than **far**.

IN EXPRESSIONS OF DISTANCE

1 far or far away?

You use **far** by itself mainly when thinking of a distance from the point of view of the journey. When you are thinking about a place and its distance from a point, you generally use **far away**. In an affirmative, or positive, context, you use **a long way** and **a long way away** with just the same distinction:

How far is Denver from here?
How far away is Mars?
There's a flower shop not far from the house.
The children will get tired; it's a long way.
The hospital is a long way away.

> ⓘ When stating a *specific* distance you do not use **far**. You have to say that a place is a certain distance **away**, or a certain distance **from** or **away from** somewhere:
> *He was standing only a few feet away.*
> *New York is 400 miles from Montreal.*

2 too far

Too, **so**, **as** and **enough** can be used with **far** in a positive context:

She was too far away to see his face clearly.
They are so far away from their families.
Kasmin wanted to get as far away from home as possible.
In two days they would be far enough south for the nights to be warm.

ⓘ You will sometimes find **far** used in positive contexts, especially with **very** or a moderator such as **quite**:
Inverness is actually quite far away.
The noises of the evening streets seemed very far away.

IN EXPRESSIONS OF TIME

You can use **far** and **a long way** in expressing length of time from the present to some time in the past or future:

The exams are not far off.
The boom years of the 1980s now look a long way away.

IN EXPRESSIONS OF EXTENT OR DEGREE

1 You can use **far** and **a long way** to express extent, degree, and state of progress:

He wondered how far he could trust Barnes.
Ten dollars would not get her very far.
He has made good progress, but still feels he has a long way to go.

2 **Far** is used like **much** as an intensifier with comparatives and superlatives. With superlatives, the intensifying expression can also be **by far**:

It would be far better to concentrate on the home market.
I have a far greater affection for them than for my own family.
The first step is considered by far the most important.

3 You can also use **far**, like **much**, to intensify **too**:

The slopes are far too steep for climbing without a rope.
To be in fashion this year, just put on a jacket that is far too big for you.

AS AN ADJECTIVE

1 Used before the noun, **far** often sounds rather too literary. You use adjectives like **faraway**, **far-off** and **distant** instead:

He was sent off to distant Siberia.
She looked out of the window at the faraway hills on the horizon.
He had changed since those far-off days of our youth.

2 As an adjective, **far** is much more frequently used to refer to the more distant of the two sides or ends of something:

He had to swim to the far bank of the river.
The car swerved towards the far side of the road.

USEFUL IDIOMS

As far as *I'm concerned* [= if you want my opinion or permission] *you can move into the flat tomorrow.*
Don't think I disapprove; ***far from it***. [= I approve]
Their flat is ***far from*** tidy. [= not at all tidy]
She went ***so far as to*** *call me* [= she took the extreme step of calling me] *a liar.*
I've only read the introduction ***so far***.

•••• farther, further, farthest, furthest ••••

The comparative forms **farther** and **further**, and their superlatives **farthest** and **furthest**, can all be used to talk about *distance*, but only **further** and **furthest** can be used in expressions of *degree* or *extent*. **Further** has a special determiner-like use of its own.

FARTHER AND FURTHER

1 in expressions of distance

Jupiter is farther (or *further*) *away from the sun than the earth is.*
They live further (or *farther*) *up the hill.*
We found a petrol station further (or *farther*) *on.*

2 in expressions of extent or degree

You can use **further**, but not **farther**, in expressions like the following:

She tried to break away from him but just got further involved.
We have progressed several stages further since you last visited us.
She opened her mouth to speak but got no further.

3 as adjectives

The **further** or **farther** side or end of something is the one that is more distant:

He was on the pavement on the farther (or *further*) *side of the street.*
I left him fishing on the farther (or *further*) *bank.*

4 as a determiner

Before a noun **further** can have the meaning 'more', 'additional' or 'extra', in which case it behaves like a determiner:

There was no further news that day.
We returned to the meeting room for further discussions.

FARTHEST AND FURTHEST

The two superlatives reflect the behaviour of the two comparative forms. Like the comparatives, they can act as adverbs or adjectives:

Fiona was the farthest (or *the furthest*) *ahead.*
Researchers at this university have progressed furthest in this field.
The furthest he would go was to admit that there had been some sort of mistake.

•••• feel ••••

The verb **feel** has four main divisions of meaning. It can express:

- personal sensations and opinions
- the qualities of things, as noticed by the speaker
- experience of things happening around the speaker
- deliberate touching, to assess qualities

Progressive forms are possible with some meanings and not with others.

PERSONAL SENSATION; PERSONAL OPINION

1 as a linking verb

■ **I feel awful**

You can describe your own physical or emotional state using **feel** as a linking verb. The complement can take the form of an adjective or a noun; progressive forms are possible here:

I suddenly don't feel very well.
I feel much better now.
I was feeling so helpless.
Does William know you feel this way?

> ⓘ Notice that you do not use a reflexive pronoun after **feel** in this sense:
> *I feel* (not *I feel myself*) *much better.*

■ **my legs feel heavy**

The subject of **feel** can be a part of your body, or something you are wearing:

Although his hand felt sore he could move his fingers.
These shoes feel too tight.

■ **feel like... , feel as if... , feel as though...**

The construction **feel like** is possible, and is used in several ways:

My knee feels like (or, more formally, *as if* or *as though*) [= is giving me the impression that] *it's been pulled out of joint.*
I didn't feel like talking [= I didn't want to talk].
Open a bottle of wine in case he feels like [= wants] *a glass.*

2 feel + object

You can **feel** an emotion or a sensation:

I felt an enormous sense of relief.
She felt a desire to run away.
He felt no pain.

3 feel + noun clause

Feel, with or without a following **that**, can be used for introducing an opinion. The progressive form is not used here:

We feel that our function is to convey accurate information.
I feel you need a complete rest before you return to normal life.
Why do you feel you've failed?

> ⓘ A passive construction is possible, with **it** as subject:
> *It was felt that they held racist attitudes.*

4 feel + about

The way you **feel** about something is your opinion or attitude to it. You don't use the progressive form here:

You know how I feel about killing animals.

THE QUALITIES OF THINGS, AS NOTICED BY THE SPEAKER

1 this surface feels sticky

You describe something you are touching or holding by saying it **feels** a certain way. The progressive form is not used:

Your head feels hot.
Our thermal fabric feels like a natural fibre.

2 it feels...

You use **it feels** to describe the weather, or the atmosphere, or to describe experiences. You don't use the progressive forms here:

It felt strange to be back in Dublin.
With the gas fire on, it was beginning to feel like home.
It feels as if (or *as though*, or, informally, *like*) *everything's falling apart.*

3 receiving sensations

■ **I felt something touch me**

You **feel** things that are touching you or happening to you. Notice that you very frequently use **can** or **could** with **feel**, where there is an idea of continuing sensation:

He could feel the warmth of the sun on his face.
She felt the baby move inside her.
She felt her face turn red with embarrassment.

> ⓘ Notice that reflexives are possible here:
> *She could feel herself shaking.*
> *He could feel himself getting flustered.*

■ **feeling the cold**

You **feel** things when they have an effect on you; you can use progressive forms in this sense:

Old people feel the cold more than the young.
After a week on the diet you should be feeling the benefits.

4 deliberate touching

■ **feel + object**

You **feel** something when you touch it deliberately to judge its qualities. Progressive forms are possible here:

She felt his forehead.
I was just feeling the bathwater to make sure the temperature was OK.

■ **used intransitively**

You **feel** for something somewhere when you search for it with your fingers:

I felt around for the switch.
'Have you got the note?' Jack felt in his pocket. 'Yes, it's safe.'

•••• fetch ••••

➤ See **bring**.

•••• few ••••

➤ See **little, few**.

•••• fewer ••••

➤ See **less, fewer**.

•••• finally, at last, in the end, at the end ••••

WHEN ONLY 'FINALLY' IS POSSIBLE

Finally is used to introduce the last element in a series:

Finally, if I can just have your attention for a moment.
Finally, try to avoid coffee at the end of the meal.

FINALLY AND AT LAST

You can use both **finally** and **at last** to suggest that you have been waiting a long time for something. **At last** is stronger than finally:

Finally a goal came.
The meeting finally finished at nine o'clock.
'The rain's stopped at last,' Maggie stated.
I feel that at last justice has returned to the area.

> ⓘ Notice that **at last** comes either before the subject or at the end of a sentence, but **finally** can take either of these positions as well as coming before the verb.

IN THE END

You use **in the end** to give the idea of something happening after a lot of difficulties and uncertainty:

In the end I had to admit he was right.
In the end the government was forced to make a minor concession.

AT THE END

At the end refers to the point when something stops, or a period near this point. There is no suggestion of difficulties or uncertainty:

It was hard work but we all felt rewarded at the end of the day.
At the end of the class, we always discuss the plan for the following session.

•••• fine, finely ••••

The adjective **fine** has four main different meanings. The adverb **finely** shares only two of these.

FINE

1 excellent

You describe something as **fine** if you think it is splendid or excellent:

You get a fine view of the hills from here.
There's a fine show of flowers in the garden this year.

2 satisfactory

You say that something is **fine** if it is OK, satisfactory or acceptable:

If your husband would like to come too, that's fine.
'Are you cold?' 'No, I'm fine thanks.'

3 small or thin

- **Fine** particles are very small:

  Porcelain is produced from very fine clay.
  The blanket was covered in fine grains of sand.

- **Fine** threads are thin or narrow:

  They work with fine threads of silk.
  Her hair was blond and very fine.

4 precise, exact

Fine also means 'very precise, exact or subtle':

Such examples of fine workmanship are rare these days.

FINELY

The adverb **finely** corresponds to meanings **3** and **4** of **fine**:

Add some finely chopped pieces of apple.
Most of us could not afford the finely-crafted Chinese bowls.

.... first name ....

➤ See **names and titles**.

.... be finished, have finished ....

Finished is the regular past particple of the verb **finish**, which can be used intransitively. More informally, you can also use **finished** as an adjective after **be**; so the following constructions are possible:

I'm sorry, I haven't (or *I'm not*) *finished yet.*
I started writing my essay at 9 o'clock and by midnight I'd (or *I was*) *nearly finished.*
Could you wait? I'll have (or *I'll be*) *finished in five minutes.*

.... fit, suit ....

FIT

A piece of clothing **fits** you if it is the right size for you:

These shoes don't fit me properly; they really hurt.
Does the skirt fit properly over the hips?

SUIT

A piece of clothing or a colour **suits** you if it makes you look attractive:

That hat really suits you!
Green doesn't suit me at all.

•••• flammable, inflammable, non-flammable ••••

FLAMMABLE OR INFLAMMABLE?

The words **flammable** and **inflammable** are commonly confused in English. In fact, they both refer to something that catches fire easily. **Flammable** is more common than **inflammable**:

Someone had poured flammable (or *inflammable*) *liquid through his letter box.*
Don't store old newspapers or other inflammable (or *flammable*) *materials under the stairs.*

NON-FLAMMABLE, FIRE-RESISTANT

Something that does not catch fire easily is **non-flammable** or **fire-resistant**. **Fire-resistant** is more commonly used to describe materials, rather than gases or chemicals:

This glue is non-flammable when dry.
Fire-resistant paints may be clear like a varnish, or coloured like ordinary paint.
The mattress should carry a fire-resistant label. [= a label indicating that the mattress is fire-resistant].

•••• floor, ground, earth ••••

FLOOR

The **floor** is a surface indoors that you stand on and walk on:

A pile of papers fell off his desk on to the floor.

GROUND

The **ground** is the outdoor surface that you stand on and walk on:

The house was built on stony ground.
The ladder broke and she fell to the ground.

EARTH

Earth is soil, the brown substance that lies on the surface of land:

We brought big buckets full of earth to fill up the hole.

➤ See also entry at **ground floor**.

•••• following ••••

Following is used as a preposition to show that one thing happens after another, and sometimes as a result of it.

MEANING 'AFTER'

Following is sometimes used in formal contexts with the same meaning as **after**. When used like this, there is not necessarily any suggestion that one event is caused by the other:

Following the miners' strike in 1984, industrial action lessened again.
Following the introductory chapter, the fundamentals of the law are discussed.

IN PAST AND FUTURE CONTEXTS

1 the past

- When you are talking in the past about something which happened on the day or morning after the events you have been describing, you can use **the next...** or **the following...** :

  The following (or *next*) *day her father suffered a second heart attack, and died.*
  The following (or *next*) *morning she caught the first flight out of Lisbon.*

- Before **afternoon**, **evening**, or the name of a day, **following** is preferable to **next**:

  The following (not *next*) *afternoon the sale was announced.*
  He made his speech on the following (not *next*) *evening.*
  On the following (not *next*) *Tuesday he had tickets for a play.*

2 the future

When you are referring to a day, week, month or year which will come after the events you have been describing, you use **the following day**, **week**, **month** or **year**:

I don't think Paul will be present at the meeting. We'll have to make our suggestions to him the following day.

•••• fond ••••

➤ See **like** (**verb**).

•••• foot ••••

PART OF THE BODY

Your **foot** is the part of your body at the end of your leg, on which you stand and walk; the plural of **foot** is **feet**:

Pushing her foot down on the accelerator, Alice thrust the car forward.
He looked at her feet. In those shoes they looked enormous.

ON FOOT

You go somewhere **on foot** when you walk there rather than using any kind of transport:

I decided to finish the journey on foot.
The car thieves jumped out of the car and escaped on foot.

ⓘ **On foot** is a rather formal expression. In informal contexts people usually talk about **walking somewhere**:
I decided to walk home (or more formally *go home on foot*) *rather than take the bus, since it was such a lovely evening.*

MEASUREMENTS

A **foot** is a measurement of length equal to twelve inches or 30.48 centimetres. The plural is **feet**:

It consisted of a metal table that was about one foot by two feet.
There he was. A man standing about forty feet away.

1 twenty foot long

Before **long**, **high** or **tall**, you can use **foot**, even in the plural:

We're supposed to clean all these ovens and they're seven foot high!
It's twenty-eight foot long and twelve foot wide.

2 a twenty-foot drop

Before a noun, the plural is always **foot**:

They were living on a fifty-eight-foot boat with twelve people aboard.
Lewis had ignored warning signs and climbed a 10-foot fence into the building.

3 I'm five foot two

When you are saying how tall someone is, the plural is usually **foot**:

I'm only very small and under five foot; and my husband is six foot two.
I'm five foot eight and take a size nine in shoes.

• • • • for • • • •

The uses of the preposition **for** can be listed under several broad headings. **For** can also be used as a conjunction.

AS A PREPOSITION

1 introducing the person or thing at the receiving end

- **this is for you**

  Has a parcel arrived for me?
  She writes books, mainly for children.

- **employment**

  He's working for British Telecom now.

- **representation**

  She's the MP for Keighley.

- **feeling and attitude**

  I'm so sorry for them.

- **how a situation affects you**

  The job's too difficult for him.
  It's normal for children to rebel at this age.

➤ For more information on constructions using **for** + **to**-infinitive see **infinitives**.

2 aims and purposes

- **destinations**

  Is this the train for Norwich?

- **goals and preparations**

  We must fight for freedom.
  She's training for a big race.

- **needs, searches, desires and requests**
  We'll have to queue for tickets.
  I was left with a desire for revenge.
  I'm going to apply for the job.
  He appealed to the audience for silence.

- **capacity**
  There's space for a few more.
  I haven't the patience for a job like that.

- **permission**
  You need a licence for exporting the goods.

- **function**
  It's a gadget for undoing staples.

- **proposals and designs**
  Plans for a settlement are being drafted.
  I discovered this pattern for a maternity dress.

- **future roles and fates**
  I'm afraid we've already selected someone for the job.
  I've chosen some curtains for the sitting room.

- **meals**
  What's for dinner?

3 support
the arguments for and against the proposal
I'm all for teaching children grammar.
Who are you going to vote for?

4 reasons and explanations
What are you doing that for?
He's gone to Oxford for a meeting.

5 transactions and exchanges

- **thanks and apologies**
  Thank you for your letter.
  I apologize for causing all this trouble.

- **payment and exchange**
  They sold the house for some vast sum.
  I got that painting for £65.
  I wrote them a cheque for £25.

- **proportion**
  They employ one woman for every five men.

- **scoring and marking**
  I actually got full marks for that essay.

- **mistakes**
  Never mistake lust for love.

- **vocabulary**
  What's the word for 'lazy' in German?

6 with regard to
You can't beat our furniture for quality.

7 duration

- **in time**
  We lived in Preston for six years.
  I haven't seen her for ages.

> ⓘ Notice that when you are using **for** to say how long something has been so, you use a perfect tense:
> *I've been waiting here for half an hour.*
> *I've worked for them for 25 years.*

- **in space**
  roadworks for the next six miles

8 appointments and schedules
I've made a dental appointment for 12.30 on Monday 8 May.

AS A CONJUNCTION

For can be used like **because**, as a conjunction of reason, but can sound rather old-fashioned and literary:

I sat there saying nothing, for there was nothing I could say.

•••• forename ••••

➤ See **names and titles**.

•••• forget ••••

You can use both **forget** and **leave** when you are talking about something that you have not brought with you, by mistake. But there is a difference in use. If you mention the *place*, you say that you **left** the thing there, not **forgot** it there.

I'm so sorry, I've forgotten (not *left*) *my purse.*
I left (not *forgot*) *it at home.*

—— formality and informality ——

Most words in English can neither be classified as particularly formal or informal. The language we use every day to talk to people we know or don't know is generally regarded as 'neutral'. However, there are specific words and phrases that are more frequently used between people who know each other very well, as well as words and expressions that are more frequently used between strangers or by those in business or official contexts.

Many other European languages have two forms of the pronoun 'you'. The two forms are used to distinguish between formal and informal relationships between people. In English, formality tends to be expressed more in the words and phrases people use when they speak to each other.

Any good dictionary will use the labels (*formal*) and (*informal*) to draw users' attention to these kinds of words and phrases. In this book, many of the entries refer to formal and informal situations, giving appropriate phrases to be used in each.

➤ For examples of formal and informal uses of English, see:

addressing people
giving advice
agreeing and disagreeing
apologizing
compliments
criticizing
exclamations
greetings and farewells
introductions
invitations
names and titles
offering
permission
requests, orders and instructions
suggestions
thanks
warnings

.... from ....

The preposition **from** is used with reference to place and time. Its various uses are listed below. Notice that **from** is often used with the preposition **to**. It is also used in combination with the prepositions **till** and **until**, and the adverbs **on** and **onwards** with reference to time. You use **away** before **from** to express the idea of separation or distance.

PLACE

1 indicating a starting point

■ **journeys**

She arrived from Paris last night.
He drove from Dundee to Inverness in two hours.

■ **continuous progress between one thing and the next**

We went from shop to shop in search of gluten-free bread.
His mind keeps jumping from one thing to the next.

■ **origin or source**

Blood was dripping from his arm.
Where's that letter from Sarah?

■ **distances and extents**

Our village is about seven miles from York.

■ **viewpoint or source of action**:

He rang me from his hotel room.
Try and see things from my point of view.

2 separation, removal or exclusion

She's away from home just now.
She took his favourite teddy away from him.
I omitted her from my list.

TIME

1 indicating a starting point

I'll be on holiday from 20 December onwards
The Museum is open from Monday to Friday (or, in AmE, *Monday through Friday*).
She lived in Malawi from 1957 to 1967.

> ⓘ Distinguish between **from** and **since**. You use **since** when giving the starting point of something that has continued *up to the present*. **From** is not linked to the present, and can be used with the simple tenses:
> *The shop is open from eight in the morning.*
> *The shop has been open since eight o'clock this morning.*

2 repeated or continuing occurrences

Our life changes very little from one day to the next.

3 the starting point in a range

The school takes children from the age of four upwards.

OTHER CONCEPTS

1 the raw materials used to make something

Paper is made from rags or wood.
He made a toy sword from two pieces of wood.

➤ See also **made**.

2 the processes of change, transformation or translation

She's changed a lot from the girl I knew at university.
Students really don't translate at all nowadays from English into Latin.

3 attachment

There was a mirror hanging from a nail on the wall.

4 a reason or cause; the basis for an opinion

You can get the disease from eating mouldy fruit.

5 protection, hiding, prevention, freeing, remaining

We looked for somewhere to shelter from the rain.
I couldn't hide the truth from her for long.
Can we prevent them from coming?
You must have a rest from work sometimes.
May I be excused from attending this class?

6 distinction and selection

Is bravery different from courage?
You can choose from a huge range of styles.

fronting

The normal structure of a sentence in English is 'subject, verb, object'.

However, in order to emphasize a particular point, or to make a particular part of the sentence into the topic, sometimes people use **fronting**.

Fronting means taking a part of the sentence, for example, the object, the verb or an adjective or adverb, and putting it at the front of the sentence in the position where the subject would normally be.

OBJECTS AND COMPLEMENTS

1 Especially in informal speech, you can emphasize the object or complement of a sentence by putting it at the front of the sentence:

__That attitude__ I hate.
__Funny__, that film.
__Nice try__ that was.

2 The object, but not the complement, may also be fronted in a more formal context:

__This question__ we shall now examine and answer.

3 In informal speech it is very common to put a question-word clause at the beginning of a sentence, especially when you want to say how difficult you find it to understand a situation:

__How they didn't see me__ I'll never know.

DETACHED SUBJECTS AND OBJECTS

In informal speech, people often detach the subject or the object, state it at the beginning of the sentence, then use a pronoun to repeat it:

__My friend__, __she__ told me that the school's going to be closed tomorrow.
__That house you wanted to buy__, I see they've sold it now.
__That song you said you like__, I heard it on the radio this morning.

ADVERBS, ADVERBIAL EXPRESSIONS AND ADVERBIAL PARTICLES

1 Adverbs and adverbial expressions are often fronted, especially when you are telling a story:

__Behind the house__ there was a…
__In his bag__ he was carrying a…
__Suddenly__, a mouse ran out from behind the sofa.

2 **Adverbial particles**, and the demonstrative adverbs **here** and **there**, are often fronted when used with intransitive verbs, especially in giving orders to children:

Charlotte, __up__ you get, please.
Oh no, Katie, you're too heavy. __Off__ you get.
That's it, __off__ you go then.

3 After some other fronted adverbial expressions, inversion is necessary (ie the subject follows the verb):

__Under no circumstances should you__ do this without advice from your doctor.
__From the road came the sounds__ of men shouting.

ADJECTIVES

Adjectives are less commonly fronted than adverbs. However, it is possible to front them in a structure with **as** or **though**:

> ***Flattered as I am*** *by your confidence, I'm afraid the situation is getting complicated.*

The same structure can be used with nouns and noun phrases:

> ***Nice man though he is,*** *I was getting bored with him.*
> *I was getting a bit bored with him,* ***nice man though he is****.*

ELLIPSIS

1 When you are speaking very informally, you can omit articles, pronouns and auxiliary verbs, bringing a more important word to the front of the clause:

> ***Fancy*** *a coffee?*
> ***Had*** *enough?*
> ***Any*** *news?*
> ***Doorbell*** *not working?*

2 Sometimes people make comments by moving the subject away from the beginning of a clause and putting it in a tag at the end. This is a very informal use:

> *Lovely weather,* ***isn't it****?*
> *Likes his whisky,* ***he does****.*

➤ See also **emphasis**.

•••• fruit ••••

➤ See **collective nouns**.

•••• full ••••

1 Something that is **full**, or **full up**, holds or contains as much as it can:

> *The bus was already full up when it came to our stop.*
> *The tank isn't quite full.*

2 Something that is **full of** things or people contains a lot of them:

> *The cupboards were full of her clothes.*
> *I was delighted to see a warm fire and a table full of food.*

ⓘ Notice that **of** is the only preposition you can use after **full**.

•••• fun, funny ••••

FUN

Fun is a noun and an adjective.

1 noun use

You have **fun** when you enjoy yourself:

> *We had a lot of fun deciding on the colour scheme.*
> *She doesn't get much fun in her life.*

2 adjective use

- A person who is **fun**, **good fun** or **great fun** is enjoyable to be with because they are cheerful and amusing:
  Why don't we invite Jane? She's great fun.

- An activity that is **fun** is enjoyable:
  'Did you enjoy it?' 'Yes, it was fun.

- In informal English you can talk about a **fun** person or a **fun** event:
  Why don't you come? It should be a fun event.
  I met him once; he's a really fun guy.

FUNNY

Funny is an adjective.

Something that is **funny** amuses you or makes you laugh:

I heard a funny story today.
Children say some funny things, don't they?

the future: ways of expressing it

In English there are several ways of talking about future happenings:

- the modal verbs **shall** and **will**
- the present progressive tense
- the present progressive form of **go** as an auxiliary verb
- the simple present tense

In addition, you can use various other structures, for instance:

- **be about to**:
  She's about to leave school.

- **be to**:
  She is to arrive in Argentina today.

- **be due to**:
  They're due to finish this section on 28 June.

- **be bound to**:
  She's bound to object.

- **be on the point of**:
  The judges are on the point of declaring the winner.

➢ For the structure **be about to** see **about**.

SHALL AND WILL

1 possible forms

I shall or *I will*
you will
he, she, or *it will*
we shall or *we will*
they will

contractions:

I'll, you'll, he'll, she'll, it'll, we'll, you'll, they'll, there'll, this'll, that'll

negative contractions:

I or *we won't* or *shan't* *you, he, she ,it,* or *they won't*

Shall and **will** are used with an infinitive without **to**. In AmE, **shall** is rare, and BrE speakers tend to use **I shall** and **I will**, and **we shall** and **we will**, without much distinction of meaning. However, both verbs do have their own distinctive range of uses. Shared uses and individual uses are shown below.

USES OF 'SHALL' AND 'WILL'

1 information

You use **will** and **shall** to give, and ask for, information about future events:

This will be your last chance.
They will remain there for up to ten weeks.
We'll be with you in a day or two.
She will hear evidence from the neighbours and local groups.
How soon will you know for certain?
Now we shall have to find another assistant.

2 predictions

You use **will** and **shall** to make predictions:

Do you really think they'll close down your old college?
It's the first time they've been here and it'll be the last.
You will probably be nervous at the audition.
She will be missed by us all.
They will not win the World Cup.
We'll always need teachers, that's for sure.
They won't be disappointed.
You won't believe this, but I really do understand.

3 conditional situations

You use **will** and **shall** to suggest the probable result, if a certain thing happens:

Act guiltily and they'll judge you guilty.
If you make enough noise, they'll ask you to leave.
I worry that you'll get hurt [if you continue].

4 typical behaviour

You can use **will** to express the idea of typical or habitual behaviour:

He wants power at any price, and he'll say anything to get it.
Sometimes she'll lie in bed till midday.

5 announcing spontaneous decisions

You use **will** when making a decision and announcing it:

You go ahead; I'll catch (not *I catch*) *you up.*
Here's a chemist's. We'll try here.
Well, we won't argue.

> ⓘ Notice that you can substitute **let's** for **we'll** in the above examples
> *Let's try here.*
> *Let's not argue.*

6 promises and threats

You use **will**, or more rarely **shall**, when announcing firm intentions or making promises:

I've said I'll finish tonight, and I shall.
You'll get a smack if you don't behave.
I promise I won't let you down.
I'll make an effort; I really will.

7 requests

You use **will you**, and **you will ..., won't you?** to express requests, orders or instructions:

Please will you make sure these letters catch the post?
Hand me that folder, will you?
You will come back tomorrow, won't you?

8 refusals

Won't expresses refusal, or persistent disobedience, and is frequently used for referring to the failure of *things* to work:

He won't commit himself.
Why won't you tell me?
She just will not (or *won't*) *learn.*
The car won't start.

9 firm wishes

You use **will** to say firmly how you expect people to behave, usually with an implicit threat, and sometimes with an explicit one:

They'll replace the faulty goods or they'll get no more orders from us.
You'll do as you're told.

10 wondering what to do

You use **shall** when asking for instructions from someone else, or offering to do something, or wondering what to do yourself:

Shall I throw this away?
What shall I do with her if she comes?
Shall I accompany you on the violin?
Shall I call him or shan't I?

> ⓘ You can use the question tag **shall I** or **shall we** after the announcement of a decision using **I'll** or **we'll**:
> *We'll go on, shall we?*
> *I'll go and collect the dry-cleaning, shall I?*

11 stating plans and intentions

You use **shall** to state your plans and intentions formally, *eg* in the introduction to an article, a speech or lecture, or book:

I shall address the issue of serious crime later on.

12 formal orders and legal obligation

Shall is often used in legal or official language with the *third person*, to express obligation:

I insist that the job shall be completed by tomorrow night.
Every student shall have an adviser of studies or research.

THE FUTURE PERFECT

1 You use the future perfect forms **shall have** and **will have**, with a past participle, to talk about things you expect will already be the case before a particular time in the future:

The building work will have begun by then, so we won't be able to use the house.
We think we'll have completed Phase 2 by the end of 1996.
On 21 May we'll have been married for 29 years.

> ⓘ You can use a progressive form in the future perfect tense:
> *By the end of this September I shall have been teaching my exercise class for eight whole years.*

2 You also use the future perfect tense for guessing what is probably already the case by now, when you don't know for certain:

He'll have been warned by now.
Don't worry; he'll have forgotten to switch on the answering machine.

THE FUTURE PROGRESSIVE

1 You use the future progressive (**will be** + **-ing** form), to talk about continuous situations in the future, or about something that will be in progress at some point in the future:

They will be cooking all our meals.
I shall be testing you on this later.
You will be working with me on this project.

2 The future progressive is also used to talk about something that is scheduled, or expected, to happen in the normal course of things:

I'll be leaving soon.
She will be giving the third lecture at the same time next week.
They will be arriving any time now.

3 You use the future progressive to guess what is probably happening now, when you don't know for certain:

You must go home; your parents will be worrying about you.

4 You use the future progressive for asking politely about people's plans, sometimes with a request in mind:

Will you be passing a chemist's at all? I was wondering if you could get this prescription for me.

➤ For other uses of **shall** and **will**, see the entries **shall** and **will**.

the future: ways of expressing it

THE PRESENT PROGRESSIVE

1 arrangements and plans already made

You use the present progressive (**be** + **-ing** form) to talk about things that have been fixed in advance:

We're meeting next week.
This store is closing in five minutes.
Are you doing anything after work?
She's not coming.

> ⓘ Notice that, in referring to scheduled or planned future events, the future progressive can usually be used instead of the present progressive:
> *This store will be* (or *is*) *closing in five minutes.*
> *She's not* (or *won't be*) *coming.*

2 stating intentions and insisting

You can use the present progressive for firm statements of intention, or refusals, and for insisting that other people do, or do not do, something

Not another word; I'm taking you home this minute.
I'm not washing up your dirty dishes.
You're not coming out with me dressed like that.

BE GOING TO

1 intentions and decisions

You use the structure **be going to**, with an infinitive, to talk about decisions that have already been made:

We are going to live in France.
Are you going to stay in London after you've retired?
We are going to build up a commitment to science.
How are you going to get to Italy?
You're not going to do anything silly, are you?

> ⓘ Notice the difference between **will** and **going to** with regard to decisions: you use **will** *as you make* a decision, and you use **going to** if you have *already made up your mind*:
> *'Does anyone want this last sandwich?' 'I'll have it.'*
> *I've seen the catalogue already; I'm going to order a copy of the spelling guide.*

2 events not under people's control

You can use the **going to** form to predict things that are not under people's control, or do not relate to people's intentions:

I think I'm going to be sick.
They're going to find out eventually.
Are you sure you're going to be all right?
You're going to get hurt!
It's going to be dry, according to the weather forecast.

3 refusing and insisting

Going to can be used, like the present progressive, for firmly refusing to do something, and for insisting that people do, or do not do, something:

I'm not going to do all your work for you.
You're going to apologize, and you're going to do it now.

 **Going to** has a progressive, or continuous form:
I can see that we are going to be baking all day tomorrow.

THE SIMPLE PRESENT

The simple present is used in three ways to talk about future happenings:

1 timetables

You can use the simple present to refer to events that are expected to happen according to a timetable or according to normal routine:

The express train leaves in five minutes.
His committee starts work this week.
When does the film start?

2 asking for instructions

You can use the simple present when asking for instructions, or when wondering what to do:

Where do we get tickets?
The speaker hasn't arrived. What do we do now?

3 subordinate clauses

The simple present is often used with a future meaning in subordinate clauses, where the main clause has a verb in the future tense:

Who will care for my children when I die?
I'll call you as soon as I hear anything.
Thanks for the scarf; I'll think of you whenever I wear it.
I'll let you know what he says.
We'll be waiting to hear whether it succeeds.

➤ For more information on the use of the present tense in subordinate clauses, see **subordinate clauses**.

THE 'BE TO' CONSTRUCTION

You use the construction **be** + **to**-infinitive to refer to future events in various ways, for instance, to convey what is *planned*, or is *expected* to happen, what is *intended* to happen, what *fate* decides, the process of *wondering* or *deciding* what should happen, and obligation:

We're to meet the others in Old Town Square.
Decide who is to play a general or a particular part in the action.

➤ For a more detailed analysis of the uses of the **be to** construction, see **be**.

THE FUTURE IN THE PAST

Notice how you talk about the future in a past context:

1 The past progressive, and **was** or **were going to**:

I said goodbye to her when I left home, as she was catching the plane to New York later that day.
I could see that it was not going to be easy.

2 Notice that **will** and **shall** turn into **would** and **should** in a past context, and **am to**, **is to** and **are to** turn into **was to** and **were to:**

Little did I realize that I would meet Peter there.
I sat there wondering whether I should call him or not.

Gg

get

The verb **get** is irregular:

gets, getting, got, got or (informal AmE) *gotten*

Get has two main divisions of meaning. With a simple object in the form of a noun or pronoun its basic meaning is 'obtain' or 'receive'. In its various other grammatical structures, its meaning is basically 'come to be', or when used transitively, 'make or cause to be'.

GET + NOUN OR PRONOUN

1 receive or obtain:

I got this watch from my son for Christmas.
We're getting a grant for the building work.
You can get those drugs from a chemist's without a prescription.

2 fetch:

Could you get a copy for me too, please?
Would you get me another cup of tea?

3 catch, develop:

We both got flu in February.
Don't you get a headache when you work non-stop like that?

4 experience in the normal course of things:

We get very few tourists at this time of year.
You do get some strange people writing in sometimes.

5 catch scheduled transport:

I decided to get the eight o'clock flight back to Edinburgh.

6 experience:

She got a lot of pleasure from looking after the garden.
I get the impression sometimes that he's jealous.
I got such a shock when I saw them.

7 understand:

I'm sorry, I still don't get that joke.

➤ For the use of **have got** in expressing possession and obligation, see **have**.

IN OTHER STRUCTURES

1 become: **get + adjective**

Get can be used as a linking verb before an adjective, with the meaning 'become':

Marjorie's beginning to get old.
It gets really hot here in summer.

2 cause to become: **get + object + adjective**

In this structure, **get** has the meaning 'cause to become':

Did you get your clothes dry in time?
They deliberately got her drunk.

➤ See also **change**, **complements** and **linking verbs**.

3 putting yourself in a situation: **get + past participle**

You can use **get** with a past participle to express the process of deliberately putting yourself into a particular state or situation. You can express the process of things happening to you using the same construction:

It takes me only a few minutes to get washed and dressed.
They got divorced the following year.
You've taken ages. Did you get lost?
Don't be a fool. You'll probably get caught.

4 get + object + past participle

This structure conveys three different ideas:

- **accomplishing a task, or achieving a goal**:

  I want to get those letters written before I go to bed.

- **arranging for something to be done**:

  We're getting an extension built on the house.

- **accidents and misfortunes**:

  The dog got its tail caught in the car door.

5 movement: **get + preposition or particle**

You use **get** with an adverbial particle or adverbial phrase to express the idea of movement somewhere:

He got home about midnight.
I didn't get to bed at all last night.
We never got away for that holiday after all.
Would you mind getting off my bed?

> ⓘ Notice the difference between **get** and **go** as verbs of movement or travelling. You tend to use **get** when you are thinking about arrival at the destination, and **go** when you are thinking about the journey itself:
> *I thought we'd go along to the gallery and see the Cézannes.*
> *We'll probably get there about twelve, so we could have lunch first.*

6 causing movement: **get + object + adverbial particle or phrase**

You use the structure **get** + object + adverbial particle or phrase to express the idea of moving, or managing to move, something somewhere:

It's impossible to get him up in the mornings.
How are you going to get all your things across town?

7 starting: **get + -ing**

You can use this structure, rather informally, to mean 'start doing something':

It's time we got moving.
It's six-thirty. We ought to get going.

8 causing to start: **get + object + -ing**

You can use this structure to express the idea of making someone or something start doing something:

Tony managed to get the engine working.
Try and get her talking about her childhood.

9 get + to-infinitive

- **gradual development**:

  You find yourself getting to enjoy the baby instead of being scared of it.
  He's getting to know the job quite well.

- **manage**:

  Did you get to see the Cézanne exhibition?

- **ask**, **persuade or make**, **especially with difficulty**:

  I got my neighbour to give me a lift into town.
  Get them to reduce the price if possible.

•••• give + nouns of action ••••

You can use **give** followed by a noun that represents an action, as a substitute for a verb of action.

1 Instead of saying **he shouted** you can say **he gave a shout**. This alternative way of expressing action is particularly common with *sounds* and *body movements*:

She gave a shriek [= she shrieked] *and slid out of view.*
He gave a bitter laugh [= he laughed bitterly].
She gave a shrug. [= she shrugged her shoulders].

2 You can use the **give + noun** construction to replace verbs which take an object, by turning the direct object into an indirect object, so instead of saying *she hugged him*, you can say *she gave him a hug*.

You have to give the door a good kick.
It's time I gave the car a wash.

3 **Give** is used in this same construction with several nouns of 'effect':

The noise gave me a fright.
He decided to get home early and give her a surprise.

•••• given name ••••

➤ See **names and titles**.

•••• glasses ••••

➤ See **pair**.

•••• go ••••

The verb **go** is irregular:

goes, going, went, gone

As well as being a verb of movement, **go** has an important use as a 'linking' verb in which it expresses change, especially for the worse (*The milk's gone sour.*).

➤ See **change** for this use of **go**.

➤ See **come** for hints on the appropriate use of **come** and **go**.

➤ See **and** for the use of **go** and other verbs in expressions such as **go and do**, **go and see**.

The structure **be going to** is important in talking about the future.

➤ See **the future** for details about its use.

WITH ACTIVITY WORDS

1 go for a + noun

You can use the construction **go**, or **come**, **for a...** with a lot of action nouns, especially nouns representing recreational and leisure activities:

We went for a swim in the lake.
They went for a drive into the hills.
Going for a drink?

2 go + -ing

Again mainly in the area of leisure activities, you can use **go** with the **-ing** form of a verb. This structure suggests a more serious and sustained activity than the **go for a** + noun structure in the previous section:

I'm going skiing next month.
I went sailing for a week with a colleague from work.

> ⓘ Notice that when mentioning the place where the activity happens, you use prepositions of *place* rather than *direction*:
> *We used to go swimming in* (not *to*) *the river.*

•••• gone ••••

AS AN ADJECTIVE

You can use **gone**, the past participle of **go**, like an adjective after the verb **be** in two ways:

1 If someone goes out, and they haven't returned, you can say they have **been gone** for, *eg* two hours, meaning that they have been away or absent for that length of time:

How long has he been gone [= been away]*?*

2 When something disappears people sometimes say that it **is gone** rather than that it **has gone**:

After a few weeks all our money was gone.
The forest is gone forever.

ⓘ The structure **is gone** sometimes sounds old-fashioned.

ⓘ Notice that you could substitute the verb **have** (**had**) for the verb **be** in any of the examples in section 2 above.

AS A PAST PARTICIPLE

➤ For guidance on **been** used like a past participle of **go**, see **been**.

•••• granted ••••

VERB

You **are granted** something, or something **is granted to** you, when you are given or allowed it:

In 1928 the vote was granted to women over 21.

TAKE SOMEONE OR SOMETHING FOR GRANTED

1 You **take something for granted** when you assume that it is true or correct:

We tend to take technology for granted.
Teachers took it for granted that children would understand.

2 You **take someone for granted** when you fail to appreciate the effort they make to help you:

I warned you not to take me for granted, Kathleen.
I don't want him to think he can take me for granted.

CONJUNCTION

You use **granted** or **granted that** at the beginning of a clause to say that you accept something as true, before you make a comment on it:

Granted that she behaved dishonestly, what should we now do about it?

—— greetings and farewells ——

➤ See pages 240 and 241.

•••• ground floor, first floor ••••

GROUND FLOOR

In BrE, the **ground floor** of a building is the floor at, or nearest to, the level of the ground outside:

The perfume department is on the ground floor.

FIRST FLOOR

In BrE, the **first floor** of a building is the floor above the ground floor:

I took the stairs to the first floor.

GREETINGS AND FAREWELLS

'Greetings' refers to the things people say when they meet someone they already know. This section also looks at what people say when they leave each other.

➤ See **introductions** for what people say when they meet for the first time.

NEUTRAL AND INFORMAL GREETINGS

1 The commonest way of greeting someone you already know is by saying **hello**, and asking them about their health or their life in general:

Hello there, Andrew. How are you today?
Hello, Jackie. How was work?

2 More informally, you can say **Hi**, **Hi there** or **Hiya**:

Hi there! How's things?
Hiya! How are you?

3 If you haven't seen someone for a long time, you might express surprise or pleasure at seeing them:

It's great to see you again! I haven't seen you for ages.

FORMAL GREETINGS

1 When you greet people formally, you can say **Good morning** until about one o'clock, and **Good afternoon** until five or six o'clock. After that you say **Good evening**:

Good morning, ladies and gentlemen
'Oh, good afternoon. Can I speak to Jack Henderson, please?'
Good evening. Tonight's headlines ...

ⓘ

- Notice that **Good night** is not used as a greeting. You say **Good night** to people when you, or they, are going to bed. **Good night** is not a formal expression.
- You do not say **How do you do?** to someone you have met before.
- **Good day** is rather old-fashioned in BrE, but is commonly used in Australian English (pronounced 'G'day' /gə'deɪ/).

2 Slightly less formally, you might say **Morning! Afternoon!** or **Evening!** to someone you meet regularly, like your boss or teacher:

Morning everyone. Now listen carefully...

3 If someone has just arrived in your town or country, or if they have come home after being away for a while, you can greet them by saying **Welcome ...!**:

Welcome home, Chris.
Welcome back, Stefan.
Welcome to Edinburgh!

SPECIAL OCCASIONS

1 On special days or occasions, you give people your best wishes by saying **Happy** (or **Merry**) **Christmas!**, **Happy Easter!** or **Happy New Year!** To reply to these good wishes, you can thank the person and wish them the same:

'Merry Christmas!' 'Merry Christmas to you too!'
'Happy Easter!' 'Thank you. And you.'

2 On someone's birthday you can say **Happy birthday** or **Many happy returns**. The person replies by saying **Thank you** or **Thanks**.

REPLYING TO A GREETING

1 You usually reply to a greeting by saying something similar back to the person who spoke first:

'Hi there!' 'Hi! How are you?'
'Hiya Greg, how are you doing?' 'Oh, hi there, Bob, how's life?'

2 If the person who speaks first asks you a question, you can reply by just answering the question:

'Susie hi. How are you?' 'I'm fine thanks'.

> ⓘ In situations where you feel sure that the person who is asking the question really wishes to know about your state of health, you can answer by describing how you feel:
> *'Hi! How are you?' Not great actually. I'm thinking of going home.'*
> Otherwise, in more formal situations, **Fine thank you**, or **Very well thank you** are more appropriate.

SAYING GOODBYE

When you leave someone you can say **goodbye** to them. However, this is fairly formal, and is commonly used by TV and radio presenters:

That's all that we have time for today. Until next week, goodbye.

1 informally

- The most common expression used when people leave each other is **Bye! Bye-bye**, pronounced /bə'baɪ/, is common in very informal contexts:

  'Bye, love.'
  'Bye! I'll give you a call.'
  Thanks, then. Look after yourself. Bye-bye.

- If you are going to see the person again, you can refer to that day or time, or to the place where you will see them, by saying **See you!** or **See you on ...** or **See you then/there!**:

  'Oh bye, see you tomorrow at the football?' 'Sure, we'll see you there.'
  See you later. Bye!

- People sometimes say **Cheerio**, **Cheers now** or just **Cheers**:

  'Many thanks, cheerio.' 'See you. Cheers.'

- Some people, especially speakers of AmE say **So long!** as an informal way of saying goodbye.

2 formally

When you are saying goodbye in a formal situation, a longer expression is usually more appropriate:

Well, it's been nice meeting you.
'So we'll see you again on the 25th?' 'Yes. I'll look forward to that.'

ⓘ In AmE, the **first floor** is the floor at, or nearest to, the level of the ground outside:
We need a bathroom on the first floor, now that John can't get upstairs.

•••• grow ••••

➤ See **change**.

Hh

had

➤ See **have**.

had better

➤ See **better**.

half

Half occurs alone or in combinations such as **less than half**, **more than half**, **nearly half**, and **over half**. It has grammatical features in common with **all** and **both**, so it might be useful to compare this entry with the entries for these words.

BEFORE NOUNS AND PRONOUNS

1 **Half** can be used before a determiner or pronoun:
*The petrol station was **half a kilometre** away.*
*We waited **half an hour**.*
*You probably only eat an ounce of butter a day, or even **half that**.*

2 **Half** has a very limited use as a determiner. It can be used with place names, to represent either the area or its population:
***Half Aberdeen** was without electricity yesterday.*

> ⓘ Notice that **half** is often used informally, with deliberate exaggeration, to mean a large proportion:
> *Half these timetables are out of date.*

3 The form **half of** is a frequently used alternative to **half**:
More than half (of) the delegates come from abroad.
Half (of) those aged over 85 are unable to walk on their own.
Half (of) the country was already overrun by enemy troops.

4 **Half of** is the form that must be used before personal pronouns:
Perhaps half of you could form a circle in the middle?
Half of me still misses him.
Half of us are still waiting for an answer.

AS AN INDEPENDENT PRONOUN

You use **half** on its own as a pronoun:
He divided the pizza down the middle and we ate half each.
Of those cases reported, less than half went to court.

AS A NOUN

The countable noun **half** (*plural* **halves**) represents one of two equal portions that together make a whole:

Normally we spend the first half of the lesson practising conversation.

1 Instead of saying:

She divided the group into two halves.

you can say:

She divided the group in half (or *in two*).

2 You can say that an amount that has been reduced to half its former level has been reduced **by half**:

Circulation of the paper has dropped by half.

AS A FRACTION

1 In expressions of measurement, as an alternative to saying, *eg* **half a** litre of milk, you can say **a half** litre of milk:

A half pint (or *half a pint*) *of lager, please.*

> ⓘ In restaurants you would order **a half bottle** of wine [an exact measurement] rather than **half a bottle** [an approximate quantity].

2 Notice how the fraction **half** is used in expressions with numbers:

Half of fifteen is seven and a half.
We could save the lives of three and a half million children every year.
The work is going to take two and a half weeks.

3 The expression **one and a half** is plural, so takes a plural noun:

The course lasts one and a half years.
It'll be the size of one and a half football pitches when it's completed.

As an alternative, you can use **a** or **an** with a singular noun:

It lasts a year and a half.
I had an hour and a half to spend there.

AS AN ADVERB

The following examples demonstrate some adverbial uses of **half**:

The theatre was half empty.
He peered at me through half-closed eyes.
I'm only half dressed.
She's half Italian and half Irish.
I woke as usual at half past six [= 6.30].

➤ For more information about **half** in expressions of time see **time**.

•••• happen ••••

HAPPEN, OCCUR, TAKE PLACE

1 You use **happen** mostly with pronouns such as **something**, **anything**, **nothing**,

what, **it**, **this** and **that**:

Something very strange is happening here.
In fact, nothing happened in the first month.
They told the old lady what had happened.

2 Events that you specify more precisely **occur** or **take place**:

The incident occurred a minute before half time.
Flowers lie beside the track where the crash took place.

ⓘ Things that are unplanned **happen**, **occur** or **take place**. Planned events **take place**:

An interesting development took place this week.
The demonstration took place peacefully.

HAPPEN TO (SOMEONE OR SOMETHING)

1 You use **happen** with the preposition **to** to talk about circumstances or incidents affecting, damaging or injuring people or things in some way:

This can't be happening to me.
The same thing happened to my next-door neighbour.

2 You often use the **happen to** construction when something or someone has not appeared when they were expected:

Dad's very late; I hope nothing's happened to him.

HAPPEN TO (DO)

You say that a person or thing **happens to do** something as a way of expressing a chance or coincidence:

One day I happened to come across this picture in his desk.
Midge happened to be standing next to us in the queue.

AS IT HAPPENS, IT SO HAPPENS

You can also express chance circumstances using the expressions **as it happens** and **it so happens**:

I retired then, and as it happened, several of my colleagues left for other reasons.
I needed a lawyer and it just so happened that I was having lunch with one.

•••• hardly ••••

1 Things that are **hardly** so are almost not so. Where **hardly** modifies a verb it takes the 'mid position', that is, before the verb, but after an auxiliary or modal verb, or the verb **be**:

She hardly lifted her head from her books all that year.
We've hardly started.

2 **Hardly** behaves like a negative (it is sometimes called a *broad negative*) and is used with non-assertive words like **any** and **ever**.

Hardly can begin a sentence before an **any**-word:

Hardly anyone there spoke to me.

ⓘ Note that both **scarcely** and **barely** can be used in exactly the same way as **hardly** senses **1** and **2**.

3 You say that one thing had **hardly** happened (or, with inversion, **hardly** had one thing happened) **when** (or **before**) another did when you want to emphasize how quickly the second event followed the first:

He had hardly finished (or *Hardly had he finished*) *speaking when the trouble started.*

ⓘ **Hardly** is very similar in meaning to **no sooner**:
Hardly had the announcement been made ***when*** (or *No sooner had the announcement been made* ***than***) *it was withdrawn.*

•••• hate ••••

➤ See **like**.

•••• have ••••

The verb **have** is used as an *auxiliary* verb, helping to form the perfect forms of other verbs, and as an *ordinary* verb.

As an ordinary verb it is used to express possession, necessity, actions of various kinds, the process of undergoing things, and choosing or obtaining things.

The auxiliary verb **do** is used with the ordinary verb **have**. It is especially common in AmE in its 'possession' and 'necessity' senses (*Do you have the time? I don't have to go*), where in BrE it is more usual to find a construction with **got** (*She's got red hair. I've got to go*).

The parts of **have**, with their contracted forms, and their negative contractions, are:

present tense

I have or *I've*	*I haven't* or *I've not*
you have or *you've*	*you haven't* or *you've not*
he has or *he's*	*he hasn't* or *he's not*
she has or *she's*	*she hasn't* or *she's not*
it has or *it's*	*it hasn't* or *it's not*
we have or *we've*	*we haven't* or *we've not*
they have or *they've*	*they haven't* or *they've not*

past tense

I had or *I'd*	*I hadn't* or *I'd not*
you had or *you'd*	*you hadn't* or *you'd not*
he had or *he'd*	*he hadn't* or *he'd not*
she had or *she'd*	*she hadn't* or *she'd not*
it had or *it'd*	*it hadn't* or *it'd not*
we had or *we'd*	*we hadn't* or *we'd not*
they had or *they'd*	*they hadn't* or *they'd not*

present participle

having

infinitive

have

- The contraction **'s** for **has** can be used after nouns and proper names, the indefinite pronouns (**someone**, **anyone**, **no-one**, **everyone**, **somebody**, and so on), **there, where, what** and **who**:

  Her book's been published.
  Pat's left a message.
  No-one's guessed.
  Where's she gone?
  What's happened?

- The contraction **'d** for **had** can be used after **there** and **who**:

  I knew there'd been an accident.
  I couldn't think who'd mentioned it.

  You hear this form after other words too, but it is rarely used in written English:

  Nobody had (/ˈnoʊbədiːəd/) *realized.*

- The contraction **'ve** is rarely *written* in positions other than those listed above with the personal pronouns, but can be *heard* in other positions:

  Where have (/ˈwɛərəv/) *you put it?*
  What have (/ˈwɒtəv/) *you done with it?*

THE AUXILIARY VERB

You use **have** to form the perfect forms of other verbs, including those of the 'ordinary' verb **have**:

1 **the present perfect** (*I've finished*)

You use **have** and **has** with the past participles of other verbs to form the present perfect:

You and I have known each other since 1963.
She has (or *she's*) *worked for us for twenty years.*

2 **the present perfect progressive** (*I've been waiting*)

You use **have** and **has** with **been** and the present participle, or **-ing** form, of other verbs to form the present perfect progressive:

They've been trying to sell their house since April.
We've been having a most interesting discussion.

3 **the past perfect** (*I'd met her before*)

You use **had** with the past participle of other verbs to form their past perfect tense:

That was the first time I had (or *I'd*) *met him.*
She died so suddenly that I hadn't (or *I'd not*) *even realized she was ill.*

4 **the past perfect progressive** (*We'd been thinking about it*)

You use **had** with **been** and the present participle of other verbs to form the past perfect progressive:

They had (or *they'd*) *been going around together for years when they decided to get married.*

5 the perfect infinitive (*Sorry to have kept you*)

You use **to** + **have** with the past participle of other verbs to form their perfect infinitive:

It was stupid of me not to have brought my camera.

6 the future perfect (*I'll have left by then*)

You use **shall** or **will** + **have**, followed by the past participle of other verbs, to form the future perfect:

She will have arrived home by now.

7 the future perfect progressive (*They'll have been worrying about you*)

You use **shall** or **will** + **have**, followed by **been** and the present participle of other verbs, to form the future perfect progressive:

By this September, I shall have been teaching for two years.

➤ For the use of the infinitive **have** after the other modal auxiliaries, see **can**, **could**, **may**, **might**, **need**, **should** and **conditionals**.

➤ For more information about the use of **have** and **had**, see **tense**.

8 -ing clauses (*Having come so far...*)

You use **having** with the past participle of other verbs to state circumstances that precede, and sometimes explain, the main action of the sentence:

Having heard her speak previously, I knew she would be entertaining.

9 questions (*Have you finished?*)

Have normally changes places with the subject to form questions in the perfect tenses:

Have they gone?
Hadn't you realized?
Why has he changed it?
What's he done now?

ⓘ A more formal construction for the negative question form is **have** + *subject* + *negative* + *past participle*:
Has it not occurred (instead of *hasn't it occurred*) *to you?*
Have they never (instead of *haven't they ever*) *heard of safety checks?*

10 ellipsis

As with other auxiliary verbs, you can use auxiliary **have** to stand for the main verb and whatever else follows it:

She likes red roses. She always has.
'You've spelt his name wrong.' 'No I haven't.'
I didn't tell them. Would it have made any difference if I had?
I don't think you've met my husband, have you?
So it's been in the newspaper, has it?

ⓘ Notice that the contracted forms **I've**, **I'd**, **he's**, **we've**, and so on, cannot be used in final position (see **contractions**):
*I went back to see if I'd switched off the lights, and **I had*** (not *I'd*).

POSSESSION

1 in a present context

Things that you **have** belong to you, are in your possession, are available to you, or are connected with you in some way. You can use **have got** as a slightly less formal alternative to **have**, in a present context. The contractions formed with **have** (**I've**, **you've**, **we've**, **they've**) are frequent in combination with **got**, but less frequent without it; the contractions formed with **has** are nearly always combined with **got**. Progressive forms are not possible:

They have (or *they've got*) *an apartment in town.*
He has (or *he's got*) *a job in publishing.*
Who has (or *who's got*) *my box of matches?*

> ⓘ The **got** forms are not possible, in the 'possession' sense, in perfect or future structures:
> *I haven't had time to read your report.*
> *I'll have more time next week.*

- **questions**:

Have you (or *have you got*, or *do you have*) *any seats for tonight's performance?*
Has she (or *has she got*, or *does she have*) *anyone to look after her?*

- **negatives**:

Sorry, I haven't (or *I haven't got*, or *I don't have*) *the faintest idea.*
She hasn't got (or *she doesn't have*, or *she hasn't*) *enough money.*

- **elliptical uses and question tags**:

'Have you got a copy?' 'Yes I have'
You have a dictionary there, haven't you? (or *don't you?*)
She's got a twin brother, hasn't she?
They don't have equipment for hire, do they?

2 in a past context

The past tense uses **had** rather than **had got** as a positive form, but usually **did have** in questions, and **did not have**, **didn't have**, **hadn't** or **hadn't got** as negative forms. The progressive forms are not possible:

- **negatives and questions**:

She had no idea where to go.
Did you have enough food with you?
I found I hadn't got enough money for the fare.
Didn't you have her telephone number?

- **elliptical uses and question tags**

I thought I had her address with me, but I hadn't (or *I didn't*).
I hadn't a clue. Had you?
I didn't have a clue. Did you?
You had a map, didn't you (or *hadn't you*)*?*

NECESSITY

1 You use **have** or **have got** with **to** and the infinitive of other verbs to express necessity, duty, obligation, or compulsion:

I have to look after the children every afternoon.
Buy everything now and you won't have to shop later.
She has to (or *she's got to*) *take a preliminary test.*

2 Progressive forms are possible:

All departments are having to make cuts.

3 Questions and negatives are formed with **do have** and **have got**:

Does he have to (or *has he got to*) *pay for his medical treatment?*
We don't have to (or *haven't got to*) *leave till midday.*
Don't you have to book in advance?

> ⓘ In the present tense, **have to** can be used whether the obligation is a repeated one, or belongs to a particular occasion. You use **have got to** if the obligation is for a particular occasion:
> *I have to be at my desk by eight every morning.*
> *Do you have to go shopping today?*
> *I've got to ring her tonight.*

4 In a past context, the positive form is **had to**. **Did have to** is used in questions, and **did not have to**, and **didn't have to** are used as negative forms:

I had to wait half an hour for a bus.
I knew I had to be there by six-thirty.
Did you have to hurry?
Didn't you have to ask permission?

5 **elliptical uses and question tags**

As with the 'possessive' sense of **have** (see above), **do** is normally used to refer back to the **do have** forms. Both **have** and **do** can refer back to the **have** and **have got** forms in general, but in question tags **have** usually refers back to the **have** and **have got** forms:

'Do you have to see the specialist again?' 'No, I don't.'
You didn't have to say that to him, did you?
It would be nice if you wrote to her, but you don't have to.
He hasn't got to sit the exam again, has he?

> ⓘ Notice that **do not have to** and **haven't got to** express the *lack of* obligation or necessity, whereas **must not** expresses prohibition:
> *You mustn't touch the exhibits.*
> *You don't have to* (or *you haven't got to*) *come if you don't want to.*

ACTING AND EXPERIENCING

1 You **have** food, drink and meals:

I've just had a cup of coffee, thanks.
What time do you have breakfast?

2 You **have** illnesses:
He had measles very badly.
Have you ever had jaundice?

3 Women **have** babies:
She's having a baby in July.
She's just had a little girl.

4 People **have** parties when they give them:
He had a big party for his eighteenth birthday.

5 You **have** people to stay in your home, or **have** them for a meal:
We had the professor for dinner the other night.
Thanks for having me to stay.

6 You **have** a good time or a bad time:
Have an enjoyable time.
We had a successful afternoon.

7 **Have**, like **take**, is used with *action* nouns formed from verbs:
Have a drink.
Did you have your usual swim?
They were always having quarrels.
I had a good cry.
Let's have a rest.
Have you had a proper wash?
I was beginning to have doubts.
We ought to have a serious discussion.

8 People also **have** such things as accidents, operations, strokes of good or bad luck, and disappointments:
We've had a bit of luck.

HAVE SOMETHING DONE

1 You **have** something done when you arrange for it to be done, or cause it to happen:
I'm having my hair cut on Friday.
It's time I had the car serviced.

2 Something that you **have** done to you can happen without you being responsible:
He's had his bicycle stolen again.
The cat liked having its tail stroked.

• • • • he, he or she, they • • • •

In the past, in formal written contexts, it was acceptable to use the singular masculine pronouns **he**, **him** and **himself** and the possessive **his** to refer back to indefinite pronouns like **someone**, **everybody**, **anyone**, **nobody** (*Someone has left his coat behind*). Nowadays, though, this is considered by many people to be sexist.

Using the plural pronouns **they**, **them** and **themselves**, and the possessives **their** and **theirs**, is the most natural-sounding, and most common alternative, although it *is* grammatically rather strange.

Some suggestions for dealing with the situation are made below.

AFTER INDEFINITE PRONOUNS

1 **They** and its related forms can usually be used, except in the most formal contexts:

Everybody has a right to their own opinion.
No-one need blame themselves over this.

2 In question tags, and after prepositions, you *must* use **they**:

Anyone can have a go, can't they?
Someone's got to take responsibility, haven't they?
Nobody had remembered to bring a torch with them.

3 It is sometimes possible to avoid the difficulty by using the plural **people** instead of an indefinite pronoun like **everyone**:

People have their own opinions.

Instead of:

Everyone has his or her (or *their*) *own opinion.*

AFTER COMMON-GENDER NOUNS

1 In an informal, conversational context, people often refer back to common-gender nouns such as **person**, **child**, **adult**, **parent** or **teacher** with **they** and its related forms:

No child should be left on their own for as long as that.

2 In a formal written context, after a noun of general reference, such as **person**, the pronoun **they** is usually fine, but with more specific nouns, such as **teacher** or **writer**, it is safer to refer back with **he or she**:

A teacher always has his or her favourite pupils.
This was often the attitude of a writer to his or her art.

3 You can nearly always avoid having to decide between **they** and **he or she** by pluralizing the noun:

Teachers all have their favourite pupils.
Children should never be left on their own for as long as that.

➤ For more information on the pronoun **he** see **personal pronouns**.

•••• hear ••••

The verb **hear** is irregular:

hears, hearing, heard /hɜːd/

AS A VERB OF SENSING

As with other verbs of sensing, you rarely use **hear** in the progressive, but you often use it with **can** and **could** in a progressive sense, especially in BrE. Instead of saying 'I'm hearing a funny noise', you say 'I can hear a funny noise'. You use **hear** in the following grammatical structures:

1 **hear + object**

The following examples show various types of object after **hear**:

I heard a loud scream.
He could hear his Mum on the phone in the next room.
Nobody can hear a word.

> ⓘ You use either **hear** or, especially in BrE, **can** or **could hear**, when talking about continuous sounds:
> *I heard* (or *could hear*) *voices.*
> But notice that where there is a single noise, or a sudden one, you use **heard** rather than **could hear**:
> *We could hear shooting.*
> But:
> *We heard a gunshot.*

2 hear + object + -ing

You can also use the **-ing** form of a verb after the object when the sound is continuous, or something is in progress. **Can** and **could** are frequently used with **hear** in this structure:

He could hear them arguing.
One morning he woke to hear the dog barking.

Notice that the sound may be a repeated, rather than continuous one:

She could hear Gloria calling her name.

3 hear + object + infinitive without 'to'

You can use the infinitive after the object to represent a complete happening:

The telephone rang and she heard Eric pick it up.
He heard the Town Hall clock chime four.

4 hear and passive structures

- You can also use **be heard** with the **-ing** form of a verb:

  He could be heard muttering to himself from time to time.

- You can use **hear** in the active with a passive past participle after the object:

  You will hear the word used in a number of different senses.

  You can convey a more continuous idea by using **being** with the past participle:

  I heard your book being praised the other day.

5 hear used intransitively

You can also use **hear** without an object:

My mother's eighty and she can't hear very well.

HEAR AND LISTEN TO

You use **hear** to express the idea of *receiving sounds* through your ears. You use **listen to** to express the idea of *paying attention to* a sound:

We heard the news on the radio at lunch break.
He was listening to the radio.
'You're not listening to me,' she complained. 'You haven't heard a word I've been saying.'

LEARNING FACTS, GATHERING INFORMATION

1 As a verb of *receiving information*, **hear** can be used with an object, a **that-**clause, or with the prepositions **about** or **of**:

'Did you hear about the new parking arrangements?' 'Yes, I've never heard

anything so ridiculous.'
He had heard (that) my husband was in hospital.
Little more was heard of him after that.

> ⓘ You can say **So I hear** when you are told things you already know:
> *'Dad's been busy.' 'So I hear.'*
> ➤ See also **so**.

HEAR OF

You say you **have heard of** someone or something if you know they exist:
We had heard of AIDS at the time, but we didn't know much about it.

•••• help ••••

ASSIST

1 **Help** can be used with or without an object:
I helped you before, didn't I?
We're looking for volunteers. Can you help?

2 **Help** can be followed by an object and an infinitive with or without **to**:
All the girls helped her to get the fire going.
Michael helped him clear up afterwards.

3 You can also use an infinitive directly after **help** without an object:
He helped establish the party politics that we know today.

CAN'T HELP

1 You **can't help** doing something when you can't stop yourself doing it, or can't resist doing it. You use the **-ing** form of the following verb, not the infinitive:
People can't help being (not *can't help to be*) *silly.*
I couldn't help laughing.

2 **Can't help** and **couldn't help** can also be followed by the pronoun **it**, taking the place of the **-ing** form of the verb:
I'm trying not to get excited, but I can't help it [= getting excited].

•••• here ••••

HERE AND THERE

1 You use **here** to refer to the place where you are, or somewhere close to you that you are indicating or pointing to; you use **there** to refer to other places, for instance, the other end of a telephone line:
'Hello, it's Margaret here. Is Frances there?'
It feels as if spring is here at last.
It's so beautiful here.

2 When expressing movement towards a place, people naturally use **here** with **come** and **bring**, and **there** with **go** and **take**:
Come here a minute.
The nearest hospital was Waterford, so I took her there.

3 **Here** and **there** are often used at the beginning of a sentence in direct speech, and the subject and verb are inverted after them, unless the subject is a personal pronoun:

There goes the doorbell again.
Here comes the bus.

But:

Here it comes!

➤ See also **there**.

WITH PREPOSITIONS

1 **Here** as an adverb of *place* or *direction* is not normally used with any preposition:

I left it here this morning.
They moved here (not *to here*) *only two months ago.*

2 You can however use **from** with **here**, and you can use other prepositions and prepositional phrases with **here** when thinking of **here** as a point or area:

From here, on a clear day, you can see Scotland.
The station's about six miles from here.
It's so dark in here.
Is there much crime round here?

OTHER USES

1 You use **here is** or **here's** when showing someone what you have got, when giving them something, or when announcing the arrival of someone or something. **Here are** is used if the noun is plural:

Here's the key.
Here are the tickets.
Ah, here's Lilian.

> ⓘ You say **here you are** to someone when you are giving them something:
> *'Could I have a coffee, please?' 'Sure, here you are.'*

2 **Here is** can be followed by a **wh-**clause:

Here's what you must do.

3 You say **Here** when offering something to someone, or when drawing someone's attention to something:

Here, catch this.
Here, let me show you.

•••• high, tall ••••

HIGH

1 **High** is used to describe things that measure a lot from bottom to top:

The island is a mixture of high mountains, sandy beaches and deep blue sea.
They were surrounded by high walls and rows of windows.

2 **High** is also used to describe things that are a long way above the ground:
High clouds floated over the distant horizon.
I am tall for a woman, but the shelves were too high for me to reach.

TALL

1 **Tall** is used to describe objects that measure a lot from bottom to top, but are comparatively narrow:
On the tray was a tall glass of milk.
The house was built among the tall trees, well back from the road.
There was a tall mirror on the landing.

2 **Tall** is also used to describe people:
He was a tall man, with a long face.
She was tall and beautiful.

> ⓘ **High** is never used to describe people.

MEASUREMENTS

When you are giving a measurement, you use **high** for things and **tall** for people:
She was only five feet tall.
The ceilings here are about 16 feet high.

•••• him ••••

➤ See **personal pronouns**.

•••• holiday, holidays, vacation ••••

HOLIDAY

1 A **holiday** is a period of time that you have away from your work, or job. You usually spend a holiday away from home, enjoying yourself in some activity, or relaxing:
Did you have good weather for your holiday?
Are you going on holiday this year?

2 A day on which you do not have to go to work, perhaps because of a religious festival, is also a **holiday**:
Next Monday's a public holiday.

HOLIDAYS

The **holidays** are the period between two academic terms, when no classes are held:
What do the children do during the summer holidays?
We have exams before the Christmas holidays.

VACATION

In American English, the term **vacation** covers both the recreational **holiday** and the academic **holidays** of British English:
I always take my annual vacation in July.
He's going on vacation in November.
I had a lot of reading to do over the summer vacation.

•••• home ••••

The word **home** can be used as an uncountable or countable noun.

AS AN UNCOUNTABLE NOUN

Home is the place where you live, or where you belong. It can be your parents' house, or the village, city or country that you come from.

1 You can use **home** like an adverb of direction, without the preposition **to**:
He picked her up at the airport and brought her home (not *to home*).
The journey home was quicker than I'd expected.
Is Mick home [= has Mick come home] *yet?*
Why didn't I go home to my own country?

> ⓘ Notice that you use **leave**, as well as **arrive**, without a preposition before **home**:
> *What time do you leave home in the mornings?*
> *I arrived home early that day.*

2 Someone who is **at home** is in their own house:
She decided she could work better at home.

3 In AmE, you use **home** like an adverb of place, without the preposition **at**:
He thought that women should stay home and do the cooking.

4 You can use other prepositions with uncountable **home**:
We were cold and wet, and fourteen miles from home.
I spend a lot of time travelling between home and work.
Most car accidents take place within a mile of home.

> ⓘ Notice that **to** is possible with **home** if it is in combination with **from**:
> *They kindly offered to pay the cost of our transport to and from home.*

AS A COUNTABLE NOUN

You use the countable noun **home** with determiners, especially possessives, to talk about people's homes, or homes in general:
It's nice to get back to your own home.
Latvia is my real home.
Her body was found about half a mile from her home.
A whole month in an American home should improve their English.
I was attending a seminar on accidents in the home.
These are kids who've never had a home of their own.
I came from a very happy home.

AT SOMEONE ELSE'S HOME

1 To express the idea of being at someone else's home, you can use **at** with the possessive form of someone's name:
I'm just ringing to say I'm at Richard's.
She suggested going round to swim at the Smiths' on Friday.

2 The possessive pronouns are sometimes used, but it is more usual to talk about **my**

place or **your place**:

By the time we get to your place (rather than *to yours*) *it'll be eight o'clock.*
You can find them at our place (rather than *at ours*) *most weekends.*

• • • hope • • •

There are some important grammatical points to notice about the verb **hope**.

1 After **hope** you often use a present tense to refer to the future:

I hope we manage to see you again soon.
I hope it stays fine for the wedding.
I hope it doesn't rain.

2 When you are expressing a negative hope, you put **not** with the verb in the clause after **hope**:

I hope he doesn't forget (not *I don't hope he forgets*).

In this way, **hope** behaves differently from the verb **expect**, and from the verbs **think**, **believe**, **imagine**, and **suppose**.

3 Notice that you often use **I hope**, and more emphatically, **I do hope** to express wishes, *eg* polite ones for other people's success, or for their enjoyment of something they are planning. People also use the form **let's hope**, to express a common wish:

Have a nice evening; I do hope you enjoy the play.
We're going skiing next week; let's hope it snows hard.

4 You can use the various forms of the future tense after **hope**:

I hope you're going to show me your holiday pictures.
I hope I'm not going to be sick.
I hope we shall meet again.

5 You can use **hope** in the progressive:

Mum's hoping he'll come back.

6 If the subject of the clause after **hope** is the same as the subject of **hope**, you can use the structure **to** + infinitive instead of a **that**-clause:

Mr Murray hopes to make a decision this month.

7 You can use **hope** with reference to the past and the present, as well as to the future:

I hope you enjoyed our governor's speech.
I do hope someone's remembered to feed the cat.
I hope you don't mind me telling you.

8 You can use **so** as a substitute for a positive clause after **hope**, and **not** as a substitute for a negative one:

'Can you do it?' 'I hope so.'
Maybe I'll regret it, but I hope not.

• • • • hopefully • • • •

Hopefully has two uses.

1 You do something **hopefully** when you do it expecting success or a good result:

He ran into the room, smiling hopefully.
I tapped on his window. 'Taxi?' I enquired, hopefully.

2 Much more commonly, **hopefully** is used as a sentence adverb, meaning 'I hope':
Hopefully my leg will soon be better and I'll be able to play again.

•••• how ••••

IN DIRECT AND INDIRECT QUESTIONS

You use **how** to ask about, or refer to, the way something happens or is done. It is used in direct questions, and in indirect questions after verbs such as **ask**, **tell**, **wonder**, **know**, **show**:

1 in direct questions:
'How did you get here so quickly?'
How on earth did you manage to persuade him?
How do you spell 'gauge'?

2 in indirect questions:
Can you show me how to rename a file?
How do you think they found us?

ⓘ Notice that **how** can be used like **the way**:
Do you remember how (or *the way*) *we used to laugh at her?*

ⓘ Notice also that you use **the way**, **as** or **like**, rather than **how**, when comparing a manner of doing something:
Put your left foot forwards first, the way (or *as* or *like*) *I do.*

3 Sometimes **how** is used like **that**, to introduce a factual statement:
He kept telling me how everyone was against him.

IN QUESTIONS ABOUT DEGREE AND AMOUNT

1 You use **how** to ask about the degree of a quality, or the extent of a condition:
How expert is he at this?
The doctors do not know how seriously injured she is yet.

2 You use **how** in questions about amount, measurement, distance, time, age and price:
How much flour do I need for this recipe?
How tall are you?
How far is it from Cardiff to Bristol?
How much is this ring? [= what does this ring cost?]
How old is the baby?

IN QUESTIONS ABOUT THE STATE OF THINGS

1 You ask someone **how** they are, or **how** they are feeling, when you want to know about their state of health, or their emotional or mental state:
Hello, how are you? I haven't seen you for ages.
How's your mother?
How's your leg today?

2 You ask someone **how** something is when you want to know what their reaction to it is, or whether it is successful:

'How was your weekend?' 'Great, thanks.'

3 You use the form **what ... like?** rather than **how** when you are asking for a description of someone or something:

'What's the new director like?' 'Oh, he's a nice man. Tall and friendly.'

4 You ask someone **how** something is going, when you want to know if it is progressing well, or if they are enjoying it:

'How's the new job going?' 'Quite well, thanks.'
I asked how the interview had gone.

IN EXCLAMATORY EXPRESSIONS

1 You use **how** with **can** and **could** to express surprise or annoyance:

How can you possibly think he doesn't love you?
How could he have found out?
How could you be so careless?

2 You use **how** in exclaiming about a quality, as a form of emphasis. In direct speech this can sound rather old-fashioned:

How blue the sky is!
Champagne! How lovely!
He commented on how efficiently she'd organized the meeting.
We all know how easily accidents happen.

•••• however, how ever ••••

This section deals with the different uses of **however**, as an adverb, and as a conjunction. It also looks at how people use **however** or **how ever** as an emphatic way of beginning a question.

AS A SENTENCE ADVERB

You use **however** to contrast what you are saying with what has been said previously:

It was an interesting play; the acting, however, was terrible.
I didn't like him; I learnt to work with him successfully, however.
However, I'd recovered by the next day.

ⓘ Notice that **however** as a sentence adverb can be positioned at the beginning of a sentence, between the subject and the verb, or at the end of the sentence.

AS A CONJUNCTION

However is also used to indicate that a situation will not change according to the degree or extent of something.

1 **However** is used with adjectives, adverbs, and words expressing things such as amount, distance and time, to comment that the degree or amount make no difference to what you are saying:

However well she did, however hard she tried, he never said an encouraging word.
However hard she tries, Joan will never forget February 6, 1971.

2 You use **however** to indicate that the way you do something makes no difference to the situation:

You'll enjoy a cup of this coffee, however you choose to make it.
However you decide to make your journey, I suggest that you do it this year.

AS AN EMPHATIC FORM OF 'HOW'

How ever or **however** is used as an emphatic form of **how**, often expressing surprise or concern:

How ever did you know that?
However did you do it, Rosie?

.... hundred, thousand, million ....

The numbers **hundred**, **thousand** and **million** behave in the same way.

1 You can use **a** or **one** with these numbers, but they cannot stand by themselves without a determiner:

There were about a thousand marchers (not *about thousand marchers*).
They sacked one hundred civil servants.
They've sold a million books in the first year.

2 After a plural number, **hundred**, **thousand** and **million**, when used as determiners, do not add **s**. You can add an **s** if you are thinking arithmetically of individual units of a hundred, thousand or million:

five hundred workers (but *ten hundreds are a thousand*)
six thousand demonstrators (but *a thousand thousands are a million*)
ten million suns (but *a thousand millions make a billion*).

3 AmE and BrE have different ways of saying numbers such as 248 or 6543. BrE inserts **and** before the 'tens' number (*two hundred and forty eight*), and AmE doesn't (*six thousand five hundred forty three*).

.... hurt, pains, discomfort ....

Hurt may be used in many different ways. When used as a verb, sometimes it takes an object and sometimes not. You may **hurt** part of your body, or part of your body may **hurt**. You may **hurt** someone, or you may **hurt** yourself.

There are also many different ways of describing pain and discomfort. These will be dealt with in the second part of the entry.

HURT

1 with an object

When **hurt** takes an object, that object may be a reflexive pronoun, a person, or a part of the body.

- You **hurt yourself**, or **hurt** part of your body, when you do something that causes you to be injured:

Be careful or you'll hurt yourself.
I hurt my shoulder when I was having a shower.
He'd hurt his back and couldn't walk very well.

- You say that something **hurts** a part of your body if it is causing you pain in that area:
  I don't like these earphones – they hurt my ears.
- You **hurt** someone else when you make them feel pain:
  Don't hurt him!
  Has he hurt you?
  I'm sorry. I hope I didn't hurt you.

2 without an object

- Part of your body **hurts** or **is hurting** when you feel pain in it:
  My hip hurts.
  I can't understand why my chest hurts.
- Something that you do, or that someone does to you, **hurts** if it makes you feel pain:
  Ouch! That really hurts!
  Did it hurt when they gave you the injection?

3 as an adjective

Hurt also acts as an adjective, coming after a linking verb:

'He's hurt!' Jack shouted.
People were screaming. Some children were badly hurt.
Luckily, nobody was hurt.

> ⓘ **Hurt** never comes before a noun. If you want to place the adjective before the noun, you should use **injured**.

DIFFERENT KINDS OF PAIN AND DISCOMFORT

1 pain, painful

- You are **in pain**, or you **have a pain** when you have an unpleasant feeling of discomfort in your body because you are ill or have been hurt. **Pain** does not describe a specific kind of discomfort:
  On 10 May, Richard Baxter's mother died in great pain.
  Jack quickly withdrew his hand with a cry of pain.
  She felt a sudden pain across her back.
  I felt sick and I had a pain in my tummy.
- Something that is **painful** causes you pain:
  This is an extremely painful condition.
  Boris suffered a painful death.
  I can't put my socks on because of my painful ankles.

2 sore

- Something that is **sore** is very sensitive and hurts when you touch it. It may also be red in colour:
  I've got a sore throat.
  He sat back, rubbing his eyes. They looked red and sore.
  I find that using an electric shaver makes your face sore.

- People sometimes say that part of their body is **sore** if it hurts when they move, or if it is causing them any kind of pain:

  'Is your ankle still sore?' 'Only if I forget and run on it.'
  She stretched out her sore leg, leaned against the wall and closed her eyes.

3 tender

Part of your body is **tender** if it hurts when it is touched:

The doctor felt the broken ankle gently, knowing that it was tender.

4 smart

Part of your body **smarts** when you feel a sharp stinging pain there:

Her eyes smarted with tears.

5 sting

If part of your body, such as your eyes or skin, **stings**, or if a wound **stings**, you experience a sudden sharp, hot pain; something you put on your body **stings** if it causes you to feel this kind of pain:

'It stings slightly, that's all,' she said bravely.
Ouch! That stings!

6 throb

Part of your body or a pain **throbs** when it beats strongly and painfully:

My thumb was throbbing where I'd cut it on the piece of glass.
A dull pain throbbed at the back of his head.

7 ache

- You **ache**, or a part of you **aches**, when you have a continuous, dull rather than sharp, pain:

  It was a warm, sunny day and my feet were starting to ache.
  Stop now, you're making my arm ache.
  I ache all over!

- An **ache** is a continuous dull pain:

  aches and pains
  He moved again to ease the ache in his back.

- You use **-ache** with **head** and **stomach** to form countable nouns, and with **back**, **ear** and **tooth** to form usually uncountable nouns that mean pain in that part of the body:

  I had a terrible headache yesterday.
  A child with toothache was receiving treatment from the dentist.

8 You can make all the verbs above into adjectives by adding **-ing**:

Susan rubbed her smarting eyes.
They had worked in the sun, with bent backs and aching arms.

•••• hung, hanged ••••

Hung and **hanged** are both used as the past tense and past participles of the verb **hang**. **Hang** has two meanings, which behave differently from each other.

1 **hangs, hanging, hung, hung**
You **hang** something somewhere, such as on a hook, rail or line when you fix the top part of it there, leaving the rest held loosely above the ground; something **hangs** when it is held in this way:

She hung her wet raincoat on a peg in the hall.
A blue dressing-gown was hanging on the back of the bathroom door.

2 **hangs, hanging, hanged**
To **hang** a person is to kill them by tying a rope round their neck and removing the support from under their feet:

Christie was convicted of murder and hanged in London on 15 July 1953.
A young man hanged himself after arguing with his girlfriend.

hyphen

➤ See **punctuation**.

idioms and collocations

WHAT IS AN IDIOM?

The term 'idiom' is not an easily defined one – it can refer to many kinds of words and phrases. The traditional definition of an idiom is 'a group of words which has a different meaning from the sum of its parts'. This means that knowing the meanings of all the words in a phrase will not necessarily help you to understand the meaning of the whole phrase.

In some cases it is possible to make a good guess at the meaning of an idiom, because the image created is an obvious one, *eg* **look like thunder** [= look angry], but in others it is virtually impossible to do so.

Five main kinds of idiom are:

- metaphorical expressions, for example, **make someone's blood boil** [= make someone angry] or **knock it off!** [= stop doing that!]
- sayings, for example, **that's the way the cookie crumbles** [= we must accept some of the unpleasant things in life]
- some phrasal verbs which have a fixed element, for example, **live it up** [= have a good time going to parties, etc]
- proverbs and variations on proverbs, for example **a bird in the hand ...** [= it's not worth giving up something you have now, even when there's a possiblity of having something better in the future]
- some foreign or Latin phrases which are commonly used in English, for example, **fait accompli** [= something already decided] and **ad infinitum** [= for ever]

WHAT IS A COLLOCATION?

Every language contains many possible combinations of words. Some of these combinations recur more frequently than others. Learning these combinations can help you to sound much more natural when speaking a foreign language.

The most common combinations, or 'collocations' in English are structured as follows:

- adjective + noun: *grave danger*, *deep regret*
- verb + noun: *show interest*, *cancel an order*
- verb + adverb: *read avidly*, *work hard*
- noun + verb: *fears subsided*, *peace reigned*
- verb + noun: *have a bath*, *make friends*

1 **common or weak collocations**

Combinations of words such as **have lunch** or **make a cake** are known as 'weak collocations'. This means that although these words are often found together, they also appear in thousands of other combinations in the language. These are the kind of collocations that you pick up in the early stages of learning a language.

2 **medium-strength collocations**

Combinations such as **finely crafted** and **raving mad** are known as 'medium-strength collocations'. This means that when you see one of the words in the group, you can say that there is a high probability that the other one will be there too. These are the kind of collocations that make English sound natural and flowing.

3 **strong collocations**

Strong collocations are combinations of words that are firmly fixed together, and which do not change. Idioms, fixed phrases (such as **do as you please**) and some phrasal verbs (such as **live it up**) are all strong collocations. Many strong collocations appear in dictionaries of idioms; fixed phrases can usually be found in a good learners' dictionary.

•••• if ••••

The conjunction **if** usually introduces a *conditional* clause: a subordinate clause containing a *condition*.

A condition is something that, if it applies, makes the main clause a possibility (*If you bend it too far, it'll break*). Both *real* and *imagined* conditions can follow **if**.

The **if**-clause can come before or after the main clause.

The conditional-clause form with **if** is not only used for presenting conditions. It can be heard, for instance, in polite requests (*I'd be most grateful if you could give me a lift*). **If** is also used, like **whether**, to introduce indirect questions (*I wondered if I was doing the right thing.*)

➤ See also **conditional clauses** and the entry **unless**.

REAL CONDITIONS

People apply the term *real* to conditions that represent real circumstances, that is, things that actually happen in the present, or are likely to happen in the future, or actually happened in the past.

1 **the present** (regular occurrences)

If-sentences relating to the present often refer to something that *always* happens, or is *always* the case, in a particular circumstance:

If you suggest anything new, they just look at you in amazement.
If you pay by cheque, you don't need a receipt.

2 **the future**

If-sentences expressing a real condition relating to the future have a *present* tense in the **if**-clause:

I'll take a taxi if she needs the car herself.
You'll be punished if you're discovered.

3 directions and advice relating to the present and future

In a present or future context, an **if**-clause is often followed by an imperative:

If you need advice, ask an expert.
If you need to phone back, do so as soon as possible.

4 regular occurrences in the past

If-sentences relating to the past usually refer to something that *always* happened in a particular circumstance:

If it rained we took the bus.

5 There can be times when **if** has a meaning similar to **since** or **as** and it is used to introduce a situation that you know is true. These clauses may apply to the present, past or future:

If you're going to be silly [as you are being], *we'll stop the class now.*
I apologize if my remarks offended you [I realize they did].
If (or *Since*) *you get so much sleep, why are you tired all the time?*
If I have a criticism [and I do have this small one] *it is that the beer isn't cold enough.*

UNREAL CONDITIONS

The term *unreal* is applied to *imagined* conditions, that is, circumstances that do not exist in the present, did not exist in the past, and may not exist in the future. With *unreal* conditions, you move the verb tenses one stage back into the past in the **if**-clause, and you use a form of one of the modal auxiliary verbs **would**, **should**, **could** or **might** in the main clause.

1 in the present

In unreal **if**-sentences relating to the present, you use a past tense in the **if**-clause, and **would**, **should**, **could** or **might** in the main clause. **Would** is the usual modal. **Should** is sometimes used (with the same sense as **would**) with **I** and **we**, and the contracted pronoun + **'d** forms (**I'd**, **you'd**, **he'd**, **they'd**, and so on) are very frequent. **Could** is used to mean 'would be able to', and **might** to mean 'would perhaps':

If I had any energy left, I'd throw you out.
I should buy it if I needed it.
You could afford to buy some nice clothes if you stopped smoking.

> ⓘ
> - You can use either **was**, or the subjunctive **were**, after **I**, **he**, **she**, or **it** in the **if-** clause. **Were** is usual in a formal context, quite common in an informal one, and regular in AmE:
>   *'What would you have for dinner if I weren't* (or *wasn't*) *here?'*
>   *'Something easy.'*
> - Notice the use of **if I were you** to give advice:
>   *I'd drink it while it's hot, if I were you.*

2 in the past

In unreal **if**-sentences relating to the past, you use the past perfect tense in the **if**-clause and the combinations **would have**, **should have**, **could have** or **might have** in the main clause:

If I had stayed at university, I would (or *should*) *never have needed a job.*
If she had not been feeling so depressed, Celia might have laughed.
I'm sure you could have got tickets at the door if you had arrived early.

3 in the future

The form used for unreal conditions in the present (see section **1** above) often has a reference to the future (*I could afford more if I stopped smoking*), but there are also ways of showing more specifically that you are referring to the future:

- **should** (*if I should die ...*)

  You can use the combination **should** + infinitive, with second and third person as well as first person, in the **if-**clause. The use of **should** makes the possibility sound rather unlikely; this impression can be increased by adding **happen to**:

  There will be no problem if he should change his mind.
  If you should happen to pass a chemist's, could you get me some cough sweets?

- **were to**, **was to** (*if I were to die ...*)

  You can use **were** or **was** with a **to-**infinitive in the **if-**clause:

  If I were to use one word to describe his life, I would say 'colourful'.

> ⓘ You can use the 'unreal past' construction, that is, the *past perfect* tense in the **if-**clause, and a modal + **have** in the main clause, to talk about present or future situations that are not possible any longer, because things have turned out differently:
> *Dad would have been a hundred this year if he'd been alive still.*

➤ See **conditional clauses** and **inversion** for the inverted conditional forms without **if**, *eg* **were I**, **had I** and **should you**.

OTHER USES

1 polite requests

If is often used with **will**, **would**, **can** and **could** to express requests, invitations or instructions politely. The conditional form here is used for distancing effect, and there is no question of a real condition waiting to be fulfilled:

If you'd wait in the library, I'll be down in a minute.
'Shall I pass the message on?' 'Oh please, if you would.'
I'd prefer it if you could attend to this first.
I've got something to discuss with you, if you wouldn't mind listening for a minute.
We would be so pleased if you could dine with us on 15 March.

2 ellipsis

- Ellipsis is possible and common in the **if-**clause. A pronoun subject and the verb can often be omitted, and **not** and **so** can replace the whole clause:

  Remember his advice: if asked [= if you are asked] *about the incident, tell the truth.*
  Try if possible [= if it is possible] *to have a hot breakfast.*

I'll certainly call if necessary [= if it is necessary].
Does your ticket number end with a zero? If so, you've won a prize; if not, bad luck.

■ **if any, if ever**

You use **if** with words like **any** and **ever** to allow for the possibility that what you are saying may not be applicable:
It was clear that he had few, if any [= in fact, probably no], *political friends.*
I had seldom, if ever [in fact, probably never], *met anyone like him.*

3 indirect questions
You can use **if** like **whether**, in reporting questions, and to ask questions indirectly:
A few children asked if it was a 'drama workshop'.
I don't know if I'll be free then.
I wonder if you'd help me with these boxes?
Do you mind if I speak frankly?

> ⓘ You can use **if** or **whether** after a verb that implies a question or a doubt, such as **ask**, **wonder**, or **doubt** but after other verbs, such as **decide** or **discuss**, **whether** is usually preferred:
> *Decide whether* (rather than *if*) *it's really what you want.*

•••• ill, sick ••••

Both **ill** and **sick** are used to describe people who are not well, or suffering from bad health.

ILL

1 **Ill** usually comes after a linking verb, so that it is more common to say **the baby is ill**, rather than referring to *an ill baby*, for example:
She had been ill for some time.
'What is the matter?' asked Marilla. 'Are you ill?'
You were very kind to me when I was ill.

2 If speakers do place **ill** before the noun, **ill** frequently follows an adverb like **terminally, mentally** or **seriously**:
The hospice helps terminally ill people.

3 **Ill** also frequently comes before the noun in the collocation **ill health**:
It was from this time that he began to suffer from serious ill health.

SICK

1 **Sick** can come before a noun or after a linking verb. When it comes before the noun, it is most frequently found with the nouns **child, children** and **people**:
They say that too many sick people are dying.

2 Below are examples of how **sick** is used after the noun it describes:
If you're sick you have to get a medical certificate.
You'll get sick if you don't eat sensibly.

3 **Sick** frequently forms part of common phrases and collocations related to taking time off work or school because of illness. Someone who is **off sick**, for example, cannot go to work or classes because they are ill, and **sick leave** is time taken off work or school because of illness:

What should I do if an employee is off sick?
She's had five times more sick leave than any of the others.

4 When **sick** is used in certain ways, it refers specifically to *vomiting*. If you **feel sick**, you feel as if you are going to vomit, and if you **have just been sick**, you have just vomited.

When **sick** is used with the verb **be**, the speaker needs to show in some way that they are talking about an action (vomiting), rather than a state (being ill):

Maybe it was then that he started feeling sick.
They tried to drink the water, which made them sick.
Millie was sick on someone's hat when we were on the roller-coaster.

•••• immediately, the moment, the instant ••••

1 Something happens **immediately** when it happens at once or without delay:

I heard the shooting and knew what it was immediately.
The restaurant was plain, and we immediately liked it.
Immediately, Lucien stood up and put his coat on.

2 One thing happens **immediately after** another when it follows at once or without delay:

Immediately after dinner he called the hospital.
We had to leave for London immediately after breakfast.
Dry your hair immediately after you have washed it.

3 You can use **immediately** as a conjunction with the same meaning as **as soon as**:

I shall phone them immediately I've finished my lunch.
His personality seems to change immediately he gets behind the wheel of a car.

—— imperatives ——

You use **imperatives** to give people orders and instructions. The typical form of an imperative is the infinitive form of a verb without **to**:

Come and sit beside me.
Stand back, please.

You form negative imperatives with the auxiliary verb **do**:

Please do not lean on the glass.
Don't cry.

1 You can use imperatives for purposes other than to give people orders and instructions. You can use them:

- to beg, or plead with, someone, to do or not do something:

  'I'm so sorry.' 'Please forget it; it's quite OK.'

- to make suggestions:
  Stay here for the night – we have a spare room.
- to express encouragement:
  Go on, you can do it if you try.
  Don't give up now.
- to offer people things, or invite them to do something:
  Have a doughnut.
  Take a seat.
- to express good wishes, or, as a form of extreme rudeness, unpleasant ones:
  Have a lovely time.
  Enjoy yourselves.
  Get lost.
- with **do**, to express an instruction, plea or invitation forcefully. **Do** can be used to stand for the whole phrase:
  Do look where you're going.
  May I take a leaflet? Please do.

2 You use the verb **be** in the imperative when telling people how to behave; notice that you can use auxiliary **do** with imperative **be**:
Don't be shy.
Do be sensible.

3 You can put **always** and **never** before a verb in the imperative. Notice the position with **don't**:
Always make sure you are visible at night.
Never say die.
Don't ever lie [= never lie] *to me again.*

> ⓘ English verbs have no imperative form for use with the first person or third person. Instead you use **let**. With the first person plural the form is usually **let's**, or, very formally, **let us**:
> *Let's stop there.*
> *Let me think; I know what we should do.*
> *Let her try herself, if she thinks she can do it better.*
> *Let this be a lesson to you.*
> ➤ See also **let**.

IMPERATIVES WITH A SUBJECT

1 **You** can be added before an imperative to express annoyance or to give emphasis to an invitation or instruction:
You just stay still and rest for a while.
You do as you're told and don't argue.

2 You can direct an instruction at people by using a name, noun or pronoun before the imperative:
Parents with small children please come forward first.
Somebody turn off the lights.

3 Put **don't** first to form a negative instruction with a subject:

Don't you dare breathe a word.
Don't anyone move!

4 You can use a range of question tags with imperatives: *could you? would you? can you? will you? won't you?*

Help me move this table, would you?
You'll go to the doctor now, won't you?
Open the door for me, will you?

- After a negative imperative you use **will you?**:
  Don't tell them I'm here, will you?
- After **let's** you use **shall we?**:
  Let's hurry, shall we?
- **Can't you?** usually expresses impatience:
  Relax, can't you?

—— imperfect ——

The **imperfect** tense is an old name for the **past progressive** tense, as in:

*I **was washing** my hair when the doorbell rang.*

.... in ....

The preposition **in** is used in expressions about: *place* and *position*; *time*; *state, situation* and *arrangement*; *areas of activity*; and in certain numerical expressions. With certain verbs **in** can be used like **into**, as a preposition of *direction*. The adverb **in** has both *position* and *direction* senses.

➤ See also **inside**.

AS A PREPOSITION

1 place and position

As a preposition of position or place, **in** has the following uses:

- **final position** as an alternative to **into**, to suggest a final destination with verbs that indicate position as well as movement, such as **put**, **throw**, **drop**, and **fall**:
  She put the mirror back in her bag.
  She threw her coat in the corner.
  He screwed up the note and dropped it in the bin.
- **place of arrival** where **into** is not possible, after verbs that put the emphasis on arrival somewhere, such as **arrive** itself, or **place**:
  Gorbachev arrived in Berlin yesterday.
  Bowls of fresh flowers had been placed in each bedroom.
- **enclosed or covered positions**:
  The knives are in the top drawer.
  an object wrapped in brown paper
- **clothes and colours**:
  She arrived in a sweater and jeans.
  You look good in red.

- **locations**:

  She must be in the library.
  The children are in bed.
  He was in his room.
  They had a pond in their garden.
  a company with offices in London, Paris and New York
  I visited her in hospital.

- **small vehicles**:

  They arrived in a taxi.

➤ For the difference between **in** and **on** with forms of transport, see **transport**.

- **areas and surfaces**:

  He glanced at himself in the mirror.
  The tower in the painting is the Tower of London.
  As she bent over she felt a pain in her back.

- **weather and environment**:

  Don't lie in the sun for too long.
  trees bending in the wind

2 inclusion

- **groups**:

  Please wait in the queue.
  There were fifty runners in the first race.

- **books, plays and films**:

  Please read the explanation in chapter 2.
  a poignant moment in the film

3 time

- **periods, seasons, years, months**:

  in 1996
  in the early sixties
  They should be watered more in summer.
  I met her one day in December.

- **taking no longer than**:

  completed in two years
  We got there in six hours.

- **at the end of the stated time**:

  See you in two days' time.
  We'll be eating in a quarter of an hour.

- **morning, afternoon, evening, night**:

  single occurrences:

  I woke twice in the night.
  Lucy rang back in the evening.

regular occurrences or unvarying situations:

I work better in the morning.
We often play games in the evening.

But notice that you say **at night** for unvarying situations or routines:

It isn't safe to go out alone at night.

➤ For differences between **in**, **for** and **during** a period of time, see **during**.

ⓘ With dates and the days of the week, the usual preposition is **on**, not **in**:
See you on Wednesday.
His birthday's on the second of April.

➤ See **dates** and **day**.

- **distinguishing between a.m. and p.m.**:

four in the afternoon
Do you know what the time is? Four o'clock in the morning.
He called about six in the evening.

4 states

- **shapes and arrangements**:

piled in a heap
The children stood in a circle.

- **states, circumstances and conditions**:

I'm in a hurry.
They're in a panic.
furniture in very poor condition
We stood in silence.
We'll talk in private.
He must be in love.

- **during, or as a result of, states or activities**:

I knocked over the lamp in my excitement.
In the confusion three prisoners escaped.

- **in + -ing form of verb**:

In unlocking [= during the process of unlocking] *the door, she managed to bend the key.*

- **form of communication**:

It's written in code.
Please put your suggestions in writing.
Names are listed in alphabetical order.

5 specification or qualities

- **area of activity, or subject area**:

new advances in cancer research
She'd like a career in television.

- **point or aspect**:

  She was a marvellous mother in every way.

- **colour**:

  I'm looking for a suit in pale grey.
  This model comes in blue, red, white or silver.

- **dimension**:

  The pool is about ten metres in width.

6 proportions or quantities

- **division**:

  We cut the pizza in three. (see also **into**)

- **proportion**:

  One in three voters were unhappy with government policy.
  The treatment has a one-in-ten chance of success.

- **quantities**:

  Guests arrived on the lawn in twos and threes.

AS AN ADVERB

The adverb **in** expresses both position and direction.

1 position

- You are **in** when you are at a place where you belong, or are expected to be, such as your home or office:

  I stayed in on my own while the others went to the pub.
  I rang the bell, but no-one was in.

➤ See also **inside**.

- **In** often occurs as part of a phrasal verb, indicating the idea of enclosing:

  Do you shut the cat in or out at night?
  I lost the key and was locked in.

2 direction

- **As an adverb of direction, in** has a wider range of uses than the preposition. It corresponds to the preposition **into**:

  The door opened and in walked Anna.
  Go straight in; they're expecting you.
  Aren't you going to ask me in?
  Come on in! The water's lovely and warm.

- Notice also these examples of **in** expressing the idea of things arriving where they are expected:

  Her plane was late in at the airport.
  Just complete the form and send it in.

•••• in case ••••

In case is a *conjunction* which you use to introduce a *precaution*. In AmE it is sometimes used in the same way as **if**.

1 You do one thing **in case** another happens when you make arrangements for dealing with it *before* it happens, or take precautions to prevent it happening:

He always keeps a guitar near him in case he gets an idea for a song.
He was not allowed near the canal in case he had another accident.

2 In a present context, a verb in the *present* tense is used after **in case** to refer to the *future*:

She must be watched carefully in case her condition suddenly changes.

> ⓘ Notice the difference between **if** and **in case**. With **if** you wait till something happens before taking action; with **in case** you take action before it happens:
> *I always thought of an excuse if my colleagues wanted me to have a drink.*
> *I picked up my little brother in case he got hurt.*

3 You can use **in case of** like a preposition. It sometimes has a meaning close to that of **if**:

It is advisable to have some candles in case of [= if there is a] *power failure.*

•••• indeed ••••

1 You use **indeed** after an adjective or adverb to give it emphasis, normally in combination with **very**:

This is very unusual indeed.
We've done very well indeed with sales this year.
Thank you very much indeed for your help.

2 You can also use **indeed** when agreeing with, or confirming, something in a rather formal way. In this use it occurs in short replies:

'Is it the ninth today?' 'It is indeed.'
'That was fortunate.' 'Indeed it was.'

3 In its *confirming* sense, **indeed** can be used to add something that supports an argument:

The factory is not doing very well; indeed, it'll probably have to close down.

4 **Indeed** can be used in final position to express surprise, disbelief, anger or scorn at what someone has just said:

'She thinks you'll give her the money.' 'Does she indeed!'

—— indefinite pronouns ——

The **indefinite pronouns** are words such as **somebody**, **nobody**, **everyone** and **anything**, which are used to refer to people or things without saying who or which they are:

There's somebody on the phone for you.
He didn't say anything.
No-one spoke.
Everything's gone wrong.

1 The full list of indefinite pronouns is:

anybody	*everybody*	*nobody*	*somebody*
anyone	*everyone*	*no-one*	*someone*
anything	*everything*	*nothing*	*something*

➤ See the entries for the individual indefinite pronouns for more information about them.

2 **-one** and **-body**

The indefinite pronouns referring to people have two forms, ending in **-body** or ending in **-one**. There is no difference in meaning or use between these two forms:

Don't tell anyone (or *anybody*).

3 You use a singular verb with the indefinite pronouns:

Is anyone coming with me?
No-one knows what happened.
Everyone has a right to their opinion.

4 Although the indefinite pronouns referring to people (*eg* **someone**, **everybody**) are singular, the plural pronouns **they**, **them**, **themselves** and the possessives **their** and **theirs** are often used, especially in informal English, to refer back to them:

If anyone wants to come with me, they'd better hurry.

More formally, people say **he or she**, **him or her** or **his or her**:

Everybody has a right to his or her own opinion.

However, **they** is the normal form in question tags:

No-one knows what happened, do they?
Everybody has a right to their own opinion, haven't they?

➤ For more information see the entry **he, he or she, they?**

5 You can use adjectives with indefinite pronouns, but they always come *after* the indefinite pronoun:

Did you meet anybody nice?
There's nothing special to report.

indirect speech

➤ See **reporting**.

infinitives

The *infinitive* of a verb is its base form, the form by which you normally refer to verbs, *eg* **go**, **do**, **have**, **be**, **eat**.

Infinitives are often used with **to**:

She tried to scream.
The dance was lovely to watch.

INFINITIVES WITHOUT 'TO'

There are four cases where the base form without **to** is used, rather than a **to**-infinitive:

1 modal verbs

The infinitive without **to** is used after the modal auxiliary verbs:

- **will**, **shall**, **would**, **should**, **can**, **could**, **may**, **might** and **must**:

I must see you.
Would you open the door?
They may still be alive.
We shall know more tomorrow.

- **need**, **dare** and **had better**:

Need you swear like that?
I daren't look.
Hadn't you better tell me all about it?

> ⓘ Notice that **ought** and **used** are both followed by a **to**-infinitive:
> *You ought to know.*
> *She used to write poetry.*

➤ For more information, see the entries for the individual modal verbs.

2 other verbs

- **of sensing and observing**

The structure here is verb + object + infinitive:

I saw him turn left.
I didn't hear you come in.

- **let**, **help**, **make**

She helped him get (or *helped him to get*) *dressed*.
I let them use my phone.
I made him put away his toys.

3 why, why not

Why and **why not** can be combined with an infinitive without **to** to make suggestions:

Why write when you can telephone?
Why not take a break?

4 second infinitive after conjunctions or prepositions

A second infinitive after the conjunctions **and** and **or**, and after **as**, **but**, **except**, **like**, or **than** used as prepositions, needs no **to**:

I want to go home and forget all about it.
They have nothing to do but make trouble.
It was easier to keep quiet than explain the whole thing.
I always wanted to do something interesting like learn a language.

TO-INFINITIVES

1 forms

As well as the basic infinitive form, there are progressive, perfect and passive forms:

I ought to be working. [progressive infinitive]
I'm sorry not to have contacted you earlier. [perfect infinitive]
The plants have to be watered once a day. [passive infinitive]
We seem to have been waiting for hours. [perfect progressive infinitive]
It appears to have been very badly managed. [perfect passive infinitive]

2 negatives

To make a **to**-infinitive negative you usually put **not** before it:

I was anxious not to be late.
He appeared not to have heard of me.

3 split infinitives

People 'split' infinitives when they insert an adverb between **to** and the infinitive form of a verb:

He never gave himself time to properly recover before he went back to work.

Some people regard this as a mistake. They avoid it by placing the adverb before or after the whole **to**-infinitive:

He never gave himself time to recover properly.

4 grammar of the to-infinitive

- A **to**-infinitive can have various functions in a sentence:

  To give up now would be very silly. [subject]
  I want to get into town early. [object]
  My aim is to complete the work by June. [complement after **is**]

- The preparatory **it** is often used as an alternative to an infinitive subject or complement:

  It would be very silly to give up now.
  It is my aim to complete the work by June.

- A construction with **for** is used when the subject of the infinitive is being supplied or when it is different from the subject of the sentence:

  It would be very silly for us to give up now.
  My aim is for the editors to finish the work by June.
  I'm quite happy for you to use our database.
  Is it possible for us to begin by nine?

USES OF THE TO- INFINITIVE

1 with verbs

- A lot of verbs can be followed by the **to**-infinitive of another verb:

He started to laugh.
We arranged to meet next day.
I intend to try.
He refused to help.
What time do you want to leave?
She seemed to be nervous.
I decided to stop there.
She pretended not to have heard.
I'll try to mend it.
Did you remember to feed the cat?

> ⓘ The infinitive can be dropped after **to** if it is clear from the previous context:
> *I invited her to come to the pub, but she didn't want to.* [= she didn't want to come].

- A lot of verbs can be followed by an object + **to**-infinitive:

I advised her to wait.
I want you to come too.
May I remind you to lock your rooms?
We allowed them to stay.
Who taught you to cook?
I warned her not to switch the freezer off.

- Verbs that are customarily followed by **for**, or involve the use of **for**, can have the construction **for** + object + **to**-infinitive:

I arranged for her to see a specialist.
He asked for his request to be reconsidered.
They should have waited for you to catch up.

2 with adjectives

Certain kinds of adjectives can be followed by a **to**-infinitive:

- **representing attitudes and reactions**:

I was afraid to say anything.
We're all eager to help.
They were amazed to see me.
I was relieved to get your letter.

- **representing possibility or certainty**:

It's certain to fail.
She's unlikely to agree.
Were you able to adjust it?
It's liable to collapse.

> ⓘ The infinitive can be dropped after **to** if is already clear from the previous context:
> *'I suppose she'll get the job?' 'She's certain to.'*

- **assessing actions**:

It's pointless to argue about it.
It was kind of you to offer.
You're lucky to be alive.
We were wrong to suspect her.
It was stupid of me not to listen.
You're welcome to join us.

- **superlatives**

Superlative adjectives, and determiners such as **first**, **last** and **next**, and **only** are often followed by a **to**-infinitive:

I was the last person to see him alive.
I'm not the only one to have come to that conclusion.
She was the first woman to be appointed.

- **subject becomes object**

The subject of the sentence can be the object of the infinitive. Instead of saying, for instance, *it's so interesting to watch the children*, you can say *the children are so interesting to watch*:

I've got the data on a floppy disk, all ready to load.
Some of these leaves are quite nice to eat.

The construction often ends with a preposition:

He's an interesting person to talk to.
Children are so rewarding to work with.

3 with nouns

- after certain nouns related to verbs:

They respected my wish to remain anonymous.
I had no desire to stay any longer.
There's no need to reply.
We all know about her decision to quit.

- after certain nouns related to adjectives:

You were an idiot to let him have the house.
It's a pleasure to see the sun.
It's a privilege to work with you.

- after 'forward-looking' nouns such as **time, plan, idea**:

Is it really a good idea for us all to travel in the same car?
The plan is for Jim to leave first.
It's time to pack up.

- after nouns, expressing purpose or function:

I looked for a taxi to take us to the station.
There's cream to pour over your fruit, if you need it.
Fortunately I'd brought a rug to sit on.
(Formal alternative: *I'd brought a rug on which to sit.*)

- **to**-infinitives are common after indefinite (**some**, **any**, etc) or quantifying (**much**, **many**, etc) determiners and pronouns:

I don't seem to have any clean clothes to put on.
I've got nothing to wear.
Have you all got something to drink?
Leave yourself plenty of time to buy your ticket.
There's always lots for the children to do.
There was nowhere to talk privately.

4 other uses

- after **wh**-words in indirect speech:

Could you tell me which bus to take?

I couldn't think who to invite.
Show me how to do it.
Tell me when to stop.

- used like **in order to** or **so as to**, to introduce purpose:

  I'd gone into town to do some shopping.

- after **enough** and **too**:

  It was warm enough to eat breakfast outside.
  They're too stupid to know the difference.

- some set phrases:

  To put it simply, prices will go up.
  To be honest, it wasn't any of my business.
  To be fair, he was just doing his job.

•••• in front of ••••

1 in front of and before

You use **in front of** rather than **before** as the opposite of **behind**. But notice that if you are **in front of** something or someone, you can be facing towards them or facing away from them:

I stood up in front of the class.
The man in front of me turned to face me.
There's a lamp post in front of [= on the same side of the road as] *our house.*

2 in front of and opposite

When there is something such as a road, river or table *between* you and another person or thing, you say that they are **opposite** or **facing** you rather than **in front of** you:

We sat down at the table, and I looked at the man opposite (or *facing*) *me.*
There was a sweetshop just opposite [= on the other side of the road from] *the school.*

> ⓘ AmE speakers usually use **across from** where BrE speakers use **opposite**:
> *I talked to the man sitting across from me at the dinner table.*

—— -ing forms ——

The **-ing** forms of verbs fall into two grammatical classes, present participles (or **-ing** participles), and gerunds, which are called '**-ing** forms' in this book. This entry deals with these gerunds or **-ing** forms. The **-ing** participles are dealt with in more detail in the separate entry **present participles**.

THE DIFFERENCE BETWEEN PRESENT PARTICIPLES AND GERUNDS

1 present participles

- The **-ing** participles, or present participles, are used to make the progressive forms of verbs:
  Who is Natalie dancing with?

- Present participles behave like *adjectives* in that they can be used to describe, qualify, or refer to, nouns:
  He gazed down at the dancing couples. [*dancing* describes *couples*]
  She went dancing along the road. [*dancing* refers to *she*, but also describes the action *went*]

2 gerunds

Gerunds or **-ing** forms are *nouns* (they are often called *verbal nouns*) and can therefore be used as the subjects, objects or complements:

Dancing keeps you fit.
I love dancing.
She's good at dancing.

FEATURES OF -ING FORMS

1 An **-ing** form may take various grammatical forms. Apart from the simple **-ing** form (*eg* **forgetting**), there are passive **-ing** forms (*eg* **being forgotten**), and perfect **-ing** forms (*eg* **having forgotten**):
These important facts are in danger of being forgotten.
She was upset at my having forgotten her birthday.

2 You can use determiners such as **the**, **this** and **that** with **-ing** forms:
The second reading of the bill took place today.
This constant arguing doesn't help the situation.

> ⓘ Notice that the object of the **-ing** form needs **of** before it when **the** comes before the **-ing** form:
> *the singing of hymns* (not *the singing hymns*)

3 Since **-ing** forms are nouns, possessive determiners can be used with them, especially in formal English. They represent the person who is the subject of the **-ing** form:
She was upset at my forgetting her birthday. [= she was upset that I forgot her birthday]

- A possessive **'s** form can be used in place of the possessive determiner:
  I didn't like Jane's inviting herself to join us like that.

4 You can introduce the **-ing** form with **it**:
It's been lovely talking to you.

5 Notices often use **-ing** forms:
NO PARKING
No running in the corridors, please.

-ING FORMS AFTER CERTAIN VERBS

1 Here are some examples using verbs that can be followed by **-ing** forms:

She admitted stealing the disk.
Avoid getting involved.
Would you consider moving to London?
I dislike queuing.
Do you fancy going for a walk?
We gave up trying.
I can't imagine him riding a horse.
I hope you don't mind my mentioning it.
We can't risk waiting any longer.
I suggest changing the subject.
I appreciate your making this effort.
He burst out laughing.
She denies having said that.
We enjoy listening to music.
Finish doing that first.
You can't help wondering
The job will involve working with children.
Practise relaxing your face muscles.
I can't stand wasting time.
I can understand you thinking that.

2 Some verbs can be followed by an **-ing** form or a **to**-infinitive. There can be a slight or even significant difference in meaning or usage:

- After the verbs **advise**, **allow**, **permit** and **forbid**, an **-ing** form is possible when there is no object:

  I advise waiting.
  I advise you to wait.
  We do not allow (or *permit*) *smoking on our flights.*
  We do not allow (or *permit*) *passengers to smoke on our flights.*
  Running in the corridors is forbidden.
  Pupils are forbidden to run in the corridors.

- With the verbs **hate**, **can't bear**, **like**, **love** and **prefer**, the **-ing** form and **to**-infinitive can be used more or less interchangeably. But a **to**-infinitive may suggest a choice, habit or preference, and an **-ing** form the idea of enjoying or not enjoying:

  I hate [= don't want] *to disturb her.*
  Open it now. I can't bear to wait.
  I like [= choose] *to get up early.*
  I hate [= don't enjoy] *queuing.*
  I can't bear lying in the sun.
  I like [= enjoy] *living here.*

  When you use the forms with **would** (**I'd like**, **I'd prefer**, and so on), you always use a **to**-infinitive:

  I'd prefer to wait.
  Thanks, I'd love to join you.

- **Begin**, **start** and **continue** can have an **-ing** form or a **to**-infinitive:

  It started to rain (or *started raining*).
  She began talking (or *began to talk*) *at fifteen months.*
  She continued to work (or *continued working*) *till midnight.*

- Notice that use of the **-ing** form or **to**-infinitive changes the meaning of the verb **stop**:

  I stopped walking (not *stopped to walk*).
  I stopped to [= in order to] *get my breath.*

- You say you **remember doing** something, or that you'll **never forget doing** something, when you are referring to the past:

  Do you remember holidaying in Port St Mary?

I'll never forget swimming in the thunderstorm.

You use a **to-**infinitive to talk about tasks that have to be done, or should have been done:

Remember to ring Daniel.
I forgot to get toothpaste.

- You **regret doing** something that is in the past, that you are sorry about:

  She always regretted not having gone to university.

  You say you **regret to say** something usually when announcing unwelcome news:

  I regret to tell you that the job was given to someone else.

- You **try doing** something as an experiment, to see what it is like, or if it works:

  Peter tried brushing his teeth with soap.

  You **try to do** something when you see if you can do it:

  I tried to carry her, but she was too heavy.

- **Need** and **require** take a passive **to-**infinitive, or an **-ing** form with a passive meaning. You say, for example, that something **needs to be done** or **needs doing**:

  These papers need sorting (or *need to be sorted*).

-ING FORMS AFTER PREPOSITIONS

1 The **-ing** form of the verb is the form you normally use after a preposition:

Thank you for helping.
He disappeared without saying goodbye.
Why not accept the situation instead of arguing?

2 When the time words **after**, **before** and **since** are used as prepositions, they can be followed by an **-ing** form instead of a subordinate clause:

After leaving school [= after I left school] *I did a teaching course.*
Think hard before making [= before you make] *a decision.*
Since writing [= since I wrote] *to you I've had another idea.*

3 Here are some examples of common verbs which are followed by a preposition and then, quite often, an **-ing** form:

Are you accusing me of lying?
Don't depend on winning.
We must prevent them from finding out.
I prefer swimming to cycling.
I believe in experimenting first.
He insisted on waiting.
Are you thinking of marrying?
I'm looking forward to seeing you.

4 Here are some typical examples of nouns and adjectives that are frequently used with a following *preposition + noun*, which may be an **-ing** form:

I'm afraid of flying.
He's clever at finding solutions.
He's used to getting his own way.
She's fond of riding.
Congratulations on winning.
He had difficulty in making decisions.
They have no interest in living.
I hate the idea (or *thought*) *of leaving.*

You're incapable of deceiving anyone. — *the distinction between lying and not telling the whole truth*

She's responsible for running the office. — *Most flights have a ban on smoking.*

I'm sorry for causing all this difficulty. — *She has a good chance of winning.*

> ⓘ Adjectives and nouns that are followed by a preposition + **-ing** form cannot usually be followed by a **to**-infinitive. For example, you can say **I hate the thought of packing** but NOT *I hate the thought to pack*.
> Notice, however, that **proud** can be followed by **of** + **-ing** or a **to**-infinitive: *I'm proud of having been selected* (or *proud to have been selected*).

➤ For the use of a **to**-infinitive with **chance** and **opportunity**, see the entries for these words.

•••• inside ••••

AS A PREPOSITION

- **Inside** carries more emphasis than **in**:

  Inside each drum was a quantity of radioactive waste.
  He pinned the photos inside his desk.
  The dolls fit one inside the other.

- **Inside** is sometimes used with the same meaning as **into**, to express direction:

  He turned left and went inside Brown's Hotel on Albert Street.

- As a preposition of time, **inside** can mean 'in less than':
  A full report is expected inside three months.

AS AN ADVERB

- **position**

  Inside means 'in the enclosed place referred to':

  Soon I was inside, with the door locked after me.
  Inside, the church was empty.
  There was a box on the table, with a key inside.

- **direction**

  Inside means 'into the enclosed place referred to':

  The door opened and Morton walked inside.
  The box rattled when I shook it, so I looked inside.

AS AN ADJECTIVE

We had access to inside information [= information not available to the public].
He put the letter in his inside pocket.

 Notice that the **inside** lane of a motorway or dual carriageway is the one for slower traffic, nearest to the side.

AS A NOUN

Apply the product to the inside of your elbow.

•••• in spite of, despite ••••

You use **in spite of** and **despite** to introduce a circumstance that surprisingly does not prevent the rest of your statement from being true.

1 **In spite of** is a little less formal that despite:

We went to the film with them, in spite of the fact that we'd seen it twice already.

2 **Despite** has the same meaning as **in spite of**. Notice that **despite** is never followed by the preposition **of**:

Despite winning all that money, they say they'll be at work tomorrow.
He still looks young, despite the fact that he's a grandfather.

•••• instead ••••

1 **Instead** on its own is an adverb:

There's no quiche left; would you like pizza instead?
I tried to comfort her, but instead I upset her even more.

2 **Instead of** is the form you use as a preposition:

I suggested lunch at the pub instead of (not *instead*) *the Café Royal.*
Instead of improving things, the new boss has made matters worse.

3 Notice that you use the **-ing** form of a verb, not the infinitive, after **instead of**:

Why don't you just get on with the job instead of moaning? (not *instead of moan* or *instead of to moan*)

—— intentions ——

➤ See pages 288 and 289.

•••• into ••••

Into is a *preposition of direction.*

➤ See also **in** and **inside**.

You use **into** rather than **in** after verbs of movement:

She poured coffee into the cups.
I saw her going into the fish shop.
We crossed the border into Belgium.
He got into his car and drove off.

➤ For details about getting **into** or **on to** forms of transport, see **transport**.

INTENTIONS

Intentions may be expressed in a variety of different ways, depending on whether the intention is definite, vague, firm or formal.

FIXED PLANS

If you have a definite intention, you can say that **you are going to do** something. If you decide that you are going to do something just before, or just as, you mention it, you can say **I think I'll ...**:

I'm going to open a bottle of wine and ask her to marry me.
I'm going to begin by telling you everything.
I think I'll have a drink too.
I think I'll have the soup. I like soup.

1 fixed plans

You can use the present progressive or the future progressive to talk about fixed plans for which you have already made the necessary arrangements, or which you have already planned to do at a fixed time:

I'm having a party next week.
I'm having a few friends round to dinner.
I'll be leaving tomorrow.

2 talking about decisions you've made

When you state your intentions based on a decision you have taken in the past, you can say that **you have decided to do** something:

I've decided to go with Louise to America.
We've decided to get married.

3 negative forms

When you want to state an intention not to do something, you can say that you **are not going to do** something, or that **you have decided not to** do something:

I'm not going to go.
I've decided not to stay the night.

VAGUE INTENTIONS

1 If you have thought about doing something, but you have not made a final decision to do it, you can say that **you are thinking of** doing it, or that **you might** do, or be doing, it:

I'm thinking of going to London for a week.
I might come and visit you on my way home.
'Well, I don't know, I might be going out this evening,' he said.

2 very vague intentions

People sometimes say **I thought I might ...** when they are considering doing something:

I thought I might go and see Mrs Farquhar.
I thought I might move in a couple of years.

3 vague negative intentions

If you want to vaguely say that you do not intend to do something, you can say that **you might not** do it, or that **you don't think you will** do it:

I might not come on Saturday.
I don't think I'll go to the gym tonight.

FIRM DECISIONS

1 You use **I'll** + infinitive when you want to express a spontaneous decision, especially when you are making arrangements or reassuring people:

I'll make sure I'm there on time.
I'll call back later.
I'll give you the money back tomorrow.

2 You use **I won't** + infinitive when you want to state a firm intention not to do something:

We won't be late.
I've tried to persuade them, but they won't come.
I won't let you down.

FORMAL EXPRESSIONS OF INTENTION

1 To express intentions more formally, you can use **intend to**, or, less frequently, **intend + ing**:

She did not intend to argue with him.
I intend doing great things tonight.

2 If you want to emphasize that you are determined to do something, you can say that you **have every intention of doing it**:

I have every intention of marrying her, if she will have me.
Mr Howard said that he had every intention of keeping the money.

3 Even more formally, you can talk about **your intention**:

My intention is not to shock anybody.
It is my intention, as I think I told you, to shape my own life.

4 If you want to formally express a negative intention, you can say **I don't intend to ...** or **I have no intention of -ing**:

I don't intend to make the same mistake again.
I wrote a letter which I had absolutely no intention of sending.

ⓘ Notice that phrases like **I might**, **I'm going to** and **I'll** can be used for expressing unintended actions as well:
Oh no. I'm going to be sick.
I can't do that. I'll fall off!
Will you remind me? I might forget.

INTRODUCTIONS

Introductions take place between people who have never met before. When people introduce themselves or each other, they always give their names, or the names of the people they are introducing, and sometimes more information about them.

This entry deals with introducing yourself and introducing people to each other.

INTRODUCING YOURSELF

1 in neutral contexts

The most common way of introducing yourself is by offering your hand to shake the other person's, possibly greeting them, and saying **I'm ...**(here you give your name):

'Hello,' she said. 'I'm Jane Walsh – I hear you've just moved in next door.'

2 in formal contexts

When introducing yourself formally, you can begin your introduction with a short phrase such as one of those below:

***I don't think we've met**. My name's Oliver King.*
***Allow me to introduce myself**. I'm Howard Taft from The New York Times.*
*'**I'd like to introduce myself**,' said the visitor. 'My name is Peterson.'*

INTRODUCING PEOPLE TO EACH OTHER

1 in neutral contexts

The most common way of introducing two people is by using **This is ...** (here you give the name):

Peter, this is Mrs Gillingham, who is here in Venice with her husband.
Julia, this is Peter Jackson; we met yesterday.

... into continued

SOME COMMON USES

1 collisions:
The van crashed into a wall.
Someone bumped into me and made me spill my coffee.

2 change:
The old castle has been turned into a tourist centre.
Her poems have been translated into several other languages.

3 changing clothes:
I got into my jeans.

4 states and situations:
There's no need to get into such a panic.

5 division:
The country is divided into fifty-two administrative districts.

6 investigation:
There will be an enquiry into the accident.

2 in formal situations

When you are introducing people formally, you can start the introduction with a short phrase like **Let me/May I/I'd like to introduce you to ...** (here you give the name), or **I'd like you to meet ...**:

Let me introduce you to Catherine, my wife.
I'd like to introduce you to Dr Brian Smith, from the University of Sussex.
May I introduce you to Paul Jenkins? Paul, this is Michele Diomede.

3 in informal situations

When you want to introduce people informally, you can start with a short phrase like **Have you two met before?** or **Do you know each other?**:

Have you two met before? Jake, this is Malcolm.
Sorry, do you know each other? Mary, this is an old friend of mine, Trevor.

RESPONDING TO AN INTRODUCTION

In formal situations, people usually say **Nice to meet you** as a response to an introduction. **How do you do** is very formal and is used by older people. Young people, and people in informal situations often just say **Hi** or **Hello**, and sometimes shake hands:

'This is my supervisor, Tim. Tim, this is Mrs Richardson, from Croydon.' 'Pleased to meet you.'
'Lee – Meryl Armitage, my colleague from the laboratory.' 'Pleased to meet you, Meryl.'
'Helen, this is Nigel.' 'Hi.'

introductions

➤ See above.

inversion

Inversion is the way you change the order of subject and verb, for example in questions, so that the statement **She's awake**, becomes **Is she awake?** as a question. Inversion takes place in a variety of grammatical circumstances; the most important are listed and illustrated below.

AUXILIARY + SUBJECT + MAIN VERB

In questions and in certain other structures you put the auxiliary verb before the subject. If there is no auxiliary in the positive statement, use the auxiliary verb **do**. You use this inverted order for the verbs **have** and **be** (as auxiliary verbs, and also when they are acting as ordinary verbs).

1 questions

- **without wh-words**

If the question does not start with a **wh-**word, you simply invert the subject and auxiliary (or non-auxiliary **have** and **be**):

Does he feel guilty?
Are you coming?
Have you finished?
Is she a vegetarian?
Hasn't she any relatives?

> ⓘ Short 'response' questions and question tags drop the main verb:
> *'You've helped me a lot.' 'Have I?'*
> *It makes no sense, does it?*

➤ For more on response questions and question tags see **question tags**.

- **with wh-words**

You use inversion after **wh**-question words:

How does this machine work?
Why didn't you let me know?
Where are those photos?
What are you talking about?

Notice that if the **wh**-word is itself the subject of the verb, there is no inversion:

What happened?
What makes you happy?

> ⓘ Notice that there is no inversion in reported questions, whether or not **wh**-words are used:
> *I wonder what she weighs* (not *what does she weigh*).
> *He asked me where my suitcase was* (not *where was my suitcase*).
> *Do you know if she's at home* (not *Do you know is she at home*) *today?*

2 Isn't it great?

A common structure for exclamations is the *negative question* form, in which there is inversion:

Doesn't that sound childish!

3 Had I realized ...

As a rather formal-sounding alternative to using **if** to introduce a conditional clause, you can invert the subject and an auxiliary:

Had I realized [= if I had realized] *that before, I might have won the case.*

4 so do I

You invert subject and auxiliary after **so** in its elliptical use, referring back to what has just been stated:

'I'm exhausted.' 'So am I.'
Melissa worked for us, and so did her husband.
'I had a big lunch.' 'So did we.'

5 neither do I; nor is she

Inversion takes place after **neither** and **nor** when they introduce a second negative statement:

She didn't give anything away, and nor did I.
I didn't exactly refuse; but neither did I agree.

6 On no account must you tell her.

Negative expressions are sometimes put at the beginning of a clause for emphasis of a rather formal kind, and inversion takes place after them:

Under no circumstances can we agree to this proposal.
At no time was he alone with the deceased person.
Nowhere was it more obvious.

7 Hardly had he spoken ...

Inversion also happens after words that behave as negatives, such as **hardly** and **rarely**, and after expressions containing the word **only**, when they are used in initial position:

Hardly had he finished speaking when the fight started.
Little did I think that I would win.
Only now was he beginning to feel better.

MAIN VERB + SUBJECT

In the following two situations, the whole verb is placed before the subject.

1 Along came a policeman

Adverbs and adverb phrases of place or direction are sometimes placed at the beginning of a clause for emphasis, and cause inversion of any following *intransitive* verb and its subject. In direct speech **here** and **there** frequently occur in initial position:

Above her on the wall hung a portrait of a woman.
Directly opposite was the entrance to the car park.
Here's George.
In walked Lesley.

ⓘ No inversion takes place if the subject is a personal pronoun:
Nearer and nearer he came (not *came he*).
Right, off we go.

➤ See also position of adverbs, section 8, at the entry **adverbs**.

2 'Come here,' ordered the teacher

When presenting direct speech in narrative, the 'saying' verbs often come after the words that were actually said, and before their subjects, unless the subject is a personal pronoun:

'It's ironic,' said George.
'How about a walk?' suggested someone.
'What's he doing these days?' asked Jay.

But:

'Any news of Dad?' he whispered.

INVITATIONS

SPOKEN INVITATIONS

1 The usual way of inviting someone politely is to say **Would you like to...?**, or **I was wondering if you... ?** When you invite someone to come in, help themselves to a drink, etc, you can say **Please ...** + imperative:

Would you like to work for us?
I was wondering if you'd like to come and have a drink?
Please have another glass of champagne.

2 More informally, you can just use the imperative form or the structures **Why don't you ...?** or **How about ...?**:

Have another drink.
Sit down and make yourself at home.
Why don't you come round and I'll cook you a meal?
How about a piece of that chocolate gateau before you go?

3 To add more emphasis, you can use the structures **Do** + imperative or **You must** + infinitive:

Do sit down. What'll you have to drink?
Julian, do come again. And bring Amanda with you next time.
You must come to tea again. I'll ring you.

4 When you want to be very polite and persuasive, you can say **Won't you ...?** or **You will ...?**:

Won't you have another drink?
But you will come again? Soon?

5 When you are speaking formally, or on behalf of a group of people, you can use the phrase **I do hope ...** or **We would like to invite you to ...**:

I do hope you will come up here to visit us.
We would like to invite you to have a look round now.

WRITTEN INVITATIONS

A very formal invitation card is normally written in the third person, using the formula **So-and-so requests the pleasure of the company of so-and-so**. In a letter, you can describe the event, and then add **We do hope you will be able to join us**:

Mr Richard Wilson requests the pleasure of Mr and Mrs David Wright on the occasion of the opening of the Wilson Gallery.
We are giving a cocktail party on ... We hope that you will be able to join us and look forward to seeing you then.

inverted commas

➤ See **punctuation**.

invitations

➤ See above.

irregular verbs

Irregular verbs are verbs in which the past tense and past participle are not formed by adding -**ed** to the base form. Irregular verbs can be grouped into four types.

In all the tables below, which give examples of the various irregular verb types, **A** = the base form, **B** = the third person present singular, **C** = the present participle, **D** = the simple past tense, and **E** = the past participle.

TYPE 1

Verbs that have the same form in their base form, their simple past tense, and their past participle.

A	B	C	D	E
cast	casts	casting	cast	cast
cut	cuts	cutting	cut	cut
let	lets	letting	let	let
put	puts	putting	put	put
split	splits	splitting	split	split

TYPE 2

Verbs that have the same irregular forms in the simple past tense and the past participle.

A	B	C	D	E
bind	binds	binding	bound	bound
bleed	bleeds	bleeding	bled	bled
buy	buys	buying	bought	bought
catch	catches	catching	caught	caught
hear	hears	hearing	heard	heard
keep	keeps	keeping	kept	kept
make	makes	making	made	made
say	says	saying	said	said

TYPE 3

Verbs that have irregular forms, ending in -**t** rather than -**ed**, in the simple past tense and the past participle but also have regular -**ed** forms in the simple past tense and the past participle.

A	B	C	D	E
burn	burns	burning	burnt/burned	burnt/burned
learn	learn	learning	learnt/learned	learnt/learned
spell	spells	spelling	spelt/spelled	spelt/spelled
spoil	spoils	spoiling	spoilt/spoiled	spoilt/spoiled

TYPE 4

Verbs in which the base form, the simple past tense, and the past participle all have different forms.

A	B	C	D	E
begin	begins	beginning	began	begun
bite	bites	biting	bit	bitten
break	breaks	breaking	broke	broken
fly	flies	flying	flew	flown
give	gives	giving	gave	given
know	knows	knowing	knew	known

ring	rings	ringing	rang	rung
see	sees	seeing	saw	seen
shrink	shrinks	shrinking	shrank	shrunk
take	takes	taking	took	taken
write	writes	writing	wrote	written

•••• it ••••

- You use the pronoun **it** as a *substitute* for things already mentioned (*you should read it*).
- You use **it** to talk about such things as the weather and the environment (*It must be at least 40° in here*).
- You use **it** to refer forward, for a variety of purposes, to circumstances you are about to mention (*It's odd that he hasn't telephoned*).
- You use **it** to bring something forward to the beginning of a sentence in order to emphasize it. (*It's Jack I worry about.*)

AS A SUBSTITUE WORD

1 You use **it** to refer to a thing, animal, or even a baby, that has just been mentioned, or that you hearer or reader knows about; **it** has the possessive form **its**:

There's the bank. You walked right past it.
He hit the dog and it bit him.
You should read it; it's an excellent book.
'What's that bright star up there?' 'It's not a star; it's a planet.'

2 You use **it** when asking, or referring to, the identity of someone who is present, or who is speaking on the telephone:

'Who's there?' 'It's me.'
'Hello, it's Anna here.'

ⓘ When identifying people using **it** and a personal pronoun, the objective form is usual:
When the phone rang I thought it might be Mum, but ***it*** *wasn't* ***her*** (not *it wasn't she*) after *all*.

3 You use **it** to refer to a situation, circumstance, fact or proposal:

She was getting tired, but wouldn't admit it.
Don't worry, it doesn't matter.
If it's possible, I'd like to leave by seven.
I don't like it [= *I don't like being*] *in London.*

4 **It** is used to refer back to the indefinite pronouns **everything**, **something**, **anything** and **nothing**, for instance in question tags:

Something always goes wrong, doesn't it?
Nothing's settled yet; it won't be for quite a while.

5 You use **it** as the subject of a clause stating, describing, or asking about, *weather, date, time, distance, environment* or *surroundings*:

It's so cold.
Has it started snowing there?
When we arrived it was thirty degrees below.
Is it half past ten yet?
I keep forgetting what day it is.
It's at least another thirty miles to Norwich.

AS PREPARATORY SUBJECT OR OBJECT

1 You can use **it** as the subject of a clause, to refer forward to something that you are about to mention. **It** can be followed by **be** and an adjective (*It's marvellous ...*), a noun (*It's a shame ...*), or by a verb (*It worries me ...*).

Various constructions are possible after this:

- **a to-infinitive**:

  It's lovely to see you again.
  It'd be a shame not to see the castle.
  It worries me to see errors like this.

- **for + to-infinitive**:

  It would be a good idea for you to have a holiday.

- **an -ing form**:

  It's no good sitting there complaining.

- **a that-clause, wh-clause or adverbial clause**:

  It's strange that he's not back yet.
  It's extraordinary what doctors can do nowadays.
  It's nice when the evenings get lighter.

- **if, as if or as though**:

  Is it OK if I leave early?
  It was as though we'd never met before.

2 **It** can be the object of a verb:

I found it difficult to keep going.
We can leave it to them to decide.
I take it that you agree?

3 You use **it takes** with a **to**-infinitive, or **for** and a **to**-infinitive, to talk about the length of time necessary for something to happen:

It only takes five minutes to fill in the form.
It took a year for her to recover.

4 **It** can be used with **seem** or **appear**, or a passive reporting verb:

It appeared that he had gone home.
It was believed that he had escaped to France.

FOR EMPHASIS

You use **it is** or **it was**, followed by a clause (very often a relative clause referring to a noun), to bring forward and highlight a particular element in your statement. For example, instead of saying **Mum reminded me**, you can stress the subject by saying **It was Mum who reminded me**:

It's Jack I'm worried about.
It wasn't till I saw his face that I realized something had gone wrong.

•••• its, it's ••••

These two words confuse native speakers as well as learners.

1 **Its** is a possessive determiner, corresponding to other possessive determiners such as **my**, **your**, **her**, **their**:

The teapot has lost its lid.

2 **It's** is the contraction for both **it is** and **it has**:

It's [= it is] *getting cold.*
It's [= it has] *got much colder in the past two days.*
It's raining; it's been raining for hours.

•••• it's time ••••

➤ See **time**.

Jj

.... just ....

The adverb **just** is used in various ways in expressions of time, and has a range of other functions, especially in conversation. It usually occurs in mid position, that is, before the verb, but after auxiliary verbs and the verb **be**.

AS AN ADVERB OF TIME

1 he's just left

Something that has **just**, or **only just** happened, happened a short time ago. BrE speakers use a present perfect tense in a present context, and a past perfect in a past context:

Hannah has just returned from working in Australia.
I've only just heard the news.
I'd just put down the telephone when it rang again.

> ⓘ Notice that AmE speakers use a simple past rather than a perfect tense after **just**:
> *'Shall I call them and book a table?' 'I just did* (BrE *I just have*)*.'*

2 I'm just making some tea

You are **just doing** something when you are doing it now, or are going to do it in the immediate future:

I'm just serving dinner. Do stay and eat with us.

3 I'm just going to put the kettle on

You are **just going to** do something, or are **just about to** do something, if you are going to do it immediately:

I'm just about to leave.
I was just going to wash up when you came in.

4 just as we were leaving ...

One thing happens **just as** another does if they happen at the same time:

The telephone rang just as I walked through the door.

5 just last week

Just is used like **only** to mean 'as recently as':

Just last week he told me how much he likes your work.

6 just before, just after

Just is used with **before** and **after** to mean 'immediately before' or 'immediately after':

Just before serving, lightly whip the cream.

7 just now

This has two meanings:

- at the present time:
  Life is pretty difficult just now.
- a short time ago:
  Dianne rang just now. She wants you to go and fetch her.

CONVERSATIONAL USES

1 exactly, precisely:

A nice cup of tea; just what we all need.
A holiday's probably just the thing for you.
She just the same.

> ⓘ **Just the** person, or **just the** thing, is someone or something absolutely suitable for a purpose:
> *I've found just the person for the job.*
> *I know just the place for a picnic.*

2 barely:

There was just enough speed for the aircraft to take off.
I just managed to catch her as she was going over the edge.
The water was just warm enough for a bath.

> ⓘ Notice that **only** often precedes **just** in this sense:
> *The stone only just missed my ear.*

3 exactly and no more:

It's just two o'clock now.
He's just six feet.

4 used for focus and emphasis:

Just be quiet for a second.
Just think what might have happened!

5 only, merely:

It's just a scratch.
Practise for just ten minutes every day.
You just add cold water.

6 used as a minimizer:

People often use **just** to make things or actions sound small or unimportant, or to soften a statement:

She'll be free soon, if you could wait just a little bit longer.
I was just making sure you were OK.
I've just got one more call to make.

Kk

•••• keep ••••

The verb **keep** is irregular:

keeps, keeping, kept, kept

Keep is used with an object to mean 'have and continue to have'. It can act as a linking verb, with or without an object. It can also be used with the **-ing** form of a verb to mean 'continue doing'.

CONTINUE TO HAVE, OWN OR PRESERVE

1 keep this pen if you want

You **keep** something when you continue to have it, or when you preserve it instead of throwing it away:

I'll lend you my scarf, but you can't keep it.
I won't be able to keep my job if we move.
He'd kept every postcard he'd ever received.

2 I keep my CDs in an old shoe box

You **keep** something somewhere if you put it there when it is not being used:

Where do you keep the carving knife?
The first-aid kit is kept under the passenger seat.

3 other similar uses

- You **keep** a family when you support it.
- You **keep** animals when you own them and care for them.
- You **keep** a diary or a record if you write it or add to it regularly.
- You **keep** a secret when you tell it to no-one.
- You **keep** a promise, your word, or an appointment, when you do as you promised, or as you arranged to do.
- If you say that a certain food, *eg* lettuce, doesn't **keep** well, you mean that it doesn't stay in good condition for long.

AS A LINKING VERB

1 He kept us waiting

You **keep** people or things in a certain state when you make them stay like that:

The noise from the street kept her awake
I apologize for keeping you waiting.
Keep all medicines hidden.
Keep her off school till the rash goes away.

2 Keep still!

You **keep** in a certain state when you stay like that:

I couldn't keep awake.
Are you keeping well?
There was a notice on the gate saying 'Keep out.'

3 I keep forgetting

You use **keep** with the **-ing** form of other verbs to express the idea of continuous or repeated actions or happenings:

He keeps smiling, even though he's in a lot of pain.
You should see your doctor if you keep fainting like that.
I keep forgetting to buy a new light bulb.

> ⓘ Notice how a negative behaves with **keep** + **-ing**: *Don't keep interrupting!*

•••• kind, sort, type ••••

People sometimes have difficulty over singulars and plurals with these three words.

USED IN THE SINGULAR

1 with a singular determiner

Use a singular noun *if the determiner is singular*:

That sort of system is not so easy for actors.
This kind of accident is relatively common.
He sent me to another sort of specialist.

But if the determiners **what** or **the** are used, the noun can be either singular or plural:

What kind of person should carry out these tasks.
They didn't say what sort of people they require.
I was surprised at the kind of things people bought.

2 with a plural determiner

You can say **those sort of people**, where **those** is behaving as the determiner of **people** rather than **sort**:

Those sort of people annnoy me.
These sort of things sometimes come as a surprise.
Nobody thought to ask those kind of questions.

> ⓘ The forms in **2** are sometimes regarded as ungrammatical. AmE speakers rarely use them at all.

USED IN THE PLURAL

After the plural forms **kinds of**, **sorts of** and **types of**, you can use a singular or plural noun. The singular sounds more formal:

There are, basically, only two types of actor.
Water can form several different kinds of crystals.

•••• know ••••

The verb **know** is irregular:

knows, knowing, knew, known

After **know** you can use a direct object, a report clause with or without **that**, or a clause introduced by a **wh-**question word or **if**. You can also use an object + **to-**infinitive construction.

Know can also be used with the prepositions **about** and **of**, and in responses can stand for a whole clause. You never use **know** in the progressive forms.

BE AWARE OF FACTS

1 know + report clause:

I know you don't like him, but you shouldn't make it so obvious.
Donna knew that this was impossible.

> ⓘ **Know** is not used to refer to the *process* of becoming aware of something. The verbs you use are **find out**, **learn** and **hear**:
> *Sam found out that I was seeing Paula.*

> ⓘ **Know** can be used elliptically to stand for a clause:
> *'We can all make mistakes like this.' 'I know, I know.'*
> *He never said anything, but I knew.*

2 know + wh- or if-clause:

Do you know what the name of the street is?
I don't know how she copes.
Do you know if Maurice is coming today?

- You **know how to** do something if you are able to do it:
  Do you know how to thread this machine?
- You **let** someone **know** something when you give them information that they need:
  I don't know how much the tickets are. I'll let you know.

3 know + object + to-infinitive:

Once we knew them to be artificial, we were no longer interested.
We knew him to be cowardly.

> ⓘ The object + infinitive construction is rather formal, but is more frequent in its passive form:
> *There are 15 people known to be dead.*

4 know + about or of

You **know about**, or **know of**, someone or something if you have heard about them:

Obviously she didn't know anything about it.
Most people know of Madonna and Elton John.

5 know + object

You **know** something such as a fact, or someone's name, when you have learnt it and remember it:

I don't know her telephone number.
I'm afraid I don't know the details.

> ⓘ You **know** a language if you can speak it and understand it:
> *Fortunately I knew some Spanish.*

BE ACQUAINTED WITH

1 people

You **know** a person if you have met them, and have become familiar with them:

I've known him about four years.
Robin, do you know my sister? Marian, this is Robin.

2 places, books, plays, music

You can say you **know** a place if you have been there and are familiar with it; and that you **know** literary or musical works if you have read them or heard them:

I've lived in Paris; I know it well.
I know all his operas.

> ⓘ You use the form **get to know** for the process of becoming acquainted with someone or something:
> *We got to know each other on holiday in the Lake District.*

3 you know...

People use **you know** in various ways:

- to introduce a person or thing that they are going to say something about:
  You know our German friends? They're moving to Switzerland.
- to add information that helps to identify something:
  I'm going to wear my new suit, you know, the grey one.
- to add emphasis, or to scold:
  This is becoming a problem, you know.
- as a way of holding someone's attention:
  So I thought I'd better tell him about it, you know.

Ll

•••• last, at last ••••

LAST

1 **Last** describes the most recent occasion, period of time, event or thing, or the one before the present one:

We went to France for our holidays last year.
I saw her only last week.
The last book I read was a biography.
Our last party was a disaster.

2 The **last** thing can be:

- the one that comes at the end of a series or row of things:

  We caught the last train back to town.
  Their house is the last one on this side of the street.

- the only remaining one:

  He ate the last cake.
  I'm giving you one last chance.

AT LAST

Something that happens **at last** happens after a long time, or after a long period of waiting:

At last I can relax.
At last the rain stopped and we could go outside.

> ⓘ Note that in the examples above, **finally** can be used instead of **at last**. Use **finally**, not **at last**, to introduce the last in a series of points or happenings:
> *Finally* (not *at last*), *I would like to thank you all for coming.*
> *We spent a few years in Bangor, then moved to Manchester, and finally* (not *at last*) *settled in Glasgow.*

•••• late, lately ••••

Late and **lately** can cause difficulties because they look like an adjective and its related adverb, when in fact they do not behave in this way.

LATE

Late is an adjective and an adverb. Something that is **late**, comes, arrives, or happens after others, or after the expected, normal or proper time:

The train was late.
We had a late breakfast at about eleven.
She arrived late for her appointment.
We got up late this morning.

LATELY

Something that has happened **lately** has happened in the recent past or not long ago:

I haven't seen him much lately.
I haven't been sleeping well lately.
Lately he's been very much in love.

•••• later, in ••••

This sections looks at how to use **later** and **in** with time expressions.

LATER

Later is used after an expression of time with the meaning 'after that time'. The verb is usually in the simple past:

Three days later the stock market crashed.
Two months later she was transferred to another hospital.

IN

In is used before a time expression with the meaning 'after now'. The verb is usually in the future:

I'll be back in three days.
We'll see you in two weeks.

> ⓘ Notice that if you do not specify a particular length of time, you can use **later** with the meaning 'after now':
> *See you later!*

•••• latest, last ••••

You use **latest** and **last** to talk about a recent event in a series of events which is continuing to happen. There is a small difference in meaning between the two.

LATEST

The **latest** thing or event in a series is the most recent thing or event in that series:

The latest survey suggests that neither party will have a majority.
I bought the latest edition of the journal.

> ⓘ Notice that if the most recent thing was produced some time ago, you use **last**:
> *He finished his last book four years ago.*

LAST

Last often has the meaning of 'the one before the current one':

I didn't enjoy his last film, but this one is really good.
I didn't like her last boyfriend much.

• • • • lay, lie • • • •

- The verb **lay** takes an object, but **lie** does not.
- **Lay** is the past form of one of the senses of the verb **lie**.
- **Lie** has two very different meanings.

LAY: LAYS, LAYING, LAID

You **lay** something somewhere, or in a certain position, when you place it there so that is lies flat or rests there:

Laying her basket down, she ran towards the noise.
She laid the cloth on the table and collected the knives and plates.

LIE

Lie has two meanings.

1 relax in a horizontal position (lies, lying, lay, lain)

You **lie** somewhere, or **lie down** somewhere when you are in, or get into, a flat or horizonal position:

He lay down on the bed.
Lie down and relax for a few moments.
I had lain awake most of the night.

2 not tell the truth (lies, lying, lied)

You **lie** when you say things that you know are not true:

'Did the woman tell you this?' 'No,' Adam lied.
'That's ridiculous,' she shouted. 'You're lying.'

• • • • learn • • • •

The past tense and past participle of **learn** can be either **learned** (/lɜːnd/) or **learnt** (/lɜːnt/).

You **learn** facts, subjects and skills.

FACTS AND SUBJECTS

Learn can be used in a variety of constructions:

- **learn** + **that** + report clause:
  I've learnt that getting angry can be effective.
- **learn** + **wh-**word + clause:
  We are still learning how our planet was formed.
- **learn** + direct object:
  How long have you been learning Italian?
- **learn** + **of** or **about** + **fact**:
  This is usually rather formal:
  I was so sad to learn of his death
- **learn** + **about** + subject:
  We've been learning about the First World War.

SKILLS AND BEHAVIOUR

1 skills

With skills you can use the construction **learn how to** + infinitive or **learn to** + infinitive:

She doesn't want to learn how to cook (or *learn to cook*).

2 behaviour

You **learn to do** something if it is the most practical or sensible way of behaving:

You have to learn to be patient.

USED INDEPENDENTLY

You can use **learn** independently with reference to knowledge, skills or behaviour:

We need memory in order to learn.
Children must be allowed to make mistakes, or they'll never learn.
There's still so much intolerance in the world. When will people learn?

•••• left-hand, right-hand; left-handed, right-handed ••••

LEFT-HAND, RIGHT-HAND

Left-hand and **right-hand** are adjectives that always come before the noun they describe. They are used to talk about things which are on, or towards, the left (left-hand), or the right (right-hand):

The date is on the right-hand side of the page.
Open the cupboard on the left-hand side and look on the fourth shelf from the top.
The drawing was signed and dated in the bottom right-hand corner.

> ⓘ Notice that **left** and **right** on their own cannot normally be used in this way. They tend to be used as adverbs, as in **keep left** or **turn right**. However, when referring to either of a pair of body parts, you can use simply **left** or **right** before the noun:
> *his left ear*
> *my right arm*
> *my left hand*

LEFT-HANDED, RIGHT-HANDED

A **left-handed** person is someone who uses their left hand to perform manual activities such as writing; a **right-handed** person uses their right hand to perform these activities:

Writing letters backwards is common in young children, particularly if they are left-handed.
Most right-handed people are unaware of the difficulties experienced by left-handed people.

•••• least, fewest ••••

➤ See **less**.

less, fewer, least, fewest

In principle, you use **less** and **least** with uncountable nouns, and **fewer** and **fewest** with plural countable nouns.

LEAST OR FEWEST?

Use **least** with uncountable nouns and **fewest** with plural countable nouns:

Jackie had the least trouble with the job.
I usually choose the method that causes fewest problems for students.

> ⓘ In practice, **least** is quite often used with plural countable nouns to mean 'the smallest quantity of':
> *the product that has attracted the least complaints*

LESS OR FEWER?

1 Where there are no specified quantities, use **less** with uncountable nouns and **fewer** with plural countable nouns:

We experienced less difficulty than we had expected.
This measure led to fewer prosecutions.

2 Where quantities are specified in reference to plural countable nouns, both **fewer** and **less** are usually possible:

We have less/fewer than ten minutes to wait.
Fewer/less than ten of the bars have escaped 'improvement'.
Today there are less/fewer than fifty thousand Indians living there.

> ⓘ **Less** is usually preferable where the quantity refers to *age, money, time* or *distance*:
> *The offer is open to people who are 65 years of age or less* (not *fewer*).
> *You can see Scotland, less than* (not *fewer than*) *thirteen miles away.*
> *The machine prepares bread in less than two hours.*

➤ See also the entry **little, few**.

lest

Lest is a fairly old-fashioned word which is rarely used in modern BrE. It is a little more frequent in AmE.

1 You do something **lest** something unpleasant or unwanted should happen when you do it in case that thing should happen, or to prevent that thing from happening:

He cut the remark out of the programme lest it should offend viewers.
We've been warned not to make a sound, lest we disturb him.

> ⓘ Notice that **lest** is often followed by a verb in the subjunctive.

2 After adjectives like **worried, anxious** or **concerned, lest** can be used like **that** to introduce a clause:

Worried lest she be misunderstood, Anna hastened to correct herself.

• • • let • • •

The verb **let** is irregular:

lets, letting, let, let

Let is less formal than **allow**, **permit** or **enable**. It is used with an infinitive without **to**. It is also used in expressions such as **let's**, **let's see**, and **let go**, which are dealt with in this entry.

➤ For more details on the differences between **allow, permit** and **let**, see **allow**.

LET + OBJECT + INFINITIVE

1 When you **let** something happen, you cause it to happen, or fail to prevent it happening:

She raised her hand and let it drop.
I've let the garden get rather untidy.

2 You **let** someone do something when you allow them to do it, or do not prevent them from doing it:

You mean they'll let him go free?
They let the older girls go shopping by themselves.

> ⓘ Notice that **let me** is often used to make offers, and to announce politely what you intend to do:
> *Let me carry your case for you.*
> *You must let me pay for lunch this time.*
> *Let me introduce you to some of the other guests.*

> ⓘ Passive constructions are not possible with **let**. Instead you can use the passive of **allow**:
> *They were allowed to take a small piece each.*

LET + OBJECT + ADVERBIAL PARTICLE OR PHRASE

You can use an adverb or a prepositional phrase with **let** and its object:

I knocked at the door and a young man let me in
Please could you remember to let the cat out?

> ⓘ Passive forms are possible with phrasal verbs formed with **let**:
> *I've been let down.*
> *He was let off with a fine.*

FORMING IMPERATIVES

English verbs have no imperative form for use with the first and third person. Instead you use **let**, keeping the objective case of the personal pronouns.

1 the third-person imperative

The third-person imperative with **let** can express three different things:

- **warnings**:

  They're threatening to take the childen away from me, but just let them try!

- **lack of concern**:

  Let them think what they like. I know I'm right.

- **formal wishes or instructions**:

  Let them wait their turn, like everyone else.

2 the first-person imperative

- You use **let's**, and more formally, **let us**, to suggest what you and the people you are addressing should do, and also to put your decisions in the form of suggestions:

  Let's wait another five minutes.
  And now let us all get some sleep.
  Let us assume that the change will cost the company nothing.

> ⓘ You use **let's not** and **let us not** as the negative forms. **Don't let's** is possible:
> *Let us not forget what the company is really interested in.*
> *Let's not waste time*
> *Don't let's worry about it now.*

- You use the form **let me ...** typically when thinking aloud, in phrases such as **let me see** and **let me think**:

  Does that mean, let me see, that only 1.01 of the population will be considered suitable?

OTHER USEFUL IDIOMS

1 let ... know

If you say you will **let** someone **know** about something, you mean you will give them the information they need about it:

But you'll let us know when you're ready, won't you?
Perhaps you could let me know when you've decided.

2 let go

- You **let go of** someone or something when you stop holding them:

  He let go of her hand, and stepped back.
  She let go of the door.

- You **let** someone **go** when you stop holding them:

  She would not let him go and dragged him out of the boat.

3 let alone

If one thing is not the case, **let alone** another, the second thing cannot be so, since it is the less likely or possible of the two:

There's no room for her, let alone her children and animals.

4 let ... have

You tell people to **let you have** something when you are asking for it:

Let me have your comments in writing by Friday.

letter-writing

All letters written in good English will have some features in common: the writer's address and the date of writing should be clear, a suitable *salutation* should be used, and after some appropriate closing words, the writer should sign the letter. It is necessary to include additional information, like the address of the person or company the letter is being sent to, in a formal, or business letter. The rules for writing this kind of letter are stricter.

INFORMAL LETTERS

1 When you write to friends or relatives you can use an informal style very like speech, if you wish.

➤ See entry for **formality and informality**.

2 It is usual to include your address (but not your name) in the top right-hand corner of the page.

3 The date of writing appears under the sender's address.

4 Personal letters nearly always begin with **Dear** + name + comma, although **My dear** + name or other minor variations are also possible:

Dear Mum and Dad,
Dear Charlotte,
Dear Mrs Brown,

Notice that you say **Dear** + given name or **Mr**, **Ms** etc + family name:

Dear Fiona or *Dear Ms Langdon* (not *Dear Ms Fiona Langdon*)

5 You close an informal letter with your signature, usually preceded by **Love**, **Love from**, **Best wishes**, **Yours**, or other similar closing words:

Love from Julie
Love, G & L
With best wishes, Peter.
Yours, Dorothy.

ⓘ Letters expressing personal feelings, such as condolences, apologies or thanks should, if at all possible, be hand-written, not typed or written on a word-processor.

FORMAL OR BUSINESS LETTERS

1 If you are not using paper that already carries your company's name and address, you should write your address (not your name) in the top right-hand corner of the page.

2 Any reference that you can quote should appear on the left of the page. If you are replying to a letter with an internal reference, for example, comprising the initials of the person who signed the letter and the person who typed it, you should quote this as well as your own if you have one:

Your reference: …
Our reference: …

3 You can write the date under your address on the right, or on the left of the page. Write the date in full:

21st December 1999

➤ See also **dates**.

4 The *salutation* of a formal letter may be **Dear Sir**, **Dear Madam**, **Dear Sir or Madam**, or **Dear** + name. If you are not writing to an individual, but to a company, then you may begin **Dear Sirs**:

Dear Mr Braithwaite,
Dear Prof. Gibson,
Dear Ms Frobisher,

5 The text of a good business letter should consist of three parts:

- An introductory paragraph should mention any previous correspondence and state the subject of the letter:

  I should like to confirm the booking I made by telephone on 19 December.
  Thank you for your letter of 12 May. I should like to clarify two points for our records.
  Thank you for your order, which I received this morning.

- The main part of the letter (one or more paragraphs) deals with the subject referred to in the introduction. If there are several points to cover, it may be helpful to number the paragraphs according to the different subjects, arguments or topics.

- The concluding paragraph usually contains a reference to the future - either to success of some kind or to further communication:

  I look forward to receiving your reply.
  We wish you every success in your next project.
  Please do not hesitate to contact us again with any further queries.

6 You should end the letter with **Yours faithfully** if you used **Sir**, **Sirs**, or **Madam** in the salutation. If you used a name in the salutation, you should end with **Yours sincerely**. Your signature should then appear above your printed name and, if appropriate, your position in your organization.

• • • • life • • • •

This entry deals with **life** used as a countable noun and as an uncountable noun.

AS A COUNTABLE NOUN

When **life** refers to the whole of a person's life, it is usually countable:

'She had a good life.' 'She had a hard life,' said Rose sharply.
He had not had an easy life, especially towards the end.

AS AN UNCOUNTABLE NOUN

When **life** refers to a particular way of living, it is usually uncountable:

Some people find it hard to adapt to country life.
He began adult life selling cigarettes in a New York cinema.

EXCEPTIONS

When **life** refers to the situation someone is living in, it is usually an uncountable noun. However, the article is common if **life** is preceded by an adjective or other qualifying expression:

They're really enjoying life at the moment.
They're living an idyllic life in the foothills of the Alps.

• • • • like (preposition, conjunction and interjection) • • • •

Like can be used as a *preposition*, a *conjunction*, or an informal *interjection*. As a preposition or conjunction it expresses *similarity.*

➤ For the verb **like**, expressing fondness or preference, see the following entry.

AS A PREPOSITION

Like has a function somewhere between an adjective and a preposition in expressing similarity.

1 It feels like spring

Like can follow verbs of acting and behaving, as well as linking verbs such as **be**, **look**, **feel**, **sound**, **taste**:

It was a big black bird, like a crow.
I was feeling more and more like a little child.
You've always looked like your Aunt Margaret.
Her hair smelt like wet grass.
Your third gear acts like a brake.

ⓘ Notice that you can intensify or moderate **like** with adverbs such as **very**, **quite**, **rather**, **a bit**:
At night a cat can sound rather like a baby crying.

2 It smells like burning

You often use structures such as **it sounds like**, **it looks like** to say you what you *think* is the case, from what you hear or see:

That sounds like Robert coming upstairs now.
The building looked like a library or some other public institution.
It feels like rain [= I think it's going to rain].
It smells like burning.

3 What is it like?

You use **like** with **what** to ask for a description of someone or something, or an opinion about how nice, or how good they are:

'What's she like?' he asked. 'Pretty?'
What's it like living in London?
What are they like? To work with, I mean?

4 He was shaking like a leaf

Like is used in idiomatic expressions that compare one thing to another:

He was shaking like a leaf.
He smokes like a chimney.

➤ See also the entry **as ... as**.

ⓘ Notice the distinction between **like** and **as**. You use **as** when you are specifying the role, job or function or a person or thing, as distinct from making *comparisons*:
She works like a horse. But: *She works as a financial consultant*

5 somewhere exciting, like Alaska

Like can be used to introduce examples of something you have just mentioned:

We thought of going somewhere hot like Crete or Cyprus.
The whole idea is to stop people like you and me asking questions.

6 people like him

You can use **like** in constructions such as **someone like him**, or **problems like this** to mean 'someone of his kind', or 'problems of this kind':

Situations like this need careful handling.
She just talks about herself all the time; I hate people like that.

6 Stop yelling like that!

You can use **like this** and **like that** to mean 'to this or that extent', or 'in this or that way':

There's no need for us to argue like this.
I hate it when you go quiet like that.

7 I can't cook like my mum

You do something **like** someone else if you can do it as well as they can:

OK, if you can dance like Ginger Rogers.
I want to paint like Picasso.

8 Like the rest of us, she's worried

You use **like** to say that someone's behaviour is typical of a certain group or other person:

Like many people, she would spend all evening in front of the TV.
Like his brother, he tried to hide his feelings.

> ⓘ Notice that **unlike** can also be used in this construction, to mention someone that behaves differently from the one you are talking about:
> *Diana needed people; unlike some, she wasn't very good at being alone.*

9 It's nothing like finished

Something that is *eg* **nothing like** complete, or **not anything like** as good as it should be, is not nearly complete, or as good as it should be:

England was nothing like the country I had expected.
She wasn't anything like her photograph.

10 There's nothing like winning

If something is unique in some way, especially in producing a certain result, you can say there is **nothing like** it:

There's nothing like sea air to wake you up.

11 That's just like Marie

Behaviour that is **like** someone is typical of them:

It was just like Denise to continue when she was exhausted.

AS A CONJUNCTION

Like as a conjunction is common in AmE, but is rather informal in BrE.

1 They aren't made like they were

You can use **like** to mean 'as' or 'the way'. It is less formal than **as**:

They don't seem to talk about their hopes and fears like we do.

2 He looks like he's going to faint

You can use **like** informally, especially with **sound**, **look** or **feel**, to mean 'as if' or 'as though'. It is less formal than **as if** or **as though**:

- **unreal comparisons**:

  I woke up feeling like I'd been sleeping on the floor all night.

- **real probabilities**:

  You look like you need a rest.

➤ For the expression **feel like** doing something see **feel**.

• • • • like (verb) • • • •

The verb **like** has a wide range of uses in English, and a variety of constructions are possible. A lot of these constructions are also used with other verbs of liking and disliking. These verbs are listed here in the order 'like very much' to 'dislike very much':

- adore
- love
- like, be fond of, be keen on
- don't mind, don't object to
- dislike, don't like, object to
- hate
- loathe, detest, can't bear, can't stand

APPRECIATION, ENJOYMENT

1 like + object (*I like Greek food*)

You **like** someone or something if you are fond of them. You also **like** a thing if you prefer it, or if you enjoy it. **Like** in these senses usually has an object, and is not normally used in the progressive forms:

'What do you think of my plan?' 'I like it.'
'Do you like my new picture?' 'I love it.'
I like you a lot, but I'm not in love with you.

> ⓘ The progressive forms are possible for **like** in the sense of 'enjoy', especially in questions:
> *How are you liking the new job?*

> ⓘ **Very much** is often used to intensify **like**, but notice that it does not come between **like** and its object:
> *I like my room very much* (not *I like very much my room*).

2 like + -ing form *(I like talking to her)*

You **like doing** something if you *enjoy* it:

I like going to parties. Other people's parties.
He likes working alone.

3 like + object + -ing form *(Do you like me brushing your hair?)*

An object is possible before the **-ing** form:

She doesn't like anyone being late for her lectures.

> ⓘ Notice that other 'liking' and 'disliking' verbs can have the same constructions with an **-ing** form:
> *I hated wearing a uniform.*
> *I adore looking at you.*
> *She can't bear people seeing her without make-up.*

IN CHOICES, PREFERENCES, HABITS AND DECISIONS

1 like + to-infinitive *(I like to know what's going on)*

You **like to do** something if you normally choose to do it, or do it as a habit:

She likes to keep the place clean and tidy.

2 like + object + to-infinitive *(I like him to be on time)*

An object is possible before the *to*-infinitive:

She liked everyone to be happy.

> ⓘ Of the other 'liking' and 'disliking' verbs listed above, only **love**, **hate** and **can't bear** can be followed by a **to**-infinitive:
> *It's such a beautiful day; I can't bear to waste a minute of it.*
> *I love to get up really early and get lots of work done.*
> *I'd hate anything bad to happen.*

3 if you like, when you like

Like can be used in clauses after conjunctions or pronouns such as **if**, **as soon as**, **when**, **whenever**, **where**, **wherever**, **how**, **however**, **what**, **whatever**, **who**, **whoever**, and **any**:

'When will I see you then?' 'Whenever you like.'
People think that I work when I like.
I think we're allowed to start as soon as we like.
Some people think they can say what they like.
There's some apple tart afterwards, if you like.

> ⓘ Notice the similar use of **want**, **prefer**, and **wish**:
> *We're not expecting any further developments, so you can leave if you want.*
> *We can give you a different table, if you wish.*
> *You can pay by cheque if you prefer.*

WOULD LIKE

You use **would like** with an object or a **to**-infinitive, or an object with a **to**-infinitive, for various purposes.

1 I'd like to apologize

You can express your own desires or wishes, or express your intentions politely, or make requests, using **I would like**, **I should like** or **I'd like**:

I'd like a second opinion.
I'd like to get back to my hotel without delay.
First of all I should like to apologize for the long delay in replying.

> ⓘ The form **would like** + -**ing** is not possible:
> *I'd like to see* (not *I'd like seeing*) *the Statue of Liberty.*

2 Would you like more coffee?

You use **would you like** to enquire about other people's wishes or desires, and to make offers or issue invitations:

What would you like to do?
Would you like to come fishing with me?
Would you like me to help you with your bags?
Would you like a drink before going to bed?

> ⓘ Notice that you do not use the form **do you like** to offer people things:
> *Would you like* (not *do you like*) *an ice cream?*
> People often respond to an offer using the form **would you like** with the verb **love**:
> *'Would you like a cup of tea?' 'I'd love one.'*

3 would have liked to ..., or would like to have ...

To express a wish about something you did not do in the past, you can use either of two forms: you can say, either **I would have liked to stay longer** or **I would like to have stayed longer**:

She would have liked to kiss him, but she knew she shouldn't.
I would like to have discussed the question with him.

.... likely ....

1 Is it likely?

Something that is **likely** is probable:

For most of the match a draw had looked the most likely result.
'But we might need these things if we go camping again.' 'Well, that's not very likely.'

2 It's likely that ...

Still with the sense 'probable', **likely** can be followed by a **that**-clause, with **it** as the subject of the main clause:

It is likely that the candidate has not understood the question.
It was likely that the President would deny the affair.

3 He'll very likely disagree

Likely can be used as an adverb, with the sense 'probably'. It is always used with an intensifier such as **very** or **most**, or occurs in the combinations **more than likely**, **as likely as not** or **more likely than not**:

If he saw you now, he would very likely not recognize you.
Any attempts would most likely fail.
More than likely she's missed the bus.

4 Is it likely to rain?

Likely can be followed by a **to-**infinitive; you use the form **likely to have** + past participle to refer to what probably happened in the past:

Overweight parents are likely to overfeed their children.
There are likely to be two main changes.
He is the man most likely to have killed the British girl.

ⓘ The adjective **unlikely** is used in the same constructions as the adjective **likely**:
It's unlikely that we'll get a grant towards the repairs.
Clients are unlikely to complain.
There are unlikely to be any developments before tomorrow.

linking verbs

➤ See also the entries **change** and **complements**.

The name **linking verbs** or **copular verbs** is given to verbs such as **be**, **seem**, **feel**, **look**, and **become**, which *link* the subject of a sentence with an adjective or a noun. The adjective or noun is called a *complement.*

In a sentence such as *The two children both became doctors*, the noun *doctors* is the complement, and the linking verb is *become.*

You use linking verbs to say something about the *subject* of the sentence. So you don't use adverbs with linking verbs. Compare the following two sentences:

Anna always dresses smartly.
Anna always looks smart.

In the first sentence the adverb **smartly** is used to describe the 'action' verb **dresses**. In the second sentence, the adjective **smart** is used to describe the subject **Anna**, after the linking verb **looks**.

TWO KINDS OF LINKING VERBS

There are two main types of linking verbs. Verbs such as **be**, **seem**, **feel**, and **look** are used to talk about the *state* of people or things; verbs such as **become**, **grow** and **get** express *change*. Some linking verbs express 'no change'; these are **keep**, **remain** and **stay**.

Below are some examples of the commonest verbs in these categories.

state	**change**
*John **is** a historian.*	*We **became** friends.*
*George **seemed** worried.*	*My dream **came** true.*
*The doctor **appeared** unconcerned.*	*It**'s getting** cold.*
*The future **looks** gloomy.*	*I**'m going** crazy.*
*The carpet **feels** damp.*	*The shadows **grew** longer.*

Dinner ***smells*** *good.*
This coffee ***tastes*** *funny.*

Emily ***turned*** *pale.*

no change
Keep *calm.*
We ***stayed*** *seated.*
He ***remained*** *a bachelor.*

Some linking verbs function also as ordinary 'action' verbs. Notice that as action verbs they are used with adverbs, not adjectives. Compare the pairs of examples shown below:

- *He remained bravely* (not *brave*) *at his post*
  She always remained cool (not *coolly*) *in a crisis.*
- *He looked intently* (not *intent*) *at her.*
  He looked pale and thin (not *palely and thinly*).

OTHER VERBS WITH A LINKING SENSE

1 Certain intransitive 'action' verbs have a sense in which they function as a linking verb and can be followed by an adjective. The following examples show the verbs **stand**, **sit**, **lie**, **fall** and **run** behaving as linking verbs:

I stood quite still.
Do sit straight.
She lay unconscious for several hours.
He fell ill early in 1996.
Someone left the hot tap on, and the water's run cold.

3 **verb + object + complement** (*We painted the bedroom yellow*)

Some transitive verbs can be followed by an object and an adjective or noun complement, so are a type of linking verb:

I decided to ***paint the door green.***
He ***pushed the door shut.***
The new detergent ***washes your glasses really clean.***
You've ***made me very happy.***
They ***made her manager.***
She started ***calling me a thief.***

•••• listen ••••

➤ See **hear**.

•••• little, few, a little, a few ••••

Little and **a little** are used with uncountable nouns. **Few** and **a few** are used with plural countable nouns. **Little** and **few** mean, respectively, 'not much' and 'not many', and function as negatives. **A little** and **a few** have a positive meaning, like 'some'.

All four expressions can act as determiners or pronouns. **A little** and **little** can also be used as adverbs.

DETERMINERS

1 **a little, a few**

Use **a little** with uncountable nouns, and **a few** with plural countable nouns:

There is evidence that a little alcohol, can guard against heart disease.
He was staying with friends, a few miles away.

2 little, few

Little means 'not much' and is used with uncountable nouns. **Few** means 'not many' and is used with plural countable nouns:

People have little time to learn everything they need to know.
They showed very little interest.
Few animals or plants can withstand such temperatures.

PRONOUNS

1 followed by 'of'

You use the forms **a little of**, **a few of**, **little of** and **few of** before pronouns and determiners:

Scrape back a little of the top soil.
A few of us protested.

2 used independently

Little, **a little**, **few** and **a few** can be used independently as pronouns:

'More whisky, Sally?' 'Yes, a little, please.'
Hurry if you want a programme. There are only a few left.

3 little and a little (*I'm a little concerned*)

You can use **a little** and **little** to modify verbs, adjectives, and comparatives:

Try to rest a little.
We were all feeling a little tired and confused.
Now she had stopped work, she felt a little lighter on her feet each day.
We slept very little that night.

•••• live ••••

1 You **live** in a particular place if that is where your home is:

They live in Scotland.
We live twenty miles from the border.

2 You say that someone **is living** somewhere if they have just moved to that place, or if that place is their home only for a limited period of time:

Now living in Miami Beach, he is enjoying life in car racing.
The boy and his family are living outside Liverpool under assumed names.

3 To talk about the length of time that a particular place has been your home, you say that you **have been living/have lived** there **for** that length of time, or that you **have been living/have lived** there **since** a particular date:

They have been living there for two years.
She has been living with her mother since her husband's arrest.

4 A **living** person, plant or animal is alive. The adjective **living** usually comes before the noun it describes:

All living things are composed of cells.
She had no living relatives.

• • • • loathe • • • •

➤ See **like (verb)**.

• • • • long • • • •

As an adverb of time, **long** is used with negatives and in questions, but is not generally used in positive statements.

POSITIVE CONTEXTS

1 It takes a long time

In a positive context, you use **a long time** rather than **long**:

She sat for a long time (not *sat for long*) *staring into space.*
In country areas people have to wait a long time for buses.
It all happened a long time ago.

2 It takes too long

You can use **long** in combinations such as **as long**, **so long**, **too long** and **long enough**:

I waited as long as I could.
Sorry to keep you waiting so long.
We can't check it. It'll take too long.
You've thought about it long enough. What's your decision?

3 long before, long after

Long can modify **before** and **after**:

We knew about it long before the workers were informed.
Long after this incident the sight of a dog would fill me with terror.

4 She'll be walking before long

Before long means 'in a short time':

You'll be married before long.
We expect some very interesting results before long.

5 all day long

The expressions **all day long** and **all night long** mean 'throughout the whole day, or night':

He had been drinking all night long.

6 It takes longer than you think

You use **longer** rather than **a longer time** as a comparative form:

They talk longer than necessary on the phone, and they don't help in the house.

NEGATIVE CONTEXTS

You can use **long** with negatives and in questions, and with words like **rarely**:

How long will I have to stay in hospital?
He rarely stayed very long with any one orchestra.
We haven't lived here long.

IN MEASUREMENTS

Long is used in expressions of physical dimension:

Expect a long thin parcel throught the post.
How long should I have my hair?
The ruler I have at home is three metres long.

➤ For the uses of **long** in measurement, see **measurement**.

•••• as long as, so long as ••••

➤ See **as long as, so long as**.

•••• look ••••

The verb **look** has two main divisions of meaning. It means both 'direct your eyes' and it acts as a *linking verb*, meaning 'seem or appear'.

AS AN ORDINARY VERB

1 look at

You cannot use a direct object after **look**.

- You use **look** with the preposition **at** to express the idea of turning your eyes towards something:

Come and look at this.
She looked at her watch.

- **Look at** also means 'examine' or 'investigate':

Let me look at your throat.
We're looking at ways of cutting costs.

- People **are looking at** an option or possible procedure when they are considering it:

We're looking at the end of August for publication.

2 Look over here

Look is often used with adverbial or prepositional phrases, and can be used independently:

He was still looking out of the window.
She looked up from her work.
Look! Isn't that Jack?

ⓘ **Look** and **look here** are used informally in conversation to draw attention to a point, or to complain or protest:
Look, shouting won't do any good.
Look here, that's not fair.

3 Look what's happened!

Look is often followed by a clause introduced by a **wh-**question word, to draw attention to something, or to express surprise, anxiety or anger:

But look how much money you save by walking everywhere.
Now look what you've done!

4 Look and see, look to see + if or wh-word

You **see if** or **whether** something is happening. You can also use **look and see** when you use **look** in its unmodified form, or **look to see** with the inflected forms of **look**:

Look and see if there are any spare boxes.
Everyone looked to see what was happening.
They will be looking to see how well you work with others.

5 look for, look after

- To **look for** something is to seek it or search for it:

  Where are we going? Mum will be looking for me.
  If you are looking for a job, where do you start?

- To **look after** someone or something is to take care of them:

  I'm capable of looking after myself.
  Looking after other people's children can be very tiring.

AS A LINKING VERB

As a linking verb, **look** is followed by an adjective or a noun.

1 She looked anxious; He looked a mess

You use **look** in commenting on, or describing, physical appearance and facial expression:

The house looks tidier than usual.
You look nice in red.
What has she done to herself? She looks a mess.

> ⓘ The progressive forms are possible in describing temporary appearance:
> *You're looking tired today.*

2 Things look depressing

You use **look** to say how things or people seem, or what impression they give:

The situation is looking brighter.
That looks an interesting book.

3 look like

Look like has various meanings and uses:

- **comparisons**

  You use **look like** in making comparisons:

  You look like that French actress.
  My eldest son looks like me.

- **impressions**

  You use **look like** to say what impression you get from the appearance of things:

  Beryl was beginning to look like an old woman.
  Do I look like a criminal or something?

ⓘ When judging the qualities of something or someone from their appearance, **look** and **look like** are often both possible:
That looks like (or *looks*) *a nasty wound.*
It looks like (or *looks*) *an interesting project.*

- **What does it look like?**

  When someone asks **what** a person or thing **looks like** they are usually asking for a description:
  'What did he look like?' 'Oh, he looked nice, actually.'

- **It looks like being a success**

  Look like + *-ing* is often used in predictions:
  The conference looks like being a success.
  The film's budget looks like being bigger than expected.

- **look as if, look as though, look like**

  Look can be followed by a clause introduced by **as if** or **as though**, or, in AmE, and increasingly in informal BrE, by **like**. This structure is used to talk about the impression something or someone gives you:
  It looks as if the product will have to be withdrawn from the shops.
  It doesn't look as though he'll be available till June.
  Now I'm here it looks like I'll stay for a while.

•••• -looking ••••

The adjectival suffix **-looking** is used a great deal in English to describe people and things, especially in cases where you are deducing a quality from the appearance of someone or something:
Up on the roof there was a nervous-looking teenager holding a gun.
They were suddenly surrounded by a group of tough-looking soldiers.

•••• loose, lose ••••

Distinguish between the adjective **loose** (/luːs/), which is the opposite of **tight**, and the irregular verb **lose** (/luːz/: **loses**, **losing**, **lost**, **lost**). Because of its pronunciation, rhyming with **choose**, people sometimes make the mistake of spelling the verb wrongly:
I continued to wear loose clothing till I managed to lose (not *loose*) *a bit of weight.*

•••• a lot of, lots of ••••

People use **a lot of** and **lots of** mainly in positive sentences. They replace **many** and **much**, which belong mainly to negative sentences and questions. **Many** and **much** can sound rather formal and unnatural in a positive context.

A lot and **lots** have to be followed by **of** before a noun or pronoun.

1 **A lot of** and **lots of** are both used before uncountable nouns and plural nouns:
We have a lot of fun.

You may have to spend lots of money on the hotel.
There's always lots of talking and laughing.
You're asking a lot of stupid questions.

A lot of and **lots of** are rather informal. To avoid them in formal situations use

- **a great deal of** and **a large amount of** with uncountable nouns:
  We've spent a great deal of time discussing your case.
- **a large number of** and **a great many** with plural nouns:
  We encountered a large number of (or *a great many*) *difficulties.*

➤ See also **plenty**.

ⓘ Notice that the verb agrees with the uncountable or plural noun, and is not affected by whether you say **lots of** or **a lot of**:
Lots of reliable information is available.
A lot of boys come to see her.

ⓘ **Quite** and **rather** can be used before **a lot of**:
There have been rather a lot of complaints.
We've received quite a lot of encouragement.

2 The following examples show **a lot of** and **lots of** used before determiners and before pronouns:
Lots of my friends have admired these flowers.
A lot of those pigs are sold for meat.
A lot of our material is exported.
The food is good: plain and simple, and lots of it.

ⓘ Notice that it is possible to use **a lot of** with a singular pronoun:
*You've seen **a lot of him** in action.*

3 **A lot** and **lots** can be used independently as pronouns:
I don't know how many brothers and sisters she has, a lot, anyway.
It's a fantastic place for a holiday. Lots to do and see.

ADVERBIAL USES

1 **A lot** can be used with verbs as an adverb meaning 'often' or 'a great deal':
I remember he used to laugh a lot.
We played together a lot as children.

2 **A lot** and **lots** are used as intensifiers with comparative adjectives and adverbs:
In half an hour she felt a lot better.
There are lots more facts like that.

•••• love ••••

➤ See **like** (**verb**).

•••• luck, fortune; lucky, fortunate, happy ••••

LUCK

1 **Luck** is success that comes by chance:
He got that job through luck rather than hard work.

2 You wish someone **luck** when you tell them that you hope things will go well for them:
I wished her luck for the future.

3 **Luck** is also those events in life that cannot be controlled, and seem to happen by chance:
You've been having a lot of bad luck recently.

FORTUNE

Fortune is chance, seen as a force in human affairs. It corresponds most closely to the third meaning of **luck**, above. **Fortune** is a more formal word than **luck**:
He was aware of his good fortune, and helped others where possible.
Throughout his life he was troubled by accidents and ill fortune.

LUCKY, FORTUNATE

You are **lucky** or **fortunate** when you are successful, more by accident than by hard work:
I know I'm lucky to have such a good job.
We must help those people who are less fortunate than ourselves.

> ⓘ Note that **fortunate** is a more formal word than **lucky**.

HAPPY

You are **happy** when you are feeling pleased or contented:
She gave a happy smile.
He was never very happy at school.

> ⓘ Note that **happy** and **lucky** do not have the same meaning.

•••• lunch ••••

➤ See entry for **meals**.

Mm

•••• made + of, out of, from, with ••••

You use **made of**, **made out of**, **made from**, and **made with** to refer to what is used to make something.

1 You use **made of** to say what *material* an article is:

All our bottles are made of reinforced glass.
She was presented with a set of suitcases made of finest leather.
What are these shoelaces made of?

2 You use **made from**, or **made out of**, when thinking of the *process* of turning one thing into another:

She had one of those bags made out of odd pieces of leather sewn together.
This paper is made from rags.

3 You use **made with** to refer to *ingredients*:

This dessert is made with cream and eggs.
The cake will last longer if it's made with real butter.

•••• majority ••••

The majority refers to more than half of the group or class that a particular number of people or things belong to. **The majority of** is followed by a plural noun or a pronoun:

The majority of our members are not actually journalists.
The majority of students have to take on holiday jobs.
Domestic violence goes unreported in the majority of cases.
The majority of us are against Sunday working.

•••• make ••••

A VERB OF CREATION

1 **Make** most basically means to 'produce' or 'create':

I'll make the sandwiches.
This is the skirt I made in my dressmaking class.

2 **Make** can have an indirect object as well as a direct one:

Shall I make you a cup of tea?
That's the suit I made my grandson.

> ⓘ Instead of an indirect object by itself, you can use the preposition **for** + indirect object:
> *I remember you used to make milkshakes for us* (or *you used to make us milkshakes*) *when we got back from school.*

➤ See also the entry **made + of, out of, from, with**.

AN ACTIVITY VERB

There is a wide variety of objects relating to behaviour or activity that are frequently used with **make**. The following list may be helpful:

you make comments, remarks, suggestions, statements, jokes, speeches
you make appointments, arrangements, plans, decisions, claims, accusations, excuses
you make a fuss about something
you make someone an offer
you make attempts, efforts, mistakes, errors
you make preparations, contributions, improvements, alterations
you make enquiries, discoveries
you make noises
you make progress, an impact, an impression
you make a start, you make a journey somewhere, and you make your escape from somewhere
a certain circumstance makes a difference to a situation
you make your own bed
you make phone calls

➤ See the entry **do** for the other main 'activity' verb, which has its own set of common objects.

A LINKING VERB

1 showing effect

You can use **make** as a linking verb with an object, an adjective or noun complement:

I'm sorry if I've made you unhappy.
You'll make yourself ill if you go on working like this.
It's not my fault - I didn't want to be made president.
We've decided to make this room the nursery.

> ⓘ **Let me make it clear that...**
> The pronoun **it** is often the object of **make**, referring forward to a noun clause introduced by **that**:
> *Let me make it clear that I do not blame you for the mistake.*

> ⓘ **I can usually make myself understood**
> You can use a reflexive pronoun after **make** followed by a limited range of past participles, such as **understood, heard, liked** and **disliked**:
> *Everyone started shouting, and I gave up trying to make myself heard.*
> *He could make himself understood in most European languages.*

2 expressing suitability

You can use **make** to talk about the suitability or success of a person or thing in a particular role. **Good** is often used before the 'role' word:

A quotation always makes a good ending.
You'll never make a chess-player.
He should make a fine lawyer.

> ⓘ Notice that an indirect object is possible:
> *She would make him an excellent wife* [= She would be an excellent wife for him].
> *She made him the ideal partner.*

CAUSING AND FORCING

You **make** someone or something *do* something if they do it because of you, or if you get them to do it, or force them to do it. The construction is **make** + object + infinitive without **to**:

- **cause**:

  You've made me forget what I was going to say.
  Waiting for Emily had made them miss their train.
  What makes you think that?
  Don't blow your nose, or you'll make it bleed again.

- **force**:

  I made him clean up the mess.
  He made us get under the table and lie down.
  I couldn't make the lights work last night.

> ⓘ A **to**-infinitive is used if the structure is put into the passive:
> *We were made to learn a lot of poetry by heart.*

male and female

➤ See the entry **he, he or she, they** for use of pronouns relating to both women and men.

1 You generally use the pronoun **it** to refer to objects and concepts, but people sometimes use **she** and **her** to talk about ships, cars and countries:

The ship was built in 1945. She was a fine example of her type.
Britain and her economy have not changed so much in these last years.

2 Generally, nouns in English have no gender, that is they are not masculine, feminine or neuter. However, some nouns refer specifically to men or women.

- Here is a list of nouns which only refer to women:

bride	*bridesmaid*	*fiancée*
girl	*girlfriend*	*lady*
schoolgirl	*widow*	*woman*

- Here is a list of nouns that only refer to men:

bachelor	*boy*	*boyfriend*
bridegroom	*chap*	*fiancé*
gentleman	*guy*	*lad*
man	*schoolboy*	*widower*

3 Many words for jobs or rank that refer to women end in -**ess**, for example, **waitress** and **actress**. They may also end in -**woman**. Examples of this are **policewoman** and **chairwoman**.

- Here is a list of words relating to jobs or rank, which only refer to women:

actress	*air hostess*	*barmaid*
baroness	*chairwoman*	*chambermaid*
duchess	*headmistress*	*hostess*
housewife	*manageress*	*nun*
policewoman	*princess*	*queen*
spokeswoman	*stewardess*	*usherette*
waitress		

ⓘ Some of the words above sound old-fashioned now, and are being replaced by words that can refer to both males and females. So, **actress** is being replaced by **actor**, **chairwoman** by **chair**, **headmistress** by **headteacher** and **policewoman** by **police officer**. Although **fireman** has never really had a female equivalent, **firefighter** is now more common as more women work in the fire service.

- Here is a list of words relating to jobs or ranks, which only refer to men:

barber	*barman*	*baron*
businessman	*craftsman*	*duke*
fisherman	*headmaster*	*host*
king	*lord*	*monk*
policeman	*postman*	*prince*
salesman	*serviceman*	*sportsman*
steward	*waiter*	*workman*

4 If you need to indicate the sex of the person you are referring to, and the noun you use is neutral, you can use **woman** or **female** before the noun for a woman, or **male** (but not **man**) for a man:

She is one of the leading female jockeys in France.
This report was written by a woman factory inspector in Glasgow in 1898.
Maurice, the male dancer, went out to sit at the bar.

5 Most names of animals can be used to refer to both males and females. Specific names for each gender do exist, but not many are used in everyday language. Some of these are **hen** (a female chicken), **ram** (a male sheep), and **bull** (a male of the cattle family).

•••• male, masculine ••••

MALE

As an adjective, **male** means belonging to the sex that does not give birth to young or lay eggs:

They didn't have any male friends at all.
The male rats were the first to show signs of the disease.

As a noun, **male** refers to animals that do not give birth to babies or lay eggs:

The females select the male of their choice, mate with him and then rear the young on their own.
The adult male develops large muscular cheeks.

The noun **male** sometimes refers to humans, but in highly official or technical texts, or in humorous styles:

A young male was found guilty of 45 offences.
I'm a 19-year-old female wanting to get to know a good-looking male.

MASCULINE

Masculine describes things that relate to men, or things that are typical of men, or considered to be more suitable for men than women:

Boxing is often seen as a manifestation of courage and masculine strength.
Western philosophy has been consistently masculine in orientation.

In some languages, **masculine** nouns are nouns that belong to the group which contains usually, amongst others, words referring to males:

'Waiter' and 'bull' are masculine nouns.

•••• man, mankind ••••

Man and **mankind** can both be used to talk about people or the human race in general.

MAN

Man, without an article, refers to human beings in general:

They argue that man is by nature aggressive.
But man is not made for a solitary, self-sufficient existence.

> ⓘ The plural form **men** can be used to refer to human beings as individuals:
> *The law says all men are free in England.*
> *All men are equal.*

MANKIND

Mankind is sometimes used to refer to human beings as a group:

His entire work reflects his constant faith in mankind.
The greatest danger to mankind is not science, but ignorance.

Some people do not like the use of **man** and **mankind** to talk about human beings, because they think it suggests than men are more important than women. Words you can use instead are **people**, **humankind**, **human beings**, or **the human race**:

History is the story of humankind's attempt to impose order on chaos.

Let us think for a few moments of the wonderful achievements of the human race.
Human beings, he found, were not nearly as interesting as animals.

•••• manage ••••

1 You **manage to** do something when you succeed in doing it:
They managed to find time to visit Disneyland.
They managed to look cheerful, even in the pouring rain.

> ⓘ Notice how **manage to** is used instead of **could** when you are referring to a single instance of being able to do something in the past. **Could** is used only for general ability or permission in the past:
> *She managed to* (not *could*) *hide her anger.*

➤ See also **could**.

2 You **arrange for** something to happen, not **manage that** it happens:
He kindly arranged for us to use the new machines.
Mother left the parcel at the station and arranged for it to be collected.

•••• many ••••

The comparative of **many** is **more**, and its superlative is **most**.

➤ See the separate entries **more** and **most**. See also **much**.

AS A DETERMINER

1 You use **many** with plural nouns. It is the opposite of **few**:
Many parents still prefer to pay for their children's education.
We decided not to move house, for many reasons.

> ⓘ **Many**, like **much**, sounds rather formal in positive statements. In conversation people often use **a lot of** or **lots of** instead.
> **Many** is common in negative contexts, however, whether formal or informal, and in questions:
> *We've received a lot of donations, but not very many* [= only a few] *offers of help.*
> *Were there many errors?*

2 Although **many** on its own is not usual in positive contexts in conversational English, it is frequently combined with words such as **too**, **so**, **as**:
Take as many brochures as you want.
There are far too many people who just don't care.
There are so many advantages to having your own car.

3 You use **how** and **however** with **many** to ask and talk about numbers and quantities:
How many guests are we expecting?
I'm need to get this right, however many hours it takes.

AS A PRONOUN

1 You use the form **many of** before **the**, **these**, and **those**, and before pronouns and possessive forms:

Many of us in the health service are worried about these changes.
Many of today's young people face unemployment.
Many of these problems can be easily solved.
Many of our students become teachers.

2 **Many** can be used independently as a pronoun:

Take these, and if there are too many, bring the extra ones back.
'Were there a lot of objections?' 'No, not many.'

•••• marry, divorce; marriage, wedding ••••

1 marry, divorce

- The verbs **marry** and **divorce** are both usually followed by an object:

In 1982 he married a young student teacher.
Are you going to divorce him?

- When you are talking about two people together, you can use the structure **get** + **past participle**, or you can use **marry** and **divorce** without an object:

When are you two getting married?
They got divorced six months after the wedding.
They married in 1967 and divorced in 1977.

2 marriage, wedding

- **Marriage** is the state or relationship of being husband and wife:

Don't enter into marriage without thinking about it seriously.
The marriage ceremony lasted two hours.
We have always had a very happy marriage.

- A **wedding** is a marriage ceremony:

We've been invited to a wedding in June.

Note that it is possible to refer to a **wedding** as a **marriage**, but this is less common, and very formal.

•••• matter ••••

Matter can be used as a *noun* or a *verb.*

NOUN

1 You use **the matter** after **what**, **something**, **anything** and **nothing** (indefinite pronouns) when you are identifying problems or difficulties:

Is anything the matter? [= Is anything wrong?]
She was crying, and I asked her what the matter was.
You look worried. Is something the matter?
What's the matter with your leg?
There's nothing the matter with me. I'm fine.

> ⓘ Notice that, as with **wrong**, you use **the matter** only with the indefinite pronouns, as shown in the examples above. When explaining what the problem is you refer to it as **the trouble**, **the difficulty** or **the problem**:
> *The trouble* (not *the matter*) *is that I can't find the receipt.*

2 You use **no matter** before **wh**-words such as **what**, **how**, **where**, **when** and so on to give them the same meaning as **whatever, however, wherever, whenever** and so on:

They won't hear you, no matter how [= however] *loud you shout.*
No matter what [= whatever] *the problem is, she can usually help.*
You'll have to pay the fine, no matter who [= whoever] *you are.*

3 A **matter** is any situation, issue, incident or affair that you have to deal with:

May I speak to you about a personal matter?
There's still the matter of the fees to discuss.
That is a matter for yourself and your husband to decide.

4 You use the plural **matters** to refer to the present situation, or the situation you are discussing:

Matters have reached crisis point.
It won't help matters if you lose your temper.
To make matters worse, the banks were shut.

VERB

1 Something **matters** to you if it is important to you:

Concentrate on getting well; only your health matters now.
Your opinion matters, so tell me what you think.

2 Something that **doesn't matter** is not important, because it does not make any difference to the situation:

It doesn't matter which method you use.
The spelling doesn't matter.

> ⓘ **It doesn't matter** is often used as a reply to an apology:
> *'I'm so sorry I'm late.' 'It doesn't matter at all. Don't worry.'*

•••• may ••••

May is one of the *modal* verbs which are used with the infinitives of other verbs to express such ideas as possibility and probability. They always keep the same form, rather than inflecting (you say *she may*, not *she mays do something*).

The modal verb **might** is used as the past tense of **may** in past indirect speech, and shares many of the same senses, but because **might** has uses of its own, it has its own entry in this book.

The chief uses of **may** are to express the idea of *possibility*, and to ask and give *permission*.

➤ See also **might** and **modal verbs**.

POSSIBILITY

1 Something that **may** be the case is a possibility in the present:
They've got the same surname. They may be [= perhaps they are] *brother and sister.*
I think she's here, but I may be wrong.

2 Something that **may** happen is a possibility in the future:
You may change [= perhaps you will change] *your mind when you hear the price.*
I may not come if my cold gets worse.
You may be asked to give a speech.

> ⓘ Notice that you rarely use **may** in direct questions about possibilities:
> *Are we likely to* (not *may we*) *need the tent?*

3 You use **may have** with a past participle to express the possibility that something happened in the past:
He may have felt [= perhaps he felt] *unwelcome.*
I may have given [= perhaps I gave] *him the wrong impression.*

> ⓘ Notice that the standard traditional form for expressing unreal possibilities in the past has always been **might have**:
> *You stupid thing! You might have* (rather than *may have*) *been killed!* [you weren't killed]
> *If you'd come a moment later we might not have* (rather than *may not have*) *survived.* [we did survive]
> *If he'd had a friend or two, he might not have* (rather than *may not have*) *taken his own life.* [he did take his own life]

4 You use **may have** to express the possibility that something will have happened by a certain time:
You never know; I may have [= perhaps I will have] *retired by then.*

> ⓘ Notice that **may not** has a different meaning from **cannot**:
> *You may not have heard* [= it's possible that you didn't hear] *the news.*
> *You can't have heard* [= it's not possible that you heard] *the news.*
> *Those figures may not be accurate.*[= perhaps those figures are inaccurate]
> *Those figures cannot be accurate.* [those figures must be inaccurate]

5 You can add **well** after **may** to emphasize a possibility:
You may well be right.
I may well have given him the wrong impression.

6 In short answers, **may** can be followed by **be**, **do**, or **have** and **may have** by **been**, **done**, or **had** in referring back to verbs that use these auxiliaries:
'Aren't you reacting a bit unfairly?' 'I may be.'
'Was it you that made the suggestion?' 'It may have been.'
'Have we got any of those crisps left?' 'We may have.'

'Does it matter?' 'It may do (or *it may).'*
Did I say this last week? I may not have done (or *I may not have).*
'Didn't Orwell fight in Spain?' 'He may have done (or *he may have).'*

➤ See also the entries **do** and **ellipsis**.

PERMISSION

You use **may**:

1 to ask for permission. **May** is politer and more formal than **can**:

Please may I use your telephone?
Hallo. May I speak to James?
May I smoke?
May I use the car this evening?

2 to give permission:

You may unfasten your seatbelts and smoke if you wish.
'May I leave the table?' 'Of course you may.'

3 with **not**, to refuse permission:

'May I borrow your PC?' 'No, you may not.'

4 to make polite offers:

May I help you?

ⓘ Notice that **may** is part of the process of asking and giving permission. You use **be allowed to** or **can** where permission has already been given or refused:
I'm allowed to (not *I may*) *go to the shops on my own.*

OTHER USES

1 You can say that something **may** be the case, meaning that although it is, there is a more important fact to consider:

You may think it's silly, but it works.

2 You use **may** in the formal expression of wishes, often at the beginning of the sentence:

May you both be very happy!
These profits are most satisfactory. Long may it last!

3 You say you **may as well** do something if there is nothing better to do:

She's obviously not going to answer the door. We may as well go home.

•••• maybe, perhaps ••••

Both **maybe** and **perhaps** mean that something is possibly the case. **Maybe** is much more common than **perhaps** in spoken English. When **perhaps** is used in spoken English, it is usually in more formal contexts:

You never know, maybe the sun will come out this afternoon.
I think I'd like the chicken – and maybe a green salad.
There are teachers who perhaps haven't had the right sort of training.

He was perhaps the most interesting Scottish bishop of his day.
Too many students came (and perhaps still come) to university for social reasons.

- When people use **perhaps** in spoken English, they often pronounce it /praps/.

meals

Different meals can have different names, depending on the person who is speaking:

- **breakfast**

This is the first meal of the day, eaten in the morning. There are no regional or social variations in the name for this meal.

- **lunch**

This is the most usual term for the meal you eat at midday.

- **tea**

This is the small meal, sometimes called **afternoon tea**, of tea, biscuits and cakes that some people still take at about 4 or 5pm. The custom is less common nowadays.

Some people use this word for their early evening meal, especially one eaten as soon as they arrive home from work or school.

- **dinner**

This is a main meal, eaten in the evening. It is the meal you invite guests to, or that you eat in a restaurant in the evening. It is also the name of the main meal on a special occasion like Christmas, even if it is eaten in the middle of the day.

Some people use this word for the main meal of their day, whatever time they eat it.

- **supper**

This is the last meal of the day. It can be tea, dinner, or a late-night snack before you go to bed.

1 Names of meals are usually uncountable and are often used with **some** or **any**:

She prepared herself some lunch.
Would you like some breakfast?
'I haven't had any lunch,' she complained.

2 When names of meals are qualified by an adjective, they are usually countable:

We usually have a cooked breakfast.
After this, a light lunch will be served.
After a delicious dinner, there were several speeches.

3 More informally, and in certain regional dialects, people use the possessive pronoun before names of meals:

What did you have for your breakfast this morning?
Take one pill after your breakfast in the morning.
I'm going to have a steak for my tea tonight.

4 When you talk about eating a particular meal, you say that you **have** breakfast, lunch, tea, etc:

Lunchtime? I've only just had breakfast!
Our son may come down and have breakfast with us.

We had lunch together in town.
Haven't you had dinner yet?

5 When you are talking about the food that you eat as part of a particular meal, you say that you eat that particular food **for** breakfast, lunch, tea, etc:

I want to ask him what he eats for breakfast.
I've got a tuna sandwich for lunch.
We had a pint of beer and a bag of crisps for lunch in the pub.
What's for tea tonight?

6 When you invite someone to share a meal with you in your home, you can ask them if they'd like to **come over**, or **round**, **for dinner**, **lunch**, etc. More formally, you can invite them to **come to dinner**, **lunch**, etc. When you want to know if they'd like to have a meal in a restaurant with you, you ask them if they'd like to **go out for a meal**. If you are intending to pay for them, you can say that you'd like to **take them out for a meal**:

Why don't you come round for lunch on Saturday?
We'd like to invite you both to dinner next Friday.
How about going out for a meal instead of cooking tonight?
Can I come over and take you out for dinner?

•••• mean ••••

The verb **mean** is irregular:

means, meaning, meant /ment/

Mean has a range of senses, from 'have a particular sense' (*'Breadth' means the same as 'width'*) to 'intend' (*I didn't mean to be unsympathetic*). **Mean** does not, however, have the sense 'think'. When expressing an opinion you say, *eg 'I think* (not *I mean*) *you're right.'*

1 When you don't understand something, you can ask **What does it/this/that** etc **mean?**:

What does 'duress' mean?
It sounded like a French word; I didn't know what it meant.
The name Isaac means 'he laughs'.
In Greece, tipping your chin upwards means 'no'.

> ⓘ Notice that questions about meanings have the form **What does such-and-such mean?** (not *What means such-and-such?*)

2 You ask a person what they **mean** when you want them to explain what they are trying to say:

What do you mean when you say 'he's been under the weather'?
'I'm not sure.' 'What do you mean, you're not sure?'
She doesn't look like Jane to me, but I know what you mean.
'Wait till I tell my sister!' 'You mean she doesn't know?'

3 You ask someone which person or thing they **mean** when you want to know which one they are referring to:

'I can't remember her name, but she was a tall girl.' 'I know the one you mean.'
'I thought you meant the pub on the corner, not this one.'

4 People use **I mean** for various purposes in conversation:

- to make something clearer:

  What does he do? Her father, I mean.

- to correct a mistake:

  Are you taking Heather with you? Sorry, I mean Hazel.

- to add information or an explanation:

  You can't ring them now. I mean, they'll all have gone to bed, won't they?

5 You say you **mean** what you say to emphasize that you are serious, not joking, pretending, or being insincere:
'Please come again.' 'Do you mean that, or are you just being polite?'
I mean what I say, Tom; any more noise and you go straight to bed.

6 One thing **means** another:

- if it involves it:

  The higher cost of organic farming means higher food prices.
  Building this pipeline means working at temperatures well below zero.
  I started talking about how love means different things to different people.

- if it implies it:

  Fewer teachers means larger classes.

- if it is a sign of it:

  The green light coming on means it's finished.

7 Things that **mean** a lot to you are important to you:
You mean a lot to me.
Time means nothing to her.

INTENTIONS

1 You **mean** to do something when you intend to do it:
I don't think they meant to hurt him.
I didn't mean to stay all evening, but I was enjoying myself.

> ⓘ Notice that although **mean** is not usually used in the progressive forms, the present perfect progressive is common in the 'intending' sense:
> *I've been meaning to call you for ages.*

2 The structure **mean** + object is also possible in the 'intend' sense:
He didn't mean any harm.
He walks like a man who means business.

3 Someone who **means well** has good intentions:
He has courage and he means well, but I don't really like him.

4 You will sometimes hear the phrase **be meant to** used in the same way as **be supposed to**:

- to talk about what is intended to happen:
  What's this dot meant to represent?
  'The colours don't match.' 'They're not meant to.'
  It's a joke! You're not meant to take it seriously.
- to talk about what is expected to happen or be the case, according to some rule, arrangement, or understanding:
  We spent our money on beer, and then couldn't afford the books we were meant to read.
  We're not meant to know about this – it's classified information.

.... means ....

1 **Means** is a countable noun that ends in an **-s** both in its singular and plural forms:
Laws are not the only means available to governments for shaping policy.
But have we no alternative means of reaching an agreement?
Different groups have different ways and means of operating.

2 **By all means** is an expression people use to give permission. It can stand alone as a response, or it can form part of a sentence, meaning 'it is all right to… ':
'May I make a suggestion, sir?' 'By all means.'
'Can I do that?' 'Of course you can, by all means.'
If you feel well enough to do it, then by all means do it.

3 Something that is **by no means** the case is definitely not the case:
Single parents are by no means unusual nowadays.
It's by no means a problem, but we must remember it's there.
He's by no means alone in thinking that.

> ⓘ Notice that **by no means** is not the opposite of **by all means**.

—— measurements ——

➤ See also entries for **abbreviations, far, many, much, nouns, numbers and fractions, comparatives and superlatives**.

ASKING ABOUT MEASUREMENTS

1 You can ask about the weight of something by saying **how heavy is it?** but it is more usual to say **how much… ?** and to use a suitable verb:
How much does it weigh?
How much sugar do we need?
How much (weight) have you lost?

2 When you ask about liquid measurements, you always use **how much… ?** or, if the liquid is in closed containers, **how many… ?**:
How much petrol did you use on the journey?
How much salad dressing is there?
How much do you get in this bottle?
How many cans shall we get?
How many pints of blood are left?

3 Measurements of length can also apply to width, height and depth. You use **how** with **long**, **wide**, **high** and **deep** to ask about these dimensions. To ask about distance, you use **how far?**:

How long is that piece of wood?
How wide is the space for the washing-machine?
How high is the tower?
How deep is the pool?
How far is the chip shop?

4 You use **what temperature?**, **how hot?** or **how cold?** to ask about temperature and climate:

What temperature is the water in the test tube?
At what temperature will the rock melt?
How hot do you like your bath water?
How cold should the fridge be?
What temperature is it in Madrid at this time of year?

EXPRESSING MEASUREMENTS

1 A measurement can behave like an adjective if it is hyphenated and placed before a noun, but note that only the *singular* form can be used in this way:

a ten-pound (not *ten-pounds*) *turkey*
an eighty-five kilo boxer
a three-litre bottle
a one-pint jug
six-inch nails
a twenty-five-yard pool
a three-mile run
a two-kilometre race

2 When you specify a quantity of something, you use the plural form and **of**:

twenty metres of wire
three litres of milk
ten tons of sand

3 When the measurement comes after a linking verb or in an adverbial phrase, you use the plural or singular form, depending on the number:

The wall is ten metres high.
The table's about a yard across.
Plant the bulbs at least ten centimetres deep.

EXCEPTIONS

There are some exceptions to the points above:

1 Although the plural form **stones** is possible, the singular **stone** is more common:

She only weighs four stone.

2 **Hundredweight** is always singular:

two hundredweight of sand

3 **Foot** is used in the singular when there is no following adjective:

He's over six foot now.
I'm five foot three.

But when an adjective is added, you can use the plural:

He's over six feet tall.

•••• middle ••••

Although **middle** and **centre** are synonyms, they are used for different purposes.

1 The **middle** of something can be quite a large, vague area:

She put the vase of flowers down in the middle of the table.
The ball struck her in the middle of her forehead.
The motorway is likely to go through the middle of their farmland.
Why don't you sit in the middle [= between us] *and then we can both talk to you?*

2 **Centre** suggests a precise point, and is used, for instance, in geometry.

People commonly talk about the **centre line** on a road, or the **central reservation** on a motorway:

Measure the radius of a circle in a straight line from its centre to its circumference.
a journey to the centre of the earth
The road is only a minor one, but has the luxury of a white centre line.

> ⓘ Note, though, that we talk about the **city centre** to mean the part of a city where most of the shops and offices are.

3 You talk about the **middle**, not the **centre**, of a period or an event:

I take a lunch break round about the middle of the day.
She was called 'Storm' because she was born in the middle of a thunderstorm.

4 People say they are **in the middle of** doing something when they are still in the process of doing it and have not nearly finished:

We were in the middle of moving house when my daughter had her second child.

> ⓘ You use **busy doing** something to mean the same as **in the middle of**:
> *We were busy looking at some photos when you came in.*

•••• might ••••

Might is one of the *modal* verbs which are used with the infinitives of other verbs to express such ideas as possibility and probability. They always keep the same form, rather than inflecting (you say *she might*, not *she mights do something*).

➤ See the entry **modal verbs** for more information about their grammatical behaviour.

The negative contracted form is **mightn't**.

POSSIBILITY

1 in the present and future

Might can be used, like **may**, to express a possibility, or to suggest that there is a chance of something happening. The traditional idea is that **might** represents a less definite possibility than **may**, but modern speakers often use them interchangeably. **May** is slightly more formal than **might**.

The situation might not be as hopeless as you think.
You might be asked to make a speech.
The alarm mightn't go off for twenty-five years.

> ⓘ Notice that **might not** has a different meaning from **could not**:
> *It might not be true* [= there is a possibility that it isn't true].
> *It couldn't be true* [= it's impossible that it's true].
> You can emphasize a possibility by adding **well** after **might**, as you can with **may**:
> *Alterations in diet and hygiene might well produce indigestion.*

2 in conditions

When you use **might** rather than **would** in the main clause of a conditional sentence, it has the same effect as adding **perhaps** to **would**:

You might (or *perhaps you would*) *think more clearly if you took a break.*

3 in indirect speech

You use **might** after a past reporting verb to represent both **may** and **might** in the original direct speech. For example:

original words:

'I may work late, so I might stay in town overnight.'

reported words:

She said she might work late, so she might stay in town overnight.

other examples:

The doctors thought I might not be able to walk again.
There were fears that the government might raise taxes.
I thought we might need more cash if we were going to eat out.

4 **Might** also represents present **may** or **might** after past structures such as **looked as if** or **sounded as if**, which are used to report an impression:

The weather looked as if it might clear up.

5 in the past

You do not usually use **might** with a past meaning. Instead, you can choose words such as **maybe** or **perhaps**:

She said nothing. Maybe she was annoyed (not *She might be annoyed*).

- **real possibilities**

You can use **might have** with a past participle to say that it is possible that something happened, or has happened, or was the case:

'They're very late.' 'Yes, they might have [= it's possible that they have] *got lost.'*

I don't remember my exact words. I might have said [= it's possible that I said] *'Cheers'.*
She was tall and dark and might have been about thirty-five.

- **unreal possibilities**

You use **might have** to express the situation where something that could have happened did not actually happen:

I might have had a different husband [but I've got this one], *and then you and Paul might never have existed* [but you do].
It was a simple mistake that might have happened to anyone [although it didn't].

- **Might have** is often used in unreal conditional sentences referring to the past:

If proper care had been taken the catastrophe might have been avoided [but it wasn't].
If she had warned us we might not have had all this trouble [but we did].

➤ See **may** for the distinction between **may have** and **might have**.

6 possibilities in the future

You can use **might have**, like **may have**, to express the possibility that something will have happened by some future time:

He might have changed his mind by this time next week.

ELLIPSIS

In short answers, **might** can be followed by **be**, **do**, or **have** and **might have** by **been**, **done**, or **had** in referring back to verbs that use these auxiliaries:

'Will you take me with you?' 'I don't know. I might do (or *I might*).*'*
'Did you leave your gloves in the car?' 'I might have done (or *I might have.*)*'*
'Was he sent abroad?' 'I don't know. He might have been.'

OTHER USES

1 You can use **might** to ask permission very politely. People generally use the form **I wonder if I might...** rather than **Might I... ?**:
I wonder if I might use your telephone?

2 You use **might** and **might have** to complain that someone is not doing something, or didn't do something:

You might help me carry this luggage.
You might have asked me before borrowing money from my purse.

3 People say that something **might** be the case, meaning that although it is, there is something more important to consider:

Your work might be boring, but at least you have a job.

4 You use **might** to make gentle suggestions:

You might like to consider giving a little more.
It might be a good idea to leave separately.
I thought we might perhaps have lunch.

5 You use **I might have known** or **I might have guessed** to comment that what has happened is typical, or was to be expected:

I might have known you would get the message wrong.

6 You say you **might as well** do something if there is nothing more interesting to do:

We might as well go home. Everything's finished.

•••• million ••••

➤ See **hundred**.

•••• mind ••••

The verb **mind** is used, especially in negative sentences and questions, and especially in the structure **mind** (+ object) + **-ing** form.

1 You **mind** something if you object to it, or are upset or annoyed by it:

The boss didn't mind if we were a bit late in the morning.
I don't mind you (or *your*) *taking notes if that helps.*
I'm sure he won't mind us going into his kitchen.
I hope you don't mind my (or *me*) *asking, but are you perfectly all right?*

2 **Mind** can also be followed, like the verb **care**, by a clause introduced by a **wh-** question word. You use a present tense in the subordinate clause when you refer to the future:

I don't mind what he does, as long as I know where he is.
I really don't mind which day we have the meeting.

> ⓘ People use **I don't mind** when they don't care enough to make a choice: *'Would you prefer a roll or a sandwich?' 'I don't mind. Either, thanks.'*

3 You use the forms **would you mind if...** and **do you mind if...** to ask permission to do something. Notice that if you use the **would** form, the verb after **if** is in the simple past. If you use the **do** form, the verb after **if** is in the present tense:

Would you mind if I asked what's for supper?
Would you mind if I went away for a few days?
Do you mind if I join you?
Do you mind if I open a window?

4 You use the forms **would you mind** and **do you mind** with **-ing** forms to ask people to do things:

Would you mind switching off the light?
Would you mind looking away for a minute?
Would you mind keeping your voices down?
Do you mind explaining why you're here?
Do you mind not using [= please don't use] *those long words?*

ⓘ Notice that when you want to give permission or agree to a request beginning **would you mind?** or **do you mind?** you should use a negative expression, like **of course not**. It's also very usual to add an additional phrase to explain your answer:
'Would you mind if I had a pudding?' 'No, of course not. I'll ask for the menu.'
'Do you mind if I come with you?' 'Not at all. I'd enjoy your company.'
To refuse permission, or refuse to do something, you don't usually answer *'Yes, I would mind'*, or *'Yes, I do mind'*, which are rather direct refusals, and can seem rude. A more polite example of refusing might be *'I'd rather not'* or *'I'd rather you didn't'.*

• • • • miss, missing • • • •

THE VERB

1 You **miss** a target when you don't hit it:
A boy threw a brick at the car, but missed.
What about the three goals you missed?

2 You just **miss** an obstacle, or **miss** being harmed when you only just avoid it or escape it:
She narrowly missed being hit when two gunmen opened fire.
His car just missed a lamp post.

3 You **miss** something when you don't notice it:
The phone box is right next to the garage; you can't miss it.
'She must know what's going on; she doesn't miss much.'
'Sorry, I missed your name; could you repeat it?'

4 You **miss** an experience or an activity when you can't be involved in it:
William's missed such a lot of school this term.
'I missed my favourite programme yesterday.' 'Well, you didn't miss much [= it wasn't very good].*'*

5 You **miss** a chance or opportunity when you fail to use it:
This is a chance not to be missed!

6 You **miss** a plane, bus or train when you are too late to travel on it:
By missing the first flight we also missed the connecting flight to the USA.

7 You **miss** a person or thing when you are sad because they are no longer with you, or available to you:
She misses her Mum and Dad, and she misses the golden stretches of beach.
I am missing her, but I know she's enjoying herself.

THE ADJECTIVE 'MISSING'

A person or thing that is **missing**

- is lost, or not in the usual place:
  Later, the body of the missing girl was washed up on the beach.

Her husband had been reported missing.
He looked in the drawer; his passport was missing.
All my money was in the missing bag.

- is non-existent or lacking:

Vitamin B12 is missing from his diet.
She noticed that there was a button missing off his shirt.
Most of the puzzles are complete, but some have one or two pieces missing.
Students have to fill in the missing words.

modal verbs

Modal verbs or *modal auxiliary verbs* are used before infinitives of other verbs, adding certain kinds of meaning to those verbs. They may indicate *probability, certainty, obligation, ability, habit* or *willingness*. The modal auxiliary verbs are:

can, could, may, might, will, would
shall, should, must, ought

Need and **dare** can also be used like modal auxiliary verbs, as can **used to**. For specific information on each modal auxiliary verb, see their separate entries.

GRAMMAR

1 Modal verbs do not have a final **-s** in the third person singular form:
He ***must*** (not *musts*) *be mad.*

2 Questions, negatives and question tags are formed without **do**:
Can *you swim?*
I ***can't*** [= cannot] *see a thing.*
Hold on a moment, ***would*** *you?*

3 Modals stand for a whole clause in short answers and other elliptical structures:
'Will she like it?' 'I'm sure she will'
You can walk faster than I can.

4 The infinitive which follows a modal does not take **to**:
They might ***be*** (not *to be*) *late.*
I couldn't ***stay*** (not *to stay*) *awake any longer.*

5 Modals themselves do not have infinitives or participles. Instead, other verbs are used:
I'm going ***to have to*** (not *must*) *work much harder this year.*
By the end of the course, you should ***be able to*** (not *can*) *write a simple business letter in French.*

6 Some modal verbs have past forms, *eg* **can–could**, **will–would**, **may–might**, **shall–should**, which can be applied in reported speech, for example. However, the 'past forms' have many of their own uses which are not related to the past at all. For details, see their separate entries.

7 Some past structures are possible with modal + **have** + past participle, especially when they are being used to express degrees of certainty about the past:
He ***must have come*** *in late. I didn't hear him.*

8 In informal contexts, contracted negative forms ending in **-n't** are often possible. **Will** and **would** have contracted affirmative forms too. These are **-'ll** and **-'d**:

*I **couldn't** unlock the door.*
*He **won't** come out of his room.*
*I'**ll** give you a ring this evening.*
*He'**d** sit in a chair watching TV all day.*

> ⓘ Notice that the contracted form of **will not** is **won't**.

MEANING

Modal verbs are used to express ideas of *certainty, possibility, ability, obligation, permission, habit* and *willingness*. Each modal can express a variety of meanings, and so an awareness of context is important for understanding a speaker's intentions.

1 degrees of certainty

- **absolute certainty**:

  *Lunch **will** be ready in five minutes.*
  *Good, that'**ll** be Richard arriving.*
  *You **must** be Charles.*
  *She **can't** be lost. She knows the area too well.*

- **probability and possibility**:

  *The bank **should** (or **ought to**) have copies of the leaflet.*
  *You **may** change your mind when you hear the price.*
  *I **might** join you later if I'm feeling better.*
  *It **could** snow tomorrow.*

- **talking about what is sometimes, or generally, true**:

  *The roads **can** get dangerous in the winter.*
  *He **can** be quite rude sometimes.*

- **certainty that is dependent on particular conditions**:

  *If I knew where I'd left it, I **wouldn't** have lost it, would I?*
  *If he really loved her, he **wouldn't** hurt her like that.*
  *Where **will** you go if you have to sell the house?*

2 obligation:

*You **must** sign out when you leave, in case of fire.*
*You **will** apologize to your mother immediately!*
***Need** I stay by the phone all day?*

3 prohibition:

*Pupils **must** not run in the corridors.*
*Drinks **may** not be taken into the auditorium.*
*I'm afraid you **can't** smoke in here.*

4 absence of obligation:

*You **needn't** come in tomorrow; there won't be anything for you to do.*

5 permission:

*'**Can** I look at this dictionary for a moment, please?' 'Of course you **can**.'*

__May__ I call you Peter?
Candidates __may__ leave as soon as they have completed the examination.

6 **recommendation and advice-seeking**:
You __should__ try that new Chinese restaurant.
You __ought__ to get someone to look at that cut.
He __might__ try being a bit nicer to people in future.
__Shall__ I bring waterproofs?

7 **willingness, wanting and offering**:
If you __would__ care to wait in the waiting room, madam, someone will come and fetch you.
__Will__ you follow me?
__I'll__ give you a lift.
__Shall__ I take that for you?

8 **ability**:
I __couldn't__ drive at that time, so I had to go all the way by bike.
__Can__ you reach that shelf?

9 **habitual behaviour**:
He__'ll__ sit at the window all day until she comes home in the evening.
She __would__ constantly interrupt you when you were trying to explain something.
We __used to__ swim there when we were kids.

> ⓘ **Used to** has the same meaning as **would** in the example above. For details of how it behaves grammatically, see the entry **used to**.

money

PRICES

1 You usually say **how much is ... ?** or **how much does ... cost?** to ask about a price:
How much is a new Rolls Royce?
How much does a sandwich cost in the college café?

2 You can say that something **costs** a certain amount of money, but more usually you simply say it **is** a certain amount, to tell somebody the price of something:
'How much is this bracelet?' 'It's £19.99.'
A car like that costs around five thousand dollars.

3 When you can buy different amounts of something, it is sold by a certain weight or some other measurement:
We sell these beans by the pound or in packets.
The sand is sold by the sack.

4 Something that is sold by weight costs a certain amount **per** unit of that weight:
The apples are 45c per pound.

In everyday speech, **a** often replaces **per**:
It's 25p a litre.

CHANGING MONEY

When you want to change your money because you don't have the right combination of coins or notes, you can say **Can you change ... ?** or **Have you got ... for ... ?**:

Can you change a fiver? I need some coins for the parking meter.
Have you got two ten-pence pieces for a twenty?
How many Euros will I get for these dollars?

EXPRESSING DIFFERENT AMOUNTS

1 When an amount comes before a noun, it is hyphenated and works like an adjective, but note that it's the *singular* form that is used in this way:

a ten-pound note
a twenty-dollar bill
a fifty-lire coin

> ⓘ Notice that although the singular of **pence** can be **a penny**, **one pence** or **one p**, you usually say **a ten-pence piece**.
> Notice however that the forms **a ten-penny piece**, **a ten-pence piece** and a **ten-p piece** are all possible, reflecting the singular forms that people use.

2 When the amount alone is given, the plural form is given where necessary:

I found five pounds!
I need another two hundred dollars.
She earns over twenty pounds an hour.
The sweets are five pence each.

3 When you express an amount of pounds and pence informally in speech, you can use the singular form **pound**:

I thought I had three pound fifty in my pocket.
The price has gone up ten pence to two pound twenty.

MONEY IN WRITING

You can use words to express an amount of pounds, dollars, etc in a sentence, but if the amount includes pence, cents, etc too, you usually write it in figures:

He sent me twenty pounds.
The yo-yo only cost 65p.
I refer to your invoice for $63.20.

> ⓘ Notice that when writing amounts which have both pounds and pence (or dollars and cents), only the **£** or **$** symbol is necessary:
> *£10.50* (not *£10.50p*)
> *$2.63* (not *$2.63c*)

months

1 The twelve months of the year are:

January, February, March, April
May, June, July, August, September
October, November, December

2 The following abbreviations are in common use in writing the date:

Jan *Feb* *Mar* *Apr* *Aug*
Sept *Oct* *Nov* *Dec*

3 Notice that the months are uncountable nouns:

Tess left home on a beautiful morning in May.

➤ For the various styles of writing the date see **dates**.

• • • • more • • • •

AS A DETERMINER

1 As the comparative of **many**, **more** is used with plural nouns, and as the comparative of **much**, it is used with uncountable nouns. **More** can have two meanings:

- **More** can mean 'a greater number of' people or things, or 'a greater amount of something':

  More people came last year.
  We had more money than we thought.

- **More** can mean 'additional' to a previous number or amount, and is often used after numbers or quantity words like **much**, **many** and **some**:

  Then two more people joined us.
  How many more nights shall we stay here?
  Would you like some more pudding?

2 You can use **many** to intensify **more** when it refers to a plural noun, and **much** to intensify it when it refers to an uncountable noun:

She showed much more interest in learning Japanese.
We've had many more applications this year.

3 Other quantifying or intensifying expressions are also possible before **more**:

- referring to either a plural noun or an uncountable noun:
  any, far, a lot, no, rather, some
- only when referring to a plural noun:
  many, several, a few, a good many, a great many
- only when referring to an uncountable noun:
  much, a bit, a good deal, a great deal, a little

AS A PRONOUN

1 You use **more of** before the determiners **the**, **this**, **that**, **those**, **these**, possessives, or pronouns:

Several more of these items will have to be returned.
I found more of her clothes in the wardrobe.
Have some more of Anna's cake.
It's time that more of you took some action.

2 You can use **more** by itself as an independent pronoun when the noun it refers to can be understood:

Three directors have resigned and three more have been appointed.
There's writing paper in the drawer if you need more.

3 You use **more than** before a number or quantity to mean 'over' that amount:

More than fifty workers have been sacked.
The baby can't be more than six months old.

AS AN ADVERB

1 After an expression like **once** or **three times**, **more** means 'again':

I looked back twice more before turning the corner.

2 **More** is used as the comparative of the adverb **much**, with the meaning 'to a greater extent':

I don't enjoy this any more than you do.

FORMING COMPARATIVES OF ADJECTIVES AND ADVERBS

You use **more** to form the comparative of most adjectives that have two or more syllables, and to form the comparative of most adverbs:

The chairs were more comfortable in the kitchen.
You could have said that more tactfully, couldn't you?

➤ See **comparatives and superlatives** for more information.

•••• morning, afternoon, evening ••••

The **morning** is the time from midnight to midday; the **afternoon** is the time from midday until about 5pm or 6pm; the **evening** is the time from 5pm or 6pm until about 10pm. In this entry, **evening** or **afternoon** can be substituted for **morning**.

1 To distinguish a specified time in the morning from the same time in the evening, you can add **in the morning**:

I couldn't get to sleep until about 2 o'clock in the morning or later.

2 The morning of today is **this morning**:

This letter came for you earlier this morning.

3 The morning of yesterday is **yesterday morning** and the morning of tomorrow is **tomorrow morning**:

I spoke to him yesterday morning.
Please report to me here tomorrow morning.

4 The morning of a particular day in the past or future can be referred to as **that morning**:

Early on 28 November Mrs Thatcher resigned, and later that morning Major was formally appointed as Prime Minister.

5 In the context of the past or future, the morning of the day before the one you are talking about is referred to as **the previous morning** or **the morning before**:

Since the previous morning they had come nearly five hundred miles.
John said he'd seen Adam the morning before.
There's a meeting on the 13th, so I'll come the morning before to discuss details.

6 In the context of the past or future, the morning of the day after the one you are talking about is referred to as **the following morning** or **the next morning**.

When I got home she was asleep. The next morning, she asked me how my evening had gone.

SINGLE AND REGULAR HAPPENINGS

1 When you are saying that something happened, or will happen, during a certain morning, you use **on**. Informally, you can omit **on** before **the**:

On the morning of 18 August, she shot her husband dead.
OK then, I'll see you the morning before the wedding.

2 When you are talking about a particular day in the past or future, you say that something happened, or will happen, **in the morning** or, as mentioned in section **4** above, **that morning**:

I can't meet you till lunchtime on Thursday; I've got a music lesson in the morning.

> ⓘ **In the morning** can also mean 'tomorrow morning', or 'on the morning of the next day':
> *Good night. See you in the morning.*
> *I was disappointed in the morning to discover that she had gone during the night.*
> This does not apply to **afternoon** or **evening**.

3 You can avoid specifying which morning, by saying **one morning**:

David asked me about my family over coffee one morning.
Why don't you come over one morning?

4 You can talk about mornings in particular months or seasons in the following ways:

On a cold and frosty morning in December, they said goodbye.
One hot summer morning I set off to climb the mountain.

5 Something that happens regularly every morning happens **in the morning** or **in the mornings**:

We used to run to school in the morning after breakfast.
He wrote poetry in the mornings, then listened to music.

6 Something that happens regularly on a particular morning of the week happens, *eg* **on a Thursday morning** or **on Thursday mornings**:

On Saturday mornings there was a film show.
I went to a dancing class on a Saturday morning.

➤ See also **night**.

• • • • most • • • •

AS A DETERMINER

As the superlative of **many**, **most** is used with plural nouns, and as the superlative of **much** it is used with uncountable nouns. **Most** is used in two ways:

- You can use **most** to mean 'the majority of' people or things, or 'the greater proportion of' something:

  Most people like the cinema.
  Most washing machines work like this.
  This product, like most chocolate, contains sugar.

■ **Most** is used as a superlative. **The most** is sometimes used in formal English:

The winner is the contestant with the most points.
Kim showed the most courage when she jumped.

AS A PRONOUN

1 You use **most of** before the determiners **the**, **this**, **that**, **these**, and **those**, possessives or pronouns, to mean 'the majority of', or 'the greater proportion of':

Most of you have a personal computer.
Most of the work can be done on a calculator.
You can delete most of these names.
Most of our clients are satisfied.
I've heard most of Bill's jokes before.

2 You can use **most** by itself as an independent pronoun when the noun it refers to can be understood:

The village people felt strongly about it and most were willing to come to the meeting.

AS AN ADVERB

1 You can use **most**, like **very**, to intensify adjectives or adverbs:

The audience were most amused.
To my surprise, he spoke most interestingly.

2 **Most** is used as the superlative of the adverb **much**, with the meaning 'to the greatest extent':

The children made a list of the presents they most wanted to receive.

FORMING SUPERLATIVES OF ADJECTIVES AND ADVERBS

You use **most** to form the superlative of most adjectives that have two or more syllables, and to form the superlative of most adverbs. **The most** is used in a situation where a group of people or things is being compared:

The most important reason is that we haven't got enough money.
How can children learn most successfully?

➤ See the entries **far** and **comparatives and superlatives** (using superlatives, paragraph **9**) for **by far** and other intensifiers used before **most**.

•••• much ••••

AS A DETERMINER

1 You often use **much** before uncountable nouns; it is the opposite of **little**:

After much hesitation he had at last begun to write.
Much thought has gone into this.
The problem can cause much unhappiness.

ⓘ **Much**, like **many**, sounds rather formal when used in positive statements. In conversation people tend to use **a lot of** or **lots of** instead. **Much** is common in negative contexts, however, whether formal or informal, and in questions. Notice that **not much** usually means 'very little':
He doesn't seem to have much interest in the subject.
Did you have much trouble finding your way?
We appear to have lots of milk but not much bread.

2 Although **much** is quite rare on its own in positive contexts in conversational English, it is often used with **too**, **so** and **as**:
I'm pleased you've done so much work.
She wants to give herself as much time as possible to prepare.
I can't concentrate during the day – the children require too much attention.

3 You use **how** and **however** with **much** to ask or talk about quantities:
How much time have you got?
I was amazed at how much rubbish I sold.

AS A PRONOUN

1 You use the form **much of** before the determiners **the**, **this** and **that** before pronouns and possessive forms:
Much of their material is borrowed.
School food was not nice; much of it was positively unhealthy.
Much of the town was without electricity last night.
I agree with much of this article.

2 You say you don't **think much of** something if you think it's no good:
He didn't think much of the course, but decided to stay on.

3 **Much** is used independently as a pronoun, without **of**:
You haven't got much to say, have you?
He asked how much I'd eaten that day.
That was as much as he felt he could do for a while.
We don't hear much about it these days but there are still problems.

4 **How much** is used to refer to amounts of money:
Do you know how much they are willing to pay?

AS AN ADVERB

1 You can use **much** to mean 'greatly' or 'to a great extent'. Notice that informally you usually intensify it with **very**:
She was very much upset.
I'm very much looking forward to meeting you.
I never enjoyed sport much.
She missed him so much that she wanted to die.
It didn't worry me as much as her.
Don't blame yourself too much.

2 **How much** is used to ask or talk about amount, degree or frequency:
How much do you actually use the club?
I would like to say how much we appreciate their hard work.

3 You use **much** to intensify or emphasize comparatives. **Much** can also intensify the adverb **too**:

Her backache was getting much worse.
The others seemed much more confident.
I arrived much sooner than I expected to.
It's much less cold than it was.
It's much too late to telephone them.

•••• must ••••

Must is one of the *modal* verbs which are used with the infinitives of other verbs to express such ideas as possibility, probability and necessity. They always keep the same form, rather than inflecting (you say *she must*, not *she musts, do something*). **Must** has two main meanings. It can express various kinds of *necessity* and *obligation*, and it can express *certainty* or *strong probability*.

The negative contracted form is **mustn't** (/ˈmʌsənt/).

NECESSITY AND OBLIGATION

1 **Must** can express various kinds of necessity and obligation:

- legal or other requirements:

  Any correspondence must be made public.
  All passengers must show their passports at the desk.

- necessity:

  Asian children here must learn English.
  A company like ours must be concerned about safety.
  We must first consider the question of expense.

- reminders:

  Our instructions must not be too difficult for children to understand.
  It must be remembered that time is money.

- urgency:

  'I can't stay here any longer. I must get back to the hospital.'
  This is between you and me. No one else must be involved.

- personal resolutions:

  I must lose some weight.
  I mustn't eat so much.
  I must remember to send them the keys.

- encouragement and reassurance:

  You mustn't be shy.
  You mustn't continue to think badly of yourself.

- recommendations:

  You must see the world while you're young.
  You must read this book; I loved it.

- invitations:

  You must come over and hear my new CDs.

- considerate or reasonable behaviour:

  Well, I mustn't keep you talking on the phone.
  You mustn't treat people like that.

- pleas and protests:

  I've seen this film already; must I watch it again?
  'Martin, you write to her this time.' 'Must I really?'
  Why must you always argue with me?
  Must you bother me when I'm thinking?

> ⓘ **alternatives to 'must'**
>
> ■ You can also use **have to** (especially in AmE), **have got to** (especially in BrE), **ought to**, **should** and **need** to express necessity and obligation in some of the situations shown above:
> *All passengers have to* (or *have got to*) *show their passports.*
> *Of course Asian children here have to* (or *have got to*, or *need to*) *learn English.*
> *It should be remembered that time is money.*
> *I've got to get back to the hospital.*
> *You ought to* [less strong than *must*] *read this book.*
> *I oughtn't to keep you talking on the phone.*
> *Do I have to* (or *have I got to*) *watch this film again?*
>
> ■ **Have to** and **have got to** are usually preferred where the obligation is not connected with your immediate situation or conversation:
> *Sorry, I must go. I've got to meet Giles at two-thirty.*

2 To express a lack of obligation or necessity you use **do not have to**, **need not** or **do not need to**:

I don't have to (not *I must not*) *agree with everything you say.*
You don't need to (or *you needn't*, but not *you mustn't*) *come if you don't want to.*

For lack of obligation in the past:

We didn't have to stay.

3 As there is no past tense of **must** (you can't say *I musted*), you use **had to**:

I had to go out and buy a birthday present for Millie.
We all had to work hard in that place.

4 **Must** can, however, be used to refer to the past in *indirect speech*:

I was told I must pay for my own reference books.

5 **Must**, **have to** and **have got to** can express obligation in a present or future situation:

I must ring the tax office tomorrow.
I've got to (or *I have to*) *be in Paris on Friday.*

You can also use **will have to** and **shall have to** for future obligation:

You'll have to pay a deposit.
I shall have to speak to them about this.

PROHIBITION

1 Something that you **must not** (or **mustn't**) do is something you are forbidden to do, or not allowed to do. In AmE, **cannot** and **can't** are used to forbid or prohibit, and are also possible in BrE:

You mustn't (or *can't*) *blame people before they can defend themselves.*
Well, we mustn't (or *can't*) *sit around here all day doing nothing.*

2 For prohibition in the past you can say, *eg*:

We weren't allowed to leave (or *We couldn't leave*).

CERTAINTY OR STRONG PROBABILITY

1 You say something **must** be the case if it is unlikely not to be the case:

If it's a hundred miles to Newcastle, it must be two hundred to Edinburgh.
You must be very proud of your daughter.
He must wish he had passed those exams.
'Our heater's broken' 'That must be a nuisance.'
That must be Julie at the door.

ⓘ As with the 'obligation' sense of **must**, the alternatives **have to** and **have got to** are possible:

This has to (or *has got to*) *be the coldest day of the year.*
You have got to be joking.

2 **Can** is usually used instead of **must** in questions and with negatives:

Who can that be, phoning so late?
It can't be eight o'clock already.

But:

I'm so sorry I left you standing outside in the cold. What must you think of me?

3 Notice that **mustn't** is regular in question tags after **must** in the main clause, and it is used in negative questions:

He must think we need extra help, mustn't he?
Mustn't it be great to be retired?

ⓘ If something is *not necessarily* so, you use **need not** or **do not have to** rather than **must not**:

'There are always several reasons for something happening.' 'There needn't (or *don't have to*) *be.'*

4 You use **must have** with a past participle to say that something probably happened, or has probably happened:

I must have dropped my keys when I got out of the car.
But it's ten-thirty. They must have arrived by now.
She must have been in love without even knowing it.
The road's wet – it must have been raining.

5 You use **can have** in questions and negatives relating to probability in the past, rather than **must have**:

She can't have meant that.
What can have happened?

6 In indirect speech in the past **must** is used to refer to the time of speaking, and **must have** to refer to a time earlier than that:

I was sure she must be lying.
I felt a sharp pain, and thought I must have been stung.

ELLIPSIS

In short answers, **must** is often followed by **be**, **do**, or **have** and **must have** by **been**, **done**, or **had**, in referring back to verbs that use these auxiliaries:

'Have you got a pen?' 'I must have, somewhere.'
'Does that area have good weather?' 'It must do (or *it must*)*, it's on the south coast of Spain.'*
'Were you dreaming?' 'I must have been.'
'Did you drop your key?' 'Yes, I think I must have done (or *I must have*)*.'*

Nn

names and titles

FIRST NAMES

There is a variety of ways of referring to the name or names that your parents give you when you are born, as distinct from the name that you share with the other people in your family.

In BrE these names are referred to as **Christian names** or **first names** and in AmE as **first names** or sometimes **given names**. On official forms the term **forename** is often used: you may be asked to fill in your **surname** and **forename(s)**:

Hungarians put their surname before their Christian names.
Everyone called him by his first name.
Please print your forename(s) in full.

TALKING ABOUT PEOPLE

When you refer to other people, you can use their first name, their first name and their surname, their title and their surname, or sometimes their surname only.

1 You use someone's **first name** when referring to them if you know that person well, and if the listener knows who you are talking about:

Robert's going to be back on Tuesday.
Jane's invited us over for dinner tomorrow night.
Guess what! Nicky's going to have a baby!

2 You use **first name + surname** when you are talking about someone you do not know very well, or not personally at all, for example, a famous person. This is also a way of distinguishing between people who have the same first name:

Jacob Hartley of Gravesend said yesterday that he couldn't believe his luck.
He said he'd heard Michael Jackson sing twice.
I'm talking about James Stewart, not James Page.

3 You use someone's **title + surname** when you do not know them very well. This form is used most commonly in professional or public situations:

Can I speak to Mr Osborne in the Sales Department please?
Mrs Johnson is on the phone for you.
Mrs Davidson said we have to have our homework done by tomorrow.

4 You use the **surname** on its own to refer to public figures such as politicians, and some well-known people like sportsmen and sportswomen; it is also used to refer to very well-known people in history:

It is easy to see why Clinton wanted a tax on energy consumption.
Although Shakespeare was a writer, he also acted in his plays.

ADDRESSING PEOPLE

There are two main ways of addressing people. You can use their first name, or their title and their surname.

1 You address someone by their **first name** when you know them very well or fairly well. First names are generally used in informal situations:

Hi, Anne! How are you?
Morning, Robin. Have you got a moment for a chat?

2 You use someone's **title**+and **surname** in more formal situations, or when you want to show respect:

Ah, Mr Hamilton. Come in. What can I do for you?
Good afternoon, Mrs Jeffreys. How are you feeling today?

ⓘ Under American influence, the use of first names is growing in Britain; work colleagues, for instance, from the most junior to the most senior, may well call each other by their first names. But it is sensible to find out whether it is all right to call someone by their first name before you do so. In many companies employees still address their bosses as **Mr** or **Mrs** + **surname**.

3 Sometimes, especially in male groups, people address each other using **surnames only**. This form of address was used more in the past by some groups of male friends, such as schoolboys, or by schoolteachers addressing male pupils:

Oi! Stubbs! Get over here!
Jones, where's your homework?

4 **Sir** and **madam** are used in a very limited number of contexts. This form of address is used mainly by people working in service occupations, *ie* serving in shops, restaurants, etc. when speaking to customers. However, even this use can sound a bit old-fashioned these days:

Good afternoon, madam. Can I help you?
Would you like to try that on, sir?

ⓘ **Mr**, **Mrs**, **Ms** or **Miss**?
When you are using the title + surname form of address, you should use **Mr** (pronounced /ˈmɪstə(r)/) when addressing a man. Like **Mr**, **Ms** (pronounced /mɪz/), which you can use for a woman, does not indicate whether the person you are addressing is married or not. You use this form if you do not know, or if you feel it is not necessary to specify, the woman's marital status. Many women choose to put this title before their own name. You can also use **Mrs** (pronounced /ˈmɪsɪz/) before the surname of a married woman, and **Miss** before the name of a girl, or a woman who has never been married.

•••• near, close, next ••••

NEAR, NEAR TO AND CLOSE TO

1 **Near** and **near to** are both used like prepositions.

- **Near** is usually preferred for expressing physical closeness:

  His name is near the bottom of the list.
  We live quite near Cambridge.
  I'm sitting too near the fire.

- **Nearer** and **nearest** are sometimes followed by **to**:

  The meeting isn't till next week; I'll phone you nearer the time.
  The areas nearest the volcano should be evacuated.
  Which planet is nearest to the Sun?
  Which of the houses is nearest to a bus stop?

- **Near to** is often used to express closeness to a *state*, especially with an **-ing** form of a verb:

  She was very near to crying.

2 **Close to** is used like a preposition, with the same meaning as **near**. The word **to** is never dropped after **close**:

I'd prefer a place that is close to the shops.
They were singing a folk song, and Erika came close to tears.
Having been so close to winning last year, I thought this was my chance.

NEAREST AND NEXT

1 **Nearest** means 'closest':

We went to the nearest pub.

2 **Next** refers to the following person or thing in order, or in a series:

I hope to illustrate that point in my next lecture.
And you think I'll be the next to be arrested?

3 **Next** also expresses the idea of one thing or person being *beside* another:

An old woman lived in the next room.

4 **Next to** and **next door to** are used as prepositional phrases in the same way as **close to** and **near to**:

He was sitting next to her, holding her hand tightly.
He isn't our dog, but he lives next door to us.

•••• nearly ••••

➤ See **almost**.

•••• necessary ••••

1 The adjective **necessary** can come before or after the noun it qualifies:

We can provide the necessary equipment.
Trainees learn the skills necessary for the job.
Protein is necessary for cell renewal.

2 Things that are **necessary to** you or your existence are things that you need or must have:

Money is necessary to our plan.
Protein is necessary to life.

3 You can express the idea of necessity by using the form **it is necessary** with a **to**-infinitive. This is a more formal alternative to **we have to**, or **we must**:

Sometimes it is necessary to be cruel before being kind.
It will soon be necessary to renew your contract.

4 The construction **it is necessary** + **for** + object + **to-**infinitive is common:

Of course it's not necessary for a nursery nurse to be a woman.

5 **Necessary** can be used after **if** and **than** to represent a clause:

If necessary [= if it is necessary] *we'll stay the night in London.*
They threatened to use force if necessary [= if it became necessary].
His smile seemed to stay on his face for slightly longer than necessary [= than was necessary].

.... need ....

The verb **need** can be either an ordinary verb or a *modal* verb.

AS AN ORDINARY VERB

As an ordinary verb, **need** inflects in the normal way:

needs, needing, needed

negative forms:

don't need, didn't need

1 **need + object**

You say you **need** something when it is necessary for you to have it:

All these plants need is sun and careful feeding.
My life has changed and I need time to adjust.

2 **need + to-infinitive**

You say you **need** to do something when it is necessary for you to do it. **Need to** can be used in positive or negative contexts, and in questions:

The players need to feel confident with each other.
How do we need to improve?
You don't need to be an expert to see that it wouldn't work.
You didn't need to swear like that.

■ The structure **need** + **object** + **to-infinitive is also possible:**

I don't need her to tell me how to behave.
We urgently need you to share the responsibility.

➤ See also **need** as a modal verb.

3 **need + -ing form**

You can say that something **needs** *dealing with* in a certain way:

The public need educating in this matter.
The floor needs cleaning, so please do it.

AS A MODAL VERB

negative forms

need not, needn't

1 **need + infinitive without to**

Need is used with an infinitive without **to**, with negatives, in questions expecting the answer 'no', after **if**, with **only** and with words such as **hardly** and **rarely**, to talk about what is **not** necessary, or what can be **avoided**:

We needn't go into details yet.
Energy needn't cost the earth.
We needn't worry about that now.
No one need know.

> ⓘ Distinguish between **needn't** and **mustn't**:
> *You needn't* [= it is unnecessary to] *tell the whole truth, but you mustn't* [= it is wrong to] *lie.*

2 **need have + past participle**

You use the form **need have** + past participle, to talk about what was unnecessary, or could have been avoided, in the past:

She needn't have worried – we wouldn't have told anyone what really happened.
I see now that I needn't have taken so much trouble.

3 In indirect speech in the past, **need** refers to the time of speaking, and **need have** to an earlier time:

He was told that he needn't waste his time calling again.
I realized that I needn't have worried.

4 You can use either the modal **need** or the ordinary verb **need + to** when *making decisions* about the future:

I doubt if you need attend the meeting tomorrow.
You don't need to attend tomorrow's meeting.

5 You use the form **will**, or **shall need to** to talk about what is necessary in the future:

We shall need to look at this again at our next meeting.
You will need to go on taking this medicine for two weeks.
You'll need to hurry if you want to catch that train.

> ⓘ Notice that with reference to the present there is no difference in meaning between the modal verb **need** and the ordinary verb:
> *You needn't* (or *you don't need to*) *stay.*
> But with reference to the past, there can be a difference:
> *I didn't need to get up early after all* [= it was unnecessary to get up early, so I didn't].
> *I needn't have got up early after all* [= I got up early unnecessarily].

•••• neither ••••

Neither is used either alone or in combination with **nor**, to present negative alternatives. One difficulty people have with certain uses of **neither** is whether it is followed by a singular or plural verb.

➤ See also **either** and **nor**.

AS A DETERMINER

Neither is used before singular countable nouns, with a singular verb, to mean 'not the one nor the other of two':

He could have jumped, or simply waited for help to arrive; neither option seemed very attractive.

AS A PRONOUN

1 The preposition **of** must follow **neither** before a pronoun or determiner + noun. The pronoun or noun is always plural:

Neither of us drives, so we use the bus a lot.
Neither of his parents (or *neither parent*) *came to the wedding.*
Neither of these problems (or *neither problem*) *is impossible to solve.*

> ⓘ **Neither of**, although always followed by a plural pronoun or noun, strictly takes a singular verb. In practice, however, people often use a plural verb:
> *Neither of his children have* (or, more formally, *has*) *inherited Peter's talents.*
> *The two men, neither of whom were football fans* (or, more formally, *was a football fan*), *recognized his name.*

2 **Neither** can stand independently as a pronoun to refer back to two possibilities that have already been mentioned:

To succeed, you needed to have a lot of money and some rich friends. Jackie had neither.
We looked at two flats, but neither was suitable.

AS AN ADVERB

You can use **neither** with the meaning 'also not', to introduce the second of two negative alternatives. Notice that if **neither** begins the sentence, it causes inversion, so that the word order is **neither** + auxiliary verb + subject:

'I can't remember, I'm afraid.' 'Neither can I.'
Felix wasn't there on that occasion, and neither was I.

> ⓘ Notice the different word order when you use the alternative form **not either**:
> *'I don't think I'll be free that day.' 'I won't either, unfortunately.'*

You can use **nor** in the same way as **neither**:

'I've seen the film. I've never read the novel, though.' 'No, nor (or *neither*) *have I.'*

AS A CONJUNCTION

Neither ... nor can be used rather formally to link two negative ideas:

I had neither the time nor the energy to argue.

I had neither heard nor seen the tiger, and yet I knew it was there.
Neither she nor her partner was (or *were*) *free to come.*

> ⓘ Notice that where you have a combination of *eg* third and first person, or second and third person, a plural verb sounds better than a singular one:
> *Neither Roger nor I are sure.*
> *Neither you nor he have been put on the short list.*

There are three alternatives to using **neither ... nor**:

- **not** (or another negative) **... neither**:
  I've never swum in the sea here, and neither has Mark. (rather than *Neither Mark nor I have swum...*)
- **not ... or**:
  I hadn't met my cousin or his wife previously. (rather than *I had met neither my cousin nor his wife.*)
- After a pause, **nor** is possible after a negative as a more emphatic alternative to **or**:
  We didn't see him on Friday evening at the lecture, nor on Saturday.

Neither ... nor is the opposite of **both ... and**. See **both** section **7** and the accompanying note.

➤ See also **nor**.

•••• never ••••

Never means 'not at any time' or 'not ever'. It is the negative of **always**.

1 **Never** is used with reference to the future, past or present:
Never do that again!
I never get up before 10am.
I never hear from her any more.
I've never heard such nonsense!
He never tried to impress people.

2 **Never** can mean 'not under any circumstances':
It's never right to hit a child.

3 **Never** is sometimes used with a simple past tense as an informal alternative to **not**:
'I bet you told her.' 'I never said a word to her.'

POSITION

1 **Never** is used in *mid position*, that is, before the verb, but after an auxiliary verb or the verb **be**:
We never go into those shops.
I'd never dream of wearing a skirt as short as that.
She was never on time for anything.

Where there is more than one auxiliary verb, **never** usually goes after the first:
You would never have realized Susan was depressed.

2 Like **always**, **never** comes before a verb in the imperative:
Never take electrical appliances into the bathroom.

3 **Never** comes before auxiliaries that refer to a previous clause:
I don't find that easy and never will.

4 **Never** can sometimes begin a clause for dramatic effect in speeches or narratives. Notice that it causes inversion; the order is **never** + auxiliary verb (or **be**) + subject:
I found plenty of cows, but no people; indeed, never was I anywhere so rural.

WITH OTHER NEGATIVES

Never is used with **any**-words, but not with other negatives:
I've never told anyone (not *no-one*).
Perhaps I shall never (not *I shan't never*) *see him again.*

> ⓘ Notice that you can use **not ever** as a weaker form of **never**, except where **never** introduces the sentence:
> *I haven't ever* (or I've *never*) *thought about that.*
> But:
> *Never give up hope.*

newspapers

There is a style of writing that newspaper reporters use, which is covered very briefly here. The language of newspapers must be brief and descriptive; it is possible to identify some of the usual ways of achieving this style in terms of vocabulary and of grammar.

VOCABULARY

There are particular words that appear in newspaper headlines, which are short, but carry a lot of meaning. They are not always the most common words in everyday language, but they are used frequently in headlines because they are dramatic and therefore catch the reader's attention. Below is a list of some of these words and a more everyday explanation of their meanings:

aid	*help*
axe	*abolish* or *reduce*
back	*support*
ban	*prohibit(ion)*
bid	*attempt*
blast	*explosion*
blaze	*fire*
blow	*disappointment*
boost	*increase*
clash	*argument* or, in sport, *match*
curb	*restrict(ion)*
drive	*campaign*
flee	*run away*
hurdle	*obstacle*
link	*connect(ion)*
mob	*uncontrolled crowd*

ordeal	*unpleasant experience*
plea	*strong request*
pledge	*promise*
probe	*investigation*
rap	*criticism*
riddle	*mystery*
row	*argument*
slam	*criticize*
soar	*increase suddenly*
toll	*number of people killed*
urge	*recommend*
vow	*promise*
wed	*marry*

GRAMMAR

Newspaper headlines usually simplify grammar so that sentences become shorter, they attract attention more effectively and they sound more dramatic. There are five important ways that are used to do this:

1 omitted words

Small words that do not carry a lot of information, such as **a**, **the**, **be** and **is**, are often simply left out:

TEACHER GIVEN WARNING [= a teacher has been given a warning]
HOSPITAL TO CLOSE [= a hospital is going to close]
QUEEN DUE IN DELHI [= The Queen is due to arrive in Delhi]

2 shortened words

Abbreviations are used wherever possible:

BA [= British Airways] *MAKES HUGE PROFIT*
PM [= the prime minister] *VISITS BELFAST*
QUAKE [= earthquake] *KILLS THOUSANDS*

3 fewer prepositions

A sentence or phrase is formed so that a preposition is not necessary:

GLASGOW GIRL CHARGED [= a girl from Glasgow has been charged]
FATAL ACCIDENT INQUIRY ENDS [= the inquiry into a fatal accident has finished]

4 more nouns

Several nouns are often used together to form a headline. To change the headline into everyday language, you might need to add several other words, such as verbs, articles and prepositions:

PEACE TALK DEADLOCK [= the peace talks have reached a deadlock]
TERRORIST HOSTAGE ESCAPE [= somebody who was taken hostage by terrorists, has escaped]

5 fewer verb forms

Most verbs in headlines are in the simple present:

MINISTER DIES
UNIONS REJECT OFFER
POLICE CHIEF QUITS

- Words that look like verbs in the simple past are often passive forms without **be**:

  FLATS (have been) WASHED AWAY BY FLOOD
  DRUGS (were) SEIZED IN PRISON

- A **to**-infinitive is usually used to express the future:

  TAXES TO RISE
  AIRPORT TO CLOSE

- When the passive form is used for the future, **to be** is *not* omitted:

  AIRPORT TO BE CLOSED

• • • • next, the next • • • •

This entry deals with **next** in expressions of time.

➤ See **near, close to and next** for the distinction between **nearest** and **next**, and for **next** in an order or series

1 You use **next** rather than **the next** when referring by name to days, months, seasons or festivals:

I'll see you after the meeting next Friday.
Next week we're going to start a new course.
Arsenal are playing Manchester United next month.
The conference isn't till next summer.

> ⓘ References to days of the week of the form **next Friday** can be confusing, because people may not be sure whether you mean Friday in the present week or Friday in the week after this one. In general, people tend to refer to the Friday of the present week as **this Friday**, or **this coming Friday**, or to say that something is happening **on Friday**:
> *Your entry should arrive here no later than this coming Friday.*
> *I've got two tickets for the concert this Friday at the Royal Concert Hall.*
> *We leave here on Friday.*
> **Next Friday** and **Friday next** usually refer to the Friday of next week:
> *'When's he coming back?' 'Next Friday.'*
> *On Friday next, September 17, a demonstration will take place on the university campus.*

2 You use **the next** to refer to a length of time from now into the future:

The next few months will be very busy.
I'll be working at home for the next couple of days.
The car park will be out of use for the next three weeks.

> ⓘ Notice that **the next week** means the seven days from today until the same day in the week after this; **the next month** means four weeks starting from today, and **the next year** means the twelve months from now till the same time in the year after this:
> *He intends to concentrate on writing for the next year.*

• • • • nice, nice and ... • • • •

You call something **nice** if you think it is pleasant, good, attractive or satisfactory:

If the weather's nice we'll eat outside.
That's a nice tie you're wearing.
Did you have a nice holiday?
How nice to see you again. Are you well?
These oranges are nice, aren't they?

TALKING ABOUT PEOPLE

You call someone **nice** if they are kind, pleasant and friendly, and you like them:

We've got plenty of nice relations you could stay with.
He was not a very nice man.

1 You say that it is **nice of** someone to do something if you think they have been kind, helpful or considerate in doing it:

And it was nice of you to think of me.
'He inquired after you and Daisy.' 'How nice of him!'
It's nice of you to call, Melissa.

2 You are **nice to** someone when you treat them kindly or politely:

She was quite nice to me and gave me a cup of tea.
I decided to try to be nice to him.

TALKING ABOUT PREFERENCES

You say that it's **nice to** do, see, etc. something when you prefer, like or get pleasure from doing, seeing, etc. that thing:

All the same, it's nice to see them so much in love.
It's nice to have somebody else to cook the dinner sometimes.

NICE AND...

You say that someone or something is **nice and** (+ adjective), when you want to indicate that you like them because they have that quality:

She's nice and cheerful. I like people like that.
This printer's nice and simple to use.
The room looks nice and bright.

> ⓘ Notice that **nice** occurs most frequently in spoken English. Because it is such a general word, it is used less often in written English. In writing, people tend to prefer adjectives like **pleasant**, **delightful** and **attractive**.

• • • • night • • • •

A **night** is one of the periods of darkness between the time the sun goes down and the time it rises, during which most people sleep, but **night** can also refer to the evening, or the period between late afternoon and bedtime:

I stayed with a friend for three nights.
We all go down to the club on Friday nights.

> ⓘ To distinguish a specified time during the night from the same time in the morning, you can add **at night**:
> *We were expected to keep quiet after nine o'clock at night.*
> When referring to a time after midnight you can add **in the morning**, to distinguish it from the same time in the afternoon:
> *The accident happened at four in the morning.*

1 You can use **the night** to refer to a particular night, or to the night that has just passed. You can say that something happened **in the night** or **during the night**:

My flight was at 7am, so I stayed the night at the airport.
We got home sometime in the middle of the night.
We were woken twice in the night.
It must have rained during the night.

2 You also use **last night** to refer to the night or evening that has just passed:

You snored terribly last night.
Thousands of demonstrators turned out last night.

3 You refer to the night that follows today as **tonight**, and to the evening of today as **this evening** or **tonight**:

I've got two tickets for the theatre tonight.

The night that follows tomorrow is **tomorrow night**, and the night between yesterday and the day before yesterday is **the night before last**:

What are you doing tomorrow night?
Where were you the night before last?

4 When you are talking about a day in the past or future, you refer to the night following it as **that night**:

He was very ill during the day and died that night.

5 You can say that things that happen regularly during the period of darkness happen **at night** or **by night**:

Tigers are most active at night.
He slept by day and walked by night.

➤ See also **morning**, **afternoon**, **evening**.

•••• no ••••

➤ See **yes** and **no** for the negative reply **no**.

AS A DETERMINER

1 **No** is used before uncountable nouns, and before countable singular or plural nouns, to mean 'not any':

The course is for students with no (or *without any*) *previous knowledge of German.*
He has no (or *he hasn't any*) *children.*
There is no (or *there isn't any*) *need to pay today.*
No politician has ever acted like this before.
No more tickets were given away after that.

ⓘ From the examples above you see that you can use **not any** instead of **no** except when **no** and its noun are the subject of the sentence or clause, and are placed at the beginning of it:
No (not *Not any*) *students turned up.*

2 You use **no** rather than **not any** if you want more emphasis:
At no time should the patient be left unattended.

You can use **no** emphatically in statements like *She's no fool*, which means 'She's quite clever', rather than just 'She isn't a fool':
He may be young, but he's no child when it comes to business.
It is no exaggeration to say that the weather saved the country from a catastrophe.

3 **No** is used in notices that express prohibitions:
No Smoking *No Entry* *No Parking* *No Photography*

AS AN ADVERB

1 **No** has special uses with comparative forms:
You say, for example, *She's no better today*, meaning 'Her condition hasn't improved at all.' (You can also say *She isn't any better today.* See also **any**):
We are no closer to a solution than when we started.
This particular research can go no further.

ⓘ Notice that you cannot use **no** + comparative *before* a noun. You cannot, for example, say *a no better situation*.

2 You can also use **no** with **different** and **differently**:
Sunday is no different from a normal working day for many people.
He will be treated no differently from anyone else.

•••• none, not one ••••

None is a pronoun. You do not need a negative verb after **none**. You say, for example, *None of them heard the explosion.*

And you do not use **none** if the sentence already has a negative in it. You use **any**:
She was offered food, but she didn't want any (not *she didn't want none*).

NONE OF

1 **None of** is used before determiners, possessive forms and pronouns. It means 'not one' before plural nouns or pronouns and 'not any' before uncountable nouns, or pronouns that represent them:
He'd written quite a lot of poetry, none of it very good.
I had hoped to see all my friends, but in fact saw none of them.
She had none of the enthusiasm I'd been told about.
I've got some red pens left, but none of the green ones.
None of his relatives knew he was ill.

2 When **none of** + a plural noun or plural pronoun is the subject of the verb, the verb can be singular or plural. Some people regard a singular verb as 'correct', at least in a formal context:

We want to buy her a present, but none of us knows (or *know*) *what she'd like.*
None of his children were (or *was*) *at the funeral.*
None of them have (or *has*) *ever forgotten about that.*

> ⓘ Although **none of** is usually followed by a plural or uncountable noun or pronoun, it may be followed by a singular noun or pronoun in certain cases:
> *It's a convincing story, but practically none of it is true.*

AS AN INDEPENDENT PRONOUN

1 You can use **none** by itself when the noun it is referring to can be understood:

The children ate all the food and there was none left for me.
He looked for footprints, but found none.

> ⓘ When **none** is the subject, and refers to a *plural* noun, a singular or plural verb can be used. Especially in formal English, some people prefer a singular verb:
> *The soldiers were taken to hospital, but none was* (or *were*) *seriously injured.*
> *Some of these snakes can bite, but none is* (or *are*) *really dangerous.*

2 You can use the more emphatic **not one**, or the even more emphatic **not a single one**, in place of **none**:

Not one of the faces showed any sympathy.
There were 20 British players at the start, and not a single one got into the final.

3 You can also use the less emphatic **not any** in place of **none**, unless **none** is the subject of the sentence or clause, and is placed at the beginning of it:

'Where's that cake we were eating yesterday?' 'Sorry, there's none (or *there isn't any*) *left.'*

But:

'I saw that thing about you in the paper.' 'Well, none of it (not *not any of it*) *was true.'*

> ⓘ When **none** represents a plural, it must refer to three or more people or things. You use **neither** in reference to a group of only two:
> *Neither of the twins wanted to leave home.*

•••• no matter ••••

➤ See **matter**.

•••• no more, any more, no longer, any longer ••••

NO MORE

No more is used as a *quantifying* expression with *nouns*:

I've no more money left.

NOT ANY MORE, NO LONGER, NOT ANY LONGER

Not any more, no longer and **not any longer** can be used to express the idea of things that have stopped being the case:

You no longer need to show you passport at the frontier.
I refused to stay any longer.
You don't need me any more.
Don't you love me any more?

> ⓘ **Any more** is sometimes written **anymore** in AmE.

—— non-assertive words ——

➤ See **assertive**.

•••• no-one, nobody ••••

1 **Nobody** and **no-one** are singular pronouns meaning 'no person' or 'not anybody':

Nobody asked my opinion.
No-one was hurt in the explosion.
We thought no-one would come.
Karen told nobody about her secret.

> ⓘ You can use the less emphatic form **not anyone** or **not anybody** instead of **no-one** and **nobody**, except where **nobody** or **no-one** is the subject of the sentence or clause, and comes at the beginning of it:
> *I've got nobody* (or *I haven't got anybody*) *to help me.*
> *No-one* (not *Not anyone*) *told me you'd arrived.*

2 **Nobody** and **no-one** are negative words and do not, therefore, need a negative verb:

Nobody volunteered (not *Nobody didn't volunteer*).

You use **anybody** or **anyone** in a sentence that has a negative in it already:

She didn't tell anybody (not *She didn't tell nobody*).

3 Adjectives used with **no-one** and **nobody** come after them:

There was nobody interesting at the conference.

> ⓘ Although **nobody** and **no-one** are singular, both are often followed by the pronoun **they**, *eg* in question tags:
> *No-one's allowed in yet, are they?*

•••• nor ••••

1 **Nor** is used after **neither** to introduce the second possibility, where both possibilities are denied:

I neither know nor care where she's gone.

➤ See **neither** for more information.

2 **Nor** is used, like **neither**, with the meaning 'and not', or 'also not', to introduce a second negative statement. Notice that inversion follows **nor**. The order is **nor** + auxiliary (or **be**) + subject + main verb:

I'm not interested in gossip and nor should you be.
They had not thought about it much, nor did they intend to.

3 You can introduce a negative response to a negative statement with **nor**:

'I'm not joking.' 'Nor am I.'

•••• not ••••

➤ See **contractions** for a list of the negative contracted forms, and details about their use.

NEGATIVE STATEMENTS

You make negative statements by using **not** or **n't** with the verbs **be** and **have**, the modal verbs (**will**, **shall**, **can**, and so on), and the auxiliary verb **do** when there is no other auxiliary or modal verb.

1 You use **not** and **n't** with **be** and **have** when they are acting as ordinary verbs:

It isn't (or *it's not*) *fair.*
They're free, but I'm not.
We were not (or *we weren't*) *very happy.*
We haven't any more news.

> ⓘ The contracted forms **haven't**, **hasn't** and **hadn't** are used as negative forms of the ordinary verb **have**, rather than the full **have** + **not** forms:
> *I haven't* (not *have not*) *a clue.*
> The forms **don't have** and also, in BrE, **haven't got**, are frequently used:
> *I haven't got* (or *I don't have*) *a clue.*

2 **Not** or **n't** comes after an auxiliary or modal verb, or after the first, if there is more than one:

I haven't finished yet.
I'm not complaining.
You won't succeed.
They should not have been asked.

3 Where there is no other auxiliary or modal verb, you combine **not** or **n't** with auxiliary verb **do, does** or **did** to form negative statements:

Don't expect him to agree.
I didn't notice you standing there.

4 The verbs **be** and **have**, and the auxiliary and modal verbs, can be used 'elliptically' with **not** or **n't** to represent a whole negative clause, within a sentence, or as a reply:

They are coming, but I'm afraid I can't [= can't come].
'Are you sure you locked the door?' 'No, perhaps I didn't' [= didn't lock it].
'Hey, you cheated!' 'I did not!'

➤ See also **ellipsis**.

ⓘ Remember that **not** and **n't** are used with words like **any**, **anyone**, **anything**, and **anywhere**, rather than with a second negative:
I don't trust any (not *I don't trust none) of them.*

QUESTIONS

1 You use **n't**, and much more formally, **not**, to form negative question tags after a positive statement:

You've read this, haven't you?
He died in 1914, didn't he?
You should apologize, should you not?

2 Negative questions using **n't** or **not** are used to make enquiries, especially enquiries expressing surprise or annoyance, and also to make suggestions:

Didn't you find her address?
Isn't she awake yet?
Couldn't we go tomorrow instead?
Why don't we take the car?
Should we not wait for her?

REPLACING A NEGATIVE CLAUSE

Not often stands for a whole negative clause. This happens frequently in the following cases:

1 after verbs of thinking and reporting

Verbs such as **assume**, **guess**, **hope**, **imagine**, **presume**, **reckon**, **suppose**, and expressions such as **I'm afraid**, **it seems**, **it appears** can be followed by **not** representing a whole clause:

'I think I may have caught your cold.' 'Oh, I hope not.' [= I hope you haven't caught my cold]
'Did the car pass its test?' 'I'm afraid not.'

2 after sentence adverbs

Not can stand for a clause after sentence adverbs such as **apparently**, **evidently**, and **unfortunately**:

'Had they met before?' 'Apparently not.'
'Can you join us this evening?' 'Unfortunately not.'

ⓘ **So** can replace a clause in a similar way to **not**.
➤ See **so** for more information about **so** and **not** used like this.

3 after **if**, **or** and **why**

Not is also used for a whole clause after **if**, **or** and **why**:

We've probably got enough, but if not, we can get more.
I'll see you at Christmas, if not before.
Are you coming with us, or not?
'I didn't really enjoy the book.' 'Oh, why not?'

OTHER USES

1 You use **not** when making corrections or distinctions:
You say 'lice' and 'mice', not 'louses' and 'mouses'.
She's in the maths department, not the physics department.

2 **Not a thing** is an emphatic expression meaning 'nothing at all':
I have to get eight hours' sleep or I can't do a thing the next morning.

Other 'small unit' words can follow **not a**, with the same meaning:
She didn't say a word.
There isn't a grain of truth in that story.
I haven't a clue what she meant.
There wasn't a sound from the children.
We haven't had a drop of rain all week.

3 You use **not** to put the present participle into the negative:
Not wishing to disturb them, I silently closed the door.
I was feeling nervous, not having met him before.

4 You put **not** *before* **to** when you are making a **to**-infinitive negative:
I asked him not to tell anyone.
It was difficult not to laugh.

• • • • nothing • • • •

Nothing means 'no things', or 'not anything'.

1 **Nothing** takes a singular verb:
Nothing is more important than your health.
Nothing was mentioned yesterday about this.

2 You do not use a negative verb after **nothing**:
Nothing came (not *nothing didn't come*) *in the post this morning.*

You do not use **nothing** in a sentence that already contains a negative. Instead, use **anything**:
When he had finished, she didn't say anything (not *she didn't say nothing*).

ⓘ You can use the less emphatic form **not anything** instead of **nothing**, except when **nothing** is the subject of the sentence or clause, and comes at the beginning of it:
I couldn't hear anything (or *I could hear nothing*).
There's nothing (or *there isn't anything*) *in the fridge.*
But:
Nothing (not *Not anything*) *is impossible.*

3 Adjectives used with **nothing** always follow it:

I had nothing special planned for the afternoon.
I'm glad there was nothing seriously wrong.

4 **Nothing but** a certain thing is that thing and that thing only:

There was nothing but make-up and a little money in her bag.

➤ See **like** for the use of **nothing like**.

· · · · not only · · · ·

You use **not only** to introduce the first of two circumstances of which the second is more surprising or significant than the first. **Not only** can be used in several kinds of structures:

AT THE BEGINNING OF A SENTENCE

1 When **not only** occurs at the beginning of a sentence, the order of the following subject and verb is reversed:

Not only had they made some mistakes, they had omitted some important details too.

2 When there is not already an auxiliary verb, use **do** or **does**:

Not only does the book list the new products, it also gives help about using them.

IN MID POSITION

1 **before verbs**:

In mid position before verbs, the auxiliary **do** is not necessary:

He not only wrote it, he published it as well.
It not only smells good, it also tastes delicious.

2 **before adjectives**:

The system is not only difficult; it's also expensive.
I was not only tired; I was ill as well.

3 **before nouns**:

She disliked not only the smell of it, but also the taste.

—— nouns ——

This entry looks at the different kinds of nouns that exist, and deals with the way they behave grammatically.

COUNTABLE NOUNS

Countable nouns are nouns that refer to things that can be counted.

They have two forms; a plural form and a singular form.

1 The singular form always has a determiner, such as **a**, **the**, **this**, **my**, **every**, or **one**, before it. The corresponding verb form is also in the singular:

Every student will receive a welcome pack.
My car won't start.
We went for a walk in the village.
My dog wakes the neighbours at night.

2 The plural form can be used with or without a determiner. You use a determiner such as **the**, **these** or **my** if you want to refer to a specific group of things. You use a quantifying determiner like **several**, **some** or **many** if you want to draw attention to the quantity of things you are talking about. You do not use a determiner at all if you want to talk about things or people in general. The corresponding verb is also in the plural:

The workers say they'll strike.
My children are all grown up now.
Parents tend to worry too much.

3 Countable nouns can also follow numbers:

I read one page and fell asleep.
Only six customers have complained in the last six months.

UNCOUNTABLE NOUNS

1 Nouns that refer to substances, qualities, feelings and types of activity, rather than to individual things or people are called *uncountable nouns*. They only have one form, and they always take the singular form of the verb:

Add some more milk.
Is there any bread?
We haven't much time.
Poverty causes misery.

2 Some nouns which are uncountable in English are countable nouns in other languages.

➤ See the entry **countable and uncountable nouns** for a list of common uncountable nouns, and ways of expressing them in units.

3 Some uncountable nouns end in **-s**, but since they are uncountable, they do not take a plural verb. Most of these fall into the categories of (i) fields of study, *eg* **linguistics**, (ii) activities and games *eg* **aerobics**, **darts**, and (iii) illnesses, *eg* **diabetes**.

4 Many nouns that are normally uncountable can be used in a countable way. This commonly happens with nouns relating to food and drink that is available in units or portions. Nouns referring to types of food and drink that are available in different varieties are also often used in a countable way:

I've got some beers in the fridge [= some cans of beer].
We sell a wide variety of cheeses.
Italian wines and a choice of beers are served here.

➤ See the entry **countable and uncountable nouns** for more detailed information on the subject.

SINGULAR AND PLURAL NOUNS

1 There are some nouns, and some particular meanings of nouns that are only ever used in the singular. These nouns usually need **the** before them:

The moon is full tonight.
Just think about the future.

2 There are some nouns that are only used in the plural, *eg* **clothes**. Certain items of clothing, too, fall into this category. These plural nouns generally refer to single items made up of two parts that are joined together, *eg* **knickers**, **trousers**, **tights**,

jeans. Words for some other things, such as tools, behave in a similar way, *eg* **scissors**, **pliers** and **tweezers**. These words are always used with a verb in the plural form:

These jeans are too small for me.
Where are the scissors?

> ⓘ Note that the two-part plural nouns mentioned above cannot be preceded by a number. If you want to specify a number, you should insert **pair(s) of** before the noun:
> *I need three pairs of trousers.*
> *It says 'one pair of scissors' on my order form, not 'two.'*

ABSTRACT AND CONCRETE NOUNS

1 An *abstract noun* is a noun which refers to a quality, an idea, or an experience, rather than something that can be seen or touched. Abstract nouns are usually uncountable, but you can use **a** or **an** before them if they are qualified by an adjective:

I've noticed his increasing unhappiness.
These things take time.
There is a strange beauty about her.

2 A *concrete noun* is a noun which refers to something that can be seen or touched, such as a person, an animal or an object.

COLLECTIVE NOUNS

There are three classes of nouns that can be regarded as *collective nouns*. These are:

1 **groups**:

These are singular nouns representing a unit consisting of a number of individuals, especially individual people, *eg* **audience**, **staff**, **government**, **orchestra**. These nouns can be used with either a singular or a plural verb, depending on whether the group is seen as a single unit or as a group of individuals.

2 **classes of articles**:

These are singular nouns representing a category containing a variety of different objects, *eg* **baggage**, **clothing**, **furniture**. Nouns like this are not used in the plural.

3 **plural groups**:

These are plural nouns without an **-s**, *eg* **cattle**, **police**, **people**. They take a plural verb and have no singular form.

➤ See the entry **collective nouns** for more detailed information.

PROPER NOUNS

Names of people, places, books, companies, etc are *proper nouns*. They are spelt with an initial capital letter and rarely have a plural form. Examples of proper nouns are:

Sophie
Walt Disney
Berlin
The Bible
Rolls Royce

NOUN MODIFIERS

There are three ways in which you can put nouns together so that one modifies the other:

1 **noun + noun**

In this structure the first noun modifies the second:

a shoe shop
a burger bar
a police officer

- Notice that even if the first noun has a plural meaning, it is represented in the singular form, *eg* **a shoe shop** is a shop that sells *shoes*.
- Notice also that the article belonging to the first, modifying, noun, is dropped, *eg a minister in the government* – **a government minister**.

2 **noun + 's + noun**

In this structure, the first noun also modifies the second:

cow's milk
a bird's nest
a doll's house
a child's toy

This structure is usually used to refer to something that is used by, or produced by or from, a person or animal.

Usually, either both nouns are singular, or both nouns are plural, *eg* **a child's toy**, or **children's toys**.

3 **noun + preposition + noun**

Sometimes it is necessary to use a structure with **of**, or another preposition:

the top of the page
the edge of the table
a paper on tropical diseases

This structure is often used to talk about position, or parts of things.

• • • • now • • • •

Now means 'the present time', or 'at the present time':

The time is now 7.30 pm.
We are now waiting for him to phone back.
Now is a good time to ask these questions.
We must act right now.

1 There are several useful phrases in which **now** is combined with prepositions or adverbial particles:

Le Bugue is a place I've never heard of before now.
I should have learnt that by now [= before now].
From now on [= starting from now] *I'm going to be more careful.*
The boss has, until now [= always before now] *been very reasonable.*
She's been a good daughter up till now[= until now].

2 People telling stories, or narrating past events, often use **now** to mean 'then', 'next' or 'at that point':

Crowds were now gathering in the square.
The previous day's fog had now disappeared.

3 **Now** is sometimes used in combination with the perfect or perfect progressive forms of verbs to update the situation, or to say how long something has been going on:

It has now been raining for three days.
He had now been her lover for nearly three years.

4 People use **now** in conversation to focus the listener's attention, *eg* when becoming impatient, or when moving on to another subject or activity:

Now, please don't think I'm criticizing.
Now, where can we find a taxi?

•••• now that ••••

You can use **now that**, and more informally **now**, as a conjunction meaning 'since' or 'seeing that', to introduce an adverbial clause of reason, relating to something that has happened or been achieved:

We could do well now that last year's champions have decided not to take part.
Now the decision was made I felt more relaxed.

•••• nowhere ••••

1 **Nowhere** means 'no place', or 'in or to no place':

The herb grows here and nowhere else.
That road goes nowhere.

2 In a rather formal style you can say that someone or something that is lost is **nowhere to be found** or **seen**:

Her husband was nowhere to be seen.

> ⓘ Notice that although you never use the prepositions **in** and **to** before **nowhere**, you can use **from**:
> *These buildings just seem to appear from nowhere.*

3 You can use **nowhere** rather like a noun, and you can use an adjective after it:

He has nowhere to go.
'Where were you?' 'Nowhere exciting.'

4 **Nowhere** is sometimes put at the beginning of a statement for emphasis, especially in a formal or literary context. Notice that the word order is **nowhere** + auxiliary verb (or **be**) + subject:

Nowhere is this more obvious than in his last symphony.

5 **Nowhere near** is an emphatic form of **not**, and means the same as **not nearly**:

The city has nowhere near enough nursery schools.
Volleyball is nowhere near as easy as it looks.

ⓘ You can use the less emphatic form **not** (or **n't**) **anywhere** instead of **nowhere** except where **nowhere** introduces the sentence:
She goes nowhere (or *she doesn't go anywhere*) *nowadays.*
But:
Nowhere (not *Not anywhere*) *have I found any other reference to this.*

numbers and fractions

There are three main types of numeral: **cardinal numbers**, **ordinal numbers** and **fractions**.

Exact quantities are represented by numbers. Words like **about**, **nearly**, **over**, **under**, **some**, **almost**, **less than**, **more than** and **fewer than** are used with numbers to indicate approximate quantities.

CARDINAL NUMBERS

Cardinal numbers, *eg* **one, two, three,** are used to indicate an exact quantity or a range. They may be written out as words (**zero**, **ten**, **eighty-six**, **a thousand**) or using the figures or digits 0 to 9 (**0**, **10**, **86**, **1000**). Note that the compound numbers, *eg* **twenty-one**, **fifty-five**, **seventy-two**, are written with a hyphen.

Cardinal numbers take the following forms:

1 They can function as nouns:
Have you got a five in these slippers?
Six tens are sixty.
Those zeros look like eights.
He's in his fifties.

2 They can function as adjectives:
He is fifty.
zero gravity

3 They can function as quantifiers:
one bottle
three girls and two boys

4 They can also function as pronouns:
We have two children and they have three.
The policeman caught one boy but the other two ran off.

ⓘ Note that singular forms of the cardinal numbers **hundred**, **thousand**, **million** and **billion** cannot stand alone without a determiner. They are always preceded by an article or another cardinal number:
ten thousand men
forty million dollars

ORDINAL NUMBERS

The ordinal numbers, *eg* **fourth** and **hundredth**, indicate the position of something in a series. They may be written out as words (**first**, **second**, **third**) or as figures followed by letters (**1st**, **2nd**, **3rd**, **4th**, **5th**, **30th**).

Most ordinal numbers (except **first**, **second** and **third**) are formed by adding **-th** to the corresponding cardinal number. When the **-th** ending is added to certain cardinals the ending of the cardinal changes (eg **fifth**, **twelfth**, **twentieth**), or a letter is dropped (*eg* **eighth**, **ninth**).

Ordinal numbers take the following forms:

1 They can function as quantifiers:

the third Duke
This is the sixteenth time she's rung me today.
the 30th of October

2 They can function as pronouns:

We're going on holiday on the fifth.
I got the first prize and he got the second.

3 They can function as adjectives or adverbs:

He was ninth.
He came in ninth.

FRACTIONS

A fraction is a quantity that is less than one, or less than a whole, *eg* **a half**, **a third**, **a quarter**, **three-fifths**. Fractions may be written out as words (**half**, **three-quarters**, **five-sixths**), or as two figures, one above the other and separated by a horizontal line ($\frac{1}{2}$ $\frac{3}{4}$ $\frac{5}{6}$ $\frac{1}{20}$).

When a fraction representing only one part (*eg* $\frac{1}{2}$ or $\frac{1}{5}$) is written out, it can be preceded by **one** or **a**:

one half or *a half*
one fifth or *a fifth*

Fractions take the following forms:

1 They can function as nouns:

Two quarters make a or *one half.*
What answer do you get when you add one third (or *a third*) *and one sixteenth* (or *a sixteenth*)*?*

2 They can also function as quantifiers:

three-quarters of the population
ten thousandths of a second
half a loaf
a one-hundredth part

3 Cardinal numbers and fractions are often combined:

two and a half pounds
three and three-quarter litres

DECIMALS

1 A **decimal** is a fraction written as a dot or a comma followed by numbers representing tenths, hundredths and thousandths, in that order:

7.3 [*seven point three*]
2.5 [*two point five*]

Notice that in BrE, the dot is centred above the line; it is expressed as a **point**.

2 A zero that comes before the point can be referred to as **zero** or **nought**. A zero that comes after the point can be referred to as **zero**, **nought** or **oh**. The numbers after the point are always said separately:

0.03 [*nought point nought three*]
0.04 [*zero point zero four*]
0.05 [*nought point oh five*]
6.66 [*six point six six* (not *sixty-six*)]

• • • • a number of • • • •

➤ See **amount**.

Oo

objects

In grammar, the noun that is the *subject* of a verb *performs* the action. The noun that is the *object* is *affected by* the action. There are two kinds of object, a **direct object** and an **indirect object**. Also, a noun following a preposition is referred to as the **object** of the preposition.

1 The **direct object** of a verb may be a noun, a noun phrase, a proper noun, such as somebody's name, or a pronoun. The direct objects in the following sentences are in bold type:

*'Can I have **a hamburger**?'*
*The child put **her wet hand** in mine.*
*I phoned **Larry**, who sounded tired. I told him I loved **him**.*

2 The **indirect object** is typically someone who receives the direct object, or somehow benefits by the action. The indirect object normally comes *before* the direct object. In the following sentences the indirect objects are in bold type:

*Give **me** a hamburger.*
*I told **Jack** I loved him.*
*Mother read **us** The Children's Encyclopaedia.*

Verbs such as **give**, **tell**, and **read**, which can have a direct object and an indirect object, are called *ditransitive verbs* at the entry **verbs**.

3 The noun or pronoun that follows a preposition is its **object**. In the following sentences the objects of prepositions are in bold type:

*The child put her wet hand in **mine**.*
*A man in **a blue suit** came out of **the building**.*
*Our grandmother read to **us** from **the Bible**.*

of

This entry divides the uses of the preposition **of** into sections, each containing a range of typical uses illustrated by examples.

POSSESSION AND BELONGING

1 You talk about a part **of** something:

the base of his skull
the fruit of the coconut palm

2 You talk about a member **of** a group, and the inhabitants **of** a place:

members of the club
citizens of Rome

3 You talk about the events or developments **of** a time, the features **of** a place, and a disease **of** a part of the body:

the poetry of the nineteenth century
the vineyards of France
cancer of the liver

> ⓘ You refer to the capital **of** a country, but you refer to other towns or cities **in** it:
> *Lilongwe, the capital of Malawi*
> *Rumpi, a town in northern Malawi*

4 You talk about the aim, cause or result **of** something:

the aim of the expedition
the causes of war
the results of the poll

5 You can talk about the works **of** a writer or artist:

the plays of Shakespeare

Notice however, that when not referring to an artist's complete works, you usually use **by**:

The course always includes at least one play by Shakespeare.

> ⓘ When you are talking about what belongs to, or relates to, a *person*, as distinct from a *thing*, you normally use the possessive **'s** rather than **of**:
> *Howard's keyboard* (not *the keyboard of Howard*)
> *my father's plans* (not *the plans of my father*).
> A country can also have a possessive form:
> *France's vineyards*

6 You can use the possessive pronouns (**mine**, **yours**, **his**, **hers**, **ours**, **theirs**) after **of**, to identify a member of a *group* belonging to, or associated with, someone. Instead of '*He's one of my colleagues*' you can say '*He's a colleague of mine*':

That's a special interest of hers.

7 You can also use a possessive form with **'s** after **of**:

Yes, I know Eva; she's a friend of Marie's.
Michael was a schoolfriend of the children's.

> ⓘ The possessive **'s**, or possessive apostrophe after a plural, is sometimes dropped:
> *an acquaintance of my parents* (instead of *of my parents'*)

➤ For more information see the entry for **possessive 's**.

QUANTITY AND CONTENT

Of is used in expressions about amounts and quantities, and about the things that compose a group.

> ⓘ After a quantifying determiner or pronoun (such as **most**, **some**, or **none**) **of** is followed by a word like **the**, **those** or **my**, or a pronoun (such as **us**, **it** or **that**):
> *some of the food*
> *none of the staff*
> *most of us*
> *I'll have one of those.*

1 **quantities**:
a kilo of apples
a litre of wine
a cup of sugar
a lot of trouble
plenty of excitement

2 **contents**:
a book of poetry
a box of matches

3 **things composing a group**:
a crowd of people
a bunch of flowers

4 **units**:
a piece of paper
a drop of water

5 **class**:
a type of bird

6 **subjects**:
a true account of the incident
the science of genetics

IN DESCRIPTIONS

You can use **of** when describing people or things in terms of the following things:

1 **qualities**:
children of unusual talent
The jewellery was of little value.

2 **possessions or reputation**:
a woman of wealth

3 **physical appearance**:
people of average height

4 **age**:
a boy of twelve
She had no friends of her own age.

DATES AND OTHER POINTS OF REFERENCE

1 **dates**

You say:
the nineteenth of January

But you write:

19 January

➤ See **dates** for more details.

2 order

You use the ordinal numbers or determiners with **of** to specify one in a series of things:

the fourth year of the war
on the second morning of their honeymoon

3 points in time:

on the morning of their wedding
in the moment of victory

4 extremes:

at the beginning of term
in the depths of despair

LINKING ACTIONS, SUBJECTS AND OBJECTS

You use **of** in various ways to talk about actions, *eg*:

1 to link an action with the thing performing it:

the rising of the sun
the constant movement of traffic

2 to link the action with the thing or person it affects:

the destruction of Troy
a review of the situation

3 to link someone who does something with the thing they do:

the writer of the note

OTHER USES

1 behaviour

You use **of** in the combination adjective + **of** + noun or pronoun to talk about particular people's behaviour:

It was kind of you to write.
It was stupid of me to leave the car unlocked.
That was most thoughtful of you.

2 Of occurs as the usual preposition after various verbs and adjectives. Here are some common combinations:

- **verbs**:

I'm thinking of resigning.
The house smells of tobacco smoke.
This tastes of lemon.
I've never heard of him.
She reminds me of someone.
Are you accusing me of cheating?
Hundreds are dying of starvation.

- **adjectives**:

I'm frightened of spiders.
We got bored of waiting.
You should be ashamed of yourself.

I'm proud of you.
She's too sure of herself.
The sky's full of birds.

•••• of course ••••

Of course can cause difficulty for some learners, because if it is used wrongly it can sound rude.

1 You use **of course** as a polite way of giving permission or agreeing to do something:
'Is it all right if I go five minutes early, Bob?' 'Of course.'
'Could you explain this to me, please?' 'Of course.'

2 You also use **of course** when you think that the person you are speaking to probably knows what you are telling them already:
There are of course many exceptions.
She's much younger than he is, of course.

3 You can use **of course** when stating something that is not surprising:
They were late, of course.

4 **Of course** is also used for emphasis:
'I wonder if you will remember it?' 'Of course I will.'

5 **Of course not** is used to add emphasis when you accept or agree with a statement or question in the negative:
'You're not sleeping?' 'Of course not.'

ⓘ Notice that since **of course** means 'as everybody knows' or 'obviously', it is rude to use it as an answer when someone states a fact, as this suggests that you think the person's remark is very obvious. Instead, use **it certainly is** or **yes, that's right**:
'That's expensive.' 'It certainly is (not *of course*)*'*.

•••• off ••••

Off can be a *preposition* or an *adverb*. It can express departure, removal, absence, distance, non-operation or failure, and completion.

DEPARTURE

1 **Off** is used like **away** to express departure. A driver or vehicle moves **off** when it leaves a place:
The bus started moving off as I reached the bus stop.
I shouted at the dog and it ran off.

2 You can also say that you *are* **off** when you are about to leave:
I'm off to bed.
We must be off in five minutes.

3 **Off** is used in expressions about falling asleep:
I must have dozed off.
I couldn't get off to sleep.

4 You turn **off** a road when you turn right or left into another road. A place that is **off** one road is on another one that leads away from it:

Turn off the M90 at Kinross.
My flat's in a lane off Rose Street.

REMOVAL

1 tearing, cutting, breaking and becoming detached:

The cover had been torn off the directory.
Don't let the hairdresser cut too much off.
They found an old jug with the handle broken off.
Let's pick the apples before they fall off.

2 clothes and covers:

Take off your wet anoraks.
Peel the plastic label off the top before use.

3 from a surface:

You'll have to take all your posters off the wall.
We ate all our meals off paper plates.

4 discounts:

You take a sum **off** a price when you reduce it by that amount:

They say they'll take £20 off if we pay cash.

5 vehicles and vessels:

We got off the train at Crewe.
I'm getting off at the next stop.

> ⓘ Notice that although you can get **off** a train, you get **out of** a car.

ABSENCE

You take time **off** work, or you are **off** work or school, when you are not working there:

I'm taking a few days off work.
I've got the whole of next week off.
She's been off school for ages.
She's off sick.

> ⓘ Notice the difference between being **off** [= absent from] **work**, and **out of work** [= being unemployed].

DISTANCE

Off can express distance or separation, like **away**.

1 place:

Tenerife lies a few hundred miles off the coast of Africa.

2 time:

Christmas was only a few weeks off.

3 avoiding things:

Keep off the grass.
Please keep off the subject of holidays.

NON-OPERATION

1 things using a power supply:
Electrical appliances and other things using a power supply are **off** when they are not connected to the supply, and so are not working:

Switch the engine off.
Make sure all the lights are off.

2 cancellation:

Tomorrow's meeting is off.
The match was rained off.

3 deterioration:
Things go **off** when they get worse or go bad:

Milk goes off quickly if it's not kept in the fridge.

4 dislike:
You are **off** something when you no longer like it:

I'm off aerobics.
The cat's off its food.

COMPLETION, FINALITY OR THOROUGHNESS

Off is used with verbs such as **finish**, to add an extra sense of completeness or finality to them:

He finished off his drink and put the glass down.
The disinfectant will kill all the bacteria off.

offering

➤ See pages 394 and 395.

often

Often can have two pronunciations. Some people pronounce it /ˈɒfən/ and others pronounce it /ˈɒftən/.

Often is an adverb of *frequency* (see **adverbs** for more details) and goes in 'mid position', that is, before the verb, but after the verb **be**, and after an auxiliary verb (or after the first auxiliary verb if there are several).

USES

The main problem with **often** is knowing when to use it, and when to use other expressions, such as **several times, repeatedly**, or **keep doing something**.

1 Something that happens **often**, happens many times, or frequently:

Our feet often became sore; we often cried with pain.
Laing has often been accused of being a workaholic.

2 You can use words such as **very**, **quite** and **fairly**, with **often**:

Despite trying to leave early I quite often get home late.

3 Although **often** is usually in mid position, it can come at the end of a short sentence, or at the beginning of a long one:

'Do you use the fitness club?' 'Yes, I go there often.'
Very often the day starts clear and bright, and this continues until about eleven, when the mist develops.

OFFERING

OFFERING THINGS

1 If you want to offer something to someone politely, you can say **would you like ...?**:

Would you like a cup of tea or coffee?
Would you like some breakfast?

2 If the thing that you are offering is not immediately available, you can say **can I get you ...?**:

Can I get you something?
Can I get you some tea?

3 Less formally, you can say **do you want ...?**:

Do you want coffee, Dave?
Do you want anything to eat?

4 If you know the person you are speaking to quite well, and you want to encourage them to take what you are offering, you can use the form **have ...**:

Have some more wine.
Have some peanuts.
Have a biscuit.

5 In informal situations, you can use the noun on its own, with a questioning tone in your voice:

Who wants pudding? Yoghurt? Fruit? Ice cream?

6 If you want people to feel that they can take something when they want, you can say **help yourself to ...**:

Help yourself to a drink.
Help yourself to anything you want.
Help yourselves to salad, won't you?

7 If someone needs or wants something, and you want to give it or lend it to them, you can say **you can have** or **borrow**, **my ...**, and add **if you like**:

You can have my room, if you like.
'Have you got a pen?' 'Here, you can borrow mine.'

OFFERING TO DO THINGS FOR PEOPLE

1 A polite way of offering to do something for someone is **shall I** + infinitive?:

Shall I walk back with you, Francisco?
Shall I come and help you?
Shall I make a cup of tea?

2 You can also make a polite offer with **would you like ...?** followed by a noun representing an action:

Would you like a lift?
Would you like a hand? [= some help]

3 If you feel fairly sure that the person you are speaking to will want you to do the thing that you are offering, you can say **let me** + infinitive:

Let me do that for you.
Let me get you another coffee.

4 If you are not sure whether the person you are speaking to will want you to do the thing you are offering, you can say **would you like me to** + infinitive or **do you want me to** + infinitive:

Would you like me to find out for you?
Do you want me to make some enquiries?

5 Another tentative way of offering to do something is to say **I'll** or **I can** + infinitive and add **if you want**:

I'll go home and get it for you if you want.
I can bring the car if you want.

> ⓘ People who work in shops, or information offices often ask **can I help you?** or **what can I do for you?** to show that they are ready to serve you.

ACCEPTING AND DECLINING OFFERS

1 If you want to accept an offer of a thing, especially one in the form of a question, you can say **yes please**, or **thank you, that'd** [= that would] **be lovely**:

'Would you like a cup of tea?' 'Oh thanks, that'd be lovely.'
'Tea?' 'Mm, yes please.'

If you want to accept an offer that is made in the imperative, you usually just say **thank you**:

'Help yourself to salad.' 'Thank you.'
'Have some crisps' 'Thank you.'

2 The usual way to decline things is to say **no, thanks**, **no, I'm fine thanks**, or more formally **no, thank you**. If you are declining an offer of more food, you can say **it's lovely but I've had enough, thanks**:

'Coffee, anyone?' 'No, I'm fine thanks.'
'Would you like another sandwich?' 'They're very nice, but I've had plenty, thanks.'

3 You can accept someone's offer to do something for you by saying **are you sure? that's very kind of you, thanks** , or just **oh, that's kind of you, thank you** or less formally **oh, that'd be great**:

'Let me carry those bags for you.' 'Oh, that's kind of you. Thank you.'
'Would you like me to help you?' 'Oh, are you sure? That'd be great.'

4 You can decline someone's offer to do something for you by saying **no, I'm fine, thank you** or **that's very kind of you, but ...** or **no, it's all right, thanks. I don't mind doing it**, or **no, don't worry, I can do it**, or **I can manage, thanks**:

'Shall I help you?' 'No, I'm fine thank you.'
'Would you like a lift?' 'That's very kind of you, but I'm going with John.'
'Shall I get those things down for you?' 'No, don't worry, I think I can do it, thanks.'
'Can I get those for you?' 'Well, I think I can manage, thanks.'

... often continued

4 **Often** is normally used in the context of a long period of time, such as a period of your life. When you are talking about a short period, such as a day, you use expressions such as **several times** or **repeatedly** or you use the structure **keep doing something**:

He had noticed the same man several times during the day.
She glanced repeatedly at her daughter.
During the flight I kept asking her about life in England.

5 You use **how often** to ask questions about frequency:

How often does luggage get completely lost?
She asked how often she should see the doctor.

6 **Often** is also used to mean 'in many cases':

The children are often [= lots of children are] *seriously ill.*
Losing a bit of weight will often [= in many cases] *cure arthritis.*

> ⓘ Notice a difference in sense with a change in the negative word order:
> *Students often don't understand* [= often fail to understand] *what is being said.*
> *These shoppers very often don't even wear* [= in many cases never wear] *the clothes they buy.*
> *We don't often see you* [= we see you rarely] *nowadays.*

•••• old ••••

➤ See **age**.

•••• on ••••

On can be used as a *preposition* or an *adverb*. It can, among other things, express contact with a surface, inclusion, location, date or day of occurrence, use of instruments, spending resources, use of a system, the state of operating progress.

SUPPORT, CONTACT OR ATTACHMENT

1 **position**

Things are **on** a horizontal surface when they rest in contact with it, and **on** a vertical surface, or any kind of object, when they are attached to it:

She preferred to sit on the floor.
A portrait of Jane hung on the wall.
See that fly on the ceiling?
The sheets were drying on the line.
There was no stamp on the envelope.

> ⓘ You use the preposition **on top of** or the adverb **on top**, rather than **on**, where the object is tall or high:
> *My suitcase was on top of the wardrobe.*
> *We saw a little hill with a castle on top.*

2 marks, print or writing

Something that marks a surface is **on** it:

You've got a dirty mark on your skirt.
I wrote the number on the back of an envelope.
See the map on page six.

3 clothes and covers:

She put on her jacket.
There was no carpet on the stairs.

4 supporting weight

Your weight is **on** a certain part of your body when that part is supporting it:

standing on one leg
Should babies sleep on their fronts or their backs?

POSSESSION

You have something **on** you when you are carrying it with you, *eg* in your pockets:

I hadn't got enough money on me to pay for a taxi.

DIRECTION

> ⓘ You use **on to** or **onto** rather than **on** to express movement or direction resulting in a final position **on** something:
> *She lowered herself on to a chair.*
> *We carried him out on to the verandah.*

1 With a lot of verbs of movement that emphasize the final position, rather than the process of moving, *eg* **put**, **throw**, **drop**, **fall**, and various verbs of 'attaching', you can use **on** or **on to**:

She threw another log on (or *on to*) *the fire.*
He was sewing a button on (or *on to*) *his shirt.*

2 You **get on** or **on to** a bus, train, boat or plane; you are **on** a horse, bicycle or motorbike when you are riding it:

The bus doesn't stop here unless anyone wants to get on or off.
He was on the five o'clock train.

> ⓘ You get **in** or **into**, not **on** or **on to**, a car.

INCLUSION

1 You talk about the items **on** a list, timetable or schedule:

What's on the agenda for this morning?

2 Representatives are **on** committees or councils:

He promised to consult his colleagues on the board.

➤ Compare the entry for **in**.

LOCATION

1 You talk about places or points being **on** a street or river, or anything else long and narrow:

the shops on (or *in*) *the high street*
a hotel on the sea front

2 You use **on** with limited areas of land:
wildlife on the island of Hoy
Helmets must be worn on the building site.

TIME

1 **dates and days**:
Dad died on 29 August, 1975.
Are you going to the talk on Thursday evening?
on the last day of her holiday

2 You can use **on** in various structures with the meaning 'immediately after', or 'as a result of' doing something:
She became extremely angry on reading these words.
He telephoned her on his return.

USING MACHINES AND INSTRUMENTS

1 **computers**:
Our work is backed up on to the network every night.
I could work it out on the computer, I suppose.

2 **recording machines**:
She did not mind being filmed on video by two students.
I've got the interview on tape.

3 **television and radio**:
I was watching the news on television.
There was a play on the radio.

ⓘ People usually say **on television** but **on the radio**.

4 **musical instruments**
You play a tune **on** a musical instrument:
She managed to play the tune on the piano.

5 **telephone**:
I spent the next few hours on the telephone.
Contact Jane on 0171 345 6789.

OPERATION

1 Electrical and other appliances using a power supply are **on** when they are operating:
The oven switches itself on and off automatically.
Shall I turn the radio on?
Who left all these lights on?

2 **Films, plays, operas,** etc are **on** when they are being shown or broadcast:
What films are on this week?
What's on at the Festival Theatre?

3 Something is **not on** if it is not possible or practicable:
We hoped the company would pay our expenses, but apparently that isn't on.

COURSES AND SYSTEMS

1 You can say that you are **on** a course of study:
They're all sent off on management courses.

2 Your doctor can put you **on** a course of treatment, or pills, and you can go **on** a diet:
He's already on pills for his heart.
He seems to live on hamburgers.

WORK AND RESOURCES

1 **work**
You work **on** tasks and projects:
We need more people on this job.

2 **time and money**:
Don't spend too long on the first question.
He spends a lot on clothes.

3 **taxes, profits and losses**:
We expect to make a profit on some products and a slight loss on others.

4 **expense**:
Drinks are on me [= I'm paying for the drinks].

PROGRESS

On is used with some verbs to express progress, continuation, or movement onward or ahead:

1 **progress**:
She stopped to look in a window, then walked on.
She just went on with what she was doing.

2 **On** is used with **earlier** and **later** to mean before or after the present moment, or the time mentioned:
I'll see you later on.
I'd noticed the parked car earlier on.

FURTHER USES

Other uses of **on** may be useful to note:

1 **influences and effects**:
She had a lasting influence on me.

2 **targets and schedules**:
We just arrived on time.
The work is on schedule.

3 Buildings or furniture are **on fire** when they are burning:
Some boys had set the shed on fire.

4 **injury**:
I cut my foot on some broken glass.
She said she'd burnt herself on the iron.

5 **subjects**
In a formal context, you talk or write **on** a subject:
an article on international trade

More informally, you talk or write **about** a subject.

➤ See **about**.

6 **systems and principles**:

It works on the same principle as a watch.
The factory workers are now on a three-day week.

•••• once ••••

Once can be an *adverb* or a *conjunction*.

AS AN ADVERB

1 **Once** means 'a single time':

Most people break their diet not just once, but many times.
Johnson has scored only once in six games.

2 **Once** can be used with the indefinite meaning 'at some time in the past':

The island was once famous for its cheese.
Rob once had a beard; and he's thinking of growing it again.

> ⓘ To refer to an indefinite time in the future you use **one day** or **sometime** rather than **once**:
> *You must come round sometime.*
> *I'll take you to the Museum one day.*

3 Something that happens **once** a month, or **once** a year, happens regularly at a certain time every month or year:

I had to make the trip to the clinic once every two weeks.

AS A CONJUNCTION

You can use **once** as a conjunction, meaning 'as soon as' or 'after'. You frequently use it with a perfect tense:

Once we have paid back the money we'll think about expanding the premises.
We all get a bit lazy once we're over thirty.

•••• one ••••

As well as being a *number*, **one** functions as a *determiner* and as a *pronoun*. As a pronoun it can be used as a 'substitute' word for nouns already mentioned, with the plural **ones**. You can also use **one** as a rather formal *personal pronoun*, meaning people in general, including yourself.

AS A DETERMINER

1 **One** person or thing is a single person, thing, unit, etc:

There's only one train per day.
The population of the island is at least one million.

2 You normally use the determiner **one** either for special emphasis:

He composed this symphony in one week.

or for contrast with other figures in a numerical context:

There were about one hundred people in favour, and two hundred against.

Otherwise you use the indefinite article **a** or **an**:

I'll see you in a week.
There were about a hundred people there.

AS A PRONOUN

1 When stressed, the pronoun **one** refers to a single member of a group just mentioned:

Masses of people have applied, but we can only appoint one.
The directors were so angry that all but one resigned.

2 **One of** a group of people or things is a member of it. **One of** is followed by a determiner and a plural noun or pronoun:

One of my brothers is a lawyer.
I hope you feel that you're one of us, now.

3 **One of** is often followed by a superlative:

Let's look at one of Europe's most successful companies.
I'm one of her biggest fans.

ⓘ Where **one of** forms part of the subject group, the verb is singular:
One of the major costs was the need to train for new skills.

AS A SUBSTITUTE PRONOUN

You frequently use **one** and its plural **ones**, as substitute pronouns for previously used nouns.

1 **One** substitutes for singular countable nouns or noun phrases:

'Which is your bed?' 'The one by the window.'
He changed his diet to one of [= a diet of] *fresh fruit and vegetables.*
I've had an idea, though it isn't much of one, I'm afraid.

ⓘ Notice that you never use **one** to refer back to an *uncountable* noun. You use **some** in a positive context, and **any** in a negative one:
'Shall I get milk?' 'There's some in the fridge, isn't there?' 'No.' 'Oh, maybe the milkman didn't bring any today.'

2 **Ones** substitutes for plural countable nouns:

'Are there any spare disks?' 'You can use the ones in the drawer.'

ⓘ You do not use the plural pronoun **ones** on its own. When there is no adjective or defining phrase or clause you use **some** in a positive context and **any** in a negative context, rather than **ones** on its own:
I was looking for screws, because I was sure we had some (not *ones*)*, but there don't seem to be any.*

3 Notice that 'pair' words such as **glasses**, **trousers** or **scissors** are referred to by the plural pronoun **ones**:

'Are my scissors over there?' 'Which ones do you want?' 'The silver ones.'

4 The question determiner **which** can be followed by **one** or **ones**:
Here are the rucksacks. Which one (or *which*) *is yours?*
Perhaps it's in my trouser pocket, if I can remember which ones [= which trousers] *I was wearing yesterday.*

5 Superlatives can stand by themselves, so you do not need **one** or **ones** after them:
We educate boys up to the age of twelve and the cleverest go on to Eton.

6 When referring back to a possessive + noun (*eg* **my children**), you do not use a structure with **one** or **ones**. You use either a possessive noun or pronoun, or, more formally, **that of** or **those of**:
My children are older than Mary's.
Her memory is more accurate than mine.
My CV and that of another applicant had been lost.

REFERRING TO PEOPLE

Ones is sometimes used to mean 'people', and, more informally, **one** is used to mean 'person', without any backward-looking reference:
They remembered their loved ones fighting abroad.
You're a strange one!

AS A PERSONAL PRONOUN

1 You can use **one** as an indefinite personal pronoun to refer to people generally, including yourself. People also use it to refer to themselves indirectly:
One doesn't hear that phrase very often.

2 **One** has the possessive form **one's** and the reflexive form **oneself**:
One's religion can be a comfort at such times.
It's necessary to ask oneself this question from time to time.

3 **One** is rather formal. **You** is used in the same way, but is less formal:
One must learn to honour the past.
Some drugs hook you almost instantly.

ⓘ Notice that you only use **one** and **you** to refer to people generally, that is, anyone in any situation. To refer to a particular, but unidentified, person, you use **someone** or **somebody**:
Did somebody (not *one*) *mention ice cream?*

•••• only ••••

Only can act as an *adjective* or an *adverb*. There are some traditional rules about where to put the adverb **only** in a sentence, but these are usually ignored by native speakers of English.

AS AN ADJECTIVE

You use **the** or the possessive determiners (**my**, **her**, and so on) with **only** to say something about a person or thing that doesn't apply to anyone or anything else:
Ours were the only huts with glass windows.
Annabelle is our only daughter.

> ⓘ You don't use the **a** or **an** before **only** except in the expression **an only child**, meaning someone who has no brothers or sisters.

AS AN ADVERB

Only is a *focusing* adverb (see **adverbs**). You use **only** to focus what you are saying on a particular word, or on a particular part of the sentence.

The traditional rule is that **only** comes before the word it focuses on, but in fact most speakers use it in mid position, and stress the 'focus' word:

I was only going to look at it, not touch it.

However, **only** is used next to the 'focus' word in the following cases:

1 If **only** focuses on the subject of a sentence, it comes before it:
Only God can forgive sin.

2 For emphasis, you can put **only** after the word or phrase it focuses on:
These files are for reference only, and cannot be edited.

3 You can put **only** at the beginning of a sentence, followed by the word or phrase it focuses on, followed by an inverted auxiliary verb and subject:
Only very slowly did we see where these policies would lead.

4 You can use **only** to mean 'as recently as', or 'no longer ago than':
He was in New York only last week.

• • • • on to, onto • • • •

The combination **on to** acts as a preposition of direction, and some people write it as one word, **onto**, to correspond with **into**. It does not matter which alternative you use, but there are some grammatical situations where you must use the two-word spelling, *eg* where **on** is an adverbial particle attached to the verb:

His job was to stick labels onto (or *on to*) *the boxes.*

But:

Let's move on to the next topic.
She went on to mention the noise problem.

It is never wrong to write **on to**, and this is the form used throughout this book.

• • • • open, opened • • • •

Open is both a *verb* and an *adjective.*

1 You **open** something such as a door or a window, when you move it so that it no longer fills the gap that it is intended to cover:
We can't open the window.
She opened the door and stared at him.

Especially in a literary or story-telling style, you can also use **open** as an intransitive verb, and say that a door or window **opens**:
The window opened, and in came George.
We heard a door open and close again in the next room.

EXPRESSING AN OPINION

This section deals with the different ways people use language to express their opinions and attitudes.

SHOWING HOW CERTAIN YOU ARE

1 You can express how certain you are about something you are saying by using a modal verb, for example **can**, **could**, **may**, **might**, **should** or **would**:

They can be a bit boring.
Yes, you could be right.

2 You can also show how certain you are by using a sentence adverb. Listed below is a selection of these, beginning with the least certain and ending with the most:

possibly
perhaps, maybe
hopefully
probably
presumably
almost certainly
no doubt, doubtless
definitely

I suppose he could, possibly, be at work still.
Maybe we've been wrong about him.
It's definitely too late to phone her.

3 The following adjectives are commonly used to show that the speaker is certain about what he or she feels:

certain	convinced
positive	sure

I'm positive my grandmother worked there.
I'm sure you'll manage.

GENERALIZING

If you want to indicate that what you are saying is a general, or approximate, statement, you can use one of the adverbs or adverbial phrases listed below:

as a rule	basically
by and large	essentially
for the most part	fundamentally

... open, opened continued

2 A door or window that is **open** is not shut or closed:

She looked in through the open door at the children.
The bathroom window was open.

3 **Open** can be used as an adjective after certain 'linking' verbs such as **lie** and **stand**:

Her book lay open on the table.
The door was standing open.

4 **Open** can also be used after certain verbs of movement such as **push**, **slide**, **swing** and **burst**. They describe the manner of opening:

The door flew open.

generally	in general
on average	on balance
on the whole	overall
ultimately	

On the whole, self-help groups are a good thing.
On balance, then, it seems as if the change is working well.

INDICATING PERSONAL OPINION

You can emphasize that you are giving your own personal opinion by beginning with one of the phrases below:

in my opinion	in my view
personally	to my mind
I'd say (*informal*)	if you ask me (*informal*)

I'd say it's one of the hardest decisions you'll have to make.
The Internet, to my mind, is a wonderful resource.

VERBS OF OPINION

Some verbs show how you feel about the opinion you are about to give. They may show that you are sure about the way you feel, or that you are still in the process of forming your ideas. Some of the commonest ones are listed below:

agree	assume
believe	guess
hope	imagine
realize	presume
reckon	suppose
think	understand

I reckon it should be stopped.
I assume that in America, if you have children, you get some help?
I think we need to consider this more carefully.

One of the most common verbs used in giving opinions is **should**. By using **should**, you indicate what you think is the best course of action:

They should spend more on education.
I think they should try a bit harder.

... **open, opened** continued

You have to push the door open.
The back door burst open and Sally came running into the room.
There was a gust of wind and the window swung open.

ⓘ You do not use **open** to mean 'switch on' (electrical appliances), 'turn on' (taps) or 'undo' (clothes):
Could you switch on (not *open*) *the television?*
I turned on (not *opened*) *the tap, but nothing came out.*
'I'm too hot!' 'Undo (not *open*) *your jacket, then.'*

expressing an opinion

➤ See pages 404 and 405.

opportunity, possibility

OPPORTUNITY

1 You can say that you **have an opportunity to** do something, or that you have been **given an opportunity of** doing something:

He will have an opportunity to examine the data.
They will be given an opportunity of defending themselves.

2 You **take an opportunity to** do something, or, more rarely **of** doing it:

May I take this opportunity to thank you all for the good work you are doing?

POSSIBILITY

Possibility is used to talk about possible happenings, not about openings or opportunities. A **possibility of** something happening, or **that** something may happen, is a slight probability that it will happen:

There was no possibility of my passing Latin.
We should now consider the possibility that other creatures may be equally intelligent.

opposite

Opposite can be an *adjective, preposition,* or *adverb.*

1 You put the adjective **opposite** *before* the noun if it is one of a pair of things that naturally face each other, such as the banks of a river, or the sides of a street or table:

On the opposite bank, Greenwich Palace shone in the sunlight.
The two leaders sat at opposite ends of the table.

2 The adjective **opposite** also goes before nouns such as **opinion** and **direction**, where there is a total contrast between two things:

I agree but my wife takes the opposite view.

➤ See also **contrary**.

3 **Opposite** can also act as a preposition or adverb:

The soldier sitting opposite me had a rifle.
The family living opposite noticed that our garage had been broken into.

ⓘ AmE uses the expression **across from** rather than **opposite**:
He found himself sitting across from a very pretty girl.

•••• or ••••

Or is a *conjunction*. It is used as a link between possibilities and alternatives, and can also be used with *whether* and *either* to introduce the second of two alternatives.

BETWEEN MATCHING WORD CLASSES

You use **or** to link word groups of the same grammatical class, *eg* nouns, pronouns, adjectives, adverbs, verbs or clauses:

1 between nouns

Or often links nouns and noun phrases:

She's looking for a teenager or young adult to help her.

> ⓘ Determiners that apply to both nouns linked by **or** can be omitted before the second noun:
> *Get your husband or (your) children to help.*

> ⓘ When **or** links singular nouns as the subject of a sentence, the verb is regularly singular:
> *A night porter or security guard is always on duty.*
> But a plural verb is sometimes used in informal English, especially where there is a combination of *eg* third and first person:
> *Alice or I are usually available to deal with queries.*

2 between pronouns

You can link personal pronouns, or a combination of nouns, proper nouns and pronouns, with **or**:

You or I could meet him at the airport.
You or your wife may be losing income.
Frank or I will do it.

> ⓘ Notice that **Frank or I** becomes **Frank or me** when used as the object of a verb or preposition:
> *You can let Frank or me know later.*
> *Hand your books in to the teacher or me.*

3 between adjectives or determiners:

Do you want fried or boiled potatoes?
A doctor can add to his or her income by taking private patients.

4 between adverbs, prepositions or adverbial phrases:

Was she acting strangely or unnaturally?
You can spell 'judgement' with or without an 'e'.

5 between verbs, modal verbs, or clauses:

The people in the shop couldn't or wouldn't cope
Are you coming with me or [are you] *staying here?*

> ⓘ After **or**, you can use **not** in place of a whole negative clause:
> *Are you coming with me or not?* [= or aren't you coming with me]

AFTER A NEGATIVE

Or is usually used after a negative word where you would use **and** in a positive context:

We then found we had no torches or candles.
It's very quiet here; you never see or hear a soul.

IN A LIST: MORE THAN TWO POSSIBILITIES

Where there are more than two possibilities, **or** is used between the last two, and commas usually separate the previous ones; a comma may be used before **or**, especially if the listed possibilities are in the form of fairly long phrases:

If you have a problem, do mention it to your doctor, health visitor or midwife.
The staff were tired from working long hours, lacked adequate training, or simply couldn't be bothered.

WHETHER ... OR, EITHER ... OR

Or introduces the second of two alternatives, where the first is introduced by **whether** or **either**:

1 **whether ... or**:

I didn't know whether I was coming or going.
He'll have to sign whether he wants to or not.

2 **either ... or**:

Is either Monday or Tuesday possible for you?

➤ For more information about **either ... or** and **whether ... or** see **either** and **whether**.

IN APPROXIMATIONS

You use **or** between numbers or other quantifying expressions to indicate an approximate amount:

We knew the forty or fifty people around us.
That marriage only lasted a year or two.

IN WARNINGS

You use **or**, sometimes with **else**, with a meaning like **otherwise**, to say what the consequences will be of failing to do something:

Hold on to me, or we may get separated.
We'll have to work overtime, or else this will be late.

➤ See also **else**.

TO CORRECT YOURSELF

You can use **or**, sometimes with **rather**, to make an adjustment to what you have just said:

He was brought up in Rhodesia, or Zimbabwe as it is now called.
She's my cousin, or rather, my second cousin.

•••• other ••••

AS A DETERMINER

1 other methods, other work

You use **other** before plural nouns and uncountable nouns to mean 'different from the things or people already mentioned'. You can use a determiner such as **some**, **a few**, **several**, **no**, **any** or **what**, or a number, before **other**:

You're not like other women.
You can get copies of certificates and other documents.
Then he confessed to five other murders.

> ⓘ Notice that **other people** can mean your fellow human beings:
> *You've got to consider other people.*

2 no other way

When **other** is used before a singular countable noun, it always has a determiner such as **some**, **any**, **no** or **what** before it:

Some other method of production must be found.

> ⓘ **Other** is never used by itself before a singular countable noun. Instead you use **another**:
> *Annie had another reason for hiding the truth.*

3 the other things, the other shoe

You use **the**, or another determiner such as **these** or **my**, with **other**, to mean:

- 'the rest' of a known group or class of people or things:

  She made friends with the teachers as well as the other pupils.
  Our other children loved Shanti dearly.

- the second of two:

  One eye was fully closed, and now the other eye was beginning to swell.

> ⓘ Notice that **the other** can mean 'the opposite':
> *Then we came to a river so wide I couldn't see the other side.*

AS A PRONOUN

1 You do not use **other** by itself as a pronoun to refer to a singular countable noun; you use **another** or **another one**:

She didn't like the hat. She would buy another (not *other*) *soon.*
If we don't get this house, we'll find another one.

Any other is possible without a following **one**:

'That's probably the worst solution.' 'I know, but I couldn't think of any other.'

2 **The other** is the second of two:

He stood on one leg for a while, then on the other.

You can also use **the other one** to refer to the second of two, especially with a possessive or demonstrative determiner:

I got this passport last summer because my other one was stolen.

OTHERS

1 You can refer to people or things different from those already mentioned as **others**:

Some people sat down and cried, but others were too shocked to do anything.

> ⓘ Notice that **others** can be used like **other people**:
> *Concern for others is becoming a priority again.*

2 You can refer to the rest of a group of people or things as **the others**:

All the others thought it was wonderful, so why didn't I?
Reply to these two letters and file the others.

USEFUL PHRASES

1 **Every other** applies to alternate items in any kind of series:

The exhibition is held every other year (or *every two years*).
They had painted every other house in the street pink.

2 You add **or other** after words like **someone**, **somewhere** and **sometime** to make them seem even more vague:

I've seen that face somewhere or other.

3 Used with nouns or pronouns, **other than** means 'different from' or 'besides' the one mentioned:

Was your bag packed by anyone other than yourself?

4 After a negative, **other than** usually means 'except':

There isn't much we can do other than wait.

➤ For information on **each other** and **one another** see **each**.

•••• otherwise ••••

1 **Otherwise** is used like **or else** to introduce the consequences of not doing what is suggested:

I want a house with a garden; otherwise I shall not be satisfied.

2 **Otherwise** can be used to say what the alternative course is, if one thing turns out to be impossible:

Print this in colour if you can; otherwise you can do it in shades of grey.

3 You can use **otherwise** to say what might happen, or might have happened, if circumstances were different:

Fortunately I'm very strong; otherwise I might have dropped dead.
These businesses might otherwise have to close down.

4 You use **otherwise** to say how things are generally, apart from the circumstance mentioned:

My headache's getting worse. Otherwise I'm fine.

5 **Or otherwise** is used as a short way of saying 'or in any other way', 'or of any other kind', 'or the opposite':

She tried not to smudge her lipstick or otherwise ruin her make-up.
No assistance, military or otherwise, has been given.
Their success or otherwise is not within their control.

•••• ought ••••

Ought is one of the *modal* verbs. Modal verbs always keep the same form, rather than inflecting (*she ought*, not *she oughts*). Unlike the other modal auxiliary verbs, **ought is used with to** before a following infinitive (*We ought to get up*).

Ought has two main divisions of meaning. It can express various kinds of *duty* or *morality*, and it can express *expectation*. **Ought** and **should** are very close to each other in meaning and use. The negative form **ought not** has the contraction **oughtn't**, which is not very widely used, and is avoided in AmE.

DUTY, MORALITY OR GOOD SENSE

1 You say someone **ought to** do something, or something **ought to** happen if you think it would be morally right:

I don't want to apologize, but I suppose I ought to.
People like that ought to be locked up.
She ought not to neglect her family.

2 You say someone **ought to** do something if it would be sensible, or a good idea, to do it:

You really ought to see your doctor.
Perhaps we ought to discuss this in more detail?

3 You say someone **ought to** do something when you recommend it:

It's a film you ought not to miss.
You ought to try windsurfing.

4 You say that something **ought to** happen or be done if it is according to the rules, *eg* of grammar, style or spelling:

This sentence ought to have a verb in it.
Oughtn't there (or, more formally, *ought there not*) *to be a 'u' in 'manoeuvre'?*

EXPECTATION

1 You say that something **ought to** be the case if you expect that it is, or expect that it will be:

They ought to be in Plymouth by now.
I posted the cheque today, so you ought to get it tomorrow.

2 You say that something **ought to** be the case, although it isn't, when you can see no reason why it isn't:

This ought to be simple; I don't know why it's taking so long.

ⓘ In short elliptical replies you can use **ought** with or without **to**:
'You ought to see your doctor.' 'Mmm, perhaps I ought (or *ought to*).'
However, you do not use **to** in question tags:
We ought to warn them, oughtn't we? (not *oughtn't we to*)

OUGHT TO HAVE + PAST PARTICIPLE

You use the form **ought to have** + past participle in two different ways:

1 to talk about something that didn't happen, or hasn't happened, in spite of its being right, sensible, or expected:

I'm sorry; I ought to have told you sooner.
You ought to have seen her face!
They ought to have arrived two hours ago.

2 to make guesses about what has happened or is now the case:

They ought to have taken off by now.

ELLIPSIS

Ought to is often followed by **be** or **have**, and **ought to have** by **been** or **done**, in referring back to verbs that use these auxiliaries:

'Was he sent to prison?' 'He ought to have been, but he wasn't.'

ⓘ An adverb that normally takes 'mid position', that is, after an auxiliary or modal verb, can come before or after **ought**:
You always ought (or *ought always*) *to warn people before arriving.*

•••• out, out of ••••

Out is an *adverb* and is the opposite of the adverbial sense of **in**. **Out of** is a *preposition*, and is the opposite of the preposition **into** and the prepositional sense of **in**. **Out** and **out of** can both be used in expressions of *position* and *direction*, and both have their own range of idiomatic uses, which are listed briefly in the last section of this entry.

POSITION

1 People are **out**, as opposed to **in**, when they are not in the place where they belong, or are expected to be, such as their home or office. You can also say that someone is **out of the house**, **the office**, or **the room**, as opposed to **in** it:

I called but you were out.
She'll be out all afternoon.
I was only out of the room for a minute.

2 **Out** and **out of** can also express position after verbs like **keep**, **stay**, **shut** and **lock**:

I've locked myself out twice already.
Keep the other children out of his bedroom.

3 **Out** is used as an alternative to **outside**, usually with a prepositional phrase:

It's really warm out.
The children have been out in the fresh air all day.

4 **Out of** can express distance from, or removal from, something:

We live out of town.
The hospital says that she's out of danger.

DIRECTION

1 **leaving rooms or buildings**:

She walked out of the room.
He ran out into the street.

2 **vehicles**, **bed**:

The car pulled up and the driver got out.
She got out of bed and stretched.

➤ See also note on vehicles at **off**.

3 **doors and windows**

You can go **out of** a door, and you can **look**, **climb**, **lean**, or **throw** something, **out of** a window:

She rushed out of the door and into his arms.
I glanced out of the window at the wet street.

> ⓘ You can also go **out through** a door, and look **out through** a window. The opposite of **out of** and **out through** is **in through**:
> *Two faces were peering in through the window.*

4 **getting or removing things**:

The policeman got out his notebook.
Let's move the furniture out of the sitting room.
I've got to get some money out of the bank.
Do you mind drinking out of plastic cups?

> ⓘ You don't use **from** after **out** except in combination with another prepositional phrase:
> *The dog crawled out from under the table.*

5 **marks and stains**:

There was a greasy mark on my skirt which I couldn't get out.

6 **sources**:

We didn't get much information out of him.

IDIOMATIC USES

1 **out of**

- **manufacture and construction**:

The best-quality paper is made out of rags.

➤ See also **make**.

- **motives**:

I only visit them out of duty.

- **lack of supply**:

  I seem to be out of beer.

- **unemployment**:

  How long have you been out of work?

- **not in the proper state**:

  The telephone's out of order.
  He sang out of tune.
  I'm very out of practice.

- **beyond a range or limit**:

  The best fruit was just out of reach.

- **persuading and cheating**:

  I talked him out of resigning.
  I feel I've been done out of my afternoon off.

2 out

- **not alight, not burning**:

  The fire's out.
  They talked with the lights out.

- **in bloom**:

  The daffodils aren't out yet.

- **published**:

  The book will be out in April.

> ⓘ As a particle used with verbs, and forming phrasal verbs, **out** has the following senses: spreading and distributing (**hand out**, **spread out**, **send out**); deleting (**cross out**, **rub out**); excluding (**leave out**); completeness or finality (**tire out**, **knock out**, **work out**); projecting (**stick out**, **poke out**); speaking aloud (**call out**, **speak out**).

•••• outside ••••

Outside can be used as a *preposition*, *adverb*, *adjective* or *noun* and is the opposite of **inside**. As a preposition it is used for position, rarely direction; but as an adverb it can, like **inside**, express both position and direction.

AS A PREPOSITION

1 physical position

You are **outside** a room, building or place when you are close to it, or close to its entrance:

He parked the car outside their house.
Harriet stood outside the door, listening.
She had rented a house outside Glasgow.

2 direction

Outside is sometimes used for direction, expressing the idea of movement out of a place to an area close to it:

I asked the parents to step outside the room for a moment.

> ⓘ Where there is no idea of staying close to a place, you use **out of**:
> *Crowds were pouring out of the cinema.*

3 other uses

- You are **outside** a community or organization if you are not part of it:

  The trade deficit with countries outside the EC grew to £3.4 billion.

- You can say that things that are not within a certain range or limit are **outside** it:

  We're open for business outside normal office hours.

AS AN ADVERB

1 position

Outside means close to, or outside the entrance of, the room or building you are in, or the one mentioned; it can also mean 'out of doors', as distinct from **inside** or **indoors**:

William, there's a car outside with a dog in it.
It wasn't quite warm enough to sit outside.

2 direction

Outside can express movement out of a place to an area close by:

I went outside and walked round to the back of the house.

> ⓘ Where there is no idea of staying close by, you use **out**:
> *'Where's Sophie?' 'Don't know. She went out.'*

AS A NOUN

The **outside** of something is its outer side or surface:

I've only seen the palace from the outside.
There are full instructions on the outside of the packet.

AS AN ADJECTIVE

Outside has a range of adjectival uses:

We've painted the outside walls of the cottage.
We had an outside toilet in those days.
He enjoys his work, but has plenty of outside interests.
The monks knew very little of the outside world.

> ⓘ Notice that the **outside** lane on a motorway or dual carriageway is the one nearest the central division.

•••• over ••••

Over can be a *preposition* or *adverb* and is the opposite of **under**. Some of the prepositional and adverbial senses overlap, and are dealt with together in the first two sections below. The adverb **over** has some uses of its own, which are dealt with separately in the section FURTHER USES OF THE ADVERB.

POSITION AND MOVEMENT IN RELATION TO SURFACES

1 directly above:

The cook lives in a flat over the garage.
He had a cut over his left eye.

➤ For more detail about this meaning of **over** see **above**.

2 extending above:

They have no roof over their heads.
Fritz held an umbrella over us.

3 covering:

He was wearing a green coat over his tweed suit.
She put her hand over his.
Lucy pulled the bedclothes up over her head.

4 supported by, and hanging down from:

I put my towel over the radiator to dry.
He was carrying an umbrella over one arm.

5 across a surface:

I watched a blush spread gradually over her face and neck.
He strode over the fields.

> ⓘ **Over** can be intensified by **all**:
> *You've got jam all over your face.*

6 from one side to the other, across the top of:

We flew over the Alps.
Jump or step over the puddles.
I fell over the cat.
He drove over a cliff.

7 position on one side or the other:

The Rayners used to live over the road.
How long is the Canadian team over here for?

8 leaning and bending:

She leant over his cot.
My back hurts when I bend over to the left.

➤ For more detail about these meanings of **over** see **across**.

FURTHER USES

1 telephone and radio:

I can't answer questions over the telephone.
I heard a familiar voice over the radio.

➤ See also **on**.

2 more than:

The fare comes to over £200.
Children of twelve and over must pay.

➤ See also **above**.

3 during:

Tell me about it over lunch.
We can discuss it over a glass of red wine.

4 about:

Let's not argue over details yet.

5 spending time and trouble:

Don't spend too long over the first essay.
She'd taken a lot of trouble over her speech.

6 power, influence and control:

He appears to have no influence over their decisions.
He certainly had a mysterious power over women.

7 recovered from:

He's been quite ill but he's over it now.

FURTHER USES OF THE ADVERB

1 considering and examining:

Think this over carefully.
Could you read this over and check the grammar?

2 falling and knocking

People or things fall **over** or are knocked **over** when they fall, or are knocked, from a standing position into a lying one:

She fell over on the pavement.
He knocked over a lamp.

3 rolling and turning:

She rolled over and yawned.
I turned over two pages at once.

4 finished:

You can use the verb **be** with **over** rather like a perfect tense, to say that something has finished:

Thank goodness the exams are over.
'Are you still going out with Harry?' 'No, it's over.'

> ⓘ You can intensify **over** with **all**:
> *When this is all over, we'll have a holiday.*

5 remaining:

We've got some potatoes left over from lunch.

6 **repetition**
You do something **all over again**, or in AmE, start **over**, when you start again from the beginning:

Will we have to count them all over again?
Sometimes the only way is to start over.

•••• over- ••••

The prefix **over-** means 'too', or 'too much', and can be used before adjectives, adverbs, nouns or verbs, with or without a hyphen (this can be checked in a good dictionary):

We need to move away from over-intensive agriculture.
These learners tend to overuse the present perfect.

Over- is most frequently used before adjectives and verbs, and can provide a brief way of expressing your meaning. For instance, instead of *'parents who protect their children too much'* you can say *'overprotective parents'*, or *'parents who overprotect their children'*.

The opposite of **over-** is **under-**.

•••• own ••••

Own can be a *determiner* or a *pronoun*. You always use a possessive determiner (**my**, **your**, etc) or the possessive form of a noun or proper name, before **own**:

This was Mother's own copy.
Is this your own car?

AS A DETERMINER

1 Your **own** things are the things that are individual to you, or belong to you exclusively. You often add **own** after a possessive determiner (**my**, **your**, etc) for clarity or emphasis:

Sally's saving up to buy her own flat.
I prefer to take my own car, thanks.

- You can use a number after **own**:

  He's an adult now, and must stand on his own two feet.

- You can intensify **own** with **very**:

  She finally had her very own home.

2 **Own** has a kind of reflexive use. You **make your own bed**, or **clean your own room** if you do it *yourself*:

She can dress herself and do her own hair.
I saw it with my own eyes [= I saw it myself].
I did all my own cooking and washing when Mum was in hospital.

AS A PRONOUN

1 Although you cannot use determiners such as **a**, **some**, **any**, **no** or **enough** before **own**, you can use these determiners before the structure **of your own**:

They've got enough troubles of their own
He has no friends of his own.

2 You can use **my own**, **our own**, and so on, without a following noun, to refer to a noun already mentioned:

We like beer, and we make our own.

3 The expression **on your own** reflects both uses of **by yourself**:

- When you are **on your own** you are alone; no-one else is with you:

  The child was left on her own for hours at a time.
  I am not going on my own. Murphy will take me.

- When you do something **on your own** you do it without help from anyone else:

  We'll be able to manage on our own now, thanks.
  I've given you all the help I can; now you're on your own.

pair

There are two kinds of objects that come in pairs:

1 two objects of the same size, and corresponding shape, intended to be used together, such as gloves, shoes or earrings

2 a piece of clothing or a tool consisting of two corresponding parts joined together, such as trousers, scissors or glasses.

SINGULAR OR PLURAL VERB?

A singular or plural verb can follow **a pair of**, whether it refers to type **1** or type **2**. If a singular determiner such as **every** or **each** precedes **pair of**, the verb is usually singular:

A pair of eyes were caught in his torch beam.
Every pair of eyes was fixed on her.
A pair of glasses was balanced on the arm of the chair.
She wore a pair of jeans that were a bit too tight for her.

WITHOUT 'OF'

You can use **pair** or **pairs** with a number or other determiner, and often an adjective or clause, to refer back to the pair word:

'Are my scissors over there?' 'Which pair do you want? There are two pairs here.'
'The small pair with blue handles.'

PLURAL PRONOUNS AND DETERMINERS

Notice that you use plural pronouns and determiners to refer back to pair words:

I need a new pair of jeans; just look at the state of these.
I've got reading glasses already. I want some distance ones.

part

'PART OF' OR 'A PART OF'?

When **part** is followed by **of** people often use it without **a**:

An earth tremor had caused part of the building to collapse.
They spend part of the year abroad.
Sports and games form part of the school curriculum.

However, if you put an adjective before **part**, you have to use **a**:

Prevention of infection is a major part of our response to the problem.

> ⓘ You use **part of** only with singular countable nouns and uncountable nouns, not with plural nouns:
> *Some of* (not *part of*) *her conclusions are wrong.*

particles

➤ See **past participles** and **present participles**.

particles

The name **particles** is given to the word class of short adverbs and prepositions such as **up**, **down**, **away**, **back**, **with**, **by**. Many of them have an important role in the formation of phrasal verbs, *eg* **dress up**, **pull down**, **fade away**, **hit back**, **stick with**, **stand by**.

➤ For a list of particles that are used to form phrasal verbs, see **phrasal verbs**.

part of speech

In grammar, the **parts of speech** are the grammatical classes of words, *eg* nouns, pronouns, verbs, adjectives, determiners, participles, adverbs, prepositions and conjunctions. A more modern term for these groups is **word classes**.

the passive

➤ See also the entry **active sentences**.

You use the *passive* forms of transitive verbs where the person or thing that *is affected by* the action is the subject of the verb.
The person or thing that is the *object* of an active transitive verb, becomes the *subject* of a passive verb. Compare the following pairs of sentences:

active:	*Delmer & Co* ***are checking*** *our accounts.*
passive:	*Our accounts* ***are being checked*** *by Delmer & Co.*
active:	*Susan and Rob* ***have invited*** *us to their party.*
passive:	*We****'ve been invited*** *to Susan and Rob's party.*

The subject of the active verb sometimes appears in the passive structure as the *agent*, after the preposition **by**. But it is common not to mention the agent at all. (See **agents and instruments** below.)

PASSIVE FORMS

You form passives by using some form of the verb **be** with a past participle. A list of all the passive forms is given below, using the verb **move**:

1 present

simple present	*I am moved*
	he, she, it is moved
	you, we, they are moved
present progressive	*I am being moved*
	he, she, it is being moved
	we, you, they are being moved

2 past

simple past	*I, he, she, it was moved*
	we, you, they, were moved
past progressive	*I, he, she, it was being moved*
	we, you, they, were being moved
present perfect	*I have been moved*
	he, she, it, has been moved
	we, you, they, have been moved
past perfect	*I, he, she, it, we, you, they, had been moved*

3 future

- with **will** or **shall**:

simple future	*I shall* (or *will*) *be moved*
	he, she, it, will be moved
	we shall (or *will*) *be moved*
	you, they, will be moved
future perfect	*I shall* (or *will*) *have been moved*
	he, she, it, will have been moved
	we shall (or *will*) *have been moved*
	you, they, will have been moved

- with **going to**

I am going to be moved
he, she, it, is going to be moved
we, you, they are going to be moved

AGENTS AND INSTRUMENTS

1 the agent

In a passive construction, you can draw attention to the person or thing that does the action (the *agent*) using the preposition **by**:

He was met at the airport by the manager herself.
The gallery was designed by James Stirling and Partners.
The village was destroyed by an avalanche.

2 the instrument

If the agent uses an instrument, it is usually introduced by **with**:

Hattersley was hit on the head with a chair by a demonstrator.
Splinters can be removed with a clean sharp needle.

WHY USE PASSIVES?

1 focus

You can keep the same person or thing as the subject of a series of statements:

Lucy was returning from an evening at a friend's house when she was knocked down by a van.

2 distancing

To give a 'distancing' effect, and sometimes to avoid specifying the person responsible for an action:

Application forms must be returned (rather than *you must return your application form*) *by 4 June.*
I was told (rather than *She told me*) *about the changes in the company.*

COMPLEX STRUCTURES

1 **compound transitive verbs**

You can turn transitive phrasal verbs and other compound verb structures into the passive:

- **knock over**:
  She was knocked over by a drunk driver.
- **laugh at**:
  I won't be laughed at.
- **take notice of**:
  Perhaps the newspapers should be taken less notice of.
- **make a fuss of**:
  We all like being made a fuss of from time to time.

2 **verbs with two objects**

With verbs that can take a direct and indirect object (such as **give**, **show**, **offer**, **pay**, **promise**, **read**, **refuse**, **tell**) two constructions are possible in the *active*. The indirect object can come before the direct object:

- **verb + indirect object + direct object**:
  She sent Clive a copy of her report.
  You put this into the *passive* by making the indirect object the subject:
  Clive was sent a copy of her report.
  Alternatively, the indirect object can become an object after a preposition such as **to** or **for**:
- **verb + direct object + preposition + object**:
  She sent a copy of her report to Clive.
  You put this into the *passive* by making the direct object the subject:
  A copy of her report was sent to Clive.

3 **report clauses**

When a report clause follows a phrase such as **experts think**, **they say**, or **we feel**, the sentence can usually be put into the passive using a construction with **it** as subject:

active: *Experts think that the fumes are coming from the drains.*
passive: *It is thought that the fumes are coming from the drains.*
active: *They say that he has invested his own money in the firm.*
passive: *It is said that he has invested his own money in the firm.*

4 **infinitive constructions**

- **reporting**
  The subject of a report clause can be made the subject of a passive 'reporting' verb, with a following infinitive, as in the following pairs of examples:
  active: *The police believe he is armed.*
  passive: *He is believed to be armed.*
  active: *We understand that he is staying with a friend.*
  passive: *He is understood to be staying with a friend.*
  Notice that the infinitive after a passive verb can be:

a perfect infinitive:

The dead man was presumed to have committed suicide.

a progressive infinitive:

The project is believed to be receiving generous grants.

- **other infinitive constructions**

Verbs that are followed by an object and a **to-**infinitive can be put into the passive, *eg*:

active: *The woman told us to wait in the queue.*
passive: *We were told to wait in the queue.*

The verbs **make** and **help**, and the 'observing' verbs **see** and **hear**, are used in the active with an infinitive without **to**. When they are put into the passive they take a **to-**infinitive:

active: *A nurse helped her sit up in bed.*
passive: *She was helped to sit up in bed by a nurse.*

- **object + complement**

Some verbs take complements after their objects:

We painted the door red.

A sentence like this can be put into the passive:

The door was painted red.

The complement can be an adjective, like **red** in the example above, or a noun:

active: *The insult rendered her speechless.*
passive: *She was rendered speechless by the insult.*
active: *They falsely branded him a criminal.*
passive: *He was falsely branded a criminal*

USING 'GET' TO FORM PASSIVES

You can use the verb **get** informally to form passives:

You'll probably get caught (or, more formally, *be caught*).
My glasses got broken (or, more formally, *were broken*) *at school today.*
We kept getting burgled (or more formally, *being burgled*).

➤ For this use of **get** see the entry **get**.

•••• past, passed ••••

PASSED

Passed is the past tense and past participle of the verb **pass**. You never use **past**:

'Hungry?' he asked, as we passed the chip shop.
We passed the evenings on the balcony in quiet conversation.

PAST

Past can be a noun (*forget the past*), a preposition (*she walked past me*), an adverb (*a taxi went past*) and an adjective (*past times*).

As an adjective it describes time that has gone, and is also used to refer to a period of time extending up to the present:

During the past year 1.5 million more men, women and children have been affected.

the past

There are six different past tenses or forms in English:

1 the simple past tense:
I moved

2 the past progressive:
I was moving

3 the present perfect:
I have moved

4 the present perfect progressive:
I have been moving

5 the past perfect:
I had moved

6 the past perfect progressive:
I had been moving

Each of these forms has its own function in referring to the past.

SIMPLE PAST

1 **forms of the simple past**:

positive	question	negative
I moved	*did I move?*	*I did not* (or *didn't*) *move*
you moved	*did you move?*	*you did not* (or *didn't*) *move*
he moved	*did he move?*	*he did not* (or *didn't*) *move*

and so on.

2 **uses of the simple past**

The simple past is the tense you normally use to report past events. The other past tenses have special functions. You use the simple past to refer to past happenings and past situations:

- **single occasions**:
The next day he drove us to the airport.
- **repeated occasions**:
Every morning he drove us to work.
- **a continuous situation**:
He knew that we were all interested and so he made us work hard.
- **stories and narratives**:
I opened the door. The long room was dark, but there was a tiny light behind the bar. I took a seat and watched.

PAST PROGRESSIVE

1 **forms of the past progressive**:

positive	question	negative
I was moving	*was I moving?*	*I was not* (or *wasn't*) *moving*
you were moving	*were you moving?*	*you were not* (or *weren't*) *moving*
he was moving	*was he moving?*	*he was not* (or *wasn't*) *moving*

and so on.

2 uses of the past progressive

- activity in progress:
  What were you doing when President Kennedy was shot?
- activity over an extended period:
  I was working in the office all weekend.
- interrupted activity:
  We were just sitting down when the phone rang.
- the current situation at the time of an event:
  At the time of his death his housekeeper was receiving £32.50 per week for her services.
- temporary conditions:
  I looked up and saw that he was smiling at me.
- vagueness:
  I was discussing this question with someone the other day.
- frequently repeated situations:
  He was always correcting people.

PRESENT PERFECT

1 forms of the present perfect:

positive	**question**	**negative**
I have (or *I've*) *moved*	*have I moved?*	*I have not* (or *I haven't* or *I've not*) *moved*
you have (or *you've*) *moved*	*have you moved?*	*you have not* (or *haven't* or *you've not*) *moved*
he has (or *he's*) *moved*	*has he moved?*	*he has not* (or *hasn't* or *he's not*) *moved*

and so on.

2 uses of the present perfect

- **past events with a present relevance**
  A present perfect used for an action or event in the past suggests that it affects the present situation. News announcements often use the present perfect:
  US agents have arrested fourteen people.
  At last he has won the World Formula-One title.
  Edward Bowen has died aged 86.

> ⓘ But notice that if the time of the happening is mentioned, the simple past is used:
> *Actor, Frank Chalmers, died yesterday, aged 71.*

- **in combination with the present tense**
  The present perfect combines naturally with the present tense:
  Kit Johnson has injured an ankle and is out of the competition.
- **ongoing, repeated, and completed activities**
  The present perfect is also used to talk about situations that began in the past and still exist:

I've always been a worrier.
I've learnt never to expect anything.

It is used to talk about repeated action in the past that is relevant to the present:

The 37-year-old has won the race four times.

It is used to talk about completed activity, the completion being relevant to the present situation:

The University has completed its own survey.
I'm wondering what to read next; I've finished all these books.

- **with 'already', 'yet' and other time expressions**
  You use the present perfect with **already**, **before**, **ever**, **never**, **yet**, and **since**:

  I know, you've already learnt all about police procedures.
  I've been here nine times before.
  I don't think I've ever been treated so badly in my life.
  The group has never tried to mislead anyone.
  I've been out of work since returning from the tour last summer.
  Has your builder started yet?

> ⓘ You use the simple past with **ago** or an expression like **yesterday** or **last week** that refers a period in the past:
> *The builder started last Monday.*

- **how long... ?**
  You use the perfect forms in questions starting **how long?**, and in stating how long something has been the case:

  How long have you been (not *are you*) *at work, John?*
  I've worked here for seven years now and I really enjoy my job.

- **It's the first time I...**
  You use the present perfect with expressions such as **it's the first time...**, **that's the fifth...** :

  This is the first time I've been to the cinema for years.

> ⓘ AmE uses the simple past in many contexts where BrE uses the present perfect:
> *This is the first time I ever tried this drink.*

PRESENT PERFECT PROGRESSIVE

1 **forms of the present perfect progressive**:

positive	question	negative
I have (or *I've*) *been moving*	*have I been moving?*	*I have not* (or *I haven't* or *I've not*) *been moving*
you have (or *you've*) *been moving*	*have you been moving?*	*you have not* (or *you haven't* or *you've not*) *been moving*
he has (or *he's*) *been moving*	*has he been moving?*	*he has not* (or *he hasn't* or *he's not*) *been moving*

and so on.

2 **uses of the present perfect progressive**

- **a situation that started in the past; the situation up to now**
  You use the present perfect progressive to talk about a situation that started in the past and is still continuing, or has just stopped. It focuses on the situation *so far*, or *up to now*:
  Sorry to be so late. Have you been waiting long?
  I've been marking the errors in red. Is that what you want?
- **recent activities**
  You use the present perfect progressive to talk about *recent activities*, often when you are referring to their results in the present:
  I've been reading your report and I'm quite impressed.
  Sorry about my appearance. I've been cleaning the house.
- **how long + verb of activity**
  You use the present perfect progressive form of activity verbs after **how long?**:
  How long have you been looking for work?
  How long have you been playing the guitar?
- **temporary situations**
  Temporary situations are expressed by the present perfect progressive, in contrast to permanent ones expressed by the present perfect:
  She's been lying in bed all day.
- **continuous increase**
  The present perfect progressive is used to express continuous increase:
  At all levels of education the ratio of women to men has been increasing steadily.

PAST PERFECT

1 **forms of the past perfect**:

positive	**question**	**negative**
I had (or *I'd*) *moved*	*had I moved?*	*I had not* (or *I hadn't* or *I'd not*) *moved*
you had (or *you'd*) *moved*	*had you moved?*	*you had not* (or *you hadn't* or *you'd not*) *moved*
he had (or *he'd*) *moved*	*had he moved?*	*he had not* (or *he hadn't* or *he'd not*) *moved*

and so on.

2 **uses of the past perfect**

- **the earlier past**
  You use the past perfect when you are referring to something that happened *before* the time in the past that you are talking about:
  I reached the place where I had seen her.
  He noticed she had hardly eaten anything.
- **unreal situations**
  You use the past perfect in unreal situations, *eg* with **I wish**, **if only**, **would rather**, conditions with **if**, or unrealized hopes:

I really wish you hadn't got involved.
If only you had stopped driving when you started feeling sleepy.

PAST PERFECT PROGRESSIVE

1 forms of the past perfect progressive:

positive	**question**	**negative**
I had (or *I'd*) *been moving*	*had I been moving?*	*I had not* (or *I hadn't* or *I'd not*) *been moving*
you had (or *you'd*) *been moving*	*had you been moving?*	*you had not* (or *you hadn't* or *you'd not*) *been moving*
he had (or *he'd*) *been moving*	*had he been moving?*	*he had not* (or *he hadn't* or *he'd not*) *been moving*

and so on.

2 uses of the past perfect progressive

The uses of the past perfect progressive correspond to those of the present perfect progressive, but in a past context:

Her eyes were red. She had obviously been crying.
We had been living together for a few weeks when he became ill.

past participles

Past participles are the forms of verbs which combine with **have** to form the perfect tense, and with **be** to form the passive, *eg*:

Prices have risen.
I had burnt the milk.
You're wanted on the telephone.
Her book will be published soon.

The past participle of a verb often has the same form as its past, but with irregular verbs it may be different.

➤ For information on irregular past participles see **irregular verbs**.

Past participles have a lot of uses independent of the auxiliaries **be** and **have**. They behave like adjectives, and qualify, or refer to, nouns or pronouns. They are used in four main ways:

- like an adjective, before a noun or after a linking verb:

  a lost child
  We are lost.

- coming immediately after a noun, and qualifying it like a relative clause:

  the four students selected [= who have been selected] *for the quiz team*

- standing for the whole verb structure of a subordinate clause, with or without a conjunction:

  Left on their own, [= when they are left on their own] *children can get into danger.*
  When cooked [= when it is cooked], *the pastry should be brown and crisp.*

- as a complement after the object of a linking verb:

  I want to get this finished.

USED AS AN ADJECTIVE

1 passive and active

- Most past participles are *passive*:

  a revised timetable [= a timetable that has been revised]

- There are a few past participles that have an *active* meaning:
  advanced English-learners [= English-learners who *have advanced* a long way]
  a retired bank-manager [= a bank-manager that *has retired*]
  swollen legs [= legs that *have swollen*]
  an increased appetite [= an appetite that *has increased*]

➤ For classified lists of **-ed** adjectives, and a list of 'active' past participles, see **the -ed ending**.

2 compound past participles

Past participles in the form of two-word compounds are quite common. They can be composed of:

- adverb + participle:

  a well-known writer

- noun + past participle:
  blood-stained clothing [= clothing stained with blood]

- adjective or number + past participle:

  a four-legged animal
  a short-sleeved dress

- past participle + adverbial particle:
  grown-up children

3 attributive and predicative use

- A lot of past participles can be used both before a noun, and after a linking verb, such as **be** or **become**:
  bored children
  The children became bored.
  two grown-up sons
  My sons are both grown up.

- You can also use past participles after other verbs, *eg* when you are describing feelings or reactions:

  She went off satisfied.
  Sorry to send you away disappointed.

PAST PARTICIPLES USED AFTER NOUNS

Past participles can be used immediately after nouns to identify or define them, like relative clauses:

> *There were some cases of malnutrition among the children studied* [= who were studied].

OTHER CLAUSE-LIKE FUNCTIONS

Past participles can be used like adverbial clauses, *eg* of time or reason.

1 active participles: the perfect participle

You can use a perfect-participle construction instead of a subordinate clause containing an *active* verb, *eg*:

Having eaten her tea [When she had eaten her tea], *she went out to play.*
Having broken my ankle [Because I had broken my ankle], *I vowed never again to ski.*

2 passive participles

The participle can be used with or without auxiliary participles. This happens in fairly formal English, and in narratives:

Having been released from prison [= When he had been released from prison], *he went back into the community and immediately re-offended.*
Preserved in a sodium solution, the eggs would last us through the winter.

PAST PARTICIPLES AFTER AN OBJECT

1 as complements

After transitive linking verbs such as **get** and **make** the object may be followed by a past participle:

There was so much noise that I couldn't make myself heard.
We'll have to get the burst pipes mended urgently.

2 after 'observing' verbs

Past participles can be used after the objects of some 'observing' or 'sensing' verbs:

I've rarely seen her flustered.
You sometimes hear this word used wrongly.

•••• perfect forms: present perfect and past perfect ••••

➤ See **the past**.

—— permission ——

See pages 432 and 433.

•••• personal pronouns ••••

Personal pronouns are words such as **I**, **you**, **it**, **they**, which you use for referring to yourself and the person you are talking to, and to things and people that have already been mentioned, or are known about.

FORMS AND FUNCTIONS

There are two sets of personal pronouns, *subject pronouns* and *object pronouns*:

	subject	**object**
singular		
first person	*I*	*me*
second person	*you*	*you*
third person	*he, she, it*	*him, her, it*

PERMISSION

This section deals with the language used to ask for permission, to give permission, and to refuse permission.

ASKING FOR PERMISSION

The form you use to ask for permission to do something depends on how formal a situation you are in and how big your request is.

1 Can I have a look at your paper?

One of the commonest and most neutral ways of asking for permission is to say **Can I ...?** or, a little more politely, **Could I ...? Please** is sometimes included.

Please, can I come in?
Can I suggest something?
Could I have your name, please?
Could I borrow a pound from you?

> ⓘ **Could I ...?** is sometimes followed by **possibly**. This has the effect of making the request for permission more polite:
> *Could I possibly use your phone?*

2 May I make a suggestion?

May I ...? now sounds rather old-fashioned and formal. It is still common, however, in situations where people ask permission in order to sound polite:

May I join you?
May I ask why?

3 Please let me see!

An insistent way of asking for permission is (**Please**) **let me ...**:

Christopher, please let me stay and watch the film.
Please let me finish what I was saying.

4 Do you mind if I smoke?

When you are asking permission to do something which might disturb people, it is usual to use an indirect form:

I was wondering if I could *paint the room?*
Do you mind if I *watch the news at six?*
Would it be all right to *stay here till my bus comes?*
Is it all right to *use her computer while she's not here?*

5 Okay if I borrow this?

If you know the person you are speaking to well, and you are quite sure that they will let you do the thing you are asking, you can shorten one of the more polite expressions:

Okay if I *eat it all?*
All right if I *use the phone?*
Mind if I *sit here?*

GIVING PERMISSION

1 informal responses

In informal situations, you can say **yeah, go ahead** or **sure** when giving permission to do something. **Sure** is more typical of AmE:

*'Okay if I use the phone?' '**Yeah, go ahead**.'*
*'Can I borrow ten pounds?' '**Sure**.'*

> ⓘ **All right** or **okay** can sound reluctant if they are not said enthusiastically or positively enough.

2 more formal responses

More formally, you can use **of course**, **please do** and **by all means** to give permission:

*'Could I possibly borrow this umbrella?' '**Please do**.'*
*'Would it be all right to leave a bit early today?' '**Of course**.'*
*'Could I use this chair?' '**By all means**.'*

> ⓘ Notice that you should not reply **Yes** or **of course** to a request for permission that begins with **Do you mind ...?** An affirmative reply like this would suggest that you were rudely refusing permission. Suitable answers to such a request would be **Not at all – go ahead**, or **No, please do**.

3 giving permission reluctantly

You can show reluctance or show that you think the request is quite a big one by using **I suppose so**:

*'Mum, can I play on the swings?' '**I suppose so**, darling.'*

REFUSING PERMISSION

When you refuse someone permission to do something, you usually say **Sorry ...**, or **I'm afraid not**, and then give an explanation:

*'Can we have our meeting in here?' '**I'm afraid not**. There's a management meeting at 12.'*
*'Can I pay for this tomorrow.' '**I'm sorry sir, but** we're not allowed to give credit.'*

1 indicating that you do not want someone to do something

If someone has asked permission to do something and you do not really want them to do it, you can say **I'd rather you didn't**:

*'Do you mind if I smoke?' 'Well, **I'd rather you didn't**.'*

2 refusing permission in an angry or informal way

In very informal situations, people who know each other very well sometimes use impolite expressions to refuse permission:

*'Go on! Let me try!' '**No way**! You'll break it!'*
*'Mum, can I have some money for sweets?' '**No, you can't**.'*

	subject	object
plural		
first person	*we*	*us*
second person	*you*	*you*
third person	*they*	*them*

➤ For the personal pronoun **one** see the entry **one**.

➤ For the use of **it** as a preparatory subject see the entry **it**.

You use the subject pronouns as the subject of a verb, and object pronouns as the direct or indirect object of a verb, or the object of a preposition, *eg*:

subject pronouns:
Sally rang this morning about Dad. ***She*** *says that* ***he****'s feeling fine after the operation and* ***we*** *can all go round tonight.*

object pronouns:
Dad was pleased to see ***us****, Sally said, and the doctors had told* ***her*** *it would be OK for* ***him*** *to leave hospital on Thursday.*

> ⓘ Remember to use a reflexive pronoun for an object or indirect object that is the same as the subject of the verb:
> ***I*** *forced* ***myself*** *to work a bit harder.*
>
> ➤ See **reflexive pronouns**.

NOTES ON INDIVIDUAL PERSONAL PRONOUNS

1 It's me

- In answer to the question **Who's there?** or **Who's that?** it is normal to use the object pronouns after **It's**:
  'Who's there?' 'It's ***me*** (not *It's I*).*'*
  'Who's that?' 'It's ***us****.'*

> ⓘ When a relative clause follows the personal pronoun, you can use the subject pronouns:
> *It is we who should be thanked.*
> An easier and commoner way is to say:
> *We're the ones who* (or *the people who*) *should be thanked.*

- You use the object pronouns in exclamations consisting of an adjective + personal pronoun:
  Lucky ***you****!*
  Clever ***me****!*
  Poor ***him****!*

2 Peter and I

- Remember that a combination such as **you and I** or **James or I** can only be the subject of a verb. Use **you and me** or **James or me** as the object of a verb or preposition:
  She and I agree on most things.

John or I will collect you.
This is just between you and me.
Let John or me know.

- It is considered polite to put yourself second in combinations such as **you and I** or **Mary and me**. It is also polite to put your hearer first in such combinations as **you and he** or **you and your doctor**.

3 you and **they**

You can use **you** like the pronoun **one** to refer to people generally, including yourself, and **they** to refer to unspecified people not including yourself:

You never quite know how the market will react.
They think the recession will end quite soon.

➤ See also the entry **one**.

4 we

You can use **we** and **us** in two ways, to *exclude*, or *include*, the person you speaking to:

Your performance really impressed us. [excluding]
We like your work a lot. [excluding]
Shall we meet for lunch next week? [including]

5 they

They and **them** are often used to refer back to singular indefinite pronouns such as **someone**, **anyone** and **no-one**:

Anyone can go to the party, can't they?

➤ For more information see the entry **he**, **he or she, or they?**

—— phrasal verbs ——

WHAT IS A PHRASAL VERB?

A **phrasal verb** may consist of one of the following structures:

- a verb and adverb
- a verb and preposition
- a verb, an adverb and a preposition.

The adverbs and prepositions that combine with verbs to form *phrasal verbs* are often called *particles*.

The combination of verb and particle has a meaning that cannot be guessed from the individual meanings of the verb and the particle.

*They **let** him **off*** [= excused him from severe punishment].	[verb + adverb]
*I wondered what **lay behind*** [= was the reason for] *her remark.*	[verb + preposition]
*They must **come up with*** [= find] *a solution.*	[verb + adverb + preposition]

POSITION OF THE OBJECT

1 A lot of phrasal verbs are *intransitive*, so have no object:

*Fortunately our supplies **lasted out** till help came.*
*I spent a year **messing about** and enjoying myself.*

With phrasal verbs consisting of an intransitive verb + preposition, the preposition is followed by an object:

*I used to **dip into** the big dictionary from time to time.*

2 With *transitive* verbs it is difficult to know where to put the object. The following guidelines may help:

- **transitive verb + adverb**

  With phrasal verbs that are composed of a transitive verb + adverb, you can usually put the object before or after the adverb particle:

  *You must set **your personal views** aside.*
  *Let us set aside **our prejudices**.*

  If the object is a pronoun, you have to put it between the verb and the particle:

  *Whatever our personal views, we must set **them** aside.*

> ⓘ There are some transitive phrasal verbs of this class that always have the object between the verb and particle, *eg:*
> *He used to knock **his younger brother** around.*
> *Don't answer **your mother** back like that!*

- **verb + preposition**

  With phrasal verbs that are composed of a transitive verb + preposition, the object of the verb comes after it, and an object follows the preposition:

  *It's the awful smell of these cheeses that puts **people** off **them**.*

- **verb + adverb + preposition**

  With phrasal verbs composed of a transitive verb + adverb + preposition, the object of the verb usually comes before the adverb, and an object follows the preposition:

  *Most parents wanted to marry **their daughters** off to **wealthy businessmen**.*
  *Even being in the same room as a cat brings **him** out in **a rash**.*

3 phrasal verb particles

Here is a list of the particles that are used to form phrasal verbs:

about	*above*	*across*	*after*
against	*ahead*	*along*	*apart*
around	*aside*	*at*	*away*
back	*behind*	*by*	*down*
for	*forth*	*forward*	*in*
into	*off*	*on*	*out*
over	*round*	*through*	*to*
together	*under*	*up*	*upon*
with	*without*		

The particles have their own range of meanings when forming part of a phrasal verb, and these established meanings are used in the creation of new phrasal verbs.

Some of the particles have their own entries in this book, and some guidance is given there on their meanings when they form part of a phrasal verb.

•••• place ••••

1 a place to stay

Place, when followed by a **to**-infinitive, can be used as though it meant 'place in which', or 'place at which', or 'place to which' so you do not need to use a preposition with it:

Have you found a place to stay?
I know a good place to go.
The best place to start is at the beginning.

2 the place we usually stay

Similarly, when followed by a relative clause, **place** can be used as if it meant 'place where' or 'place in which', or 'place to which':

There is no place we can talk in this house now.
The first place they went was Manhattan.

3 anyplace, someplace, no place

Notice that in AmE -**place** often takes the place of BrE -**where**:

I'm happy to meet them just anyplace.
A school principal cannot simply send the child someplace else.

•••• please and thank you ••••

PLEASE

1 You use **please** to make a request more polite:

Could you hold this for me, please?
Please could you all try to be on time tomorrow?

> ⓘ Notice that **please** does not make an order into a request:
> *Could you check this for me, please?* (not *Check this for me, please.*)

2 You also use **please** after **Yes...** when you accept something that someone is offering you:

'More coffee?' 'Yes, please.'

WHEN PLEASE IS NOT USED

1 asking for repetition

When asking someone to repeat something they have said, use **Pardon?** or **Sorry?**:

*'What is your date of birth please?' '**Pardon**?'* (not *Please?*)
*'Where do you think I need?' 'Er **sorry**,* (not *Please*) *what was that?'*

2 giving things to people

Use **Here you are** or **There you are** when giving someone something:

'Can I borrow your dictionary?' 'Yes. Here you are.' (not *Please.*)

3 as an answer to 'thank you'

You do not say **please** as a response when someone thanks you for something.

THANK YOU, THANKS

Thanks is more informal than **thank you**.

1 strengthening and emphasizing

- You can strengthen **thank you** by adding **very much**, **so much** or **ever so much**; you can strengthen **thanks** by adding **very much**, **ever so much** or **a lot**:

  'Here you are.' 'Oh, lovely, thank you very much.'
  'Thanks a lot. You've been a great help.'

- You can use **indeed** to strengthen **Thank you very much** or **Thanks very much**:

  Thank you very much indeed. I really appreciate everything you've done.

2 Thanks for...

Thank you for or **Thanks for** is followed by a noun or by a verb + -**ing** form:

Thanks for your help.
Thank you for coming so quickly.

ACCEPTING AND REFUSING OFFERS

When refusing something say **No thanks**, or more formally, **No thank you**. **Yes please**, or sometimes **Thanks!** shows that you want to accept something:

'Another biscuit?' 'No thank you. I'm full.'
'Coffee?' 'Oh, thanks!' (or *Yes please.*)

RESPONDING WHEN SOMEONE THANKS YOU

If someone has thanked you for a very small thing, such as passing you something at the table, it is not necessary to reply.

1 In most situations, if someone thanks you for doing something for them, you can say **That's all right**, **That's okay** or, more informally, **No problem**:

'Thanks ever so much for the lift last night.' 'That's okay.'
'Thanks for all your help.' 'No problem.'

2 More formally, you can say **Not at all**, **You're welcome** or **Don't mention it**. At the end of a formal telephone conversation, if someone thanks you for your help, the most common reply is **You're welcome**:

'Well, that's very kind of you; thank you.' 'Not at all.'
'I'm so grateful for everything you've done. Thank you so much.' 'Don't mention it.'
'Well thank you for all your help.' 'You're welcome.'

•••• plenty ••••

Plenty is a *pronoun*.

1 plenty of

Plenty is rather informal. It means 'more than enough', or 'a lot', and is used with plural nouns and uncountable nouns. **Plenty** behaves like **a lot** and is always used with **of** before a following noun:

There are plenty of children (not *plenty children*) *for her to play with.*
I've got plenty of work to keep me busy.

> ⓘ A plural verb follows a plural noun used with **plenty**, and a singular verb follows an uncountable noun:
> *Plenty of articles have been written about it.*
> *Plenty of wine was drunk.*

2 used independently

Plenty can used without **of** to refer to a noun already mentioned, or simply to mean 'plenty of things':

The food is good and there is plenty to feed hungry teenagers.
Always give children plenty to keep them busy.

> ⓘ **Plenty** can be used as an intensifier with **more**:
> *There are plenty more cakes in the tin.*

plural and singular forms

The plural of most nouns is formed by adding **-s** to the singular. However there are some variations and irregular cases.

SPECIAL RULES

1 plural of nouns ending in consonant + y

If the singular form of a word ends in a **consonant + y**, *eg* **baby**, **lady**, **cherry**, you make the plural form by removing the **-y** and adding **-ies**:

singular	**plural**
baby	*babies*
lady	*ladies*
cherry	*cherries*

The final syllable of the plural form of these nouns is pronounced /ɪz/.

2 plural of words ending in -sh, -ch, -ss, -x and -s

If the singular form of a word ends in one of the above letters or pairs of letters, you make the plural form by adding **-es**:

singular	**plural**
blush	*blushes*
torch	*torches*
kiss	*kisses*
box	*boxes*
bus	*buses*

The final syllable of the plural form of these nouns is pronounced /ɪz/. Note, though, that where **-ch** is pronounced /k/, as in **stomach** and **monarch**, the regular **-s** ending is used.

3 plural of words ending in -o

Some nouns ending in **-o** have plural forms ending in **-oes**. Some of the most common are:

singular	**plural**
potato	*potatoes*

tomato	*tomatoes*
hero	*heroes*
echo	*echoes*

Many more nouns ending in -**o** form their plurals with -**s** alone. For example:

singular	**plural**
radio	*radios*
piano	*pianos*
kilo	*kilos*
solo	*solos*
alto	*altos*
concerto	*concertos*

The final syllable of the plural form of these nouns is pronounced /oʊz/.

Some nouns can have plurals ending in either -**os** or -**oes**. Some of the most common of these are listed below:

buffalo
flamingo
manifesto
mosquito
tornado
volcano

4 nouns ending in -f or -fe

There are some nouns ending in -**f** or -**fe**, which take the ending -**ves** in their plural form. Some of the most common of these are listed below:

singular	**plural**
calf	*calves*
half	*halves*
knife	*knives*
leaf	*leaves*
life	*lives*
loaf	*loaves*
scarf	*scarves*
self	*selves*
shelf	*shelves*
thief	*thieves*
wife	*wives*
wolf	*wolves*

PRONUNCIATION

1 nouns ending in -sh, -ch, -ss, -x and -s

The plural ending **-es** is pronounced /ɪz/:

bushes /ˈbʊʃɪz/

2 nouns ending in other unvoiced sounds

The plural ending of nouns that end in other unvoiced sounds, such as /f/, /k/, or /t/ is /s/:

books /bʊks/

3 nouns ending in voiced sounds

The plural ending of nouns that end in voiced sounds, such as /m/, /g/, or /d/ is /z/:

pigs	/pɪgz/

4 irregular pronunciation of plurals

baths	/bɑːðz/ or /bɑːθs/
houses	/ˈhaʊzɪz/
mouths	/maʊðz/ or /maʊθs/
paths	/pɑːðz/ or /pɑːθs/
roofs	/ruːfs/ or /ruːvz/
truths	/truːðz/ or /truːθs/
wreaths	/riːðz/ or /riːθs/
youths	/juːðs/ or /juːθs/

IRREGULAR PLURALS

1 Some nouns have irregular plural forms:

singular	**plural**
child	*children*
foot	*feet*
goose	*geese*
louse	*lice*
man	*men*
mouse	*mice*
ox	*oxen*
person	*people*
tooth	*teeth*
woman	*women*

ⓘ ■ Note that the pronunciation of the first syllable of the plural form **women** (/ˈwɪmɪn/) is different from that of the singular form **woman** (/ˈwʊmən/).
■ It is also sometimes possible to use **persons** as the plural form of **people**. This is generally only used in official language:
Only five persons may enter the lift at one time.

2 plural and singular the same

Some words end in **-s**, and do not change in the plural, *eg* **barracks, crossroads, headquarters, means, series, species**.

Other nouns which do not change in the plural are:

- words ending in **-craft**, *eg*, **hovercraft, spacecraft.**
- nationalities ending in **-ese**, *eg* **Chinese, Japanese, Taiwanese**.
- the names of some animals and fish, *eg* **sheep, fish, deer**.
- words representing groups of numbers, *eg* **dozen, hundred, thousand, million**.

But, the last group of words relating to numbers can take a final **-s** when they are used in certain expressions, *eg* **hundreds of people**.

➤ See **hundred, thousand, million**.

3 plurals of letter and numbers

- The plural form of lower case (not capital) letters is usually **-'s**:
  Has accommodation got two c's or one?
- The plural form of capital letters, abbreviations and dates may be spelt either with **-'s** or **-s**:
  She got As (or *A's*) [pronounced /eɪz/] *in all her exams.*
  People born in the 1950s (or *1950's*) [= nineteen fifties]

> ⓘ Remember that an apostrophe is not normally used for making plural forms.

4 compound nouns

- In compound nouns which consist of a noun ending in **-er** and an adverb, such as **passer-by** or **runner-up**, the plural is usually formed by adding **-s** to the noun:
  passers-by
  runners-up
- Other compounds, such as **down-and-out** and **work book**, form their plural by adding **-s** to the final element:
  down-and-outs
  work books
- The plural form of **mother-in-law**, **brother-in-law**, etc is either **mothers-in-law**, **brothers-in-law**, *etc*, or **mother-in-laws** and **brother-in-laws**.

5 plurals with no singular form

- Some words, such as **people**, **cattle**, **police**, and **vermin** take a plural verb form and refer to groups of people or things:
  There were a few police around.
  They owned three hundred cattle.
- Other words, such as **jeans**, **glasses**, **scissors** and **binoculars** end in **-s** and take a plural verb, but they have no singular form:
  These jeans are too small for me now.
  Don't leave those scissors on the floor.

> ⓘ If you want to refer to one item, or to a particular number of items of the things mentioned above, you can use **pair of** or **pairs of**:
> *I've brought three pairs of jeans.*
> *You'll need a pair of scissors and some sticky tape.*

6 plurals of words of foreign origin

Some words that come from foreign languages have irregular plurals. Below is a list of some of the more common ones:

cactus	*cacti* or *cactuses*
fungus	*fungi*
nucleus	*nuclei*
radius	*radii*
stimulus	*stimuli*

formula	*formulae* or *formulas*
larva	*larvae*
vertebra	*vertebrae*
analysis	*analyses*
basis	*bases*
crisis	*crises*
diagnosis	*diagnoses*
hypothesis	*hypotheses*
oasis	*oases*
bacterium	*bacteria*
datum	*data**
medium	*media**
memorandum	*memoranda*
criterion	*criteria*
phenomenon	*phenomena*
appendix	*appendices*
index	*indices*

ⓘ *The words **data** and **media** (referring to TV, radio and the press) are often used as uncountable nouns; the singular forms are rare:
How did you go about collecting this data (or *these data*)*?*
The media pervades (or *pervade*) *our lives these days.*

•••• point of view, view, opinion ••••

There is a small difference between your **point of view** and your **view** or **opinion**.

1 point of view

- You look at a situation **from** a particular **point of view**, when you concentrate on that particular aspect of the situation:
  It changed the study of language from a scientific point of view.
- You look at a situation **from** a particular person's **point of view** when you take into account their job, nationality, status, etc, and the way that the situation affects them:
  From the employer's point of view, wouldn't it be better if they had personal insurance cover?
  From the students' point of view, the teacher's involvement in research is quite irrelevant.

2 view, opinion

- Your **view** or **opinion** is what you think about something:
  She wanted my opinion on his progress.
  His view is that consumers should be told the whole truth.

> ⓘ Notice that you use the prepositions **on** or **about** with **view** and **opinion**:
> *They asked us our views on the subject.*
> *What's your opinon about all this?*

- Someone's **views** are the set of ideas they have regarding a subject:

  Her political views were regarded as radical.
  Tell me, what are your views on this?

- You use **In my view** or **In my opinion** when you want to indicate that what you are saying is only what *you* think:

  In my opinion the man is innocent.
  This is unpleasant and, in my view, wrong.

•••• possession, possessive expressions ••••

You use possessive expressions when referring to things that belong to people.

Possession can be expressed in three main ways:

- using a **possessive determiner** such as **my**, **your** or **our**:

  my opinions
  our products

- adding **'s** (or just the apostrophe in the case of plurals) to the noun that is the 'possessor':

  Harry's luggage
  the cats' food

- using **of**:

  the walls of the bedroom
  the wines of France

➤ For more detailed information, see the entries **possessive determiners and pronouns**, and **possessive 's**.

This entry shows which ways of expressing possession are suitable for which kinds of possessing.

THE RELATIONSHIP OF BELONGING

1 something belonging to a person or animal

- You can use a possessive determiner:

  *She enjoyed **her** work as a statistician.*
  *I really admire **their** courage.*
  *Britain treats **its** athletes with too little respect.*

- If the possessor is a short name, noun or noun phrase, you can use the possessive **'s**:

  ***Miss Pinkie's** father was a solicitor.*
  *We followed **the animal's** tracks.*
  ***Philip's** bed had not been slept in.*

- You can use **of**; notice that you normally have to use **of** if the possessor noun phrase is a long one:
  She was the daughter of the manager of the local supermarket.
  The needs of the local community must be considered.

> ⓘ In informal situations you will sometimes hear possessive **'s** used after a longer noun phrase:
> *That's the people next door's cat.*

2 something belonging to a thing

- When referring to something that belongs to a thing, you usually use **of** or a possessive determiner:
  *The measurements **of the room** are as follows.*
  *I've written down **its** measurements.*
- The possessive **'s** is sometimes used with things:
  The play's real strength (or *the real strength of the play*) *is the exploration of relationships.*
  The pub's original name (or *the original name of the pub*) *has been lost.*

PARTS

1 parts of a person or animal

- When referring to parts of a person or animal you normally use possessive **'s** or a possessive determiner:
  I almost tripped over someone's feet.
  I trod on the dog's tail.
  What's the first word that comes into your head?
- You can also use **of**, *eg* when you are making a general statement about a class of animals or people:
  The ears of a dolphin (or *a dolphin's ears*) *are highly sensitive.*
- You usually need to use **of** when the possessor noun phrase is a long one:
  The body of the missing child was discovered yesterday.

2 parts of a thing

- When referring to a part of a *thing* you normally use **of**:
  They camped out on the roof of the prison.
  He was holding the leg of a chair.

> ⓘ You can also use the noun referring to the part as an adjective or 'modifier':
> *the **prison** roof*
> instead of :
> *the roof **of the prison***

➤ See the section NOUN MODIFIERS at the entry **nouns**.

- Occasionally people use possessive **'s** when referring to part of a thing:
  All but the building's external wall will be destroyed.

> ⓘ You normally use **of** with position words like **top, middle, end, edge, corner**:
> *I banged my hip on the corner of the table.*
> *Eventually his passport turned up at the back of a drawer.*

possessive determiners and pronouns

The forms of the possessive determiners and pronouns are:

	possessive determiners		possessive pronouns	
	singular	plural	singular	plural
1st person	*my*	*our*	*mine*	*ours*
2nd person	*your*	*your*	*yours*	*yours*
3rd person	*his*	*their*	*his*	*theirs*
	her	*their*	*hers*	*theirs*
	its	*their*		
Also:				
	whose	*whose*	*whose*	*whose*
	one's		*one's own*	

You use possessive determiners and pronouns to say who *owns* something, or who or what something *belongs to* or is *connected with*.

POSSESSIVE DETERMINERS

This section explains some important points about the way possessive determiners behave. For more general information about their use, see the entry **possession**.

1 choosing a possessive determiner

- Possessive determiners correspond to the person or thing that is the *owner* or *possessor* of the thing referred to:
  ***I** chained **my** bicycle to a lamp post.*
  *We compared **the novels** and discussed **their** plots.*
- Possessive determiners stay the same, whether what is *owned* is singular or plural, or is a person or thing:
  *Colin says **his knee** hurts.*
  *Colin says **his colleagues** don't like him.*

> ⓘ Notice that a *plural* possessive determiner is followed by a *plural* noun in cases where everyone referred to owns one of the things mentioned:
> *We were asked to be at **our desks** (not desk) by 8.45.*

2 possessive determiners are not used with other determiners

- You do not use **the** or other determiners with possessive determiners:
  *Where are **my** (not the my) shoes?*
- You can use the determiners **a, this** and **that** in a construction with **of** and a possessive pronoun:
  *It's just **a theory of hers**.*
  *I've been considering **that idea of yours**.*

➤ For more details, see POSSESSIVE PRONOUNS below.

3 'the' instead of a possessive determiner

- **The** is often used instead of a possessive determiner in *prepositional phrases*:
  *He tried to kiss me **on the mouth**.*
  *I punched him **in the eye**.*

> ⓘ If the *part of the body* affected is the direct object, you use a possessive determiner:
> *I've broken **my** arm.*
> *The arrow pierced **his** chest.*

- You use **the** for a part of a part:
  I've got a bald patch on the top of my head.

4 its and **it's**

Distinguish between the possessive determiner **its** and the contraction **it's**, which is the short form of **it is** or **it has**:

*The dog always brings me **its** lead when **it's*** [= it has] *eaten **its** lunch and **it's*** [it is] *time for **its** walk.*

5 their

People often use **their** when referring back to a singular indefinite pronoun such as **someone**, **anyone** or **no-one**, where the sex is not specifed, to avoid using *his* or *her* or the rather formal **his or her**:

*Has **anyone** brought **their** textbook with them?*

6 whose and **who's**

Distinguish between the possessive determiner **whose**, and the contraction **who's**, which is the short form of **who is** or **who has**:

*Give me a list of the people **whose*** (not *who's*) *names I ought to include.*

7 one's

One's is used as the possessive determiner of the personal pronoun **one**:

*One must look after **one's** reputation.*

➤ See the entry **one**.

POSSESSIVE PRONOUNS

1 **Mine**, **yours**, **his**, **hers**, **ours** and **theirs** are the pronouns corresponding to the determiners **my**, **your**, **his**, **her**, **our** and **their**:

*It's your responsibility to lock up, not **theirs**.*
*Can I borrow your alarm clock? **Mine's** not working.*
*I'm out of coffee. Could I use some of **yours**?*

> ⓘ You don't use **its** as a pronoun.

2 theirs

People often use **theirs** to refer back to a singular indefinite pronoun such as **someone**, **anyone** or **no-one**, where the sex is not specified:

*We need access to a word-processor, so if **anyone** isn't using **theirs**, could they let me know?*

3 whose

Whose is a possessive pronoun as well as a possessive determiner:

'Whose is this hat?' 'I've no idea whose it is.'

4 a friend of mine

The possessive pronouns have an important use with **of** in phrases such as *a friend of mine, that dog of hers, this awful weather of ours.* You use this form of words because you can't use possessive determiners with other determiners:

Shall we consider this suggestion of hers?
Any friend of yours is a friend of mine.

> ⓘ Notice that **one of my friends** has a very similar meaning to **a friend of mine**.

➤ See also the entry **possessive 's** for the similar construction using the possessive form of a name (*eg a friend of Peter's*).

possessive 's: rules and uses

RULES

You make possessive forms of nouns and proper names either by adding **'s** or by adding an apostrophe (**'**) on its own.

1 basic rules

- You add **'s** after singular nouns and names:

  the manager's office
  Peter's shoes

- You add an apostrophe alone after plural nouns and names:

  my friends' addresses
  the Johnsons' house

- You add **'s** after irregular plural nouns that do not end in **-s**:

  the children's playroom
  people's opinions
  women's clothes

2 singular nouns ending in -s

- People have difficulty with singular nouns and names that already end in **-s**. But it is never wrong to add **'s** in the regular way:

  My boss's (/ˈbɒsɪz/) *schedule*
  James's (/ˈʤeɪmzɪz/) *family*
  Mrs Jones's (/ˈʤoʊnzɪz/) *car*

- With some Greek, Latin and biblical names ending in **-s** people sometimes just add an apostrophe:

  Socrates' (/ˈsɒkrətiːz/) *death*

But you can add **'s** to these names, if you prefer to stick to the regular rule for singular nouns:

Jesus's (/ˈʤiːzəsɪz/) *parents*

THE BEHAVIOUR OF POSSESSIVE 'S FORMS

➤ For more general information about the use of possessive **'s** forms see the entry **possession**.

1 possessive 's forms are determiners

You do not need an article before the possessive form of a name:

Michael's room (not *the Michael's room*)
Shakespeare's plays (not *the Shakespeare's plays*)

But the possessor may be an ordinary noun used with an article:

the captain's cabin
What are a project manager's duties?

2 two possessors

To form the possessive of a noun group consisting of two names joined by **and**, such as **Susan and Rob**, you usually put ***'s*** after the second name only:

I was round at Susan and Rob's house yesterday.

3 a friend of Peter's

When you want to refer to one of the things belonging to someone, you do not use articles or determiners before the possessive **'s** form. You have to use a construction with **of**:

It was a habit of Alan's to say nothing when he disagreed with you.

ⓘ Notice that **a friend of Peter's**' has a similar meaning to **one of Peter's friends**.

4 using possessive forms independently

- You can use possessive **'s** forms like pronouns, without a following noun, if the meaning is clear:

  'Whose is the red car parked outside?' 'It's Maggie's.'

- You can refer to people's homes using a possessive **'s** form:

  I'm just going round to Susan and Rob's.

- Shops and churches can be referred to like this too:

  You can buy one at Fraser's or any other department store.
  We can hear the bells of St Michael's from here.

- The premises of *eg* a grocer, butcher or baker or a doctor or dentist can also be referred to by possessive **'s** forms:

  I'm just going out to the grocer's.
  I picked up an out-of-date magazine at the dentist's.

5 time expressions

- You can use possessive **'s** forms of some time expressions, to refer to events:

  next week's meeting
  Sunday's performance of 'The Messiah'

- Possessive **'s** forms are often used, mainly with uncountable or plural nouns, for saying how long something takes or lasts:
  Five hours' work had been wasted.
  She was sentenced to two years' imprisonment.

•••• possibility ••••

➤ See **opportunity**.

•••• prefer ••••

GENERAL PREFERENCE

When you want to say that you generally enjoy doing one thing more than doing another, you use the **-ing** form of both verbs:

I prefer hill-walking to rock-climbing.

A PARTICULAR OCCASION

When you want to say that you have a particular preference now, you use **I'd prefer** + noun, or **I'd prefer to** + verb:

'Tea, coffee, or something stronger?' 'I think I'd prefer something stronger if you've got it.'
'Do you want something to eat?' 'Well, I'd prefer to wait until I've had a wash actually.'

You can also use **I'd rather** + verb:

'Shall we eat out tonight?' 'Well, to tell you the truth I'd rather have a night in.'

INTRODUCING A LESS DESIRABLE ALTERNATIVE

When you use **I'd prefer to** + verb, you can introduce the less desirable alternative with **rather than**:

I think I'd prefer to stop somewhere overnight rather than drive all that way in one go.

➤ See also **rather**.

•••• prepositions ••••

Prepositions are words you use to show position or movement, and to express different kinds of relationships and connections. The words in bold type in the following passage are all prepositions:

*The meeting scheduled **for** Monday has been postponed **till** Tuesday. There will be a discussion **of** the relevant issues **before** the meeting **on** Tuesday morning **at** eight-thirty **in** the boardroom.*

Prepositions are followed by an 'object' consisting of a noun or noun phrase, *eg* in the passage above: the object of **for** is **Monday** and the object of **in** is **the boardroom**.

➤ For details about particular prepositions, see their individual entries. The commonest prepositions have their own entries in this book.

> ⓘ Notice that some prepositions consist of two or more words used together. Some examples are:
>
> | | | |
> |---|---|---|
> | *along with* | *away from* | *in front of* |
> | *on top of* | *out of* | *together with* |

AFTER VERBS, ADJECTIVES AND NOUNS

Certain verbs, adjectives and nouns are normally followed by a preposition. A good learners' dictionary will show the most frequent combinations at the entry for the verb, adjective or noun in question.

PREPOSITIONS THAT CAUSE DIFFICULTY

Prepositions have their own idiomatic uses. Some common situations that require a particular preposition are listed below:

1 places of activity

talk to someone ***at*** *a party*
see a good film ***at*** *the cinema*
attend an event ***at*** *the sports complex*
go to a play ***at*** *the theatre*
study a subject ***at*** *university*

2 transport and travel

go somewhere ***by*** *bicycle, boat, bus, car, taxi, plane, train*
go ***by*** *air, land, sea*

But:

go somewhere ***on*** *your bicycle,* ***on*** *a boat,* ***on*** *a bus,* ***in*** *a car or taxi,* ***on*** *a plane,* ***on*** *a train*
go somewhere ***on*** *foot*

3 in the end, at the end

achieve success ***in*** *the end*
The novel has a surprising twist ***at*** *the end.*

4 on time, in time

The train arrived ***on*** *time* [= at the scheduled time] *for once.*
The train was about to leave but I got on it just ***in*** *time.*

5 on

speak to someone ***on*** *the phone*
watch something ***on*** *television*
listen to something ***on*** *the radio*
look at the picture ***on*** *page 49*

6 in

look at the horse ***in*** *the picture*
See that lady ***in*** *the red jacket?*
lie ***in*** *the sun too long*
write your name ***in*** *pencil, or* ***in*** *ink*
see yourself ***in*** *the mirror*
walk somewhere ***in*** *the rain*
talk ***in*** *a loud voice*

PREPOSITIONS THAT REFER BACK

There are four cases in which a preposition can come at the end of a clause, separated from its object, but still referring to it:

1 wh-questions

- In the statement '*I was talking to Peter*' the preposition **to** is followed immediately by its object, **Peter**. When a **wh-** word is the object of a preposition, the preposition usually comes at the end of the clause:

Who were you talking to? *What are you so scared of?*
Where did that idea come from? *Which chair did she sit on?*

ⓘ You can also put the preposition before the **wh-**question word (*To whom were you talking?*). Some people prefer this structure, but it sounds rather unnatural in conversation. It can sometimes be appropriate in a formal written style. Notice that **whom**, the object form of **who**, is used immediately after a preposition.

- Indirect **wh-**questions, and **wh-**exclamations, also put the preposition at the end:

  Let me know which train you'll be arriving on.
  What a mess this place is in!

- Short questions in conversation can consist simply of a **wh-**question word and a preposition:

  'I'm going out tonight.' 'Oh, yes. Who with?'
  'We could open a tin.' 'What with? There's no tin-opener.'
  'You ought to apologize.' 'Maybe, but who to?'

2 relative clauses

When a *relative pronoun* is the object of a preposition, the preposition usually comes at the end of the clause. The relative pronoun itself is however often omitted:

I found the quotation [that] *I was looking for.*
That's what I was scared of.

ⓘ A more formal style is possible, putting the preposition before the relative pronoun:
*I found the quotation **for which** I was looking.*
Notice that you use **which**, not **that**, after a preposition.

3 infinitive constructions

A **to-**infinitive can be used after a noun to qualify it, and may have a preposition with it:

Have you got a cloth to wipe the table with?
I couldn't find anyone to talk to.
It's an excellent project to be associated with.

ⓘ A formal alternative construction puts the preposition before the **to-**infinitive, followed by a relative pronoun:
It's an excellent project with which to be associated.

4 passive constructions

In passive constructions, the object of the preposition becomes the subject, and goes to the beginning of the sentence, but the preposition stays with the verb or verb phrase:

'People are staring at you.' 'I don't mind being stared at.'
They've made a fool of me. I hate being made a fool of.

OMITTING PREPOSITIONS: TIME EXPRESSIONS

1 You normally use prepositions with days and months (*in December, on Monday*), but you omit them when you are using a determiner such as **this**, **that**, **some**, **next**, or **last**, and in expressions such as **yesterday morning** or **tomorrow evening**:

We're leaving this (not *on this*) *Friday.*
I'll be back next Tuesday.
Are you free any morning next week?
I went to bed early that evening.
We moved house last February.
I phoned her yesterday afternoon.

> ⓘ Even without a determiner **on** is sometimes omitted before the name of a weekday, especially in AmE:
> *See you Friday afternoon.*
> *I'm due to be in Amsterdam Wednesday.*
> Similarly, people sometimes informally omit **at** before a specified time, especially with **about**:
> *He said he'd arrive about three-thirty* (or, more formally, *at about three-thirty*).

2 You normally leave out **at** in questions beginning **what time… ?**, and you leave out **on** in questions beginning **which day… ?**, **which evening… ?** and so on:

What time does the post go? (rather than *'What time does the post go at?'* or *'At what time does the post go?'*)
What time is your appointment?
Which evening are you going out?

PREPOSITIONS THAT CAN ALSO BE ADVERBS

A lot of prepositions can also be adverbs, that is, they can be used without a following noun object. **In** is an example of a preposition that can also be an adverb:

She's not in her room. [preposition]
I called at your house but you weren't in. [adverb]

The following prepositions can all be used as adverbs:

aboard	*about*	*above*	*across*
after	*against*	*along*	*alongside*
around	*before*	*behind*	*below*
beneath	*in between*	*beyond*	*by*
down	*in*	*inside*	*near*
off	*on*	*opposite*	*outside*
over	*past*	*round*	*since*
through	*throughout*	*under*	*underneath*
up	*within*		

PREPOSITIONS USED BEFORE -ING FORMS

Prepositions are frequently followed by objects that consist of -**ing** forms:

I'm no good at singing.
I insist on paying.
I'll ask them about paying by cheque.

— the present —

There are two forms of the present tense in English, the *simple present* (*eg she moves*) and the *present progressive*, also called the *present continuous* (*eg she is moving*). These two forms have their own particular uses in referring to present time, although in a few situations, they are interchangeable.

THE SIMPLE PRESENT

1 The forms of the simple present, illustrated by the verb **move**, are:

positive	**question**	**negative**
I move	*do I move?*	*I do not* (or *don't*) *move*
you move	*do you move?*	*you do not* (or *don't*) *move*
he, she or it moves	*does he, she, it move?*	*he, she, it does not* (or *doesn't*) *move*
we move	*do we move?*	*we do not* (or *don't*) *move*
they move	*do they move?*	*they do not* (or *don't*) *move*

2 third person singular

You usually just add -**s** to the infinitive form of the verb for the third person:

*she leave**s*** *he leap**s*** *it pay**s***

➤ For more on forming verbs in the simple past, see **spelling rules**.

3 the uses of the simple present

- **general facts**

  You use the simple present for general facts, for permanent situations, and for regular happenings:

  We breathe oxygen.
  Marie attends the local school.
  I swim every Sunday morning.

- **speech acts**

  Verbs that state your attitude or make declarations, such as **like, agree, object** or **promise**, are usually in the simple present:

  I promise to say nothing.
  I agree with you completely.
  I don't believe you.
  I apologize for disturbing you.
  Do you like my tie?

- **instructions**

  You use the simple present when you are asking what to do, or telling someone what to do:

  'How do I open my file?' 'First you select the drive and directory you want, then you double-click on the filename.'

- **plans and timetables**

  You use the simple present with a future meaning when talking about scheduled events:

  Paula starts at her new school in September.
  My plane leaves in half an hour.

➤ See also **the future**.

- **why don't you... ?**

  Notice the use of the simple present in this form of suggestion, which again has a future meaning:

  Why don't you try turning off the computer and starting again?

> ⓘ In spite of the use of the simple present to refer to future scheduled events, or make suggestions, you don't usually use the simple present to refer to the future: *'Is that someone at the door?' 'I'll go* (not *I go*).*'*

- **commentary**

  Normally you use the present progressive to report on what is happening at the moment of speaking:

  Mr Thompson is making a telephone call at the moment.

  But sports commentators use the simple present to deal with fast-moving events:

  Agassi returns the ball and forces his opponent to play a backhand.

- **quoting**

  Use the simple present when you quote from something written:

  'Murder most foul,' as the ghost says to Hamlet.
  She says in her postcard that Jack's been ill.

THE PRESENT PROGRESSIVE

1 forms

The forms of the present progressive, illustrated by the verb **move**, are:

positive	**question**	**negative**
I am (or *I'm*) *moving*	*Am I moving?*	*I am not* (or *I'm not*) *moving*
you are (or *you're*) *moving*	*Are you moving?*	*You are not* (or *you aren't*, or *you're not*) *moving*
He is (or *he's*) *moving*	*Is he moving?*	*He is not* (or *he isn't* or *he's not*) *moving*

and so on.

2 uses

- **present happenings**

  You use the present progressive to talk about what is happening now:

  'What are you doing?' 'I'm checking these figures.'
  Is something burning?
  Why are you all staring at me like that?
  Come on! Everyone else is waiting on the coach.

➤ For lists of non-progressive verbs, see the entry **progressive forms**.

- **temporary, not permanent or regular**

  The present progressive expresses a *temporary* activity or situation, as distinct from a *permanent* or *regular* one:

  'Where's Mum?' 'She's sitting in the car.' [temporary]
  'Where's the telephone directory?' 'It usually sits beside the telephone.' [permanent]

'Where's Susan?' 'She's playing tennis down at the club.' [temporary]
She plays tennis down at the club every Friday. [regular]

- **change and development**

You use the present progressive to express change and development:

The baby's growing fast.
The situation's getting worse.

- **referring to the future**

There are three ways in which you use the present progressive to refer to the future. You use it to refer to *plans and arrangements* that have already been made; you use it to refer to things that *have just begun to* happen; and you use it as a firm way of expressing your intentions:

I'm having lunch with Joan tomorrow. [plan]
I'm taking the dog out. Are you coming? [action just beginning]
I'm not staying here to be insulted. [firm intention]

➤ For more details about the use of the present progressive to refer to the future, see **the future**.

THE PROBLEM OF NON-PROGRESSIVE VERBS

There are some verbs that you do not normally use in the present progressive. These are verbs such as **know** and **realize**, which represent states of mind, or **like** and **hate**, which represent attitudes, **promise** and **insist**, which you use to declare what you intend or want, **mean**, **include** and **contain**, which represent a fact or truth:

I know (not *am knowing*) *it's difficult.*
We realize (not *are realizing*) *your position.*
I like (not *am liking*) *your hat.*
I hate (not *am hating*) *loud music.*
What does this memo mean (not *what is this memo meaning*)?

WHERE THE SIMPLE PRESENT AND PRESENT PROGRESSIVE ARE BOTH USED

1 letters

In formal letters people often use the simple present where, in informal correspondence, they would use the present progressive:

I enclose (or, less formally, *am enclosing*) *a cheque for £5.*
I look (or, less formally, *am looking*) *forward to hearing from you.*

2 feel

You can use either the simple present or present progressive of **feel** to enquire about, or report on, physical health:

How do you feel (or *how are you feeling*) *now?*
I feel (or *I'm feeling*) *better, thanks.*

• • • • presently • • • •

1 You use **presently** in BrE usually with **will** or **shall** to mean 'in a while', or 'not immediately':

Tell them I'll be there presently.
You can attend to that presently.

You use **presently** with a past tense to mean 'after a while', 'a little later':

Presently she remarried.
Presently the nurse returned to collect the tray.

> ⓘ Notice that when it is used with a future tense, **presently** comes towards the end of the sentence. With a past tense, it usually comes at the beginning of the sentence, before the subject.

2 In AmE, and increasingly in BrE, **presently** means 'now', or 'at the moment':

A committee is presently working on the problem.
My son is presently in Scotland.
A questionnaire will be given to all students presently studying Arabic.

Presently only occurs in this meaning with a present tense. The verb is nearly always either the verb **be**, or in the present progressive, and **presently** is in mid position.

present participles

Present participles are the -**ing** forms of verbs, which combine with **be** to make the progressive forms:

*She **was smiling***	*I'**m working***
*It'**s snowing***	*You'**re joking***

➤ See also the entry -**ing forms** for information about verbal nouns ending in -**ing**.

There are five other main ways in which you will find present participles being used. They behave like adjectives, and qualify, or refer to, nouns or pronouns.

AS ADJECTIVES

1 Present participles, or -**ing** forms, are active, in contrast to -**ed** forms, which are passive. **A deafening noise**, for instance, is a noise that deafens you, and **smiling faces** are faces that are smiling.

➤ See also **past participles**.

2 A large number of present participles are well-established as adjectives. These -**ing** adjectives typically mean *causing* a certain feeling or reaction in people. Most can be used both before a noun, as well as after a linking verb such as **be** or **become**:

a terrifying prospect	*The prospect is terrifying.*

Here are some other typical reaction-related -**ing** adjectives:

amazing	*amusing*	*annoying*	*astonishing*
boring	*challenging*	*confusing*	*demanding*
disgusting	*displeasing*	*encouraging*	*enthralling*
exciting	*fascinating*	*frustrating*	*infuriating*
interesting	*irritating*	*pleasing*	*refreshing*

3 Compound -**ing** adjectives are possible. They are mainly used before a noun. They can be composed of:

- a noun object + participle:

  a sightseeing tour
  a fact-finding mission

- an adverb + participle:

  far-reaching results
  a good-looking man

AFTER NOUNS

Present participles can be used immediately after nouns or pronouns, to identify or define them, like relative clauses. The participle may be followed by a prepositional phrase, or an object:

Who's the woman talking [= who is talking] *to Malcolm?*
You're not the person making the decision.
Anyone listening would think we were quite mad.
Which trousers do you mean? The ones lying on the bed?

DESCRIBING ACTIONS

Present participles can have the function of modifying the verb, or describing an action, in the same way as an adverb:

She ran down the street shouting.
Maggie stood there staring at him.

ⓘ The action described in the participle construction may actually occur just before the action represented by the main verb:
Kneeling down beside the girl he tried to see if she was injured.

INSTEAD OF SUBORDINATE CLAUSES

1 Present participles can take the place of adverbial clauses, *eg* of time or result:
Tidying up [= while I was tidying up] *one day, I found the letter.*

ⓘ The subject of the participle should be the same as the subject of the main verb.

2 Some verbs, such as **know**, **realize**, **want**, **be** and **have**, which are rarely used in the progressive forms, can be used as present participles:
Realizing the danger she was in, she ran away fast.
Not wanting to disturb him I dressed quietly.

3 You can use present participles immediately after certain conjunctions of time or concession:
While driving home the other day I heard this music on the radio.
When choosing [= when you are choosing] *a bed, remember these points.*

➤ For similar constructions using **-ing** forms after prepositions such as **after**, **since**, and **before**, see the entry **-ing forms**.

AFTER THE OBJECTS OF OBSERVING OR LINKING VERBS

1 **observing verbs**

A present participle can follow the object of an *observing* or *sensing* verb:

I noticed her coming out of the house.
Can you smell something burning?

2 linking verbs

After the transitive linking verbs **get** and **have** the object may be followed by a present participle:

It'll take quite a while to get everything working smoothly again.

•••• previous ••••

When you are talking about something that happened in the year, month, or week before one you have already mentioned, you use **previous**, not **last**. You can also use **before**.

For example, if you are talking about something that happened in 1990, and you want to mention something that happened in 1989, you refer to 1989 as **the previous year** or **the year before**:

The minutes of the previous year's meeting were read and signed.
Many people reported that they had had flu the month before.

•••• principal, principle ••••

These two words have the same pronunciation but different meanings. It is important not to confuse the spellings.

PRINCIPAL

1 As an *adjective*, **principal** means 'chief' or 'main':

The principal aim of the campaign is to encourage walking.

2 As a *noun*, **principal** means the head of a school or college, and as a title is often spelt with a capital initial:

The Principal agreed to three new courses.

PRINCIPLE

1 A **principle** is a rule by which people choose to behave, or a law, *eg* a law of physics, according to which things happen:

It is against all my principles to give money to charity.
Einstein discovered the principle of relativity.

2 in principle, on principle

- You use **in principle** to mean 'as a general rule', without reference to particular cases:

  I'm in favour of public transport in principle, but I use my car when I need to.
  Foreign ministers agreed in principle to open negotiations.

- You use **on principle** to mean 'because of a particular moral belief', without reference to practical reasons:

  They buy second-hand clothes on principle.

progressive forms

FORMS

The *progressive* verb forms, also called the *continuous* forms, are made by using a part of the verb **be** with an -**ing** form. There are progressive forms to refer to the *present*, *past* and *future*; there are progressive *passive* forms, and progressive *infinitives*:

*I **am trying** to do this crossword.* [present progressive]
*I've **been trying** to do it for the last three hours.* [present perfect progressive]
*I **was doing** the crossword when you came home.* [past progressive]
*I **had been doing** it for ten minutes when the phone rang.* [past perfect progressive]
*I **will be doing** it all night at this rate.* [future progressive]
*I **will have been doing** it then for fifteen hours.* [future perfect progressive]
*My watch **is being repaired**.* [present progressive passive]
*Are you likely **to be passing** the jeweller's?* [progressive infinitive]

➤ For full lists of the progressive forms, and more details of their functions, see **the past**, **the present**, **the future**.

USES

The progressive forms express activities that are:

1 *ongoing* or *continuous* as opposed to finished or complete:
I've been making myself an evening dress.[it probably isn't finished yet]

2 *temporary* as opposed to permanent:
Marie was standing outside the shop, counting her change.

3 *repeated* as opposed to happening once:
People were walking across the square.

VERBS NOT USED IN THE PROGRESSIVE

Some verbs represent *states*, especially states of mind, as opposed to activities. They are not normally used in the progressive forms. You say, for example, that you **know** something, not that you *are knowing* it, and that you **recognize** someone, not that you *are recognizing* them.

Non-progressive verbs can be subdivided into certain categories:

1 **states of the mind or the emotions**

admire	*adore*	*believe*	*desire*
despise	*detest*	*dislike*	*envy*
feel	*forget*	*hate*	*imagine*
know	*like*	*love*	*prefer*
realize	*recognize*	*remember*	*see* [= understand]
suppose	*suspect*	*think*	*understand*
want	*wish*		

2 **sense impressions**

appear	*hear*	*look* [= seem]	*resemble*
see	*seem*	*smell*	*sound*
taste			

3 reactions

agree	*amaze*	*astonish*	*deny*
disagree	*impress*	*interest*	*please*
promise	*satisfy*	*surprise*	

4 others

be	*belong*	*concern*	*consist*
contain	*depend*	*deserve*	*fit*
have	*include*	*involve*	*keep*
lack	*last*	*matter*	*mean*
measure	*need*	*owe*	*own*
possess	*weigh*		

EXCEPTIONAL SITUATIONS

1 special senses

Some of the verbs listed above have senses in which they can be used in the progressive. Contrast the following pairs of examples:

He feels [= thinks] *he could have done better.*
He's feeling better.

What do you think of [= what is your opinion of] *the design?*
I'm still thinking about that incident.

I like and admire her.
How are you liking [= enjoying] *your present job?*

The floor measures 5 metres by 3.5 metres.
I'm just measuring the floor.

I see your point.
I'll be seeing [= meeting] *Dave this evening.*

The milk smells funny.
I'm smelling [= sniffing] *the milk to see if it's gone off.*

These apples taste sour.
I'm just tasting the apples to see if they're sweet enough.

2 present participles

Most of the first category of verbs above can be used as present participles:

Realizing that they wanted to be left alone, I went out of the room.
Not wanting to disturb him, I closed the door quietly.

3 'be' and 'have'

You can use the verb **be** in the progressive when it refers to *behaviour*, and you can use 'non-possessive' **have** in the progressive:

You're being stupid.
We were having an interesting chat.

EXPRESSING FREQUENCY

You use the frequency adverbs **always**, **constantly**, **continually** and **forever** with the progressive form to mean 'often', 'repeatedly' or 'again and again':

He once had a beard, and he is forever touching his chin as though he missed it.
Helen was constantly complaining about her husband.

ⓘ **Always** with a progressive form expresses the idea of something that happens a lot, but is not planned or expected. **Always** with a non-progressive verb suggests a regular, planned arrangement:
She always rang if she was going to be late.
He hated the way people were always ringing her up.

pronouns

➤ See **indefinite pronouns**, **personal pronouns**, **possessive determiners and pronouns**, **reflexive pronouns**, and **this, that, these, those**.

punctuation

Punctuation marks help to make written or printed text clearer, by giving information that is conveyed by intonation, pauses, etc. in speech. The various punctuation marks are dealt with here in alphabetical order.

THE APOSTROPHE

1 used to show omissions

An apostrophe (') is often used to show that one or more letters have been omitted from a word:

cannot	*can't*
it is	*it's*
I would, I had	*I'd*
I have	*I've*

2 used to show possession

An apostrophe + **s** is used after a noun to show possession:

the child's dog [= the dog that belongs to the child]
the children's dog [= the dog that belongs to the children]
James's dog [= the dog that belongs to James]
Robert Burns's dog [= the dog that belongs to Robert Burns]

If the noun is plural and already ends in **s**, add only the apostrophe:

the boys' dog [= the dog that belongs to the boys]
in two months' time

3 in plural forms

Apostrophes are not normally used in the formation of plural nouns. In some cases, though, they can be used to make understanding easier:

How many l's are there in 'fulfil'?

BRACKETS

1 Brackets ( ) are used to separate comments from the rest of the text:

Essays (two copies) should be given to your teacher before Friday 5pm.
The result of the match (3-2 to France) was announced on the news.

2 Brackets are also used to indicate alternatives or options:

Any candidate(s) for the position must be formally proposed.

COLON (:)

1 expansions

A colon is used to introduce a part of a sentence that explains or expands on the part of the sentence before it:

I've got something important to tell you: Andrew is coming home.
There is one thing I would really like: a much larger house.

2 lists

A colon is used to introduce a list of items:

We'll need the following things: string, paper, glue, scissors and a pencil.

3 direct speech

A colon is often used to introduce speech in plays:

John: *Look out! He's coming back!*
Peter: *Where can we hide?*

> ⓘ Note that a comma, rather than a colon is usually used to introduce other, more common, forms of direct speech:
> *John suddenly shouted, 'Look out! He's coming back!'*

4 American usage

- In AmE, a colon is used between the hours and the minutes in writing the time (*eg* 3:45) where in BrE a full stop would be used (3.45).
- AmE also uses a colon after the initial salutation in a business letter:

  Dear Mr Forsyth:
  Thank you for...

COMMA

1 indicating a pause in a sentence

A comma is used to indicate a pause or slight break in a sentence:

I don't want to go, but I'm afraid I must.
If you want to say something, say it now.
No, thank you.

2 lists

Items in a list are usually separated by commas:

We need sugar, flour, eggs, milk and cocoa powder.

> ⓘ Notice that in a list, a comma is not necessary before **and**, but it is used more commonly in long lists, and in AmE.

3 direct speech

A comma is often used to separate direct speech from the rest of the sentence:

Peter said, 'I want to come too.'
'I wouldn't stay now,' she said, 'even if you paid me.'
'I want to come too,' said Peter.

4 with 'but' and 'so'

A comma is used when there is a balance or contrast between the parts of a sentence, or when the second part of the sentence expresses a consequence or result of what is said in the first part:

It's smaller, but more expensive.
She works in the evenings, so her husband looks after the children.

5 non-defining relative clauses

Commas are used before and after non-defining relative clauses.

Whereas a defining relative clause identifies the noun it refers to, a non-defining relative clause gives additional information about a noun.

Compare:

The boy who was here last night is her brother.

with:

The boy, who was here last night, is her brother.

- In the first sentence, the words *who was here last night* identify which boy is being talked about, that is, not *the boy who was here today*, for example.
- In the second sentence, the clause *who was here last night* is a non-defining relative clause. It gives additional information about the boy and must be separated from the rest of the sentence by commas.

6 subordinate clauses

A comma is used after a subordinate clause, when the subordinate clause begins the sentence:

When he arrived home, the children ran to kiss him.
If you have time, could you have a look at this report?

7 to clarify meaning

In some cases, it would be difficult to understand a sentence without a comma:

Compare:

Throughout January only, customers with loyalty cards can earn double points.

with:

Throughout January, only customers with loyalty cards can earn double points.

DASH

1 A dash may be used to expand or explain something that comes before it:

The house was ideal – just what we'd been looking for.

2 A dash may be used in a sentence in order to emphasize what follows:

He can do it – and he will!
There is nothing – absolutely nothing – that I would like better.

3 A dash with no space on either side is used to indicate ranges between certain limits:

pages 346–387
An A–Z Guide to Birds

➤ See also the section on hyphens below.

EXCLAMATION MARK

1 An exclamation mark (!) is used after short interjections, and at the end of sentences or statements that are emphatic or express strong emotions such as fear, anger, pleasure or surprise:

Yuck! This pizza tastes of soap.
Help! Fire!
I dont believe it!
What a beautiful picture!

2 If the exclamation is a quotation in the actual words of the speaker, the exclamation mark is placed at the end of the exclamation, inside the closing quotation mark or marks, as in:

She screamed at the top of her voice, 'I hate you!'
'Don't you dare touch me!' he shrieked.

3 Notice that after an imperative, there may or may not be exclamation mark, depending on the degree of emphasis used by the speaker:

Sit down now and get out your books.
'Everybody freeze! Put your hands in the air!' he shouted.

> ⓘ Exclamation marks are used in informal writing, for example in personal letters (but not following the greeting). They should never be used in formal letters or documents.

FULL STOP

1 A full stop (.) is used at the end of a sentence when the sentence is not a question or an exclamation. A sentence that ends with a full stop always begins with a capital letter:

Where are you going?
What a mess!
It started to rain.

2 Full stops are sometimes used in abbreviations and contractions; however fewer and fewer are used in BrE texts. They are still frequent in AmE usage.

➤ For more details on abbreviations see the entry **abbreviations**.

3 A series of three full stops (...) is used to show that a sentence or statement has not been completed, or that something has been omitted from a quoted passage:

Oh no, I feel dizzy; I think I'm going to ...

HYPHEN (-)

> ⓘ Modern English uses hyphens to join compound words less and less often, although the hyphen is still more common in BrE than in AmE.

It is advisable to look words up in a good dictionary if you are in any doubt about their spelling.

1 Multi-word phrases that are used as nouns are usually hyphenated:

I know his mother-in-law.
Are these flowers forget-me-nots?

2 A hyphen is used to join two or more separate words which together form an adjective, when the adjective comes *before* the noun it describes:

a sixteenth-century church
my next-door neighbour
a well-known writer
an up-to-date report

Notice that the hyphen is omitted from many compound adjectives when they are used *following* the nouns they describe:

The problem is well known.
The report was surprisingly up to date.

3 A hyphen is often used in a noun or adjective that has been formed from a phrasal verb, but some compounds formed with the longer adverb particles are often written as a single word:

One look at the show's line-up and I knew it would be very funny.
I'd always wanted to go to a drive-in movie.
We listened to the countdown from NASA on the radio.
The latest breakthrough in cancer research

> ⓘ A hyphen should never be used between the parts of a phrasal verb:
> *He says he is going to give up* (not *give-up*) *his job.*

4 If a compound word is very common and built up from words of only one syllable each, it is very likely to be written as one word, without a hyphen:

bedroom
teacup

5 Numbers from 21 to 99 and fractions should be hyphenated:

twenty-three
three-quarters

6 Compound words beginning with **half** and **self** are usually hyphenated:

half-brother
self-respect

QUESTION MARK

A question mark (?) is used at the end of direct questions. Notice that a question mark should not be used at the end of sentences that contain an indirect question:

Compare:

Do you take your coffee black or white? (direct question)

with:

He asked me if I took my coffee black or white. (indirect question)

QUOTATION MARKS

Quotation marks – also known as quotes or inverted commas – are always used in pairs. There are two types: single quotes ('…') and double quotes ("…").

1 Quotation marks are used around direct speech or quotations, that is, the exact words someone has spoken or written:

'Why can't I go?' asked Rosie.
He said, 'You must help her.'

ⓘ In direct speech, it is very important to remember that the quotation marks enclose only the exact words used by the speaker, and not a reported version of these words:
Compare: *'Are you ready?' she asked him.*
with: *She asked him if he was ready.*

ⓘ When there is a second quotation inside the first one, the first quotation is marked by single quotes, and the quotation within it is surrounded by double quotes:
The manager said, '"These are circumstances beyond my individual control", as Mr Micawber said.'

2 Quotation marks can also be used to highlight certain words and phrases in a sentence:

What does 'vice versa' mean?
Should 'English' always have a capital letter?

3 Titles of books, plays, articles, etc. may appear in bold or italic type, or they may be enclosed in quotation marks, to separate them from the rest of the text:

Have you seen my "Grammar and Usage"?
I think I'll buy a **21st Century Dictionary**.
a quotation from *Hamlet*

SEMICOLON (;)

1 A semicolon may be used because it marks a stronger break in a sentence than a comma would. It therefore emphasizes the contrasting ideas in the two clauses it separates:

A crocodile is a reptile; a whale is a mammal.

2 A semicolon can represent a weaker break between two sentences than a full stop would. It therefore emphasizes the close relationship between them:

I will say no more about your behaviour; the subject is closed.

3 A semicolon is sometimes used to mark off main sections of a list whose individual elements are separated by commas:

Copies of the report have been sent to our offices in Lagos, Nigeria; Nairobi, Kenya; and Harare, Zimbabwe.

CAPITAL LETTERS

Ordinary sentences begin with a capital letter. This also applies to so-called 'sentence fragments' (sentences containing one or two words, sometimes without a verb):

I don't think I've ever worked so hard in my life.
Will he ever be able to find a decent job? Somehow, I doubt it.
I have to find five hundred dollars before next week. No chance!

1 proper names

A capital is used for the first letter of proper names: that is, for the names of people and places. Here are some examples:

Paul
Donald Macpherson
Asia
Mexico
Lake Winnipeg
the Pacific Ocean
Mars

Capitals are used for the titles of books, plays, films, newspapers, etc. When the title is made up of several words, it is usually only the most important words that are given capitals, unless an unimportant word such as an indefinite or definite article is the first word of the title. Here are some examples:

Hamlet
The Sunday Times

In the same way, capitals are used for each important element in the official titles of people, institutions, organizations, buildings, etc:

His Royal Highness, the Prince of Wales
the Foreign Secretary
the Archbishop of Canterbury
the Pope
the House of Lords
Westminster Abbey
the White House.

2 words derived from proper names

In general, words that are derived from proper names also have an initial capital letter, as in:

the Napoleonic system
the Brazilian national squad
Victorian architecture
Shakespearean tragedies

The names of days of the week, months and festivals start with a capital letter:

Good Friday
He'll be fifteen in March.
Easter Sunday
Diwali or the Festival of Lights

Notice, however, that the seasons **spring**, **summer**, **autumn** and **winter** do not require a capital letter.

The names of languages and their related adjectives start with a capital:

He's studying French, Italian, Latin and Greek.
a Spanish phrasebook
They speak Urdu at home.

quantifiers

This group of determiners is used to indicate how much of something, or how many people or things you mean.

Quantifiers include **some**, **any**, **all**, **enough**, **several**, **many**, **a lot of**, **few**, **much**, **little**, **more**, **most**, **half**, **double**, **both** and **no**.

Some, **all**, **any** and **enough** are used before an uncountable noun, or a plural countable noun. **Several**, **most** and **many** are used before plural countable nouns. **No** is used before a singular or plural countable noun, or an uncountable noun:

*I planted **some** flowers.*
*Would you like **some** chocolate?*
*We don't have **any** bread left.*
*I need some help carrying these boxes. **Any** volunteers?*
*You're not having **much** luck, are you?*
*There are **no** dry towels in the bathroom.*
*There is **no** reason to doubt her.*

Certain quantifiers behave rather like gradable adjectives in that they can be used to express comparison between amounts. For example, the quantifiers **few**, **fewer** and **fewest** may be used to indicate graded amounts on a scale ranging from higher to lower, as in:

***Few** people understand the theory fully.*
***Fewer** people are using public transport.*
*Which system is likely to involve the **fewest** problems?*

➤ See also individual entries for **some**, **any**, **all**, **enough**, **many**, **a lot of**, **little and few**, **much**, **more**, **most**, **half**, **both** and **no**.

quantities, units, bits and pieces

You sometimes need to refer to a unit, piece or quantity of a food or substance, such as *bread*, *milk*, *cloth* and *glass*. Words such as **piece** and **bit**, followed by **of**, are frequently used for solid substances, and **drop of** for liquid ones.

There are other appropriate, specific terms that you can use in some cases. Some typical uses are listed below:

a **bar** of:	*chocolate, soap*
a **bit** of:	*cake, bread, paper, rubbish*
a **block** of:	*ice, wood, chocolate*
a **drop** of:	*milk, oil, rain, water, wine*
a **length** or **width** of:	*cloth, material, fabric*
a **loaf** of:	*bread*

a **lump** of:	*coal, sugar*
a **piece** of:	*bread, cake, chocolate, cloth, paper*
a **sheet** of:	*paper, glass*
a **slice** of:	*bread, cake, meat*
a **stick** of:	*chalk, chewing gum*

SETS

1 Certain things belong together in groups containing particular items. Groups like this can usually be referred to as **sets** of things:

a set of cutlery
a set of tools
a set of drums
a set of criteria
a set of statistics
a set of data

2 With things or people in groups, you can often use the terms **batch** or **lot**:

I went back into the kitchen to bake another batch of loaves.
This is the third lot of antibiotics they've given me.
I teach a different lot of students every year.

ABSTRACT NOUNS

You use **bit**, **piece**, and other terms, with abstract uncountable nouns such as *information* and *advice*, *eg*:

*a **piece** or a **bit** or a **word** of advice*
*a **piece** or a **bit** or an **item** of information or news*
*a **bit** or a **stroke** of luck*

5 You use words meaning 'the smallest possible bit', such as **scrap**, **trace**, **grain** after a negative, to indicate that there is not even the smallest bit:

*They haven't got a **scrap** of evidence.*
*There's not a **trace** of an accent in his speech.*
*There probably wasn't a **grain** of truth in the propaganda.*
*It was a cold bright morning without a **breath** of wind.*

➤ For more information see **countable and uncountable nouns**.

question mark

➤ See **punctuation**.

questions

There are two types of question. First, there are 'yes-or-no' questions, that is, questions that expect the answer **yes** or **no**. Second, there are **wh-**questions, that is, questions beginning with a **wh-**word such as **what**, **when**, **where** or **why**.

A process called *inversion* is usual in questions. This means that the subject changes places with the auxiliary verb:

***Has he** finished?*
*What **is she** saying?*

YES-OR-NO QUESTIONS

1 purpose

You ask yes-or-no questions when you want the answer **yes** or **no**:

'Will we see you tonight?' 'Yes, I expect so.'
'Were you worried?' 'No, not really.'

2 word order

- You form yes-or-no questions by changing the order of the subject and the auxiliary verb:

  Have the children completed their project?
  Will you meet him tomorrow?
  Is Jim getting the tickets?

- If you want to ask a question in the simple present, or simple past, you have to use the auxiliary verb **do** to help form the question.
  Does she swim a lot?

You use **did** when you are asking a question in the simple past:
Did he telephone them last night?

> ⓘ Notice that it is only the auxiliary verb that changes places with the subject, not the whole verb structure.

3 the verb 'be'

The verb **be** when used as an ordinary linking verb, changes places with the subject. You don't use the auxiliary **do**:

Are you upset?
Were they still in bed?

4 the verb 'have'

When you are using the verb **have** in its possession sense, there are three possible question forms:

Do you have the time?
Have you got the time?
Have you the time? (formal, and rarely used)

➤ For more information see the entry **have**.

5 negative yes-or-no questions

You can use a negative question form to indicate that you are expecting the answer **yes**:

Wasn't Dave hoping to come too?
Aren't you going to kiss me goodbye?
Can't you explain it more simply than that?

6 yes-or-no questions without inversion

You sometimes ask a yes-or-no question using the form of a statement when you are checking whether your information is correct, or expressing surprise:

Your advice is stay here and wait, then?
You don't mind them calling you 'Miss Piggy'?

WH-QUESTIONS

1 purpose

You use **wh-** questions to ask for specific facts or details. **Wh-**questions start with **wh-** words:

What did he say?
Where are you staying?

The full list of **wh-**words is:

pronouns	*what*	*which*	*who*	*whom*	*whose*
determiners	*what*	*which*	*whose*		
adverbs	*how*	*when*	*where*	*why*	

➤ For more information about **wh-**words see their individual entries in this book.

2 word order

In **wh-**questions the subject and auxiliary verb change places. You use **do** as the auxiliary in the simple present and simple past, when there is no other auxiliary, as you do in yes-or-no questions:

How was he yesterday?
When do you want to see us?
What shall I tell her?
Who (or formally, *whom) did you appoint?*
Which day would you prefer?

When the **wh-**word is the object of a preposition, the preposition usually comes at the end of the question:

What are you staring at?

➤ See also **prepositions**.

When a **wh-**word is the *subject* of the question, the word order is the same as in a statement:

What's your problem?
Who told you that?
Which buses go there directly?

ⓘ Since there is no inversion of subject and auxiliary, you do not need to use **do** to form questions.

3 answering wh-questions

Answers to **wh-**questions often contain only the information that the questioner wants. You do not usually repeat any part of the question:

'***What time*** *should we start?*' '***About ten***.'
'***What*** *gave you that impression?*' '***Your attitude***.'
'***Where*** *are the children?*' '***At my mother's***.'
'***When****'s the meeting?*' '***At ten o'clock***.'
'***Why*** *did you say that?*' '***Because it's true***.'

INDIRECT QUESTIONS

In indirect questions you do not put an auxiliary verb before the subject, and you do not use **do** to form questions:

*He asked me **where I had** (not where had I) been.*
*Let me know **what you think** (not what do you think).*

2 An indirect-question form is often used to ask someone politely for information:
***Do you know** what time the public library opens?*
***Could you tell me** which buses go to the city centre?*

question tags

Question tags are short yes-or-no questions that you can add to a statement. You do this to get people to agree with you, or to ask for confirmation of what you have just said, but you don't always expect a reply:

*You remember the Robertsons, **don't you**?*
*The map's still in the car, **isn't it**?*
*Goodness, she's quite an expert, **isn't she**?*

FORMING QUESTION TAGS

Question tags are composed of the same form of the auxiliary verb, or the verb **be**, that is in the statement, followed by a personal pronoun that refers to the subject of the statement:

***That song was** pretty popular in our day, **wasn't it**?*
*But **Helen and I haven't** had our turn yet, **have we**?*

If you have not used an auxiliary verb in the statement, you form the question tag with the auxiliary **do**:

***Those clouds look** a bit threatening, **don't they**?*
***You noticed** it too, **didn't you**?*

POSITIVE + NEGATIVE, NEGATIVE + POSITIVE

1 You normally use a negative tag after a positive statement:
*Hello. You'**re** the new girls, **aren't** you?*
*We'**ve** got to get this right, **haven't** we?*
*We'**ll** have to hurry, **won't** we?*

2 And you use a positive tag after a negative statement:
*The course **didn't** help you much, **did** it?*
*You **don't** mind, **do** you?*
*Well, we **mustn't** waste time, **must** we?*

3 Negative words such as **never**, and words like **hardly** or **scarcely**, may be used in the statement. They are also followed by positive tags:
*We'll **never** know, **will we**?*
*I suppose it's **no use** telephoning her, **is it**?*
*But we've **hardly** begun, **have we**?*

FURTHER POINTS

1 aren't I?

Aren't I is used as the question tag corresponding to **I am**:
***I'm** being a nuisance, **aren't I**?*

2 don't you? or **haven't you?**

You can use question tags with **do** or **have** after non-auxiliary **have**:
*I **have** a right to my opinion, **haven't I**? (or **don't I**?)*

3 Nothing ever happens, does it?

You use **it** in question tags to refer to the indefinite pronouns **nothing**, **everything**, **something** and **anything**:

*Something's sure to go wrong, **isn't it**?*

4 Anybody can try, can't they?

You use **they** in question tags to refer to the indefinite pronouns **no-one**, **everyone**, **someone** and **anyone** (and **nobody** and the other **-body** forms):

*Nobody's allowed in yet, **are they**?*

5 There's a problem, isn't there?

There in its pronoun sense is used in question tags:

*There wasn't enough food, **was there**?*

6 I like it, don't you?

You can use tags with **you** after introducing your own opinion with something like **I think** or **I like**:

***I love** this weather, **don't you**?*
***I'm looking forward** to this evening, **aren't you**?*

FURTHER USES OF QUESTION TAGS

1 requesting

You can use negative questions, with positive question tags, to make tentative requests:

*You **couldn't** give me a lift home, **could you**?*

To make more positive requests you can use an imperative, with the verb **will** or **would** in the question tag:

***Open** the door for me, **would you**?*
***Don't let** me forget, **will you**?*

2 responding with interest

You use positive question tags after positive statements to express interest, surprise, or sometimes annoyance, or just to check your information:

***You've driven** this car before, **have you**?*
*She **makes** all her own clothes, **does she**?*
*So **he's** leaving all the work to us, **is he**?*

You also use question tags in conversation, to show that you are paying attention, and to encourage the speaker to continue:

*'**I thought** the film was a bit long.' '**Did you**?'*
*'**It wasn't** a very brilliant evening.' '**Wasn't it**?'*

•••• quite ••••

Quite has three distinct meanings.

FAIRLY, REASONABLY

1 with adjectives

Quite can come before gradable adjectives used both predicatively (after a linking verb) and attributively (before a noun):

That's quite good.
Some quite interesting results have come up.

The order before a singular countable noun is **quite** + **an** + adjective + noun:

*That's **quite an effective way** of treating the problem.*
*I need to catch **quite an early train** from Liverpool Street.*

2 with adverbs and verbs

With gradable adverbs **quite** has the meaning 'fairly, reasonably', and with verbs it has the meaning 'to a certain extent':

I reached the final quite easily; then everything went wrong.
I quite admired her determination.
I'd quite like a rest soon.

COMPLETELY

Quite has the meaning 'completely' when it is used with non-gradable adjectives or adverbs, or verbs with a non-gradable quality:

You're quite right.
She quite obviously wasn't listening.
I quite agree.

1 with adjectives

Quite can come before non-gradable adjectives, and also certain 'extreme' or 'exaggerated' adjectives:

A reaction like that is quite normal.
I tried the diet myself, with quite amazing results.

ⓘ Notice that the order before a singular countable noun is **a** + **quite** + adjective + noun:
That's a quite ridiculous idea.

2 with adverbs and verbs

With non-gradable adverbs and verbs, **quite** means 'completely' or 'absolutely':

I can quite honestly say it was a pleasure.
I've quite finished, thank you.

3 not quite

Not quite means 'not, but almost', or 'not exactly':

It's not quite wide enough.
Are you ready?' 'Not quite.'
Sorry, I didn't quite catch your name.

4 with superlatives

Quite can be used with the meaning 'completely, absolutely' before superlatives, and before other adjectives representing extremes:

Pierre Alexis is quite the finest eating place in town.
New things are not all bad; quite the opposite.

ⓘ **Quite** is not usually used with comparatives. But you can say that you are **quite better** after an illness, meaning that you are completely cured or recovered.

CONSIDERABLE, STRIKING

1 **with singular countable nouns**

Someone or something that is **quite a** thing, or, especially in AmE, **quite some** thing is a considerable or significant thing of its kind:

Prison was quite a shock for this 15-year-old schoolboy.
This is quite an insult.
Old Darlington was quite some place in those days.

2 **with quantifying expressions**

Quite a lot, **quite a bit** and **quite a few** all mean 'a considerable quantity':

Quite a few people turned up.
There's been quite a lot of interest.

quotation marks

➤ See **punctuation**.

Rr

rarely

➤ See **seldom**.

rather

Rather has two main uses. It is used as a *moderating* adverb of degree, similar to **quite**, and it is used to express preference, in the forms **would rather** and **rather than**.

MODERATING ADVERB

1 before adjectives and adverbs

- **Rather** is sometimes used to moderate the negative effect of adjectives or adverbs that have a negative or critical meaning:

  *That was **rather silly** of you.*
  *Indexing is **rather boring** work.*
  *He made some **rather unhelpful** comments.*

- When used with positive or approving adjectives or adverbs, **rather** has an emphatic effect:

  *I heard some **rather interesting** news today.*
  *I thought I handled the situation **rather well**.*

- When you use **rather** before a singular countable noun, it can come after the article or before it:

  *I thought that was **rather an odd** thing to say.*
  *In the drawing-room was **a rather lovely** fireplace.*

2 before singular countable nouns

Like **quite**, **rather** can be used directly before a noun phrase, without an adjective:

*In the office they think I'm **rather an idiot**.*

3 before verbs

Rather can be used with verbs, especially verbs of feeling or thinking:

*Jill felt sorry for him and **rather wished** she hadn't spoken so pointedly.*
*I **rather like** some of his plays.*
*I've **rather wasted** your time, I'm afraid.*

4 before 'like'

Rather is often used before the preposition **like**:

It was an ugly-looking fish, rather like an eel.

5 with comparatives and 'too'

Unlike **quite**, **rather** can be used with comparative. It is also used with **too**:

*We've done **rather more** than half.*
*It's **rather** colder today.*
*He seemed to be **rather too** pleased with himself.*

EXPRESSING PREFERENCE

1 would rather

- 'I **would rather** do something' means the same as 'I *would prefer to* do something':

  'Would you like a beer?' 'I think I'd rather have a glass of red wine.'
  I'd rather not speak in front of so many people.
  We'd rather keep the money than spend it on something we don't need.

- You can use a clause after **would rather**, with the verb in the past tense:

  I'd rather she stayed in the car.
  'Do you mind if I smoke?' 'I'd rather you didn't.'

- The rest of the clause can be dropped after **would rather**, as it can after **would prefer**, if the meaning is clear:

  We can deliver it tomorrow or, if you'd rather, you can come back and collect it.

2 rather than

- You use **rather than** to talk about preferring one option to another, or about one thing being closer to the truth than another:

  Women should be thought of as workers rather than as housewives and mothers.
  The gossip and speculation have intensified rather than diminished.
  For the bedroom we chose yellow rather than blue.

- A **to**-infinitive is usually contrasted with an infinitive without **to**:

  I wanted to move on rather than wait.

➤ See also the entry **prefer**.

3 or rather

You can use **or rather** to correct yourself:

I've spent a lot of time on this, or rather, wasted a lot of time.

—— reacting ——

➤ See page 479.

• • • • real, really • • • •

Real and **really** have several different uses which can overlap.

REAL

1 A **real** thing or person actually exists, as distinct from existing only in imagination, theory or pretence:

They reached the top of the slope. Here lay the real danger.
It now seems that war is a real possibility.
What was the real reason for his behaviour?

GENERAL REACTIONS

1 A common way of expressing your first reaction to something you see or hear is to say **How** + adjective**!** or **What** + noun**!**:

How awful!
How funny!
What an idiot!
What fun!

➤ For more details about constructions with **what** and **how** see **exclamations**.

2 You can say, **That's interesting** or **stupid** or **clever**, *etc*, as a direct way of reacting to something, but it's very usual to soften the directness of such a statement by making it into a negative question:

Isn't that interesting?
Isn't that ridiculous?

MORE SPECIFIC CONTEXTS

There are certain words and phrases that are frequently used in particular contexts. Below are some of the most usual:

1 **surprise**:

Really?
Good heavens!
I don't know what to say!
You're joking!
I can't believe it!
You don't mean that!

2 **sympathy**:

Oh dear!
I'm so sorry.
Oh bad luck!
Hard luck!
You poor thing!
What a shame!
What a pity!
Never mind.

3 **distress**:

Oh no!
Ouch! That hurt(s)!
Help!
Look out!

...real, really continued

2 Something that is **real** is genuine, as distinct from being an imitation or a copy:

It suits you. It doesn't matter that it's not real silk.
It is cheaper than real leather.

3 **Real** can also mean 'in the true sense of the word', but is sometimes used just for emphasis:

We knew that we had a real crisis on our hands.

In AmE, **real** is commonly placed before an adjective with the meaning 'very'; in BrE, **really** would be more common here:

I got some real (or BrE *really) nice things for my birthday.*

REALLY

1 **in statements**

You use **really** informally, to emphasize the truth or strength of what you are saying:

If you follow a few basic rules, you really can't make a mistake.
Thanks. I really needed that.

In informal styles, when **really** precedes an adjective, it has a similar meaning to **very**:

We had a really good day.
She gets really annoyed when you can't answer her questions.

2 in questions

- You can add **really** to a question to which you expect the answer 'no':

  Do you really think he would ever hurt you?
  Is it really possible to learn to drive in such a short time?

- People sometimes reply to what someone says by saying **really?** Depending on the context and the speaker's intonation, this may indicate surprise or disbelief, or polite interest:

  'My son's doing very well at university now, you know.' 'Really?'

3 in negatives

People often use **really** after **not** as a polite or less severe way of saying 'no' or making a negative statement:

She's not really confident about her thoughts and opinions.
'Do you like these earrings?' 'Well, not really, no.'

•••• reason ••••

The reason **for** something is the situation or facts which explain why it exists or happens:

The reason for the fall in sales was increased competion.

1 When **reason** is followed by a clause, the clause may be introduced by **why**, or less commonly by **that**:

There is no good reason why traditional methods should be abandoned.
The reason that they are opposed to a road is that they do not consider it necessary.

2 Most commonly, however, **why** or **that** is omitted, giving **The reason I ...**:

The reason I'm calling is that I've lost my wallet.

3 When you are introducing the reason itself, you can use **that** or **because**:

The reason I'm calling is that we're thinking of going out tomorrow night.
The reason he killed the woman was because he lost control.

Notice that the use of **because** in this position is more common in spoken English and informal writing; **that** is more common in formal language.

Notice that the structures presented above are all emphatic ways of saying **because**:

The reason I'm here is because ... [= I'm here because ...]
I did it for the simple reason that ... [= I did it because ...]

reflexive pronouns

FORMS

The reflexive pronouns are:

	singular	**plural**
first person	*myself*	*ourselves*
second person	*yourself*	*yourselves*
third person	*himself*	*themselves*
	herself	
	itself	

USES

1 as objects

- You use a reflexive pronoun as the object of a clause when it is the same as the subject:
  *What's the matter? Have you hurt **yourself**?* [direct object of *hurt*]
  *After rubbing **themselves** dry, they dressed and had breakfast.* [direct object of *rubbing*]
  *I decided I needed more exercise, so I bought **myself** a bike.* [indirect object of *bought*]
- The reflexive pronoun may be the object of a preposition:
  *I had another look **at myself** in the mirror.*
  *Many children talk **to themselves** when they're alone.*
  *He was feeling pretty proud **of himself**.*

2 reflexive verbs

- Some verbs are frequently used with a reflexive pronoun, *eg*:
  cut enjoy express help hurt
  *Try to **express yourself** clearly.*
  *We **enjoyed ourselves** at the party.*
  ***Help yourselves** to a plate and some food.*
  *I **cut myself** on a piece of broken glass.*
- The verbs **busy**, **content** and **pride** are always used with a reflexive pronoun:
  *He **contented himself** with pulling a face at her departing back.*
  *Mum turned away and **busied herself** with setting the table.*
  *She **prided herself** on her slim figure.*
- Other verbs have common reflexive senses or uses:

*The children can **amuse themselves**.*	*Learn to **apply yourself** to your work.*
*You mustn't **blame yourself**.*	*Give me time to **compose myself**.*
*Try to **distance yourself** from your job.*	*She got out and **dried herself**.*
*You've **excelled yourself** this time.*	*He doesn't **exert himself** enough.*
*Let me **introduce myself**.*	*To commit suicide is to **kill yourself**.*
***Prepare yourselves** for bad news.*	*We must **restrict ourselves** to one suitcase each.*
*Don't **strain yourself**.*	*She **taught herself** Hungarian.*

The plural reflexive pronoun **themselves** is sometimes used with **someone, no-one, anyone** and **everyone**, especially in informal English. In formal English **himself or herself** is likely to be used:

*Has someone **hurt themselves**?*
*I admire anyone who can **express themselves** so fluently in public.*

- **verbs not used with a reflexive pronoun**
  Although the verbs **wash**, **dress** and **shave** have a reflexive sense, they are used without reflexive pronouns:
  *When is he going to **wash** and **dress**?*
  *I **shaved** in the kitchen, as there was someone in the bathroom.*
  But you may add reflexive pronouns if you want to emphasize the independent action:
  *She's only two and she can already dress **herself**.*

3 used for emphasis

You can use reflexive pronouns to give emphasis to the subject or object of a sentence or clause, with a variety of senses:

*The only person who can make this decision is the prime minister **himself*** [and no-one else].
*You can't go into the palace **itself*** [the main attraction].
*If I had his address I would write to him **myself*** [= and not rely on you].

4 by yourself

You use **by yourself** in the same way as **on your own**:

- You do something **by yourself** if you do it without help or interference from anyone else:
  *I want to learn to manage **by myself**.*
- You are ***by yourself*** when you are alone:
  One in three elderly people live by themselves.

reinforcement tags

In informal English, people sometimes use **reinforcement tags** to emphasize what they are saying. Reinforcement tags repeat the subject and auxiliary verb of the statement they follow. They are formed in the affirmative if they support an affirmative sentence, and in the negative if they support a negative sentence. However, they are much more commonly used in the affirmative:

*You're stupid, **you are**!*
*He's great, **he is**.*
*I'll get you, **I will**!*
*You're all right, **you are**.*

Reinforcement tags are sometimes used to move the subject of the sentence to the end, so that the verb or complement is emphasized:

*Ooh, love it, **we do**.*
*Phew! Exhausted, **I am**.*

Some tags consist only of the subject and complement, without a linking verb:

*Very nice, **that bag of yours**.*
*Really bad, **that train crash**.*

•••• relative clauses and relative pronouns ••••

RELATIVE CLAUSES

Relative clauses are clauses that typically begin with **wh-**words such as **who** or **which**, and are used to identify, or tell you something about, a person or thing just mentioned.

There are two kinds of relative clauses:

- One type *identifies* a person or thing so far unidentified:

  I telephoned the couple [which couple?] ***who had offered the best price***.

  Relative clauses like these are called *identifying* or *defining* clauses.

- The other kind of relative clause *adds information* about a person or thing that is already identified:

  I tried phoning my mother, ***who was out***.

  Relative clauses like these are called *non-identifying* or *non-defining* clauses.

  The two kinds of relative clauses are dealt with in separate sections in this entry.

RELATIVE PRONOUNS

The relative pronouns have the same forms as the **wh-**question words, but instead of asking for information, they give information. Besides the **wh-**words, **that** is also widely used as a relative pronoun.

The relative pronouns are:

who, whom, which, that

➤ See also the individual entries for **who**, **whom**, **which**, **that**, **what** and **whose**.

1 defining clauses

- **Who**, **which** and **that** are used as the subjects of defining relative clauses.

  Who refers to people:

  Obviously not all elderly patients ***who*** *live alone are in need of assistance.*

  Which refers to things:

  She talked about the ideas and places ***which*** *had influenced her work.*

  That can refer to both people or things:

  She searched among the books ***that*** *stood in piles all over the floor.*
  Most children prefer teachers ***that*** *don't shout.*

- You can use **who** or **whom**, **which** and **that**, as the objects of defining relative clauses. **Whom** is used rather than **who** in formal English, and is considered 'correct' by a lot of people:

  Try to find an adult ***whom*** (or ***who***) *you can trust.*
  I didn't recognize the people ***who*** (or ***whom***) *I saw there.*
  A doctor is obliged to report any cases ***that*** *he sees.*
  She let me read the essay ***which*** *she had been writing.*

- Relative clauses can be introduced by **when** after 'time' words, by **where** after 'place' words, and by **why** after the word **reason**:

  Adolescence is ***a time when*** *many people rebel.*
  This is ***the place where*** *the tragedy occurred.*
  There's ***no reason why*** *they should like me.*

➤ See also the entries for **place**, **time**, **reason**.

- **What** as a relative pronoun means 'the thing that' or 'the things that'; it does not refer back to a previously used noun:

  *I think you can probably provide me with **what** I'm looking for.*
  ***What** amazed me was her arrogance.*

- You can drop the relative pronoun if it is the object of the relative clause:

  Where's that drink (that) you promised me?
  We eventually found the kind of mattress (that) we were searching for.
  Who was that woman (whom) you were talking to?

- When you want to identify someone in terms of something that belongs or relates to them, you use **whose**:

  *There are arrangements for dealing with doctors **whose** performance is consistently poor.*

  You will also hear **whose** used for identifying *things*:

  *Put on one side any books **whose** covers are falling off.*

2 non-defining clauses

- You use non-defining clauses to add a point about someone or something that is already known or identified:

  *They are wonderful people, **whom** I will never forget.*
  *Our victory was heartening for the fans, **whose** support so far this season has been fantastic.*

- A comma always comes before a non-defining relative clause:

  *I contacted Mary, **whom** I had last seen in October.*

  If the non-defining clause comes in the middle of the sentence, you put commas on each side of it:

  *Mary, **whom** I had last seen in October, wrote to me from Germany.*

3 prepositions in relative clauses

- **defining clauses**

  You can place the preposition before the relative pronoun, at the beginning of the clause:

  *This is the chair **in which** she used to sit.*
  *The girl **to whom** I gave the message had a Scottish accent.*

> ⓘ Notice that you always use **whom**, not **who**, after a preposition in this position.

  You can also put the preposition after the verb, at the end of the clause:

  *This is the chair **that** she used to sit **in**.*
  *The woman **who** I was talking **to** suddenly screamed.*

  A third possibilitiy is to omit the relative pronoun:

  *This is the chair she used to sit **in**.*

■ **non-defining clauses**

You can place the preposition before the relative pronoun (**which** or **whom**) at the beginning of the clause:

*I'm so sorry about the mistake, **for which** I can offer no excuse.*
*I have referred the matter to my lawyers, **to whom** all future correspondence should be addressed.*

The other possibility is to put the preposition after the verb, and introduce the clause with **which** or **who(m)**:

*I'm so sorry about the mistake, **which** I can offer no excuse **for**.*
*This is Marie, **who(m)** I rely **on** totally to organize my life.*

You can use **which** to refer back to a circumstance or situation that has just been mentioned

*He said he could speak Russian, **which** was untrue.*

•••• remember, remind ••••

Remember and **remind** are often confused by learners.

REMEMBER

1 remember + noun or **+ -ing**

You **remember**, or can **remember**, something from the past when you still have an impression of it and can bring it back into your mind:

She could still remember it all intensely.
I can't remember the word; it begins with a P.
I remember having to wash and bathe in the river.

Remember is not normally used in the progressive form.

2 remember + to-infinitive

You **remember to do** something when you do it as you intended:

Did you remember to feed the cat?
Remember to remove your jewellery before you do this kind of work.
I must remember to get that phone number for you, Peter.

REMIND

Remind means 'to cause someone to remember something'. There are three different structures possible.

1 remind + that-clause

Something may **remind** you, or someone may say something to **remind** you, **that** something is the case:

Someone reminded him that she was only fourteen years old.
The smell reminded Sarah that she hadn't eaten since early morning.

2 remind + to-infinitive or **about**

You **remind** someone **to do** something or **about** something when you mention to them that they should do it:

Remind me to get a card on Wednesday.
I reminded him to talk in English.
She reminded me about signing the register.

3 remind + of

- You **remind** someone **of** something when you mention it to them in case they have forgotten about it:

  He reminded me of the problems I was going to face.

- One thing or person **reminds** you **of** another if there is a particular characteristic about one that makes you think of the other:
  He reminded me of his father, James.

• • • • reporting • • •

There are two ways of reporting people's speech and thoughts. You can either quote the exact words used:

'Have you been swimming?' asked Bill.
'Why is he so interested?' I wondered.

This is called *direct speech.*

Or you can include or 'edit' the speaker's or thinker's words into your own account of things:

Bill asked if I'd been swimming.
I wondered why he was so interested.

This is called *indirect speech*, but is also often referred to as *reported speech.*

DIRECT SPEECH

Direct speech is found mostly in stories

1 The *reporting* verb (*eg* **said**, **asked**, **answered**) comes before or, more frequently, after the quoted words:

*I **said**, 'Just you try.'*
*'Don't worry,' he **answered**.*

2 When the reporting verb comes after the quoted words, its subject, the speaker or thinker, can come before or after it:

*'It's still raining,' **my mother said**.*
*'Has the post arrived yet?' **asked Ellen**.*

But if the subject of the reporting verb is a pronoun, it must come before the reporting verb:

*'You can do it,' **he insisted**.*

3 punctuation

- When the subject + reporting verb come before the direct speech you can introduce the direct speech with a comma or a colon, but it is not really necessary to use any punctuation:

  She said, 'Well, now we all know where we stand.'
  She said: 'As I opened the door he slid to the ground.'
  She said 'You evidently think it amusing to dress like that, Donald.'

- You use quotation marks, which can be single or double, to open and close direct speech:

  'Be very careful,' she warned.
  "But he likes me," I protested.

- A comma replaces a full stop at the end of quoted speech, unless the end of the quotation is also the end of the whole sentence.

  'Write to me sometimes,' he pleaded.

  But:

  Tom said, 'Don't be upset.'

- As a general rule, punctuation marks that belong to the direct speech stay inside the quotation marks:

  'Where's my anorak?' wailed Paul.
  'Watch out!' yelled Jenny.

- When the reporting phrase interrupts the direct speech, the direct speech re-opens after a comma, unless a new sentence is starting:

  'They'll be looking for you,' she said, 'up there.'

  But:

  'I can't keep silent,' she said. 'It's not fair to ask me.'

4 verbs for reporting direct speech

- In spoken English, when you are quoting direct speech or thoughts, you use very simple reporting verbs, such as **said**, **asked** and **thought**:

- Some reporting verbs indicate what kind of communication is being made, or how it links with what has just been said:

  'Any chance of a meal?' he ***enquired****.*
  'I've just finished the washing-up,' she ***protested****.*
  'And anyway,' she ***continued****, 'It's bedtime.'*
  'Oh, go on,' ***pleaded*** *Tom.*
  'Absolutely not,' ***insisted*** *Ellen.*
  Then she ***added****, 'There's some food in the freezer.'*

- Other reporting verbs indicate the kind of voice the communication is made in:

  'Alice!' ***called*** *Jean.*
  She ***whispered*** *'Look, they're just behind her.'*

INDIRECT SPEECH

1 The most usual way of reporting what people say is by indirect speech, using a reporting verb such as **say**, followed by a **that**-clause, with or without the word **that**.

Often a tense change is needed, but other changes may be needed too:

I like the shoes you're wearing tonight. [Peter's original words to Alice, one evening]
Peter said he liked the shoes I was wearing last night. [Alice's report, next day]

After using the simple past reporting verb **said**, Alice changes:

- the simple present **like** into the simple past **liked**
- the present progressive **are wearing** into the past progressive **was wearing**
- the pronoun **I**, used by Peter, into the pronoun **he**
- the pronoun **you**, used by Peter, into the pronoun **I**.
- the time reference from **tonight** to **last night**

TENSES

1 the past

After a reporting verb in the past tense, the tenses used in the orginal words usually go one stage back into the past:

	original words	**reported words**
Anne:	*You'**re** right.*	*Anne said I **was** right.*
Bob:	*She'**s looking** very well.*	*Bob said she **was looking** very well.*
me:	*I **tried** to be friendly.*	*I said I **had tried** to be friendly.*
Bill:	*I'**ve found** my wallet.*	*Bill said he **had found** his wallet.*
Angie:	*I'**ve been playing** a lot of tennis.*	*Angie said she **had been playing** a lot of tennis.*

However, a *simple past* in the original words may remain a simple past in the reported version, instead of turning into the past perfect, if it is not important to show the time sequence between the event and the words that report it:

The guide told us that Queen Mary was beheaded in 1567.

- **modal verbs**

Can in the original words usually becomes **could** in past reporting; **will** becomes **would**. Notice that **shall** also usually becomes **would** rather than **should**. **May** becomes **might**:

*'You **can** borrow my bike.'*	*I said she **could** borrow my bike.*
*'I'**ll** let you know.'*	*She said she **would** let me know.*
*'We **shall** be delighted to help.'*	*They said they **would** be delighted to help.*
*'I **may** be delayed.'*	*He said he **might** be delayed.*

Notice that when the modals **would**, **could**, **might**, **must**, and **need** are used in the original words, they keep the same form in past reporting.

2 the present and the future

After reporting verbs in the *present*, *present perfect*, and *future*, the tenses of the original words remain the same:

*'It'**s** too early to know.'*	*He **says** it'**s** too early to know.*
*'I'**ll join** you later.'*	*He **says** he'**ll join** us later*
*'You **were** a great help.'*	*He **says** I **was** a great help.*
*'I **respect** her.'*	*He **has** often said he **respects** you.*
*'She'**s** very busy.'*	***I'll say** you'**re** very busy.*

VERBS USED IN REPORTING

Verbs used in reporting may be 'saying' or 'thinking' verbs.

1 'saying' verbs

admit	*agree*	*announce*	*claim*	*confess*	*deny*	
hint	*insist*	*mention*	*report*	*say*	*suggest*	*warn*

He didn't mention (that) you were coming.
You're not suggesting (that) I was drunk, are you?

- The following verbs need the hearer as object:
  assure, convince, inform, notify, persuade, reassure, remind, tell
  She persaded me that she could do the job.
  He told us there was no need to worry.

➤ See also **say, tell**.

2 'thinking' verbs

- The following 'thinking' verbs can be used with or without **that**:

assume	*believe*	*decide*	*expect*
feel	*hope*	*imagine*	
know	*notice*	*presume*	*realize*
remember	*think*		

  I thought you were still at home.
  I realized that she was ill.

- With some 'thinking' verbs, when you are reporting a negative thought, you make the 'thinking' verbs negative, instead of making the **that**-clause negative. The verbs that behave like this are:

believe	*expect*	*feel*	*imagine*
suppose	*think*		

  I don't believe you two have [= I believe you two haven't] *met, have you?*
  I don't think he can [= I think he can't] *hear you.*
  I don't imagine there will [= I imagine there won't] *be any problems.*

USING THE PASSIVE FOR REPORTING

With verbs that require the hearer as object, the hearer can be made the subject of a passive verb:

*I **was assured** that the ambulance would arrive within a few minutes.*

You can also use **it** as the subject of a passive reporting verb, followed by a **that**-clause:

***It is believed** that the fumes are coming from the drains.*

The person or thing that the report concerns can be made the subject of a passive reporting verb, with a following **to**-infinitive:

***She is said to be** an expert on wines.*

You use these passive constructions usually in formal English, or when you want to avoid saying whose opinion you are reporting.

➤ See the entry **the passive** for use of passive verbs in reporting.

REPORTING QUESTIONS

1 In a reported question there is no inversion of subject and auxiliary verb as there is in direct questions. The order is the same as in a statement:

	original question	**reported question**
Jim:	*What **are you** doing?*	*Jim asked **what I was*** (not *what was I) doing.*
Sue:	*Where **do you** want to have lunch?*	*Sue asked where **I wanted*** (not *where did I want) to have lunch.*

2 If there is a **wh-**question word, such as **what**, **when**, **where**, **why** in the original question, you use the same **wh-**word in the reported question:

Why are you upset?	*I asked why she was upset.*
Which trousers do you want to wear?	*She asked which trousers I wanted to wear.*

3 When you are reporting a question that expects the answer yes or no you use **if** or **whether**. People tend to use **whether** when a choice is mentioned:

Would you like a sandwich?	*He asked **if** I'd like a sandwich.*
Do you want a cheese or ham?	*He asked **whether** I wanted cheese or ham.*

4 **verbs used for reporting questions**

- **Ask** is the normal verb for reporting questions. You can mention the hearer as a direct object:

  A man came and asked me where the car park was.

  More formally, you can use **enquire** or **inquire**. With these you cannot mention the hearer:

  *A man approached me and **enquired** when the train was due.*

- When reporting *unspoken* questions you normally use **wonder**, or a negative expression such as **don't know** or **can't think**, or **have no idea**:

  *I **wondered** if I would have time to finish the project.*
  *I **couldn't think** how we were going to cross the river.*
  *We **had no idea** where he was.*

- You use reporting verbs like **say**, **tell** and **know** when you are referring to the *answer* to a question:

  *You **haven't said** yet whether you like it.*
  *He **told** me where it was and I fetched it.*
  *I **know** why it isn't working.*

5 **to-infinitives after a reporting verb + wh-word**
You often use a **to-**infinitive after a reporting verb + **wh-**word:

*This lady wants to know **how to get** to the post office.*
*Tell me **what to do** next.*

7 **reporting verbs referring to actions**
Reporting verbs that refer to future actions, such as **promise**, **threaten** or **offer**, are often followed by a **to-**infinitive:

She promised to be back by five o'clock.
He's threatening to withhold payment
I offered to help her.

Here are some common reporting verbs that are followed by a **to-**infinitive:

agree, demand, offer, promise, refuse, swear, threaten, vow

Except for **offer** and **refuse**, these verbs can also be followed by a **that-**clause, in which you use a modal verb, or a subjunctive:

*I **agreed that** I **would** complete the book by December.*
*We **demanded that** they **return** the money immediately.*

Other reporting verbs that refer to future actions take an object + **to**-infinitive:

*He **encouraged me to apply** for the job.*
*A policeman **ordered us to stop**.*

Common reporting verbs that have an object + **to**-infinitive are:

advise	*ask*	*beg*	*command*
encourage	*forbid*	*instruct*	
invite	*order*	*persuade*	*remind*
tell	*urge*	*warn*	

requests, orders and instructions

➤ See pages 492–494.

the rest, the remains, the remainder

The rest, **the remains** and **the remainder** all describe the things or part that is left after something has been taken away. They can all act as nouns and as pronouns. However, they have own individual uses.

THE REST

The rest of something, or **the rest** of a group, is the part that is left after someone or something has been mentioned, taken, or has gone away:

Only Trevor arrived at 9am; the rest were all late.
The rest of the day passed quickly.
She tried to remember the rest of the story.

Notice that whether the verb is in the singular or plural depends on the noun following, or implied by, **the rest**:

The rest of us were given various different tasks to complete.
The rest of the day was devoted to private study.

THE REMAINDER

The remainder is used in the same way as **the rest**, but is far more commonly used in written and formal English:

The remainder of these examples come from spoken English.
In the remainder of the book, the focus is on activities.
The company paid for the first part of my course. The remainder was paid for by the education authority.

THE REMAINS

The **remains** of something are the parts left after other parts have been taken away or lost, used up or destroyed:

I scattered the remains of the food on the window ledge.
In the garden lay the remains of a snowman.
The man's body was discovered among the burnt remains of his cottage.

REQUESTS, ORDERS AND INSTRUCTIONS

REQUESTS

1 asking someone to do something

Most polite requests are yes-or-no questions, which give people the chance to refuse. The commonest polite forms are **Could you (possibly) ...?, Would you mind ...-ing?, I wonder if you could (possibly) ...?**, and **Do you think you could (possibly) ...?**:

> ***Could you possibly*** *go a little slower?*
> ***Could you*** *pick me up here at about five thirty?*
> ***Would you mind moving*** *slightly? I can't see the screen very clearly.*
> ***I wonder if you could*** *help me with a problem.*
> ***Do you think you could possibly*** *come back later?*

More informally, people use **Will you ...?** and **Can you ...?**, or they may introduce a request with **I wonder if you could do me a favour?** or **Will** (or **Could**) **you do me a favour?**:

> ***Will you*** *give me a lift to Doris's house?*
> *Becky,* ***will you*** *please go and do your homework?*
> ***Can you*** *speak up a bit?*
> *Now,* ***can you*** *pack your things up, please?*
> ***Will you do me a favour*** *and answer the phone when I'm out?*

Another way of asking someone to do something is to use a negative statement, followed by tag:

> ***You wouldn't*** *just hold this for me,* ***would you****?*
> ***I don't suppose you'd*** *be able to video that film for me tonight,* ***would you****?*

Very formally, you can use **Would you kindly ...?**:

> ***Would you kindly*** *stand and raise your glasses?*
> ***Would you kindly*** *write your ideas down on a sheet of this paper?*

When making a request in a formal letter, you usually use **I would (or should) be most grateful if you could ...**:

> ***I would be most grateful if you could*** *pass this information on to your colleagues.*
> ***We should be most grateful if you could*** *let us have your ideas as soon as possible.*

2 asking for something

When you are asking for something, the commonest polite form is **Can** (or **Could**) **I have ...?**:

> ***Could I have*** *a drink?*
> ***Can I have*** *a fork, please?*

When you are asking for something in a shop or a restaurant, you can use the structures presented above, but you can also say **I'd like ..., I'll have ...** or **Have you got ...?**:

I'd like *ten first-class stamps, please.*
I'll have *the steak, please.*
Have you got *anything for removing stains?*

In shops, bars and restaurants where service is fast, people often just state what they want, followed by **please**:

A glass of red wine, please.
Two first-class stamps, please.
Return to Glasgow, please.

GIVING ORDERS

People only usually give orders when they are angry or when there is some danger that they need to avert. Orders are generally given in the imperative form:

Hurry up!
Look out!
Don't switch it off!
Be quiet!

You can make an order sound more polite by adding **please**. However, this can still sound impatient:

Write this down, please.
Open wider, please.
Right, stand on the scales, please.
Come here, please.

You can also use an imperative with the tag **... will you?** at the end. This can sound rude when one adult is speaking to another, but is commonly used by adults speaking to children:

Jonathan, ***put*** *that straight in the bin for Mum,* ***will you*** *please?*
Fetch *Miss Chester some hot coffee and warm rolls,* ***will you****, Kay?*

Adding **... won't you?** or beginning with **Do ...** makes an imperative sound more like a request:

Remember *to turn the lights off,* ***won't you****?*
Do *ask him if it's all right before you go in.*

People in authority, such as teachers, often politely tell others what to do by saying **I'd like you to ...**, or **What I'd like you to do is ...**:

I'd like you to *take notes in the new form that we've learnt.*
What I'd like you to do is *take a clean sheet of paper and write your name on it.*

1 emphasis

You use **You must ...** or **You mustn't ...** to emphasize the importance of an order:

You must *come to the hospital for your medicines.*
Graham! You ***mustn't*** *do that!*

2 showing anger

Using **Will you ...?**, **Can't you ...?** or the tags **...will you?** and **...can't you?** when giving orders shows that the speaker is angry or impatient:

Will you stop interrupting and listen to me?
Leave me alone, will you?
Can't you be a bit quieter?
Try a bit harder, can't you?

3 official notices

Signs in public places often give orders. Typical examples are:

No smoking.
Dogs must be kept on a lead.

Some official notices are worded as if they were requests, but they are still orders:

You are kindly requested to refrain from smoking.

INSTRUCTIONS

Instructions may be in the imperative form, or, more informally, the second person singular, that is, **You ...** They are frequently used in recipes, manuals, and by people giving directions:

***Add** the milk and **stir**.*
***You go** along here, **turn** left at the traffic lights, and it's on the left.*

Must be and **should be** are both used to instruct people what to do with something. **Should be** is not as strong as **must be**:

All rooms must be vacated before 9.30a.m.
Passengers should be at the airport at least one hour before their flight.

REPLYING TO REQUESTS

1 agreeing

You can agree to a request by saying, **OK**, **All right**, or **Sure**. More formally, you can say **Certainly** or **Of course**:

'Will you give me a hand?' 'OK.'
'Would you do me a favour?' 'Sure.'
'Could I possibly have a glass of water?' 'Yes, of course.'
'Could you send some breakfast up to my room?' 'Certainly, madam'.

2 refusing

When you refuse someone a request, you usually apologize and give a reason why you cannot do what they want:

*Could you give me a hand with this case, please?' **'I'm really sorry, but I've got a bad back**.'*
*'Could I borrow your dictionary, please?' '**Well, I'm afraid I'm using it at the moment**.'*
*'Have you got the Cambridge text of 'Othello?' '**I'm afraid we're out of stock at the moment, madam**.'*

...the rest, the remains, the remainder continued

When **the remains** is used alone, it usually refers to the body of a dead person or objects from past periods in history which have been found or dug up:

After a short religious ceremony, the remains were buried in the churchyard.
The remains include parts of an Anglo-Saxon church and a medieval monastery.

The remains always takes a plural verb.

• • • • road, street • • • •

ROAD

Road is a general word for any route for vehicles:

a road map
It's a long way, but most of it's on the same road.

STREET

A **street** is a road in a town or village, with pavements or buildings on either side:

He owned a shop on the main street, selling groceries and some garden produce.

You can also refer to a **street** as a **road**:

What's the name of the main road that goes through the town?

> ⓘ Remember that you cannot refer to a road that goes through the country, or to a motorway, as a **street**.

Ss

•••• same, similar ••••

MEANING

1 Two or more things that are **the same** are exactly alike:

They were the same height and almost the same build.

2 Things that are **the same** compared with how they were in the past have not changed:

I hadn't seen her for ten years, but she seemed exactly the same.

3 **The same** thing or person is that particular thing or person in each case, or over a particular period:

They all have the same surname.
I saw the same girl again, an hour later.

> ⓘ **Same** is almost always preceded by **the**.

STRUCTURES

1 the same as

You can say that one thing or person is **the same as** another thing or person:

It costs about the same as an ordinary bottle of wine.
He claims that his objectives are the same as mine.

2 the same (noun) as...

You can also put a noun between **the same** and **as**:

She would be coming home at the same time as Gina.

3 the same (noun) that...

The same can also be followed by a noun or pronoun and a **that**-clause, with or without **that**:

It was the same one (that) I'd seen earlier.

AS AN ADVERB

In informal contexts, **the same** can be used to describe a verb:

Everyone's treated the same here.
He felt the same about me as I felt about him.

MODIFIERS

Certain emphasizing adverbs appear particularly frequently before **the same**:

*We've got one **exactly** the same as that, except that it's wooden.*
*The tune is **basically** the same as the old one, but jazzed up.*
*The first argument is **essentially** the same as the second.*

SIMILAR

Two people or things are **similar** if they have certain features in common:

I've been in a similar situation.
Similar results were obtained in other experiments.

1 similar to...

You can say that one person or thing is **similar to** another:

Her ideas on punishment are similar to mine.
They were found in a rubbish sack similar to this one.

2 a similar (noun) to...

As with **the same**, it is possible to insert a noun between **similar** and the preposition **to**:

She's got similar views to mine.
I saw a similar car to yours today.

.... say, tell ....

You **say** something when you express yourself aloud in words. You **tell** someone something when you give them information. You **tell** someone **to do** something when you give them an order or an instruction.

➤ See also **reporting**.

SAY

1 reporting speech

- **Say** is used when you are quoting the words someone said:

'Look,' she said, 'Why don't we go back and start again?'
He said, 'Dammit!' and left.
'It looks like it's going to rain,' she said.

- **Say (that)** is used when you are reporting indirectly what someone has said:

She said she would be there early.
The Prime Minister said that he was deeply shocked.

2 When you are commenting on the words someone has used to express themselves, you talk about the way they said **it**:

She said it softly, but with certainty.

3 When you want to say that someone had certain thoughts or feelings, and also expressed them, you can say that they felt a certain way and they said **so**:

Well, I never liked him. I always said so.
Her father disagreed, and had said so.

4 If you want to mention the hearer as well as the speaker, use **to** after **say**:

He said the same thing to each of us as we left.

TELL

1 Tell someone (that)... is used to talk about giving information, when the hearer is mentioned as well as the speaker:

He told me (that) he'd loved me for years.
She once told us, 'I just like to enjoy myself, that's all.'
He had told her (that) he didn't want to go out that night.

2 **Tell someone to...** is used to talk about giving orders and instructions:

He told me to come back after I'd lost ten kilos.
The doctor told him to have a few weeks off work.

3 **tell lies, tell jokes, tell the truth**

Tell also occurs frequently in certain combinations:

You can't sing, you can't dance and you can't tell jokes.
Tell me a story.
If they ask you, tell the truth.

4 **tell the difference**

Tell used with **can** also means 'distinguish' or 'judge':

Can you tell the difference between a French Cabernet and a South African one?
'Unfortunately the paint here is a different colour.' 'Really? I can't tell.'

•••• scarcely ••••

➤ See **hardly**.

—— the seasons: spring, summer, autumn, winter ——

1 When making a general remark about any of the four seasons, you can use the season name with or without **the**:

He doesn't go out much in (the) winter.
I think (the) autumn is the prettiest season.

> ⓘ AmE **fall** is normally used with **the**:
> *New England in the fall is just as beautiful as everyone says.*

2 When referring to a particular spring, summer, autumn or winter you usually use **the**:

Those few weeks in the winter of 1981–82 were colder than usual.

3 You can refer to a season of the present year as **this summer** (**autumn**, **winter**, etc.) or **the summer**. The summer of last year is **last summer** and the summer of next year is **next summer**:

We're hoping to go to Spain in the summer.
I've got till next summer to decide.
Last autumn, I flew to New England to visit my sister.

4 **Winter** and **summer** have rather literary possessive forms, but **spring** and **autumn** do not:

One beautiful summer's evening we were all sitting on the verandah.

But:

He set off one chilly autumn afternoon.
It happened on a spring day in 1995.

•••• see, look at, watch ••••

See, **look** and **watch** are all related in that they refer to being aware of things through your eyes. They do, however, have their own individual uses and meanings.

SEE

1 You **see** something when you notice it, observe it, witness it or look at it:

I've seen him several times on television.
I saw her throw the gun over the wall.
He was seen leaving the house at 4.30.

ⓘ Notice in the last two examples that **see** can be followed by a verb in the infinitive (without **to**) or a verb + -**ing**. You use the infinitive if you are talking about a completed action, and the verb + -**ing** when you mean that the person was in the middle of the action when you saw them.

2 You say that you **can see** something when it is within your range of vision:

Can you see that ship on the horizon?
We could see her waving to us.
I can't see what he's holding.

ⓘ The progressive form is not normally used with **see**, unless you are using **see** in another sense, such as 'meet' (see below).

3 **other meanings of 'see'**

- See is often used with the meaning 'understand'. You can use **can** or **could** with it:

  I see, so this is the best way.
  Yes, yes, I can see what you mean.
  I couldn't see why she was so worried.

  You cannot use the progressive form of **see** when it has this meaning.

- You **see** someone when you meet them, or have an appointment with them:

  I'm seeing my mother this weekend.
  He called round to see me the other day.
  Do they know we're seeing each other?

  The progressive form is common with this sense of **see**, especially when you are talking about plans to meet someone.

LOOK AT

You **look at** someone or something when you deliberately turn your eyes towards it, so that you can see it:

Look! Someone's coming!
We looked at each other in horror.
Look at that!
She's been looking at that painting for an hour.

ⓘ Notice that **look** does not need **at** + object when it is used in the imperative.

WATCH

1 You **watch** someone or something when you look at them moving, changing, developing or doing something:

By watching an expert, you can learn a lot.
He watched my father walk across the lawn.
'How did you do that?' 'Watch again'

2 You **watch TV** and you **watch sport:**
She watches television, plays music and reads.
There's something I want to watch at 6.30.
They always come to our house to watch the football.

> ⓘ Notice that **see** is used more than **watch** to talk about watching the whole of a film, match, *etc*:
> *Did you see that film on telly last night?*

•••• seeing ••••

Seeing, **seeing that**, and sometimes, informally, **seeing as**, are used with the meaning 'since' or 'because' to introduce the reason for saying or doing something; **seeing** on its own is a little more informal than **seeing that** and **seeing as**:
Seeing as you refuse to change your mind, I give up.
Well, seeing that you are her husband, I shall tell you.
I'll go, seeing it's only for one night.

•••• seldom, rarely ••••

Seldom and **rarely** belong to a small number of adverbs called **broad negatives**. They are used to make a clause almost negative:
She rarely arrives at work on time.

The **broad negatives** are:

barely *hardly*
rarely *scarcely*
seldom

➤ See also entry for **hardly**.

1 **position**
Seldom and **rarely** usually take the adverbial mid position, but they may begin a clause, for emphasis:
Her mother seldom asked her for anything.
Rarely have I seen such awful behaviour.

> ⓘ Notice that when placed in initial position, broad negatives cause inversion of subject and auxiliary verb:
> *Rarely **had she** felt quite so helpless.*

2 **used with any-words**
Seldom and **rarely**, like full negatives such as **not** and **no**, are used with **any-**words and words such as **any** and **ever**:
She rarely went anywhere without her dog.
*There was seldom **any** time for having fun.*

3 question tags

Notice that a question tag after a sentence using **seldom** or **rarely** is positive, in the same way that it is after a full negative:

*Girls seldom went into pubs alone then, **did they?***

•••• shall ••••

Like **will**, **shall** is used with an infinitive without **to**. However, it differs from **will** in that it can only be used with the first person singular and plural, **I** and **we**.

In AmE, **shall** is rare, and BrE speakers tend to use **I shall** and **I will**, and **we shall** and **we will**, without much distinction of meaning. Although **shall** is used to talk about future actions, this use is limited to fairly formal contexts. For information about how **shall** can be used to refer to future actions, see the section **the future: ways of expressing it**. Below, you will find other uses of **shall**. These are all cases where **will** is *not* possible.

MAKING SUGGESTIONS

You can make a suggestion about what you and someone else should do, by asking a question starting with **shall we… ?**:

Shall we go for a drink tonight?
Shall we meet by the pool in about an hour?

> ⓘ More assertive suggestions starting with **Let's...** take **...shall we?** as a question tag:
> *Well, let's go in, shall we?*

ASKING FOR ADVICE AND SUGGESTIONS

You can ask for advice or suggestions from other people by asking a question beginning with a **wh-**word, followed by **... shall I...?** or **... shall we...?**:

Where shall we go?
What shall I wear for this party tonight?
Which film shall we go and see?

ASKING FOR INSTRUCTIONS

You can also use **... shall I...?** and **... shall we...?** to ask for instructions:

Shall I start this now?
Now what shall we do?

MAKING OFFERS

Shall I...? and **shall we...?** are also used to introduce offers:

Shall I hold it for you?
Shall we help you with these bags?

> ⓘ Notice that although **shall** is not used systematically in forming the future, it is widely used in conversation to form questions of the type shown above.

•••• should ••••

Should is a *modal* verb. Its negative form is **should not** or **shouldn't**. **Should** has several uses.

Firstly, it is sometimes used in formal and literary contexts with first-person pronouns (**I** and **we**) to form conditionals (see **if**):

If I should die, please take care of her.

Its other uses are dealt with below.

EXPRESSING OBLIGATION

1 **Should** is used, like **ought to**, to express ideas of *obligation* and *duty*. It is not as strong as **must**, and is usually used to talk about what is advisable, rather than what is absolutely necessary:

I don't want to give it back, but I suppose I should.
They shouldn't leave that child on her own in the house, should they?
People like that shouldn't be allowed to look after old people.

2 You use **should** to give advice, make suggestions, or to say that you think something would be a good idea:

You should prepare yourself for bad news.
Perhaps we should ask an expert.
You should try that Thai restaurant on Nicolson Street.

3 You also use **should** to ask for advice and suggestions:

Shouldn't we buy a mobile phone while they're still cheap?
Should I telephone the police?

TALKING ABOUT PROBABILITY, MAKING DEDUCTIONS

You say that something **should** be so, or **should** happen, if you think it is probably so, or if you expect it to happen:

They should be in Lisbon by now.
The bank should have copies of the leaflet.
She should make an excellent head teacher.
You shouldn't have any difficulty getting seats.

SHOULD HAVE

You use **should have** to talk about something that wasn't done, but that would have been the right thing to do:

I should have been kinder to her.
I know I've done it wrong, but how should I have done it?

ⓘ **Should** can be replaced by **ought to** in all the above cases, with very little change in meaning, except that **ought to** is slightly less formal than **should**.

- **Should have** is used to talk about things that you think have probably already happened or things that you expected to happen, which have not happened.

  They should already have received an application form.
  It's ten o'clock. They should have arrived by now.

IN SUBORDINATE CLAUSES

In fairly formal contexts, **should** is used in **that**-clauses after certain kinds of main clause:

1 **after main clauses expressing reactions**:

It's sad that he should feel so bitter.
It's funny that he should say that.
I wasn't surprised that she should disapprove so strongly.

2 **after main clauses reporting or expressing suggestions, requests and requirements**:

His family suggested that his invention should be named after him.
It's important that she should avoid politics for a while.

Less formally, **should** is left out of this kind of clause, and the following verb agrees with the subject of the **that-**clause:

It's important that he comes to see me.

Another way of expressing the same idea is to use the *subjunctive* (see **the subjunctive**). In this case, **should** is left out and the base form of the verb is used:

They suggested that it ***be*** *named after him.*

Remember that in ordinary conversational English, other forms are possible:

I want him to come *and see me.* (rather than *I insist that he come/should come and see me*).

ELLIPSIS

Should often stands on its own for the main verb in question tags, short answers and other elliptical structures:

There should be a 'u' in 'manoeuvre', shouldn't there?
'Are you going to invite them?' 'I don't know; perhaps we should.'

Should is sometimes followed by **be**, **have** or **do**, and **should have** by **been** or **done** in referring back to verbs that use these auxiliaries:

You're giving her far more than you should (or *should be*).
'I've switched off your computer.' 'Oh no, you shouldn't have (or *shouldn't have done*)*!'*

•••• since ••••

Since can be a *preposition*, a *conjunction*, or an *adverb*. **Since** can also be a conjunction of *reason*, similar in meaning to **because**.

This entry demonstrates four main senses of **since** as a preposition, conjunction and adverb of time, and shows the tenses that are possible with each.

1 Something that has been so, or has happened, **since** a certain time in the past has been so, or happened, from that time until the present, or has happened between then and now:

Since that murder, we've been scared to go out at night.
I've been working here since I gave up teaching in 1991.
He's lost a lot of weight since her death.
He hasn't written since he left for the States.
He came to my 21st birthday party and I haven't heard from him since.

- With this sense of **since** you normally use a perfect form for the main verb:
  I've been thinking about you a lot since I heard the news.
  I had been living on my own since my husband died (or *had died*).

> ⓘ Notice that you use **for** when referring to a period of time that continues into the present as distinct from the particular time in the past that **since** refers to:
> *I've been living on my own **for** five years* (not *since five years*).

2 You can use **since** with an **it**-construction and a time phrase to say how long ago something happened:
It's twenty years since I last saw them.
How long is it since your husband died?

➤ See also **ago**.

3 **Since** is often used after superlatives:
It's the most important discovery since Darwin.
Unemployment figures are the highest since 1974.

•••• single ••••

Apart from being used to mean 'one and only one', **single** is frequently used for emphasis after singular determiners such as **one**, **every** and **a**:

They produce 5 billion packets annually – that's one for every single person in the world.
Nine centimetres of rain fell in a single hour.
Not one single person spoke to me during the time I was there.

➤ For **whole** used in a similar way see the entry **whole**.

—— 's showing possession ——

➤ See **possessive 's**.

—— size ——

➤ See **measurements**.

—— slang ——

The word 'slang' is used to refer to several different types of language. It may be used to refer to the sort of language used within particular social groups, such as criminals, or professional groups such as soldiers or actors. The function of this kind of slang, often called 'jargon', is usually to reinforce group identity. In most dictionaries, the label *slang* is used to signal a wide range of non-standard language, from colloquial to vulgar. Slang words often express strong feelings, and a great number can be found covering such subjects as sex, race and religion.

It is extremely important in any language to be aware of how easy it is to offend people if a slang word is not used in precisely the right context. For this reason, it is often best to avoid using slang completely. If you are eager to learn about, and use, slang expressions, make sure you try them out only when in conversation with people you know very well.

•••• small, little ••••

Both **small** and **little** refer to size – they are opposites of **big** or **large**. They are, however, used in different ways.

SMALL

Small refers only to size, and is the opposite of **big** or **large**:

I arrived early and waited in a small living-room.
A small number of companies are competing.
We're all quite small in my family.

LITTLE

1 **Little**, like **small**, also refers to size, but the use of **little** often indicates an emotional reaction on the part of the speaker. **Little** usually indicates some kind of affection, but it can also be part of an insult:

I love your sweet little nose.
When are you going to get the facts into your stupid little brain?

2 Sometimes **little** is used instead as an informal way of saying **small**, **short**, **young**, *etc*:

Could you stay here for a little while?
The big hand is on the twelve and the little hand is on the five – so it's five o'clock.
A little girl came into the room.

•••• smell ••••

The past tense and past participle of the verb **smell** can be **smelt** or **smelled** /smɛlt/ or /smɛld/ in BrE. The AmE form is **smelled**.

Smell is used in four ways:

INTRANSITIVE VERB

Something that **smells** has an unpleasant smell:

That fish is beginning to smell.
Raw onions make your breath smell.

LINKING VERB

You use **smell** as a linking verb to talk about the kind of smell something has:

■ **You smell nice**

You use adjectives, not adverbs, after **smell**:

What are you cooking in there? It smells delicious (not *deliciously*).
The milk smells bad.

■ **The place smelt of cigarette smoke**

You can use the structure **of** + noun after **smell**:

His breath smelt of whisky.

■ **smell like, smell as if**

You can use **smell like** and **smell as if** to say what impression you get of from the smell of something:

It smells as if something's burning.
This smells like brandy, not whisky.

TRANSITIVE VERB MEANING 'DETECT'

You **smell** something such as burning when you detect it, or become aware of it through your nose. Progressive forms are not used here, but **can** and **could** are frequent:

We could smell the meal cooking upstairs.
Can you smell bacon?
I smelt something strange.

TRANSITIVE VERB MEANING 'DELIBERATELY SNIFF'

You **smell** something when you deliberately sniff it by way of investigating it; progressive forms are possible:

Smell this! Doesn't it remind you of something?
I'm just smelling this meat to see if it's OK.

•••• so ••••

So is an *adverb* and a *conjunction*.

AS AN ADVERB OF DEGREE

So can intensify adjectives, quantifiers such as **much**, **many**, **little** and **few**, adverbs and certain verbs.

1 Result can be expressed by the structures **so...that** + clause, and (more usual with negatives) **so...as to** + infinitive:
I was so tired (that) I fell asleep standing up.
So little food was provided that most of us were hungry.
I'm not so stupid as to believe that.

2 **So** can mean 'to such an extent'. It refers to facts already known, and is usually used with negatives and in questions. It can be replaced by other expressions:
I'm sorry to be so late (or *as late as this*).
Do you really have to work so hard (or *as hard as this*)?
I didn't realize she was so young (or *as young as she is*).

3 **So** can be used as an intensifier, like **very**. This use of **so** is similar to an exclamation:
You've been so kind.
Thank you so much.
I've behaved so stupidly.

> ⓘ You use **so** with *adjectives* that are not followed by nouns, and before *adverbs*. You use **such** with **nouns**, whether or not they are used with adjectives:
> *You've got such* (not *so*) *lovely hair*
> *He's such a sweet person.*

4 **Not so** is used like **not very**, as a less direct form of **not**:
'How is he?' 'Not so well, I'm afraid.'
The future doesn't look so great now.

5 **So** can be used instead of **as** in negative comparisons:
It wasn't quite so difficult the second time.
I like the green plates; the blue aren't so pretty.
She isn't quite so fit as she once was.

6 You use **so much**, not **so**, before comparative adjectives and adverbs:

She's so much prettier than she used to be.
You'll work so much more efficiently if you take a rest.

AS A SUBSTITUTE WORD

So has five uses in which it occurs in various combinations with verbs, and it can stand for a whole **that**-clause.

1 **subject + verb + so**

- This is used especially in response to a question, after verbs of thinking and reporting, such as:

assume	*expect*	*fear*	*guess*	*hope*
imagine	*presume*	*reckon*	*suppose*	*think*
I'm afraid	*it seems*	*it appears*		

'Are you going home at the weekend?' 'I expect so.'
'Will we get help?' 'I hope so.'

ⓘ The negative forms usually have **not** replacing **so**, *eg I hope not*, but there is an alternative form using **so** with a negative verb, *eg I don't think so.* This is frequent with the verbs **believe**, **expect**, **imagine**, **suppose**, and **think**:
'Is it worth waiting for them?' 'I don't suppose so (or *I suppose not*).'

- You use **so** with **say** and **tell** to ask for, or give the authority or reason for, a statement:

'You can't go in there!' 'Who says so?'
She likes you. She told me so herself.

ⓘ The verb **know** can't be used with **so**:
You're the strongest one here; everyone knows that (not *knows so*).

2 **so + subject + verb**

You use **so** with verbs such as **hear, see, gather**, and **understand** to indicate that you are already aware of something you are told:

'Simon's working for us again.' 'So I hear.'
'They're digging up the road again.' 'So I see.'

3 **so + subject + auxiliary**

You use **so** with **be, have** and the auxiliary and modal verbs, to express agreement and often surprise:

'There's Philip now.' 'Oh, so it is.'
'You've dropped something.' 'Thanks, so I have.'

4 **so + auxiliary + subject**

You use **so** with **be, have** and the auxiliary and modal verbs to say that what has been said also applies in another case:

'I'm exhausted.' 'So am I [= I am too].'
Melissa worked for us then, and so did her husband.
'I'd love to get out in that sunshine.' 'So would I.'

I've got three kids, and so has (or *does*) *my sister.*

Notice that the auxiliary after **so** is the same auxiliary as in the main clause. If there is no auxiliary in the main clause, you use **do** after **so**.

5 further substitute uses

- **Do so** can take the place of a verb and whatever follows it:

  'Did you phone the doctor?' 'I was just about to do so.'
  I picked up the book, and as I did so, a note fell out.

  Notice that in both the first mention of the action, and in the substituted **do so**, the same person is the performer of the same action.

- **So** can represent a whole clause after **if**, **even**, **maybe** and **perhaps**:

  I know it doesn't matter. Even so [= even if it doesn't matter] *it upsets me.*
  'Was he taking drugs?' 'If so, he didn't tell me.'

- **So** can replace an adjective or adverb, or a prepositional phrase:

  She was angry, and rightly so [= she was right to be angry].
  The company is in chaos and will probably remain so [= in chaos] *for a few days.*

- Something that is **so**, is true, or is the case:

  You say you don't care. That may be so, but the rest of us still want to succeed.

AS A CONJUNCTION

1 **So** is used to bring the facts together, to check that you have understood, and to introduce what follows next, or happens as a result:

So we were wrong after all?
Her baby's ill, so she can't come to work.

2 **So that** introduces clauses of purpose:

We'd packed the night before, so that we could leave early.

Less formally, you can use **so** by itself:

Go to bed early, so you get a good night's sleep.

—— social occasions ——

➤ For appropriate expressions to use on social occasions, see the individual entries for **introductions**, **greetings and farewells**, **meals**, **drink**, **reacting**, **offering**, **apologizing**, **invitations**, **thanks** and **telephoning**.

.... some ....

Some can be a *determiner* or *pronoun*. You use **some** mainly to refer to an indefinite number of things or amount of something, but it can also be used with the meaning 'particular' or 'certain', and has other uses as well.

AS A DETERMINER

1 with plural nouns and uncountable nouns

- **Some** is used with plural nouns or uncountable nouns:
  In the square some children were kicking a ball about.
  Some money was found under his bed.
  There's some more tea in the pot.

- **as the plural of 'a'**
  Some acts as the plural of **a** or **an**:
  There's a hook on the door, and there are some coat-hangers in the wardrobe.
  There's some bread in the freezer.

ⓘ Notice **some** is used with *pair* words:
I bought some new jeans (or *a new pair of jeans*).

- **no determiner**
  There is a difference between using **some** and using *no determiner*. You use *no determiner* when you are not thinking of a limited number or quantity:
  People wear clothes to keep themselves warm.
  You use **some** when you are thinking of a limited number or amount without actually specifying it:
  She quickly packed some clothes.

- **negatives**
  Any, not **some**, is used with negatives:
  We haven't got any (not *some*) *coffee in the house.*

- **questions**
  A general rule is that you use **any** rather than **some** in questions. But **some** can be used in questions expecting a *positive* answer, including polite offers, and is also possible after **if**:
  Would you like some more tea?
  Isn't there some cake left from yesterday?
  Contrast the last example with the following one, which asks an 'open' question:
  Have you read any good books lately?

- You can stress **some** to give it the meaning 'a considerable amount or number of', especially with 'time' words:
  We drove around for some time before finding a suitable hotel.
  He's going to be in hospital for some weeks yet.

- **Some** is often used in contrast to **other** or **all**, to refer to certain things or people out of the total number, or a certain proportion of something. **Some** is usually stressed in this sense:
  Some people never learn.
  Of course some children learn faster than others.

2 with singular countable nouns

Some is used with a singular countable noun to refer to a certain indefinite, or unspecified, person or thing:

I hope to see you some day soon.
They arranged to meet at some bar in Rome.

You can add **or other** to express a lack of interest in the person or thing referred to:

She's living with some boy or other in Birmingham.

3 You can use **some** before a *number* to make it sound approximate:

They held a dinner for some forty guests.
He was trapped some thirty metres below the ground.

AS A PRONOUN

1 You use **some of** before determiners like **the**, **these**, **that** and **those**, and pronouns:

Some of the new boys were homesick.
There's still some of that meat left.
Some of us thought he was right.

2 You can use **some** independently as a pronoun when it is clear what it is referring to:

If you want a biscuit there are some in that tin.
Some people like her and some don't.

•••• somebody, someone ••••

There is no difference in meaning between **somebody** and **someone**.

1 You use **somebody** and **someone** (there is no difference in meaning between the two) to refer to an unspecified person:

There's someone on the phone for you.
'Who was that?' 'Oh, just somebody I know.'

2 You do not use **somebody** and **someone** with negatives. You use **anyone** or **anybody**:

But I didn't give anybody (not *somebody*) *my address.*

3 You can, however, use **somebody** and **someone** in questions that expect a positive reply:

'Have you got anyone for that job, yet?' 'No, why? Have you thought of somebody?'

4 Adjectives that are used to qualify **somebody** and **someone** always follow them:

I met someone interesting at your wedding.

5 **Somebody** and **someone** are *singular*:

Someone has moved my glasses.

If you need to use a plural form, you say **some people**:

I have an enormous flat and I need some people to share it with me.

6 Although **someone** and **somebody** are singular, you can use the plural pronoun **they**, rather than **him or her** to refer back to them. In a question tag, **they** is the only possible form:

When someone insults you like that, you should try to ignore them.
Somebody's obviously made a mistake, haven't they?

➤ For more information see the entry **he, he or she, they.**

•••• someplace ••••

➤ See **place**.

•••• something ••••

1 **Something** refers to an unspecified thing or situation:
We'll have something to eat when we get home.
There was something I wanted to tell you.

2 You do not use **something** with negatives. You use **anything**:
She didn't say anything (not *something*) *for a minute or two.*

3 You can use **something** in questions that invite a *positive* reply:
Isn't there something we can do to help?

4 Adjectives that are used to qualify **something** always follow it:
You can't just sit there waiting for something exciting to happen.

•••• sometime, sometimes, some time ••••

SOMETIME

Sometime (/ˈsʌmtaɪm/) means 'at an unknown or indefinite time in the future', or more rarely, 'the past':
I'll tell you sometime when you aren't so busy.
I'm supposed to arrange a meeting with him sometime soon.
They started the building work sometime last July.

SOMETIMES

Sometimes (/ˈsʌmtaɪmz/) is an adverb of *frequency* and means 'occasionally':
'You never get headaches, do you?' 'Yes, I do sometimes.'
'Sometimes I hate you, Paula,' Sally said.

SOME TIME

Some time (/ˈsʌm ˈtaɪm/), spelt as two words, has an equal stress on both words and means 'quite a long time':
It took some time for him to relax in the water.

•••• somewhere ••••

1 **Somewhere** is used to refer to an unspecified place:
I realized I was somewhere near the town centre.
I think I should go and live somewhere else.

> ⓘ You use **anywhere** rather than **somewhere** with a negative:
> *I can't find my notes anywhere.*
> But you can use **somewhere** in questions, especially ones that invite or expect the answer 'yes':
> *Oh, you're all dressed up. Are you going out somewhere?*

ⓘ Although you do not use the prepositions **to** or **in** with **somewhere**, you can use **from**:
He could hear music coming from somewhere in the distance.

2 You can use **somewhere** rather like a noun, and you can use an adjective after it:
He told me he had to find somewhere new to live.

3 People often use **somewhere** in approximate expressions about amounts:
His age was somewhere between 45 and 55; it was difficult to tell.
So a woman of 5ft 5in. (1.65 m) should be somewhere around 8st 13lb. (56.7 kg.)

•••• soon ••••

1 You use **soon** in relation to now, or the time when you are speaking. Something that is going to happen **soon** is going to happen a short time from now:
Anyway, you'll be twenty-one soon.

You can use **soon** when talking about the past, to mean 'a short time after that':
He soon changed his mind.

ⓘ **Soon** is sometimes confused with **early** and **quickly**, but neither of these is linked to the present moment in the way that **soon** is:
I invited them for seven-thirty, but they came early [= before seven-thirty].
Lenny quickly [= in a short time] *learnt how to play the guitar.*

2 Like other time adverbs, **soon** can go at the beginning or end of the sentence, but it often takes 'mid position', before the verb, or after the first auxiliary verb (or the verb **be**):
Soon you'll be taller than me.
It'll be winter soon.
Things soon began to go wrong.
Shops will soon have to put their prices up again.

3 **Soon** is gradable: you can use **very** and **too** with **soon**, and it also has comparative and superlative forms, **sooner** and **soonest**:
I'll be seeing you very soon.
It is too soon to be very optimistic.
His train arrived sooner than expected.
The doctor could see you at 3.30; that's the soonest she can manage.

4 You use **how soon** to ask how long it will be before something happens:
How soon can we expect a decision?

5 You say that **no sooner** does one thing happen **than** another does, to emphasize that the second quickly follows the first. **No sooner** usually comes at the beginning of the sentence, followed by *auxiliary + subject*:
No sooner had the announcement been made than it was withdrawn.

➤ For the use of **as soon as** see the entry **as soon as**.

sorry

Sorry is an *adjective.*

You say **I'm sorry** or, more briefly, **sorry**.

CONSTRUCTIONS

Sorry can be followed by the following structures:

1 a **that-**clause, usually without **that**:
Sorry I forgot to tell you.
I'm sorry I'm a bit late.

2 a **to**-infinitive:
I'm very sorry to disappoint you.
Sorry not to have replied earlier.

3 an **if**-clause:
Sorry if I sounded rude.

4 the prepositions **for** or **about** + noun phrase or an **-ing** form:
I'm sorry for being so disorganized.
I'm awfully sorry about the terrible mess.
Sorry about getting so angry the other day.

➤ See also the entry **apologizing**.

EXPRESSING REGRET

You can use **sorry** to express regret about things you are not responsible for:
I was so sorry to hear about your grandmother's death.
Sorry you didn't get the job.
I'm sorry to tell you that your application has been unsuccessful.

sort

➤ See **kind**.

sound

1 **Sound** is used as a linking verb. You use it to talk about the impression you get from hearing something or someone, or from being told about them:
He didn't sound worried.
'I have to go and meet a journalist.' 'That sounds interesting.'
He sounds the type who is ambitious.

2 You can use **like** and **as if** or **as though** after **sound**, to make comparisons, or to talk about the impression something makes:
That sounds like the train coming now.
It sounds as if (or *as though*) *the party's started.*

3 You use the adjectival suffix **-sounding** after an adjective, to say what quality something gives the impression of having, from the way it sounds:
She wrote from the innocent-sounding address 'Old Church Farm'.
He had one of those odd-sounding first names.

•••• speak, talk ••••

Speak and **talk** have similar meanings, but they are used in different ways.

SPEAK

Speak means 'to say words':

He didn't speak all night.
Don't turn away before I've finished speaking!
The students need confidence in speaking and listening.

TALK

Talk refers to two-way communication – conversations and discussions:

How do you stop them from talking in class?
We always have to talk about his children.
Talk together about any problems as honestly as possible.

SPECIFIC USES

Speak is often used in the same way as **talk**, but is also used to refer to more formal or serious situations.

If you **speak to** someone, it is more likely that you have something specific and rather important to say to them; if you **talk to** them, you will probably have a less formal conversation or discussion:

I must speak to the students about keeping their rooms tidy.

1 lectures

You **talk** to a group of people about a subject when the atmosphere is informal and the subject is not academic or too technical; you **speak** about a subject in more formal and intellectual circumstances:

I've been invited to talk about my holiday in Moscow.
The Professor will speak about teaching English abroad.

2 languages

It is usual to use **speak** when referring to people's abilities with, and use of, different languages:

They were speaking in a foreign language.
Do you speak German?
I can speak a bit of Chinese.

3 on the telephone

When you ask for a particular person in a telephone conversation, you ask if you can **speak** to them:

Hello. Can I speak to Mike, please?

—— spelling ——

VERBS

1 In most cases, you can add -**ing** and -**ed** without changing the spelling of the first part of a verb:

walk	*walking*	*walked*
stay	*staying*	*stayed*

2 But if a verb consists of only one syllable, with a single short vowel, and ends in a consonant, you must double this final letter before adding **-ing** or **-ed**:

stop	*stopping*	*stopped*
grin	*grinning*	*grinned*
hum	*humming*	*hummed*

3 If a verb has two or more syllables, and the last one contains a single short vowel and ends in a consonant, double this final letter, but only if the stress comes on the last syllable:

pre'fer	*pre'ferring*	*pre'ferred*
ad'mit	*ad'mitting*	*ad'mitted*
e'quip	*e'quipping*	*e'quipped*

If the stress is not on the last syllable, the final letter is not doubled:

'enter	*'entering*	*'entered*
'gossip	*'gossiping*	*'gossiped*

4 If the last syllable of a verb has a short vowel and ends in **-l**, double the **l**, regardless of where the stress comes:

'equal	*'equalling*	*'equalled*
re'pel	*re'pelling*	*re'pelled*

5 If the verb ends in **-c**, add a **k** before adding **-ing** or **-ed**:

picnic	*picnicking*	*picnicked*
panic	*panicking*	*panicked*

6 If the verb ends in **-e**, remove the **-e** before adding **-ing**. Instead of adding **-ed**, just add **-d:**

stare	*staring*	*stared*
bake	*baking*	*baked*
issue	*issuing*	*issued*

7 But notice that verbs ending in **-oe**, **-ee** and **-ye** are exceptions to this rule:

agree	*agreeing*	*agreed*
dye	*dyeing*	*dyed*
hoe	*hoeing*	*hoed*
eye	*eyeing*	*eyed*

8 If the verb ends in **-y**, and there is no vowel before the **y**, change the **y** to **i** before adding **-es** or **-ed**:

cry	*crying*	*cries*	*cried*
hurry	*hurrying*	*hurries*	*hurried*

But if a verb has a vowel before the **y**, keep the **y** when you add **-s** and **-ed**:

stay	*staying*	*stays*	*stayed*
play	*playing*	*plays*	*played*

9 If the verb ends in **-ie**, you change **ie** to **y** before adding **-ing**:

tie	*tying*	*tied*
die	*dying*	*died*

10 If the verb ends in **-s**, **-x**, **-z**, **-ch** or **-sh**, add **-es** in the third person present tense, rather than just **-s**:

miss	*misses*

fix	*fixes*
buzz	*buzzes*
fetch	*fetches*
rush	*rushes*

ADVERBS

1 Most adverbs are formed by adding -**ly** to the adjective:

foolish	*foolishly*
strange	*strangely*
initial	*initially*

Note that adjectives ending in -**e** keep the **e** before adding -**ly**, but in the following four cases, it is removed:

true	*truly*
due	*duly*
whole	*wholly*
eerie	*eerily*

2 If an adjective ends in -**ic**, you add -**ally** to form the adverb:

basic	*basically*
economic	*economically*

An exception to this rule is:

public	*publicly*

3 If an adjective ends in -**y**, you change the **y** to -**i** before adding -**ly**:

happy	*happily*
hungry	*hungrily*

4 If an adjective ends in -**le**, you remove the -**e** and add -**y**:

simple	*simply*
double	*doubly*

5 Adjectives ending in a -**y** that is pronounced /ai/, often have two possible adverb forms:

dry	*drily* or *dryly*
sly	*slily* or *slyly*

IE OR EI?

A well-known and useful way of remembering this rule is the rhyme '**i** before **e**, except after **c**'. This means that the order is **ie** except when a **c** comes first – then the order is **ei**. Have a look at these words:

chief	*brief*	*conceit*
siege	*grief*	*deceive*
achieve	*thief*	*deceit*
belief	*ceiling*	*receive*
relieve	*conceive*	*receipt*

split infinitive

A **split infinitive** is a **to-**infinitive which has an adverb placed between **to** and the verb, *eg*:

*Finally, the patient is told **to gradually** open her eyes.*

Some people think that it is incorrect to split an infinitive in this way, and therefore try to avoid it.

USING SPLIT INFINITIVES

1 Sometimes, splitting an infinitive can make a sentence clearer:

Part of the job is to really get to know all the staff.

In the example sentence, **really** emphasizes the verb. Placed in any other part of the sentence, **really** would simply emphasize the speaker's opinion:

Part of the job is really to get to know all the staff.

2 In some cases, it is even necessary to split an infinitive. For example, the structure **more than** has to come immediately before the verb it refers to, and therefore must split the infinitive:

The management intends to more than double the workforce.

stand: can't stand

➤ See **like** (**verb**).

subjects

The subject of a clause or sentence is the word, or word group, representing a person or thing, that *performs* the action of an *active* verb. The subject is usually a noun or pronoun:

***The building** faces the sea.*
***We** are hoping for a quick answer.*

> ⓘ You do not repeat the subject by adding a pronoun after it:
> *My husband works terribly hard* (not *my husband he works terribly hard*).

➤ See the entries **concord**, **inverson** and **passives** for more information about subjects.

substitution

Substitution is using a simple all-purpose word instead of a longer, more specific, expression that has been used in the immediately previous context.

You substitute pronouns for nouns or noun phrases; you substitute the general action verb **do** for ordinary lexical verbs; and you can substitute **so** and **not** for whole clauses.

➤ See also **ellipsis**.

PRONOUNS

1 personal pronouns and possessives

You use personal pronouns and possessives to refer back to people or things mentioned in the preceding context:

*Is this the bottle? There's no label on **it**.*
*Betty's worried because **she**'s lost **her** watch, but **she** won't borrow **mine**.*

2 **one** and **ones**

The substitute pronoun **one** and its plural **ones** are very frequently used, often with determiners, in place of previously used countable nouns:

- **One** substitutes for a singular countable noun:

He asked me for my fax number, but I haven't got one.
There are two desks free: this one and the one in the art department.
You must look after this copy; it's the only one we've got.

> ⓘ Notice that you do not use **a** before **one** unless you add an adjective:
> *Is this one of your jokes?*
> *The old door had been replaced by a brand-new one.*

- **Ones** substitutes for plural nouns, including 'pair' words like **glasses** or **pants**:

The public hospitals are old but there are many new private ones.
'It's in the pocket of my trousers.' 'Which ones?'

➤ For detailed rules on the use of **one** and **ones** as substitute pronouns see the entry **one**.

3 **it, this, that**

All three of these pronouns refer back to a previously-mentioned circumstance that you are going to make a comment about:

She resigned later in the year. It came as no surprise.
Tell them you're pregnant; that'll surprise them.

'DO' AS A SUBSTITUTE VERB

1 **Do**, as a general action verb, is used as a substitute for a previously used verb (see also **do**):

I must ring Philippa. I'll do that [= ring Philippa] *first.*

2 **Do so** substitutes for a verb and whatever follows it:

Would any passengers who have not yet checked in, please do so now.

> ⓘ **Do** and the other auxiliary and modal auxiliary verbs can stand for a complete verb phrase:
> *I warned him he might get bored, and he **did**.*
> This is dealt with in the entry **ellipsis.**

'SO' AND 'NOT'

You can use **so** and **not** to stand for a whole clause:

'Are you going to the meeting tomorrow?' 'I expect so [= I expect I will be going].
'Are we in time?' 'I'm afraid not.'
Are you going into town? Because if so, I'll give you a lift.

➤ For more information see the entries **so** and **not**.

'THERE' AND 'THEN'

You use **there** as a substitute for a place that has been mentioned, and **then** as a substitute for a time that has been mentioned:

William's at the library. He works there.
'I'm having lunch at about one.' 'OK, see you then.'

•••• the subjunctive ••••

The **subjunctive** is a form of the verb which is used in a limited number of, usually formal, cases. Its form is the same as the base form of the verb. The use of the subjunctive is sometimes regarded as old-fashioned, but in certain situations it is fairly common.

THAT-CLAUSES

The subjunctive is commonly found in **that**-clauses, after main clauses in which the speaker is making a suggestion, giving advice, or saying that something is important or desirable:

*We recommend that he **be** promoted to head teacher.*
*We demand that this product **go** through proper testing procedures.*
*The adults insisted that she **not be** left behind.*

Many speakers still prefer to use the **should** + infinitive, or ordinary present and past tenses, instead of the subjunctive in this context:

The adults insisted that she should not be left behind.
We demand that this product goes through proper testing procedures.

➤ See entry for **should**.

IF-CLAUSES AND WISHES

Another type of subjunctive use is **were**. This form of the verb **be** is found in the **if** clauses and in wishes:

If I were you, I'd stop and go home now.
If he were a bit more friendly I'd like him better.
I wish I were taller.

Was is also possible in these conditional clauses.

FIXED PHRASES

There are certain fixed phrases in English where the subjunctive has remained. Some of the most common ones are listed below:

as it were [= 'in a sense'; used to show that you are speaking figuratively]
be that as it may [= whether that is true or not]
so be it [= We can't do anything to change it.]
Long live the Queen!
God save the Queen!

•••• subordinate clauses ••••

A **subordinate clause** is a clause which completes the information given in the main clause of a sentence. It cannot stand on its own, and is dependent on the main clause for meaning. Many subordinate clauses begin with a subordinating conjunction, such as **if**, **that** or **because**.

Subordinate clauses can be of three types; this entry looks mainly at different kinds of *adverbial* clauses.

➤ For information about *relative* clauses and **that**-clauses, see the entries **relative clauses** and **that**.

ADVERBIAL CLAUSES

Adverbial clauses tell you more about the action of the main clause, for instance, its time or place, or the reason for it. They are introduced by a 'subordinating' conjunction, such as **when, where** or **because**. They can come before or after the main clause.

There are several different types of adverbial clause. For a list of conjunctions that can be used with each type, see **conjunctions**:

1 **time clauses**:

*Wash your hands **before** you start doing that.*
***The moment** I saw him I knew there was something wrong.*

2 **place clauses**:

***Everywhere** we went, people stared.*
*I'm quite happy **where** I am, thank you.*

3 **manner clauses**:

*He treated me **as if** I was a child.*
*So she got up for work **the way** she always did.*

4 **reason clauses**:

*I can't go **because** my car won't start.*
***Considering** she doesn't speak French, she's doing very well.*

5 **concession clauses**:

*She never complained, **although** she was always in pain.*
***While** I see your point, I still don't agree.*

■ The subject of concession clauses with **although**, **though**, **while** and **whilst** is sometimes omitted when it is the same as the main subject. The following verb then becomes a participle:

***Whilst disagreeing** on many questions, we do agree on this.*

■ You can put a complement before **though** in formal contexts:
Clever though the invaders were, they still lost the final battle.

6 **purpose clauses**:

*Come here **so that** we can see you properly.*
*Pens were chained to the counter **so** they wouldn't be stolen.*
*In **order that** everyone gets a turn, we'll have to limit our time to five minutes each.*

If the subject of the main verb is the same as the subject of the subordinate clause, you can use a **to**-infinitive, by itself or after **in order** or **so as**, to express purpose:

*I went to the shop **to** get some milk.*
*You must register now **in order to** be sure of a place on the course.*
*I set off early **so as to** arrive in time for lunch.*

> ⓘ You cannot use **not** with a simple **to**-infinitive to express a negative purpose; you have to use **in order not to** and **so as not to**:
> *I opened the door quietly, **so as not to** (or **in order not to**) wake him.*
> An alternative is to use verbs like **avoid**, **prevent** and **stop**:
> *I opened the door quietly to avoid waking him.*
> *The pens were chained to the counter to prevent them from being stolen.*

7 **result clauses**:

*The workforce was cut **so that** people lost their jobs.*
*She landed badly **so that** she broke her ankle.*

8 **conditional clauses**:

***Unless** we talk to these people, we'll never find a solution.*
***If** you see her, could you tell her I called?*
*I don't mind if you stay out late, **as long as** you ring me.*
***Provided** it doesn't rain, we can have the party outside.*

> ⓘ In formal and literary styles, the conditional conjunction **if** can be dropped, and an auxiliary verb put before the subject. This most commonly happens with **were**, **had** (auxiliary) and **should**:
> ***Had I** known I would have come earlier.*
> ***Should there** be any problem, please do not hesitate to call again.*
> ***Were I** in your position I would probably resign.*

TENSES

Tenses are often simplified in subordinate clauses, because if the main clause makes it clear what time is being talked about, it may not be necessary to repeat it.

1 **present instead of future**

Present tenses are commonly found instead of future forms after conjunctions of time:

We'll stay here till the sun goes down.
Will you ring me before you leave?
I'm going to leave as soon as I get my certificate.

- When there is an idea of completion, the present perfect may be used instead of the simple present:

  We'll stay until we've finished.

- This kind of simplification also takes place in the **if**-clause of conditional sentences relating to the future:

  Will you tell me if you decide to go?
  If it rains we'll play cards indoors.
  I'm not sure what she'll do.

2 **past instead of conditional**

In the same way that **will** does not appear in the **if**-clause of conditional sentences relating to the future, **would** does not appear in **if**-clauses expressing unreal conditions. Instead, past forms are used:

*If we **had** some tools, this would be a lot easier.*

*If I'**d known** [= had known], I would have stayed in.*

3 simple forms instead of perfect

Simple forms are often found in subordinate clauses in the place of more complex perfect forms:

*She had been taken ill while she **was** travelling home.*
*She'd been learning the language while she **was** abroad.*

• • • • such • • • •

REFERRING TO SOMETHING JUST MENTIONED

1 **Such** is used to refer to the kind of thing or person that has just been mentioned. Notice that you put **such** before **a** or **an** when using it with a singular countable noun:

I'm not mad! I don't know how you can say such things.
There's no excuse for such behaviour.
You can't argue with such a person.

2 You can use determiners like **all**, **any**, **no**, **many**, **few**, **other** and **some** before **such**:

All such incidents should be reported at once.
I didn't mean that. I said no such thing.
You don't get many such opportunities.

ⓘ Notice that you do not use **such** when you are indicating things around you in your immediate environment. You use **like this** or **that**, or **like these** or **those**, or you can use **this** or **that sort of** or **kind of**:

You're lucky to live in a house like this (not *such a house*).
Clouds like those (not *such clouds) usually mean rain.*
That kind of hat (not *such a hat) is just what you need on a day like this* (not *such a day*).

EMPHASIS

1 with adjectives

Such can be used to emphasize adjectives. When **such** is used before an *adjective* + *noun* the order is:

- **such** + adjective + plural noun or uncountable noun:

such warm evenings
such lovely weather

- **such** + **a** + adjective + singular countable noun:

such a beautiful day

2 with nouns

Such can also intensify nouns:

such a nuisance
such idiots
such luxury

3 when to use 'such' for emphasis

You use **such** for emphasis in two slightly different ways:

- **Such** can refer to a situation that is known about from what has just been said, or is obvious. This is how it is used, for example, in questions and negative sentences, after **if**, and in report clauses:

  How can you believe such obvious lies?
  I'd never been in such terrible danger before.
  No-one will feel sorry for you if you make such a fuss.
  I'm glad you had such an enjoyable evening.

- **Such a** can also be used informally as an emphasizer, rather like **really** with adjectives, or **real** with nouns:

  It's such a [= a real] *pleasure to see you.*
  We've had such [= really] *terrible winds recently.*

4 'such' followed by a result clause

Such can be followed by a clause of result introduced by **that**:

It was such a warm night that we were able to sleep outside.

> ⓘ **a reminder about 'so' and 'such'**
> You use **such** with *nouns*, whether or not they are used with adjectives:
> *You've got such* (not *so*) *lovely hair.*
> *He's such a sweet person.*
> *I've never heard such nonsense before.*

You use **so** with adjectives that are not followed by nouns, and before adverbs:

You've been so kind.
She walked so quickly that I couldn't keep up.

FURTHER USES

1 Not such a is used to mean 'not very':

Maybe it's not such a brilliant idea after all.

2 Such and **such a … as** are used in negative comparisons:

It isn't quite such a problem as I thought it'd be.
Last year was great, but we didn't have such good weather this year.

3 Such as introduces examples:

a profession such as architecture or engineering
such problems as poor housing and unemployment

suggestions

➤ See pages 524 and 525.

superlatives

➤ See **comparatives and superlatives**.

SUGGESTIONS

This section deals with two main types of suggestion: when you want to advise someone what to do, and when you want to know if someone would like to do something with you, such as go for a walk, for example.

SUGGESTING A COURSE OF ACTION

One of the commonest ways of suggesting a course of action is to say **You could ...**. A little more informally, you can say **How** (or **what**) **about -ing?**, or **How** (or **what**) **about** + noun**? Another typical, and fairly informal way of suggestiong is Have you thought of -ing?** or **Why don't you ...?**:

'You could ask the doctor,' suggested George.
How about ringing the library? They might have it.
What about a smaller car than this?
Have you thought of getting her a CD?
Why don't you go by plane?

1 firm suggestions

If you want a suggestion to sound stronger or more direct, either because you feel strongly about what the person should do, or because you know the person well, you can say **Couldn't you ...?**, **Can't you ...?**, **Why not ...?** or **Try -ing**:

Couldn't you just get up a bit earlier?
Can't you go by bike?
So why not have another glass of champagne?
Try putting an ad in a local paper.

2 unenthusiastic suggestions

If you do not feel very strongly about an idea, but you suggest it anyway, you can use **You may** (or **might**) **as well ...**, or **I suppose you could ...**:

Well, you may as well come in now you're here.
I suppose you could ring the Editor's secretary and check.

3 formal and polite suggestions

In written English, and in formal situations where people give advice, such as on the TV or radio, or in lectures, common ways of making suggestions are **You might consider ... -ing**, **You might like** (or **want**) **to ...**, **It might be a good idea to ...** or, most formally of all, **Might I suggest ...?** and **I suggest ...**, both followed by a **that-**clause (from which **that** is sometimes omitted):

You might consider changing the name of the shop.
It might be a good idea to keep a bucket of water by the fire.
I suggest you use this version because it's clearer.

SUGGESTING DOING SOMETHING TOGETHER

If you know the person you are speaking to fairly well, you can suggest doing something together in a confident and informal manner, using **Let's ...**, **How** (or **what**) **about ... -ing?**, **Shall we ...?** or, more formally, **I suggest we ...**:

Come on, let's go then, shall we?
How about going for a swim?
Shall we go and see Tom?
OK, I suggest we take a five minute break.

1 tentative suggestions

If you do not know the person you are speaking to very well, or you are not completely sure about the idea you are suggesting, you can say **We could ...**, **I thought we might ...** or **I wonder whether we could ...**:

We could try asking her again – it might work.
I thought we might perhaps have lunch together.
I wonder if we could perhaps meet to talk about this.

2 unenthusiastic suggestions

If you do not feel very strongly about the idea you are suggesting, or if you feel unenthusiastic about it, you can say **We might as well ...**:

I think we might as well start.

SUGGESTIONS ABOUT THE BEST COURSE OF ACTION

If you want to say what you think would be best, you can say **We** (or **you**) **ought to ...**, **We'd better ...**, **I think we** (or **you**) **should ...**, **Shouldn't we** (or **you**) **...? I suppose we'd better ...**, or **Don't you think we'd better ...?**:

We ought to see if we can do it better in future.
We'd better be getting back.
I think we should have dinner together and talk.
Shouldn't you get something a bit cheaper?

> ⓘ The **'d** in the expression **We'd better...** stands for **had**.
> Notice that **You'd better...** is used as a criticism or reproach, rather than a suggestion.

RESPONDING TO SUGGESTIONS

1 agreeing

You can agree to a suggestion by saying **Okay**, **All right**, **Why not?**, or **That's a good idea**:

'Let's have some lunch.' 'Okay.'
I think you should stop now.' 'All right.' '
How about going for a Mexican?' 'Why not?'
'Have you thought of taking a break?' 'That's a good idea.'

2 agreeing reluctantly

If you do not feel very enthusiastic about someone's suggestion, but you do not want to be too negative about it, you can say **I suppose I could**:

'You could take up rock-climbing too.' 'Yeah, I suppose I could.'

3 disagreeing or responding negatively

If you do not want to do what someone suggests, you can say **I don't think that's a very good idea**, or **Yes, but...** and then give an explanation of why you do not want to do the thing they suggest:

'Let's ring them now' 'I don't think that's a very good idea. It's very late.'
'You could get a car.' 'Yes, but I can't afford one.'

•••• suppose ••••

This section deals with the different meanings and uses of the verb **suppose**.

You say that you **suppose** that something is so if you think it is likely to be so:

I suppose they're all the same underneath.
The car keys? I suppose they're in my coat pocket.

OTHER STRUCTURES WITH SUPPOSE

1 You say that you **don't suppose** that something is the case when you think it is unlikely. You can also use **I don't suppose...** as a way of introducing a tentative suggestion or request:

I don't suppose we'll be there before 5 p.m.
I don't suppose you could help me, could you?

2 You say **I suppose not** as a way of agreeing with a negative statement or a question:

'Does it make a difference?' 'I suppose not.'
'You don't seem very worried.' 'I suppose not.'

3 You say **I suppose so** as a way of agreeing, often reluctantly, with a positive statement, or when giving a positive, but reluctant, answer to a question:

'Shall we go home?' 'I suppose so.'
'I expect they'll tell you what to do.' 'I suppose so.'

AS A CONJUNCTION

Suppose is also a conjunction. You say **'Suppose... ?** or **Supposing...** a certain thing is the case', to mean the same as **What if... ?** when you are wondering what effect it would have. People often use this structure as way of making suggestions:

Suppose we do what he says, what happens then?
And supposing he comes back? Then what do we do?
Supposing I give you some money; would that help?

> ⓘ **Suppose...** and **Supposing...**, when followed by a verb in the past perfect, are used to speculate about things that might have happened, but didn't:
> *That was a silly thing to do. Supposing he had heard you phoning the police?*

BE SUPPOSED TO

1 Someone or something that **is supposed to** be or do something is:

- intended to be that thing or to do that thing:

  What's that picture supposed to be?
  'The colours don't match.' 'They're not supposed to.'

- expected to be or do that thing, according to some rule or arrangement:

  You're supposed to talk quietly in here.
  Aren't we supposed to be in the gym?

- believed or reported to be or to do that thing:

  This shampoo is supposed to cure dandruff.
  Have you been there yet? It's supposed to be quite nice.

2 If you **are not supposed to** do something, you are not allowed to do it:

You're not supposed to come up here.
You're not supposed to speak with your mouth full.

3 **Supposed to ...** is often used to contrast between what happens and what is actually the case:
Amanda was supposed to be looking after the baby [= she wasn't].
He was supposed to be at the church by ten. [= he wasn't]

.... sure ....

➤ See **certain**.

.... surely ....

You use **surely** differently from **certainly** and **definitely**. You use **certainly** and **definitely** to emphasize statements:
Now is certainly the time for change.
She definitely said she was getting the five-forty train.

1 You use **surely** to appeal for agreement or confirmation, especially when your opinion is being challenged, or when you are challenging someone else's opinion. Sentences with **surely** are usually questions, and **surely** often comes at the beginning, but it can also come in 'mid position':
Surely you remember her?
You surely remember that occasion?

2 **Surely** sometimes expresses desperation:
Surely there's someone around who knows what happening?

3 People use **surely not** when they can hardly believe something:
Margot Iverson died in the night.' 'No! Surely not!' exclaimed Tom.
Surely you're not frightened of me?

.... sympathetic ....

Although the word **sympathetic** may look like similar words in other European languages, in English it is used to describe someone who easily understands how other people think or feel about things.

You are **sympathetic** to someone when you understand their feelings of sadness or distress and try to help them by doing or saying kind or comforting things:
I tried to be sympathetic when they fell in the water but it was difficult not to laugh.
Thank you for being so sympathetic – I feel much better now I've told someone.

Tt

taste

1 **linking verb**:

You use **taste** as a linking verb to describe something when you eat it or drink it. Various constructions are possible:

- **taste + adjective:**

  This wine tastes funny.
  The fish looked and tasted quite delicious.

- **taste + of + noun:**

  The tea is awful. It tastes of disinfectant.
  Wine doesn't actually taste of grapes.

- **taste + like, as if** or **as though**:

  You use **taste like**, **taste as if**, and **taste as though** to make comparisons, or when describing tastes:

  Gently cooked, this vegetable tastes rather like spinach.
  The coffee tasted as if it had been boiled.

2 You **taste** something when you are able to detect it with your tongue in what you are eating or drinking. Notice that like other sensing verbs, **taste** is often used with **can** and **could**:

I think you can taste the heather in this honey.
I stood by the sea and could taste the salt on my lips.

3 You **taste** something when you eat or drink a small amount, *eg* to find out what it is, or whether the flavour is right. Progressive forms are possible:

Here, taste this. Is it sweet enough?
I'm just tasting the cream to make sure it hasn't turned.

-tasting

You can add **-tasting** after an adjective to form a compound adjective describing the taste of something:

We had some of that sweet-tasting Norwegian cheese.

telephoning

➤ See pages 530 and 531.

telling the time

➤ See page 547.

tense

A verb tense is a particular form of a verb that shows at what time, past, present or future, the action of the verb takes place. English has only two basic tenses. These two tenses are the **present tense** *eg talk, talks; go, goes; come, comes; am, is, are; have, has; run, runs*; and the **past tense** *eg talked; went; came; was, were; had; ran.*

Even though there are, strictly speaking, only two main English tenses, various combinations of these two tenses with the various forms of the auxiliary verbs **be** and **have** can also be broadly defined as tenses. These combinations are known as compound tenses. References to future time are also possible in English using compound tenses, or using **will** or **shall** + the base form of a main verb.

SIMPLE PRESENT TENSE

The table below shows the forms of the simple present tense using the verb **make**:

	singular	**plural**
first person	I make	we make
second person	you make	you make
third person	he, she, it makes	they make

The simple present tense is used in:

1 statements about timeless truths or facts:
*The moon **orbits** the earth.*
*Hot air **rises**.*

2 statements about habitual actions, or actions or events that occur repeatedly over a period of time:
*I **catch** the bus at 7.30am.*
*My son **phones** me every Sunday.*

3 statements about permanent or unchanging actions or situations:
*He **farms** three hundred acres.*
*Do you **take** sugar in your tea?*

4 expressions of opinion or attitude, observations and declarations:
*I **like** your tie. Is it silk?*
*Harriet **hates** waiting.*
*I **hope** you're mistaken.*

5 when giving instructions:
*To open a bottle of champagne, first **take** the wire off the cork, then **put** a cloth over the top of the bottle, **grip** the cork firmly, and **turn** and **pull** it slowly and carefully upwards.*

6 with adverbials of time to refer to future scheduled events:
*Our plane **leaves** at six in the morning.*
*The film festival **starts** next week.*

7 to convey a sense of immediacy, *eg* in sports commentaries:
*Gascoigne's got the ball. He **shoots**. Yes, he **scores**. A brilliant goal!*

TELEPHONING

ANSWERING THE PHONE

When you answer a private phone, you usually either say **Hello?** or you give the number of the phone you are answering. Some people just give their name:

Hello?
Six five seven, six seven double oh?

> ⓘ Notice that when you give you telephone number, you give each figure separately. Speakers of BrE usually say **oh** for **zero**. When two figures are the same and next to each other, you say **double**:
> *six double oh three* [= 6003]

If you are answering the phone for a company, you usually say the name of the company, possibly followed by **Good morning** or **Good afternoon** and your own name, and maybe **Can I help you?**:

Shanghai Bank, good afternoon. Lynda Smith speaking. Can I help you?

1 finding out who is calling

If the caller wants to speak to you, and you don't know who it is, you can say **Sorry, who is this?** If you want to know the name of a caller who wants to speak to someone else, you can ask **Who's calling, please?**:

'Hello?' 'Hello. How are you?' 'Sorry, who's this?'
'Hello. Can I speak to Hannah, please?' 'Sure, who's calling, please?'

2 passing the call to someone else

If the person who has called would like to speak to someone else in the building, you can say **I'll just get him** (or **her**) if you are using a private phone, or **Hold on please, I'll put you through**, if you are answering the phone for a company:

'Hello. Could I speak to Francis, please?' 'Yes, I'll just get him for you.'
'I'd like to speak to Neville Ashe in Marketing, please.' 'Hold on please, I'll just put you through.'

3 asking people to wait

Below are several ways of asking people to wait while you find, or put them through to, the person they want to speak to:

Could you hold on, please?
Could you hold the line, please?
Hang on. (very informal)

4 when the person is not available

If a person is not available to speak on the phone, it is usual to ask the caller to **call back later** or to offer to **take a message**:

I'm sorry, he's busy just now. Could you call back in an hour?
I'm afraid she's not here/at lunch/in a meeting at the moment. Can I take a message or would you like to phone back later?

MAKING A CALL

1 When you make a telephone call and you are sure that the person answering the phone knows you, you can say **Hello, it's ...** (**here**). If they do not know you, you can introduce yourself by saying **Hello, this is ...** or **my name is ...** :

'Hello, it's Ginny here.'
'Hello. This is Deidre Fairweather. I'm calling about my reservation.'

2 When you are making a phone call to get some public information, you do not need to give your name at all:

'Hello. Could you tell me the time of the first train to Glasgow, please?'

3 If you are not sure that you recognize the voice of the person who has answered the phone, you can ask **Is that ...?** or say **Sorry. Who's that?**:

'Hello?' 'Hi. Is that Nina?'

4 asking to speak to someone

When you are calling someone specific, you say **Can I speak to ..., please?** or more formally **Could I speak to ... ?** or **I'd like to speak to ...** :

Hi. Can I speak to Cathy, please?
Good afternoon. I'd like to speak to Nick Rodgers, please.

ⓘ If you have asked to speak to the person who is already speaking to you, they will say **Speaking**:
'Hello.' 'Oh hello. I'd like to speak to Jim Owens, please.' 'Speaking.'

5 leaving a message

When the person you want to speak to is not available, you can ask the person who answered the phone to **take a message**:

Would you take a message, please? Could you tell her Julie called?
Can I leave a message?
Could you ask him to call me back, please?

6 ending a call

At the end of a personal call, people might say **Bye for now** or **Speak to you soon**. The person who received the call can say **Thanks for ringing**, or, in more formal situations, **Thank you for calling**. The person who made the call can say **Thank you for your help** if this is appropriate.

POSSIBLE PROBLEMS

1 wrong numbers:

Sorry, I think I've got the wrong number. (caller)
I think you've got the wrong number. (receiver of call)

2 difficulties hearing people:

Can you speak up a bit please?
This is a really bad line. I'll hang up and call you again.

3 spelling:

Is that 'S' for Susan or 'F' for Frederick?

8 in headlines in newspapers and headline captions in television news programmes to refer to events in the very recent past:

*Farmers **march** through London.*
*Brit **wins** Wimbledon.*

➤ For more on the simple present tense see the entry **the present**.

SIMPLE PAST TENSE

The forms of the simple past tense using the verb **make** are:

	singular	**plural**
first person	I made	we made
second person	you made	you made
third person	he, she, it made	they made

The simple past tense is used generally for references to past time. Specific uses of the simple past are:

1 when referring to particular actions that were performed in the past:
*They **mowed** the lawn and **tidied** the borders.*

2 when referring to past actions that were completed at a particular time in the past:
*He **moved** to Australia last year.*
*Years ago, I **broke** my ankle playing hockey.*

3 when referring to actions or events that occurred as a matter of habit or routine in the past
*He never **played** football as a boy.*
*They always **had** roast beef on Sundays.*

4 when referring to the point where the main action being described was interrupted:
*She was laying the table when the doorbell **rang**.*

5 when referring to an action that goes on at the same time as another:
*He was whistling cheerfully as he **mowed** the lawn.*
*Janine dusted while I **washed** the floor.*

6 as a 'distancing' device, with verbs of thinking or wondering to express one's attitude or to make polite or tentative requests:
*I just **thought** you might need a break.*
***Did** you **want** to try one of our new products?*

➤ For more on the simple past tense see the entry **the past**.

COMPOUND TENSES

There are six compound tenses. These are aspects of the simple present and the simple past tense rather than true tenses referring to actual time.

1 The **present perfect** is formed from the present tense of the auxiliary **have** + the **-ed** form (past participle) of a main verb. The present perfect is used to refer to a situation or an action that began at some time in the past, and was completed in the recent past, or the result of which continues to be relevant (from the point of view of the speaker or writer):
*He **has gone** home.*
***Have** you **eaten**?*
*He **hasn't eaten** today.*

➤ For more on the present perfect see the entry **the past**.

2 The **past perfect** is formed from the past tense of the auxiliary **have** + the **-ed** form (past participle) of a main verb. The past perfect is used to refer a situation or an action that happened or began at some point and was already completed at the point in the past being referred to by the speaker or writer:

*He **had gone** home by the time I arrived at the office.*
*I felt ill. I **had eaten** far too much.*

➤ For more on the past perfect see the entry **the past**.

3 The **present progressive** (or **continuous**) is formed from the present tense of the auxiliary verb **be** + **-ing** form (the present participle) of the main verb. It is used to refer to something that is in progress now from the point of view of the speaker or writer:

*'What **are** you **doing**?' 'I'm **planting** trees.'*
*He **is** always **making** mistakes like that.*

➤ For more on the present progressive see the entry **the present**.

4 The **past progressive** (or **continuous**) is formed from the past tense of the auxiliary verb **be** + **-ing** form (the present participle) of the main verb. It is used to refer to something that was in progress at some time in the past from the point of view of the speaker or writer:

*'What **were** you **doing** when you cut yourself?' 'I **was chopping** vegetables.'*
*He **was putting** the car in the garage when I arrived.*

➤ For more on the past progressive see the entry **the past**.

5 The **present perfect progressive** is formed from the present tense of the auxiliary **have** + **been** + the **-ing** form (present participle) of a main verb. It is used to refer to actions or situations that began in the past and are still continuing in the present from the point of view of the speaker or writer:

***Have** you **been waiting** long?*
*We **have been sitting** here for more than two hours.*

➤ For more on the present perfect progressive see the entry **the past**.

6 The **past perfect progressive** is formed from the past tense of the auxiliary **have** + **been** + the **-ing** form (present participle) of a main verb. It is used to refer to actions or situations that began at one point in the past, went on for some time, and were already completed before the point on the past being referred to:

*I **had been working** round the clock for days.*
*He asked if we **had been waiting** for a long time.*

➤ For more on the past perfect progressive see the entry **the past**.

FUTURE TIME

There are several ways in which future time is indicated in English.

1 Future time is commonly expressed using the modal verbs **will** or **shall** (or their contracted forms or negative contracted forms) and the base form of a main verb:

*She **will ring** you back tomorrow.*
*I'**ll give** him your message when I see him later.*
*They've gone and they **won't be** here tomorrow.*
*I **shan't use** that shampoo again.*

2 The present progressive form of the verb **go** (**is going/are going**) + the

to-infinitive of a main verb is another common way of referring to future time especially when something has been decided and the intention is to carry it out, or when predicting what will happen:

*At the moment he says he**'s going to study** architecture, but he might change his mind.*
*There **are going to be** some pretty radical changes in the very near future.*

3 The present progressive form of certain main verbs can be used to refer to planned activities or events:

*He**'s making** a big speech on Friday.*
***Are** you **having** your baby at home or in hospital?*

4 As was mentioned earlier, the simple present tense is used with a future meaning when talking about future scheduled events:

*Kirsty **moves** into her new flat in December.*
*Hurry up. Our plane **leaves** in twenty minutes.*

5 The present progressive form is also used to talk about future scheduled events:

*Kirsty **is moving** into her new flat in December.*
*Hurry up. Our plane **is leaving** in twenty minutes.*

6 The future progressive is formed with the modal verb **will** + auxiliary **be** + the present participle of a main verb, and is used to refer to something that will, or is likely to, happen at some indefinite time in the future:

*I**'ll be moving** into my new flat sometime soon.*
*He**'ll be telling** me how to do my job next, I expect.*

7 The auxiliary **be** + **to-**infinitive of a main verb is used in formal English to refer to something that has been arranged or planned for some time in the future. This usage often has the implication of compulsion or obligation and can be used for giving instructions in a firm manner:

*He **is to appear** at the Crown Court on April 5th at 10 a.m.*
*You **are to let** him know that this is his last warning.*

8 The future perfect formed from the auxiliaries **will** and **have** + the **-ed** (past participle) form of a main verb is used to talk about actions that will be completed at a time in the future that is being referred to:

*Let's have a party next week. We **will have finished** the decorating by then.*
*She **will have prepared** a big meal as usual.*

➤ For more on the future see the entry **the future: ways of expressing it**.

•••• than ••••

Than is used with comparative adjectives and adverbs:

Your name's longer than mine.
She managed more successfully than I did.

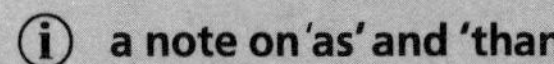

> ⓘ **a note on 'as' and 'than'**
> You use a comparative followed by **than** to express the idea of *difference* or *inequality* between things. **As** is sometimes confused with **than**. But the expressions **as ... as** and **the same ... as** are used in comparisons of *equality*, and you do not use comparatives with them. Compare the following examples:
> *I'm heavier than you are.*
> *You're not as heavy as I am.*
> *Are you the same weight as me?*

> ⓘ Notice also that you don't use **that** with comparatives:
> *I suppose she has more time than* (not *that*) *I have.*

POSSIBLE CONSTRUCTIONS

Than can be followed by various grammatical forms:

1 **Than** can be a *preposition*, so can be followed by:

- a noun or noun phrase:
  The brown suit was more expensive than the black one.
  Faisal was nicer than Gamal.
- an **-ing** form:
  Preventing disease is easier than curing it.
- a pronoun:
  Can't we think of something more original than that?
  Their house is bigger than ours.
  You're more sensible than me.

> ⓘ Personal pronouns are used in the objective case (*me*, *him*, *us*, and so on). Personal pronouns used by themselves in the subjective case (*I*, *he*, *they*, and so on) after **than** sound very formal. They are usually followed by an auxiliary verb, or **be**:
> *They had suffered a good deal more than us* (or *than we had,* but not *than we*).

2 **Than** can be a *conjunction*, and can be followed by:

- a full clause with subject and object:
  They know more about it than I did at their age.
  You can put a clause beginning with **if** or **when** after **than**:
  Use the train; you'll get there quicker than if you go by bus.
  I earn less now than when I was twenty.
- a prepositional phrase, past participle, adjective, or adverb, standing for a whole clause:
  Sales are better than in any previous year. [= than they have been in any previous year]

They deliberately keep you waiting longer than necessary.
Profits were lower than expected.

ⓘ Notice that non-assertive words such as **any** and **ever**, the kind of words you use after a negative, are used after **than**:
The puppy was better than any present she had ever had before.

MORE THAN, LESS THAN

More than and **less than** are used with numbers or amounts to mean 'over' or 'under' a certain amount:

More than a thousand delegates attended.
The work should have taken less than three months.

➤ For constructions with **rather than** see **rather**.

➤ For **no sooner than** see **soon**.

➤ For the use **different than** see **different**.

•••• thankful, grateful ••••

1 You use the word **grateful** to describe the way you feel when you want to thank someone for doing something for you:

I'm really grateful for all your hard work.
I'm grateful to Mr Johnson for the advice he gave me.

This is a polite and formal way of thanking someone.

ⓘ Notice that you say you are **grateful to** someone **for** something.

2 You use the word **thankful** to describe the relief someone feels after having avoided or survived an accident, or some other unpleasant experience:

She was thankful when the session was over and she could go home.
We watched the building burn, thankful that we were all safe.

—— thanks ——

➤ See pages 538 and 539.

•••• that ••••

That has two main uses:

It is used as a *demonstrative determiner* and *pronoun*, and is the opposite of **this**. Its plural is **those**.

➤ For the use of **that** as a demonstrative see the entry **this, that, these** and **those**.

That is also used as a connecting word between main and subordinate clauses. It acts as a *relative pronoun*, introducing relative clauses, and it acts as a *conjunction* introducing indirect speech, usually after a reporting verb; it also has other uses as a conjunction. These uses of **that**, as a relative pronoun and conjunction, are dealt with in this entry.

That has two pronunciations. As a demonstrative it is pronounced /ðat/, and as a relative pronoun and conjunction it is pronounced /ðət/.

AS A RELATIVE PRONOUN

1 In *defining* relative clauses, **that** can be used in place of **which**, **who** and **whom**:

We had a call from the lady that (or *who*) *lives across the road.*
I must find someone that (or *who* or *whom*) *I can rely on.*
I prefer the blackcurrant jam that my aunt makes.
This is the best method that I know of.

> ⓘ **That** can be omitted when it is the object of the verb or a preposition:
> *I prefer the jam my aunt makes.*
> *She's someone I can rely on.*

➤ For more information see **relative clauses**.

2 **That** is used to introduce the relative clause that follows **it is** or **it was**, when you use **it is** or **it was** to highlight, and comment on, some aspect of a situation:

It's the waste that horrifies me.

➤ For more information see the section FOR EMPHASIS at the entry for **it**.

AS A CONJUNCTION

Clauses introduced by **that** are mainly clauses containing reported speech or thought. **That** can be used in this way after some verbs, adjectives and nouns, and after certain other structures. **That** can be omitted after certain verbs, adjectives or nouns. Where **that** may be omitted in the examples below, brackets have been used around it:

1 **after verbs**:

She told me (*that*) *she didn't want a baby just yet.*
I've warned them (*that*) *I'll be late.*
I know (*that*) *there's something seriously wrong.*
I hope (*that*) *I can help you.*
He suggested that I should contact you.

➤ For more information see **reporting**.

2 **after adjectives**:

- *I'm disappointed* (*that*) *you can't come.*
  I'm afraid (*that*) *our decision is final.*
  I'm amazed (*that*) *it works.*
  I'm sorry (*that*) *you're still ill.*
- The adjective may follow **it is** or **it was**:
  It's vital that help reaches them immediately.

3 **after nouns**:

- *There's no doubt that she's losing her memory.*
  What gave you the idea (*that*) *I was a feminist?*
- The noun may follow **it is** or **it was**:
  It's a pity (*that*) *you don't agree.*

4 **following other structures**

THANKS

You thank someone to show that you are grateful to them for doing something for you or giving you something. You say **Thank you** or, more informally, **Thanks**.

You use the preposition **for** when you want to say why you are thanking someone:

Thank you for bringing this to our attention, Miss Connor.
Thank you for your support.
Thanks for all you've done.

EMPHASIS

1 You can emphasize your thanks by adding **very much**, or **very much indeed**; to **thanks**, you can also add **a lot**:

Thanks very much.
Thank you very much indeed.
Thanks a lot.

ⓘ Notice that you cannot say **Thank you a lot**.

2 Other emphatic ways of thanking people are **That's very kind of you**, **That's very good of you**, **That's wonderful** and **Great**:

You've been to a lot of trouble over this; thank you. It's very kind of you.
Can I give it back to you on Thursday? Yeah? That's wonderful. Thanks.

FORMAL THANKS

In formal situations, you use **I want ...** or **I'd like ...** with the verb **thank**:

I'd like to thank you for being so understanding.
First of all I want to thank John for all his help.

THANKING PEOPLE FOR DIFFERENT THINGS

1 an offer

If someone offers you something, such as a cup of coffee, you can accept by saying **Thank you** or **Thanks** or **Yes, please**. If you do not want what is offered to you, you should say **No, thank you** or **No, thanks**:

'A biscuit?' 'Oh. Thank you.'
'Another cup?' 'Erm. No thanks.'
'Would you like one of these?' 'Oh, yes, please!'

... that continued

- A **that**-clause can be a complement after **be**:

  The stupid thing was that nobody warned me.

- A **that**-clause as the subject of a sentence is formal and unusual, but can be used for emphatic effect:

  That such creatures existed at all is amazing.

2 a present

Thank you or **thanks** is not usually enough when you are receiving a present from someone. People usually add some other comment like **It's lovely. That's really kind of you**:

Oh, thank you. They're lovely. What a beautiful colour.
Thank you very much. I've always wanted one of these.

3 an enquiry

If someone asks how you are, or how your holiday or weekend was, you answer them, and add **... thanks** or **... thank you**:

'How are you?' 'Fine, thanks.'
'Nice holiday?' 'Oh, great, thanks.'

REPLYING TO THANKS

1 It is not normal to reply when someone thanks you for a small service, such as passing the salt.

If someone thanks you for helping them, you say **That's all right** or **That's OK**:

'Thanks for organizing the lunch, Catherine.' 'That's okay.'
'Thank you for your help.' 'That's all right.'

2 A very polite and friendly way of replying to someone's thanks is to say **It's a pleasure**:

'It's very kind of you to invite us.' 'Oh, it's a pleasure.'

3 If someone thanks you very emphatically, you can say **No trouble**, **It's nothing** or **Not at all**:

'Thank you so much for doing that.' 'No trouble.'
'We really appreciate the care you've taken to get every detail right.' 'Not at all, sir.'

4 If you thank someone for their help at the end of a business phone call, they often say **You're welcome**:

'Right. Thank you for your help.' 'You're welcome. Goodbye.' 'Goodbye.'

ⓘ **You're welcome** is very common as a reply to all kinds of thanks in AmE. In BrE, it is treated more as a polite formula, as in the example above.

... that continued

- Using **it** as a subject is more frequent:

It's surprising that they didn't know.

- **The fact that** is used after prepositions, and after verbs that can't take **that**-clauses:

I was referring to the fact that the sun is shining.

5 **introducing a clause after 'it is' or 'it was', to highlight a point**:

It was much later that he took up golf.

➢ See also the entry **it**.

6 **introducing clauses of result after 'so'**:

- *She spoke so fast that I couldn't understand her.*
- Notice that **that** can be omitted:

It was so cold the water froze in the pipes.

➢ For more information see **so**.

7 **'so that' introducing clauses of purpose**

We should get there early, so that we can welcome the guests as they arrive.

➢ For more information see **so**.

•••• the ••••

There are two pronunciations for **the**. You say /ðə/ before a consonant, and /ðɪ/ before a vowel, *eg*:

the doctor /ðə 'dɒktə/
the office /ðɪ 'ɒfɪs/

This entry sums up the uses of the definite article **the** and mentions some special uses. For more information about **the**, and about the use of articles generally, see the entry **articles**.

1 You use **the** to refer to things or people when you expect your hearer to know which you mean:

I've got to go back to the office tonight.
Where's the dog?
I'm going to see the doctor.
The dinner was going fine until I realized I'd forgotten the wine.

2 **The** is used to refer for the second time to someone or something that has already been mentioned using **a**:

A boy and a girl were sitting opposite her. The boy spoke first.

3 **The** is used for someone or something that you are in the process of specifying or identifying:

The candidates we interviewed yesterday seemed better.
Who's the girl in the green jacket?

4 You use **the** when there is only one such thing *eg* **the sun**, **the moon**, **the sky**:

Isn't it nice to see the sun?

➢ For the use of **the** with proper names see the entry **articles**.

5 **The** is used with a singular countable noun to refer to classes of things or people:

In those days people relied on the horse for transport.

6 You use **the** to refer to familiar features of life:

The weather is always a safe topic.
The trains don't run at the weekend.

7 You can use **the** with an adjective such as **poor** or **unemployed**, or a nationality adjective such as **British** or **Dutch** to form a plural noun representing all the people belonging to that class or nationality:

The Dutch are a much taller race than the British.

➤ For lists of adjectives commonly used in this way see **adjectives**.

8 You usually use **the** before the first noun in a group such as *the leg of a chair*, even though the second may be preceded by **a**, **the** or a possessive determiner, or have no determiner:

the wheel of a car
the death of a child
on the fourth finger of his left hand
lying in the path of the storm
the pursuit of wealth

9 **The** is sometimes used to mean 'enough', 'sufficient' or 'adequate', especially with negatives, or in questions:

He hadn't the strength to argue.

➤ For the use of **the** with comparatives, *eg The more she resisted, the angrier he got,* see paragraph 8 of USING COMPARATIVES at **comparatives and superlatives**.

•••• there ••••

There has two very different uses. It can be used as a *demonstrative adverb*, to refer to a place within your surroundings, or a place that has just been mentioned; or it can be used as a *pronoun* with the verb **be**, to say that something exists or is available. The two uses have different pronunciations.

AS A DEMONSTRATIVE ADVERB

When **there** is being used as a *demonstrative adverb*, its pronunciation is /ðɛə/.

1 You use **there** to indicate a place some distance away, but within your view or surroundings. It is the opposite of **here**:

'Where's my notepad.?' 'You left it over there.'
'Here I am, on the roof.' 'How did you get up there?'

➤ For the differences between **here** and **there** see **here**.

2 In direct speech, **there** often comes at the beginning of a sentence, with inversion of the subject and verb, except when the subject is a pronoun:

There's Dad talking to Mr Jeffries.
'Where's the newspaper?' 'There it is, on the floor.'
There goes the bell at last.

ⓘ You can say **there you are** when you are handing something to someone:
Would you like some chocolate? There you are.

3 You use **there** to refer to any place, other than where you are, that has just been mentioned:

'Is Philip in his office?' 'He was there a minute ago.'

Just go to the reception desk and the lady there will help you.
You mentioned the Lyceum Theatre; we used to go there a lot.

As an adverb or place of direction, **there** is not normally used with any preposition. But you can use **from** with **there**, and other prepositions are possible when you are thinking of **there** as a point, space or area:

We visited Naples and from there we went on to Rome.
This is our spare room; no-one sleeps in there just now.

4 **There** can refer to a point or stage in a sequence of events, or a point in a discussion:

Don't stop there. What happened next?
Sorry, I can't agree with you there.

5 You can say that something is **there**, meaning that it is in existence, or is real:

'Has your headache gone?' 'No, it's still there.'
Macbeth reaches out for a knife that isn't really there.

AS AN INTRODUCTORY SUBJECT

When **there** is used as an introductory subject, its pronunciation is /ðɛ/ or /ðə/.

1 **There** is used with the verb **be** like a pronoun, to talk about things existing or happening, or being available. You use **there is** before a singular noun:

There's a dirty mark on your skirt.

There are is used with plurals:

There are three good reasons why this won't work.

2 **There is** and **there are** are often used with indefinite pronouns and indefinite determiners, like **some** and **any**, and with **what**:

There are some loaves in the freezer.
I'm afraid there are no vacancies left.
Is there any mail to collect?
Let me know if there's anything you want.
What is there to do in a town this size?

3 **There is** is used with indefinite pronouns + **wrong** or **the matter**:

There's nothing wrong with enjoying yourself.
Is there something the matter?

> ⓘ Notice that you don't use **there is** or **there are** with **since**. You say **it's** (not **there is**) **a few days**, or **a month, since...** :
> *It's twenty years since he died.*

4 **tenses**:

You can use any tense of **be**:

There were only a few visitors this morning.
Has there been an accident?
There'll be someone to collect you at the station.

5 **modal verbs**:

There + modal verb + **be** is possible. Verbs that are followed by a **to**-infinitive *eg* **be going**, **seem**, **appear** and **tend** can be used too:

There must be a record of it somewhere.
There would be trouble if she found out.
Isn't there going to be some sort of celebration?
There appears to be some mistake here.

6 Notice that **there** can be the object after verbs like **expect** or **want**:
I don't expect there to be any phone calls.

7 Question tags are common after the **there is** or **there are**:
There are a lot of people here, aren't there?

8 **with other verbs**:
A few other verbs can be used in place of **be** after **there**:
There remains the matter of the price.
There followed a long section about her childhood.

.... these ....

These is a *demonstrative determiner* and *pronoun*. It is the plural of **this** and the opposite of **those**.

➤ For the uses of **these**, see the entry **this, that, these** and **those**.

.... this, that, these, those ....

This, **that**, **these** and **those** are *demonstratives*, or 'showing' words. They are used as *determiners* and as *pronouns*. You use them to refer to, or identify, things and people within your view or surroundings, and also to refer to things and people just mentioned. As a rough rule, you use **this** and its plural **these** to refer to things *close* to you in space or time, and you use **that** and its plural **those** to refer to things *further away* from you in space or time. All four words have some special uses of their own.

THINGS AND PEOPLE IN YOUR SURROUNDINGS

Examples follow of the use of all four demonstratives to refer to things and people within view, or in the immediate environment:

1 **this, these**
You use **this** and **these** for things on your body, or being held by you, as well as for things or people close to you:
I don't often wear this ring.
Who made all this mess?
My mum gave me these gloves.
Compare these two diagrams.
These are my books.

2 **that, those**
You use **that** and **those** for referring to things that other people are wearing or holding, as well as things further away from you:
That hairstyle suits you.
Who's that lady with the dark hair?
What's that funny noise?

Where did you get those nice earrings?
Haven't you got a cleaner pair of trousers than those?

ⓘ You can refer to things using the pronouns **this, that, these** and **those**, but you do not refer to people in this way:
Carry this for me, would you?
Put those on the kitchen table.
But:
Can you help this lady (not *this*)*?*
Could you find chairs for these people (not *these*)*?*

3 identifying and introducing people

Although you don't refer to people using the pronouns **this** and **that** in the way shown in the note above, you can use **this** to introduce people, and **that** to identify people:

Susan, have you met Marion? Marion, this is Susan.
Isn't that one of your pupils?

You also identify yourself on the telephone using **this**, and refer to the person at the other end with **that**:

Hello, is that you, Neil? This is Anne.

SUBSTITUTION

This, **that**, **these** and **those** are all used to refer to things being spoken about. As a rough guide, you use **that** and **those** in reference to things that have been said; you use **this** and **these** to refer to things that have been mentioned and will continue to be discussed. And you use **this** or **these** to refer to things you are about to mention:

1 that, those

'I passed!' 'That's great!'
That's the story so far.
He's been ill; that's why we haven't heard from him.
Those are just some of the complaints we received about the programme.

2 this, these

This is where we can use your talents.
There's something you're forgetting, and it's this.
There was a sheet of paper on the desk, and on it were these words.

➤ For more information about this use of **this**, **that** and **it**, see the entry **substitution**.

TIME

You use **this** and **these** to refer to the present, and **that** and **those** to refer to the past and the future:

1 You use **this** to refer to the present situation:

This is terrible; they just don't understand.
It's great having everyone together like this.

2 before this, after that

You can use **this** to mean 'now', and **that** to refer to a point in the past or future, with the prepositions **after** and **before**:

I expected to be finished before this.
Before that we'd always gone abroad for our holidays.
Where are you going after this?
This job finishes on 20 April, and after that I'll be free.

3 these days, those days

- **These times** refer to the present. **These days** means the same as **nowadays**:

  These are difficult times for everyone.
  Nobody knows how to waltz these days.

- You use **those days** to refer to some period in the past:

  Of course we had no electricity in those days.

4 this week, that day

- **This** week, month or year is the present one. **This** Friday is the one coming in the present week. **This** weekend is the approaching one. **This** summer is the one in the present year. **This** morning, afternoon or evening are the morning, afternoon or evening of today:

  I'm too busy this week.
  We're going away this weekend.

➤ See also the entries for **day**, **morning**, **evening**, **night**, **seasons** and **year**.

- You use **that** to refer to particular days, weeks, months, seasons, years, in the past or future:

  Later that evening he proposed to me.
  We shall be moving house that week.

DEFINING CLAUSES OR PHRASES

1 You use **that** and **those** with a relative clause, or identifying phrase, to identify a part or group:

in that part of the town which lies close to the river
Would those delegates who have just arrived please go to the office?

2 As pronouns, **that** and **those** have a similar meaning to **the one** and **the ones**:

A dog's sense of hearing is better than that of humans.
Many of those present had no idea how to behave properly.

•••• those ••••

Those is a *demonstrative* determiner and pronoun. It is the plural of **that** and the opposite of **these**. For the uses of **those**, see the entry **this, that, these** and **those**.

•••• thousand ••••

➤ See **hundred**.

•••• time ••••

UNCOUNTABLE AND COUNTABLE USES

1 **Time** is uncountable when you are thinking of it as a resource:

Who knows how much time will be needed to complete the work?
I like to have plenty of time to spare at the airport.

> ⓘ **Time** or **the time** is often used with the meaning 'enough time':
> *We haven't got time to argue now.*

2 **Time** is used countably, usually with an adjective, to mean a period of a certain length:

She took a long time to dress.
The wounds will take quite a time [= a long time] *to heal.*

➤ See also the entry **long**.

OCCASIONS OR POINTS IN TIME

1 You use **time** to refer to an occasion, often with **last** or **next**. You do not need prepositions:

Are you busy? Shall I come back another time?
Last time I saw him he was drunk.
You take a risk every time you cross the road.
This time you'll have to go on your own.
There are times when being single is lonely.

2 You use **time** to refer to a point in time when something happens. You need prepositions with **time** in this sense:

She was over fifteen stone by the time of her marriage.
There was a fire, but fortunately we were out at the time.

3 **on time, in time**

- Something happens **on time** when it takes place just when it was planned, neither early nor late:

  She reached the restaurant at ten to one, precisely on time.

- You are **in time** for something when you are not too late for it:

  The train was just leaving but I managed to jump on just in time.

4 You use **it's time**, not only to say what is due according to a plan or schedule, but to talk about practical or moral necessities. You can use **it's time** with:

- a **to-infinitive:**

  It's time to get up.

- **for** + **object**, and **for** + **object** + **to-infinitive:**

  It's time for a review of the situation.
  I think it's time for us to forget the past.

ASKING FOR THE TIME

There are several acceptable ways of asking what the time is:

What's the time?
What time is it?
Have you got the time?
Can you tell me the time, please?

GIVING TIMES

1 When someone asks what the time is, the subject of the answer is always **it**:

It's three o'clock.
It's just gone half past four.

2 When you say what time an event happens or happened, you use the preposition **at**:

The meeting's at ten o'clock.
We'll meet at three thirty then, shall we?

3 There are usually at least two ways of expressing a time in words:

11.00 :	*eleven o'clock*		
11.05 :	*five past eleven*	or	*eleven oh five*
11.10 :	*ten past eleven*	or	*eleven ten*
11.15 :	*a quarter past eleven*	or	*eleven fifteen*
11.20 :	*twenty past eleven*	or	*eleven twenty*
11.25 :	*twenty five past eleven*	or	*eleven twenty-five*
11.30 :	*half past eleven*	or	*eleven thirty*
11.35 :	*twenty five to twelve*	or	*eleven thirty-five*
11.40 :	*twenty to twelve*	or	*eleven forty*
11.45 :	*a quarter to twelve*	or	*eleven forty-five*
11.50 :	*ten to twelve*	or	*eleven fifty*
11.55 :	*five to twelve*	or	*eleven fifty-five*
11.12 :	*twelve minutes past eleven*	or	*eleven twelve*
11.48 :	*twelve minutes to twelve*	or	*eleven forty-eight*
12.00 :	*twelve o'clock*	or	*midday*, *noon* or *midnight*

4 If you feel it is necessary, you can specify which part of the day you are referring to when you give a time before twelve o'clock. You add **a.m.** for times between midnight and midday, and **p.m.** for times between midday and midnight (the use of full stops is optional):

The meeting finished at 4 pm.

... **time** continued

- a clause containing a subject and a verb in the simple past or past progressive, with reference to the present:

It's time we sent the children to bed.
It's time you sorted yourself out.
It's time I was getting home.

•••• to ••••

To has two main uses. It is used as a *preposition* (*We are moving to the States*), and it is used as a *particle*, or *infinitive-marker*, before an infinitive (*We have decided to move*).

This entry deals mainly with the preposition **to**, but includes a section on the difference between *verb* + **to** + **-ing** form (*I object to paying*) and verb + **to**-infinitive (*I refuse to pay*).

> ➤ See the entry **infinitives** for more information about **to**-infinitives.

USES OF THE PREPOSITION

1 physical direction

- movement somewhere, or arrival there, sometimes with **from**:
  Which is the quickest way to Dundee from here?
  She's gone round to Sarah's.
  Are you invited to the wedding?
- facing or pointing in a certain direction:
  She pointed to an empty seat.
  She sat with her back to the fire.
- position in relation to you:
  To the east the sky was brightening.
- close connection:
  He tied the dog to the lamp post.

2 a resulting state

- progress in the direction of a state or situation:
  her sudden rise to fame
- result of an action:
  We rocked the baby to sleep.
- alteration in state:
  The rain turned to snow.
- reaction or response:
  Are the arrangements to your satisfaction?

3 ranges, often with 'from'

In some cases, **to** could be replaced by **till**, or, more formally, **until**. These alternatives are given in the examples below:

- telling the time:
  It's twenty minutes to six.
- range in time or space:
  We serve breakfast from eight to (or *till* or *until*) *ten.*
  There's only a fortnight to (or *till* or *until*) *the exam.*
  The job will take from six to eight weeks.

- scores, proportions and rates:

We were winning by two goals to one.
How many Singapore dollars are there to the pound?

4 giving and communicating

- with indirect objects

When you put the indirect object of a verb such as **give** or **send** after the direct object, you need **to** before it:

Could you give this envelope to Jack?
I'll send the photos back to you.

- communicating:

I still haven't written to Shirley.
I saw her talking to Jamie.

5 after various verbs, adjectives and nouns

To is used with certain verbs, adjectives and nouns to express relationships of various kinds:

How did he react to the news?
I object to that remark.
He listened to the tape again.
Who were you referring to?
Does this belong to you?
I'm glad I'm not married to him.
Where's the key to the door?
There's no obvious solution to the problem.
Please be nice to Mum.

TO + -ING FORM

Some verbs, phrasal verbs, and other expressions that are followed by preposition **to** + noun object can have an **-ing** form as their noun object:

He's used to getting his own way.
I object to paying for you.

These should be distinguished from verbs and expressions that are followed by a **to**-infinitive:

I tried to ring you.
He's lost the will to live.

Some verbs and other expressions that can be followed by **to** + **-ing** form are shown below:

I object to waiting.
I look forward to starting work.
He prefers reading to watching television.
I never got round to filling up the form.
He's not used to being independent.
He was bleeding in addition to being badly bruised.

➤ For more information see the section -ing forms after prepositions at the entry **-ing forms**.

today

1 You use **today**, not **this day**, to refer to the present day:
Today is St Patrick's Day.
I'll call you later today.

2 You refer to the morning, afternoon and evening of today as **this morning**, **this afternoon** and **this evening**:
I'm seeing the doctor later this afternoon.
There's a letter for you; it came earlier this morning.
I'll phone you later on this evening.

tonight

1 You refer to the night that follows today as **tonight**:
I don't think I'll get much sleep tonight.

2 You refer to the night between yesterday and today as **last night**:
He spent last night at the police station, answering questions.

too

Too has three uses. It can be used like **also** or **as well** to make an addition; it can be used to mean 'more than necessary or desirable'; and it is sometimes used as an intensifier like **very**.

INDICATING AN ADDITION

1 You use **too** to add or include someone or something:
You too can have the trip of a lifetime.
He used to hit his wife, and sometimes the children too.
'I'm fed up.' 'Me too [= I am too].'
'She's nice.' 'Yes, clever, too.'

2 People also use **too** to draw attention to a striking aspect of a situation:
I was amazed that such things could happen, and in our village, too.

➤ See the entry **also** for more information about **too** meaning 'also' or 'as well'.

MORE THAN NECESSARY OR DESIRABLE

1 **Too** is used before *adjectives* and *adverbs* to mean 'more than necessary':
He's too pleased with himself.
Don't go too far ahead, or we'll lose sight of you.

2 Things that are **too** something **for** someone are impossible for them:
Some of the tasks are too difficult for children.

3 **Too much** and **too little** are used before *uncountable nouns*, and **too many** or **too few** before *plural nouns* to mean 'an excessively large', or 'undesirably small' quantity:
They give us too much work.
You read too many dieting articles.
There's too little evidence.
We have too few supporters.

4 Intensifiers and moderators that can be used before **too** are the same as the ones used before comparatives: **far**, **much**, **a lot**, **a little**, **a bit** and **rather**.

All the intensifiers and moderators mentioned above, including **much**, can be used before **too** + adjectives and adverbs, and before **too** + **much** + uncountable noun, but only **far** and **rather** are normally used before **too** + **many** + plural noun:

You're being a little too optimistic.
I arrived rather too early.
You've given me much too much pudding.
Most people have far too many clothes.

TOO+ TO-INFINITIVE

Too is followed by a **to**-infinitive, or by **for** + **to**-infinitive, to form a clause of result similar to one using **so ... that**:

There was too little snow to go skiing. [= so little snow that we couldn't go skiing]
It isn't too late to refuse.

> ⓘ The order **too** + adjective +**a** + noun is used in formal English:
> *It was too obvious a clue to miss.*

There are the following grammatical points to note:

- The first subject may become the subject or object of the infinitive:

  It's too good an opportunity to waste [**it** becomes the object of the infinitive **to waste**].
  You're too good a teacher to lose [**you** becomes the object of **to lose**].
  She was too frightened to call for help [**she** remains the subject of the infinitive **to call**].

- A change of subject before the infinitive is introduced by **for**. Personal pronouns after **for** are in the object case:

  It was too cold and windy for us to eat our picnic on the summit.
  He was too heavy for me to carry down the hill.

AS AN INTENSIFIER

1 you're too kind

Like **so**, but more rarely, **too** is used informally as an intensifier like **very**, *eg* when showing appreciation or sympathy. This use is rather old-fashioned in positive sentences:

'Could I drive you home?' 'Oh that's really too kind of you. I should be most grateful.'

2 not too happy

You can use **not too** like **not very** as a weak form of **not**, usually as an alternative to using an opposite expression:

They don't look too cheerful. [= they look miserable]
I didn't feel too good myself. [= I felt awful]
It wasn't too hard [= it was easy] *to guess what she was thinking.*

3 **'only too' and 'all too'**

Only too and **all too** are both used to mean 'very' or 'extremely', with various extra meanings according to context:

Lambert was only too [= acutely] *aware of the dangers.*
We're only too [= naturally very] *willing to help.*
It was all too [= painfully] *obvious that he didn't care.*

—— transport ——

PREPOSITIONS

1 When you walk or run, you are going somewhere **on foot**:

You should really see the Old Town on foot.
When the traffic's this bad, you can get there quicker on foot.

2 You use **by** with the name of a vehicle or with **air**, **rail**, **road** or **sea** to describe different ways of travelling:

They came by car.
The only way to get to the island is by sea.

> ⓘ It is more usual to say **go overland** than **go by land**:
> *I'd always wanted to go overland to India.*

3 When you are thinking of a vehicle as part of a journey process, you use the preposition **on**:

I left my umbrella on the bus.
He met a very nice girl on the plane to Dublin.

However, when you want to emphasize a location, you use **in**:

They opened the doors to try to lower the temperature in the train.

VERBS

1 The verb you choose can describe your means of transport:

go by car = *drive*
go by bicycle = *ride, cycle*
go on horseback = *ride*
go by ship = *sail*
go by air = *fly*

2 If you get a lift by signalling to the driver of a passing car, you **hitch**, **hitch a lift** or **hitch-hike**:

We hitched home at the end of each term.
I hitched a lift into town.

3 You **get in** or **into** a car or boat, but you **get on** or **onto** a bicycle, bus, train, plane or ship:

Fiona just jumped into the car and drove off without another word.
You'd better get on the bus now and find your seat.
We had to get off and push our bikes through the muddy field.

4 You **get out of** a car or boat, but you **get off** a bicycle, bus, train, plane or ship:

She finds it hard to get out of the car with her bad back.
Where do you get off the bus?

5 When you get on a bus or train that is going somewhere, you **catch** it:
If I run I might be able to catch the 3.30 bus.

■ If you fail to catch a bus, train or plane, you **miss** it:
The taxi got stuck in the traffic and we missed the train.

NOUNS

1 travel

Travel is a verb and an uncountable noun, but *not* a countable noun (so it is wrong to say *a travel*):
The boys spent the summer travelling around Europe.
Air travel is so much cheaper than it used to be.

2 journey

The verb **journey** is not used as much as the noun, which is very common. You make a **journey** when you travel from one place to another:
The journey had been long and hot and we were all very tired.
The journey won't take long at this time of day.
How was your journey?

3 trip, tour

A journey to a place and back again is a **trip**. A journey on which you visit several or many different places before returning is a **tour**:
Have a good trip!
I'll be away on a business trip for the rest of the week.
The highlight of this term is the school trip to Austria.
Coach tours are very popular at this time of year.

4 voyage, cruise

Any long journey on a ship or a spacecraft is a **voyage**. A holiday on a ship is a **cruise**:
The voyage would be dangerous and could take months.
We went on a cruise round the Bahamas.

•••• trouble ••••

You use **trouble** in some expressions about effort or difficulty:

1 You **take the trouble to do** something that requires an effort, when you make the effort and do it:
How many people take the trouble to check their restaurant bills these days?

2 To **go to the trouble of doing** something is also to do something that requires a special effort:
Why would he go to the trouble of booking himself on a flight, and then not go?

3 You **have trouble doing** something when you have difficulty in doing it:
I'm very tall and have trouble finding clothes that fit.

•••• type ••••

➤ See **kind**.

Uu

•••• un- ••••

1 You use adjectives that start with **un**- (and their related adverbs and nouns) when you want to express an opposite or negative idea. Here are a few examples:

unconscious	*unconsciously*	*unconsciousness*
unfair	*unfairly*	*unfairness*
unhappy	*unhappily*	*unhappiness*

2 You use verbs that begin with **un**- for talking about reverse processes, removals or releases of some kind. Here are some examples:

undo *uncork* *unfold* *unload* *unzip*

3 You can add **un**- to the past participle of some verbs to indicate that a process has not happened. For example, although the verb *unhear* does not exist, the past participle **unheard-of** is common. Here are some more examples:

unannounced	*unattached*	*unauthorized*	*unknown*	*unfit*
unidentified	*uninhabited*	*unoccupied*	*unsaid*	*unspoken*
unused	*unwritten*			

4 You can add **un-** to the beginning of many adjectives ending in **-able** to express an impossibility or a process that cannot happen. Here are some common examples:

unacceptable	*unavailable*	*unavoidable*	*unbearable*
unbelievable	*uncontrollable*	*uncountable*	*unforgettable*
unimaginable	*unpredictable*	*unpronounceable*	*unthinkable*

•••• unless ••••

Unless is often used with the meaning 'except if', to introduce the only circumstance that will stop something taking place, or being the case:

Don't drive in the fog unless [= except if] *your journey is absolutely necessary.*
Don't try this yourself unless you are expert with the computer.
Unless it rains tonight, the race will take place in the morning.

> ⓘ Sometimes the pronoun subject and verb can be omitted from the **unless** clause:
> *Unless* [= except if it is] *otherwise stated, delivery is included in the price.*

But sometimes **unless** simply means 'if … not':

Unless you [= if you do not] *talk to people regularly, you cannot claim to know what they are thinking.*

Not unless usually means 'only if':

'Would you like a drink?' 'Not unless [= only if] *you're having one yourself'.*

TENSES WITH 'UNLESS'

1 If the **unless** clause refers to the future, you usually use a simple present in it:

Unless food reaches [= if food doesn't reach] *the areas soon, many more will die.*

2 If the **unless** clause refers to the past, a simple past is usually used:

They threatened to kill me unless I changed my mind [= if I didn't change my mind].

WHEN YOU CAN'T USE 'UNLESS'

You don't use **unless** in unreal conditions:

If you hadn't (not *unless you had*) *caught me, I would have fallen.*

•••• until ••••

Until is used to talk about *time*. It has an alternative, **till**, whch is slightly less formal. The two words have no difference in meaning. AmE prefers the spelling **'til** to **till**. Both words can be used either as *prepositions* or as *conjunctions*.

1 I worked until ten

Something that happens **until** a certain time, or **until** a certain thing happens, goes on happening up to that point:

I waited for you until one-thirty.
We sat talking till after midnight.
The child used to scream until her parents gave her what she wanted.

> ⓘ Sometimes the subject pronoun and verb can be omitted from the clause after **until** when it is used as a conjunction, *eg* in recipes:
> *Whisk two egg whites until* [= until they are] *firm.*

2 from nine till five

You use **from ... until** to say how long a situation or event lasts:

The programme is on air from 11pm till 2am.
He taught at Oxford University from 1860 until 1882.

> ⓘ You can also use **from ... to** in 'time-range' expressions:
> *The exhibition will be on view from 12 July to* (or *until*) *14 August.*

3 one month till the exams

You can use **until**, **till** or **to** when calculating how much time you have before some future event:

It's only a fortnight till (or *to*) *the exams.*

NOT UNTIL

1 The meaning of **not until** is similar to 'not before'. Something that does **not** happen **until** a certain time, or **until** a certain thing happens, happens at that time or point, but not before:

The car won't be ready till Friday.
He was not promoted until 1958.

2 In a formal or literary style you can begin the sentence with **Not until**. If you do this, the order in the main clause is auxiliary verb (or **be**) + subject:

Not until his death did she begin to appreciate him as a person.

TENSES WITH 'UNTIL'

1 You use a simple present in **until** clauses that refer to the future:

The casualty should not be moved until help arrives.

2 You can use a simple past in an **until** clause referring to the past:

She waited till the applause died down, then spoke again.

3 You can also use a present perfect, or a past perfect, to convey the idea of one thing being over before another starts:

Just sit down, and don't move on until you've got your breath back.
She waited until the applause had died down, then spoke again.

•••• used to ••••

Used to forms part of two different structures with two distinct meanings.

USED TO + INFINITIVE

1 **Used to** is a verb which occurs only in the past tense. When it occurs with the infinitive, it refers to past habits and states that are no longer the case:

When I was a child, I used to live with my grandparents.
We used to go to church every Sunday.

2 **Used to** can be treated like a modal verb for creating negative and question forms:

The people used not to be so unfriendly.
Used you to live here?

But these forms are considered very formal, and so **used to** is more commonly treated as an ordinary verb:

The people didn't use to be so unfriendly.
Did you use to live here?

> ⓘ Note that you do not use **used to** to talk about how many times something was done in the past.

BE/GET USED TO + NOUN OR -ING FORM

You **are used to something** or **are used to doing something** when you have become very familiar with it. You **get used to something**, or **get used to doing something** when you *become* very familiar with it:

I'm used to living alone now.
'How can you work with all that noise?' 'I'm used to it.'

I'm getting used to living in the city now, but it's taken a long time.
I didn't like his funny habits at first, but I'm getting used to him now.

> ⓘ **Used to** is pronounced /juːstuː/ before vowel sounds and /ˈjuːstə/ before consonants.

Vv

verbs

A **verb** is a word that states what someone or something does, what happens to them, or that describes the state they are in. Verbs can be divided into categories, depending partly on meaning, but also on the way they behave grammatically. This entry looks at the different kinds of structures that are possible.

GRAMMATICAL PATTERNS OF ALL REGULAR VERBS

Regular verbs have the following forms:

- a base form, *eg* **work**
- a final -**s** in the third person simple present tense, *eg* **works**
- a present participle with a final -**ing**, *eg* **working**
- a past form with a final -**ed**, *eg* **worked**

➤ For information on irregular verbs, see the entry **irregular verbs**.

Questions and negatives are formed with the auxiliary **do**:

__Do__ you work?
__Does__ he work?
I __don't__ work any more.
I __didn't__ know you were getting married.
__Did__ they see us?

TRANSITIVE AND INTRANSITIVE VERBS

1 Many verbs can be followed by a noun or a pronoun. A noun or pronoun in this grammatical position is called a *direct object*. Verbs which work like this are *transitive* verbs:

I've got to __write a letter__.
She __hates dogs__.

2 Other verbs are not normally followed by a direct object. These verbs are called *intransitive* verbs:

Sorry, I was __dreaming__. What did you say?
'How did you get home?' 'I __walked__.'

3 Some verbs can be used either with or without an object, depending on the kind of subject that precedes them:

transitive use	**intransitive use**
She opened the door.	*The door opened.*
The bomb shook the building.	*The building shook.*
They've changed the rules.	*The rules have changed.*
I'll boil an egg.	*The water's boiling.*

4 Some verbs take two objects. These verbs are called *ditransitive* verbs. Usually the indirect object refers to a person, and comes first:

*Tell **him a story**.*
*Could you lend **me your car**?*
*She showed **us her new flat**.*

- **position of indirect object**

It is also possible to position the indirect object after the direct object, as a way of placing emphasis on that part of the sentence. If you do this, you usually need to add a preposition, *eg* **to** or **for**:

*He bought a house **for** her.*
*I sent the letter **to** the head office.*

- **two pronouns**

If both the direct and the indirect objects are pronouns, and the direct object pronoun is **it** or **them**, it is common to put the indirect pronoun last, with a preposition (**to** or **for**). With other pronouns like **one** or **some**, both structures are possible:

*Could you give **it to me**, please?*
*Shall I buy **them for you**?*
*I'll lend **you some**.*
*I applied for a visa but they refused **me one**.*
*If you could leave **some for me**, I'd be grateful.*

- **wh-questions**

When ditransitive verbs are used in **wh-**questions, the preposition **to** or **for** is necessary at the end:

*Who did you write **to**?*
*Who should I buy it **for**?*

- **passives**

When ditransitive verbs are used in passive sentences, the indirect object is commonly given subject status, and the preposition is not needed:

*I **was lent** some clothes for the day.*
*They **were offered** a house and a boat, but they refused it.*

VERBS WITH PREPOSITIONS AND PARTICLES

Many verbs can be followed by a preposition or an adverbial particle:

*Look **at** this!*
*We sat **down** by the river.*

Some verbs can regularly be found with certain prepositions or particles. The meaning of the two parts cannot always be guessed from the meaning of the individual parts. These word groups are called *phrasal verbs*:

*If you don't know a word, **look** it **up** in a dictionary.*
*He **takes after** his father.*

➤ For details on how phrasal verbs work grammatically, see the entry **phrasal verbs**.

LINKING VERBS

Some verbs are not followed by an object, but by an adjective or a noun complement that describes the subject. These verbs are called *copular verbs* or *linking verbs*. Common linking verbs are **look**, **appear**, **seem**, **sound**, **feel**, **taste**, **become**, **get**, and **be**:

➤ For more detailed information on linking verbs, see the entry **linking verbs**.

VERBS FOLLOWED BY OTHER VERBS

1 Many verbs can be followed by other verbs, even when they themselves are not auxiliaries. The second verb may be in the form of an infinitive, with or without **to** or an **-ing** form:

*She finally **agreed to appear** in public.*
*I **hated being** on social security and I tried everywhere for a job.*
*The treatment will **help ease** the tight muscles causing the pain.*

2 Some verbs, such as **try**, **like**, **remember**, and **regret** have a different meaning, depending on whether they are followed by an **-ing** form or an infinitive:

Try taking an aspirin. [= to see if it has any effect]
I tried to unblock the sink. [= I made an attempt at unblocking the sink]

I like listening to jazz. [= I enjoy it]
I like to brush my teeth three times a day. [= I think it's a good thing to do]

I remember hearing the bombs.
Remember to lock the door.

I regret leaving university. [= I wish I hadn't left]
We regret to inform you that … [= We are sorry to have to announce that …]

Depending on the verb, many different structures are possible. For example, with some verbs, it is possible to put an object between the two verbs:

*I want **you** to make an effort today.*
*I don't know how to stop **him** crying.*

➤ For more details on these structures, see entries for **infinitives** and for **-ing** forms.

PASSIVE STRUCTURES

*Shakespeare **wrote** these two poems.* (active)
*These two poems **were written** by Shakespeare.* (passive)

You can use a *passive* structure of a verb if you want to talk about an action, but you do not want to mention who or what did it.

1 The use of the passive is common in the writing of academic papers and journalistic texts:

Subjects from each social category were tested.
During the night of March 23–24 alone, 17 people were arrested.

2 The passive form is also used when you wish to focus on new information. If that information is the person or thing carrying out the action, you introduce it with the preposition **by**:

This book was written by one of my lecturers.

> ⓘ Notice that in the last example, the passive structure is used not in order to avoid mentioning, but to draw attention to, the agent.

➤ For more detailed information on passive structures, see the entry **the passive**.

MODAL VERBS

Modal auxiliary verbs are verbs like **can**, **could**, **may**, **might**, **shall**, **should**, **will** and **would**. They are used together with other verbs to express ideas such as certainty, probability, obligation, habit, willingness and ability.

➤ For more information about uses of modals and how they behave grammatically, see the entry **modal verbs**, or the separate entry for each modal verb.

verbs forming nouns

The **-ing** form of a verb often functions like a noun, as in:

Seeing is believing.
Fishing is very popular .

When the **-ing** form functions in this way it is known as a *gerund* or *verbal noun*. Most gerunds are uncountable nouns, but some gerunds are countable nouns and can be used in the plural:

***Swimming** is a great form of exercise.*
*She has this great **liking** for offbeat comedy.*
*All these **comings** and **goings** upset her.*

The gerund is also often used to form compound nouns. In such nouns, the gerund is used to specify the function of an item:

*It takes a while to break in a new pair of **climbing** boots.*
*He has a small **recording** studio at the back of his house.*

very

Very is the adverb most commonly used for intensifying adjectives or adverbs:

The house was very dirty.
I've just heard some very interesting news.
She was walking very slowly.

People use **not very** before adjectives and adverbs as a less direct form of **not**; it actually has the effect of quite a strong negative:

I wasn't very impressed.
That's not a very good adea.
You haven't explained it very well.

You can use **Not very** as a short reply:

'Did you have a nice time?' 'Not very.'

vocative

➤ See **addressing people**.

Ww

wait

You **wait** when you do nothing, or delay doing something, or remain in the same place, until the thing happens that you are expecting to happen.

1 wait + to-infinitive

Wait can be followed by a **to**-infinitive:

I'm waiting to see the doctor.
The mail lay on her desk waiting to be opened.
I waited to hear what he was going to say next.

2 wait + for + object

Wait is used with the preposition **for** before a following object:

I'm waiting for my husband.
He had to wait half an hour for the bus.
Day after day we waited for his arrival.

> ⓘ You never say *wait something*. Always use the preposition **for**.

3 wait + for + object + to-infinitive

A **to**-infinitive can follow **for** + object:

We waited for him to speak.
He waited for the woman to sit down.
He waited for the two customers in front of him to pay.

> ⓘ Notice that **wait** is never followed by a **that**-clause. You cannot say *He waited that someone answer.*
> The correct form is:
> *He waited **for** someone **to** answer.*

4 wait + expressions of time

Wait can be followed by an expression of time, with or without **for**:

We waited (for) weeks, but nothing happened.
She waited (for) hours before being told it had been cancelled.

•••• want ••••

You **want** something when you desire it, or feel you need it:

I don't want a very big car.

Want can be used in several different grammatical constructions.

1 want + object

You can use **want** simply with a direct object:

Does he want two copies?

After the object, you can use **for** or a **to**-infinitive to add the purpose:

I suppose they'll want bacon and egg for breakfast
Ask the others if they want anything to drink.

> ⓘ You do not usually use **want** in the progressive forms:
> *I want* (not *am wanting*) *a bit of peace.*

2 want + to-infinitive

You can use **want** with a **to-**infinitive:

Why does he want to see me?
Angela did not want to get involved.

> ⓘ Notice that you cannot drop **to**:
> *She just wants to die* (not *wants die*) *in peace.*

3 want + object + to-infinitive

You can have an object before the **to-**infinitive:

The management doesn't want things to go wrong.
I wanted you to know that we understand the situation.

> ⓘ **That-**clauses are not possible after **want**:
> *Naturally we want everything to go* (not *want that everything goes*) *smoothly.*

4 want + object + complement

You can also have an adjective, past participle, or adverb acting as a complement after the object. For example, instead of saying you **want something to be returned** to you, you can say you **want it returned**:

I want the matter settled by this evening.
He's my dad, and I want him back.
No shooting. We want them alive.

You don't put a noun as complement directly after the object. You say, for example:

I want her to be project manager or *I want her as project manager.*

You can't say *I want her project manager.*

a note about politeness

In general, forms such as **could I have** or **would you like** are more polite than **I want** or **do you want**, unless you are in an informal situation or know the other person very well:

Could I have (not *I want*) *four brown rolls, please.*
Would you like (rather than *do you want*) *to come with us?*
I'd like you (rather than *I want you*) *to start work on this tomorrow.*
I'd like (rather than *I want*) *the job completed by Friday.*

• • • • -ward, -wards • • • •

ADJECTIVES

You can form adjectives of direction or position by adding -**ward** to nouns or to adverbial particles such as **in**, **out**, **up** and **down**:

a backward look
an eastward direction
the homeward journey
inward thoughts
outward appearances

ADVERBS

You can form adverbs of direction by adding -**ward** or -**wards** to nouns or to adverbial particles such as **in**, **out**, **up** and **down**:

going homeward(s)
looking inward(s)
We were travelling northward(s).

-**wards** is more usual in BrE.
-**ward** is more usual in AmE.

TOWARD, TOWARDS

Towards (or more commonly in AmE, **toward**) is a preposition of direction. It can refer to space, time or attitude:

He leant towards Bill and whispered something.
Towards dawn, he finally fell asleep.
She's been behaving oddly towards me lately.

AFTERWARDS, AFTERWARDS

Afterwards (or more commonly in AmE, **afterward**) is an adverb of time:

I'm going shopping now but I'll join you afterwards.

—— warnings ——

➤ See pages 566 and 567.

WARNINGS

This section deals with how to warn people about things, depending on how dangerous a situation is, how formal the circumstances are, and whether the warning is written or spoken.

CONVERSATION

If you want to warn someone casually about something, you can say **I wouldn't ... if I were you**, or, less forcefully, **I don't think you should** (or **ought to**) **...** :

I wouldn't touch that if I were you; it's very hot.
I don't think you should drive by yourself yet.

1 direct warnings

A very direct way of warning someone informally is to tell them what will happen if they do something, by saying **You'll ... if you ...**, or **Don't ... or you'll ...** . You can also make a direct warning more forceful by saying **Don't ... whatever you do**:

Don't! They'll fly away if you do that.
If you do that to it you'll break it.
Don't pull that or you'll cut off the electricity.
Whatever you do, don't touch these papers.

2 warning of immediate danger

- If you want to warn someone about something that might be about to happen you can say **Careful!**, **Be careful!**, **Watch it!**, **Watch out!** or **Look out!**
- If you want to tell someone to be careful about where they are walking, you can say **Mind the ...**:

Mind the gap.
Mind the step.

3 explicit warnings

You can use the words **I warn you**, or **I must warn you** as a way of warning someone about something:

•••• way ••••

Way is used to mean both 'direction' and 'method'.

➤ For the use of **a long way** instead of **far** in positive sentences, see the entry **far**.

ROUTE OR DIRECTION

1 When you are using **way** to mean 'route' or 'direction', you do not need the preposition **by**:

We went a different way home.
'Which way did you come?' 'The usual way.'

2 **on my way** and **in my way**

Notice the difference between these two expressions:

I'd love to learn, but I warn you now that I'm very stupid.
I must warn you that at six o'clock the door locks itself automatically.

4 threats

The words **I'm warning you** usually suggest that the speaker is making a threat:

So, I'm warning you: come near me and there'll be trouble.
I'm warning you, I'll tell your mother if you're rude again.

WARNINGS USED IN BOTH SPOKEN AND WRITTEN CONTEXTS

1 If you think that someone might hurt themselves in some way, you can warn them against doing so by saying (or writing) **Be careful not to...** or **Take care not to**:

Be careful not to eat too much fat.
It's not hard; you just have to be careful not to hit anything.
Drill a small hole (take care not to split the wood).

2 In written texts, especially those which instruct on how to do something, and in public situations, people often give warnings by saying **Never ...** or **Beware of ...**:

Never leave your plants overnight in freezing conditions.
Beware of these so-called 'sugar-free' commercial products.
Beware of putting too much of your money in one area.

WARNINGS ON PRODUCTS AND NOTICES

Many products which are poisonous or which can cause damage have labels on them with the words **Warning, Caution** or **Danger**. Signs in public places which warn you of dangers may say **Beware** or **Danger**:

Warning. Keep out of the reach of children.
Caution. Keep in a dry place.
Danger. Poison.
Beware of the dog.
Danger. Falling rocks.

... way continued

- You are **on your way** or **on the way** somewhere when you are going there. You do something **on your way** if you do it as you go:

I noticed the ambulance on my way to work this morning.
Could you call in on your way into town?
I've rung the doctor. She's on the way now.

- Something that is **in your way** or **in the way** is an obstacle, blocking your path:

It was difficult cleaning the house, with the children getting in her way.
She moved the bike out of my way.

3 Notice these expressions for talking about the position of things:

the wrong way up	*the wrong way round*
the right way up	*the right way round*
the other way up	*the other way round*

... way continued

Something that is, for example, **the wrong way up**, is upside down. You hold something **the wrong way round** when you hold it facing or pointing in the wrong direction:

You're holding your chopsticks the wrong way round.
Shouldn't that lampshade be the other way up?

MANNER, METHOD, OR MEANS

1 You can use the preposition **in** with **way** in this sense, but you can often omit it, especially if you are using possessives such as **my** or **your**, or determiners such as **this** or **that**:

She died in a rather mysterious way.
You can cook rice in several different ways.
You must deal with the problem your own way.
Make a list of points before we start. That way we'll save time.

2 You can use an **-ing** form or a **to**-infinitive after **way**:

What's the quickest way of getting fit?
This isn't the only way to do it.

3 **Way** is often followed by a relative clause, with three possible structures. You can talk about **the way in which** something is done, or **the way that** it is done, or **the way** it is done:

I noticed the way in which he always looked for the most important person.
I can't cook the way my mother used to.
I like the way you have your hair cut.
I approved of the way he dressed.

ⓘ **How** can be used after **at** similarly to **the way**:
We were amazed at how the smaller children kept going.
However, you cannot use **how** after **the way**:
I admire the way you (not *the way how you*) *cope.*

4 **used as a conjunction**

The way is sometimes used informally as a conjunction, meaning 'considering how':

The way I'm playing at the moment, I'm confident I'll win.

weak and strong forms

Some words in English have two pronunciations, depending on whether they are stressed or not, for example:

'What's it for?' [for = /fɔː(r)/]
'It's for measuring temperatures.' [for = /fə(r)/]

These words are usually 'grammatical' words, like prepositions, pronouns, articles, conjunctions and auxiliary verbs. Since such words are not usually stressed, the weak form is generally the commonest one.

Below is a list of the most important words which change their pronunciation when they are stressed:

	unstressed	stressed
a	/ə/	/eɪ/
am	/(ə)m/	/am/
an	/ən/	/an/
and	/(ənd)/	/and/
are	/ə(r)/	/ɑː(r)/
as	/əz/	/ɑz/
at	/ət/	/at/
be	/bɪ/	/biː/
been	/bɪn/	/biːn/
but	/bət/	/bʌt/
can	/k(ə)n/	/kan/
could	/kəd/	/kʊd/
do	/d(ə)/	/duː/
does	/dəz/	/dʌz/
for	/fə(r)/	/fɔː(r)/
from	/frəm/	/frɒm/
had	/(h)əd/	/had/
has	/(h)əz/	/haz/
have	/(h)əv/	/hav/
he	/(h)ɪ/	/hiː/
her	/(h)ə(r)/	/hɜː(r)/
him	/(h)ɪm/	/hɪm/
his	/(h)ɪz)	/hɪz/
is	/z, s/	/ɪz/
must	/m(ə)s(t)/	/mʌst/
not	/nt/	/nɒt/
of	/əv/	/ɒv/
our	/ɑː(r)/	/aʊə(r)/
shall	/ʃ(ə)l/	/ʃal/
she	/ʃɪ/	/ʃiː/
should	/ʃ(ə)d/	/ʃʊd/
sir	/sə(r)/	/sɜː(r)/
some	/s(ə)m/	/sʌm/
than	/ð(ə)n/	/ðan/
that	/ð(ə)t/	/ðat/
the	/ðə, ðɪ/	/ðiː/
them	/ð(ə)m/	/ðem/
there	/ðə(r)/	/ðeə(r)/
to	/tə/	/tuː/
us	/əs/	/ʌs/
was	/w(ə)z/	/wɒz/
we	/wɪ/	/wiː/
were	/wə(r)/	/wɜː(r)/
who	/hʊ/	/huː/
would	/wəd, əd/	/wʊd/
will	/(ə)l/	/wɪl/
you	/jʊ/	/juː/
your	/jə(r)/	/jɔː(r)/

THE WEATHER: TALKING ABOUT IT

ASKING ABOUT THE WEATHER

You can ask about weather conditions by saying **What's the weather like?**

If you are indoors, and you want to know about the weather outside, you ask **What's it like out?** or **Is it cold** (or **hot**) **out?**:

'What's the weather like where you are?' 'Oh it's gorgeous!'
'What's it like out?' 'It's lovely.'

DESCRIBING THE WEATHER

When describing some weather conditions, you can use a verb in the present progressive. For others, you use the construction **It's ...** + adjective.

1 temperature

Below is a list of adjectives you can use to describe temperature. The list begins with the coldest, and ends with the hottest temperature:

icy, freezing
cold
chilly
cool
mild
warm
hot
boiling

It was a chilly November day.
It's very warm for March, isn't it?
It's boiling out there!

Some of the above adjectives can be modified, for example, you can say that it is **freezing cold** or **bitterly cold**, or that it is **boiling hot**.

Do you want some tea? [= /s(ə)m/]
Some people prefer coffee. [= /sʌm/]

There's someone at the door. [= /ðə(r)/]
Who's there? [= /ðeə(r)/]

Don't forget your scarf. [= /jə(r)/]
That's your scarf, not mine. [= /jɔː(r)/]

•••• what ••••

What is used as a question word, as a relative pronoun and determiner, and in exclamations.

AS A QUESTION WORD

1 You use **what** to ask for something to be specified or identified:
'What's the time?' 'Quarter to four.'

THE WEATHER: TALKING ABOUT IT

ⓘ Notice that **weather** is an uncountable noun. You cannot say *We are having a fine weather.*

2 sun, wind and clouds

When you are talking about the weather conditions created by the sun, wind and the clouds, you use the adjectives **sunny**, **windy** and **cloudy**:

It's a lovely sunny afternoon.
That Monday morning was particularly wet and windy.
You can still get sunburn on a cloudy day.

3 rain and snow

When you are talking about rain and snow, you use a verb in the present progressive (*eg It's snowing*). There are many different ways of saying that it is raining hard:

It was a cold, windy night, and it was raining heavily.
The sky is black and it's pouring with rain.

COMMENTING ON THE WEATHER

It is fairly common to comment on the weather, especially when you meet someone you know, and you want to make friendly conversation. Below are some typical expressions that people use to comment on weather conditions:

Isn't it cold?
It's freezing, isn't it?
What awful weather we're having!
Lovely weather, isn't it!
Looks like rain. [= I think it's going to rain.]
Looks like it might be brightening up. [= I think the clouds are going to move away.]

'What's the matter?' 'There's a mistake here.'
'What's her name?' 'Gloria, I think.'
What else do you remember?
What happened?

2 When **what** is the object of the verb, the word order is **what** + auxiliary + subject:

What did you say next?
What have I done with my purse?

3 When **what** is the object of a preposition, the preposition usually comes at the end of the question:

What are you making so much fuss about?
'Try hammering it down.' 'What with?'

4 You use **what** with **be** to ask about people's jobs:

'What do you want to be?' 'A surgeon.'

5 When you use **what** with **do** in a progressive form, you are expecting a verb in reply:
'What are you doing?' 'Trying to fix my glasses.'

You use a simple tense of **do**, not a progressive, when asking about someone's job:
'What does your mother do?' 'She's a statistician.'

6 **What** is also used before singular or plural nouns:
What time is it?
What sort of clothes would be suitable?
What qualifications shall I need?

> ⓘ You use **what** rather than **which** when you are not referring to a limited range of choices.
> ➤ For more information on the different uses of **what** and **which** see the entry **which**.

IN REPORTED QUESTIONS

1 In reported questions, the word order after **what** is the same as in a statement:
Do you remember what his surname is (not *what is his surname*)?
I wondered what she thought (not *what did she think*) *of me.*

2 A **to**-infinitive often follows **what**:
I'd no idea what to say.
I wasn't sure what temperature to cook the cake at.

➤ See also the entry **reporting** for more information.

IN CONVERSATION

1 In informal situations, people sometimes say **what?** in response to being addressed:
'Granny?' 'Yes, what?' 'How do you spell your name?'

2 You also use **what** informally to ask the speaker to repeat something because you haven't heard or understood. Sometimes **what** is used simply to express incredulity or disbelief:
'Are you going by bus or car?' 'What, sorry?'
'It's fitted with a catalytic converter.' 'It's fitted with a what?'
'Jill's broken her ankle.' 'She's done what?'

➤ See also the entry **questions**.

SOME IDIOMS

1 You say **what about** something when you are reminding someone about something:
What about the tickets? Who's going to get them?

2 You ask **what** a thing or action is **for** to enquire about its purpose:
What's this lever for?
What are you standing there for?

3 You use **what if** in the same way as **suppose** and **supposing** to mention a possible difficulty:
What if she objects?

➤ For more information see the entry **suppose**.

4 You use **what** with **like** to ask for a description:

What was the road like? Busy?

➤ For more information see the entry **like**.

AS A RELATIVE PRONOUN

1 **What** is used to introduce relative clauses in which it acts not only as a relative pronoun, but also the thing that is being referred back to. Its meaning is something like 'the thing that' or 'the things that':

Thanks for the information; it's just what I needed.
He usually says what he means.
Make sure you get what you want out of life.

2 The **what-**clause can be made the subject of the verb **be**, to highlight some aspect of a situation:

What you need is a good night's sleep.
What annoyed me most was the bureaucracy.

MEANING 'WHATEVER'

What can often be used with the same meaning as **whatever**:

I've eaten what was left of the food.
I'll do what I can to help.
They provided what assistance they could.
I've spent what money there was.

> ⓘ You do not use **what** as a relative pronoun in relative clauses of either the defining or non-defining kind:
> *Everything that* (not *what*) *could be done has been done.*
> *The one thing I need* (not *the one thing what I need*) *is a bit of peace.*
> *They announced that they were getting married, which* (not *what*) *surprised us after all these years.*
> ➤ For more information see the entry **relative clauses**.

➤ For exclamations using **what**, see **exclamations**.

•••• whatever ••••

PRONOUN OR DETERMINER

I'll do whatever I can

Whatever usually has the meaning 'anything or everything that':

I'll do whatever I can to stop her worrying.
We'll help in whatever way you need.
They'll vote for whatever he advises.

CONJUNCTION

1 **whatever happens ...**

You also use **whatever** to convey the idea of something being the case in any circumstances:

Whatever happens, you can rely on me.

Whatever his faults [= whatever his faults may be, or in spite of his faults], *I still love him.*
Whatever excuse he had, he shouldn't have insulted her.

➤ For more information about uses of the pronoun **whatever**, see the entry **wh-ever words**.

2 nothing whatever
Whatever can be used to emphasize **nothing** or **not anything**, or some other negative noun expression:
I remember nothing whatever about the match.
Has this got anything whatever to do with me?
There's no reason whatever to be anxious.

•••• when ••••

When can be an *adverb*, a *conjunction* or a *relative pronoun*.

AS AN ADVERB IN QUESTIONS

1 You use **when** to ask questions about the past or the future:
When does the train arrive?
'She's off to Budapest.' 'Oh, when?' 'Tomorrow.'
'When did miniskirts come into fashion?'

2 In reported questions beginning with **when**, the word order is the same as in a statement:
Have you any idea when you'll (not *when will you*) *be finished?*

- **When** is often followed by a **to**-infinitive in reported questions:
People often don't know when to seek expert advice.
- **When** can stand by itself in place of the whole report clause, if the meaning is clear:
I'm going to be posted abroad, but they haven't told me when.

➤ For more information see the entries **reporting** and **questions**.

AS A CONJUNCTION OF TIME

1 **When** sometimes means 'every time that':
I always lock the door when I go to bed.

2 **When** can also mean 'during the time that':
It happened when I was abroad.
What were you doing when I was on the phone?

> ⓘ **As** and **while** are also used with the meaning 'during or at the time that':
> *As I was walking round she followed me closely.*
> *We were burgled while we were on holiday.*

3 **When** can mean 'as soon as'. You do not use the future in the **when**-clause:
Wait for me when you get to the corner.
I'll come when I've done the washing up.

> ⓘ **If** is used differently from **when**. You use **if** for happenings that are possible but not certain, and you use **when** for *expected* happenings:
> *They'll let me do a PhD if I get a first-class degree.*
> *I'm going to have a holiday when my exams are over.*

4 You can use a **when-**clause to report an event that *interrupts* an activity. **When** here has the meaning 'but just then':

I was about to leave when the telephone rang.

5 People sometimes use **why-**questions to say that some action is pointless, followed by a **when-**clause giving the reason for saying so:

Why stand when you can sit?

6 When the subject in the **when-**clause is the same as in the main clause, you can sometimes omit the subject and verb:

I always carried a whistle when walking [= when I was walking] *at night.*
Some people work better when under pressure [= when they are under pressure].
Mention names only when necessary [= when it is necessary].

AS A RELATIVE PRONOUN

When can be used as a relative pronoun in both defining and non-defining relative clauses.

1 In non-defining relative clauses **when** may add more information about the time mentioned, or it may have the meaning 'because then', in referring back to the time mentioned:

He sometimes went jogging long after dark, when most people were in bed.
Ring tomorrow, when I'll have more information.

2 You can use **when** to introduce a defining relative clause referring back to a word like **day**, **time**, or **occasion**:

I can remember two other occasions when you lost your keys.

•••• whenever ••••

➤ See **wh-ever words**.

•••• where ••••

Where can be an *adverb*, a *conjunction* or a *relative pronoun*.

AS AN ADVERB IN QUESTIONS

1 You use **where** to ask questions about the position or location of something or someone:

'Where's my wallet?'
'Where do you live?'
'Where's Mum?'
'There's a shooting star!' 'Where?'

2 You also use **where** to ask about direction. You use **from** with **where** when asking about the place someone or something comes from. You can use **to** with **where** when asking about the place someone or something is going to, but the meaning is usually clear without it. However, **to** is normally kept in the short question **where to?**

Where are these books being delivered to?
Where did you get these plates from?
'We've got some foreign guests.' 'Oh, yes. Where from?'
'Do you want to come with me?' 'Where to?'

3 **Where** is sometimes used to ask about a stage or point in a series of events:

Where did our marriage go wrong?

4 **in reported questions**

In reported questions after **where** the word order is the same as in a statement:

I think I can remember where the station is (not *where is the station*).
Who can tell us where we got to (not *where did we get to*) *in chapter 3?*

- In reported questions, **where** is often followed by a **to-**infinitive:

  Can you tell me where to get a good map?

- **Where** can sometimes stand by itself in place of the whole report clause, if the meaning is clear:

  I've got those photos somewhere, but I can't think where.

➤ For more information see **reporting** and **questions**.

AS A CONJUNCTION OF PLACE

1 **Where** can mean 'in the place that':

He left her where she was and went home.
The was an empty space where the house had stood.

2 **Where** can be used like **wherever** to mean 'in, or to, any or every place that':

Just sit where you want.

3 **Where** can also refer to a situation, or to a step in an argument:

That's where you're wrong.
This is a good example of where you should use 'might', not 'may'.

4 **Where** can be used like **wherever** to mean 'in all situations in which'. You can reduce clauses such as **where it is necessary** to **where necessary**:

We try to keep families together where we can.
Where possible, real names have been given.

AS A RELATIVE PRONOUN

As a relative pronoun **where** can be used in both defining and non-defining clauses:

1 In defining relative clauses, **where** can refer back to a place or a situation:

We went to see the village where I was born.
It was one of those situations where you had to be very tactful.

2 In non-defining clauses, **where** may add information about the place mentioned, or it may mean 'and there', giving the next point in a story or account:

I wanted to visit Pontefract, where 'Pontefract cakes' are supposed to come from.
We stopped at Bradford, where we collected Jane.

• • • • wherever • • • •

➤ See **wh-ever words**.

• • • • whether • • • •

Whether is a *conjunction*. You can use it like **if** to introduce reported questions, and it can be used with **or** to introduce alternatives.

IN REPORTED QUESTIONS

1 You use **whether**, like **if**, to introduce reported questions of the **yes** or **no** kind, after verbs like **know**, **ask**, **find out** and **wonder**:

I must find out whether (or *if*) *the train is on time.*
I wonder whether (or *if*) *Rosemary's been told.*

> ⓘ **differences between 'whether' and 'if'**
> ■ **Whether** can be followed by a **to**-infinitive; **if** cannot:
> *We weren't sure whether to tell Bob.*
> ■ **Whether** can be preceded by prepositions; **if** cannot:
> *His release will depend upon whether he is fully recovered.*
> *I felt some uncertainty as to whether she was really suitable.*

2 You can use **whether ... or ...** for alternatives (often two opposites) in reported questions:

I didn't know whether to laugh or cry.

When the second alternative is negative, you use **or not**. Notice the two possible word orders:

Could you let me know by Friday whether or not you're interested?
It'll soon become clear whether we're making a profit or not.

In the last example you could also use **if ... or** but it is less common:

I wasn't sure if he was joking or not.

INTRODUCING ALTERNATIVES

1 You use **whether ... or ...** when something is the case in either of two possible circumstances:

The rules, whether fair or unfair, are the same for everyone.
You must tell her the truth, whether or not she suspects it.

> ⓘ When the second alternative is negative you can also use both the following structures:
> *whether she suspects it or not*
> or:
> *whether she suspects it or whether she doesn't.*

2 **Whether ... or ...** is sometimes used to present more than two possibilities:

Whatever form of transport you use, whether car, bus, train or bicycle, you'll need at least an hour.

wh-ever words

There are six **wh-ever** words. They are: **however**, **whatever**, **whenever**, **wherever**, **whichever** and **whoever**.

You use **wh-ever** words to avoid specifying something definite out of a range of possibilities. There are five different ways of using **wh-ever** words:

LINKING CLAUSES;

1 In the sentence *'Buy whichever costs the least.'* **whichever** is taking the place of the words 'the one that', so it is linking the main clause to the subordinate clause, and playing a part in both. More examples follow, using other **wh-ever** words:

Pay however [= in any way that] *you like: cash, cheque or card.*
Whatever [= the thing that] *is causing the error is not at all obvious.*
I visit Mum whenever [=at any time that] *I can.*
I think you should take it back to wherever [= the place that] *it came from.*
I'll do my best to be nice to whoever [= the person that] *you marry.*

2 **Whatever** and **whichever** can be used as determiners before nouns:

We slept in whatever clothes [= the clothes that] *we were wearing.*
I'll have whichever room [= the room that] *you don't want.*

3 After **wherever** and **whenever**, adjectives such as **necessary** and **possible** can stand for a whole clause:

Boys and girls are taught together wherever possible [= wherever it is possible].

4 You can refer back to a choice of possibilities with a clause like **whichever you prefer** or **whichever is more convenient**:

I won't come by plane. I'll take the bus or train, whichever is cheaper [= depending on which is cheaper].

IT DOESN'T MATTER...

1 You also use **wh-ever** words like conjunctions to say that something remains the case in all possible circumstances. The **wh-ever** word means 'it doesn't matter where, how, what', and so on, and the main clause states the fact that doesn't change:

Wherever he's gone, he'll come back when he's hungry.
However you pay – cheque, cash, card – you'll benefit from the discount.
Whatever is causing the problem, we'll sort it out.

- You can use **however much** and **however many** to mean 'it doesn't matter how much', and 'it doesn't matter how many':

  However many books you read, you'll never read them all.

- You can use an adjective or adverb with **however**:

  You'll have to do it now, however tired [= it doesn't matter how tired] *you are.*
  Something always goes wrong, however carefully you organize things.

2 The verb **be**, or the combination **may be**, can sometimes be dropped in clauses introduced by **whatever**:

We'll find a solution, whatever the difficulties [= no matter what the difficulties are, or may be].

EXPRESSING IGNORANCE

You can also use **wh-ever** words to express your ignorance about something that has been mentioned, or your lack of interest in it:

We've all been told to write a haiku, whatever that is [= though I've no idea what that is].
You're supposed to sing it to the tune of 'Greensleeves', however that goes.
It happened at the Battle of Rumbling Bridge, whenever that was.
We're to meet at St Bridget's Church, wherever that is.
It was built by the Albigensians, whoever they were.

TWO WORDS FOR EMPHASIS

You use **what ever**, **how ever**, **where ever**, **who ever** and so on, written as two separate words, for emphasis, to convey amazement or irritation:

What ever do you think you're doing?
Where ever did I put those keys?
How ever am I supposed to get this done by tomorrow?

•••• which ••••

Which can be a question word or a relative pronoun.

AS A QUESTION WORD: PRONOUN OR DETERMINER

You use **which** when asking for a particular person or thing, or particular people or things, to be selected or identified from a group of possible ones.

1 **Which** can stand by itself as a pronoun:

Train or plane: which is really quicker?
Which is your room?
There's ice cream or fruit salad; which would you prefer?

- When **which** is the object of the verb the word order is: **which** + auxiliary + subject:

  Which do you recommend?
  Which has she chosen?

- There is no inversion with an auxiliary when **which** is the subject:

  Which makes a better sound?

> ⓘ Especially in conversation, people often use **which one** rather than **which** by itself:
> *These are my latest drawings. Which one shall I give to Mum?*

2 **Which** can come before a noun as a determiner:

Which colour do you prefer?
Which restaurant shall we take them to?
Which members of staff are attending the conference?

3 You use the form **which of** before determiners, and before pronouns:

Which of your sons is studying medicine?
Which of these letters do you want to keep?

> ⓘ You use **which of**, not **what of**, when referring to a group of things, and you use **which of**, not **who of**, before a group of people:
> *Which of the speakers did you find most interesting?*
> *Which of the three houses did you prefer?*

4 When **which**, or **which** + noun, is the object of a preposition, the preposition is usually at the end of the question:

Which train will you be arriving on?
Your job or your family: which do you care more about (or *about more*)*?*

5 In reported questions, the word order after **which** is the same as in a statement:

Let me know which train you'll be arriving (not *will you be arriving*) *on.*

- In reported questions, **which** is often followed by a **to-**infinitive:

  I didn't know which to choose.

- **Which** can be used after the reporting verb to represent the whole report clause, if the meaning is clear:

  He's going to be posted to Prague or Vienna, but he hasn't heard which, yet.

➤ For more information see **reporting** and **questions**.

AS A RELATIVE PRONOUN

As a relative pronoun, **which** refers only to *things*, never to *people*. It can be used in both defining and non-defining clauses:

1 Introducing defining relative clauses:

This is the kind of thing which increases costs.
Nocturnal animals are animals which are active at night.

- When **which** is the object of its clause, it can be omitted:

  I made a list of the topics we had discussed (or *which we had discussed*).

- In a formal style, a preposition can come before **which**. In this case **which** cannot be omitted:

  He was keen to meet us and visit the areas in which we lived.

> ⓘ **Which** can be replaced by **that** except when **which** follows a preposition:
> *They gave us a bedroom which* (or *that*) *looked out over the bay.*
> But:
> *Look again at the plays in which* (not *in that*) *that character appears.*

2 A non-defining clause after **which** may add information about the thing referred to, or it may add the next point in a story:

This very interesting idea, which he mentioned yesterday, is not new.
I switched on the computer, which immediately began to go wrong.

3 You can use quantity expressions such as **some of**, **any of** or **many of** before **which**:

He made fifty-four films, some of which have been shown on television.

4 **Which** can be used to refer back to a situation or circumstance:
She may not be able to babysit after all, which will be most inconvenient.

5 **Which** is rarely used as a *relative determiner*, but notice some common expressions beginning with prepositions, where **which** comes before a noun as a determiner:

- **In which case** is used to link a possible circumstance with its result:
  She may be unable to babysit, in which case you'll have to go on your own.
- **By which time** and **at which point** are used to link parts of a narrative:
  A discussion on price increases began, at which point [= and at that point] *I left.*
  We talked till about midnight, by which time [= and by that time] *the other guests had left.*

•••• whichever ••••

➤ See **wh-ever words**.

•••• who, whom ••••

PRONOUNS

Who is used as a question word and as a relative pronoun.

Who has an object form **whom**, which is used in formal English.

Who also has a possessive form, **whose**, which has its own entry in this book.

IN QUESTIONS

You use **who** to ask for a person's identity:

1 **in direct questions**

- **Who** is always the form used as the subject of a question:
  Who told you that?
  Who made this delicious cake?
- **Who** and, very formally, **whom**, are used as the object in a question. The word order is **who** or **whom** + auxiliary + subject:
  Who (or *whom*) *do you recognize in this photo?*
  Who (or *whom*) *have you invited?*
- **Who** is often the *complement* of the linking verb **be**. The order is **who** + **be** + subject:
  Who is the girl in the blue sweater?
  Who are their lawyers?
- **Who** can be the object of a preposition. The preposition usually comes at the end of the question, or after the verb:
  Who is this postcard from?
  Who were you talking to on the phone?

> ⓘ The form **whom** is very rarely used when the preposition comes at the end of the question. But sometimes in formal English the preposition may be placed at the beginning of the question. In this case, **whom** is always used after it:
> *To whom was she referring?*

2 in reported questions

- In reported questions the word order after **who** and **whom** is the same as in a statement:

  There's a man at the door but I've no idea who he is (not *who is he*).
  I wondered who I could turn to (not *who could I turn to*) *for help.*
  You know perfectly well to whom I'm referring (not *to whom am I referring*).

- **Who** and **whom** can be followed by a **to-**infinitive:

  Tell your children who (or *whom*) *to contact in an emergency.*

- **Who** and **whom** can stand by themselves in place of the whole reported question, if the meaning is clear:

  Someone has betrayed us, but I don't know who.
  She obviously suspected someone, but she wouldn't say whom (or *who*).

AS RELATIVE PRONOUNS

As relative pronouns, **who** and **whom** can be used in both identifying and non-identifying clauses. If you put a preposition at the beginning of the clause, you must use **whom** after it, not **who**:

1 Examples follow of **who** and **whom** in identifying clauses:
Where's the waitress who served us?
There are people in this organization whom (or *who*) *you can't trust.*
I made a list of the members from whom I'd received replies.

> ⓘ ■ You can drop **whom**, except when it comes after a preposition placed at the beginning of the clause, and you can drop **who** when it is the object:
> *There aren't many people I really trust* (or *whom or who I really trust*).
> But:
> *He was a man in whom I placed absolute trust.*
> ■ You can replace **who** and **whom** with **that**, except after a preposition:
> *There's the waitress that served you.*
> *I'm glad I met you. There's nobody to whom* (not *that*) *I'd rather talk.*

2 When **who** and **whom** are used in non-defining clauses, they sometimes give more information about the person they refer to, or they can add the next happening in a story:
That music was by Bellini, who was born 190 years ago.
I telephoned Inga, who answered straight away.
She lived with her sister, whom (or *who*) *she secretly hated.*
I telephoned the Jessops, from whom I'd just received a postcard.

3 It is possible to use quantity expressions such as **some of**, **many of**, **both of**,

neither of, before **whom**:

We rang Jane and Susan, neither of whom were able to help.

➤ For more information see **relative clauses and relative pronouns**.

•••• whoever ••••

➤ See **wh-ever words**.

•••• whole ••••

You use **whole** in various ways to mean *all* of something.

1 When you have a noun phrase beginning with **the**, such as **the week**, or **the roof**, you can either say **the whole of** before **the** + noun, or you can say **the whole** + noun:

The whole of the roof had to be renewed.
We spent the whole day on the beach.

> ⓘ Notice that in reference to a particular period of time, you can also use **all** + noun:
> *It took all morning* (or *the whole morning or the whole of the morning*) *to clean up.*

2 Before a proper name, *eg* the name of a place, you have to use the form **the whole of**:

By this time the whole of Northern Somalia was in their hands.

3 You can use determiners such as **my**, **your**, **this** and **that** with **whole** in the same way as **the**:

I feel as if I've wasted my whole life.
I'm afraid that whole subject bores me stiff.

4 With noun phrases beginning with **a**, or **one**, **whole** is used for emphasizing the length of time, or the amount of something:

He hasn't cried at night for a whole week.
We spent the whole of one lesson discussing this.

5 You can use **whole** before a plural noun. It means 'entire' or 'complete':

Whole cities had been destroyed.

Notice the difference between this and *Every city had been destroyed.*

6 **'on the whole' and 'as a whole'**

- You use **on the whole** to sum up a situation or give a general impression:

  On the whole he has succeeded.
  People's lives are pretty dull on the whole.

- You use **as a whole** especially after words that represent a community, such as **country** or **school**, to emphasize that you mean the community generally, not just the individuals in it:

  The community as a whole will benefit from these changes.

•••• whose ••••

Whose is the possessive form of **who**. Like **who**, **whose** occurs in questions and relative clauses.

IN QUESTIONS: DETERMINER OR PRONOUN

Whose asks who a certain thing belongs to or relates to.

1 in direct questions

Since **whose** is a possessive form, it is asking for a possessive form - a possessive pronoun or the possessive form of a name - as a reply:

'Whose watch is making that noise?' 'Mine, I'm sorry.'
'Whose story would make the best play?' 'Amanda's.

- When **whose**, or **whose** + noun, is the object of the verb, the word order is **whose** (+ noun) + auxiliary + subject:

  Whose story did you enjoy most?
  His tent is still here. So whose has he borrowed?

- If **whose** (+ noun) is the object of a preposition, the preposition may come at the end of the question or, more formally, before **whose**:

  Sorry, whose essay were you talking about?
  From whose play are these words taken?

2 in reported questions

The word order after **whose** in a reported question is the same as in a statement:

I enquired whose the car was (not *whose was the car*).
We had to guess whose voice he was imitating (not *whose voice was he imitating*).

- A **to-**infinitive can follow **whose**:

  I stood outside wondering whose offer to accept.

- **Whose** can stand by itself in place of the whole reported question, if the meaning is clear:

  She said a name had been mentioned, but she wouldn't tell me whose.

AS A RELATIVE DETERMINER

As a relative, **whose** can be used in both defining and non-defining clauses.

1 in defining clauses

- You use **whose** to identify or describe a person, people, thing or things in terms of someone or something associated with them or belonging to them:

  Children whose parents are working often have stronger ambitions.
  I was joined by a lady whose face I recognized.

- When **whose** + noun is the object of a preposition, the preposition may come at the end of the clause, or, more formally, it may be placed before **whose** at the beginning:

  We were met at the station by the students whose families we were staying with.
  Why not join a local group in whose cause you believe?

2 in non-defining clauses

You use a non-defining **whose-clause** to add more information about the person or thing mentioned, or to add the next point in a story:

I rang Sarah, whose answering machine was switched on.
My thanks to my parents, without whose help I couldn't have coped.
Meet Deborah, whose new book everyone's so enthusiastic about.

•••• wh-words ••••

➤ See entries for individual words **what, when, where, why, how, who, whom, which** and **whose**.

•••• why ••••

Why is a question word, but is also sometimes used as a relative after the word **reason**.

AS A QUESTION WORD

1 direct questions

You use **why** to ask the reason for something:

'Why won't this printer work?' 'It's not switched on.'
'Why aren't you asleep?' 'Because I'm not tired.'
'Why did you say that?' 'No particular reason.'

> ⓘ The word order with **why** in direct speech is always **why** + *auxiliary* + *subject*:
> *Why haven't you told me this before?*

- **Why** and **why not** are often used on their own in conversation. You use **why** to question a positive statement, and **why not** to question a negative one:

  'I'm feeling really depressed.' 'Why?'
  'I don't want to discuss it.' 'Why not?'
  'Sorry, but I can't come with you.' 'Oh, why not?'

- You can make a suggestion using **why don't ...?** and agree to one using **why not?**:

  Why don't you come round to my place?
  Why don't we go and get a pizza?
  'Come and have a drink.' 'OK, why not?'.

- You can use **why** with an infinitive without **to** to say that something is pointless:

  Why stand when you can sit down?
  Why wait? Let's get on with it.

- **Why not** is used with an infinitive without **to** to make suggestions:

  'I'm so tired.' 'Well, why not take a break?'

2 reported questions

In reported questions, the word order after **why** is the same as in a statement:

I know why it isn't (not *why isn't it*) *working.*
I wondered why I hadn't (not *why hadn't I*) *heard from him.*

- **Why** and **why not** can stand by themselves in place of the whole reported question, if the meaning is clear:

  She's very pleased with herself, and I don't know why.

- You use **that's why** to say that what has just been mentioned is the reason for something:

  My father was a doctor. That's why I'm studying medicine.

AS A RELATIVE PRONOUN

1 You can use **why** as a relative pronoun after **reason**:
Is there any good reason why I should get involved?

2 If you use **the** before **reason** you can use **that instead of why**, or you can omit the relative pronoun:
The reason that I rang (or *the reason I rang) was to make sure you were OK.*

➤ See also the entry **reason**.

• • • • will • • • •

Will is widely used in its contracted form **'ll** for giving information about the future (see section entitled **the future: ways of expressing it**). But it is not only used in this way. It has a wide range of other uses. In these other cases **will** expresses such ideas as willingness, wishes and strong intentions.

ANNOUNCING DECISIONS

You use **will** (or **'ll**) when making a decision and announcing it:

You go ahead: I'll catch (not *I catch) you up.*
We'll have the steak, please.
Well, we won't argue.
I'll call him later.
Er, no. I won't come in, thanks.

ⓘ Notice that the contracted form of **will not** is **won't**.

SHOWING WILLINGNESS

1 You use **will** when showing that you are willing to do something:
That was the doorbell–I'll go.
'Nobody's offered to help yet.' 'I will.'
I'll sort everything out. You sit down.

2 You use **will** if you want to show that you are determined to do something:
We will never give in.
'What if you forget?' 'I won't.'
Promise you'll write to me.

3 In its negative form, **will** is used to talk about refusal:
I've tried telling her, but she won't change her mind.
They won't let you in if you arrive late.
The door won't open.

> ⓘ Notice that objects can be referred to as if they had the human ability to refuse to do something:
> *The car won't start.*
> *My computer won't save this file.*

PERSISTENCE, HABITS AND CHARACTERISTICS

1 You use **will** to talk about what is typical or characteristic:

Accidents will happen.
A good teacher will know if a child is unhappy.
He'll try anything to make you buy it.

2 You can also use **will** to express criticism of the way someone keeps behaving, emphasizing the word **will**:

She will leave her clothes all over the floor.
You will keep forgetting things.

REQUESTS AND INSTRUCTIONS

Will is used in its interrogative form to make requests, or to tell people what to do:

Will you post this for me?
Will you pass the salt, please?
Will you give me a hand with this translation?
Will you get back to me as soon as possible?

OFFERS AND INVITATIONS

The interrogative form of **will** is also used in making offers and issuing invitations:

Will you have some more coffee?
What will you have to drink?
Will you come round for dinner on Saturday?

CERTAINTY

You use **will** when you make a deduction that something must be the case:

That'll be John phoning.
It's not worth it; they'll have left by now.

ELLIPSIS

Will often stands on its own for the main verb in question tags, short answers and other elliptical structures:

You'll be punctual, won't you?
I'll phone soon. I promise I will.

•••• without ••••

WITHOUT + NOUN

The noun after **without** can be someone or something you do not have, or do not have with you, or something that does not happen:

He's better-looking without his beard.
It's difficult to bring up a child without a partner.
She agreed without hesitation.

WITHOUT + -ING FORM

You often use an -**ing** form of a verb after **without** to say what doesn't happen at the same time as the main verb:

Ruth managed to lift the baby without waking him.
He went on with his work without looking up.

WITHOUT + NOUN + -ING FORM

You do one thing **without** another thing *happening* when the second thing does not happen:

How did they get into the building without the alarm going off?

Notice that **without** acts like a *negative* word, and is followed by non-assertive words like **any** and **ever**:
We got down the mountain without anyone getting hurt.
People can get jobs without ever making a positive decision.

•••• wonder ••••

EXPRESSING UNCERTAINTIES

You use **I wonder** to express queries, doubts and uncertainties. **Wonder** can be followed by a **wh-**clause or by **if** or **whether**:

I wonder what he's doing now?
I wonder how many of us have had this experience?
I wonder if I ought to forget the whole thing?
I wonder whether they realize the danger they're in?

IN REPORTING

Wonder has an important use in reporting *unspoken* questions:

He wondered where he'd left his glasses.
I wondered if I should ring her.

IN POLITE REQUESTS

People use **I wonder**, particularly in the simple past tense or past progressive, to introduce polite requests and invitations:

I wonder if I could possibly have my book back?
I was wondering if you'd like to come to the opera with me?

—— word class ——

➤ See **part of speech**.

•••• worth ••••

Worth is used as a *preposition* and as a *noun.*

AS A PREPOSITION

1 Something is **worth** a certain amount of money if it has that value, or can be sold for that amount:

The house must be worth at least £100,000.
I didn't realize his old books were worth so much.
How much is this chair worth?

2 Something that is **worth it** or **worth the trouble** is a good thing to do, usually because you get the result you want:

He thought he might apologize, but decided it wasn't worth it.

3 You can use **-ing** forms after **worth** in two ways. You can say, for example, *It's worth trying every possibility*, or you can make the object of the **-ing** form the subject, and say *Every possibility is worth trying*:

They may have reductions for children. It's worth asking.
He didn't think the television set was worth repairing.

■ **Worth** can be intensified by **well**:

These ancient sites are well worth visiting.

4 As well as being able to say **it's worth doing** something, you can also say **it's worthwhile doing** it:

I told them it wasn't really worthwhile coming for less than three days.

AS A NOUN

You can use the possessive form of a sum of money + **worth** when estimating the value of such things as commodities, or the loss caused by damage:

I've got over a thousand pounds' worth of brandy here.
The fans caused thousands of pounds' worth of damage in the town centre.

•••• would ••••

Would is a modal verb. It is the past form of **will**. When **would** follows a pronoun in speech, it is usually pronounced /d/ (spelt **'d**). The negative form of **would** is **would not** or **wouldn't**.

Although **would**, like **should**, has a large role to play in forming conditionals (see **conditionals**), it has other uses, many of which it shares with **will**.

In general, although **would** has much in common with **will**, it is less direct, and therefore used in more formal contexts.

TALKING ABOUT THE PAST

1 **Would** is used to talk about past habits, with the same meaning as **used to**:

Wherever she happened to be she would always phone me at six.
We would get up, go for a swim, then come back to a big breakfast.

2 You can also stress **would** in speech to show that you are criticizing someone's behaviour in the past:

He was nice, but he would keep trying to tell me what to do.

3 **Would not** is used to talk about refusal in the past:

He wouldn't give up smoking.

INDIRECT SPEECH

Would is used in indirect speech where **will** was used in the original, direct, speech:

She said she'd be leaving at 10 a.m.
I hoped they wouldn't notice.
I asked him to write to me every week and he promised he would.

FUTURE IN THE PAST

You use **would** when you are talking about a past action which had not yet happened at the time you are referring to:

Later on, he would see his mistake.

REQUESTS, INVITATIONS, OFFERS

Like **will**, **would** can be used to make requests and offers, and to issue invitations. **Would**, however, has more of a distancing effect than **will**, and is therefore more tentative, friendly and polite:

Would you hold this for a moment, please?
Would you like anything to eat?
Would you like to come over at the weekend

ELLIPSIS

Would often stands on its own for the main verb in question tags, short answers and other elliptical structures:

'I expect you'd like a rest, wouldn't you?' 'I certainly would.'
I tried to get him to give up smoking, but he wouldn't.

Would is sometimes followed by **be, have** and **do**, and **would have** by **been** and **done** in referring back to verbs that use these auxiliaries:

'Are you going to the lecture?' 'I would be but I've got too much work.'
'Did you realize she was over 70?' 'I wouldn't have (or *wouldn't have done*) *if someone hadn't told me'.*

Yy

•••• year ••••

1 A **year** is the period of 365 days, or twelve months, from 1 January to 31 December:

During the whole of 1963 and the following year she was living abroad.
Was 1969 the year men first landed on the moon?
Is it this year or next year that she starts at university?
We didn't get away for a holiday at all last year.
Deaths reached 23,000 in 1994, an increase of 15 per cent on the previous year.

2 A **year** can also be any period of twelve months:

We've arranged to hold a reunion here, one year from today.
Her husband wasn't due to retire for several years.
Twenty years ago nobody had heard of Boris Becker.

3 You use **year** in giving the age of a person or thing. You say that someone or something is so many **years old**:

These carvings are thousands of years old.
a two-year-old child

➤ For more details see **age**.

•••• yes, no ••••

1 **Yes** is used as a positive reply, and **no** is used as a negative reply:

'Are you going to the party tonight?' 'Yes. What time are we supposed to be there?'
'Did you do your homework?' 'No, I didn't have time.'

2 A negative question expects the answer 'yes'. So you give a positive response to a negative question by answering 'yes', and a negative response by anwering 'no':

'Haven't you met him yet?' 'Yes, I met him last night.'
'Aren't you enjoying yourself?' 'No, not really.'

3 When you agree with a negative statement, which may be followed by a positive tag, you use **no** + short response, and when you agree with a positive statement, which may be followed by a negative tag, you use **yes** + short response:

'It's not very attractive, is it?' 'No; it isn't really.'
'She seems friendly.' 'Yes; I think I'll enjoy working with her.'

4 When you contradict a negative statement, you use **yes** + short response; when you contradict a positive statement, you use **no** + short response:

'Her name isn't on the list.' 'Yes, it is.'
'Mum, Jack called me a horrible name!' 'No, I didn't!'

> ⓘ Note that a short **yes** or **no** contradiction can sound rude. People use words and phrases like **Well ...**, **I'm not sure ...**, **actually ...** and **I (don't) think ...** to soften their replies:
> *'It's really cold outside.' 'Oh, I didn't think it was too bad, actually.'* (not *No it isn't.*)
> *'She's German.' 'Erm, I'm not sure she is; I think she's Austrian, actually.'* (not *No she isn't.*)

•••• yesterday ••••

1 **Yesterday** is the day before today:
It was so cold yesterday that she didn't go out at all.

2 You can refer to the morning, afternoon and evening of yesterday as **yesterday morning**, **yesterday afternoon** and **yesterday evening**. But you say **last night**, not **yesterday night**, for the night between today and yesterday:
I didn't sleep at all last night.

3 You can also use **last night** to mean the same as **yesterday evening**:
I watched the most extraordinary programme last night.

•••• yet ••••

➤ See **already**.

Other titles available in the Chambers ELT range are: